FOURTH EDITION

Educational Psychology
Theory and Practice

ROBERT E. SLAVIN

Johns Hopkins University

ALLYN AND BACON

Boston ▪ London ▪ Toronto ▪ Sydney ▪ Tokyo ▪ Singapore

Editor-in-Chief, Education: Nancy Forsyth
Series Editorial Assistant: Christine Nelson
Develpmental Editor: Mary Ellen Lepionka
Composition Buyer: Linda Cox
Manufacturing Buyer: Louise Richardson
Editorial-Production Service: Margaret Pinette
Eletronic Manuscript Manager: Andrew Walker
Text Designer: Ron Kosciak
Photo Researcher: Susan Duane
Cover Administrator: Linda Dickinson
Cover Designer: Studio Nine

Copyright © 1994, 1991, 1988, 1986 by Allyn and Bacon
A division of Paramount Publishing
160 Gould Street
Needham Heights, Massachusetts 02194

Previous editions of this book were published under the title *Educational Psychology: Theory into Practice.*

Library of Congress Cataloging-in-Publication Data

Slavin, Robert E.
    Educational psychology: theory into practice/Robert E. Slavin.
       p.   cm.
    Includes bibliographical references (p.   ) and index.
    ISBN 0–205–15161–2
    1. Educational psychology. I. Title.
LB1051.S615   1994
370.15—dc20   93–37334
                                                                            CIP

Printed in the United States of America

10 9 8 7 6 5 4 3 2   98 97 96 95 94

BRIEF CONTENTS

CONTENTS

CHAPTER 3

Development During Childhood and Adolescence 70

CHAPTER 4

Student Diversity 112

CHAPTER 5

Behavioral Theories of Learning 150

CHAPTER 6

Cognitive Theories of Learning Basic Concepts 184

CHAPTER 7

Cognitive Theories: Constructivist Approaches 222

CHAPTER 9

Accommodating Instruction to Individual Needs 306

CHAPTER 12

Students at Risk and Exceptional Learners 434

CHAPTER 13

Assessing Student Learning 484

CHAPTER 14

Performance Assessments and Standardized Tests 528

When I first set out to write *Educational Psychology: Theory and Practice*, I had a very clear objective in mind. What I wanted to do was to give tomorrow's teachers the intellectual grounding and practical strategies needed to be effective as instructors. In looking at the texts that existed then, I felt that most fell into two categories: stuffy and lightweight. The stuffy books were full of research but ponderously written, losing the flavor of the classroom and containing few guides to practice. The lightweight texts were breezy and easy to read, but lacking in research and the dilemmas and intellectual issues brought out by research. They contained suggestions for practice of the "Try this!" variety, without considering evidence about the effectiveness of the strategies suggested.

What I wanted to do was see if it was possible to write a text that was as complete and up-to-date as the most research-focused texts, but was readable, practical and loaded with examples and illustrations of key ideas. I wanted to include suggestions for practice based directly on classroom research (tempered by common sense), so that I could have confidence that if teachers actually tried what I suggested, it would be likely to work. I wanted to write the kind of book that I would like to read myself—even though I have been doing educational research for two decades, I find that I really never understand theory or concepts in education until someone writes me a compelling classroom example, and I'm willing to bet that most of my colleagues (and certainly students) feel the same way. As a result, the words "for example" or their equivalent must appear hundreds of times in this text. I have tried to write this book in a way that the reader will almost hear children's voices and smell the lunch cooking in the school cafeteria. I believe that if there is any chance that students will transfer what they learn in educational psychology to their own teaching, texts (and instructors) must make the connection between theory and practice explicit by the use of many realistic examples.

I can't say I have succeeded in what I have set out to do; that is for the reader to judge. But in this fourth edition I have continued to try to achieve the objectives I had in the earlier editions. I have made changes throughout the text, adding examples, refining language, deleting dated or unessential material. I am a fanatic about keeping the text up-to-date. The text has about fifteen hundred citations, about 80% since 1980. I know that students don't usually care much about citations, but I want them and their professors to know what support exists for any statements I've made and where to find additional information.

The field of educational psychology and the practice of education have changed a great deal in recent years, and I have tried to reflect this in the text. Only a few years ago, direct instruction and related teacher effectiveness were dominant in educational psychology. Today, discovery learning, authentic assessment, and other humanistic strategies are once again coming to the fore. In the first and second editions of this text I had a statement to the effect that we shouldn't discard discovery learning and humanistic methods, despite the (then) current popularity of direct instruction. In revising the text this statement seemed oddly anachronistic (even though it is only six years old!).

This edition presents new research and practical applications of these and many other topics. It contains a substantially expanded chapter on student diversity, including an extended discussion of multi-cultural education and programs for students at risk. It is the first educational psychology text to devote an entire chapter to constructivist theories of learning. Throughout, this edition reflects the "cognitive revolution" that is transforming educational psychology. It has new sections on authentic assessment, new conceptions of intelligence and motivation, learning styles, cooperative learning, prevention of learning problems, and new approaches for exceptional children.

Given the developments of the past two decades, no one can deny that teachers matter, that their behaviors have a profound impact on student achievement. To have a positive impact, teachers must have both a deep understanding of the powerful principles of psychology as they apply to education and a clear sense of how these principles can be supplied. Effective teaching is neither a bag of tricks nor a set of abstract principles; rather, it is intelligent application of well-understood principles to solve practical problems. I hope this edition will help give teachers the intellectual and practical skills needed to do the most important job in the world.

How this Book is Organized

The chapters in this book are arranged in terms of three principle themes: Students, Learning, and Teaching. Each chapter discusses important theories, with many examples of how these theories apply to classroom teaching.

This book emphasizes the intelligent use of theory and research to improve instruction. The chapters on teaching occupy about one-third of the total pages in the book, and the other chapters all relate to the meaning of theories and research practice. Whenever possible, the guides for practice in this book are specific programs or strategies that have been evaluated and found to be effective, not just suggestions for things to try.

This edition has been revised to place a greater emphasis on critical thinking, engaging the reader with dilemmas, controversial issues, and opportunities for reflection and problem-solving. In addition, several of the book's major elements have been integrated into a self-regulated learning program, new to this edition, that will help readers to succeed in the course and transfer their learning to professional teaching practice.

Features

The goal of helping teachers acquire and develop the tools they need to be good teachers is addressed by the Theory into Practice sections in each chapter. These sections, twice as many as in the last edition, present specific strategies for applying information in the text to the actual classroom.

On the all-new Teachers on Teaching pages, practicing master teachers contribute personal essays describing how they faced and met particular teaching challenges. In each chapter, two teachers respond in depth to the same question relating concepts in educational psychology to classroom practice. Their responses show the relevance of educational psychology theory and research and the rich variety of teachers' reflection and problem-solving approaches.

The new Focus On... feature in every chapter presents a balanced discussion of controversial topics in education that are in the news. Critical thinking questions invite readers to apply chapter content as they analyze, compare and contrast, and evaluate views that will affect the future of teaching and learning.

At the end of each chapter, the Case to Consider presents a realistic dialogue among teachers and students, or between teachers and students, parents, administrators, or specialists. The cases, mostly new, present authentic dilemmas or conflicts for readers to discuss and resolve. Problem-solving questions guide readers in modeling their proposed solutions by extending the dialogue through writing or role-play.

Self-Regulated Learning

The integrated self-regulated learning component of this text reflects a major trend in education toward putting students more in charge of their own learning and meaningful constructions of reality. Self-regulated learning approaches promote individual success through self-motivation, self-monitored practice, and self-assessment. In each chapter the following elements are closely interrelated to assist students of educational psychology in self-regulated learning:

- A chapter outline, with main headings framed as questions
- A list of learning outcomes or objectives keyed to main headings
- A Self-Check after each main section to determine if the objective has been mastered and to suggest study strategies that will lead to understanding
- A scenario reinterpretation feature in which readers reinterpret a chapter opening scenario in terms of chapter content
- Photo captions framed as questions that invite readers to apply information and concepts in the chapter to interpret the images
- Glossary annotations in the margins defining boldfaced key terms in the text
- Connections annotations that point out interrelationships between concepts and topics within a chapter or between one chapter and another
- A Summary that answers the questions posed in the main headings
- A list of Key Terms with page references at chapter end
- A Self-Assessment quiz with eight multiple choice, matching, and short essay items
- An Answer Feedback section at the back of the book with correct answers or answer guidelines to the Self-Assessments, plus explanations and page references
- A Glossary, Name Index, Subject Index, and list of References at text end
- A student Success Guide that is especially designed to co-ordinate with and support this self-regulated learning program

These aids to self-regulated learning are discussed further in Chapter 1 of the text.

Acknowledgments

I wish to thank my many colleagues who served as reviewers for this edition. Their comments provided invaluable information that helped me revise and augment the text. I would also like to thank those who contributed material for text features, including Theory Into Practice and Case to Consider. Reviewers and contributors are listed alphabetically below, including the supplements authors. I would especially like to thank Pamela George, author of the instructor's section and annotations in the Annotated Instructor's Edition; Steven Ross, Test Bank author; and Catherine McCartney, who wrote the student Success Guide:

Jean Blomenkamp
Wayne State College

Elena Bodrova
Metropolitan State College of Denver

Helen Botnarescue
California State University —Hayward

John Clark
University of Vermont

Lynne Diaz-Rico
California State University—San Bernadino

Ricardo Garcia
University of Idaho

Marisal Gavilan
Florida International University

Pamela George
North Carolina Central University

Ajaipal Gill
Anne Arundel Community College

Kevin Hughes
Western Kentucky University

Fintan Kavanaugh
Marywood College

Deborah Leong
Metropolitan State College of Denver

Catherine McCartney
Bemidji State University

Peg Perkins
University of Nevada—Las Vegas

Mary Ann Rafoth
Indiana University of Pennsylvania

Steven Ross
University of Tennessee

Ruth Sandlin
California State University—San Bernadino

Duane Shell
Western Kentucky University

Deborah Smith
University of New Mexico

Stephen Strichart
Florida International University

Anthony Truog
University of Wisconsin–Whitewater

James Turner
University of North Texas

Jane Wolfle
Bowling Green State University

Douglas Yarbrough
Boise State University

Vicky Zygouris-Coe
Towson State University

I would like to thank contributors to previous editions, such as Stacie Goffin, William Zangwill, Thomas Andre, and Sandra Damico, and the people at Prentice-Hall who helped me with the first three editions, especially Susan Willig and Jane Ritter. At Allyn and Bacon I'd like to thank Nancy Forsyth, Education Editor–in–Chief, and Mary Ellen Lepionka, Developmental Editor, for their help with the fourth edition. In particular Mary Ellen Lepionka put hundreds of hours into helping me with everything from reviewers to references to wording. In addition to a thousand other tasks, she planned and co-ordinated the Annotated Instructor's Edition and all the supplements.

I would also like to thank others on the Education Team and at Allyn and Bacon who helped bring this project to fruition: Mary Beth Finch, Editorial–Production Supervisor; Margaret Pinette, Copyeditor and Production Coordinator; Ellen Mann, Marketing Manager; Linda Dickinson, Cover Administrator; Laurie Frankenthaler, Permissions Researcher; Susan Duane, Photo Researcher; and Christine Nelson, Editorial Assistant. In addition, I'd like to thank Cherie Jones and Gretta Gordy of Johns Hopkins University for their help with typing and references.

I also want to thank the classroom teachers and education specialists from Alaska to the nation's capitol who contributed illustrated essays for the Teachers on Teaching feature: Julie Addison, Randall Amour, Margaret Ball, Robert Coleman, Gail Dawson, Joyce Flaxbeard, Louis Gotlib, Gail Hartman, Janie Hill, Elonda Hogue, Gemma Hoskins, Karen Kusayanagi, Nancy Letts, Jodi Libretti, Rosa Lujan, Lynne McKee, Ricardo Morris, Terry Olive, Vicki Olsen, Dorothy Paulsen, Melissa Scott, Deanna Seed, Audrey Seguin, Benetta Skrundz, Melissa Smith, Sandra Taylor, Gloria Thompson, Richard Thorne, Thomas Welch, and James Williams.

Finally it is customary to acknowledge the long-suffering patience of one's spouse and children,. In my case, this acknowledgment is especially appropriate. My wife, Nancy Madden, not only read and commented on every word, but also as my co-worker kept our classroom research going while I was in the throes of writing. Our children, Jacob, Benjamin, and Rebecca (who were not particularly patient or long suffering) did, however, contribute to this work by providing examples for sections of chapter 3. They also provided me with a sense of purpose for writing; I had to keep thinking about the kind of school experience I want for them, as a way of making concrete my concern for the school experiences of all children.

This book was written while I was supported in part by grants from the Office of Educational Research and Improvement, U.S. Department of Education (No, OERI-R-117-R90002). However any opinions I have are mine alone and do not represent OERI positions or policy.

Robert Slavin is currently the director of the Elementary School Program of the Center for Research on Effective Schooling for Disadvantaged Students, Johns Hopkins University. He received his Phd. in Social Relations from Johns Hopkins in 1975, and since that time has authored more than 150 articles and book chapters on such topics as cooperative learning, ability grouping, school and classroom organization, desegregation, mainstreaming, and research review. Dr. Slavin is the author or co-author of twelve books, including *Cooperative Learning, Educational Psychology, Theory and Practice, School and Classroom Organization, Effective Programs for Students at Risk,* and *Preventing Early School Failure.* In 1985 Dr. Slavin received the Raymond Cattell Early Career Award for Programmatic Research from the American Educational Research Association, and in 1988 he received the Palmer O. Johnson Award for the best article in an AERA journal.

Educational Psychology

1

Educational Psychology: A Foundation for Teaching

Chapter Objectives

▲ List some characteristics of a good teacher.

▲ Explain how research in educational psychology is applied to teaching and give examples of research findings that contribute to teaching effectiveness.

▲ Compare and contrast experimental, correlational, and descriptive research, provide an example of each type of research, and explain the differences between correlational and causal relationships.

Ellen Mathis was baffled. She was a new teacher who had been trying to teach creative writing to her third-grade class, but things were just not going the way she'd hoped. Her students were not producing very much, and what they did write wasn't very imaginative and was full of errors. For example, she recently assigned a composition on "My Summer Vacation," and all one of her students wrote was "on my summer vacation I got a dog and we went swimming and I got stinged by a bee." Ellen wondered whether maybe her kids were just not ready for writing, and needed several months of work on such skills as capitalization, punctuation, and usage before she tried another writing assignment. One day, however, Ellen noticed some compositions in the hall outside of Leah Washington's class. Her third-graders were just like Ellen's, but their compositions were fabulous! The students wrote pages of interesting material on an astonishing array of topics.

At the end of the day, Ellen caught Leah in the hall. "How do you get your kids to write such great compositions?" she asked.

Leah explained how she first got her children writing on topics *they* cared about, and then gradually introduced "mini lessons" to help them become better authors. She had the students work in small groups to help each other plan compositions, and then the students critiqued each other's drafts, helped each other with editing, and finally "published" final versions.

"I'll tell you what," Leah offered, "I'll schedule my next writing class during your planning period. Come see what we're doing."

Ellen agreed. When the time came, she walked into Leah's class and was immediately overwhelmed by what she saw. Children were writing everywhere—on the floor, in groups, at separate tables. Many were talking with partners. Ms. Washington was conferencing with individual children. Ellen looked over the children's shoulders and saw one student writing about her pets, another writing a gory story about Ninjas, and another writing about a dream. A Mexican-American child was writing a funny story about her second-grade teacher's attempts to speak Spanish. One student was even writing a very good story about his summer vacation!

After school, Ellen met with Leah. She was full of questions. "How did you get students to do all that writing? How can you manage all that noise and activity? How did you learn to do this?" "I did go to a series of workshops on teaching writing," Leah said, "but if you think about it, everything I'm doing is basic educational psychology."

Ellen was amazed. "Educational psychology? I got an A in that course in college, but I don't see what it has to do with your writing program."

"Well, let's see," said Leah. "When I started my writing instruction this year, I read students some funny and intriguing stories written by other classes, to arouse their curiosity. I got them motivated by letting them write about whatever they wanted, and also by having "writing celebrations" in which students read their finished compositions to the class for applause and comment. I adapt to the needs of each learner by conferencing with students and helping them with the specific problems they're having. I use cooperative learning groups to let students give each other immediate feedback on their writing, to let them model effective writing for each other, and to get them to encourage each other to write. The groups also solve a lot of my management problems by keeping each other on task and dealing with many classroom routines. I use a flexible form of evaluation. Everybody eventually gets an A on his or her composition, but only when it meets a high standard, which may take many drafts. I adapt to students' developmental levels and cultural styles by encouraging them to write about things that matter to them—if dinosaurs or Nintendo is important right now, or if children are uncomfortable about being Muslim or Jewish at Christmas time, that's what they should write about!"

Ellen was impressed. She and Leah arranged to visit each other's classes a few more times to exchange ideas and observations, and in time Ellen's writers began to be almost as good as Leah's. But what was particularly important to her was the idea that educational psychology could really be useful in her day-to-day teaching. She dragged out her old textbook and found that concepts that seemed theoretical and abstract in ed psych class actually helped her think about problems of teaching.

---

educational psychology:
the study of learning and teaching.

What is **educational psychology**? An academic definition would perhaps say that educational psychology is the study of learners, learning, and teaching. However, for students who are or expect to be teachers, educational psychology is something more. It is the accumulated knowledge, wisdom, and seat-of-the-pants theory that every teacher should know to intelligently solve the daily problems of teaching. Educational psychology cannot tell teachers what to do, but it can give them the principles to use in making a good decision. Consider the case of Ellen Mathis and Leah Washington. Nothing in this or any other educational psychology text will tell teachers exactly how to teach creative writing to a particular group of third-graders. However, Ms. Washington uses concepts of educational psychology to consider how she will teach writing, to interpret and solve problems she runs into, and to explain to Ellen what she is doing. Educational psychologists carry out research on the nature of students, principles of learning, and methods of teaching to give educators the information they need to think critically about their craft and to make teaching decisions that will work for their students.

What Makes a Good Teacher?

What makes a good teacher? Is it warmth, humor, and caring about people? Is it planning, hard work, and self-discipline? What about leadership, enthusiasm, a contagious love of learning, and speaking ability? Most people would agree that all of these qualities are needed to make someone a good teacher, and they would certainly be correct. But these qualities are not enough.

Knowing the Subject Matters.   There is an old joke that goes something like this:

Q. What do you need to know to be able to teach a horse?

A. More than the horse!

> **Connections**
> Effective instruction is the topic of Chapter 8. Pedagogical strategies are also presented in Chapters 7 and 9 and throughout the text.

This joke makes the obvious point that the first thing a teacher must have is some knowledge or skills that the learner does not have; teachers must know the subject matter they expect to teach. But if you think about teaching horses (or children), you will soon realize that while subject matter knowledge is necessary, it is not enough. A cowboy might have a good idea of how a horse is supposed to act and what a horse is supposed to be able to do, but if he doesn't have the skills to make an untrained, scared, and unfriendly animal into a good saddle horse, he's going to end up with nothing but broken ribs and teeth marks for his troubles. Children are a little more forgiving than horses, but teaching them has this in common with teaching horses: Knowledge of how to transmit information and skills is as least as important as knowledge of the information and skills themselves. We have all had teachers (most often college professors, unfortunately) who were brilliant and thoroughly knowledgeable in their fields, but who could not teach. Ellen Mathis may know as much as Leah Washington about what good writing should look like, but she has a lot to learn about how to get third-graders to write well.

For effective teaching, subject matter knowledge is not a question of being a walking encyclopedia. Effective teachers not only know their subjects, they can also communicate their knowledge to students. In the movie *Stand and Deliver*, math teacher Jaime Escalante is teaching the concept of positive and negative numbers to students in a high school in a Los Angeles barrio. He explains that when you dig a hole, you might call the pile of dirt +1, the hole -1. What do you get when you put the dirt back in the hole? Zero. Escalante's ability to relate the abstract concept of positive and negative numbers to the experiences of his students is one example in which the ability to communicate knowledge goes far beyond simply knowing it.

Mastering the Teaching Skills.   The link between what the teacher wants students to learn and students' actual learning is called instruction, or **pedagogy.** Effective instruction is not a simple matter of one person with more knowledge transmitting that knowledge to another. If telling were teaching, this book would be unnecessary. Rather, effective instruction demands the use of many strategies. For example, to teach a lesson on long division to a diverse class of fourth-graders, teachers must accomplish many things. They must make sure that the class is orderly and that students know what behavior is expected of them. They must find out whether students have the multiplication and subtraction skills needed to learn long division, and if any do not, they must find a way to teach students those skills. They must present lessons on long division in a way that makes sense to students, using teaching strategies that help students remember what they have been taught. The lessons should also take into account the intellectual and social characteristics of students in the fourth grade and the intellectual, social, and cultural characteristics of their particular students. Teachers must make sure that students are interested in the lesson and are motivated to learn long division. They may ask questions or use quizzes or other assessments to see if students are learning what is being taught, and they must respond appropriately if these assessments show that students are having problems. After the series of lessons on long division ends, teachers should review this skill from time to time to ensure that it is remembered. These tasks—motivating students, managing the classroom, assessing prior knowledge, communicating ideas effectively, taking into account the characteristics of the learners, assessing learning outcomes, and reviewing information—must be attended to at all levels of education, in or out of schools. They apply as much to the training of astronauts as to the teaching of reading. *How* these tasks are accomplished, however, differs widely according to the ages of the students, the objectives of instruction, and other factors.

What makes a good teacher is the ability to accomplish all the tasks involved in effective instruction. Warmth, enthusiasm, and caring are essential, as is subject matter knowledge; but it is the successful accomplishment of *all* the tasks of teaching that makes for instructional effectiveness.

Can Good Teaching Be Taught?

Some people think that good teachers are born that way. Outstanding teachers sometimes seem to have a magic, a charisma, that mere mortals could never hope to achieve. Yet research over the past twenty years or so has begun to identify the specific behaviors and skills that make up the "magic" teacher. There is nothing an outstanding teacher does that any other teacher can't also do—it's just a question of knowing the principles of effective teaching and how to apply them. Take one small example. In a high school history class, two students in the back of the class are whispering to each other—and they are *not* whispering about the Treaty of Paris! The teacher slowly walks toward them without looking at them, continuing his lesson as he walks. The students stop whispering and pay attention. If you didn't know what to look for, you might miss this brief but critical interchange, and believe that the teacher just has a way with students, keeping their attention. But the teacher is simply applying principles of classroom management that anyone could learn: Maintain momentum in the lesson, deal with behavior problems using the mildest intervention that will work, and resolve minor problems before they become major ones. When Jaime Escalante gave the example of digging a hole to

pedagogy: the study of teaching and learning with applications to the instructional process.

illustrate the concept of positive and negative numbers, he was also applying several important principles of educational psychology: Make abstract ideas concrete by using many examples, relate the content of instruction to the students' background, state rules, give examples, and then restate rules.

Can good teaching be taught? The answer is definitely yes. Good teaching has to be observed and practiced, but there are principles of good teaching that teachers need to know, which can then be applied in the classroom. These principles are summarized in Figure 1.1.

Figure 1.1 Components of Good Teaching

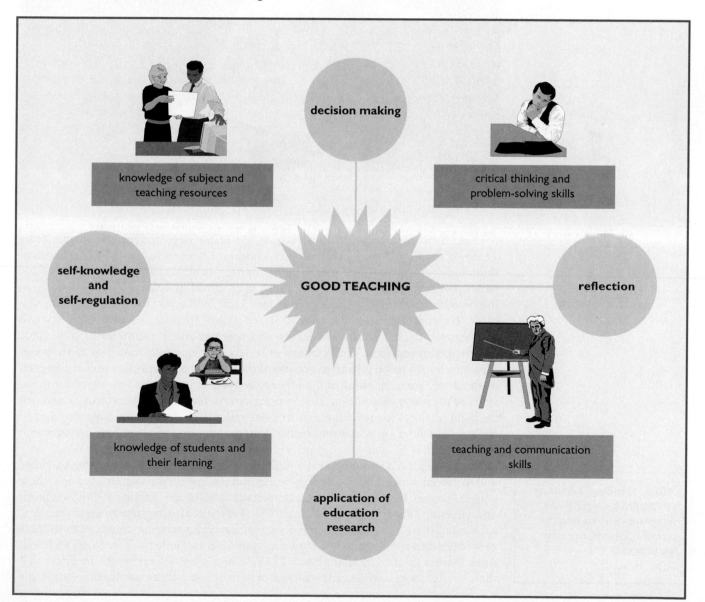

What characteristics of good teaching might this expert teacher possess? What behaviors might distinguish this teacher's attitudes and practices from those of a novice?

Teaching as Critical Thinking

There is no formula for good teaching, no seven steps to Teacher of the Year. Teaching involves dozens of decisions each hour. Effective teaching requires **critical thinking:** seeing situations clearly, identifying problems, and exploring possible solutions. A primary goal of this book is to develop critical thinking skills in tomorrow's teachers. This goal is addressed both by the text itself and by other features. The text highlights the ideas that are central to educational psychology and the research related to these ideas. It also presents many examples of how these ideas apply in practice. The emphasis is on teaching methods that have been evaluated and found to be effective, not just theory or suggestions. The text is designed to develop critical thinking skills for teaching by engaging the reader with discussions of the many dilemmas found in practice and research. No text can provide all the right answers for teaching, but this one tries to pose the right questions and to engage the reader by presenting realistic alternatives and the concepts and research behind them.

Many studies have looked at the differences between expert and novice teachers, and between more and less effective teachers. One theme comes through these studies: Expert teachers are critical thinkers (Floden and Klinzing, 1990; Leinhardt and Greeno, 1986; Swanson *et al.*, 1990). Teachers are constantly upgrading and examining their own teaching practices, reading and attending conferences to learn new ideas, and using their own students' responses to guide their instructional decisions (Sabers *et al.*, 1991; Shulman, 1987). There's an old saying to the effect that there are teachers with twenty years of experience and there are teachers with one

critical thinking: evaluating conclusions by logically and systematically examining the problem, the evidence, and the solution.

year of experience twenty times. Teachers who get better each year are the ones who are open to new ideas and who look at their own teaching critically. Perhaps the most important goal of this book is to start the habit of informed reflection with tomorrow's expert teachers.

Critical Thinking Features of This Text. Each feature in this text has components that support the theme of teachers as critical thinkers. The THEORY INTO PRACTICE feature, for instance, set off by a vertical rule in the margin, gives practical suggestions for classroom applications of theory and research in educational psychology. On the TEACHERS ON TEACHING page, real-life applications of theory and research are described by practicing teachers and school counselors from all over the country, including many recipients of "Teacher of the Year" awards. In each chapter teachers at different grade levels describe in some depth specific instances when they identified and ultimately met a teaching challenge. These inspiring true stories model teacher reflection and problem solving using principles of educational psychology.

The FOCUS ON . . . feature in each chapter includes Critical Thinking questions. FOCUS ON . . . focuses on controversial issues in educational psychology that have an impact on teaching effectiveness.

Problem Solving Practice. The CASE TO CONSIDER, which appears near the end of each chapter, presents a realistic dilemma in dialogue form. After reflection and discussion with classmates, you will have an opportunity to creatively express your solution to the case dilemma by extending the dialogue through writing or role play.

Teachers as Self-Regulated Learners

In addition to being critical thinkers and creative decision makers, good teachers are lifelong learners. They practice self- regulation. This means they take responsibility for their knowledge and skills. They set learning goals, motivate themselves to learn, monitor their own progress, assess their own mastery of new knowledge and skills, and continually redirect the course of their own learning. They also teach their students the study skills, thinking skills, and strategies that promote self-regulated learning.

This textbook applies the principles of self-regulated learning to model good teaching for you and to help you succeed in this course. Several text features address these goals. Suggestions follow for your optimal use of these features as you read each chapter.

1. *Outline:* The outline gives you a quick overview of the chapter content and sequence and includes all the headings and titled features.

2. *Main Headings:* The main headings in the outline and in the text are phrased as questions, which are keyed to the chapter objectives. The outline and objectives together let you know what to expect and prepare you for learning chapter content.

3. *Objectives:* In this text, the objectives are critical, because several other elements in the text and its supplements are directly keyed to them. The text itself teaches to the outcomes stated in the objectives. There is one general objective

Connections

Chapters 5, 7, and 8 also address topics in self-regulated learning and how to help your students become self-regulated learners.

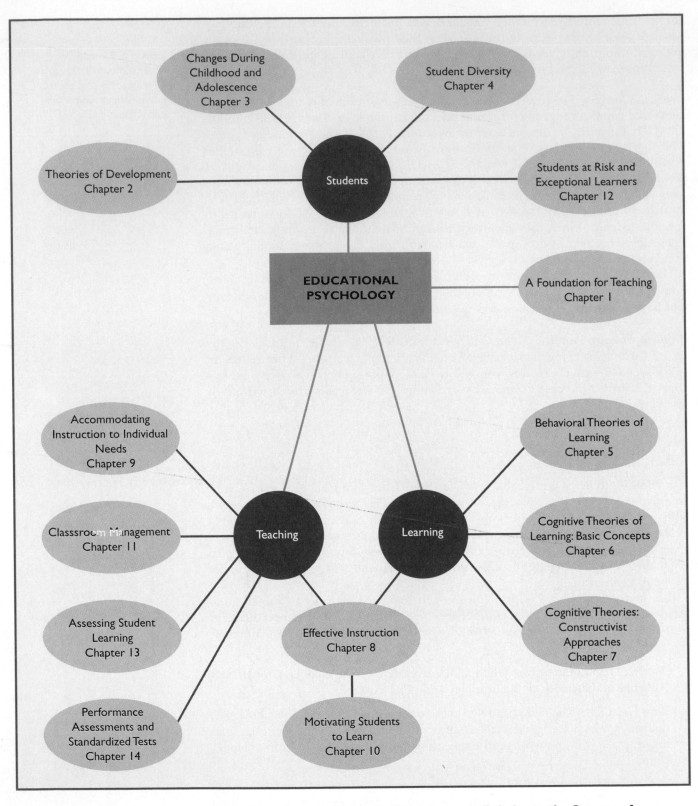

Figure 1.2   Concept Map: Text Organization in Relation to the Concept of Educational Psychology

for each main heading in the chapter. The objectives state the parameters of answers to the questions posed in the chapter's main headings.

4. *Self-Checks:* A good practice before reading the chapter is to skim for the main headings and read the "Self-Check" that appears at the end of each main section of text. It gives you a way to determine if you have mastered the objective and often suggests study strategies that will lead to understanding.

   This self-checking feature highlights the value of self-regulated learning, because you will be demonstrating or applying your learning to your own satisfaction. In addition, specific suggestions for creating your own study aids, such as comparison charts, concept maps, or diagrams, should help you understand the material. Figure 1.2 is an example of a concept map that illustrates the organization of this text in relation to the concept of educational psychology.

5. *Chapter Opening Scenarios:* As you begin to read the chapter, don't skip the opening scenario. This element introduces themes and challenges addressed in the chapter in real-life teaching contexts. The specific situation in the case study is reiterated in the body of the chapter as new concepts are brought to bear, ever enlarging your understanding. By the end of the chapter you should be able to reinterpret the situation in the scenario in terms of chapter content. A Self-Check in each chapter guides your reinterpretation.

6. *Student Annotations:* As you read the chapter, use the student annotations, printed in the margins, to clarify meanings of concepts and interrelationships among topics. The "Glossary" annotations define key terms that are boldfaced in the text. These same terms are listed alphabetically under KEY TERMS at the end of the chapter and in the GLOSSARY in the back of the book. The "Connections" annotations relate what you are reading to topics you have read previously and also refer you to other relevant topics or chapters.

7. *Summary and Key Terms:* After reading the chapter you will come to the chapter summary, which is in paragraph form and answers the questions posed in the main headings. The summary succinctly covers the chapter's main points and helps you review and prepare for tests. Particular sections of the summary may also be used in conjunction with their matching Objectives and Self-Checks, because all these elements are based on the questions posed in the main chapter headings. Following the summary, page references serve as study aids to help you locate definitions of key terms in the text.

8. *Self-Assessment with Answer Feedback:* The self-regulated learning theme of this text is brought to completion at the end of the chapter in a brief quiz. The eight items include multiple choice, matching, and short essay forms. Correct answers and answer guidelines for essay questions are provided in a section at the back of the book. In addition, ANSWER FEEDBACK is provided for objective items— an explanation of why each answer is correct and page references where explanations of answers may be found. You will find the answer feedback section in the back of the book.

9. *Success Guide:* The STUDY GUIDE for this text is closely integrated with the text objective and self-checking feature. For example, for each objective, the SUCCESS GUIDE provides a sample quiz, mastery criteria for your self-assessment, activities for mastering learning tasks, and suggested study strategies.

Focus On

Future Education Issues

New and not-so-new ideas about American education are likely to affect the teaching profession and the political economy of schooling. Three developments that so far have resisted a clear consensus of opinion are for-profit schools, school choice, and national testing.

The idea of privatizing public schools was proposed during the 1980s by the CEO of Whittle Communications, known controversially for beaming Channel One cable television, including commercial advertising, into classrooms. Disbelieving in the possibility of real education reform, Whittle and a consortium of private corporations have backed a plan to build an entirely new educational system to replace the old one. The Edison Project, which boasts a development team of educators, technology specialists, entrepreneurs, and journalists, plans to open 200 for-profit schools nationwide by 1996.

According to the plan each school will operate on a per-pupil budget no greater than the per-pupil cost to public schools. Random selection will govern admission, need-based scholarships will be awarded, and information about the new techniques developed will be available to everyone. Yet critics fear that privatizing public education will lead to even greater inequities than presently exist and that control over the curriculum will pass to private interests as well.

Voucher systems would enable parents to enroll their children in Whittle schools. In a related development, school-choice programs have proven popular, especially for parents whose neighborhood schools offer little promise of equal opportunity or upward mobility for their children. School-choice programs presently operate on the district level through alternative schools, magnet schools, and schools within schools. School choice is supposed to upgrade education through competition by making schools

try harder to attract students. The most divisive issue is whether to include private schools in school-choice plans. Milwaukee and Detroit are the first to use public funds to pay tuition at private schools on a limited basis. Generally, members of the public education establishment are strongly opposed to the idea.

Developments stimulating innovations such as for-profit schools and school-choice programs include reports of declining student achievement, which affects the workplace and international standings, among other things. Another response to the knowledge and ability gap is a growing movement toward national standards and national testing of students. Since the 1980s professional organizations, such as the National Council of Teachers of Mathematics and the National Science Teachers Association, have been working to develop nationwide curricula and standards. Meanwhile, routine national testing of teachers for recertification is in the wings. Critics ask if the federal government is the right party to dictate what and how teachers should teach and kids should learn.

Critical Thinking

What is your position on the issues of for-profit schools, school choice, and national standards? What more would you want to know about each issue before taking a stand?

John Coons, "Choice Plans Should Include Private Option," *Education Week*, January 17, 1990. Lynn Olsen, "Changing the System," *Teacher*, May/June 1992.

SELF-CHECK

Reassess the chapter opening scenario. In terms of the concepts introduced in this section, what qualities identify Ms. Washington as a good teacher?

What Is the Role of Research in Educational Psychology?

Teachers who are critical thinkers and self-regulated lifelong learners are likely to enter their classrooms equipped with knowledge about research in educational psychology. One problem educational psychologists face is that almost everyone thinks he or she is an expert on their subject. Most adults have spent many years in schools watching what teachers do. Add to that a certain amount of knowledge of human nature, and *voila!* everyone is an amateur educational psychologist. For this reason, professional educational psychologists are often accused of studying the obvious.

However, as we have painfully learned in recent years, the obvious isn't always true. For example, it was considered obvious that schools that spent more per pupil would produce greater student achievement than other schools, until Coleman *et al.* (1966) found this was not always so. Most people assume that if students are assigned to classes according to their ability, the resulting narrower range of abilities in a class will let the teacher adapt the instruction to the specific needs of the students, and, thereby, increase student achievement. This also turns out to be false. Many teachers believe that scolding students for misbehavior will improve student behavior. This is true for many students, but for others, scolding may be a *reward* for misbehavior and will actually increase it.

Some "obvious" truths even conflict with one another. For example, most people would agree that students learn better from a teacher's instruction than by working alone. This belief supports teacher-centered direct instructional strategies, in which a teacher actively works with the class as a whole. On the other hand, most people would also agree that students often need instruction tailored to their individual needs. This belief, also correct, would demand that teachers divide their time among individuals, or at least among groups of students with differing needs—which results in some students working independently, while others receive the teacher's attention. Now, if schools could provide tutors for every student, there would be no conflict; direct instruction and individualization could coexist. In practice, however, classrooms typically have twenty or more students and, as a result, more direct instruction (the first goal) almost always means less individualization (the second goal).

Goals of Research in Educational Psychology

The goal of research in educational psychology is to carefully examine obvious as well as less than obvious questions using objective methods to test ideas about the factors that contribute to learning. The products of this research are principles, laws, and theories. Principles explain relationships between factors, such as the effects of alternative grading systems on student motivation. Laws are simply principles that have been thoroughly tested and found to apply in a wide variety of situations.

Theories are sets of related principles and laws that explain broad aspects of learning, behavior, or other areas of interest. Without theories, the facts and principles discovered would be like disorganized specks on a canvas. Theories tie together these facts and principles to give us the big picture. However, the same facts and principles may be interpreted in different ways by different theorists. As in any science, progress in educational psychology is slow and uneven. A single study is rarely a breakthrough, but over time evidence accumulates on a subject and allows theorists to refine and extend their theories.

principle: explanation of the relationship between factors such as the effects of alternative grading systems on student motivations.

theories: sets of principles that explain and relate certain phenomena.

The Value of Research in Educational Psychology to the Teacher

It is probably true that the most important things teachers learn they learn on the job—in student teaching or during their first years in the classroom. However, teachers make hundreds of decisions every day and each decision has a theory behind it, whether or not the teacher is aware of it. The quality, accuracy, and usefulness of those theories are what determine, ultimately, the teacher's success. For example, one teacher may offer a prize to the student with best attendance, on the theory that rewarding attendance will increase it. Another may reward the student whose attendance is most *improved*, on the theory that it is poor attenders who most need incentives to come to class. Which teacher's plan is most likely to succeed? This depends in large part on the ability of each teacher to understand the unique combination of factors that shape the character of their classroom and, therefore, to apply the most appropriate theory.

Teaching as Decision Making.   The aim of educational psychology is to test the various theories that guide the actions of teachers and others involved in education. Here is another example of how this might work.

Mr. Harris teaches an eighth-grade social studies class. He has a problem with Tom, who frequently misbehaves. Today Tom makes a paper airplane and flies it across the room when Mr. Harris turns his back, to the delight of the entire class. What should Mr. Harris do?

Some actions Mr. Harris might take, and the theories on which are based, are as follows:

Action	*Theory*
1. Reprimand Tom.	1. A reprimand is a form of punishment. Tom will behave to avoid punishment.
2. Ignore Tom.	2. Attention may be rewarding to Tom. Ignoring him would deprive him of this reward
3. Send Tom to the office.	3. Being sent to the office is punishing. It also deprives Tom of the (apparent) support of his classmates.
4. Tell the class that it is everyone's responsibility to maintain a good learning environment, and if any student misbehaves, five minutes will be subtracted from recess.	4. Tom is misbehaving to get his classmates' attention. If the whole class loses out when he misbehaves, the class will keep him in line.
5. Explain to the class that Tom's behavior is interfering with lessons that all students need to know, and that his behavior goes against the rules the class set for itself at the beginning of the year.	5. The class holds standards of behavior that conflict with both Tom's behavior in class and the class's reaction to it. By reminding the class of its own needs (to learn the lesson) and its own rules set at the beginning of the year, the teacher may make Tom see that his behavior is not really supported by the class.

Connections

Connections: This example of teacher reflection and decision making is drawn from theory and research discussed in Chapter 5 (Behavioral Learning Theories) and Chapter 11 (Classroom Management).

Each of these actions is a common response to misbehavior. But which theory (and, therefore, which action) is correct?

The key may be in the fact that his classmates laugh when Tom misbehaves. This is a clue that Tom is seeking their attention. If Mr. Harris scolds Tom, this may increase his status in the eyes of his peers and may reward his behavior. Ignoring misbehavior might be a good idea if a student is acting up to get the teacher's attention, but in this case it is the class's attention that Tom is apparently seeking. Sending Tom to the office does deprive him of his classmates' attention, and thus might be effective. But what if Tom is looking for a way to get out of class to avoid work? What if he struts out with a chip on his shoulder, to the obvious approval of his classmates? Making the entire class responsible for each student's behavior is likely to deprive Tom of his support and to improve his behavior. But some students may feel it is unfair to punish them for another student's misbehavior. Finally, reminding the class (and Tom) of its own interest in learning and its usual standards of behavior might work if the class does in fact value academic achievement and good behavior.

Research in education and psychology bears directly on the decision Mr. Harris must make. Developmental research indicates that as students enter adolescence, the peer group becomes all-important to them and they try to establish their independence from adult control, often by flouting or ignoring rules. Basic research on behavioral learning theories shows that when a behavior is repeated many times, there must be some reward that is encouraging the behavior, and that to eliminate a behavior, the reward must first be identified and eliminated. This research would also suggest that Mr. Harris consider certain problems concerning the use of punishment to stop undesirable behavior. Research on specific classroom management strategies has identified effective methods to use both to prevent a student like Tom from misbehaving in the first place and to deal with his misbehavior when it does occur. Finally, research on rule setting and classroom standards indicates that student participation in setting rules can help convince each student that the class as a whole values academic achievement and appropriate behavior, and this can help keep individual students in line.

Armed with this information, Mr. Harris can choose an effective response to Tom's behavior that is based on an understanding of why Tom is doing what he is doing and what strategies are available to deal with the situation. Research does not give Mr. Harris a specific solution; that requires his own experience and judgment. But research does give Mr. Harris basic concepts of human behavior to help him understand Tom's motivations, and an array of proven methods that might solve the problem.

Research + Common Sense = Effective Teaching. As the case of Mr. Harris illustrates, no theory, no research, no book can tell teachers what to do in a given situation. Making the right decisions depends on the context within which the problem arises, the objectives the teacher has in mind, and many other factors, all of which must be assessed in the light of educated common sense. For example, research in mathematics instruction usually finds that a rapid pace of instruction increases achievement (Good *et al.,* 1983). Yet a teacher may quite legitimately slow down and spend a lot of time on a concept that is particularly critical, or may even let students take time to discover a mathematical principle on their own. It is usually much more efficient to directly teach students skills or information than to let them make discoveries for themselves, but if the teacher wants students to know how to

These teachers are discussing
instructional approaches to meet
the challenges of student diversity in their school. How will they
know which approaches are likely to work best for them and
their students?

find information or to figure things out for themselves, then the research findings
about pace can be temporarily shelved.

The point is that while research in educational psychology can sometimes be
translated directly to the classroom, it is best to apply the principles with a hefty
dose of common sense and a clear view of what is being taught to whom for what
purpose.

Theory Into Practice

Tracing Your Development as a Teacher

The art and science of teaching implies a need to continually blend new information from educational research into daily practice through thoughtful evaluation and reflection of daily experiences and choices in the classroom. Only by
reviewing your actions in the classroom can you formulate better approaches for
the future. How can teachers review their skill development and become truly
reflective practitioners? There are many ways and tools:

1. Create a portfolio of classroom activities: Include your directions, listing of
   materials, and examples of student products (good, average, and poor
   examples). Compare student products as you experiment with refining
   directions, materials, and presentation.

2. Videotape your presentations looking for the amount of eye contact you
   make with students, your nonverbal expressions and body language, your
   movements around the room, and the reactions of your students to the lesson. Compare videotapes as you target certain behaviors for improvement.

3. Audiotape your lessons and listen to your voice quality. Listen for vocabulary;
   clarity; intonation; use of "signal words" such as *listen, look, first, second,
   most importantly, especially,* which cue students to relevant information; and
   loudness. Again, compare tapes as you target areas for improvement.

4. Ask another teacher to observe you, recording key factors such as your
   student questioning patterns, your pattern of movement around the room,

your responses to student questioning, and the overall pace of the lesson. Discuss this quantitative data as well as overall qualitative impressions of your class with your peer observer.

5. Use a "magic circle" in your classroom to keep in touch with your teaching effectiveness. Choose four or five students to meet briefly with you (perhaps on a rotating basis) concerning how the class is feeling about instruction, assignments, and morale. Alter your approaches based on their feedback. Record their comments for future reference.

6. Keep a journal of your feelings and classroom failures and successes. Writing helps to refine and clarify our thoughts and leads to effective problem solving. Your journal will chronicle your development as a teacher.

7. Put aside five minutes at the beginning and end of each day to mentally review your goals for the day and evaluate your success.

SELF-CHECK

Suggest some commonsense ways that the following findings from educational psychology research might help you be more effective as a teacher:

- Children are generally not capable of formal logic and hypothetical reasoning before the age of 11.
- Students better observe rules they have helped to set and are better motivated to learn topics they have helped to select.
- Misbehavior for which attention is the reward will diminish if attention is not given. What does research tell us about teaching effectiveness?

What Research Methods Are Used in Educational Psychology?

How do we know what we know in educational psychology? As in any scientific field, knowledge comes from many sources. Sometimes researchers study schools, teachers, or students as they are, and sometimes they create special programs, or **treatments,** and study their effects on one or more variables (a **variable** is anything that can have more than one value, such as age, sex, achievement level, or attitudes). The following sections discuss the principal methods used by educational researchers to learn about schools, teachers, students, and instruction (see Slavin, 1992).

Experiments

In an **experiment,** researchers can create special treatments and analyze their effects. For example, Lepper *et al.* (1973) set up an experimental situation in which children used felt-tipped markers to draw pictures. Some children were given a prize (a "good player award") for drawing pictures, and others were not. At the

treatment: a special program that is the subject of an experiment.

variable: something that can have more than one value.

experiment: procedure used to test the effects of a treatment.

If these students are among 30 students participating in a study on the effectiveness of a computer program in aiding instruction—in which the participants are tested before and after using the program—what type of research is being conducted? What type of research would be involved if participants' results were compared to those of the students in a control group who did not use the program?

---

random assignment: selection by chance into different treatment groups to try to ensure equality of the groups.

laboratory experiment: experiment in which conditions are highly controlled.

internal validity: the degree to which an experiment's results can be attributed to the treatment in question, not to other factors.

---

end of the experiment, all students were allowed to choose among a number of activities, including drawing with felt-tipped markers. The children who had received the prizes chose to continue drawing with felt-tipped markers about half as frequently as did those who had not received prizes. This was interpreted as showing that rewarding individuals for doing a task they already liked could reduce their interest in doing the task when they were no longer rewarded.

Several important aspects of experiments are illustrated by the Lepper study. First, the children were randomly assigned to receive prizes or not. For example, the children's names might have been put on slips of paper that were dropped into a hat and then drawn at random for assignment to a "prize" or "no-prize" group. **Random assignment** ensured that the two groups were essentially equivalent before the experiment began. This is critical, because if we were not sure that the two groups were equal before the experiment, we would not be able to tell if it was the prizes that made the difference in their subsequent behavior.

A second feature of this study that is characteristic of experiments is that everything other than the treatment itself (the prizes) was kept the same for the "prize" and "no-prize" groups. The children played in the same rooms with the same materials and with the same adults present. The researcher who gave the prize spent the same amount of time watching the non-prize children draw. Only the prize itself was different for the two groups. The goal was to be sure that it was the treatment, and not some other factor, that explained the difference between the two groups.

Laboratory Experiments. The Lepper *et al.* (1973) study is an example of a **laboratory experiment.** Even though it took place in a school building, a highly artificial, structured setting was created that existed for a very brief period of time. The advantage of laboratory experiments is that they permit researchers to exert a very high degree of control over all the factors involved in the study. Such studies are high in **internal validity,** which is to say that any differences they find can, with confidence, be attributed to the treatments themselves (rather than other factors). The primary limitation of laboratory experiments is that they are typically so artificial and so brief that their results may have little relevance to real-life situations. For example, the Lepper *et al.* (1973) study, which was later repeated several times, was used to support a theory that rewards can diminish individuals' interest in an activity when the rewards are withdrawn. This theory served as the basis for attacks on the use of classroom rewards, such as grades and stars. However, later research in real classrooms using real rewards has generally failed to find such effects. This does not discredit the Lepper *et al.* (1973) study itself, but does show that theories based on artificial laboratory experiments cannot be assumed to apply to all situations in real life but must be tested in the real settings.

Randomized Field Experiments. Another kind of experiment often used in educational research is the **randomized field experiment,** in which instructional programs or other practical treatments are evaluated over relatively long periods in real classes under realistic conditions. For example, Good and Grouws (1979) used a randomized field experiment to test their Missouri Mathematics Program, or MMP (discussed in Chapter 8). Forty fourth-grade teachers volunteered to participate. These teachers were randomly assigned to receive training in the MMP or to continue teaching as before. In experiments, the group that receives a treatment is called the **experimental group,** while the one that receives no treatment is called the **control group.**

In the Good and Grouws (1979) study, all teachers' classes took a mathematics pretest. Sixteen weeks later, they took the same test again. Experimental classes, whose teachers had received the MMP training, gained more on the second tests than did the control classes, so the experimenters concluded that the MMP was more effective than traditional methods of teaching mathematics.

Note the similarities and differences between the Good and Grouws (1979) randomized field experiment and the Lepper *et al.* (1973) laboratory experiment. Both used random assignment to make sure that the experimental and control groups were essentially equal at the start of the study. Both tried to make all factors except the treatment equal for the experimental and control groups, but the Good and Grouws study was (by its very nature as a field experiment) less able to do this. For example, experimental and control teachers taught in different schools with different principals and students. Random assignment made it likely that these factors would balance out, but the fact remains that in a field setting control is never as great as in a laboratory situation. On the other hand, the fact that the Good and Grouws study took place over a long period of time in real classrooms means that its **external validity** is far greater than that of the Lepper *et al.* study. That is, the results of the Good and Grouws study have direct relevance to instruction in fourth-grade mathematics, and probably to mathematics instruction at other grade levels as well.

Both laboratory experiments and randomized field experiments make important contributions to the science of educational psychology. Laboratory experiments are primarily important in building and testing theories, while randomized field experiments are the "acid test" for evaluating practical programs or improvements in instruction. For example the "writing process" method Leah Washington was using has been evaluated many times in comparison to traditional methods and found to be highly effective (Hillocks, 1984). This is not a guarantee that this method will work in every situation, but it does give educators a good direction to follow to improve writing.

Single-Case Experiments.   One type of experiment often used in educational research is the **single-case experiment** (Hersen and Barlow, 1976). In one typical form of this type of experiment, a single student's behavior might be observed for several days. Then a special program is begun, and the student's behavior under the new program is observed. Finally, the new program is withdrawn. If the student's behavior improved under the special program, but the improvement disappeared when the program was withdrawn, it suggests that the program affected the student's behavior. Sometimes the "single case" can be several students, an entire class, or a school that is given the same treatment.

An example of a single-case experiment is a study by Barrish *et al.* (1969). In this study, a fourth-grade class was the single case. Observers recorded the percent of time that at least one student in the class was "talking out" (talking without permission) during reading and math periods. After ten days, a special program was introduced. The class was divided into two large teams, and whenever any student on a team misbehaved, the team was given a check mark. At the end of each day, the team with the fewest check marks (or both teams if both received fewer than five marks) could take part in a thirty-minute free period.

The results of this study are illustrated in Figure 1.3. Before the "Good Behavior Game" began (baseline), at least one student in the math class was talking out 96 percent of the time, and at least one student was out-of-seat without permission 82 percent of the time. When the game was begun in math, the class's behavior improved dramatically. When the game was withdrawn, the class's behavior got worse again but improved once more when it was reintroduced. Note that when

randomized field experiment: experiment conducted under realistic conditions in which individuals are assigned by chance to receive different practical treatments or programs.

experimental group: group that receives treatment during an experiment.

control group: group that receives no special treatment during an experiment.

external validity: degree to which results of an experiment can be applied to real-life situations.

single-case experiment: study of a treatment's effect on one person or one group by contrasting behavior before, during, and after the treatment is applied.

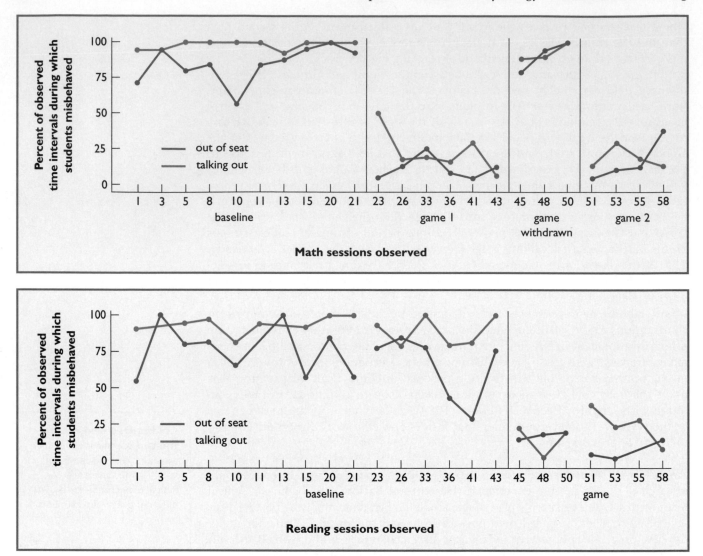

Figure 1.3   Results of Successful Single-Case Experiments

The effect of rewarding good behavior in fourth-grade math and reading classes is clear from these graphs. They show that misbehavior was high during the baseline period (before the "Good Behavior Game" was introduced), but fell during the game. For instance, in reading session 13, before the game was introduced, students were out of their seats during nearly 100 percent of the observed time intervals. In reading session 53, however, when the game was in use, the percentage of time intervals in which students were out-of-seat approached zero. In single-case experiments on treatments affecting behaviors that can be frequently measured, graphs like these can prove a treatment's effectiveness.

Adapted from Barrish *et al.,* 1969.

the game was introduced in reading class, the students' behaviors also improved. The fact that the program also made a difference in reading gives us even greater confidence that the "Good Behavior Game" is effective.

One important limitation of the single-case experiment is that it can only be used to study outcomes that can be frequently measured. For this reason, most single-case studies involve observable behaviors, such as talking out and being out-of-seat, which can be measured every day or many times per day.

Correlational Studies

Perhaps the most frequently used research method in educational psychology is the **correlational study.** In contrast to an experiment, where the researcher deliberately changes one variable to see how this change will affect other variables, in correlational research the researcher studies variables *as they are* to see whether they are related. Variables can be positively correlated, negatively correlated, or uncorrelated. An example of a **positive correlation** is the relationship between reading achievement and mathematics achievement. This means that, in general, someone who is better than average in reading will also be better than average in math. Of course, there are students who are good readers but not good in math, and vice versa, but *on the average,* skills in one academic area are positively correlated with skills in other academic areas; when one variable is high, the other tends also to be high. An example of a **negative correlation** is days absent and grades. The more days a student is absent, the lower his or her grades are likely to be; when one variable is high, the other tends to be low. When two variables are **uncorrelated**, there is no correspondence between them. For example, student achievement in Poughkeepsie, N.Y., is probably completely unrelated to the level of student motivation in Portland, Oregon.

One example of correlational research is a study by Lahaderne (1968), who investigated the relationship between students' attentiveness in class and their achievement and IQ. She observed 125 students in four sixth-grade classes to see how much of the time students were paying attention (for example, listening to the teacher and doing assigned work). She then calculated attentiveness with achievement in reading, arithmetic, and language, and with students' IQs and attitudes toward school. The advantage of correlational studies is that they allow the researcher to study variables as they are, without creating artificial situations. Many important research questions can only be studied in correlational studies. For example, if we wanted to study the relationship between gender and math achievement, we could hardly randomly assign students to be boys or girls! Also, correlational studies let researchers study the interrelationships of many variables at the same time.

The principal disadvantage of correlational methods is that while they may tell us that two variables are related, they do not tell us what *causes* what. The Lahaderne study of attentiveness, achievement, and IQ raised the question: Does student attentiveness *cause* high achievement, or are high-ability, high-achieving students simply more attentive than other students? A correlational study cannot answer this question completely. However, correlational researchers do typically use statistical methods to try to determine what causes what. In Lahaderne's study, it would have been possible to find out whether among students with the same IQ, attentiveness is related to achievement. For example, given two students of average intelligence, would the one who is more attentive tend to achieve more? If not, then we might conclude that the relationship between attentiveness and achievement is simply the result of high-IQ students being more attentive and higher-achieving than other students, not to any effect of attention on achievement.

Figure 1.4 illustrates two possible explanations for the correlation between attentiveness, achievement, and IQ. In Explanation A, attentiveness causes achievement. In Explanation B, both attentiveness and achievement are assumed to be caused by

correlational study: research into the relationships between variables as they naturally occur.

positive correlation: relationship in which high scores on one variable correspond to high scores on another.

negative correlation: relationship in which high scores on one variable correspond to low scores on another.

uncorrelated variables: lack of relationship between two variables.

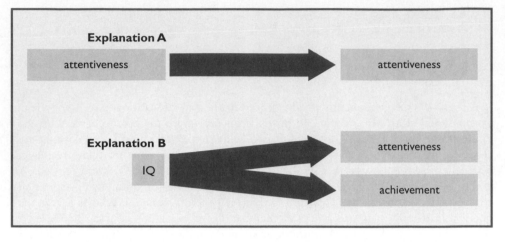

Figure 1.4   Possible Explanations for Correlations Among Attentiveness, Achievement, and IQ

Correlational studies can show that variables are related, but such studies cannot prove what causes what. In Lahaderne's (1968) study, for example, did the attentiveness of the students cause higher achievement scores (Explanation A), or did a third factor, intelligence, determine both attentiveness and performance on achievement tests (as diagrammed in Explanation B)? Both explanations are partially correct.

a third variable, IQ. Which is correct? Evidence from other research on this relationship suggests that both explanations are partially correct, that even when the effect of IQ is removed, student attentiveness is related to achievement.

Descriptive Research

Experimental and correlational research look for relationships between variables. However, some research in educational psychology simply seeks to describe something of interest. One example of **descriptive research** is a survey or interview. Another, called ethnography (Taft, 1987; Bogdan and Biklen, 1982), involves observation of a social setting (such as a classroom or school) over an extended period. An example of descriptive research that combined observation with interviews is a study by Metz (1978) of three newly desegregated junior high schools. The author observed students and teachers in and out of class; interviewed students, teachers, principals, counselors, and others; attended assemblies and faculty meetings; and obtained and analyzed handbooks, yearbooks, and other written materials. In this way, she was able to describe the meaning and consequences of desegregation in extraordinary detail.

Jonathan Kozol (1991) wrote a descriptive study of life in well-funded and poorly funded schools that paints a devastating portrait of inequality in America's educational system. Jeannie Oakes (1985) described teachers' practices in tracked and untracked middle schools. These and many other descriptive studies provide much more of a complete story of what happens in schools and classrooms than could a study that boiled down the findings into cold, hard numbers. Descriptive research usually does not have the scientific objectivity of correlational or experimental research, but it makes up for this in richness of detail and interpretation (Bogdan and Biklen, 1982; Strauss and Corbin, 1990).

descriptive research:
study aimed at identifying and gathering detailed information about something of interest.

Teachers on Teaching

How has educational psychological theory and research helped you In your teaching?

A few years ago, I was selected to participate in a national research project being implemented in my school district—a five-year study of the effects of cooperative learning among Hispanic students using a program known as CIRC (Cooperative Integrated Reading and Composition). Educational researchers are working with teachers like me to develop a process for effective bilingual and second-language instruction through cooperative learning. My students and I have helped in piloting, giving feedback, and experimenting with assessments. Originally, CIRC was developed to be used with monolingual English students, but this model is now being adapted to classrooms with large numbers of language-minority students. This adaptation has required extensive teacher and staff development so that I and other teachers could become researchers in our own classrooms. My involvement in this research has made me more analytical about what I observe in the classroom and more appreciative of the importance of educational psychology theory and research in what I do. The greatest result, through, has been the increased self-esteem and achievement of my students. Even the most reluctant learner becomes actively involved in learning. Students know they are important, a part of the classroom *familia*. Academically, they are now reading and writing in two languages. As a professional, my commitment and excitement for teaching and learning is stronger. I'm on fire!

Rosa E. Lujan, Bilingual Teacher, Grades 5–6
Ysleta Elementary School, El Paso, Texas
1992 Texas Teacher of the Year

I teach mainstreamed children with mild disabilities. Much educational research supports the teaching principles I have followed. When planning for the year, for example, establish classroom procedures and structure that will accommodate the learning styles and ability levels of a variety of students. Also enlist the support of parents before the beginning of the school year. Establish a firm, sensible, and consistent discipline plan with negative consequences and positive group and individual rewards. Teach the children how they are expected to behave at learning centers, when lining up, during seatwork time, and so on.

Be eclectic. Integrate the best of all instructional modes and teaching techniques. Keep taking classes and reading research so you can keep learning how to teach. Provide appropriate basic skills instruction. Plan instruction so all students can have active participation and can also work at their own ability levels. Use real books for reading instruction. Be sure seatwork is meaningful, interesting, and tied to specific curriculum goals and objectives. Train students to help each other when difficulties arise. Be a strong content-area teacher. Assessments should be brief, directly related to the goals, and, when possible, performance-based. All reading and content areas should have writing components and real-life situations for practicing writing skills. Homework should be directly related to content and skills being taught and should also have a parental component. Finally, it is critical to approach each year with the notion that all students can learn and that how you teach can and will make a difference in student success.

K. Janie Hill, Teacher, Grade 2 Dillingham Elementary School,
Dillingham, Alaska Alaska 1991 Teacher of the Year

Descriptive research is extensively used in developmental psychology (see Chapters 2 and 3) to identify characteristics of children at different ages. The most important research in developmental psychology was done by the Swiss psychologist Jean Piaget (1952b), who began by carefully observing his own children. As a result of his observations, he developed a theory that describes the cognitive development of children from infancy through adolescence.

SELF-CHECK

Construct a comparison chart for "Experimental," "Correlational," and "Descriptive" research, and enter information in the following four categories: goals of research, forms studies take, kinds of findings, examples. Then write a paragraph explaining why correlations must not be confused with causes.

Why Is Teaching the Hardest Job in the World, and Why Do Teachers Secretly Love It?

This book was written to communicate what we know about students, about the learning process, and, most importantly, about classroom instruction to people who are now or will soon be doing one of the most important jobs in the world—teaching the next generation. Teaching is one of the toughest jobs there is because a teacher must do so many things well. A teacher must be a leader, an effective speaker, a quick diagnostician, a tactful diplomat, and a firm but fair disciplinarian. Teachers must know their subject and, even more importantly, know their craft. Teachers have to be "on" all the time and they do not leave their jobs behind when they go home at the end of the day.

Yet most teachers love what they do. Society may not always give them the respect they deserve, nor pay them adequately, nor provide them with the facilities they need to do their job well. But it always gives teachers its children. Let's face it, children are fun. Their changes, their challenges, their successes, are fascinating to watch and to participate in. Teachers matter, and they know they matter. It is a humbling experience to write a book for people who will make such an important difference to our future. This book is dedicated to teachers, in the hope that the information and tools it contains will help the next generation of teachers do the best possible job with the next generation of students.

Summary

What Makes a Good Teacher?
Good teachers know their subject matter and have mastered pedagogical skills. They accomplish all the tasks involved in effective instruction with warmth, enthusiasm, and caring. They are critical thinkers and self-regulated and use principles of educational psychology in their decision making and teaching. They combine research and common sense.

What Is the Role of Research in Educational Psychology?
Educational psychology is the systematic study of learners, learning, and teaching. It focuses on the processes by which information, skills, values, and attitudes are communicated between teachers and students in the classroom and on applications of the principles of psychology to instructional practices.

What Research Methods Are Used in Educational Psychology?

Experimental research involves testing particular educational programs or treatments. Random assignment of experimental subjects into groups before the testing helps ensure that groups are equivalent and findings will be valid. An experimental group receiving the treatment is matched with a control group whose members do not receive treatment. Laboratory experiments are highly structured and short-term. All the variables involved are strictly controlled. Randomized field experiments are less structured and take place over a long period of time under realistic conditions in which not all variables can be controlled. A single-case experiment involves observation of one student or group of students over a specified period before and after treatment. Correlational studies examine variables to see whether they are related. Variables can be positively correlated, negatively correlated, or uncorrelated. Correlational studies provide information about variables without manipulating them or creating artificial situations. They do not indicate, however, the causes of relationships between variables. Descriptive research uses surveys, interviews, or observations to describe behavior in social settings.

Key Terms

control group, 18
correlational study, 21
critical thinking, 8
descriptive research, 22
educational psychology, 4
experiment, 17
experimental group, 18
external validity, 19
internal validity, 18
laboratory experiment, 18
negative correlation, 21

pedagogy, 6
positive correlation, 21
principles, 13
random assignment, 18
randomized field experiment, 18
single-case experiment, 19
theories, 13
treatment, 17
uncorrelated variables, 21
variable, 17

Self–Assessment

1. Write a paragraph that begins with the following topic sentence: Effective teaching requires critical thinking.

2. A product of educational psychology research that explains relationships between factors that influence behavior or its outcomes is called a
   a. fact.
   b. principle.
   c. theory.
   d. law.

3. Which of the following pairs correctly matches a type of research to an advantage that it offers?
   a. laboratory experiment: has high internal validity
   b. randomized field experiment: exercises rigorous control
   c. descriptive study: shows relationships between variables
   d. single-case experiment: involves infrequent assessments

4. Match the following types of experiments with the situations that illustrate each (a situation may be used more than once or not at all).

   _____ randomized field experiment
   _____ descriptive research
   _____ laboratory experiment
   _____ correlational study
   a. observing and noting how preschoolers play
   b. recording the number of times a student misbehaves before, during, and after the administration of a special reinforcement program
   c. determining the relationship between reading ability and math achievement
   d. evaluating a new teaching technique for several months under typical classroom conditions
   e. evaluating a new teaching technique for a short period of time under highly controlled conditions

5. Students in Ms. Jameson's class receive a check mark for each day they *fail* to turn in homework. How is the number of check marks received by midterm likely to correlate with midterm test scores in that class?
   a. positively
   b. negatively
   c. no correlation

6. Studies in educational psychology that offer the greatest internal validity are
   a. randomized field experiments.
   b. laboratory experiments.
   c. ethnographies.
   d. correlational studies.

7. In a hypothetical school-wide correlational study, the relationship between the number of days a student was absent during a marking period and decreases in the student's class ranking from one marking period and the next was shown on average to have a negative correlation. This would mean that
   a. absenteeism causes lower class rankings.
   b. the study does not have external validity.
   c. class rankings tend to rise as attendance increases.
   d. class rank decreases absenteeism.

8. During reading circle, Mr. Traub usually calls on children randomly rather than in the order they are sitting. This simple practice seems to make perfect common sense, so he never gives it much thought. He assumes that random calling makes the children pay attention and that such a small thing could not possibly affect his students' achievement in reading. Suggest a research design for finding out if Mr. Traub is right. What do you think your research would show?

2

Theories of Development

Chapter Objectives

▲ Give an overview of some factors involved in human development and identify Piaget, Vygotsky, Erikson, and Kohlberg as key theorists.

▲ Identify the behaviors and thought processes of preschool, elementary school, middle school, and secondary school children in terms of Piaget's stages of development.

▲ Evaluate Piaget's theory and apply Piagetian principles appropriately in teaching contexts.

▲ Compare and contrast the views of Vygotsky and Piaget, and apply Vygotskian principles appropriately in teaching contexts.

▲ Identify the behaviors and relationships of people at different ages in terms of Erikson's stages of psychosocial development, and evaluate and apply Eriksonian principles appropriately in teaching contexts.

▲ Compare and contrast the views of Piaget and Kohlberg on the development of moral reasoning, identify the characteristics of moral reasoning at each stage, and evaluate theories of moral development and their implications for teachers.

In the first week of school Mr. Jones tried to teach his first-graders how to behave in class. He said, "When I ask a question, I want you to raise your *right* hand, and I'll call on you. Can you all raise your right hands, as I am doing?" Thirty hands went up. They were all *left* hands.

• Because her students were getting careless about handing in their homework, Ms. Lewis decided to lay down the law to her fourth-grade class. "Anyone who does not hand in all his or her homework this week will not be allowed to go on the field trip." It so happened that one girl's mother became ill and was taken to the hospital that week. As a result of her family's confusion and concern, the girl failed to hand in one of her homework assignments. Ms. Lewis explained to the class that she would make an exception in this case because of the girl's mother's illness, but the class wouldn't hear of it. "Rules are rules," they said. "She didn't hand in her homework, so she can't go!"

• Ms. Quintera started her eighth-grade English class one day with an excited announcement: "Class, I wanted to tell you all that we have a poet in our midst. Frank wrote such a wonderful poem that I thought I'd read it to you all." Ms.

Quintera read Frank's poem, which was indeed very good. However, she noticed that Frank was turning bright red and looking distinctly uncomfortable. A few of the other students in the class snickered. Later Ms. Quintera asked Frank if he would like to write another poem for a citywide poetry contest. He said he'd rather not because he really didn't think he was that good, and besides, he didn't have the time.

What Are Some Views of Human Development?

Development refers to the ways people grow, adapt, and change during their lifetimes. People grow, adapt, and change through physical development, personality development, socioemotional development, cognitive development (thinking), and language development.

Aspects of Development.   Children are not miniature adults. They think differently, they see the world differently, and they live by different moral and ethical principles than adults do.

The three scenarios just presented illustrate a few of the many aspects of children's thinking that differ from those of adults. When Mr. Jones raised his right hand, his first-graders imitated his action *as they perceived it;* they were unable to see that since he was facing them, his right hand would be to their left. The situation in Ms. Lewis's class illustrates a stage in children's moral development when rules are rules and extenuating circumstances don't count. Ms. Quintera was surprised that her praise of Frank's poem had an effect opposite to what she intended. Had she paused to consider the situation, she might have realized that highlighting Frank's achievement could cast him in the role of "teacher's pet," a dependent role that students in early adolescence strongly resist.

One of the first requirements of effective teaching is that the teacher understand how students think and how they view the world. There are ages at which children simply do not have the maturity to learn certain concepts no matter how well or how long the concepts are taught. Effective teaching strategies must take into account students' ages and stages of development. For example, Ms. Quintera's public recognition of Frank's poetry might have been quite appropriate if Frank had been three years younger or three years older. A bright fourth-grader might appear to be able to learn any kind of mathematics, but, in fact, might not have the developmental readiness to do the abstract thinking required for algebra. This chapter presents three major theories of human development that are widely accepted: Jean Piaget's and Lev Vygotsky's theories of cognitive development, Erik Erikson's theory of personal and social development, and Lawrence Kohlberg's theory of moral development. Each of these theories describes a set of stages through which children and adolescents go as they grow and develop. Chapter 3 discusses human development from a different perspective, describing the development of language and physical, social, cognitive, and other skills in early childhood, middle childhood, and adolescence.

development: orderly and lasting growth, adaptation, and change over the course of a lifetime.

Continuous and Discontinuous Theories.   Long ago human development was assumed to follow a smooth progression from infancy to adulthood. By the age of six or seven children were believed to think in much the same way as adults, and it was assumed that all they lacked was experience and education. This belief in a smooth progression is called a **continuous theory of development.**

In this century, however, developmental psychologists discovered that children do not develop gradually, but rather go through a series of stages of development. The abilities that children gain in each subsequent stage are not simply "more of the same"; at each stage children develop qualitatively different understandings, abilities, and beliefs. Skipping stages is impossible, although at any given point the same child may exhibit behaviors characteristic of more than one stage (Epstein, 1990).

A view of development that emphasizes these steps is called a **discontinuous (stage) theory of development.** Piaget, Vygotsky, Erikson, and Kohlberg each focus on a different aspect of development. Nevertheless, all are stage theorists because they share the belief that distinct stages of development can be identified and described. This agreement does not extend, however, to the particulars of their theories, which differ significantly in the numbers of stages and in their details.

After decades out of favor, continuous theories of development are returning to prominence as developmental psychologists find that development, especially cognitive development, proceeds at different rates on different tasks (see Gelman and Baillargeon, 1983; Siegler, 1991). This chapter emphasizes discontinuous theories of development, but it is important to keep in mind the fact that the question of continuous versus discontinuous development is by no means settled.

Self-Check

Begin a four-column comparison chart, listing PIAGET, VYGOTSKY, ERIKSON, and KOHLBERG, each at the head of a column. As the first bit of information in the chart, identify the theory each proposed, the type of development involved, and whether the theory is continuous or discontinuous. After you finish reading the chapter, explain the three opening scenarios in terms of the theories and concepts presented in the chapter.

How Did Piaget View Cognitive Development?

Jean Piaget is probably the best known child psychologist who ever lived. He was born in Switzerland in 1896, and by age eleven had already published his first scientific paper, about birds. His education was as a biologist, and he became an expert on shellfish. After receiving his doctorate in biology he became more interested in psychology, basing his earliest theories on careful observation of his own three children. Piaget thought of himself as applying biological principles and methods to the study of human development, and many of the terms he introduced to psychology were drawn directly from biology.

Piaget saw the development of a child's intellectual, or **cognitive,** abilities as progressing through four distinct stages. Each stage is characterized by the emergence of new abilities, which allows for a major reorganization in the child's thinking. For Piaget, development depends in large part on the child's manipulation of and

continuous theory of development: theory based on the belief that human development progresses smoothly and gradually from infancy to adulthood.

discontinuous theory of development: theory based on the belief that human development occurs through a series of distinct stages.

cognitive development: gradual, orderly changes by which mental processes become more complex and sophisticated.

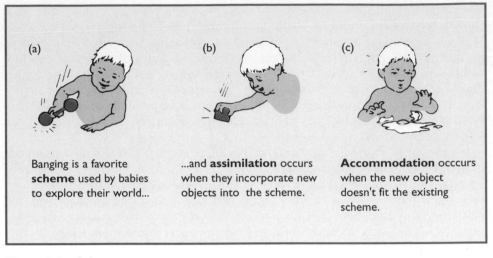

Figure 2.1   **Schemes**

Babies use patterns of behavior called schemes to learn about their world.

active interaction with the environment. In Piaget's view, knowledge comes from action (see Ginsburg and Opper, 1988; Wadsworth, 1989).

Schemes

The building blocks of Piaget's theories are his ideas about how children and adolescents organize their thinking and behavior and how they change their thinking as they grow. The patterns of behavior or thinking that children and adults use in dealing with objects in the world are called **schemes**. Schemes can be simple, as when a baby knows how to grasp an object within reach, or complex, as when a high school student learns how to attack mathematical problems. Schemes can also be classified as behavioral (grasping, driving a car) or cognitive (solving problems, categorizing concepts). A scheme is something like a computer program that people construct for dealing with the world. Like a computer program, each scheme treats all objects and events in the same way. For example, most young infants will discover that one thing you can do with objects is bang them. When they do this, the object makes a noise and they see the object hitting a surface. This tells them something about the object. Babies also learn about objects by biting them, sucking on them, and throwing them. Each of these behaviors is a scheme. When babies encounter a new object, how are they to know what this object is all about? According to Piaget, they will use the schemes they have developed and will find out if the object makes a loud or soft sound when banged, what it tastes like, whether it gives milk, and maybe whether it rolls or just goes "thud" when dropped (see Figure 2.1a).

Assimilation and Accommodation

Assimilation occurs when the baby uses a scheme (such as banging or biting) on a new object. Assimilation is basically the process of incorporating a new object or

---

Connections

The concept of schemes is developed further in Chapter 6 in connection with "schema" in information processing and memory.

---

schemes: mental patterns that guide behavior.

assimilation: interpreting new experiences in relation to existing schemes.

event into an existing scheme. It's similar to putting new data into a computer. But just as data must be correctly coded before being entered into the computer, the object or event to be assimilated must fit an existing scheme. Therefore assimilation involves more than simply taking in new information. It also involves the "filtering or modification of input" (Piaget and Inhelder, 1973) so that the input fits. Give young infants small objects that they have never seen before but that resemble familiar objects and they are likely to grasp them, bite them, and bang them—in other words, they will try to use existing schemes on these unknown things (see Figure 2.1b). Similarly, a high school student may have a well-developed scheme for studying, which she may then apply and adapt to a novel type of course, such as driver's education.

Sometimes, however, old ways of dealing with the world simply don't work. For example, give an egg to a baby who has a banging scheme for small objects and it's obvious what will happen to the egg (Figure 2.1c). Less obvious, however, is what will happen to the baby's banging scheme. Because of the unexpected consequences of banging the egg, the baby might change the scheme. In the future the baby may bang some objects hard and others softly. Piaget used the term **accommodation** to describe this changing of an existing scheme to fit new objects. Another example of accommodation would be the actions of a high school freshman who has always breezed through routine worksheets given as homework, but then encounters assignments requiring creativity or initiative. Accommodation of the existing "homework scheme" must occur for the freshman to achieve a passing grade.

Equilibration

The baby who banged the egg and the freshman faced with a different kind of homework had to deal with situations that could not be fully handled by existing schemes. This, in Piaget's theory, creates a state of disequilibrium, or an imbalance between what is understood and what is encountered. People naturally try to reduce such imbalances by focusing on the stimuli that cause the disequilibrium and developing new schemes or adapting old ones until equilibrium is restored. This process of restoring balance is called **equilibration.** According to Piaget, learning depends on this process. When equilibrium is upset, children have the opportunity to grow and develop.

Teachers can take advantage of equilibration by creating situations that cause disequilibrium and therefore spark students curiosity (Moshman, 1990). Science teachers who introduce new concepts by presenting startling experiments use this technique. Social studies teachers use it when they introduce students to provocative ideas. For example, a teacher who asked American students to defend the position of loyalists in the American Revolution might be introducing a state of disequilibrium in students' minds. To resolve this disequilibrium, students must accommodate a new perspective and grow in understanding. However, not all students can detect the discrepancies in new words, images, or ideas that might create disequilibrium. This is a skill that improves as a person's cognitive abilities develop. For example, Inhelder and Piaget (1958, p. 22) describe a five-year-old who stated the belief that small objects float and large ones sink. When shown a large piece of wood floating, he pushed it under the water with all his strength, saying, "You want to stay down, silly!" The child resisted experiencing disequilibrium by denying it, because he was not ready to form a more abstract and sophisticated explanation of why things float.

> **accommodation:** modifying existing schemes to fit new situations.
>
> **equilibration:** the process of restoring balance between present understanding and new experiences.

Piaget's Stages of Development

Piaget divided the cognitive development of children and adolescents into four stages: sensorimotor, preoperational, concrete operational, and formal operational. He believed that all children pass through these stages *in order,* and that no child can skip a stage, although different children pass through the stages at somewhat different rates. It is also important to note that the same individuals may perform at different stages on different tasks at different times, particularly at points of transition into a new stage (Crain, 1985). Table 2.1 summarizes the approximate ages at which children and adolescents pass through Piaget's four stages. It also shows the major accomplishments of each stage.

Sensorimotor Stage (Birth to Age Two).   The earliest stage is called **sensorimotor** because during it babies and young children explore their world by using their senses and their motor skills.

All infants have inborn behaviors, which are often called **reflexes.** Touch a newborn's lips and the baby will begin to suck; place your finger in the palm of an

Table 2.1

Piaget's Stages Of Cognitive Development

People progress through four stages of cognitive development between birth and adulthood, according to Jean Piaget. Each stage is marked by the emergence of new intellectual abilities that allow people to understand the world in increasingly complex ways.

Stages	Approximate Ages	Major Accomplishments
Sensorimotor	Birth to 2 years	Formation of concept of "object permanence" and gradual progression from reflexive behavior to goal-directed behavior.
Preoperational	2 to 7 years	Development of the ability to use symbols to represent objects in the world. Thinking remains egocentric and centered.
Concrete operational	7 to 11 years	Improvement in ability to think logically. New abilities include the use of operations that are reversible. Thinking is decentered and problem solving is less restricted by egocentrism. Abstract thinking is not possible.
Formal operational	11 years to adulthood	Abstract and purely symbolic thinking possible. Problems can be solved through the use of systematic experimentation.

sensorimotor stage: stage during which infants learn about their surroundings by using their senses and motor skills.

reflexes: inborn, automatic responses to stimuli (e.g., eyeblinking in response to bright light.

infant's hand and the infant will grasp it. These and other behaviors are innate and are the building blocks from which the infant's first schemes form.

The earliest schemes that children develop help them explore their own bodies. Soon, however, they turn to external objects like rattles and cups, which they grasp, hit, and suck—discovering by accident that these actions have interesting results. Intentional behavior emerges next. No longer will infants only repeat behaviors that make interesting things happen; now they will try to solve very simple problems, such as searching for things that are out of sight. This shows that they now understand that objects continue to exist even if they cannot be seen. When children develop this notion of **object permanence,** they have taken a step toward somewhat more advanced thinking. Once they realize that things exist out of sight, they can start using symbols to represent these things in their minds so that they can think about them.

Another hallmark of the sensorimotor stage is the emergence of trial-and-error learning. Suppose a desired object is placed out of the infant's reach but on top of a blanket that can be reached. Very young infants might try a few times to reach for the object, but would soon give up. Older infants, however, having failed to reach the object directly, would try to get it in other ways. They would probably discover eventually that the object can be gotten by pulling on the blanket.

Toward the end of the sensorimotor stage, children progress from their earlier trial-and-error approach to problem solving to a more planned approach. For the first time they can mentally represent objects and events. It is now that what most of us would call "thinking" appears. This is a major advance because it means that the child can think through and plan behavior. For example, suppose a two-year-old is in the kitchen watching Mom prepare dinner. If the child knows where the step stool is kept, he or she may ask to have it set up—to afford a better view of the counter and a better chance for a nibble. The child did not stumble onto this solution accidentally. Instead, he or she thought about the problem, figured out a possible solution that used the step stool, tried out the solution mentally, and only then tried the solution in practice.

Preoperational Stage (Ages Two to Seven). While infants can learn about and understand the world only by physically manipulating objects, the preschooler has greater ability to think about things, and can use symbols to mentally represent objects. For example, the letter "a" can stand for "apple" or for the *a* sound. During the **preoperational stage** children's language and concepts develop at an incredible rate. Yet much of their thinking remains surprisingly primitive. One of Piaget 's earliest and most important discoveries was that young children lacked the principle of **conservation.** For example, if you pour milk from a tall, narrow beaker into a short, wide one in the presence of a preoperational child, the child will firmly believe that the tall glass has more milk (see Figure 2.2). The child focuses on only one aspect (the height of the milk), ignoring all others, and cannot be convinced that the amount of milk is the same. Similarly, a preoperational child is likely to believe that a sandwich cut in four pieces is more sandwich, or that a line of blocks that is spread out contains more blocks than a line that is compressed, even after being shown that the number of blocks is identical. Wadsworth (1978) presents the following interview with a preoperational child to illustrate this point.

The examiner arranges a row of nine blue blocks, each about an inch apart, between himself and the child (See Figure 2.3a).

EXAMINER: Will you make a row of blocks using the red ones just like my row, and right in front of you? [The child makes a row below the examiner's row by first placing two end

object permanence: knowing an object exists when it is out of sight.

preoperational stage: stage at which children learn mentally to represent things.

conservation: the concept that certain properties of an object (such as weight) remain the same regardless of changes in other properties (such as length).

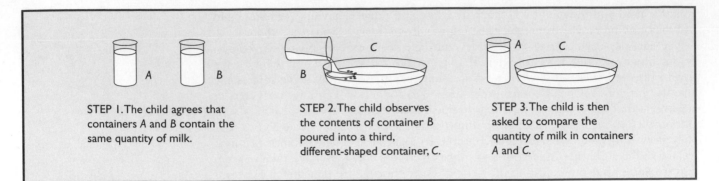

STEP 1. The child agrees that containers *A* and *B* contain the same quantity of milk.

STEP 2. The child observes the contents of container *B* poured into a third, different-shaped container, *C*.

STEP 3. The child is then asked to compare the quantity of milk in containers *A* and *C*.

Figure 2.2   The Task of Conservation

A typical procedure for studying conservation of liquid quantity.

From Wicks-Nelson and Kail, 1993 p.190

blocks in position, then placing eight blocks between those two without any careful comparison.] Does one row of blocks have more blocks than the other, or do they both have the same number?

CHILD: They're the same.

EXAMINER: Are you sure?

CHILD: Yes.

EXAMINER: How do you know they're the same number of blocks? [request for reasoning]

CHILD: I can count them. [Child proceeds to count the blocks. He counts nine for the blue row and ten for the red row.] They're different. There are more reds.

EXAMINER: Can you make them so they have the same number? [Child removes one of the red blocks from the middle of the row and lines the other red ones up corresponding to the blue ones.]

EXAMINER: Now both rows have the same number of blocks?

CHILD: Yes.

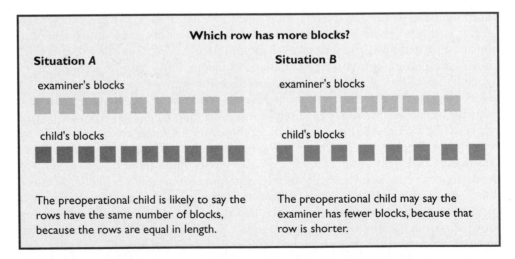

Which row has more blocks?

Situation A

examiner's blocks

child's blocks

The preoperational child is likely to say the rows have the same number of blocks, because the rows are equal in length.

Situation B

examiner's blocks

child's blocks

The preoperational child may say the examiner has fewer blocks, because that row is shorter.

Figure 2.3   Centration

Centration, or focusing on only one aspect of a situation, helps explain some errors in perception made by young children.

Adapted from Wadsworth, 1978, p. 225

EXAMINER: Okay, I'm going to move my blue blocks together like this. [The row of blue blocks is collapsed so that they are about one-half inch apart. See Figure 2.3b.] Now, are there more blocks in my row or in your row, or do we both have the same number of blocks?

CHILD: I have more.

EXAMINER: How can you tell? [request for reasoning]

CHILD: My row sticks out more. [preoperational reasoning]

EXAMINER: Okay, I'm going to make my row just like your row again. Who has more blocks now, or do we have the same number of blocks? [Examiner makes his row of blocks as long as the child's.]

CHILD: Same.

EXAMINER: How do you know? [request for reasoning]

CHILD: They both come out to here and here. [The child points to the ends of each row.]

EXAMINER: Now if I move your blocks closer together [the child's row of blocks is collapsed the way the examiner's row was previously], do we both have the same number of blocks or does one of us have more blocks than the other?

CHILD: You have more.

EXAMINER: How do you know I have more? [request for reasoning]

CHILD: Same as before; your row is bigger.

(Adapted from Wadsworth, 1978, p. 225)

One characteristic of preschoolers' thought that helps explain the error on conservation tasks is **centration**. In the example illustrated in Figure 2.2, children might have claimed that there was less milk after pouring because they *centered* on the height of the milk, ignoring its width. Similarly, in the block example just quoted, the child is focusing on one aspect of the problem (the lengths of the rows) and ignoring another, equally important one (their density).

Preschoolers' thinking can also be characterized as being irreversible. **Reversibility** is a very important aspect of thinking, according to Piaget, and simply means the ability to change direction in one's thinking so that one can return to a starting point. As adults, for example, we know that if 7 + 5 = 12, then 12 - 5 = 7.

How is this preoperational child likely to respond to the Piagetian conservation task she is attempting? As a teacher, how might you help a young child discover errors caused by centration and irreversibility?

---

centration: paying attention to only one aspect of an object or a situation.

reversibility: the ability to perform a mental operation and then reverse one's thinking to return to the starting point.

If we add five things to seven things and then take the five things away (reverse what we've done), we're left with seven things. If preoperational children could think this way, then they could mentally reverse the process of pouring the milk and realize that if the milk were poured back into the tall beaker, its quantity would not change. Likewise, they would understand that four pieces of a sandwich could be put back together to form the original one, or that the blocks could be put back to a one-to-one correspondence between the rows. Such reversible mental routines are called **operations.**

Another characteristic of the preoperational child's thinking is its focus on states. In the milk problem the milk was poured from one beaker to another. Preschoolers ignore this pouring process and focus only on the beginning state (milk in a tall beaker) and end state (milk in a wide beaker). "It is as though [the child] were viewing a series of still pictures instead of the movie that the adult sees" (Phillips, 1975). You can understand how a preoccupation with states can interfere with a child's thinking if you imagine yourself presented with the milk problem and being asked to close your eyes while the milk is poured. Lacking the knowledge of what took place, you would be left with only your perception of the milk in the wide beaker and your memory of the milk in the tall beaker. Unlike adults, the young preschooler forms concepts that vary in definition from situation to situation and are not always logical. How else can we explain the two-year-old's ability to treat a stuffed animal as an inanimate object one minute and an animate object the next? Eventually, though, the child's concepts become more consistent and less private. Children become increasingly concerned that their definitions of things match other people's. But they still lack the ability to coordinate one concept with another. Consider the following problem:

ADULT: Sally, how many boys are in your play group?
SALLY: Eight.
ADULT: How many girls are in your play group?
SALLY: Five.
ADULT: Are there more boys or girls in your play group?
SALLY: More boys.
ADULT: Are there more boys or children in your play group?
SALLY: More boys.
ADULT: How do you know?
SALLY: I just do!

Sally clearly understands the concepts of "boy," "girl," and even "more." She also knows what children are. However, she lacks the ability to put these separate pieces of knowledge together to correctly answer the question comparing boys and children. She also cannot explain her answer, which is why Piaget used the term "intuitive" to describe her thinking.

Another aspect of preschoolers' thought is that it is **egocentric.** These children believe that everyone sees the world exactly as they do. For example, Piaget and Inhelder (1956) seated children on one side of a display of three mountains, and asked them to describe how the scene looked to a doll seated on the other side. Children below the age of six or seven described the doll's view as being identical to their own, even though it was apparent (to adults) that this could not be so. Preoperational children also interpret events entirely in reference to themselves. Owen *et al.* (1981) cite a passage from A. A. Milne's *Winnie the Pooh* to illustrate the young child's egocentrism. Winnie the Pooh is sitting in the forest, and hears a buzzing sound.

operations: actions carried out through logical mental processes.

egocentric: believing that everyone views the world as you do.

That buzzing-noise means something. You don't get a buzzing-noise like that just buzzing and buzzing, without its meaning something. If there is a buzzing-noise, somebody's making a buzzing-noise, and the only reason for making a buzzing-noise that *I* know of is because you're a bee . . . and the only reason for being a bee that *I* know of is for making honey . . . and the only reason for making honey is so as *I* can eat it.

Of course, egocentrism does diminish gradually over time. Two-year-old Benjamin and his four-year-old brother Jacob were driving with their father through dairy country and admiring the cows. "Why do you think farmers keep cows?" said their father. "So my [I] can look at them!" said Benjamin. "No," said his older and wiser brother. "The farmer likes to play with them." Benjamin's egocentrism is extreme; he believes that everything that happens in the world relates to him. Jacob, at four, realizes that the farmer has his own needs, but assumes that they are the same as his.

Preoperational children also take unconventional steps in reasoning rather than using the more logical reasoning that comes later (Phillips, 1975). Consider the following description by Piaget of his daughter Jacqueline, who at the time was two years old:

> J. wanted to go and see a little hunchbacked neighbor whom she used to meet on her walks. A few days earlier she had asked why he had a hump, and after I had explained she said: "Poor boy, he's ill, he has a hump." The day before J. had also wanted to go and see him but he had influenza, which J. called being "ill in bed." We started out for our walk and on the way J. said: "Is he still in bed?" "No. I saw him this morning, he isn't in bed now." [J. replied:] "He hasn't a big hump now!" (Piaget, 1962, p. 231)

How did Jacqueline reason that the boy's recovery from influenza also meant that he had recovered from his disability? Instead of distinguishing between two *general* classes of physical condition, Jacqueline reasoned from one *particular* condition to another, treating both as equivalent. Thus, when cured of one, the boy was "cured" of the other. In effect, she created a link between two particular events where none existed. As another example, Lucienne, another of Piaget's daughters, said at four years of age, "I haven't had my nap so it isn't afternoon" (Piaget, 1962, p. 232). Here the child reasoned that one particular event (the afternoon) depended upon another particular event (the nap), and if one hadn't occurred, neither could the other.

Concrete Operational Stage (Ages Seven to Eleven). During the elementary school years the cognitive abilities of children undergo dramatic changes. The thinking of an elementary student is therefore quite different from that of a preschooler. Elementary school children no longer have difficulties with conservation problems (such as the milk and block problems) because they have acquired the concept of reversibility. For example, they can now see that the amount of milk in the short, wide beaker must be the same as that in the tall beaker because if the milk were poured back in the tall beaker, it would be at the same level as before. This means that the child is able to imagine the milk being poured back and can recognize the consequences of this—mental skills that are beyond the abilities of the preoperational child.

One fundamental difference between preoperational and **concrete operational** children is that the younger child, who is in the preoperational stage, responds to *perceived appearances,* while the older, concrete operational child responds to **inferred reality.** Flavell (1986) demonstrated this by showing children a red car and

concrete operational stage: stage at which children develop skills of logical reasoning and conservation but can use these skills only when dealing with familiar situations.

inferred reality: the meaning of stimuli in the context of relevant information.

then, while they were still watching, covering it with a filter that made it look black. When asked what color the car was, three-year-olds responded "black," six-year-olds "red." The older, concrete operational child is able to respond to *inferred reality,* seeing things in the context of other meanings; preschoolers see what they see, with little ability to infer the meaning behind what they see.

It is no coincidence that throughout the world children start formal schooling at an age close to the beginning of the concrete operational stage. Most of what children are taught in school requires the skills that appear in this stage. For example, school-aged children who have entered the concrete operational stage can make sense of the question, "If I had three candy bars and you had two, how many would we have all together?" They can visualize the situation without actually seeing the candy bars or being distracted by irrelevant aspects of the situation. They can form concepts and see relationships between things. They are no longer quite so egocentric, but are beginning to see things from another's perspective.

One important task that children learn during the concrete operational stage is **seriation**, arranging things in order according to one attribute, such as size or weight—for example, lining up sticks from smallest to largest. To do this, they must be able to compare separate but related bits of information along a scale, in this case length. Once this ability is acquired, children can master a related skill known as **transitivity**, which requires the mental arrangement and comparison of objects. For example, if you tell preoperational preschoolers that Tom is taller than Becky and Becky is taller than Fred, they won't see that Tom is taller than Fred. Logical inferences such as this are not possible until the stage of concrete operations, during which school-aged children develop the ability to make two mental transformations that require reversible thinking. The first of these is inversion (+A is reversed by -A), and the second is reciprocity (A < B is reciprocated by B > A). Since these kinds of logical inferences are important in such subjects as mathematics and science, lessons for elementary school students in these subjects must take into account the children's newly developing skills of logic. By the end of the concrete operational stage, children have the mental abilities to learn how to add, subtract, multiply, and divide, to place numbers in order by size, and to classify objects by any number of criteria. Children can think about what would happen "if . . . ," as long as the objects are in view (e.g., "what would happen if I pulled this spring and then let it go?"). Children can understand time and space well enough to draw a map from their home to school and are building an understanding of events in the past.

Children in the upper elementary grades are moving from egocentric thought to *decentered* or objective thought. Decentered thought allows children to see that others can have different perceptions than they do. For example, children with decentered thought will be able to understand that different children may see different patterns in clouds. Children whose thought processes are decentered are able to learn that events may be governed by physical laws, such as the laws of gravity.

A final ability that children acquire during the concrete operational stage is **class inclusion**. Recall the example of Sally, who was in the preoperational stage and believed that there were more boys than children in her play group. What Sally lacked was the ability to think simultaneously about the whole class (children) and the subordinate class (boys, girls). She could make comparisons *within* a class, as shown by her ability to compare one part (the boys) with another part (the girls). She also knew that boys and girls are both members of the larger class called children. What she could not do, however, was make comparisons *between* classes. Concrete operational children, on the other hand, have no trouble with this type of

---

Connections

Chapter 3 has further information on how to teach concrete and formal operational learners and accommodate instruction to the developmental characteristics of children and adolescents.

---

seriation: arranging objects in sequential order according to one aspect, such as size, weight, or volume.

transitvity: a skill learned during the concrete operational stage of cognitive development in which individuals can mentally arrange and compare objects.

class inclusion: a skill learned during the concrete operational stage of cognitive development in which individuals can think simultaneously about a whole class of objects as well as relationships among its subordinate classes.

problem because they have additional tools of thinking. They no longer exhibit irreversibility of thinking and can now re-create a relationship between a part and the whole. Second, concrete operational thought is decentered, so that the child can now focus on two classes simultaneously. Third, the concrete operational child's thinking is no longer limited to reasoning about part-to-part relationships. Now part-to-whole relationships can be dealt with as well. It is important to note that these changes do not happen all at the same time. Rather, they occur gradually during the concrete operational stage.

While the differences between the mental abilities of preoperational preschoolers and concrete operational elementary school students are dramatic, concrete operational children still do not think like adults. They are very much rooted in the world as it is and have difficulty with abstract thought. Flavell describes the concrete operational child as taking "an earthbound, concrete, practical-minded sort of problem-solving approach, one that persistently fixates on the perceptible and inferable reality right there in front of him. A theorist the elementary-school child is not" (1985, p. 103). This is where the term "concrete operational" comes from. The child can form concepts, see relationships, and solve problems, but only so long as they involve objects and situations that are familiar.

Formal Operational Stage (Age Eleven to Adulthood). Sometime around the onset of puberty children's thinking begins to develop into the form characteristic of adults. The preadolescent begins to be able to think abstractly and to see possibilities beyond the here-and-now. These abilities continue to develop into adulthood.

With the stage of **formal operational thought** comes the ability to deal with potential or hypothetical situations so that the "form" is now separate from the "content." Consider the following problem: A two-foot-tall man jogged ten miles today and five miles yesterday. How many miles did the man jog? Elementary school children in the concrete operational stage might not answer, not because they cannot add ten and five, but because they cannot imagine a two-foot-tall man. Since their thought is concrete, they are unable to draw conclusions from situations that may be possible but are unfamiliar. Another example, the transitivity problem, illustrates the advances brought about by formal thought. Recall the concrete operational child who, when told that Tom was taller than Becky and Becky was taller than Fred, understood that Tom was taller than Fred. If, however, the problem had been phrased the following way, only an older child who had entered the formal operational stage would have solved it: Becky is shorter than Tom, and Becky is taller than Fred: who is the tallest of the three? Here the younger concrete operational child, lost in the combinations of greater-than and less-than relationships, would reason that Becky and Tom are "short," Becky and Fred are "tall," and therefore Fred is the tallest, followed by Becky, and then Tom, who is the shortest. Adolescents in the formal operational stage may also get confused by the differing relationships in this problem, but they can imagine several different relationships between the heights of Becky, Tom, and Fred, and can figure out the accuracy of each until they hit on the correct one. This example shows another ability of preadolescents and adolescents who have reached the formal operational stage, namely, they can monitor or "think about" their own thinking.

Inhelder and Piaget (1958) described one task that will be approached differently by elementary school students in the concrete operational stage and by adolescents in the formal operational stage. The children or adolescents were given a pendulum consisting of a string with a weight at the end. They could change the length of the string, the amount of weight, the height from which the pendulum was released,

Connections

The ability to think about one's thinking is called metacognition. Metacognition and teaching metacognitive skills to students are topics in Chapters 6 and 7.

formal operational thought: deals abstractly with hypothetical situations and reason.

and the force with which the pendulum was pushed. They were asked which of these factors influenced the speed at which the pendulum swings back and forth. Essentially, the task was to discover a principle of physics, which is that only the length of the string makes any difference in the speed of the pendulum (the shorter the string, the faster it swings). This experiment is illustrated in Figure 2.4.

The adolescent who has reached the stage of formal operations is likely to proceed quite systematically, varying one factor at a time (for example, leaving the string the same length and trying different weights). For example, in Inhelder and Piaget's (1958) experiment one fifteen-year-old selected 100 grams with a long string and a medium-length string, then 20 grams with a long and a short string, and finally 200 grams with a long and a short string, and concluded, "It's the length of the string that makes it go faster and slower; the weight doesn't play any role" (p. 75). In contrast, ten-year-olds (who can be assumed to be in the concrete operational stage) proceeded in a chaotic fashion, varying many factors at the same time and hanging on to preconceptions. One boy varied simultaneously the weight and the impetus (push); then the weight, the impetus, and the length; then the impetus, the weight, and the elevation, etc., and first concludes: *"It's by changing the weight and the push, certainly not the string."*—"How do you know that the string has nothing to do with it?"—*"Because it's the same string."*—He has not varied its length in the last several trials; previously he had varied it simultaneously with the impetus, thus complicating the account of the experiment. (Adapted from Inhelder and Piaget, 1958, p. 71).

An easy way to see the difference between concrete operational and formal operational thought is to give children and adolescents a familiar problem: How many different sums can be made using a quarter, two dimes, a nickel, and two pennies? Notice the differences in how they attack the problem. The younger child is likely to try random combinations of coins, while the adolescent is more likely to use a systematic plan to be sure that all possibilities have been covered.

Generating abstract relationships from available information, and then comparing those abstract relationships to each other, is a general skill underlying many tasks in which adolescents' competence leaps forward. Piaget (1952a) described a task in which students in the concrete operational stage were given a set of ten proverbs and a set of statements that meant the same thing as the proverbs. They were asked to match each proverb to the equivalent statement. Again, children can understand the task and choose answers. Their answers, however, are often incorrect because they often do not understand that a proverb describes a general principle. They match statements that have similarities, but they fail to compare the meanings of the statements to find the *best* matches. Adolescents and adults have little difficulty with this task.

Hypothetical Conditions.   Another ability Piaget and others recognized in the young adolescent is the ability to reason about situations and conditions that have not been experienced. The adolescent can accept, for the sake of argument or discussion, conditions that are arbitrary, that are not known to exist, or even that are known to be contrary to fact. Adolescents are not bound to their own experiences of reality, so they can apply logic to any given set of conditions.

One illustration of the ability to reason about hypothetical situations is found in formal debate. In structured debate participants must be prepared to defend either side of an issue, regardless of their personal feelings or experience, and their defense is judged on its documentation and logical consistency. For a dramatic illustration of the difference between children and adolescents in the ability to sus-

Figure 2.4

A Test of Problem-Solving Abilities

The pendulum problem uses a string, which can be shortened or lengthened, and a set of weights. When children in the concrete operational stage are asked what determines the speed of the pendulum's swing, they will tackle the problem less systematically than will adolescents who have entered the stage for formal operations. (The answer is that only the string's length affects the speed of the pendulum's swing.)

(Inhelder and Piaget, 1958, p. 68)

pend their own opinions, compare the reactions of fourth- and ninth-graders when you ask them to present an argument in favor of the proposition that schools should be in session six days a week, forty-eight weeks a year.

The abilities that make up formal operational thought—thinking abstractly, testing hypotheses, and forming concepts that are independent of physical reality—are critical in the learning of higher-order skills. For example, learning algebra or abstract geometry requires the use of formal operational thought, as does understanding difficult concepts in science, social studies, and other subjects.

The formal operational stage brings cognitive development to a close. For Piaget, what began as a set of inborn reflexes has developed into a system of cognitive structures that makes human thought what it is. This does not mean, however, that no intellectual growth takes place beyond adolescence. According to Piaget, the foundation has been laid and no new structures need to develop; all that is needed is the addition of knowledge and the development of more complex schemes. However, some researchers (for example, Commons *et al.*, 1982; Byrnes, 1988) have taken issue with Piaget's belief that the formal operational stage is the final one.

What can you infer from this picture about the students' cognitive abilities? What operations are they likely to be able to perform? What Piagetian stage best describes their level of cognitive development?

Self-Check

Think of an original example from your own experience or observations for each of the following phenomena as described by Piaget:

scheme   accommodation
assimilation   equilibration

Add Piaget's four stages of development to the comparison chart you started in the first Self-Check. Then classify the following phenomena or capabilities in terms of Piaget's stages. At what stage is each one achieved? What is a good example of each one?

inferred reality	reflexes	abstract thinking
object permanence	egocentrism	use of symbols
centration	use of logic	reversibility
perceived appearances	conservation	goal direction
reciprocity	inversion	classification

How Is Piaget's Work Viewed Today?

Piaget's theory revolutionized and still dominates the study of human development. However, some of his central principles have been questioned in more recent research, and modern descriptions of development have revised many of his views.

Some Criticisms and Revisions of Piaget's Theory

One important Piagetian principle is that *development precedes learning.* That is, Piaget held that developmental stages were largely fixed, and that such concepts as conservation could not be taught. However, research has established some cases in which Piagetian tasks can be taught to children at earlier developmental stages (Gardner, 1982; Price, 1982). Piaget (1964) responded to such demonstrations by arguing that the children must have been on the verge of the next developmental stage already—but the fact remains that some (though not all) of the Piagetian tasks can be taught to children well below the age at which they usually appear without instruction.

Other critics have argued that Piaget underestimated children's abilities by using confusing, abstract language and overly difficult tasks. Several researchers have found that young children can succeed on simpler forms of Piaget's tasks that require the same skills (Donaldson, 1978; Black, 1981). For example, Gelman (1979) found that young children could solve the conservation problem involving the number of blocks in a row when the task was presented in a simpler way with simpler language. Boden (1980) found that the same formal operational task produced passing rates from 19 to 98 percent, depending on the complexities of the instructions (see also Nagy and Griffiths, 1982).

Similar kinds of research have also led to a reassessment of children's egocentricity. In simple, practical contexts children demonstrated their ability to consider the point of view of others (Black, 1981; Damon, 1983; Gupta and Bryant, 1989).

The result of this research has been a recognition that children are more competent than Piaget originally thought, especially when their practical knowledge is being assessed. Gelman (1979) suggests that the cognitive abilities of preschoolers are more fragile than those of older children and therefore are only evident under certain conditions.

Another area in which Piaget's work has been criticized in recent years goes to the heart of his "stage" theory. Many researchers now doubt that there are broad stages of development affecting all types of cognitive tasks, but rather argue that children's skills develop in different ways on different tasks and that their experience (including direct teaching in school or elsewhere) can have a strong influence on the pace of development (see Byrnes, 1988; Gelman and Baillergeon, 1983; Overton, 1984). The evidence is particularly strong that children can be taught to perform well on the Piagetian tasks assessing formal operations, such as the pendulum problems illustrated in Figure 2.4 (Greenbowe *et al.*, 1981). Clearly, experience matters. DeLisi and Staudt (1980), for example, found that college students were likely to show formal operational reasoning on tasks related to their majors but not on other tasks. Watch an intelligent adult learning to sail. Initially, he or she is likely to engage in a lot of concrete operational behavior, trying everything in a chaotic order, before systematically beginning to learn how to adjust the tiller and the sail to wind and direction (as in formal operational thought).

Another criticism of Piaget's stages is that they do not take into account cultural differences. Culture influences children's cognitive development in basic ways. Culture shapes the experiences children have and determines the frequency of occurrence of the contexts in which those experiences take place. Cultural values and norms make meaningful the relationships among learning contexts and dictate the timing and level of difficulty of learning cognitive and social tasks (Laboratory of Comparative Human Cognition, 1983). For example, in some cultures there may be no "terrible twos" or rebellious adolescents. For more on revisions of Piaget's theories, see Miller (1983) and Nagy and Griffiths (1982)

Educational Implications of Piaget's Theory

Piaget's theories have had a major impact on the theory and practice of education. First, they focused attention on the idea of **developmentally appropriate education**—an education with environments, curriculum, materials, and instruction that are suitable for students in terms of their physical and cognitive abilities and their social and emotional needs (Elkind, 1989). In addition, several major approaches to curriculum and instruction are explicitly based on Piagetian theory (see, for example, Berrueta-Clement *et al.*, 1984), and this theory has been influential in "constructivist" models of learning, described in Chapter 7. Berk (1991, p. 244) summarizes the main teaching implications drawn from Piaget as follows.

1. A focus on the process of children's thinking, not just its products: In addition to the correctness of children's answers, teachers must understand the processes children use to get to the answer. Appropriate learning experiences build on children's current level of cognitive functioning, and only when teachers appreciate children's methods of arriving at particular conclusions are they in a position to provide such experiences.

2. Recognition of the crucial role of children's self-initiated, active involvement in learning activities: In a Piagetian classroom, the presentation of ready-made

> **developmentally appropriate education:** instruction felt to be adapted to the current developmental status of children (rather than their age alone).

knowledge is de-emphasized, and children are encouraged to discover for themselves through spontaneous interaction with the environment. Therefore, instead of teaching didactically, teachers provide a rich variety of activities that permit children to act directly on the physical world.

3. A de-emphasis on practices aimed at making children adultlike in their thinking: Piaget referred to the question "How can we speed up development?" as "the American question." Among the many countries he visited, psychologists and educators in the United States seemed most interested in what techniques could be used to accelerate children's progress through the stages. Piagetian-based educational programs accept his firm belief that premature teaching may be worse than no teaching at all, because it leads to superficial acceptance of adult formulas rather than true cognitive understanding (Johnson and Hooper, 1982).

4. Acceptance of individual differences in developmental progress: Piaget's theory assumes that all children go through the same sequence of development, but they do so at different rates. Therefore, teachers must make a special effort to arrange classroom activities for individuals and small groups of children, rather than for the total class group. In addition, since individual differences are expected, assessment of children's educational progress should be made in terms of each child's own previous course of development, rather than against normative standards provided by the performances of same-age peers.

Theory Into Practice
Classroom Applications of Piaget's Theory

It makes sense to listen carefully to children and watch them solve problems to understand how they think and how they perceive their world. Instruction must be adapted to students' developmental levels. It is important to stimulate students to move beyond their current level of functioning, but not too far. For example, it is probably pointless to teach first-graders world geography because they have no conception of what a "country," "state," or even "city" is. It would make more sense to teach them local geography—their neighborhood, school, classroom, and so on. Teaching algebra to fourth-graders is also probably a waste of time because the subject requires more ability to deal with abstractions than students at the concrete operational stage are likely to have.

Another implication is that children in preschool and elementary school need to see examples of concepts. With young children you do not say, "Imagine that I had a pie with six slices and I took out two of the slices." Rather, you must show them a picture of a pie and physically remove the slices if you expect them to learn the underlying mathematical concepts. Applying Piaget's insights to instruction means constant use of demonstrations and physical representations of ideas. Students should be allowed to experiment with materials in order to accommodate new understandings, and to discover information for themselves through active participation. Discovery learning (Bruner, 1966), discussed in Chapter 7, is one way in which Piaget's principles have been put into action in classroom instruction.

Piagetian principles of instruction are most often applied in preschool and kindergarten programs that emphasize (1) learning through discovery and hands-on experiences, and (2) the teacher's role as one who sets up environments in which students can have a wide variety of learning experiences (see, for example, Lavatelli, 1970; Kamii and DeVries, 1978, 1980).

Joyce and Weil (1986) describe a general strategy for applying Piagetian concepts to instruction:

- *Phase 1:* Present a puzzling situation well matched to learners' development stage. For example, ask students for their theories about why things float, and then show examples of floating and sinking objects (such as heavy logs float, light paper sinks) that challenge their current understandings.

- *Phase 2:* Elicit student responses and ask for justifications. Offer counter-suggestions, probe student responses. For example, ask students to give hypotheses to explain why some things float and others sink, and confront them with additional demonstrations to further explore the phenomenon. Create an environment that is accepting of wrong but thoughtful answers. Always ask students to give reasons for their answers.

- *Phase 3:* Present related tasks and probe students' reasoning. Offer counter suggestions. The idea here is to see that the concepts learned previously transfer to new related concepts. For example, if students have acquired the concept of why things float, have them suggest why some balloons rise in the air and others do not, to see if they can generalize to a new situation.

The most obvious implication of Piaget's theory of cognitive development is that young children view the world differently from older children and adults. Consequently, Piagetian theory is often used to guide decisions about the readiness of children for specific activities. This has been especially true of the teaching of mathematics and science—subjects in which the mental operations described by Piaget are critical (Price, 1982). Attempts to apply Piaget's ideas to early education focus on encouraging children to construct more adequate concepts (Goffin and Tull, 1984). Cognitive development is not the accumulation of isolated pieces of information; rather, it is of the construction by children of a framework for understanding their environment. Teachers should serve as role models by solving problems with children, explaining the problem–solving process and talking about the relationships between actions and outcomes. Teachers should be available as resources, but should not become the authorities who enforce correct answers. Children must be free to construct their own understandings. Educators should also learn from children. Observing children during their activities and listening carefully to their questions can reveal much about their interests and levels of thinking. Children's solutions to problems and their questions reveal their point of view.

Neo-Piagetian and Constructivist Views of Development

Neo-Piagetian theories are recent modifications of Piaget's theory that attempt to overcome its limitations and address problems its critics have identified. One example of neo-Piagetian work on cognitive development is that of R. Case (1984, 1985), who believes Piaget's stages can be redefined by establishing equivalents between different kinds of cognitive tasks, such as different kinds of problems that share the same logical structures or require the same number of logical steps to solve them. Research in this direction could lead to a new conceptualization of devopmental stages that accounts for the fact that cognitive development proceeds at different rates on different tasks (see Gelman and Baillargeon, 1983; Siegler, 1991).

Alternatives to Piagetian views of cognitive development include information-processing approaches (Siegler, 1986), based on the idea that people process information in a way similar to computers. Information-processing theorists, discussed in greater detail in Chapter 6, tend to agree with Piaget's description of cognition, but, unlike Piaget, believe that thinking skills can be directly taught.

Siegler (1983, 1985b) observes, for example, that children acquire increasingly powerful rules or procedures for solving problems and can be stimulated to discover deficiencies in their logic and to apply new logical principles. They can discern rules and assess their application. In this way children develop greater capacity for abstract thought. The implications of the rule-assessment approach for education is that stimulating new methods of instruction may actually enhance children's thinking abilities (Siegler, 1988; Sternberg, 1988b).

Constructivism is a view of cognitive development as a process in which children actively build systems of meaning and understandings of reality through their experiences and interactions. In this view, children actively construct knowledge by continually assimilating and accommodating new information (Anderson 1989).

An example of a constructivist approach to development is Bronfenbrenner's (1989) ecological systems theory, which views the child as developing within a complex system of relationships. According to this theory, the child's relationships are affected by multiple levels of the environment from the intimate levels of parent-child interaction (the "microsystem") to the immediate settings of family, school, and neighborhood (the "mesosystem") to the broad contexts of society and culture (the "exosystem"). An important implication of the ecological systems theory is that changes at any level have an impact on development, which supports the idea that prevention and intervention programs or services can have significant impact on children's well-being and education (Bronfenbrenner, 1989).

Connections

Chapters 7 and 8 explore constructivist views of teaching and learning, which complement the constructivist views of human development that are presented in this Chapter and in Chapter 3.

Connections

The concept of social learning is further discussed in Chapter 5. See Chapter 7 for additional information on Vygotskian adaptations, such as scaffolding.

Self-Check

List four general teaching implications that reflect Piagetian principles. Describe in detail an example of a teaching strategy that applies Piagetian concepts in the classroom. Briefly summarize the argument against Piaget's theory of cognitive development. How do neo-Piagetian and constructivist views of development differ ?

---

constructivism: theories of cognitive development that emphasize the active role of learners in building their own understanding of reality.

How Did Vygotsky View Cognitive Development?

Lev Semanovich Vygotsky was a Russian psychologist who was a contemporary of Piaget's but died in 1934. His work was not widely read in English until the 1970s, however, and only since then have his theories become influential in North America. Vygotskian theory is now a powerful force in developmental psychology, and many of the critiques he made of the Piagetian perspective more than sixty years ago have come to the fore today.

Social Learning and Private Speech

The most important contribution of Vygotsky's theory is an emphasis on the sociocultural nature of learning (Vygotsky, 1978; Wertsch, 1986). He believed that learning takes place when children are working within their **zone of proximal development.** Tasks within the zone of proximal development are ones that a child cannot yet do alone but could do with the assistance of peers or adults. That is, the zone of proximal development describes tasks that a child has not yet learned but is capable of learning at a given time. Vygotsky further believed that higher mental functioning usually exists in conversation and collaboration among individuals before it exists within the individual.

A mechanism emphasized by Vygotsky for turning shared knowledge into personal knowledge is **private speech.** Private speech is easy to see in young children, who frequently talk to themselves, especially when faced with difficult tasks (Berk and Garvin, 1984). Later, private speech becomes silent, but is still very important. Studies have found that children who make extensive use of private speech learn complex tasks more effectively than do other children (Bivens and Berk, 1990). Vygotsky proposed that children incorporate the speech of others and then use that speech to help themselves solve problems.

Assisted Learning

Another key idea derived from Vygotsky's theories is scaffolding (Wood *et al.*, 1976). **Scaffolding** means providing a child with a great deal of support during the early stages of learning and then diminishing support and having the child take on increasing responsibility as soon as he or she is able. Mothers use scaffolding when they teach their children to play a new game or to tie their shoes, and in fact scaffolding is common whenever one-to-one instruction takes place. For example, Mark Twain, in *Life on the Mississippi,* describes how he was taught to be a steamboat pilot. At first the experienced pilot talked him through every bend in the river, but gradually he was left to figure things out for himself, with the pilot there to intervene only if the boat was about to run aground.

Applications of Vygotskian Theory in Teaching

There are two major implications of Vygotsky's theories of education. One is the desirability of setting up cooperative learning arrangements among students, so that students can interact around difficult tasks and be exposed to effective problem-solving strategies within each other's zones of proximal development (Forman and McPhail, 1989). Second, a Vygotskian approach to instruction emphasizes scaffolding, with students taking more and more responsibility for their own learning. For example, in Reciprocal Teaching (described in Chapter 7) teachers lead small groups of students in asking questions about material they have read and gradually turn over responsibility for leading the discussion to the students (Palincsar *et al.*, 1987). Tharp and Gallimore (1988) emphasize scaffolding in an approach they call

zone of proximal development: level of development immediately above a person's present level.

private speech: children's self-talk, which guides their thinking and action. Eventually these verbalizations are internalized as silent inner speech.

scaffolding: support for learning and problem solving. The support could be clues, reminders, encouragement, breaking the problem down into steps, providing an example, or anything else that allows the student to grow in independence as a learner.

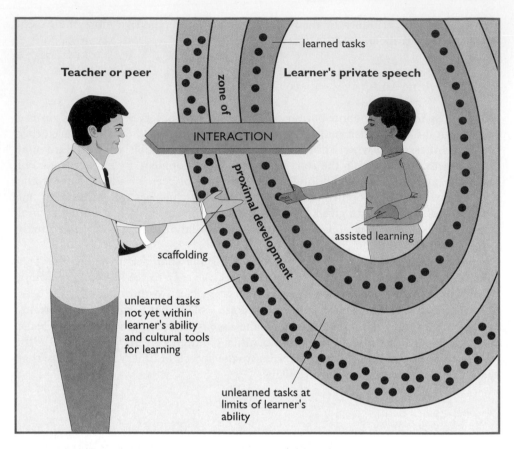

Figure 2.5   Teaching Model Based on Vygotsky's Theory

"assisted discovery," which calls for explicitly teaching students to use private speech to talk themselves through problem solving. (See Figure 2.5)

Theory Into Practice
Classroom Applications of Vygotsky's Theory

Vygotsky's concept of the zone of proximal development is based on the idea that development is defined as what a child can do independently and what the child can do when assisted by an adult or more competent peer (Wertsch, 1991). Knowing both levels of Vygotsky's zone is useful for teachers as these levels indicate where the child is at a given moment as well as where the child is going

The zone of proximal development has several implications for both assessment and teaching in the classroom.

Implications for Assessment
Most standardized and informal classroom tests deal with skills and understandings a child already possesses and therefore measure only the lower level of a child's zone of proximal development. By assessing only this lower level, teachers

miss important developmental information and underestimate the child's abilities. A Vygotskian approach advocates testing both levels of the zone so that teachers find out about a child's current status and natural level as well as how much the child benefits from certain types of assistance.

This is similar to the idea of dynamic assessment (Cronbach, 1990; Spector, 1992) in which teachers give the child hints and prompts at different levels of complexity during the assessment. Notations are made about the child's ability before and after the hints as well as about which hints and prompts were most useful. To assess the total zone of proximal development, consider the following:

- Assessment should be done on a one-to-one basis in interaction with a child.

- The items used should encompass more than one level of skill or degree of complexity.

- The teacher should develop a set of prompts and hints ahead of time to use during the assessment.

- Prompts and hints should be based on the child's actual level or current status, mistakes and errors common to child learning, child explanations of understandings and misunderstandings, and the next developmental level in the particular skill being assessed.

- The teacher should make notes on the effect of these hints and prompts on the child's answers.

As one example, Spector (1992) developed a dynamic assessment of kindergartners' abilities to identify sounds in a word that was read to them (for example, *man* contains the sounds *mmmm, aaaa,* and *nnnn*). If children could not identify the sounds, she gave them a series of prompts, such as saying the word more slowly, asking for the first sound, giving the first sound and asking for the next one, and so on. If a child could not identify the sounds in the word *man* on the first try but could do so after one or more prompts, then it is likely that identifying sounds in words is in the child's zone of proximal development, and the child will respond to appropriate teaching.

Implications for Teaching

The definition of "age appropriate" curriculum must take into account more than just the child's current level of functioning. According to Vygotsky, to be developmentally appropriate, the teacher must also plan activities that encompass the higher level of the zone. For example, when children can play with symbols and begin to use symbolic thinking at about three and four years of age, they are capable of learning about other symbols—in writing, reading, and math. These ideas are within the child's zone.

This does not mean that anything can be taught to any child. Only instruction and activities falling within the "zone" promote development. For example, if a child in Spector's study could not identify the sounds in a word even after many prompts, the child may not benefit from instruction in this skill. Practicing previously known skills or introducing concepts that are too difficult and complex have little positive impact. Information about both levels of development can be used when organizing classroom activities in the following ways.

- Instruction can be planned to provide practice at the upper levels of the zone of proximal development for individual children or for groups of children. For example, hints and prompts that helped children during the assessment could form the basis of instructional activities.

- Cooperative learning activities can be planned with groups of children at different levels who can help each other learn.

- Scaffolding (Wood *et al.*, 1976) is a tactic for helping the child in his or her zone of proximal development in which the adult provides hints and prompts at different levels. In scaffolding the adult does not simplify the task, but the role of the learner is simplified "through the graduated intervention of the teacher" (Greenfield, 1984, p. 119).

For example, in the tasks studied by Spector, a child might be shown pennies to represent each sound in a word (*e.g.*, three pennies for the three sounds in man). When this word is mastered, the child might be asked to place a penny to show each sound in a word, and finally the child might identify the sounds without the pennies. The pennies provide a "scaffold" to help the child move from assisted to unassisted success at the task.

Self-Check

On your comparison chart of theorists, enter information comparing and contrasting the views of Piaget and Vygotsky on the nature of learning and the contexts in which learning takes place. Describe in detail an example of a teaching strategy that applies Vygotskian concepts in the classroom.

How Did Erikson View Personal and Social Development?

As children improve their cognitive skills, they are also developing self-concepts, ways of interacting with others, and attitudes toward the world. Understanding these personal and social developments is critical to the teacher's ability to motivate, teach, and successfully interact with students at various ages.

Like cognitive development, personal and social development proceeds in stages. We speak of the "terrible twos," not the "terrible ones" or "terrible threes," and when someone is reacting in an unreasonable, selfish way, we accuse that person of "behaving like a two-year-old." The words "adolescent" and "teenager" are associated in our culture with rebelliousness, identity crises, hero worship, and sexual awakening. These associations reflect stages of development that we all go through. This section focuses on a theory of personal and social development proposed by Erik Erikson, which is an adaptation of the developmental theories of the great psychiatrist Anna Freud. Erikson's work is often called a **psychosocial theory** because it relates principles of psychological and social development. Like Piaget, Erikson had no formal training in psychology, but as a young man he was trained by Freud as a psychoanalyst.

psychosocial theory: a set of principles that relates social environment to psychological development.

This teacher is modeling private speech as she assists a group of students in new learning that is within their zone of proximal development. What does this mean, and what advantages might such an approach have?

Erikson hypothesized that people pass through eight psychosocial stages in their lifetimes. At each stage there are crises or critical issues to be resolved. Most people resolve each **psychosocial crisis** satisfactorily and put it behind them to take on new challenges, but some people do not completely resolve these crises and must continue to deal with them later in life (Miller, 1983). For example, many adults have yet to resolve the "identity crisis" of adolescence.

Table 2.2 summarizes the eight stages of life according to Erikson's theory. Each is identified by the central crisis that must be resolved.

Stages of Psychosocial Development

Stage I: Trust versus Mistrust (Birth to Eighteen Months).   The goal of infancy is to develop a basic trust in the world. Erikson (1968, p. 96) defined basic trust as "an essential trustfulness of others as well as a fundamental sense of one's own trustworthiness." This shows the dual nature of this crisis: infants not only have their needs met, but they also help in the meeting of the mother's needs. The mother, or maternal figure, is usually the first important person in the child's world. She is the one who must satisfy the infant's need for food and affection. If the mother is inconsistent or rejecting, she becomes a source of frustration for the infant rather

psychosocial crisis: a set of critical issues that individuals must address as they pass through eight life stages, according to Erikson.

Approximate Ages	Psychosocial Crises	Significant Relationships	Psychosocial Emphasis
I Birth to 18 mo.	Trust vs. mistrust	Maternal person	To get To give in return
II 18 mo. to 3 yr.	Autonomy vs. doubt	Parental persons	To hold on To let go
III 3 to 6 yr.	Initiative vs. guilt	Basic family	To make (= going after) To "make like" (= playing)
IV 6 to 12 yr.	Industry vs. inferiority	Neighborhood, school	To make things To make things together
V 12 to 18 yr.	Identity vs. role confusion	Peer groups and models of leadership	To be oneself (or not to be) To share being oneself
VI Young adulthood	Intimacy vs. isolation	Partners in friendship, sex, competition, cooperation	To lose and find oneself in another
VII Middle adulthood	Generativity vs. self-absorption	Divided labor and shared household	To take care of
VIII Late adulthood	Integrity vs. despair	"Mankind" "My kind"	To be, through having been To face not being

Table 2.2   Erikson's Stages Of Personal and Social Development

As people grow, they face a series of psychosocial crises that shape personality, according to Erik Erikson. Each crisis focuses on a particular aspect of personality and involves the person's relationship with other people.

Source: Adapted from Erikson, 1980, p. 178.

than a source of pleasure. This creates in the infant a sense of mistrust for his or her world that may persist throughout childhood and into adulthood.

Stage II: Autonomy versus Doubt (Eighteen Months to Three Years).   By the age of two, most babies can walk and have learned enough about language to communicate with other people. Children in the "terrible twos" no longer want to depend totally on others. Instead, they strive toward autonomy, or the ability to do things for themselves. The child's desires for power and independence often clash with those of the parent. Erikson believes that children at this stage have the dual desire "to hold on" and "to let go." Nowhere is this more apparent than during toilet training, which usually takes place in this stage. Erikson cautioned parents against strict toilet training because he believed that this led to an unfavorable resolution of the Stage II crisis and caused children to become overcompulsive adults (Thomas, 1979).

Parents who are flexible enough to permit their children to explore freely and do things for themselves, while at the same time providing an everpresent guiding hand, encourage the establishment of a sense of autonomy. Parents who are overly restrictive and harsh give their children a sense of powerlessness and incompetence. This can lead to shame and doubt in one's abilities.

Stage III: Initiative versus Guilt (Three to Six Years).   During this period children's continually maturing motor and language skills permit them to be increasingly aggressive and vigorous in the exploration of both their social and their physical environment. The "troublesome threes" are accompanied by a growing sense of initiative, which can be encouraged by parents and other family members who permit children to run, jump, play, slide, and throw. "Being firmly convinced that he is a person on his own, the child must now find out what kind of person he may become" (Erikson, 1968, p. 115). Parents who severely punish children's attempts at initiative will make them feel guilty about their natural urges both during this stage and later in life.

Stage IV: Industry versus Inferiority (Six to Twelve Years).   One might say that personality at the first stage crystallizes around the conviction "I am what I am given," at the second stage around "I am what I will," and at the third stage around "I am what I can imagine I will be." The fourth stage is characterized by the conviction "I am what I learn" (Erikson, 1980).

Entry into school brings with it a huge expansion in the child's social world. Teachers and peers take on increasing importance for the child, while the influence of parents decreases. Children now want to make things. Success brings with it a sense of industry, a good feeling about oneself and one's abilities. Failure, on the other hand, creates a negative self-image, a sense of inadequacy that may hinder future learning. Failure need not be real; it can be an inability to "measure up to" one's own standards or those of parents, teachers, or brothers and sisters.

Stage V: Identity versus Role Confusion (Twelve to Eighteen Years).   The question "Who am I?" becomes importan t during adolescence. To answer it, adolescents increasingly turn away from parents and toward peer groups. Erikson believed that during adolescence the individual's rapidly changing physiology, coupled with pressures to make decisions about future education and career, creates the need to question and redefine the psychosocial identity established during the earlier stages. Adolescence is a time of change. Teenagers experiment with various sexual, occupational, and educational roles as they try to find out who they are and who they can be. This new sense of self, or "ego identity," is not simply the sum of the prior identifications. Rather, it is a reassembly or "an alignment of the individual's *basic drives* (ego) with his endowment (resolutions of the previous crises) and his opportunities (needs, skills, goals, and demands of adolescence and approaching adulthood)" (Erikson, 1980, p. 94).

Stage VI: Intimacy versus Isolation (Young Adulthood).   Once young people know who they are and where they are going, the stage is set for the sharing of their life with another. The theme of this stage is best expressed as "to lose and find oneself in another." The young adult is now ready to form a new relationship of trust and intimacy with another individual, a "partner in friendship, sex, competition, and cooperation." This relationship should enhance the identity of both partners without stifling the growth of either. The young adult who does not seek out such intimacy, or whose repeated tries fail, may retreat into isolation.

Stage VII: Generativity versus Self-absorption (Middle Adulthood).   Generativity refers to "the interest in establishing and guiding the next generation" (Erikson, 1980, p. 103). Typically, this comes through raising one's own children. However, the crisis of this stage can also be successfully resolved through other

Connections

Chapter 3 further explores self-concept, identity formation, and teachers' roles in students' psychosocial development.

According to Erikson, what specific psychological tasks are especially important for these adolescents to accomplish? As a teacher, how might you support each task?

forms of productivity and creativity, such as teaching. During this stage people should continue to grow; if they don't, a sense of "stagnation and interpersonal impoverishment" develops, leading to self-absorption or self-indulgence (Erikson, 1980, p. 103).

Stage VIII: Integrity versus Despair (Late Adulthood).   In the final stage of psychosocial development people look back over their lifetime and resolve their final identity crisis. Acceptance of accomplishments, failures, and ultimate limitations brings with it a sense of integrity; a realization that one's life has been one's own responsibility. The finality of death must also be faced and accepted. Despair can occur in those who regret the way they have led their life and how it has turned out.

Implications and Criticisms of Erikson's Theory

As with Piaget's stages, it is important to note that not all people experience Erikson's crises to the same degree or at the same time. The age ranges stated here may represent the best times for a crisis to be resolved, but they are not the only possible times. For example, children born into chaotic homes that failed to give them adequate security may develop trust after being adopted or otherwise brought into a more stable environment. People whose negative school experiences gave them a sense of inferiority may find as they enter the work world that they can learn and do have valuable skills, a realization that may help them finally resolve the industry versus inferiority crisis others resolved in their elementary school years.

Erikson's theory emphasizes the role of the environment, both in causing the crises and in determining how they will be resolved. The stages of personal and social development are played out in constant interactions with others and with society as a whole. During the first three stages the interactions are primarily with parents and other family members, but the school plays a central role for most children in Stage IV (industry versus inferiority) and Stage V (identity versus role confusion).

Theory Into Practice

Classroom Applications of Erikson's Theory

Applying Erikson's theory to elementary and secondary education requires understanding the characteristics of Stage IV (industry versus inferiority) and Stage V (identity versus role confusion). Stage IV corresponds to the elementary school years (ages six to twelve), and Stage V to the middle and high school years (ages twelve to eighteen).

Helping Students with the Industry versus Inferiority Crisis

In working with elementary school children teachers must be aware that their students are trying very hard to maintain a positive self-concept, a view of themselves as capable, valuable individuals. Almost all children enter kindergarten or first grade believing that they can and will learn. They fully expect to succeed in school (see Entwistle and Hayduk, 1981). However, they soon have to confront reality. Almost from the beginning, they are sorted into high, middle, and low reading groups, and soon afterward they are given grades on a competitive, relative standard. Those students who are put in the lower reading groups and receive poor grades may soon lose their initial expectations that they will succeed. This causes a downward spiral: Negative evaluations from teachers lead to poor self-concept as a learner, which leads to low performance (Wattenberg and Clifford, 1964), which in turn leads to more negative evaluations. By third or fourth grade, or even earlier, students know who the winners and losers are. As they approach adolescence, the "losers" are likely to turn to activities outside of school to salvage their self-concept—perhaps sports or social activities, but all too often delinquency, drugs, and other antisocial pursuits. In Erikson's terms, this downward spiral is a case of poor resolution of the industry versus inferiority crisis of childhood. For the child, the school is the place where success and failure are defined. Erikson (1963) describes the school as providing children with the tools they need to participate in society. If students despair of being able to participate in school society (because they lack the appropriate "tools"), they may reject participation in society as a whole. Teacher must help students through the industry versus inferiority crisis. The behavior of teachers toward students, their evaluations, and the way they structure their classrooms can have important effects on student's self-concepts.

Helping Students with the Identity versus Role Confusion Crisis

We all know that adolescence is a time of turmoil. Erikson points out that because adolescents take on a completely new body im age, they must "refight many of the battles of earlier years, even though to do so they must appoint perfectly well-meaning people to play the roles of adversaries" (Erikson, 1963, p. 261). Among these "well-meaning people" are, unfortunately, teachers. Elementary school students often mistakenly call their female teachers "Mom"; the similarity between the teacher's role and the parent's role is helpful in elementary school because at this stage children generally want to please their parents and earn their approval. However, the similarity has the opposite effect in adolescence. The task of adolescents is to break away from their parents' control and establish themselves as independent, self-reliant individuals. This is a normal and desirable process. Thus the similarity between the roles of teacher and parent means that many students will reject their teachers' authority as much as they do their parents'.

The key point is that adolescents want to be treated as adults, and if they are, they are likely to respond with adultlike behavior. This principle has many implications. First, students at the middle and senior high school levels should never be referred to or treated as "children." Adolescents should never be belittled or humiliated in front of their peers, or anyone else for that matter.

Teachers of adolescents should try not to make judgments of students that appear arbitrary. They should set explicit expectations and rules, with clear consequences for achieving or failing to achieve standards. For example, a teacher might say, "To get an A in this course, you will need to hand in all assignments on time, write five book reports of at least three pages in length, and pass all tests with an average of at least 90 percent." This puts the responsibility for meeting the standards squarely on the students themselves. Most Adolescents crave responsibility. Teachers should take advantage of this and give them as much independent responsibility as they can handle, with clear guidelines for what they are to produce.

Finally, most adolescents are far more concerned about their peer group than about school. Teachers can take advantage of this by assigning well-structured group projects and by using cooperative learning strategies (see Chapter 8) in which students work together and succeed as a group.

Self-Check

Compare Erikson's eight stages of psychosocial development to Piaget's four stages of cognitive development on your comparison chart . Which of Erikson's stages pertain to preschool, elementary school, middle school, and secondary school students? Think of an example in which an individual experiences and then successfully resolves each psychosocial crisis that occurs before and during the school years. In each instance give an example of how a parent or teacher might help a child to resolve developmental crises in a positive way.

What Are Some Theories of Moral Development?

Society could not function without rules that tell people how to communicate with one another, how to avoid hurting others, and how to get along in life generally. If you are around children much, you may have noticed that they are often rigid about rules. Things are either right or wrong; there's no in-between. If you remember back to your own years in junior high or high school, you may recall being shocked to find that people sometimes break rules on purpose, and that the rules that apply to some people may not apply to others. These experiences probably changed your concept of rules. Your idea of laws might also have changed when you learned how they are made. People meet and debate and vote; the laws that are made one year can be changed the next. The more complexity you are able to see, the more you find exists.

Just as children differ from adults in cognitive and personal development, they also differ in their **moral reasoning.** Piaget studied this difference by watching children play games. First we will look at the two stages of moral reasoning described by Piaget, then we will discuss a similar theory developed by Lawrence Kohlberg. There is a relationship between the cognitive stages of development and the ability to reason about moral issues. Kohlberg believed that the development of the logical structures proposed by Piaget is necessary to, although not sufficient for, advances in the area of moral judgment and reasoning.

Piaget's Theory of Moral Development

moral reasoning: the thinking processes involved in judgments about questions of right and wrong.

Piaget spent a great deal of time watching children play marbles and asking them about the rules of the game. He felt that by understanding how children reasoned about rules, he could understand their moral development. The first thing he discovered was that before about the age of six, there were no true rules. Children of about two years old simply played with the marbles. From two to six they expressed an awareness of rules but did not understand their purpose or the need to follow them. The idea of "winning" the game also did not appear, or if it did, it was not by any "rule" that Piaget could understand.

Teachers on Teaching

How has knowledge of child development helped you in your teaching?

Knowledge of early childhood development has helped me to deal with issues of social acceptance in my kindergarten classes. As the year begins, students become acutely aware of differences among classmates in ethnic background, gender, physical appearance, and ability or exceptionality. How do I guide these young students to accept both social equality and individual differences? According to Piaget, kindergarten-age children are in the preoperational stage of cognitive development. How can I foster social acceptance when my students do not have sufficient cognitive development to deal with such an abstract concept? Lesson 1: I give students a number of different objects (a crayon, a ball, a bell) and discuss similarities and differences in their appearances and capabilities. Students talk about which objects they would choose for various purposes and eventually choose them all. Lesson 2: I have the children discuss and dramatize things they like most about familiar story characters and ratify their observations about similarities and differences among the characters and their strengths and weaknesses. Which ones would students like to visit, which could probably play games the best, which could probably tell the best stories? Again, students discover that all the characters can be chosen. Lesson 3: The students share with one another the things they do well, and also share stories about times they felt badly because of comments others made about some difference or weakness of their own. These lessons form a developmentally appropriate groundwork for other "affective education" issues that come up as the year progresses.

Deanna Seed, Kindergarten Teacher
Schnell Elementary School
Placerville, California

I planted a grapevine in the backyard. The vine grew beautifully. The grapes began to form. Suddenly, in the midst of their ripening, a spot appeared on the delicate skin. Within weeks the fruit shrivelled. A small group of students in our regional high school also began each school year full of hope. Gradually, their absences mounted, homework was not done, missed tests were not made up, and long-term assignments were abandoned. Like the grapes in my backyard, these students always seemed to wither. Most of them left school. What could we do? As a team, the faculty researched and tested possible causes and solutions. Our most successful strategies were informed by Erik Erikson's theory of psychosocial development. We rated the students in terms of the developmental tasks and issues that Erikson says adolescents must resolve before they can move on to young adulthood. The tasks of adolescence we chose to address had to do with the management of personal time and resources. We developed an alternative education program designed to meet these very specific needs. The program empowers students by teaching them the organizational and time management skills necessary for their success but lacking in their background. The program respects their responsibility for their own learning and gives them the skills they need to achieve their potential. The result has been an 80 percent graduation rate for students previously identified as likely dropouts. The grapes in my backyard still wither every August because I have not taken the time to discover why they do. Every September, however, a group of adolescents thrive and become able self-managed learners.

Robert E. Coleman, English and Social Studies, Grades 9–12
Pomperaug High School Alternative Educational Program
Middlebury, Connecticut
1992 Connecticut Teacher of the Year

Between the ages of six and ten, Piaget found, children began to acknowledge the existence of rules, though they were inconsistent in following them. Frequently several children supposedly playing the same game were observed to be playing by different sets of rules. Children at this age also had no understanding that game rules are arbitrary and something that a group can decide by itself. Instead, they saw rules as being imposed by some higher authority and unchangeable. It was not until the age of ten or twelve years that Piaget found that children conscientiously used and followed rules. At this age every child playing the game followed the same set of rules. Children understood that the rules existed to give the game direction and to minimize disputes between players. They understood that rules were something that everyone agreed upon, and therefore if everyone agreed to change them, they could be changed. Because they have no conception of rules, morality does not exist for the infant and preschooler. Piaget's stages of moral development do not begin until around the age of six, when children begin to make the transition from preoperational to concrete operational thinking. Piaget used the changes that take place in understanding and application of rules to propose that there are two stages of moral development (Table 2.3).

Table 2.3   Piaget's Stages of Moral Development

As people develop their cognitive abilities, their understanding of moral problems also becomes more sophisticated. Young children are more rigid in their view of right and wrong than older children and adults tend to be.

Source: Adapted from Hogan and Emler, 1978, p. 213.

Heteronomous Morality (Younger)	Autonomous Morality (Older)
Based on relations of constraint; for example, the complete acceptance by the child of adult prescriptions.	Based on relations of cooperation, mutual recognition of equality among autonomous individuals, as in relations between people who are equals.
Reflected in attitudes of *moral realism:* Rules are seen as inflexible requirements, external in origin and authority, not open to negotiation; and right is a matter of literal obedience to adults and rules.	Reflected in *rational* moral attitudes: Rules are viewed as products of mutual agreement, open to renegotiation, made legitimate by personal acceptance and common consent, and right is a matter of acting in according with the requirements of cooperation and mutual respect.
Badness is judged in terms of the objective form and consequences of actions; fairness is equated with the content of adult decisions; arbitrary and severe punishments are seen as fair. Punishment is seen as an automatic consequence of the offense, and justice as inherent.	Badness is viewed as relative to the actor's intentions; fairness is defined as equal treatment, or taking account of individual needs; fairness of punishment is defined by appropriateness to the offense.
	Punishment is seen as affected by human intention.

Piaget (1964) labeled the first stage of moral development **heteronomous morality**; it has also been called the stage of "moral realism" or "morality of constraint." "Heteronomous" means being subject to rules imposed by others. During this period young children are consistently faced with parents and other adults telling them what to do and what not to do. Violations of rules are believed to bring automatic punishment. Justice is seen as automatic and people who are bad will eventually "get theirs." This reasoning creates in the child the belief that moral rules are fixed and unchangeable.

The second stage is labeled **autonomous morality** or "morality of cooperation." It arises as the child's social world expands to include more and more peers. By continually interacting and cooperating with other children, the child's ideas about rules and therefore morality begin to change. Rules are now what we make them to be. Punishment for transgressions is no longer automatic but must be administered with a consideration of the transgressors' intentions and extenuating circumstances.

Kohlberg's Stages of Moral Reasoning

Kohlberg's (1963, 1969) stage theory of moral reasoning is an elaboration and refinement of Piaget's. Like Piaget, Kohlberg studied how children (and adults) reason about rules that govern their behavior in certain situations. Kohlberg did not study children's game playing, but rather probed for their responses to a series of structured situations or **moral dilemmas.** His most famous one is the following:

> In Europe a woman was near death from cancer. One drug might save her, a form of radium that a druggist in the same town had recently discovered. The druggist was charging $2,000, ten times what the drug cost him to make. The sick woman's husband, Heinz, went to everyone he knew to borrow the money, but he could only get together about half of what it cost. He told the druggist that his wife was dying and asked him to sell it cheaper or let him pay later. But the druggist said "No." The husband got desperate and broke into the man's store to steal the drug for his wife. Should the husband have done that? Why? (Kohlberg, 1969, p. 379)

On the basis of the answers he received, Kohlberg proposed that people pass through a series of six stages of moral judgment or reasoning. Kohlberg's levels and stages are summarized in Table 2.4. He grouped these six stages into three levels: preconventional, conventional, and postconventional. These three levels are distinguished by how the child or adult defines what he or she perceives as correct or moral behavior. As with other stage theories, each stage is more sophisticated and more complex than the preceding one and most individuals proceed through them in the same order (Colby and Kohlberg, 1984). Like Piaget, Kohlberg is not so much concerned with the direction of the child's answer as with the reasoning behind it. The ages at which children and adolescents go through the stages in Table 2.4 may vary considerably; in fact, the same individual may behave according to one stage at some times and according to another at other times. However, most children pass from the preconventional to the conventional level by the age of nine (Kohlberg, 1969).

Stage 1, which is on the **preconventional level of morality,** is very similar in form and content to Piaget's stage of heteronomous morality. Children simply obey authority figures to avoid being punished. In Stage 2 children's own needs and desires become important, yet they are aware of the interests of other people. In a concrete sense they weigh the interests of all parties when making moral judgments, but they are still "looking out for number one."

heteronomous morality: stage at which children think that rules are unchangeable and that breaking them leads automatically to punishment.

autonomous morality: stage at which a person understands that people make rules and that punishments are not automatic.

moral dilemmas: hypothetical situations that require a person to consider values of right and wrong.

preconventional level of morality: stages 1 and 2 in Kohlberg's model of moral development, in which individuals make moral judgments in their own interests.

Table 2.4

Kohlberg's Stages of Moral Reasoning

When people consider moral dilemmas, it is their reasoning that is important, not their final decision, according to Lawrence Kohlberg. He theorized that people progress through three levels as they develop abilities of moral reasoning. (Adapted from Kohlberg, 1969.)

I. Preconventional Level	II. Conventional Level	III. Postconventional Level
Rules are set down by others.	Individual adopts rules, and will sometimes subordinate own needs to those of the group. Expectations of family, group, or nation seen as valuable in own right, regardless of immediate and obvious consequences.	People define own values in terms of ethical principles they have chosen to follow.
Stage 1: Punishment and Obedience Orientation. Physical consequences of action determine its goodness or badness.		
		Stage 5: Universal Ethical Principle Orientation. What's right is defined by decision of conscience according to self-chosen ethical principles. These principles are abstract and ethical (such as the Golden Rule), not specific moral prescriptions (such as the Ten Commandments).
Stage 2: Instrumental Relativist Orientation What's right is whatever satisfies one's own needs and occasionally the needs of others. Elements of fairness and reciprocity are present, but they are mostly interpreted in a "you scratch my back, I 'll scratch yours" fashion.	Stage 3: "Good Boy–Good Girl" Orientation. Good behavior is whatever pleases or helps others and is approved of by them. One earns approval by being "nice."	
	Stage 4: "Law and Order" Orientation. Right is doing one's duty, showing respect for authority, and maintaining the given social order for its own sake.	Stage 6.: Social Contract Orientation. What's right is defined in terms of general individual rights and in terms of standards that have been agreed upon by the whole society. In contrast to Stage 4, laws are not "frozen"—they can be changed for the good of society.

conventional level of morality: stages 3 and 4 in Kohlberg's model of moral development, in which individuals make moral judgments in consideration of others.

postconventional level of morality: stages 5 and 6 in Kohlberg's model of moral development, in which individuals make moral judgements in relation to abstract principles.

The **conventional level of morality** begins at Stage 3. Here morality is defined in terms of cooperation with peers, just as it was in Piaget's stage of autonomous morality. This is the stage at which children have an unquestioning belief in the Golden Rule (Hogan and Emler, 1978). Because of the decrease in egocentrism that accompanies concrete operations, children are cognitively capable of putting themselves in someone else's shoes. Thus they consider the feelings of others when making moral decisions. No longer do they simply do what will not get them punished (Stage 1) or what makes them feel good (Stage 2).

At Stage 4 society's rules and laws replace those of the peer group. A desire for social approval no longer determines moral judgments. Laws are followed without question, and breaking the law can never be justified. Most adults are probably at this stage.

Stage 5 signals entrance into the **postconventional level of morality.** This level of moral reasoning is probably attained by fewer than 25 percent of adults. Here there is a realization that the laws and values of a society are somewhat arbitrary and particular to that society (Hogan and Emler, 1978). Laws are seen as necessary to preserve the social order and to ensure the basic right of life and liberty. In Stage

Affective Education

Social problems affecting children and youth and public policies for dealing with those problems increasingly affect school curricula at all grade levels. Many Americans advocate that curricula directly address problems such as alcohol and drug abuse, child abuse, teen pregnancies, the spread of AIDS, school violence, and racial conflict. In addition, there is growing demand nationwide for education to promote ethical conduct and character development. As a result, new programs have been developed not only for informing students about particular risk factors but for directly teaching basic principles of ethical conduct.

Across the nation, children as young as four and five may receive instruction in honesty, sharing, peer pressure, and health and safety risks linked to moral choices. Children may learn, for example, how to discuss their feelings, respond to namecalling, refuse offers of harmful substances, and report classmates who carry weapons. Older students, traditionally exposed to values clarification and decision-making exercises, may now receive training in confrontation management and conflict resolution.

While most Americans agree that standards of conduct should be raised, however, opinion on the role of public schools is divided. Opponents argue that moral instruction should be given at home, that morality is rooted in culture or is the province of religion. They ask, "Whose morality will be taught?" Some critics also believe that ethics instruction in the schools violates the principle of the separation of church and state that is guaranteed in the Constitution of the United States.

Advocates, on the other hand, including civic groups, parent and educator organizations, and religious bodies, such as the Jewish Synagogue Council and the National Conference of Catholic Bishops, endorse moral instruction in the schools. They argue that a common, even universal, core of secular and civic values exists that can be taught without reference to the precepts of any particular religion. They point out that even nondysfunctional families may not be up to the job because the stresses today's families undergo discourage the regular transmission of prosocial ethical codes.

Proponents also argue that many basic values, such as respecting people's rights and property, are already implicitly a part of the curriculum and a part of school life. As the debate continues, curriculum developers struggle to find an acceptable mix of affective education approaches and materials for the nation's next generations.

Critical Thinking

Do you think schools can teach ethical principles without violating the separation clause of the Constitution? To what extent is affective education, and specifically moral instruction, desirable in school? How could moral instruction be integrated into existing curricula? What stand-alone ethics classes or lessons might you advocate?

"Anti-Bias Classes in Georgia," *New York Times,* January 1, 1990, p. B7; Alex Molnar, "Judging the Ethics of Ethics Education," *Educational Leadership,* November 1990; Peter Schmidt, "Despite Controversy, Consensus Grown on the Need to Teach Values in Schools," *Education Week,* February 7, 1990.; "Teaching Tolerance," *Teacher,* February 1991.

6 one's ethical principles are self-chosen and based on abstract concepts such as justice and the equality and value of human rights. Laws that violate these principles can and should be disobeyed because "justice is above the law. " Later, Kohlberg (1978, 1984) speculated that Stage 6 is not really separate from Stage 5, and suggested that the two be combined.

Kohlberg (1969) believed that moral dilemmas can be used to advance a child's level of moral reasoning, but only one stage at a time. He theorized that the way children progress from one stage to the next is by interacting with others whose reasoning is one or, at most, two stages above their own. Thus in dealing with children, teachers must first try to determine their approximate stage of moral reasoning. They can do this by presenting them with a dilemma, like the Heinz dilemma

How would these students be likely to react if a classmate refused to perform the pledge of allegiance? How might Piaget and Kohlberg describe these reactions? As a teacher, how could you respond to such a situation to help students advance in their moral development?

discussed earlier. Once a child's level of reasoning is established, other moral dilemmas can be discussed and the teacher can challenge the child's reasoning with explanations from the next higher stage. After the child's reasoning advances to this stage, the teacher can advance again. All this must be done over an extended period of time, however. Teachers can help students progress in moral development by weaving discussions of justice and moral issues into their lessons, particularly in response to events that occur in the classroom (see Nucci, 1987). In addition, concern with moral development has led to the creation of curricula and teaching tools for affective education—teaching for greater awareness of one's own and other's feelings, social responsibilities, and ethical choices.

Limitations and Implications of Kohlberg's Theory

Kohlberg found that his stages of moral reasoning ability occurred in the same order and at about the same ages in the United States, Mexico, Taiwan, and Turkey. Other research throughout the world has generally found the same sequence of stages (Snarey, 1985). However, one limitation of Kohlberg's work is that it mostly involved boys (Aron, 1977). Some research on the moral development of girls finds patterns somewhat different from Kohlberg's; while boys' moral development revolves primarily around issues of justice, girls are more concerned about caring and responsibility for others. (Gilligan, 1982, 1985; Gibbs *et al.*, 1984). Carol Gilligan has argued, for example, that males and females use different moral

Connections

Gender issues in education are discussed in Chapter 4 (Student Diversity).

criteria and that male moral reasoning is focused on people's individual rights while female moral reasoning is focused more on individuals' responsibilities for other people. This is why, she argues, females tend to suggest altruism and self-sacrifice rather than rights and rules as solutions to moral dilemmas (Gilligan, 1982).

Kohlberg (Levine *et al.*, 1985) later revised his theory based on these criticisms. However, most research has failed to find any male–female differences in moral maturity (Thoma, 1986; Walker, 1989). The most important limitation of Kohlberg's theory is that it deals with moral reasoning rather than with actual behavior. Many individuals at different stages behave in the same way, and individuals at the same stage often behave in different ways (Walker *et al.*, 1987). In a classic study of moral behavior Hartshorne and May (1928) presented children of various ages with opportunities to cheat or steal, thinking they would not be caught. Very few children behaved honestly in every case, and very few behaved disho nestly in every case. This study showed that moral behavior does not conform to simple rules, but is far more complex. Similarly, the link between children's moral reasoning and moral behavior may be quite weak (Burton, 1976). Children may have learned to say certain things about moral decisions at various ages, but what they do may be another matter (Blasi, 1983).

Self-Check

On you comparison chart, compare Piaget's two stages of moral development to Kohlberg's five stages of moral reasoning. By what school levels do children seem capable of each level of thinking? Think of an original example of a moral dilemma and show how different individuals' judgments would illustrate each of Kohlberg's stages. In each case, how might a parent or teacher help a child to grow?

Cheating and Moral Orientations

Ms. Jackson administered a unit test to students in her eighth-grade pre-algebra class. As the class began to take the test, however, she was summoned to the office for an urgent call. Rather than interrupt the activity flow, she quickly appointed Nichole, a high-achieving student who always finished tests early, to serve as classroom monitor during her absence. Ms. Jackson expected to be back in class in only a few minutes. She thought the students might not even notice she was gone.

Unfortunately, Ms. Jackson was detained. As Nichole watched with growing alarm, Kirk and Martin began to discuss test items and compare answers. Gradually, other students became aware of their behavior.

KIRK: What did you get for number 2? Mine doesn't look right.

NICHOLE: *Shhhhh.*

MARTIN: I got $x = 4$. But I can't do the first one.

NICHOLE and SANDY: *Shhhhh.*

KIRK: I think you have to divide everything by 2.

SANDY: They're cheating! That's not fair!

NICHOLE: If you don't stop right now, I'll have to tell the teacher you were talking.

MARTIN: You better not. I'm not the only one. Look around. Vicki even has her book open.

VICKI: I'm not going to get a bad mark because of you guys cheating.

KIRK: So, if everyone does it then it's fair, right? We could all get good grades.

DAN: That's dumb. If everyone cheated, school would be a total joke. Teachers wouldn't know if we were learning anything. Grades would be worthless.

NICHOLE: Cheating is worse than dumb; it's dishonest.

CARMEN: Everybody, *shhhh.* We shouldn't go against the rules. Everybody knows you're not supposed to cheat.

SANDY: Yeah, Kirk, how can you look at yourself in the mirror? What would your father say, Martin?

MARTIN: Don't be so righteous. The main thing is not getting caught. It's getting caught that's dumb. If nobody's the wiser it doesn't matter, and if you're dumb enough to get caught then you deserve whatever you get. So just mind your own business.

SANDY: Cheater! Cheater!

VICKI: I don't want to be a cheater. See, I closed my book. My mother would die if she thought I cheated. And Ms. Jackson would be so disappointed. You're not going to tell, are you, Nichole?

NICHOLE: I want to do whatever is best for everyone.

KIRK: Well, I'm not doing detention over this.

DAN: We could all get detention over this, because it's wrong to cheat. Meanwhile, we've lost ten minutes, so if everyone would just shut up maybe we'll be able to finish. This is a test!

When Ms. Jackson returned to class she knew instantly that something had gone wrong. Nichole wore an embarrassed expression and quickly returned to her seat. Martin looked angry and had a paper balled up on his desk. Kirk looked shifty and scared. Vicki was gazing sadly out the window, and Sandy seemed to have some secret she desperately wanted to share. Only Dan was able to finish the test by the bell.

Problem Solving

1. Analyze the differences in moral reasoning evident in the dialogue. How might Piaget interpret each speech in relation to stages of moral development? How might Kohlberg classify each speech in relation to stages of moral reasoning? How might Gilligan interpret the dialogue to support her view that males and females reason differently?

2. What should Ms. Jackson do to follow up on her suspicions? Assuming she learned that cheating had taken place, how should she address cheating as a moral issue in a way that would help students?

3. Apply your solutions by writing or role playing a dialogue between Ms. Jackson and the students.

Summary

What Are Some Views of Human Development?

Human development includes physical, cognitive, personal, social, and moral development. Development can be significantly affected by heredity, ability, exceptionality, personality, child rearing, culture, and the total environment. Jean Piaget and Lev Vygotsky proposed theories of cognitive development. Erik Erikson's theory of psychosocial development and Lawrence Kohlberg's theory of moral development also describe important aspects of development.

How Did Piaget View Cognitive Development?

Piaget postulated four stages of cognitive development through which people progress between birth and young adulthood. People reorganize their schemes through assimilation (and accommodation). Piaget's developmental stages include the sensorimotor stage (birth to two years of age), the preoperational stage (two to seven years of age), and the concrete operational stage (ages seven to eleven). During the formal operational stage (age eleven to adulthood), young people develop the ability to deal with hypothetical situations and to monitor their own thinking.

How Is Piaget's Work Viewed Today?

Piaget's theory has been criticized for relying exclusively on broad, fixed, sequential stages through which all children progress and for underestimating children's abilities. In contrast, neo-Piagetian theories place greater emphasis on social and environmental influences on cognitive development. At the same time, Piaget's theory has important implications for education. Piagetian principles are embedded in the curriculum and in effective teaching practices, and the concepts of cognitive constructivism and developmentally appropriate instruction guide education reform.

How Did Vygotsky View Cognitive Development?

Vygotsky viewed cognitive development as an outgrowth of social development through interaction with others and the environment. Assisted learning takes place in children's zones of proximal development where they can do new tasks within their capabilities only with a teacher's or peer's assistance. Children internalize learning, become self-monitors, and problem solve through vocal or silent private speech. Teachers provide interactional contexts, such as cooperative learning groups, and scaffolding.

How Did Erikson View Personal and Social Development?

Erikson proposed eight stages of psychosocial development, each dominated by a particular psychosocial crisis precipitated through interaction with the social environment. In Stage I, trust versus mistrust, the goal is to develop a sense of trust through interaction with caretakers. In Stage II, autonomy versus doubt (eighteen months to age three), children have a dual desire to "hold on" and "let go," which is reflected in toilet training. In Stage III, initiative versus guilt (three to six years of age), children elaborate their sense of self through exploration of the environment. Children enter school during Stage IV, industry versus inferiority (six to twelve years of age), when academic success or failure is central. In Stage V, identity versus role confusion (twelve to eighteen years), adolescents turn from family to peer group and begin their searches for partners and careers. Adulthood brings Stage VI (intimacy versus isolation), Stage VII (generativity versus self-absorption) and Stage VIII (integrity versus despair).

What Are Some Theories of Moral Development?

According to Piaget, children develop heteronomous morality (obedience to authority through moral realism) by around age six and later advance to autonomous morality (rational morality based on moral principles). Kohlberg's five stages of moral development reflect children's responses to moral dilemmas. In Stages 1 and 2 (the preconventional level), children obey rules set down by others while maximizing self-interest. In Stages 3 and 4 (the conventional level), the individual adopts rules, believes in law and order, and seeks the approval of others. In Stage 5 (the postconventional level), people define their own values in terms of abstract ethical principles they have chosen to follow.

Critics point out that Kohlberg's study was based only on male subjects. Studies suggest there may be little connection between what children say and their actual moral behavior.

Key Terms

accommodation, 33
assimilation, 32
autonomous morality, 61
centration, 37
class inclusion, 40
cognitive development, 31

concrete operational, 39
conservation, 35
constructivism, 48
continuous theory of development, 31
conventional level of morality, 62
development, 30

Self-Assessment

1. According to Piaget, most elementary school children between the ages of seven and eleven whose thinking is decentered and reversible are in the stage of cognitive development.

   a. formal operational
   b. concrete operational
   c. preoperational
   d. sensorimotor

2. Teaching strategies based on Vygotsky's work suggest that when children are capable of learning tasks they have reached but have not yet begun to learn, teachers should assist learning through any of the following methods *except*

   a. social interaction and private speech.
   b. assisted discovery and problem solving.
   c. conservation tasks.
   d. scaffolding.

3. The psychosocial crisis associated with the high school years is

   a. identity vs. role confusion.
   b. industry vs. inferiority.
   c. intimacy vs. isolation.
   d. integrity vs. despair.

4. Which of the following situations best illustrates the process of assimilation?

   a. A student adopts a new approach to a writing assignment after realizing that an approach learned earlier won't work.
   b. A child learns that she can be noisy when Grandma visits but she must be quiet and polite around Aunt Charlotte.
   c. A student learns how to crack the security code for the school's computer.
   d. A child attempts to ice skate by moving his legs in the same way that he does when he roller skates.

5. All the following teaching suggestions are applications of Piaget's theory *except*

   a. focus on children's thinking, not just its products.
   b. accept individual differences in developmental progress.

   c. recognize the importance of children's self-initiated, active involvement in learning.
   d. intervene in children's learning to accelerate their cognitive development.

6. Piaget's principles have been criticized on the basis of findings showing that

   a. many children go through the stages in a different order.
   b. cognitive tasks such as conservation cannot be taught unless the child is in the appropriate stage.
   c. the clarity of task instructions can significantly influence young children's performance on conservation tasks.
   d. children, on the average, are actually less competent than Piaget thought and rarely reach the different stages at the designated age levels.

7. Match the following stages of cognitive development with the brief descriptions identifying each.
   formal operational stage
   concrete operational stage
   preoperational stage
   sensorimotor stage

   a. learning occurs largely through trial-and-error
   b. mental symbols can be used to represent objects
   c. reversible mental operations are developed
   d. abstract thinking is possible and problems can be solved systematically

8. Match the following stages of Kohlberg's theory to descriptions of each.

   conventional
   postconventional
   preconventional

   a. "Do what the rule says, regardless of the consequences."
   b. "If I get caught, I was bad."
   c. "Before judging her, let's consider her situation and motives."

Development During Childhood and Adolescence

(3)

At Parren Elementary/Middle School, eighth-graders are encouraged to become tutors for first-graders. They help them with reading, math, and other subjects. As part of this program, Jake Stevens has been working for about a month with little Billy Ames. "Hey, shorty!" said Jake one day when he met Billy for a tutoring session. "Hey, Jake!" As always, Billy was delighted to see his big buddy. But today, his friendly greeting turned into a look of astonishment. "What have you got in your ear?" "Haven't you ever seen an earring?" "I thought those were just for girls." Jake laughed. "Not like this one! Can you see it?" Billy squinted at the earring and saw that it was in the shape of a small sword. "Awesome!" "Besides," said Jake, "Girls wear two earrings, guys only wear one. A lot of guys are wearing them." "Didn't it hurt to get a hole in your ear?" "A little, but I'm tough! Boy, was my mom mad though. I have to take my earring off before I go home, but I put it back on while I'm walking to school."

"But didn't your mom . . ."

"Enough of that, squirt! You've got some heavy math to do. Let's get to it!"

The interaction between Jake and Billy illustrates the enormous differences between the world of the adolescent and that of the child. Jake, at thirteen, is a classic young teen. His idealism and down-deep commitment to the positive is

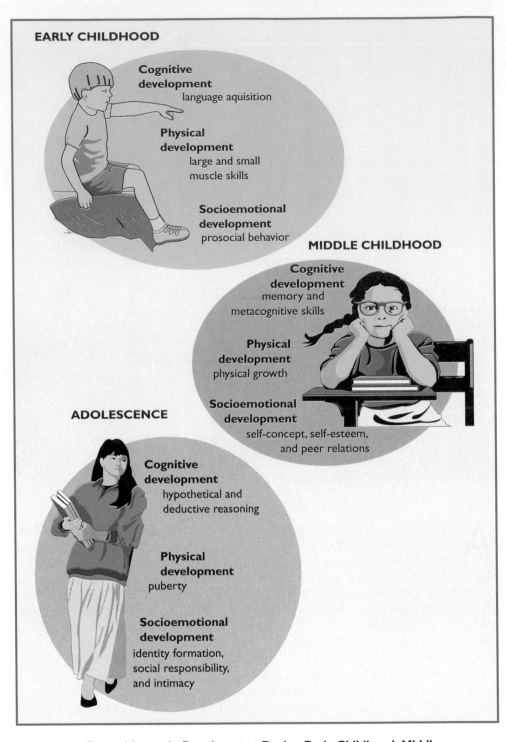

Figure 3.1   Central Issues in Development During Early Childhood, Middle Childhood, and Adolescence

These are some developmental concerns characteristically (but not exclusively) important during each of the three broad age levels discussed in this chapter.

shown in his volunteering to serve as a tutor and in the caring, responsible relationship he has established with Billy. At the same time, Jake is asserting his independence by having his ear pierced and wearing an earring, against his mother's will. This "independence" is, however, strongly supported by his peer group, so it's really only a shift of dependence from parents and teachers toward peers. His main purpose in wearing an earring is to annoy adults, and thereby show that he is not under their control. Yet Jake does still depend on his parents and other adults, and does take off his earring at home to avoid a really serious battle with his parents.

Billy, on the other hand, lives in a different world. He can admire Jake's audacity, but he would never go so far. Billy's world has simpler rules. For one thing, boys are boys and girls are girls, so he is shocked by Jake's flouting of convention to wear something usually associated with girls. He is equally shocked by Jake's willingness to directly disobey his mother; Billy may misbehave, but within much narrower limits. He knows that rules are rules, and fully expects to be punished if he breaks them.

Teachers need to understand the worlds their children live in. Educators must know the principal theories of cognitive, social, and moral development presented in the previous chapter so that they will understand how young people grow over time in each of these domains. However, teachers usually deal with children of a particular age, or in a narrow age range. A preschool teacher needs to know what preschool children are like. Elementary teachers are concerned with middle childhood, and junior and senior high school teachers with adolescence. This chapter presents the physical, social, and cognitive characteristics of students at each phase of development. It discusses how the principles of development presented in Chapter 2 apply to children of various ages, and adds information on physical development, language development, and self-concept. Figure 3.1 identifies central themes or emphases in development during early childhood, middle childhood, and adolescence.

How Do Children Develop During the Preschool Years?

Children can be termed "preschoolers" when they are between three and six years of age. This is a time of rapid change in all areas of development. Children master most motor skills by the end of this period and can use their physical skills to achieve goals. Cognitively, they start to develop an understanding of classes and relationships and absorb an enormous amount of information about their social and physical worlds. By the age of six, children use almost completely mature speech, not only to express their wants and needs, but also to share their ideas and experiences. Socially, children learn appropriate behaviors and rules and become increasingly adept at interacting with other children.

As each of these aspects of development is discussed, keep in mind the complexity of development and how all facets of a child's growth are interrelated. Although physical, cognitive, and social development can be put in separate sections in a book, in real life they are not only intertwined but are also affected by the environment within which children grow up.

Connections

The information in this chapter extends or applies the theories of development described in Chapter 2.

Physical Development in Early Childhood

Physical development describes the changes in the physical appearance of children as well as in their motor skills. During the preschool years the sequence in which all children develop motor skills is generally the same, though some gain skills faster than others.

Children's physical growth is marked by the loss of their characteristic protruding abdomen as their legs and trunk grow faster than their heads. The center of gravity—the point in the body around which weight is evenly distributed—begins to move lower, allowing children to become steadier on their feet and capable of movements that were impossible when they were top-heavy infants and toddlers (Schickedanz *et al.,* 1982). During this time children also develop a preference for one side of their body, which can be observed when they use one hand more frequently than the other. Most children will favor their right hand, but those who show a preference for their left should not be forced to change.

The major physical accomplishment for preschoolers is increased control over the large and small muscles. **Small muscle development,** sometimes called *fine motor activity,* refers to movements requiring precision and dexterity, such as tying a shoe and writing letters of the alphabet. **Large muscle development,** or *gross motor activities* involve such movements as walking and running.

By the end of the preschool period, most children can easily perform self-help tasks such as buckling, buttoning, snapping, and zipping. They can go up and down steps with alternating feet. They can perform fine motor skills such as cutting with scissors and using crayons to color a *predefined* area. They also begin learning to write letters and words. After six or seven years of age children gain few completely new basic skills; rather, the quality and complexity of their movements improve (Malina, 1982).

Physical development has implications for preschool education. Preschool children are natural wigglers. Their activity levels are very high, and they are unable to sit for long periods unless they are engaged in very interesting activities. They need (and actively seek) opportunities to run, jump, slide, and crawl.

Preschoolers' play can be structured by providing engaging equipment such as tires, walking boards, jungle gyms, and large blocks. Children gain in balance, coordination, and strength from a variety of activities, but well-chosen equipment and activities also help encourage social play, as children learn to share and have fun together (see Cratty, 1982; Poest *et al.,* 1990).

For most preschoolers (especially boys), large muscle skills far outpace small muscle skills. Children who are quite skilled at climbing or running may be clumsy and awkward at writing, drawing, cutting with scissors, tying shoelaces, and other fine motor activities. With their natural enthusiasm and love of movement, preschoolers can literally run until they drop. For this reason, they need frequent rest periods after periods of intense activity.

In addition, children's visual perception usually lags behind other aspects of their development. Preschoolers need large-print books, and have difficulty with tasks (such as threading needles) that require acute eyesight. Because of their problems with small muscle skills and visual perception, preschoolers should not be forced to master activities requiring manipulation of small objects. They need big brushes, fat crayons and pencils, and large equipment.

Language Acquisition

From birth to about two years of age, infants try to understand their world by using their senses. Their knowledge is based on physical actions, and their understanding is restricted to events in the present or the immediate past. Only when

small muscle activity: a physical action of the fine muscles of the hand.

large muscle activity: a physical action, such as running or throwing, that involves the limbs and large muscles.

children enter the preoperational stage (at about age two), and begin to talk and to use mental symbols, are they able to use thoughts or concepts to understand their world. During the preoperational stage, however, their thoughts are still prelogical, tied to physical actions and the way things appear to them. Most children remain in the preoperational stage of cognitive development until they are seven or eight years old.

Children normally develop basic language skills before entering school. Language development involves both verbal and written communication. Verbal abilities develop very early, and by age three, children are already skillful talkers. By the end of the preschool years, children can use and understand an almost infinite number of sentences, can hold conversations, and know about written language (Gleason, 1981; Menyuk, 1982, Schickedanz *et al.*, 1982).

Verbal Language. Development of verbal language—or spoken language— requires not only learning words but also learning the rules of word and sentence construction. For example, children learn how to form plurals before they enter kindergarten. Berko (1958) showed preschoolers a picture of a made-up bird, called a "Wug." She then showed them two such pictures, and said, "Now there is another one. There are two of them. There are two _____." The children readily answered, "Wugs," showing that they could apply general rules for forming plurals to a new situation. In a similar fashion, children learn to add "-ed" and "-ing" to verbs. As they learn these rules, they initially overgeneralize them, saying words like "goed" instead of "went," and "mouses" instead of "mice." Interestingly, children often learn the correct forms of irregular verbs (such as "He broke the chair"), and then replace them with incorrect but more logical constructions ("He *breaked* [or *broked*] the chair"). One four-year-old said, "I flew my kite." He then thought for a moment and emphatically corrected himself, saying, "I *flewed* my kite!" These errors are a normal part of language development and should not be corrected.

Just as they learn rules for forming words, children learn rules for sentences. Their first sentences usually contain just two words ("Want milk," "See birdie," "Jessie outside"), but soon they learn to form more complex sentences and to vary their tone of voice to indicate questions ("Where doggie go?") or to indicate emphasis ("Want *cookie!*"). Three-year-olds can usually express rather complex thoughts even though their sentences may still lack such words as "a," "the," and "did." Later, children continually expand their ability to express and understand complex sentences. However, they still have difficulty with certain aspects of language throughout the preschool and early elementary school years. For example, Carol Chomsky (1969) showed children a doll that was blindfolded and asked, "Is the doll easy to see or hard to see?" Only 22 percent of five-year-olds could respond correctly; not until age nine could all her subjects respond appropriately to the question. Many students confuse such words as "ask" and "tell" and "teach" and "learn" well into the elementary grades.

Preschoolers often play with language, or experiment with its patterns and rules (Schwartz, 1981). Frequently this experimentation involves changing sounds, patterns, and meanings. One three-year-old was told by his exasperated parent, "You're impossible!" to which he replied, "No, I'm impopsicle!" The same child said that his baby brother, Benjamin, was a man because he was a "Benja-man." Children often rearrange word sounds to create new words, rhymes, and funny sentences. The popularity of finger plays, nonsense rhymes, and Dr. Seuss storybooks shows how young children enjoy playing with language.

Connections

Language and articulation disorders are discussed in Chapter 12.

Connections

Whole language is referred to again in Chapter 8 in the contexts of curriculum and instruction and in Chapter 10 in the context of motivation.

Reading. Learning to read in the early elementary grades is one of the most important of all developmental tasks, if only because in our society school success is so often equated with reading success. The process of learning to read can begin quite early if children are read to. Research on what is called **emergent literacy** (Laminack, 1990; Sulzby and Teale, 1991) has shown that children may enter school with a great deal of knowledge about reading, and that this knowledge contributes to success in formal reading instruction. For example, young children have often learned concepts of print such as the ideas that letters represent sounds, that spaces between words have meaning, and that books have a front and a back. Many preschoolers can "read" books from beginning to end by interpreting the pictures on each page. They understand about story plots and can often predict what will happen next in a simple story. They can recognize logos on familiar stores and products; for example, very young children often know that "M" is for "McDonald's." Further, even if they have not been read to, children have developed complex language skills that are critical in reading. Children from families in which there are few literacy-related activities can learn concepts of print, plot, and other pre-reading concepts if they attend preschools or kindergartens that emphasize reading and discussing books in class (Mason *et al.,* 1992).

The formal teaching of reading is undergoing a substantial transformation. It is now understood that reading is not built up from little bits of isolated skills, but rather interacts with language, with cognitive development, and with writing. The term **whole language** (Goodman and Goodman, 1989) is used to refer to a broad range of teaching practices that attempt to move away from teaching of reading as a set of discrete skills. Whole language emphasizes having students read whole stories and novels, newspaper articles, and other "real" materials. It emphasizes integrating reading with writing, and writing for real audiences and purposes. Word attack skills (such as knowing how a silent *e* changes the sound of *a* in *can* and *cane*) may be taught in whole language classes, but usually only in the context of what students are reading.

Since whole language is not a single, well-specified practice, it is difficult to evaluate. Programs based on whole language principles do seem to be effective in kindergarten, but there is little evidence of any positive effects in first grade or beyond (Stahl and Miller, 1989). The problem is that many children need a more systematic approach to learning phonics, to crack the reading code, at the same time as they need to learn that reading has meaning. A balanced approach emphasizing "real" reading, integration of reading and writing, and systematic instruction in word attack skills in the context of meaningful materials is favored by many researchers (Adams, 1990; Ehri, 1991; Juel, 1991; Vellutino, 1991), although debate on this topic still rages.

Writing. Most children begin to grasp the fundamentals of writing during early childhood. Children as young as three years of age recognize differences between print and drawings. They gradually begin to discriminate the distinctive features of print, such as whether lines are straight or curved, open or closed, diagonal, horizontal, or vertical. But through the early elementary grades, many children continue to reverse letters such as "b" and "d," and "p" and "q," until they learn that the orientation of letters is an important characteristic (Schickedanz *et al.,* 1982). Letter reversal is not an indication of reading or writing problems if other development in these areas is normal.

Children's writing follows a developmental sequence. It emerges out of early scribbles and at first is spread randomly across a page. This reflects an incomplete

emergent literacy: knowledge and skills relating to reading that children usually develop from experience with books and other print media before the beginning of formal reading instruction in school.

whole language: an educational philosophy that emphasizes the integration of reading, writing, and language and communication skills across the curriculum in the context of authentic or real-life materials, problems, and tasks.

understanding of word boundaries as well as an inability to mentally create a line for placing letters. Children invent spellings by making judgments about English sounds and by relating the sounds they hear to the letters they know. In trying to represent what they hear, they typically use letter names as opposed to letter sounds; short vowels are frequently left out because they are not directly associated with letter names (Downing *et al.,* 1986) (see Figure 3.1). For example, one kindergartner labeled a picture of a dinosaur, "DNSR." In recent years educators have experimented with teaching kindergartners and first-graders to write stories using invented spellings, to help them learn reading as well as writing (Calkins, 1983).

Theory Into Practice
Promoting Language Development in Young Children

Many of the educational implications derived from research on children's language development transfer findings from two sources: parental behaviors that encourage oral language development and studies of young children who learn to read without formal instruction. The most frequent recommendations include reading to children, surrounding them with books and other printed materials, making various writing materials available, encouraging reading and writing, and being responsive to children's questions about letters, words, and spellings (Schickedanz, 1982; Vukelich and Golden, 1984).

What language acquisition knowledge and skills are these children likely to have by the time they enter kindergarten? As a teacher, what general approaches to formal instruction in reading and writing might you use to build on their knowledge and skills?

There are numerous props teachers can use in the classroom, such as telephone books and "office space" in a dramatic play area. Classrooms can have writing centers with materials such as typewriters, magnetic letters, chalkboards, pencils, crayons, markers, and paper (Tompkins, 1981; Vukelich and Golden, 1984). Art activities also contribute to children's understanding of print; children's recognition that their images can stand for something else helps develop an understanding of abstractions, which is essential to understanding symbolic language (Eisner, 1982).

Teachers can encourage children's involvement with print by reading in small groups, having tutors read to children individually, and allowing children to choose books to read. Intimate reading experiences allow children to turn pages, pause to look at pictures or ask questions, and read along with an adult. These experiences cannot occur as easily if the teacher sits at the front of the room reading to a large group of children (Schickedanz, 1982).

Predictable books such as *The Three Little Pigs* and *There Was an Old Lady Who Swallowed a Fly* allow beginning readers to rely on what they already know about language while learning sound-letter relationships. Stories are predictable if a child can guess what the author is going to say and how it will be stated. Repetitive structures, rhyme and rhythm, and a match between pictures and text increase predictability (Rhodes, 1977).

Children's understandings about language are enhanced when adults point out the important features of print (Harste and Burke, 1980; Dyson, 1984). Statements such as "We must start at the front, not at the back of the book"; "Move your finger; you're covering the words and I can't see to read them"; and "You have to point to each word as you say it, not to each letter, like this " (Schickedanz, 1982, p. 256), help clarify the reading process. Teachers can indicate features in print that are significant and draw attention to patterns of letters, sounds, or phrases (McKenzie, 1977). These informal experiences also teach children the words that are related to written language, such as "letter," "word," and "a, b, c" (Schickedanz, 1982).

Socioemotional Development

A young child's social life evolves in relatively predictable ways. The social network grows from an intimate relation with parents or other guardians to include other family members, nonrelated adults, and peers. Social interactions extend from home to neighborhood, and from nursery school or other child-care arrangements to formal school.

Erik Erikson's theory of personal and social development suggests that during early childhood children must resolve the personality crisis of initiative versus guilt. The child's successful resolution of this stage results in a sense of initiative and ambition, tempered by a reasonable understanding of the permissible. Early educators can encourage this by giving children opportunities to take initiative, to be challenged, and to succeed.

The Impact of Parenting Styles.   Parents usually have the earliest and strongest influence on a child. People appear to have a preferred style of interacting with their children, and these parental variations in style affect children's social development. During the last two decades researchers have tried to identify strategies used by effective parents. The best-known studies of **parenting styles** have been done by Diane Baumrind (1973). Her research identified three main styles that varied around the degree of parental control, clarity of parent–child communications, parents' maturity demands, and nurturance.

Authoritarian parents value obedience even at the expense of the child's autonomy. These parents do not encourage verbal give-and-take, believe children should accept parental authority without question, and tend to be harsh. In contrast, **permissive parents** give their children as much freedom as possible and place few expectations on them. **Authoritative parents,** however, attempt to direct their children's behavior in ways that respect children's abilities, but at the same time express their own standards of behavior and expect those standards to be met. Authoritative parents are both warm and demanding (Baumrind, 1973). Note that these two similar words, "authoritarian" and "authoritative," describe very different styles of parenting.

Baumrind (1973, 1980) concluded that the most effective parents more often chose an authoritative style. Authoritative parents tend to have children who are independent, self-assertive, friendly, cooperative with parents, high in self-esteem, and achievement-oriented. On the other hand, parents who are authoritarian or overly permissive tend to have children who lack these traits (Baumrind, 1973). Baumrind's findings emphasize the importance of parental control and warmth, of giving age-appropriate reasons for actions, of giving children responsibility when appropriate, and of expecting children to act in a mature way. These findings suggest strategies that teachers can use with children. Adults most effective in influencing children explain the reasons behind their demands. They also tell children their expectations and express their belief that these standards will be met.

Theory Into Practice

Creating Home–School Partnerships

It has long been known that children whose parents are actively involved in their schooling achieve better than those whose parents are less involved (Epstein, 1983; Scott-Jones, 1984). What can schools do to build partnerships between home and school?

Joyce Epstein (1991, pp. 1145–1146) has identified six major types of collaboration between parents and schools:

- Type 1: Basic Obligations of Families. Families are responsible for providing for children's health and safety, developing parenting skills and child-rearing approaches that prepare children for school and that maintain healthy child development across grades, and *building positive home conditions* that support learning and behavior throughout the school years. Schools help families develop the knowledge and skills they need to understand their children at each grade level through workshops at the school or in other locations and in other forms of parent education, training, and information giving.

- Type 2: Basic Obligations of Schools. The schools are responsible for *communicating with families* about school programs and children's progress. Communications include the notices, phone calls, visits, report cards, and

parenting styles: general patterns of behavior used by parents when dealing with their children.

authoritarian parents: parents who strictly enforce their authority over their children.

permissive parents: parents who give their children great freedom.

authoritative parents: parents who mix firm guidance with respect and warmth toward their children.

conferences with parents that most schools provide. Innovative communications include information to help families choose or change schools and to help their children select curricula, courses, special programs and activities, and other opportunities at each grade level. Schools vary the forms and frequency of communications and greatly affect whether the information sent home can be understood by all families. Schools strengthen partnerships by encouraging two-way communication.

- Type 3: Involvement at School. Parents and other *volunteers* who assist teachers, administrators, and children are involved in classrooms or in other areas of the school, as are families who come to school to support student performances, sports, or other events. Schools improve and vary schedules so that more families are able to participate as volunteers and as audiences. Schools recruit and train volunteers so that they are helpful to teachers, students, and school improvement efforts at school and in other locations.

- Type 4: Involvement in Learning Activities at Home. Teachers request and guide parents to monitor and *assist their own children* at home. Teachers assist parents in how to interact with their children at home on learning activities that are coordinated with the children's classwork or that advance or enrich learning. Schools enable families to understand how to help their children at home by providing information on academic and other skills required of students to pass each grade, with directions on how to monitor, discuss, and help with homework and practice and reinforce needed skills.

- Type 5: Involvement in Decision Making, Governance, and Advocacy. Parents and others in the community serve in *participatory roles* in the PTA/PTO, Advisory Councils, Chapter 1 programs, school site management teams, or other committees or school groups. Parents also may become activists in independent advocacy groups in the community. Schools assist by training parents to be leaders and representatives in decision-making skills and how to communicate with all parents they represent, by including parents as true, not token, contributors to school decisions and by providing information to community advocacy groups so that they may knowledgeably address issues of school improvement.

- Type 6: Collaboration with Community Organizations. Schools collaborate with agencies, businesses, cultural organizations, and other groups to share responsibility for children's education and future success. Collaboration includes school programs that provide or coordinate children's and families' *access to community and support services,* such as before- and after-school care, health services, cultural events, and other programs. Schools vary in how much they know about and draw on community resources to enhance and enrich the curriculum and other student experiences. Schools assist families with information on community resources that can help strengthen home conditions and assist children's learning and development (see Nettles, 1991).

Teachers and principals can promote these six types of parent involvement in a variety of ways. One is simply to communicate an openness to parent involvement in the school, to identify ways to involve parents within the school (see Epstein and Dauber, 1991), and to communicate frequently with parents in general and with each child's parents individually. Such simple strategies as providing a space on homework sheets for parents to indicate any problems students

---

Connections

For a discussion of parent involvement in classroom management, school discipline, and home-based reinforcement, see Chapter 11. For a discussion of parent involvement in prevention and intervention programs for at-risk students and in education plans for exceptional learners, see Chapter 12.

had with homework or to routinely communicate any concerns or other feedback can go a long way toward helping parents feel as though they are in a true partnership with the school (Epstein and Dauber, 1989; Kreinberg and Thompson, 1986). Giving parents specific ideas for helping their own children at home and finding ways to attract parents to school events are also important strategies. As an example of the latter, experienced teachers and administrators know that parents are much more likely to attend evening activities at the school if their children are performing or involved in some way, and if activities are provided for all children (so that parents need not worry about babysitters). Every school and community is different, but in all schools a staff that truly wants to increase collaboration with parents can find a way to do it. An ideal source of ideas for increasing parents' involvement is the parents themselves, who are of course more likely to participate in activities they have asked for.

In terms of Epstein's six types of parent involvement, which forms of parent–school collaboration may be inferred from the situation portrayed in this picture? As a teacher, how do you expect to promote parent involvement in your work?

Peer Relationships. It is during early childhood that **peers**, other children who are a child's equals, first strongly influence a child's development. Children's relations with their peers differ from their interactions with adults in several ways. Most importantly, children interact with each other as equals. This relationship lets them assert themselves, present their own views, and argue different viewpoints.

Peer play allows children to interact with other individuals whose level of development is similar to their own. When peers have disputes among themselves, they must make concessions and must cooperate in resolving them if the play is to continue; unlike in adult–child disputes, no one can claim to have ultimate authority. Peer relationships also help young children overcome the egocentrism that Piaget described as being a characteristic of preoperational thinking (Kutnick, 1988).

Peer conflicts let children see that others have thoughts, feelings, and viewpoints different from their own. Conflicts also heighten children's sensitivity to the effects of their behavior on others.

Successful interactions with peers require communication and specific social skills such as initiating interactions, maintaining relations, and resolving conflicts. Research suggests that unpopular children lack social skills and seem not to know the kinds of behavior that are most appropriate in different social situations (Asher *et al.,* 1982). Teachers can help children who are having social difficulties by arranging classroom situations that will help them improve their social skills. Peer interactions can be encouraged by use of small groups, toys and materials involving more than one child, and activities such as puppets or sociodramatic play. In particular, use of cooperative learning or peer tutoring activities can increase peer acceptance and reduce rejections (Slavin, 1983a). Also, students can be taught specific social behaviors that will help them get along with peers (Gresham, 1981).

Friendships. Friendship is the central social relationship between peers during childhood, and it undergoes a series of changes before adulthood. Using as their basis the developmental stages of Piaget and children's changing abilities to consider the perspective of others, Selman (1981, Selman and Selman, 1979) has described how children's understanding of friendship changes over the years. Between the ages of three and seven, children usually view friends as momentary playmates. Children of this age might come home from school exclaiming, "I made a new friend today; Jamie shared her doll with me," or "Bill's not my friend anymore 'cause he wouldn't play blocks with me." These comments reveal the child's view of friendship as a temporary relationship based on a certain situation rather than on shared interests or beliefs (Furman and Bierman, 1984). Later, children become more aware of the thoughts and feelings of others, and their image of a

Connections

Additional classroom applications for promoting positive, prosocial peer relations appear in Chapter 4 (Student Diversity) and Chapter 12 (Accommodating Instruction to Individual Needs). Suggestions for cooperative learning activities may be found in Chapters 7, 8, 9, 10, and 12.

peers: people who are equal in age or status.

friend becomes one of someone who will do what they want. Eventually children realize that good relationships depend upon give-and-take.

Prosocial Behaviors.   **Prosocial behaviors** are voluntary actions toward others such as caring, sharing, comforting, and cooperation. Understanding the roots of prosocial behavior has contributed to our knowledge of children's moral development.

Several factors seem to be associated with the development of prosocial behaviors (Caldwell, 1977). These include:

- Parental disciplinary techniques that stress the consequences of the child's behavior for others and that are applied within a warm, responsive parent–child relationship (Baumrind, 1973; Hoffman, 1979).
- Contact with adults who indicate they expect concern for others (Bryan, 1975; Grusec and Arnason, 1982).
- Contact with adults who let children know that aggressive solutions to problems are unacceptable and who provide acceptable alternatives.

Theory Into Practice
Modeling Cooperation for Young Children

Teachers of young children should provide a variety of materials such as puppets, blocks, water, and a dramatic play area that encourage cooperative play. Too many materials, however, can make cooperation unnecessary (Asher *et al.*, 1982). Competition that emphasizes outdoing others should be minimized; instead, you should help children learn to cooperate and should set a good example by trying to understand the perspectives of the children you are teaching.

Group games that let children develop rules and abide by them encourage cooperation and self-governance (Kamii and DeVries, 1980). Because preoperational thinking is still tied to actions, the actions necessary for cooperation should be concrete and observable. For example, three-legged stilts where two children stand next to each other and have their inside legs tied to a shared middle stilt require children to coordinate their physical movements (Goffin and Tull, 1984). Kamii and DeVries (1978) emphasize the importance of minimizing adult authority. Adult-oriented morality encourages blind obedience, whereas children's cooperative planning, decision making, and resolution of conflict promote compromise. Support for peer interactions, and peer conflict in particular, is the most frequent social application of Piaget's work. Peer play also encourages a peer-oriented morality based on cooperation, which is believed to be a developmental root of morality (Piaget, 1932; Damon, 1983, 1984).

Play.   Children spend a major portion of their time playing. Play, which contributes to development, can be characterized as follows (Krasnor and Pepler, 1980; Rosenblatt, 1982; Damon, 1983):

- Play is voluntary, pleasurable, spontaneous, and self-initiated.
- Play involves repetition or elaboration of behaviors already acquired, but it also promotes new skills and abilities.
- Play is pursued "for its own sake"; it is not goal-directed.
- Play is creative and nonliteral. It contains elements of reality interwoven with fantasy.
- Play changes as children develop.

prosocial behaviors:
actions that show respect and caring for others.

A form of play that dominates the preschool period is pretend or make-believe play. **Pretend play** involves transforming oneself or objects into other persons, places, or objects. This has been the most researched form of play because it is thought to contribute to cognitive, social, and language development. Its appearance marks the emergence of the ability to use mental symbols and images to stand for the real world of objects and actions.

Pretend play first appears during the second year of life, increases in frequency and complexity during the preschool years, and then declines in middle childhood. At first children play alone, or engage in *parallel play,* in which they play side by side without taking much notice of one another. At around three, children begin to engage in *cooperative play* in which they coordinate their activities, take turns, and work together to achieve a group goal (Guralnick and Weinhouse, 1984). One example of cooperative play is **sociodramatic play,** which includes such activities as playing "house" or "teacher," in which children act out prescribed roles. According to Piaget (1973), pretend play becomes more realistic as logic replaces preoperational thought.

Play reveals important elements of children's ability to make sense of their environment, of their linguistic, cognitive, and social skills, and of their general personality development.

Children exercise their minds when playing because they think and act as if they were another person. When they make such a transformation, they are taking a step toward abstract thinking in that they are freeing their thoughts from a focus on concrete objects. Play is also associated with creativity, especially the ability to be less literal and more flexible in one's thinking (Fein, 1979; Christie, 1980; Yawkey, 1980).

Play also gives children safe situations in which to express ideas and feelings that would be unacceptable in other settings. In play they can freely express their hostility and anger and relive hurtful events. For example, two four-year-old neighbors had new baby sisters at about the same time. Both children were affectionate toward their new sisters, but they also played a game called "bad baby," in which they scolded and punished a certain doll. This game helped them deal with their natural jealousy toward the new babies. This kind of play can help children come to grips with their feelings and with the often harsh aspects of reality (Damon, 1983).

Play plays an important role in Vygotsky's theories of development (see Chapter 2) because it allows children to freely explore ways of thinking and acting that are above their current level of functioning. He wrote, "In play a child is always above his average age, above his daily behavior; in play it is as though he were a head taller than himself" (Vygotsky, 1978, p. 102).

Self Check

Begin a three-column comparison chart with the columns headed "Early Childhood," "Middle Childhood," and "Adolescence ." Enter information concerning Early Childhood in terms of the categories listed below. Work from memory first to record what you can and then review the section to make your entries more complete.

- relevant ages
- relevant grade levels
- Piagetian stage(s)
- Eriksonian stage(s)
- characteristics of behavior
- examples of key social relationships

- physical characteristics
- examples of physical abilities
- characteristics of language and thought
- examples of cognitive abilities
- sources of impact on development

pretend play: creative activity in which children put themselves into imaginary roles or situations.

sociodramatic play: activities in which children act out prescribed roles.

What Kind of Early Childhood Education Do Children Need?

In almost all the countries of the world, children begin their formal schooling at about six years of age, a time when they have typically attained the cognitive and social skills necessary for organized learning activities. However, there is much less agreement on what kind of schooling, if any, children younger than five need. The kindergarten originated in Germany in the 1800s, but it was not until the turn of the century that this innovation gained widespread acceptance. Since World War II nursery schools and day-care programs have mushroomed, as increasing numbers of women with children have entered the work force (Scarr and Weinberg, 1986; White and Buka, 1987). For example, in the late 1980s, more than half of all women with children under three years of age were working. By contrast, the proportion of working mothers with young children in 1970 was one in four (U.S. Government, Bureau of Labor Statistics, 1988). Group day-care programs exist for children from infancy on, and organized preschool or nursery school programs sometimes take children as young as two.

Day-Care Programs.   Day-care programs exist primarily to provide child-care services for working parents. They range from a baby-sitting arrangement in which one adult takes care of several children to organized preschool programs that differ little from nursery schools.

Nursery Schools.   The primary difference between day-care and nursery-school programs is that nursery schools provide a planned program designed to foster the social and cognitive development of young children. Most nursery schools are half-day programs, with two or three adults supervising a class of fifteen to twenty children. Unlike day-care centers and Head Start programs (which are discussed in the following section), nursery schools most often serve middle-class families (White and Buka, 1987).

A key concept in nursery school education is **readiness training:** students learn skills that are supposed to prepare them for formal instruction later, such as how to follow directions, stick to a task, cooperate with others, and display good manners. Children are also encouraged to grow emotionally and develop a positive self-concept, and to gain in large and small muscle skills. The nursery school day usually consists of a variety of more and less structured activities, ranging from art projects to group discussion to unstructured indoor and outdoor play. These activities are often organized around themes. For example, a unit on animals might involve making drawings of animals, acting out animal behavior, hearing stories about animals, and taking a trip to the zoo.

Compensatory Preschool Programs.   Perhaps the most important development in early childhood education over the past thirty years has been the introduction of **compensatory preschool programs** for children from disadvantaged backgrounds. A wide variety of programs were introduced under the overall federal Head Start program, begun in 1965. Head Start was part of President Lyndon Johnson's war on poverty, an attempt to break the cycle of poverty. The idea was to give disadvantaged children a chance to start their formal schooling with the same preacademic and social skills possessed by middle-class children.

Typically, Head Start includes early childhood education programs designed to increase school readiness. However, the program also includes medical and dental services for children, at least one hot meal per day, and social services for their parents.

Connections

Compensatory and early intervention programs for students at risk are discussed further in Chapter 12.

---

readiness training: teaching the skills and knowledge necessary for a given activity.

compensatory preschool programs: programs designed to prepare disadvantaged children for entry into kindergarten and first grade.

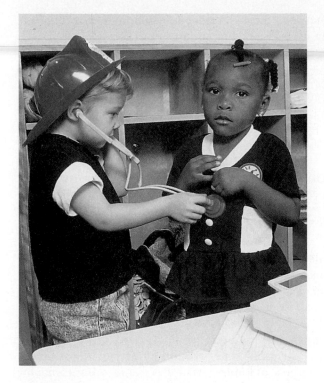

In what type of play are these children engaged? How might the children benefit from play sessions such as this in terms of their development of prosocial behaviors and peer relations?

Research on Head Start has generally found positive effects on children's readiness skills and on many other outcomes (Karweit, 1989a; McKey *et al.*, 1985; Zigler and Valentine, 1979). The effects on academic readiness skills have been greatest for those Head Start programs that stress academic achievement (Stallings and Stipek, 1986).

Research that followed disadvantaged children who participated in several such programs found that these students did better throughout their school years than similar students who did not participate in the programs (Berrueta-Clement *et al.*, 1984). For example, 67 percent of the students in one program, the Perry Preschool, ultimately graduated from high school, as compared with 49 percent of students in a control group who did not attend preschool. However, preschool programs by themselves are much less effective than preschool programs followed up by high-quality programs in the early elementary grades (Karweit, 1994a).

The research on compensatory early childhood education might seem to indicate that preschool programs are crucial for all students. However, many researchers (for example, Nurss and Hodges, 1982) hypothesize that preschool programs are more critical for lower-class than for middle-class children, because many of the experiences provided by preschools are typically present in middle-class homes but lacking in lower-class homes.

Early Intervention.   Most compensatory preschool programs, including Head Start, have begun working with children and their parents when the children are three or four. However, many researchers believe that for children who are at the greatest risk for school failure, earlier intervention is needed. A number of **early intervention programs** have been developed to start with children as young as six months. One of the most successful of these was a program for the children of retarded mothers in an inner-city Milwaukee neighborhood. An intensive program of infant stimulation, high-quality preschool, and family services made it possible

early intervention programs: compensatory preschool programs that target very young children at the greatest risk of school failure.

for the children to perform adequately through elementary school; nearly all of the children in a comparison group were assigned to special education (Garber, 1988). Several other early intervention programs have also had strong effects on students that have lasted into elementary school (Ramey and Ramey, 1992; Wasik and Karweit, 1994).

The introduction of preschool programs such as Head Start was based on the belief that the preschool years were critical to a child's cognitive development. These programs emphasized structured learning experiences designed to accelerate development by matching curriculum activities to the cognitive level of children (Zigler and Seitz, 1982).

Associated with the idea that cognitive development is shaped by early experience is the belief that later development can be predicted from early experiences (Kagan *et al.*, 1979). However, many researchers question the degree to which early experiences determine later development (Clarke and Clarke, 1976; Goldhaber, 1979; Kagan *et al.*, 1979; Thomas, 1981). Their research has shown that young children who are deprived of appropriate early experiences can catch up if given supportive environments later (Clarke and Clarke, 1976). Such findings do not imply that early environments are unimportant, but they do indicate that both early and later experiences affect development (Karweit, 1994a).

Kindergarten Programs.   Most students attend kindergarten the year before they enter first grade. However, only seven states require kindergarten attendance (Karweit, 1989b). The original purpose of kindergarten was to prepare students for formal instruction by encouraging development of their social skills, but in recent years this function has increasingly been taken on by nursery schools and preschool programs. The kindergarten has increasingly focused on academics, emphasizing prereading and premathematical skills, as well as behaviors that are appropriate in school (such as raising hands, lining up, and taking turns). In some school districts, kindergarten programs are becoming similar to what first grades once were, a trend that is opposed by most child development experts (*e.g.*, Bryant *et al.*, 1991; Elkind, 1981). One particularly distressing aspect of this trend is that many schools are failing students in kindergarten if they do not meet certain performance standards (Mantzicopoulos and Morrison, 1992).

Research on **retention** in kindergarten finds that while it improves children's performance relative to their grademates in the short run, it is detrimental in the long run (Ellwein *et al.*, 1991; Karweit and Wasik, 1994; Shepard and Smith, 1986). Many schools attempt to adjust to young students' different developmental stages by inserting an additional year between the beginning of kindergarten and the end of first grade for children who appear to be at risk. Different versions of the strategy are called junior kindergarten, transitional first grade, pre-first, and so on. Studies of these strategies find few benefits in the long run (Karweit and Wasik, 1994).

Research on kindergarten indicates that attending a full- or half-day kindergarten program is beneficial for academic readiness and increases a child's achievement in the first and second grades, but these effects diminish or disappear by the third or fourth grade (Nurss and Hodges, 1982). Recently research has indicated that lower-class students gain more from well-structured full-day kindergarten programs than from half-day programs (Karweit, 1989b; 1994b).

Developmentally Appropriate Practice.   A concept that has become increasingly important in early childhood education is called developmentally appropriate

retention: the practice of having students repeat a year of school.

practice. This is instruction based on students' individual characteristics and needs, not their ages (Elkind, 1989). The National Association for the Education of Young Children (1989, p. 4) has described developmentally appropriate practice for students ages 5–8 as follows:

> Each child is viewed as a unique person with an individual pattern and timing of growth. Curriculum and instruction are responsive to individual differences in ability and interests. Different levels of ability, development, and learning styles are expected, accepted, and used to design curriculum. Children are allowed to move at their own pace in acquiring important skills including those of writing, reading, spelling, math, social studies, science, art, music, health, and physical activity. For example, it is accepted that not every child will learn how to read at age 6, most will learn by 7, and some will need intensive exposure to appropriate literacy experiences to learn to read by age 8 or 9.

The NAEYC and other advocates of developmentally appropriate practice recommend extensive use of projects, play, exploration, group work, learning centers, and so on, and a de-emphasis on teacher-directed instruction, basal readers, phonics, and workbooks.

Along with a renewed emphasis on developmentally appropriate practice has come the re-emergence of an innovation of the 1950s, the nongraded primary or elementary school, in which students are assigned to multi-age classes and are flexibly grouped for instruction across age lines (see Katz *et al.,* 1991; Pavan, 1992). A review of studies of nongraded programs done in the 1960s and 1970s found that such programs could be beneficial for student achievement if they still emphasized instruction from the teacher. To the extent they emphasized individualized instruction, learning centers, and other work done independently of the teacher, they became ineffective (Gutiérrez and Slavin, 1992).

Self–Check

Distinguish the day-care center, nursery school, compensatory preschool, and kindergarten as alternative approaches to early childhood education. What do research findings suggest about the value of early intervention, compensatory readiness training, and kindergarten retention? What is meant by developmentally appropriate practice?

How Do Children Develop During the Elementary Years?

Children entering the first grade are in a transitional period from the rapid growth of early childhood to a phase of more gradual development. Shifts in both mental and social development characterize the early school years.

Several years later, when children reach the upper elementary grades, they are nearing the end of childhood and entering preadolescence. These "transescents," as Donald Eichorn (1966) called them, are in transition from childhood to adolescence.

Connections

Chapter 13 relates knowledge of students' cognitive, physical, and socioemotional development to the creation of cognitive, psychomotor, and affective behavioral objectives in planning and assessment.

Developmentally Appropriate Early Education

With an eye to the much publicized competitive world of the future, many parents seek opportunities to give their childre n every educational advantage, beginning even in infancy. In response, preschool private enterprises talk about the "goal-oriente d" activities and "structured-play" opportunities their services offer. Preschools are generally available only to parents who can afford them, but over the years federally funded programs for low-income children, such as Head Start, have helped even the odds for school readiness and early academic success. A new Chapter 1 program in Brooklyn, New York, called Giant Step, has served 7000 preschool-age children with spectacular results. Giant Step kids do twice as well on standardized tests as those in older preschool programs. How do they do it? Spokespersons say that the children learn how to learn in small classes assisted by teachers, aides, and social workers, who make house calls to get parents actively involved.

Demand for kindergarten space is just as great as the demand for private and public preschool programs. Traditionally, kindergartners have attended half-day sessions and in many districts across the nation these have become overcrowded because of the birth-rate bulge of the late 1980s. Even so, parents are clamoring for full-day kindergarten sessions and more rigorous academic preparation. It seems clear to such parents that good early childhood education can enhance chances of future success.

Some observers note, however, that kindergartens of today resemble what first grade used to be, and that young kids who are pushed too hard do less well in school later and often develop emotional or behavioral problems. Is accelerated learning premature in preschool and kindergarten?

Critics say the temptation to use inappropriate instructional approaches to boost educational outcomes is too great, with the chance that lectures, worksheets, and computer training will be emphasized over the time-honored picture books, blocks, and costumes and props for playing house. These critics would call attention to the words of the founder of the kindergarten movement, Frederick Frobel, who wrote, "I shall not call this an infant school because I do not intend the children to be schooled but to be allowed under the gentlest treatment to develop freely."

CRITICAL THINKING

What are the advantages and disadvantages of readiness-oriented and accelerated early childhood education programs? What guidelines would you use to determine what kind of early childhood education is the right kind and how much is too much?

Source: Colette Daiute, "All Work and No Play," Teacher, January 1992; Mary Drew, "From Garden to Hothouse," Teacher, March 1991.

Physical Development During Middle Childhood

As children progress through the primary grades, their physical development slows in comparison with earlier childhood. Children change relatively little in size during the primary years.

To picture the "typical" child in the primary grades, we must picture a child in good physical condition. Girls are slightly shorter and lighter than boys until around the age of nine, when height and weight are approximately equal for boys and girls.

Muscular development is outdistanced by bone and skeletal development. This may cause the aches commonly known as "growing pains. " Also, the growing muscles need much exercise, which may contribute to the primary-grade child's inability to stay still for long. By the time children enter the primary grades, they have developed many of the basic motor skills needed for balance, running, jumping, and throwing. During the primary years skills involving the large and small muscles are improved through practice. As development progresses, children can switch from using oversized pencils to regular-sized ones, and from activities like finger painting that use awkward whole-arm movements to building intricate models and using delicate finger movements to play the piano and stringed instruments. In addition, the eyesight of children often improves during this period. Many preschoolers tend toward farsightedness, but as the eye changes shape during the early primary grades, this condition improves.

Although this is a period of general good health, not all children fit the description of the "typical" child. Some of the childhood diseases that previous generations of children were expected to suffer through (such as measles and mumps) are now controlled through immunization programs, but not all children are protected. Other diseases now controlled by immunization programs include smallpox, diphtheria, polio, and German measles.

Nine-year-old boys and girls are similar in both height and weight. Upper elementary students are, on average, healthier than their younger brothers and sisters. Children who have entered the middle childhood period show more resistance to fatigue and disease. They are better coordinated than seven- or eight-year-olds.

During the latter part of the fourth grade, however, many girls begin a major growth spurt that will not be completed until puberty. This spurt begins with the rapid growth of the arms and legs. At this point there is *not* an accompanying change in trunk size. The result is a "gangly" or "all-arms-and-legs" appearance. Because this bone growth occurs before the development of associated muscles and cartilage, children at this growth stage temporarily lose some coordination and strength.

By the start of the fifth grade, almost all girls have begun this spurt. In addition, muscle and cartilage growth of the limbs resumes in the earlier-maturing females and they regain their strength and coordination. By the end of the fifth grade, girls are typically taller, heavier, and stronger than boys. Since males are twelve to eighteen months behind girls in development, even early-maturing boys do not start their growth spurt until age eleven. By the start of the sixth grade, therefore, most girls will be near the peak of their growth spurt and all but the early-maturing boys will be continuing the slow, steady growth of late childhood. Girls usually will have started their menstrual period by age thirteen. For boys, the end of preadolescence and the onset of early adolescence is measured by the first ejaculation, which occurs between the ages of thirteen and sixteen.

Cognitive Abilities

Between the ages of five and seven, children's thought processes undergo significant changes (Ginsburg and Opper, 1988; Osborn and Osborn, 1983). This is a period of transition from the stage of preoperational thought to the stage of concrete operations. This change allows them to do mentally what previously was done physically, and to mentally reverse the actions involved (see Chapter 2).

All children do not make this transition at the same age, and no individual child changes from one stage to the next quickly. Children will often use cognitive behaviors characteristic of two stages of development at the same time. As individuals advance from one stage to the next, the characteristics of the previous stage are maintained as the cognitive behaviors of the higher stage develop.

In addition to entering the concrete operational stage, elementary school-age children are rapidly developing memory and cognitive skills, including metacognitive skills, the ability to think about their own thinking and to learn how to learn. Cognitive skills are discussed in Chapters 6 and 7.

Theory Into Practice
Teaching Concrete-Operational Learners

Most children in elementary school are at the concrete operational stage of cognitive development and therefore lack the ability to think in abstractions. This means that classroom instruction in the elementary grades should be as concrete and experiential as possible.

- Science lessons should involve touching, building, manipulating, experimenting, and tasting.
- Social studies lessons should include field trips, guest speakers, role playing, and debates.
- Language arts and reading activities should include creating, imagining, acting out, and writing.
- Mathematics lessons should use concrete objects to show concepts, and allow students to manipulate objects to represent mathematical principles and operations.

An emphasis on the use of mathematics to solve real-life problems, as in simulations of buying things and receiving change or running a simulated bank or store, can be important. These activities give students concrete mental representations of the concepts they are learning, and these mental representations are critical in forming a solid basis of concepts on which later instruction will build.

Particularly in the early grades, elementary school children need to be able to relate concepts and information to their own experiences. For example, a "kilometer" has no meaning to students in the abstract, but may be related to the distance students walk to school. "Democracy" is a meaningless abstraction unless students can elect class leaders and live by a set of rules they had a part in developing.

Socioemotional Development in Preadolescence

By the time children enter elementary school, they have developed skills for more complex thought, action, and social influence. Up to this point, children have been basically egocentric, and their world has been that of home, family, and possibly a nursery school or day-care center.

The early primary grades will normally be spent working through Erikson's (1963) fourth stage, industry versus inferiority. Assuming that a child has developed trust during infancy, autonomy during the early years, and initiative during the preschool years, that child's experiences in the primary grades can contribute to his or her sense of industry and accomplishment.

These children are all the same age. In what ways will they vary in physical development as they grow? How might this variability affect the children's self-concepts? As a teacher, how would you support the socioemotinal development of these students during their preadolescent years?

During this stage children start trying to prove that they are "grown up"—in fact, this is often described as the "I-can-do-it-myself" stage. Work becomes possible. As children's powers of concentration grow, they can spend more time on chosen tasks and they often take pleasure in completing projects. This stage also includes the growth of independent action, cooperation with groups, performing in socially acceptable ways, and a concern for fair play.

Self-Concept. An important area of personal and social development for elementary school children is **self-concept,** or self-esteem. This aspect of their development will be strongly influenced by experiences at home, with peers, and at school. Self-concept includes the way we perceive our strengths, weaknesses, abilities, attitudes, and values. Its development begins at birth and is continually shaped by experience. Lack of a positive self-concept can severely damage a child's social development.

When children begin school, they tend to judge themselves on specific accomplishments rather than on a general sense of worth (Damon and Hart, 1982; Harter, 1982). You can understand this when you see that even the smallest failure can cause a child to feel worthless. It is also important to note that a child's self-concept can be different in different areas. For example, it is possible to have a positive self-image in school or sports but not in peer relations or physical self-image (Marsh, 1990a).

Self-esteem changes over the years of childhood and adolescence. Preschoolers and young children have extremely high self-concepts that bear no relationship to their school performance or other objective factors (Stipek, 1981). By second or third grade, however, children who are having difficulty in school begin to have lower self-concepts (Marsh, 1989; Marsh *et al.,* 1991). This begins a declining spiral; students who perform poorly in elementary school develop low academic self-concepts, and this in turn leads to poorer performance in secondary school (Marsh, 1990b). For most children, self-esteem gradually rises from fourth grade through adolescence, especially for children who are doing well in school, sports, or other activities.

The primary grades give many children their first chance to compare themselves with others and to work and play under the guidance of adults outside their family. These adults must provide experiences that let children succeed, feel good about themselves, and maintain their enthusiasm and creativity (Canfield, 1990).

Connections

For a discussion of the influences of self-concept and self-esteem on motivation, see Chapter 10.

---

self-concept: a person's perception of his or her own strengths and weaknesses.

self-esteem: the value each of us places on our own characteristics, abilities, and behaviors.

Theory Into Practice

Promoting the Development of Self-Esteem

Along with basic skills, the most important things elementary students are learning in school is whether they are "smart " or "dumb," "good kids" or "bad kids," popular or unpopular. A person's self-concept is largely formed during middle childhood, and the impact of school on self-concept can be profound.

The key word regarding personal and social development is "acceptance." The fact is, children do differ in their abilities, and no matter what teachers do, students will have figured out who is more able and who is less able by the end of the elementary years (usually earlier). However, teachers can have a substantial impact on how students feel about these differences, and on the value that low-achieving students place on learning even when they know they will never be the class star.

Teachers must accept students as they are and communicate a norm that all students are valuable and all are learners. They may also communicate the idea that there are many valuable skills. Some students are good in reading, others in math, others in sports, others in art. Particularly in the elementary school it is important to avoid setting up competition among students to be the "best" if only the most able students have a chance to win (Cohen, 1984).

If ability grouping within the class is used in reading or in mathematics, assignments to such groups should be done flexibly and changed often as students change in performance. This gets away from the idea that there are "high" and "low" students, but maintains the notion that different students need help with different skills at different times (Slavin, 1987c).

It goes without saying that teachers should never tell a student that he or she is "dumb," and should avoid implying this by word or action. For example, even if the entire class knows that the "Yellowbirds" are the low reading group, the teacher should never refer to the "Yellowbirds" as such; to do so communicates the idea that those students will *always* be poor readers, which is rarely true and is harmful to the students' self-concepts (Barr, 1992).

As one example of how teachers can help the students maintain a positive self-image, Rosenholtz and Simpson (1984) have described the *multidimensional classroom*, in which teachers make it clear that there are many ways to succeed. They emphasize how much students are learning. For example, many teachers give students pretests before they begin an instructional unit, and then show the class how much everyone gained on a posttest. Multidimensional teachers may stress the idea that different students have different skills; some are good in reading, others in math, still others in art or music. By valuing all of these skills, the teacher can communicate the idea that there are many routes to success, rather than a single path (Cohen, 1984).

To maintain positive self-concepts among all students, teachers need not lie and say that all are equally good at reading or math. However, they can avoid unnecessary distinctions among students, recognize progress rather than level of ability, and value all kinds of skills. Also, teachers should focus their praise and evaluation on *effort,* not ability. Even if not every student can get 100 percent on a test, every student *can* give 100 percent effort, and it is this effort that should be recognized and rewarded.

Growing Importance of Peers.   The influence of the child's family, which was the major force during the early childhood years, continues in importance as parents provide role models in terms of attitudes and behaviors. In addition, relationships with brothers and sisters affect relationships with peers, and routines from home are either reinforced or must be overcome in school.

However, the peer group takes on added importance. Speaking on the child's entrance into the world outside the family, Ira Gordon noted the importance of peers:

> If all the world's the stage that Shakespeare claimed, children and adolescents are playing primarily to an audience of their peers. Their peers sit in the front rows and the box seats; parents and teachers are now relegated to the back rows and the balcony. (Gordon, 1975, p. 166)

In the lower elementary grades peer groups usually consist of same-sexed children who are around the same age. This preference may be due to the variety of abilities and interests among young children. By the sixth grade, however, students often form groups that include both boys and girls. Whatever the composition of peer groups, they let children compare their abilities and skills to those of others. Members of peers groups also teach one another about their different worlds. Children learn through this sharing of attitudes and values how to sort out and form their own attitudes and values.

Groups composed of boys and those made up of girls seem to value different attitudes and behavior. Boys gain prestige by being physically aggressive, good at sports, daring, attention-getting, and friendly to other males. In female peer groups membership is related more to being attractive, popular (with girls *and* boys), friendly, optimistic, and having a sense of humor about oneself (Rubin, 1980). Boys are expected by their peers to misbehave in class, while among girls being well-behaved and courteous is usually more important.

For both boys and girls in the upper elementary grades, membership in groups tends to promote feelings of self-worth. *Not* being accepted can bring serious emotional problems. Herein lies the major cause of the preadolescent's changing relationship with parents. It is not that preadolescents care less about their parents. It is just that their friends are *more* important than ever. This need for acceptance by peers helps explain why preadolescents often dress alike. Girls' conformity may be neater, but boys are just as likely to copy one another, perhaps in wearing their shirttails out or in wearing special athletic shoes. The story of Jake Stevens's earring at the opening of this chapter illustrates how young adolescents express their belongingness with other peer group members through distinctive dress or behavior.

Partly as a result of their changing physical and cognitive structures, children in the upper elementary grades seek to be more " grown up." They want their parents to treat them differently, even though many parents are unwilling to see them differently. Nine- to twelve-year-olds still depend heavily on their families and generally report that they love their parents. They also report that though they feel their parents love them, they do not think they *understand* them.

Regarding the changing relationships of preadolescents with their parents, Hershel Thornburg in *The Bubblegum Years* writes:

> Some parents believe that their happiest years as parents were when their children were in these bubblegum years. Nine- to twelve-year-olds do not have the same time-consuming needs they do when they are younger and neither have they matured to the point where they will be active, often unmanageable—their adolescent years. At the risk of discouraging some parents, it may be that this "sense of easy childrearing" is one reason

why so many preteens have problems. At the very point in time where parents relax in their childrearing roles, their preteens are going through the most significant changes of their lives. (Thornburg, 1979, p. 57)

Thornburg suggests that parents (and teachers) of preadolescents remember two facts (1979, p. 58):

1. When change is occurring, preteens are breaking up the well-defined, predictable behaviors and attitudes of childhood. They are growing up and changing the ways they do things, ways to which their parents have become accustomed.

2. When change is occurring, preteens need additional guidance. Parents must remember that many of their children's ways of acting are as new and unpredictable to the children as they are to them. Therefore parental direction and reassurance are important to normal growth.

The middle childhood years often also bring changes in the relationship between children and their teachers. Early in primary school, children easily accept and depend on teachers. During the upper elementary years this relationship becomes more complex. Sometimes students will tell teachers personal information they would not tell their parents. Some preadolescents even choose teachers as role models. At the same time, however, some preteens talk back to teachers in ways they would never have considered several years earlier, and some openly challenge teachers.

Emotional Concerns.   Emotional problems related to the physical, cognitive, and social development of upper elementary children are common. Though preadolescents are generally happy and optimistic, they also have many fears, such as:

- not being accepted into a peer group
- not having a "best friend"
- being punished by their parents
- having their parents get a divorce
- not doing well in school
- getting hurt

Other emotions of this age group include anger (and fear of being unable to control it), guilt, frustration, and jealousy. Preadolescents need help in realizing that these emotions and fears are a natural part of growing up. Adults must let them talk about these emotions and fears, even if they seem unrealistic to an adult. Feelings of guilt often arise when there is a conflict between children's actions (based on values of the peer group) and their parents' values. Anger is another common emotion at this age. It is displayed with more intensity than many of the other emotions. Just as they often tell their preadolescents they shouldn't be afraid, parents often tell them that they should not get angry. Unfortunately, this is an unrealistic expectation, even for adults—including parents!

Self-Check

Continue the comparison chart you began earlier, adding information in each category for Middle Childhood. Later, how will you clearly distinguish features of early and middle childhood?

Teachers on Teaching

How has your knowledge of child development helped you to make instruction developmentally appropriate?

As a language arts and English teacher of high-school-aged students with specific learning disabilities, I need to be aware of students' cognitive abilities and language development. I need to be sensitive to the learning channels by which individual students learn best. For example, some students learn best if instructions are shown as well as told. Some learn best if learning is broken down into small tasks and presented as a skill-building hierarchical process. I also need to gear instruction so that each student clearly understands instructions and can successfully complete the assignments. Many modifications can help, including the use of oral tests, additional time, reduction in the number of problems or sentences, questions read to a student, or dictation received from a student who has difficulty writing. Students have combinations of capabilities and deficits that interact with one another to which teachers must respond. By using students' best modes of learning, we can maximize their success. As a teacher of adolescents I also need to know about their physical, social, moral, and emotional development. Adolescence is a time for experimentation with possible roles. Most students would be expected to have reached or approached the stage of formal operations. It is in the social and emotional areas that the turmoil of adolescence is most apparent. Knowledge of physical, cognitive, and socioemotional development enables teachers to accommodate instruction to individual needs and to help students take small steps toward greater competence, maturity, and freedom.

Randall Amour, Special Educator Grades 6–12
Special Education Cooperative School,
Columbus, Texas

Curriculum is often developmentally inappropriate for students at the middle school level. There are problems with reading, mathematics, science—even art. Perspective drawing is a good example. Perspective drawing is based on a fixed, somewhat arbitrary point of view, with a set of inflexible rules. Some students understand the existence of viewpoints other than their own, while others struggle with the idea. For many, simultaneously thinking about another point of view and manipulating a set system of rules presents a significant cognitive challenge. Perspective drawing also requires an ability to measure. I have students who are unable to read or measure in standard units. Others sigh with indignation when we stop to examine the increments on rulers. However, most students bring with them an intense desire to learn to draw realistically. That interest has allowed me to adapt the art curriculum and to teach perspective with good results. We begin with three-dimensional, concrete experiences before we attempt any drawing. Then, to get from three to two dimensions, I have students use a piece of glass as a "window on the world" and markers to trace what they see onto the glass. By the time we start drawing, they've had the opportunity to experience and to think about points of view, how we learn to read distance with our eyes, and how the real world translates to a two-dimensional surface. Developmentally appropriate practice often requires adapting the curriculum to match and to challenge the students' abilities in relation to their cognitive development. In my experience the results are truly worth the effort.

Gail C. Dawson, Art Teacher
John Muir Middle School
San Leandro, California

How Do Children Develop During the Middle School and High School Years?

The adolescent period of development begins with puberty. The pubertal period, or early adolescence, is a time of rapid physical and intellectual development. Middle adolescence is a more stable period of adjustment to and integration of the changes of early adolescence. Later adolescence is marked by the transition into the responsibilities, choices, and opportunities of adulthood. In this section we will review the major changes that occur as the child becomes an adolescent, and we will examine how adolescent development affects teaching, curriculum, and school structure.

Physical Development During Adolescence

Puberty is a series of physiological changes that render the immature organism capable of reproduction. Nearly every organ and system of the body is affected by these changes. The prepubertal child and the postpubertal adolescent are different in outward appearance because of changes in stature and proportion and the development of primary and secondary sexual features. Table 3. 1 summarizes the typical sequence of physical development in adolescence.

Although the sequence of events at puberty is generally the same for each person, the timing and the rate at which they occur vary widely. The average girl typically begins pubertal changes one and a half to two years before the average boy. In each sex, however, the normal range of onset is approximately six years. Like the onset, the rate of changes also varies widely, with some people taking only eighteen to twenty-four months to go through the pubertal changes to reproductive maturity, while others may require six years to pass through the same stage.

These differences mean that some individuals may be completely mature before others the same age have even begun puberty. The age of maximum diversity is thirteen for males and about eleven for females. The comparisons children make among themselves, as well as the tendency to hold maturity in high regard, can be a problem for the less mature. On the other hand, the first to mature are also likely to experience temporary discomfort because they stand out from the less mature majority.

Adapting to Puberty.   One of the most important challenges to adolescents is to accommodate to the changes in their bod ies. Coordination and physical activity must be adjusted rapidly as height, weight, and skills change. The new body must be integrated into the existing self-image. New routines of care must be learned and new habits developed. As adolescents become more like adults in appearance, they find themselves expected to behave more like adults, regardless of their emotional, intellectual, or social maturity.

The purpose of puberty is to make people able to reproduce. Thus the adolescent is faced with a new potential that includes increased interest in sexual activity, erotic fantasy, and experimentation. Masturbation becomes a regular activity for many adolescents, and increasing percentages of adolescents engage in intercourse (Hass, 1979). Sexual activity necessitates facing the possibility of sexually transmitted diseases, conflict with parents, and pregnancy.

Early and Late Maturing.   Researchers have long been interested in the possible differences between children who enter puberty early and those who enter it

puberty: developmental stage at which a person becomes capable of reproduction.

Girls	Boys
Initial enlargement of the breasts occurs (breast bud stage). Straight, lightly pigmented pubic hair appears. Maximum growth rate is attained. Pubic hair becomes adult in type but covers a smaller area than in adult. Breast enlargement continues; the nipple and the area around it now project above the level of the breast. Menarche occurs. Underarm hair appears; the sweat glands under the arms increase in size. Breasts and pubic hair reach adult stage.	Growth of the testes and scrotum begins. Straight, lightly pigmented pubic hair appears. Growth of the penis begins. Early changes in the voice occur. First ejaculation of semen occurs. Pubic hair becomes adult in type but covers a smaller area than in adult. Maximum growth rate is attained. Underarm hair appears; the sweat glands under the arms increase in size. The voice deepens noticeably. Growth of mustache and beard hair begins. Pubic hair reaches adult stage.

TABLE 3.1   The Typical Sequence of Physical Development in Adolesence

Source: The Committee on Adolescence, Group for the Advancement of Psychiatry, 1968; Tanner, 1978.

when they are older. Peskin (1967) demonstrated that earlier maturers have a harder time *at* puberty. Youths who mature earlier experience more anxiety and have more temper tantrums, more conflict with their parents, and lower self-esteem at puberty than do those who are older at puberty. But by the time the earlier maturers are in high school, long past puberty and having accommodated its changes, they are more at ease, popular, and mature than are later maturers, who are still experiencing pubertal changes. Problems of late maturation seem to be much greater for boys than for girls (Greif and Ulman, 1982; Steinberg and Hill, 1978). A few studies have found that even in their thirties early-maturing males are more confident and poised than males who matured later (Livson and Peskin, 1980).

Cognitive Development

As the rest of the body changes at puberty, the brain and its functions also change. Just as pubertal changes vary widely across individuals, so does the timing of intellectual changes vary. One indication of this is that scores on intelligence tests obtained over several years from the same individual fluctuate most during the period from twelve to fifteen years of age.

In Piaget's theory of cognitive development, adolescence is the stage of transition from the use of concrete operations to the application of formal operations in reasoning. Adolescents begin to be aware of the limitations of their thinking. They wrestle with concepts that are removed from their own experience. Inhelder and Piaget (1958) acknowledge that brain changes at puberty may be necessary for the cognitive advances of adolescence. They assert, however, that experience with complex problems, the demands of formal instruction, and exchange and contradiction of ideas with peers are also necessary for formal operational reasoning to develop. Adolescents who reach this stage (not all do) have attained an adult level of reasoning. For more on Piaget's theories on cognitive development in adolescence, see Chapter 2.

In terms of Piaget's classification, these teens are in the formal operational stage of cognitive development. How does the picture suggest this idea? By what processes did these students begin to acquire formal operations?

Theory Into Practice

Helping Students Become Formal-Operational Learners

The cognitive changes of adolescence have major implications for teaching and for curriculum. As young adolescents begin to sense the inadequacy of concrete operational logic, they may become frustrated with learning. They may struggle with tasks that adults see as simple, but that require new and unfamiliar assumptions. Teachers should help young adolescents explore the uses of abstract thinking, but should keep in mind that it takes students several years to fully develop their newfound intellectual skills.

Just as physical puberty occurs at different ages and rates, so do the intellectual changes of adolescence. Since grade assignment is based on age, the seventh through ninth grades typically mix students with different levels of cognitive maturity. It is the teacher's job to accommodate these student differences—and not to punish the slower-maturing pupils.

The curriculum should change as cognitive abilities change. It is no accident that algebra, with all its abstract concepts, is introduced in early adolescence. Science moves from simple content and observational skills toward experimentation and full use of logic. Mathematics is integrated into the study of science as students become able to use the two systems simultaneously. Social studies and literature increasingly emphasize interpretation, synthesis, and exploration of different forms of both creation and criticism (Becker, 1990).

Effective teachers of adolescents respect and enjoy the intellectual practices that adolescents engage in, even when, as sometimes happens, they are turned on the teacher. A primary goal of teaching, after all, is to help students learn to think.

Characteristics of Hypothetical-Deductive Reasoning

Hypothetical-deductive reasoning is one of the characteristics which mark the development of formal operational thinking that emerges by the time children are about 12 years old. Prior to formal operations, thought is concrete operational in nature. The differences between these two stages of thinking are exemplified in Table 3.2.

Piaget found that the use of formal operations depended on the learner's familiarity with a given subject area. When students were familiar with a subject, they were more likely to use formal operations. When unfamiliar, students proceeded more slowly, tended to use concrete reasoning patterns, and used self-regulation sparingly.

The Implications for Educational Practice

Consider the following general guidelines:

1. When introducing new information, particularly involving abstract concepts and theories, allow students enough time to absorb the ideas and to use formal

Table 3.2 Comparing Concrete and Formal Operations

Non–Hypothetical-Deductive Reasoning (Concrete Operational Thinkers)	Hypothetical-Deductive Reasoning (Formal Operational Thinkers)
Can form limited hypotheses, reasons with reference to actions, objects, and properties that are familiar or that can be experienced.	Can form multiple hypotheses, has combinatorial logic, reasons with concrete and formal abstract concepts and relationships; reasons about intangible properties and theories.
May memorize prominent words, phrases, formulas, and procedures but will apply them with little understanding of the abstract meaning or principles underlying them.	Can understand the abstract meaning and principles underlying formal concepts, relationships, and theories.
Has problems reasoning logically about ideas that are contrary to fact or personal beliefs, or that are arbitrary.	Can argue logically about ideas that are contrary to fact or personal belief or that are arbitrary; can reason based on testimonials.
Needs step-by-step instructions when planning a lengthy, complex procedure.	Can plan a lengthy, complex procedure given a set of conditions, goals, and resources.
Is unaware of inconsistencies and contradictions within own thinking.	Is aware and critical of own reasoning; can reflect on the problem-solving process and verify conclusions by checking sources, using other known information, or seeking a solution from another perspective.

thought patterns. Begin with more familiar examples and encourage them to apply hypothetical-deductive reasoning.

2. Students who have not yet attained formal operational thought may need more support for planning complex tasks. Pairing children who can plan with those who need support is one way of handling the situation.

3. Encourage students to state principles and ideas in their own words and to search for the meaning behind abstract ideas and theories.

4. Incorporate a variety of activities that promote the use of hypothetical deductive thinking.

   For example:

   a. Have students write a paper that requires a debate between arguments pro and con, and a discussion of the evidence that supports the two perspectives. For younger students, you may want to pair children or groups and have one write from one perspective and the other from another.

   b. Have students discuss each other's ideas—purposefully picking specific opposing positions. Debates and mock trials are two ways this can be done.

   c. Develop cooperative activities that require much planning and organization. Have children work in groups composed of children with different levels of planning and organizing skills. Provide an outline of what to think about as the planning process proceeds for those children who are still at the concrete operational level.

   d. Develop activities in which facts come from different testimonials that may be contradictory, such as television commercials. For example, use commercials in which one brand claims that brand X is the best selling domestic car and has more features than other cars. Brand Y claims that its cars are the highest-rated and have higher levels of owner satisfaction. Have the students discuss and weigh the evidence from these different sources.

   e. Have students critique their own work. Ask students to generate a list of ways one could look for flaws in thinking or other sources that might be used to verify results.

Socioemotional Development in Adolescence

One of the first signs of early adolescence is the appearance of **reflectivity,** or the tendency to think about what is going on in one's own mind and to study oneself. Adolescents begin to look more closely at themselves and to define themselves differently. They start to realize that there are differences between what they think and feel and how they behave. Using the developing intellectual skills that permit them to consider possibilities, adolescents are prone to be dissatisfied with themselves. They critique their personal characteristics, compare themselves to others, and try to change the way they are.

Adolescents may also ponder whether other people see and think about the world in the same way they do. They become more aware of their separateness from other people, and of their uniqueness. They learn that other people cannot know fully what they think and feel. The issue of who and what one "really" is dominates personality development in adolescence.

reflectivity: the act of analyzing oneself and one's own thoughts.

According to Erikson, the stage is set during adolescence for a major concern with who one is—with one's identity.

Identity. The physical and intellectual changes of adolescence disrupt the child's sense of continuity and personal wholeness. The cognitive ability to relate past to present, and to think about the future, presents the young adolescent with the problem of understanding the continuity of experience across time and projecting that continuity into the future. The adolescent's psychosocial task, then, is to create a sense of what Erikson calls ego identity. To accomplish this, adolescents usually depend on several activities.

1. They pay great attention to how other people view them: Young adolescents have sensitive antennas, tuned to receive subtle messages about themselves from other people. They listen carefully to their peers, parents, teachers, and other adults for any information that indicates how these people view them. Information obtained is chewed over, worried about, compared to other views, and inserted into their self-concept, if it can be made compatible with information already there.

2. They search the past: Young adolescents often want to know about their ancestors, family trees, their own infant and childhood experiences. Some learn basic genetics, and are concerned about the sources of their physical and psychological characteristics. All these contribute to their understanding of continuity across time and of their potential future.

3. They experiment with roles: Their attempts to find out what kind of person they are lead to trying out different ways of being. Healthy adolescents explore who they are by attempting to be different. They adopt the characteristics of other people to see if they fit themselves. They take on, and quickly cast off, the traits of peers, teachers, and other acquaintances. As they try on characters and roles, they test how they feel. They also watch carefully how other people respond to their experiments in order to see if they can fit them into their relationships with others.

4. They act on feelings and express their beliefs and opinions: Adolescents place a high value on "being honest" and on behaving in ways that are "true to oneself." Some adolescents become distressed if they think they are not presenting their real feelings or if they are not being consistent in their behavior. Gradually most come to realize that feelings, beliefs, and people can change, and that consistency is less important than accurate representation of oneself.

Erikson calls the experience of not having a sense of one's identity **identity diffusion**. This is the unpleasant awareness of continual change in oneself and of the differences between one's self-concept and how others see one. To escape this troubling situation, some adolescents adopt a role—an identity—prematurely. Such a choice, which Erikson calls **identity foreclosure**, gives a person a self-concept around which to organize feelings and behavior. The choices are usually supported by the reactions of parents and other people, because they find it helpful to know how to relate to the adolescent. Often adolescents choose a role that they know will be socially desirable—the premed scholar, for example. Sometimes, however, as in the choice of sexual promiscuity by a rebellious youth, the behavior may draw disapproval, even though it may have been "forecast" by anxious parents.

Foreclosed identities may help adolescents cope with the normal identity crisis, but may not be psychologically healthy. Eventually, the hastily chosen identity is

identity diffusion: the adolescent's inability to develop a clear sense of self.

identity foreclosure: the premature choice of a role, often done to reinforce self-concept.

establish their own identity. Teenage gossip spreads quickly. For many, the telephone provides an essential link to peers. Fads are shared, imitated, and rejected. Adolescents with similar interests and values form groups. The friendships made in adolescence may endure through life—if not in reality, at least in nostalgia.

Friendships change quickly and constantly during adolescence. Teachers encounter this phenomenon as they intercept notes passed between friends and struggle to keep the attention of young adolescents for whom, at a particular moment, nothing may be as important as telling their best friends the latest and hottest gossip. They will also see groups of friends who must sit together, do projects together, and play on the same teams.

Good teachers have a sense of humor about adolescent relationships. They know that the skills of friendship are necessary throughout life, whereas any particular school lesson is likely to have a slight long-term effect. While teachers must limit the intrusion of social activities into the classroom, they should acknowledge their importance and be respectful of their significance.

If school is to be a place where students are helped to understand the world around them and to interpret their experiences in it, educators have to pay attention to interpersonal skills and relationships. At some point in the curriculum, adolescents' experience as peers, friends, intimates, and potential mates should be addressed, though it is an unusual school that does this in a systematic way. Typically these issues are incorporated into courses on family living or health. Probably more important are spontaneous class discussions or an impromptu discussion with a particularly astute teacher. The teacher who is prepared and willing to talk about the important issues of friendship with young adolescents will be sought out by students and is sure to have challenging and rewarding interactions with them.

Schools, like families, must deal with the pressures placed on adolescents by their peer groups to conform. It is discouraging to a teacher to suspect that a student is holding back in class for fear of risking ridicule or laughter. Teachers should use such incidents to encourage appropriate risk taking and talk to students about acceptance and tolerance. It may take sensitive individual encouragement to convince a student to try an activity or a challenge that is not considered "cool" by that student's peers.

Building students' social competence and social responsibility are important ends in themselves, but there is also evidence that they have positive effects on students' academic performance as well (Wentzel, 1991). Direct teaching of universally held moral values, such as honesty, caring, and cooperation, and modeling of these values by teachers in their interactions with students, can be valuable in building students' commitments to prosocial goals (Kirschenbaum, 1992).

Intimacy.   A powerful interpretation of adolescent interpersonal relationships is provided in the classic work of Harry Stack Sullivan (1953). In his *Interpersonal Theory of Psychiatry* Sullivan presents a hypothesis to describe the changes in important relationships from infancy to adulthood. In Sullivan's view, human behavior is shaped by our attempts to maintain comfortable relationships with significant other people. We often act to avoid anxiety, the emotion we feel when one of our significant relationships—and therefore our security—is threatened. As children develop, the number and the variety of their significant relationships expand: the newborn's sole relationship is with the mother, but the older child develops relationships with other family members and caretakers. Moving on, playmates are added, then classmates, teachers, and other adults. As the circle of important relationships expands, new social skills are required, and children gradually join the larger society. Security of relationships is the most important human need, and it governs and motivates social behavior and development.

In early adolescence, according to Sullivan, two new needs arise. First is the need for intimacy, for relationships in which a person can share feelings and thoughts with an equal. Second, and less important, is the need for sexual gratification. The tasks of adolescence are to develop the skills of intimacy and to begin developing relationships that will lead to the choice of a partner for sexual gratification.

Adolescents who develop relationships with the other sex without major mishap are those who can separate their needs for intimacy and for sexual gratification. They give priority to developing friendships with peers of both sexes. They do not confuse real intimacy, which may or may not include sex, with sexual "intimacy." Wise adolescents seem to know what Sullivan proposed: Mature adult relationships are those in which intimacy is maintained, and lasting sexual gratification is achieved within an intimate relationship.

Sullivan's approach helps us understand the gradual changes in peer interactions around the time of puberty. The "gang" of playmates, chosen mainly on the basis of proximity, begins to split up into pairs. Friends spend more time talking; action becomes less necessary. Young people seek privacy from adults and peers. Friendships may shift rapidly as adolescents seek others at similar stages of development. Friendships are tested repeatedly. Exclusivity is sought—"We have to be *best* friends"—to protect the adolescent who wants to share inner feelings. But, inevitably, confidences are broken, secrets are shared, and best friends become untrustworthy enemies. Concern, trustworthiness, and loyalty characterize these early efforts at intimacy (Berndt, 1982).

Dating plays an important role in the process of identity formation because the dating "game" lets adolescents try out the male and female roles. The reaction of the partner provides the adolescent with information about how to play the role, and how well he or she is playing it. Although dating may be less formal today than in earlier generations, and may involve more equality between boys and girls, it still includes awkward moments as adolescents use dates to learn more about one another than can be learned in a group.

Seen in this way, dating is a step toward the stage beyond Erikson's identity stage. In his theory, the stage of young adulthood is marked by concern for intimacy, which is the sharing of one's identity with that of another person. Intimacy develops as the two identities come to overlap and to include as a part of each being a member of the intimate pair. As young couples date and move toward "going steady," seeing themselves and being seen by others as a couple, they gain shared experiences on which to base a shared identity.

What characteristics of adolescent development may be inferred from this picture? As a teacher, how could you make this group's interest educationally relevant? How might you build on student's social competence and social responsibility to help them improve their academic performance?

Problems of Adolescence

Adolescence is the time when a person's identity is largely established (Erikson, 1963). A group of eleven-year-olds is fairly homogeneous. However, six years later some will be delinquents, others star pupils. Some will be math whizzes, others will be interested in art or drama, and still others will be concerned with auto mechanics. High school teen groups have clear demarcations: "jocks," "grinds," "grits," "hoods," "druggies," and so on. Obviously, experiences at home and in school before adolescence play an important role in determining how an individual's adolescence will turn out, and the best approach to the problems of adolescence is

Connections

Problems of adolescence that place students at risk of failing academically or dropping out of school are discussed again in Chapter 12.

prevention in the younger grades (Zigler *et al.*, 1992). Still, junior and senior high schools play a crucial role in helping students through a period that is quite difficult for most of them (Elkind, 1984).

Most adolescents experience emotional conflicts at some point (Blos, 1979). This is hardly surprising since they are going through rapid and dramatic changes in body image, expected roles, and peer relationships. The transitions from elementary to middle or junior high and then onto high school can also be quite stressful for many students (Simmons *et al.*, 1987; Hirsch and Radkin, 1987). For most adolescents, emotional distress is temporary and is successfully handled, but for some, the stresses lead to delinquency, drug abuse, or suicide attempts (O'Neil, 1991).

Emotional Disorders.   Mild to serious emotional disorders frequently arise during adolescence. These range from depression to being overly anxious about health to suicidal thoughts or attempts (Masterson, 1967). Many adolescents who engage in delinquent, bizarre, or self-abusive behavior do so as a call for help during a difficult period. Others use drugs, alcohol, or sex as a response to emotional disorders that could have been detected and resolved.

Secondary educators should be sensitive to the stresses faced by adolescents and should realize that emotional disturbances are common. They should understand that depressed, hopeless, or unaccountably angry behavior can be a clue that the adolescent needs help, and should attempt to put such students in touch with school counselors or other psychologically trained adults. See Chapter 12 for more on emotional disorders.

Drug and Alcohol Abuse.   Drug and alcohol abuse have increased dramatically in recent years. A majority of high school students have used marijuana at least once, and increasing numbers seriously abuse alcohol. It is safe to say that most high school teachers will sooner or later encounter students who come to school drunk or stoned.

Experimentation with marijuana and alcohol is not particularly harmful in itself. However, rates of alcoholism and of daily marijuana use among high school students are at alarming levels, and the rates of cocaine use are increasing (although uses of heroin and hallucinogens are decreasing; National Institute on Drug Abuse, 1987). Not surprisingly, heavy use of alcohol and drugs has a serious impact on students' performance in school (Conger and Peterson, 1984).

Delinquency and Violence.   One of the most dangerous problems of adolescence is the beginning of serious delinquency. The problem is far more common among males than females (Dornbusch *et al.*, 1985). Delinquents are usually low achievers who have been given little reason to believe that they can succeed by following the path laid out for them by the school. Delinquency in adolescence is overwhelmingly a group phenomenon; most delinquent acts are done in groups or with the active support of a delinquent subgroup (Hirschi, 1969). Delinquency (and its prevention) is discussed in Chapter 11.

Risk of Pregnancy.   Pregnancy and childbirth are increasing among all groups of female adolescents, but particularly among those from lower-income homes (Morrison, 1985). Just as adolescent boys often engage in delinquent behavior to try to establish their independence from adult control, so adolescent girls often engage in sex, and in many cases have children, to force the world to see them as adults. Since early childbearing makes it difficult for adolescent girls to continue their schooling or get jobs, it is a primary cause of the continuation of the cycle of poverty into which many adolescent mothers were themselves born. Of course, the other side of teen pregnancy is teen fatherhood. Teen fathers also suffer behavioral and academic problems in school (Hanson *et al.*, 1989).

Risk of AIDS. In addition to all the traditional risks of early sexual activity is the rise in AIDS and other sexually transmitted diseases. AIDS is still very rare during the adolescent years but is growing rapidly among individuals in their twenties. Since full-blown AIDS can take ten years to appear, it is assumed that unprotected sex, needle-sharing, and other high-risk behavior among teens is what is causing the AIDS epidemic among young adults. The appearance of AIDS has made the need for early, explicit sex education critical, potentially a life-or-death matter.

Connections

The problems of childhood and adolescence discussed in this chapter relate to information on students at risk in Chapter 12.

Self-Check

Add information about adolescence in the last column of the comparison chart you started, using the same categories as before. Later, how will you be able to clearly distinguish features of middle childhood and adolescence? Reread the scenario at the beginning of this chapter and explain the interaction between Jake and Billy in terms of what you have learned about child development.

The Junior High Homework Dilemma

Makita Reynolds, a junior high school teacher with four years' experience, talks with Bobby Ryan, a seventh-grader,

MAKITA: Bobby, we have to talk about your last report card. I'm worried about your grades.

BOBBY: But, Mrs. Reynolds, I'm going to miss my bus.

MAKITA: Don't worry. You still have ten minutes. Bobby, your homework just isn't getting done these days, and that's your main problem. Are you giving the homework your best effort?

BOBBY: Yes; uh, no—not really. It's always too hard.

MAKITA: Now, Bobby, I have a lot of confidence that you can handle the work I assign. Do you think you might not be spending enough time on it?

BOBBY: I don't know. I just can't do it.

MAKITA: Bobby, what do you like to do after school?

BOBBY: Mostly I hang out with my friends or watch TV.

MAKITA: What do you and your friends do?

BOBBY: I don't know. Sometimes we go to the mall or over to someone's house.

MAKITA: Maybe you and your friends could spend some time doing homework together.

BOBBY: Nah, I don't think so, Mrs. Reynolds.

MAKITA: But they must have homework to do. When do they do theirs?

BOBBY: I don't know. In school, I guess.

MAKITA: In any case, what they do shouldn't have anything to do with your work. If you're finding the assignments too hard, do you think your mom or dad could help?

BOBBY: Nah. Last time I showed them some of those math problems you wanted us to do, they said they didn't understand them either.

MAKITA: Isn't there any way we can get you to do more homework?

BOBBY: I don't know, Mrs. Reynolds. I guess I could try a little harder.

MAKITA: OK, and maybe I can give you some help, too.

BOBBY: Can I go now?

MAKITA: I guess so. Go ahead.

A week later after school, Makita visits with Ann Macy, a mentor teacher with fifteen years' experience.

MAKITA: I talked with Bobby Ryan the other day about his homework. I'm not sure it did much good, though. Twice this week I've gone over homework assignments with him to make sure he understands them, but he still comes in the next day with little or nothing done. And he's not the only one of my boys who is starting to slack off on his work.

ANN: I know what you mean. Twelve or thirteen is a tough age for kids. I sometimes worry that if I grade them too hard, they may give up on school, but if I'm too easy on them, they'll figure they've outsmarted me.

MAKITA: Yeah, I've been wondering how tough to be with the grades this term. But I just don't know how else to get the attention of these kids.

ANN: You've got a particular challenge in Bobby's case, because his test scores and grades have always been good. He'd be perfectly fine if he'd only put his mind to it.

MAKITA: Ann I've got to do something to steer Bobby straight. What would you do?

Problem Solving

1. What are the cognitive and socioemotional characteristics of children Bobby's age? Does Bobby seem typical of children his age in relation to these developmental patterns?

2. Who are the various authority figures in Bobby's life? Which ones are apparently exerting the most influence at present? Is this typical with young adolescents?

3. How would you change the dialogue to model a more effective talk with Bobby on the teacher's part?

4. What can Makita do to help Bobby? Devise a plan of action for helping a student this age, including ways to approach and involve parents. Model your action plan by extending the dialogue between Ann and Makita.

Summary

How Do Children Develop During the Preschool Years?

Physically, young children develop strength and coordination of the large muscles first and then the small muscles (as in cutting with scissors or writing). Cognitive abilities corresponding to Piaget's sensorimotor and preoperational stages also include the acquisition of language. Verbal language is usually acquired by age three and includes the development of vocabulary, grammatical rules, and conventions of discourse. The foundations of reading and writing are usually acquired before formal schooling begins.

Socioemotional development in early childhood can be partly described in terms of Erikson's "initiative versus guilt" stage. Play is vital and tends to be voluntary, pleasurable, spontaneous, aimless, repetitive, imaginative, and nonliteral. Chief caregivers have the greatest impact on development, but it is during early childhood that peer relations based on equality are established. Self-expression, conflict, and cooperation contribute to social skills and moral development.

What Kind of Early Childhood Education Do Children Need?

Economic factors have led to a crisis in demand for early childhood education programs, including day-care centers, nursery schools, compensatory preschool programs, and kindergartens. Research findings have tended to support trends toward early intervention, school-readiness training, continuation of compensatory programs in the early elementary grades, targeting of students placed at risk, and avoidance of potential detriments of kindergarten retention.

How Do Children Develop During the Elementary Years?

Between the ages of five and seven, children have slower growth but greater health and skill. They think in ways described in Piaget's theory as the concrete operational stage and develop skills of conservation, classification, and number. Children can perform mathematical operations, form limited hypotheses, and understand space and time. Children in the upper elementary grades move from egocentric thought to more decentered thought. At nine to twelve years of age, children can use logical, reversible thought, can reason abstractly, and can have insight into causal and interpersonal relationships.

In middle childhood children may be seen as resolving Erikson's "industry versus inferiority" psychosocial crisis. School becomes a major influence on development, where the child develops a public self, builds social skills, and establishes self-esteem based on academic and nonacademic competencies. In preadolescence, between ages nine and twelve, conformity in peer relations, mixed-sex peer groupings, and challenges to adult authority become more important.

How Do Children Develop During the Middle School and High School Years?

Puberty is a series of major physiological changes leading to the ability to reproduce. Significant differences exist in the age of onset of puberty and early maturers and late maturers may both experience difficulties. Adolescents develop reflectivity and greater metacognitive skills, such as those described in Piaget's formal operations—combinatorial problem solving and hypothetical reasoning.

Adolescents may be seen as resolving Erikson's "identity versus role confusion" psychosocial crisis. They pay attention to how other people view them, search the past, experiment with roles, act on feelings and beliefs, and gradually seek greater autonomy and intimacy in peer relations. Identity foreclosure occurs when the individual chooses a role prematurely. Many factors, such as substance abuse and AIDS, place adolescents at risk.

Key Terms

authoritarian parents, 79
authoritative parents, 79
compensatory preschool programs, 84
early intervention programs, 85
emergent literacy, 76
identity diffusion, 101
identity foreclosure, 101
large muscle development, 74
parenting styles, 79
peers, 81
permissive parents, 79

pretend play, 83
prosocial behaviors, 82
puberty, 96
readiness training, 84
reflectivity, 100
retention, 86
self-concept, 91
self-esteem, 91
small-muscle development, 74
sociodramatic play, 83
whole language, 76

Self-Assessment

1. Which of the following cognitive abilities do children usually have when they enter first grade?

    a. understand abstract concepts

    b. understand an almost infinite variety of sentences

    c. use systematic approaches to solving problems

    d. concentrate for long periods of time

2. All of the following statements about play are true *except:*

    a. Psychologists today generally agree that play is overemphasized in kindergarten and detracts from cognitive training.

    b. Parallel play occurs when children do not interact purposefully with each other to create shared experiences.

    c. Sociodramatic play developmentally follows pretend play.

    d. Because play is spontaneous and nonreflective, it appears to stimulate creativity.

3. Participation in compensatory preschool programs has been found to

    a. benefit middle-class children more than lower-class children.

    b. increase disadavantaged children's readiness for kindergarten and first grade.

    c. have stronger effects on long-term achievement than on initial achievement.

    d. be of little benefit to children under the age of two.

4. During the elementary years, children in middle childhood typically develop all the following characteristics *except:*

    a. decentered thought.

    b. academic self-concept.

    c. preoperational thought.

    d. preadolescent peer group conformity.

    e. fear of not having a "best" friend.

5. During the middle school and high school years, most adolescents typically exhibit all the following characteristics *except:*

    a. identity foreclosure.

    b. reflectivity.

    c. ability to reason hypothetically.

    d. growing demand for autonomy.

    e. variability in the onset of puberty.

6. Physical growth patterns in upper elementary school show that

    a. the average girl experiences a growth spurt earlier than the average boy.

    b. children are more susceptible to illness than they were in lower elementary school.

    c. muscles and cartilage develop more rapidly than bones.

    d. the average girl reaches puberty at 11.5 years.

    e. the average boy reaches puberty at 11.5 years.

7. Develop an outline for an essay that would begin with the following thesis statement: "Child development has important implications for classroom instruction at each grade level." Include an example for each grade level that would help prove the thesis.

8. Match the developmental challenge below with the period of development in which it most likely first occurs.

    ___ identity diffusion

    ___ friendship

    ___ prosocial behavior

    ___ intimacy

    ___ verbal language

    ___ sociodramatic play

    ___ conflict management

    a. early childhood

    b. middle childhood and preadolescence

    c. adolescence

4

Student Diversity

Chapter Outline	Chapter Objectives
What Is the Impact of Culture on Student Learning?	▲ Discuss several impacts of culture on student learning.
How does Socioeconomic Status Affect Student Achievement?	▲ Explain how socialized values, parenting styles, and normative expectations in schools reflect social class and how low socioeconomic status may place students at risk of school failure.
How Do Ethnicity and Race Affect Students' School Experiences? Racial and Ethnic Composition of the United States Academic Achievement of Minority-Group Students Why Have Minority-Group Students Lagged in Achievement? What Has Been the Effect of School Desegregation?	▲ Explain how differences in academic achievement among different racial and ethnic groups can be traced to long-term social and economic inequalities.
How Do Language Differences and Bilingual Programs Affect Student Achievement? Bilingual Education How Effective Are Bilingual Programs?	▲ Discuss the impact of language differences on teaching and learning, and evaluate different approaches to bilingual education.
How Do Gender and Gender Bias Affect Students' School Experiences? Do Males and Females Think and Learn Differently? Sex-Role Stereotyping and Gender Bias	▲ Discuss the impact of gender differences on school experiences and achievement, and give examples of ways teachers can detect and avoid gender bias in the classroom.
How Are Students Different in Intelligence and Learning Styles?	▲ Compare and contrast different theories of intelligence, discuss the significance of debates about the origins of intelligence in relation to education, and give examples of learning style differences and ways teachers can accommodate such differences.
What Is Multicultural Education?	▲ Define multicultural education and give examples of ways teachers can meet the goals of multicultural education in the classroom.

Marva Vance and John Rossi are first-year teachers at Emma Lazarus Elementary School. It's November, and John and Marva are meeting over coffee to discuss the event dreaded by many a first-year teacher: the upcoming Thanksgiving pageant. "This is driving me crazy!" Marva starts. "Our classes are like the United Nations. How are we supposed to cast a Thanksgiving pageant? I have three Navaho children—should I cast them as Indians, or would they be offended? My Vietnamese kids have probably never seen a turkey, and the idea of eating a big bird like that must be revolting to them. I wonder how meaningful this will be to my African Americans. I remember when I was in a Thanksgiving pageant and our teacher had us black students be stage hands because she said there weren't any black pilgrims! Besides, what am I going to do about a narrator? Jose says he wants to be narrator, but his English isn't too good. Lakesha would be good, but she's often out for gifted class and would miss some rehearsals. My special ed kids also get pulled out of class a lot, so they'll miss rehearsals too. I've also been worying about the hunters. Should they all be boys? Wouldn't it be stereotyping if the boys were hunters and the girls were cooks? What about Mark? He's in a wheelchair—should I let him be a hunter?" John sighs and looks in his coffee. "I know what you're talking about. I just let my kids sign up for each part in the pageant. The boys signed up as hunters, the girls as cooks, the Indians as Indians. Maybe it's too late for us to do anything about stereotyping when the kids have already bought into their roles. Where I was in school everyone was white and no one questioned the idea that hunters were boys and cooks were girls. How did everything get so complicated?"

Students differ. They differ in performance level, learning rate, and learning style. They differ in ethnicity, culture, social class, and home language. They differ in gender. Some have various disabilities, and some are gifted or talented in one or more areas. These and other differences can have important implications for instruction, curriculum, and school policies and practices. Marva and John are concerned with student diversity as it relates to the Thanksgiving pageant they are planning, but diversity and its meaning for education is an important issue every day, not just on Thanksgiving. This chapter discusses some of the most important ways in which students differ and some of the ways teachers can accept, accommodate, and celebrate student diversity in their daily teaching. However, diversity is such an important theme that every chapter in this book touches on this issue.

Teachers are more than instructors of students. They are builders of tomorrow's society. A critical part of every teacher's role is to make certain that the equal opportunity we hold to be central to our nationhood is translated into equal opportunity in day-to-day life in the classroom. This chapter was written with this goal in mind.

What Is the Impact of Culture on Student Learning?

If you have ever traveled to a foreign country, you noticed differences in behaviors, attitudes, dress, language, and food. In fact, part of the fun of traveling is in discovering these differences in **culture.**

Even though we usually think of cultural differences as being mostly national differences, there is probably as much cultural diversity within the United States as between the United States and other industrialized nations. The life of a middle-class family in the United States or Canada is probably more like that of a middle-class family in Italy, Ireland, or Israel than it is like that of a poor family living a mile away. Yet while we value cultural differences between nations, we are often less tolerant toward differences within our own society. Our tendency is to value characteristics of mainstream, high-status groups and devalue those of other groups.

By the time children enter school, they have absorbed many aspects of the culture in which they were raised: the language, beliefs, attitudes, ways of behaving, food preferences, and so on. Many of the behaviors associated with being brought up in a particular culture have important consequences for classroom instruction. For example, the school expects children to speak standard English. This is easy for students from homes where standard English is spoken but difficult for those whose families speak other languages or significantly divergent dialects of English. The school also expects students to be highly verbal, to spend most of their time working independently, and to compete with other students for grades and recognition. However, many cultures within our society value cooperation and peer orientation rather than independence and competitiveness. Since the culture of the school reflects mainstream middle-class values, and since most teachers are from middle-class backgrounds themselves, the child from a different culture is often at a

culture: the language, attitudes, ways of behaving, and other aspects of life that characterize a group of people.

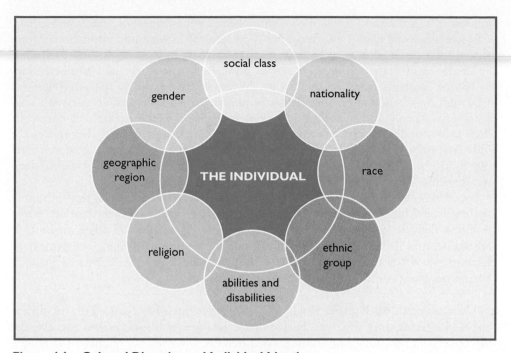

Figure 4.1   Cultural Diversity and Individual Identity
Adapted from Banks, 1993.

disadvantage. Understanding the backgrounds from which students come is critical for effectively teaching them both academic material and the behaviors and expectations of the school. (See Figure 4.1)

Self-Check

Define culture, list as many components of culture as you can think of, and then hypothesize about the impact of each one on student learning. Identify the elements in your own cultural identity, and reflect on the impact of each element on your own school experience.

How Does Socioeconomic Status Affect Student Achievement?

One important way in which students differ from one another is in social class. Even in small rural towns in which almost everyone is the same in ethnicity, religion, and basic world outlook, we can safely assume that the children of the town's bankers, doctors, and teachers have a different upbringing from that experienced by the children of farmhands or domestic workers.

Social class, or **socioeconomic status (SES)**, is defined by sociologists in terms of an individual's income, occupation, education, and prestige in society. These factors tend to go together, so SES is most often based on a combination of the

socioeconomic status: a measure of prestige within a social group most often based on income and education (often abbreviated SES).

individual's income and years of education, because these are most easily measured.

However, social class indicates more than level of income and education. Along with social class goes a pervasive set of behaviors, expectations, and attitudes. Students' social-class origins are likely to profoundly affect attitudes and behaviors in school. Students from lower-class backgrounds are less likely than middle-class students to enter school knowing how to count, to name letters, to cut with scissors, or to name colors. They are less likely to perform well in school than are children from middle-class homes (Mullis *et al.*, 1991). Of course, these differences are only true on average; many lower-class parents do an outstanding job of supporting their children's success in school, and there are many lower-class children whose achievement is very high.

Social class has little to do with **race** or **ethnicity.** While it is true that Hispanic and African-American families are lower in social class on average than are white families, there is substantial overlap; the majority of all poor families in the U.S. are white, and there are many middle-class minority families (U.S. Department of Education, 1991). Definitions of social class are based on such factors as income, occupation, and education, never on race or ethnicity.

The Role of Child-Rearing Practices.   Much research has focused on the differences in child-rearing practices between the average middle-class and the average lower-class family. One important class difference involves the quality of language parents use with their children. Hess and Shipman (1970) studied mothers of different social classes and their four-year-old children. The researchers asked the mothers to teach some simple tasks to their children. The middle-class mothers used much more expressive language, gave clearer directions, and took their children's perspective better than the lower-class mothers. For example, a middle-class mother explained one task as follows:

> All right, Susan, this board is the place where we put the little toys; first of all you're supposed to learn how to place them according to color. Can you do that? The things that are all the same color you put in one section; in the second section you put another group of colors, and in the third section you put the last group of colors. Can you do that? Or would you like to see me do it first? (Hess and Shipman, 1970, p. 182).

In contrast, the lower-class mothers used less elaborate language, gave less clear directions, and were more likely to communicate "Do it because I told you to" than to explain why and how the task was to be done. One lower-class mother's instructions were as follows:

> "I've got some chairs and cars, do you want to play the game?" Child does not respond. Mother continues: "O.K., what's this?" Child: "A wagon?" Mother: "Hm?" Child: "A wagon?" Mother: "This is not a wagon. What's this?" (Hess and Shipman, 1970, p. 182)

Hess and Shipman's (1970) findings suggest that lower-class children receive an upbringing less consistent with what they will be expected to do in school than middle-class children do. By the time they enter school, middle-class children are likely to be masters at following directions, explaining and understanding reasons, and comprehending and using complex language, while lower-class children will probably have less experience in all these areas (Hess and McDevitt, 1984).

Another important difference between middle-class and lower-class families is in the kinds of activities parents tend to do with their children. Middle-class parents are likely to express high expectations for their children and to reward them for

race: visible, genetic characteristics of individuals that cause them to be seen as members of the same broad group (*e.g*, African, Asian, Caucasian).

ethnicity: a history, culture, and sense of identity shared by a group of people.

intellectual development. They are likely to provide good models for language use, to talk and read to their children frequently, and to encourage reading and other learning activities. They are particularly apt to provide all sorts of learning opportunities for children at home, such as books, encyclopedias, records, puzzles, and, increasingly, home computers. These parents are also likely to expose their children to learning experiences outside the home, such as museums, concerts, and zoos (see Bloom, 1964).

The Link between Income and Achievement.   One very interesting study underscored the link between social class and school achievement. This study found that students from families of different social-class backgrounds achieved quite similarly during the school year. However, over the summer students from poorer families lost much of the achievement they had gained, while those in wealthier families gained in achievement level (Heyns, 1978). In fact, the poorest group students lost more than half of the word knowledge they had gained in the fifth grade in only three summer months, while the wealthiest gained a third more during the summer over their school-year gains (Heyns, 1978).

What the Heyns data suggest is that home environment influences not only academic readiness for school but also the level of achievement throughout students' careers in school. Middle-class children are learning all summer and, presumably, at other times when they are at home. Lower-class children are receiving less academically relevant stimulation at home and are more likely to be forgetting what they learned in school (Thompson *et al.*, 1992).

The Role of Schools as "Middle-Class" Institutions.   Students from backgrounds other than the mainstream middle class have difficulties in school in part because their upbringing emphasizes behaviors different from those valued in the school. The problem is that the school overwhelmingly represents the values and expectations of the middle class. Two of these values are individuality and future time orientation (see Boykin, 1986). Most American classrooms operate on the assumption that children should do their own work. Helping others is often defined as cheating. Students are expected to compete for grades, for the teacher's attention and praise, and for other rewards. Competition and individual work are values instilled early on in middle-class homes.

However, students from lower-class white families (Pepitone, 1985) and from some minority groups (Kagan, 1983) are less willing to compete and more interested in cooperating with their peers than are middle-class Anglo-Americans. These students have learned from an early age to rely on their friends and family, and have always also helped and been helped by others. Not surprisingly, students who are most oriented toward cooperation with others learn best in cooperation with others, while those who prefer to compete learn best in competition with others (Kagan *et al.*, 1985). Because of the mismatch between the cooperative orientation of many lower-class and minority-group children and the competitive orientation of the school, Kagan *et al.* (1985) have argued that there is a "structural bias" in traditional classrooms that works against these children. He recommends the use of cooperative learning strategies (see Chapter 8) at least part of the time with these students so that they receive instruction consistent with their cultural orientations.

Schools are geared to reward behavior "sometime in the future." That future may be the end of the day, but more likely is the end of the week, the grading period, or even the school year. Therefore, success in school requires the ability to

This mother is receiving training on how to help her child succeed in the culture of the school. What is meant by a culture of the school? What is happening in the picture that will help the child in that culture, and what else could this actively involved parent do to help?

forgo the gratification of doing something now for the sake of a future reward. Middle-class children are likely to have learned not only to work for a delayed reward but also to plan their own actions so that they accomplish tasks on schedule. Schools demand this type of behavior all the time. An example would be a social studies project assigned on Monday and due on Friday. Lower-class pupils may have difficulty pacing their work so that they can complete the project when required. However, all students can learn to manage their time and to develop and carry out plans if they are given many opportunities to do so.

Implications for Teachers.   Children enter school with varying degrees of skills needed for success. Their behaviors, attitudes, and values also vary. However, just because some children initially don't know what is expected of them and have fewer entry-level skills than others does not mean that they are destined for academic failure. While there is a positive correlation between social class and achievement, it should not by any means be assumed that this relationship holds for all children from lower-social-class families. There are many exceptions. Lower-class families can provide home environments quite supportive of their children's success in school. Autobiographies of people who have overcome poverty often refer to the influence of strong parents with high standards, who expected nothing less than the best from their children and did what they could to help them achieve. While educators need to be aware of the problems encountered by many lower-class pupils, they also need to avoid converting this knowledge into stereotypes. In fact, there is evidence that middle-class teachers often have low expectations for lower-class students (Rist, 1978) and that these low expectations can be a cause of low achievement (Alexander *et al.*, 1987).

Self-Check

Define socioeconomic status and explain how SES is (and is not) determined. Then identify three or more factors affecting school achievement that relate to social class background, and give specific examples showing the impact of each factor.

How Do Ethnicity and Race Affect Students' School Experiences?

A major determinant of the culture in which students will grow up is their ethnic origin. An **ethnic group** is one in which individuals have a shared sense of identity, usually because of a common place of origin (such as Swedish, Polish, or Greek Americans), religion (such as Jewish Americans), or race (such as African or Asian Americans).

Most Anglo-Americans identify with some ethnic group, such as Polish, Italian, Irish, Greek, or German. Identification with these groups may affect a family's traditions, holidays, food preferences, and, to some extent, outlook on the world. However, white ethnic groups have been largely absorbed into mainstream American society, so the differences among them have few educational implications.

The situation is quite different for other ethnic groups. In particular, African, Hispanic, and Native Americans have yet to be fully accepted into mainstream American society and have not yet attained the economic success or security achieved by the white ethnic groups. Students from these ethnic groups face special problems in school and have been the focus of two of the most emotional issues in American education over the past thirty years: desegregation and bilingual education. The following sections discuss the situation of students of different ethnic backgrounds in schools today.

Racial and Ethnic Composition of the United States

The people who make up the United States have always come from many ethnic backgrounds, but every year the U.S. becomes even more diverse. Table 4.1 shows U.S. Census Bureau projections of the percentages of the U.S. population under 25 according to ethnicity. Note that the proportion of non-Hispanic whites is expected to continue to decline; as recently as 1970, 83.3 percent of all Americans were in this category. In contrast, the proportions of Hispanics and "Other" (mostly Asians) will grow dramatically by 2010. The Hispanic population under 25 may be as much as 40 percent higher in 2010 than in 1990, and the "Other" group may grow by 33 percent. There may be 14 percent more African Americans under 25, and almost 7 percent fewer whites in absolute terms. These trends, due to immigration patterns and differences in birth rates, have profound implications for American education. Our nation is becoming far more ethnically diverse. Even the term **minority group** may have to be revised, as some states (such as California) have or will soon have a majority of "minorities"!

ethnic group: a group within a larger society that sees itself as having a common history, social and cultural heritage, and traditions, often based on race, religion, language, or national identity.

minority group: an ethnic or racial group that is a minority within a broader society.

Race/Ethnicity	1990	1995	2000	2010
Anglo-European-American	70.7	69.0	67.4	64.2
Hispanic American	10.5	11.5	12.4	14.2
African American	15.5	15.9	16.4	17.3
Other	3.3	3.6	3.8	4.3
Total	100.0	100.0	100.0	100.0

Table 4.1   Projected Percentages of the U.S. Population, Birth to Age 24, by Race/Ethnicity

Source: Adapted from U.S. Department of Education, 1991.

Academic Achievement of Minority-Group Students

If minority-group students achieved at the same level as Anglo-Americans, there would probably be little concern about ethnic group differences in American schools. Unfortunately, they don't. On virtually every test of academic achievement, African-, Hispanic-, and Native-American students score significantly lower than their Anglo-American classmates.

Table 4.2 (from Levine and Havighurst, 1989) shows the standardized test scores and socioeconomic status of high school sophomores according to their racial and ethnic groups. All scores were set at a mean of 50.0, so numbers below 50 indicate scores below the mean. There are two points to be made about Table 4.2. First, African, Hispanic, and Native Americans score below the mean for whites (and for Asian Americans) on all tests. Second, note how closely the socioeconomic status scores correspond to the achievement test scores. This suggests that the ethnic group differences shown in Table 4.2 are highly associated with differences in social-class background and upbringing.

One recent development in the academic performance of minority-group students is heartening: The achievement gap between them and Anglo-Americans is narrowing. For example, African-American and Hispanic students are gaining more rapidly than whites on Scholastic Achievement Tests (SATs) each year, as is shown in Figure 4.2. Figure 4.2 also shows the trends in performance on the National Assessment of Educational Progress (NAEP) reading tests for nine- and thirteen-year-olds in 1975, 1980, 1984, and 1988. Gains have been particularly dramatic for the lowest-achieving minority-group children (Carroll, 1987). Although African-American and Hispanic students are gaining in achievement more rapidly than whites, they still have a long way to go. Similar patterns appear in every subject assessed by the National Assessment of Educational Progress: The gap between whites and members of minority groups remains wide, but is diminishing over time (Mullis *et al.*, 1991).

Why Have Minority-Group Students Lagged in Achievement?

Why do minority–group students score so far below Anglo-Americans on achievement tests? The most important reason is that in our society African Americans, Hispanics (particularly Mexican Americans and Puerto Ricans), and

| Level and Subject | Standardized Scores | (Total 50.0) | | | | | | |
| | | | All | | Puerto | | | |
Sophomores	Anglo- American	African American	Hispanic American	Mexican American	Rican American	Cuban American	Asian American	Native American
Vocabulary	52.0	42.4	44.9	44.2	44.0	48.1	51.6	45.0
Reading	51.7	44.2	45.1	44.6	44.5	48.6	51.6	46.2
Math part 1	51.8	43.1	44.9	44.5	43.9	48.0	55.7	44.6
Math part 2	51.3	44.9	46.2	45.7	45.5	49.3	55.5	46.2
Science	52.1	41.6	44.5	44.0	42.9	46.3	51.5	46.1
Writing	51.8	43.3	44.9	44.8	43.3	46.8	53.7	46.0
Civics	51.3	45.7	45.9	45.7	46.0	45.6	51.0	45.5
Socioeconomic status	51.3	46.1	46.0	45.0	44.2	47.3	51.7	47.2

TABLE 4.2   Test Score Differences among Racial/Ethnic Groups

As groups, Anglo- and Asian-American high school sophomores were above average in performance on standardized tests and in socioeconomic status in 1980. Other racial and ethnic groups, taken as a whole, were below average.

Source: Levine and Havinghurst, 1989, p. 381.

Native Americans tend to occupy the lowest rungs of the socioeconomic ladder. Consequently, families in these groups are often unable to provide their children with the stimulation and academic preparation typical of a middle-class upbringing. Chronic unemployment, epidemic in minority communities, has a negative effect on family life, including contributing to high numbers of single-parent families in minority-group communities (U.S . Department of Education, 1991).

Another important disadvantage faced by minority-group students is that they often attend academically inferior, overcrowded urban schools (Kozol, 1991). Middle-class and working-class families throughout the United States buy their way out of center-city schools by moving to the suburbs or sending their children to private or parochial schools, leaving the public schools to serve those without the resources to afford alternatives.

Often, minority-group students perform poorly because the instruction they receive is inconsistent with their cultural background (Boykin, 1986; Kagan *et al.*, 1985; Henry and Pepper, 1990; Hilliard, 1989; Ogbu, 1987). Academic excellence itself may be seen as inconsistent with acceptance in a student's own community; for example, Ogbu (1987), Boykin (1986), and others have noted the tendency of many African-American students to accuse their peers of "acting white" if they strive to achieve. Similar attitudes have been seen among Native Americans (Henry and Pepper, 1990) and Mexican Americans (Kagan *et al.*, 1985).

Low expectations for minority-group students can contribute to their low achievement (Brophy and Good, 1986). This is especially true if, as often happens, low expectations lead well-meaning teachers or administrators to place minority-group students disproportionately in low-ability groups or tracks (see Braddock, 1989).

The low achievement of these students may well be a "temporary" problem; in a decade or two, as minority groups increasingly achieve economic security and

Connections

For a discussion of the environmental and motivational factors that affect some minority-group students and low achievers, including the role of teacher expectations and the phenomenon of learned helplessness, see Chapter 10.

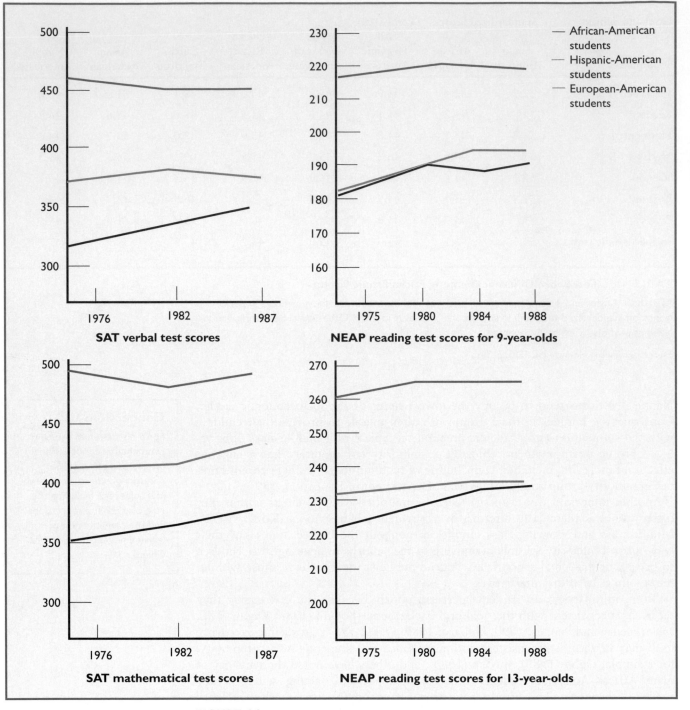

FIGURE 4.2

Trends in Standardized Test Scores by Group

As a group, European-American students score higher on standardized tests than African- and Hispanic-American students. However, the gap in achievement differences has narrowed because of relative improvements in the scores earned by African and Hispanic Americans.

From College Entrance Examination Board, 1985, and Digest of Education Statistics, 1988.

enter the middle class, their children's achievement will come to resemble that of other groups. In the 1920s it was widely believed that immigrants from southern and eastern Europe (such as Italians, Greeks, Poles, and Jews) were hopelessly backward and perhaps retarded (see, for example, Kirkpatrick, 1926), yet the children and grandchildren of these immigrants now achieve as well as the descendants of the nation's founders. However, we cannot afford to wait a decade or two. The school is one institution that can break the cycle of poverty, by giving children from impoverished backgrounds the opportunity to succeed (see Gordon, 1991).

What Has Been the Effect of School Desegregation?

Before 1954, black, white, and Hispanic students were legally required to attend separate schools in twenty states plus the District of Columbia, and segregated schools were common in the remaining states. Minority-group students were often bused miles past their nearest public school to separate schools. The doctrine of "separate but equal" education was upheld in several Supreme Court decisions. However, in 1954 the Supreme Court struck down this practice in the landmark *Brown vs. Board of Education of Topeka* case, on the grounds that separate education was inherently unequal. *Brown vs. Board of Education* did away with legal segregation, but it was many years before large numbers of racially different students were attending school together. In the 1970s a series of Supreme Court decisions found that the continued segregation of many schools throughout the United States was due to past discriminatory practices, such as the drawing of school boundary lines deliberately to separate neighborhoods along racial lines. These decisions forced local school districts to desegregate their schools by any means necessary. Many districts were given specific standards for the proportions of minority-group students who could be assigned to any particular school. For example, a district in which 45 percent of the students were African American might be required to have an enrollment of 35 to 55 percent African Americans in its schools. To achieve desegregation, some school districts simply changed school attendance areas, while others created special "magnet schools" (such as schools for the performing arts, for talented and gifted students, or for special vocational preparation) to induce students to attend schools outside of their own neighborhoods. However, in many large, urban districts, segregation of neighborhoods is so extensive that students must be bused to achieve racially balanced schools.

School desegregation is supposed to increase the academic achievement of minority-group students by giving them opportunities to interact with more middle-class, achievement-oriented peers. All too often, however, the schools to which students are bused are no better than the segregated schools they left behind, and the outflow of middle-class families from urban areas (which was well under way before busing began) often means that lower-class African- or Hispanic-American students are integrated with similarly lower-class whites (Rossell, 1983).

Perhaps for these reasons the overall effect of desegregation on the academic achievement of minority students has been small, though positive. However, when desegregation begins in elementary school, and particularly when it involves busing minority-group children to high-quality schools with substantially middle-class student bodies, desegregation can have a significant effect on the achievement of minority-group students (Crain and Mahard, 1983). This effect is not thought to result from sitting next to whites but rather from attending a better school. One important outcome of desegregation is that blacks who attend desegregated schools

School Resegregation

Often, demographic, social, and economic forces, more than court decisions, influence people's actions. Because of these forces, segregation persists in America's schools, despite court-ordered integration. The courts cannot order people to use public rather than private schools or reside in economically depressed inner cities or rural areas rather than suburbs. While school integration is the law, many public schools have remained segregated or become resegregated through shifts in the composition of neighborhood populations. Even where schools have achieved integration, students tend to maintain separate social groupings based on racial identity or ethnic pride.

The population shift that has left large concentrations of minority-group members in cities increased with the advent of court-ordered busing. In Oklahoma City, for example, at the start of busing in 1968 minority-group students composed about 22 percent of the school population. By 1982, the percentage had risen to almost 50 percent. In cities such as Washington and Detroit, the proportion of minority-group children in the schools approaches 90 percent, and in Camden, New Jersey, and East St. Louis, Illinois, as much as 99 percent.

Cities have tried various methods of achieving even nominal integration, including magnet schools, regionalized schools, controlled school choice programs, and school redistricting. Lately, however, other social forces appear to be shifting emphasis from integration to cultural pride, from melting pot to multicultural models. Some observers argue that celebration of diversity may backfire in racial separatism, isolation, even antagonism, especially in light

of the depth of racism's roots in America's history. They note that a visit to the high school cafeteria will confirm the comparative isolation of racial or ethnic groups within fully integrated schools. In nonintegrated schools in cities such as Milwaukee and Baltimore, meanwhile, new curricula in African and African-American history, art, and literature take center stage, while other communities design new curricula for their largely Hispanic-American or Native-American students. Decades after the Supreme Court ordered school desegregation, segregated schools are again a fact of American life. Providing students equal educational opportunity while promoting both cultural diversity and racial harmony are continuing challenges with outcomes that will have a significant impact on America's future.

Critical Thinking

What are the main causes and consequences of school resegregation? How can resegregation best be prevented? How are multiculturalism and separatism different? How should schools address issues of racism versus cultural pride?

Sources: Jonathan Kozol, *Savage Inequalities*, New York: Crown 1991; "School as a Model for Race Relations," *New York Times*, July 11; 1989; Thomas Sobol, "Understanding Diversity," *Educational Leadership*, November 1990; Debra Viadero, "Father Figure," *Education Week*, March 1991.

are more likely than other blacks to attend desegregated colleges, to work in integrated settings, and to attain higher incomes (Braddock, 1985).

Theory Into Practice

Teaching in a Culturally Diverse School

Following are some recommendations for promoting social harmony and equal opportunity among students in racially and ethnically diverse classrooms and schools. (See also Pine and Hilliard, 1990.)

- Use fairness and balance in dealing with students. Students should never have any justification for believing that "people like me [whites, blacks, Latinos, Vietnamese] don't get a fair chance."

- Give students equal opportunities for success and recognition in high-status groups such as the cheerleading squad or student council (Crain *et al.,* 1982).

- Do not show bias by calling on minority-group students less often in class.

- Allow students to participate in human relations committees to receive and discuss complaints from students concerning unfair treatment. The use of human relations committees is associated with positive intergroup relations (Forehand and Ragosta, 1976; Crain *et al.,* 1982).

- Choose texts and instructional materials carefully to make sure minority groups are not underrepresented or misrepresented. Themes should be nonbiased, and minority-group individuals should appear in nonstereotyped high-status roles.

- Avoid communicating bias, but discuss racial or ethnic relations openly rather than trying to pretend there are no differences.

- Let students know that racial or ethnic bias, including slurs, taunts, and jokes, will not be tolerated in the classroom and school, and institute consequences to enforce this standard.

- Help all students to value their own and others' cultural heritages and contributions to history and civilization. At the same time, avoid trivializing or stereotyping cultures merely in terms of ethnic foods and holidays. Because the United States is becoming a mosaic rather than a melting pot (Towson, 1985), students more than ever need to value diversity and to acquire a more substantive knowledge and appreciation of other ways of life.

- Avoid resegregation. Tracking, or between-class ability grouping, tends to segregate high and low achievers and, because of historical and economic factors, minority-group students tend to be overrepresented in the ranks of low achievers. For this and other reasons, tracking should be avoided (Braddock and Slavin, 1992; Rosenbaum, 1980; Slavin, 1989).

- Provide structure for intergroup interaction, because proximity alone does not lead to social harmony among racially and ethnically different groups (Gerard and Miller, 1975; Epstein, 1985). Students need opportunities to know one another as individuals and to work together toward common goals (Allport, 1954; Slavin, 1985c). For example, students who participate in integrated sports are more likely than other students to have friends who are ethnically or racially different from themselves (Slavin and Madden, 1979).

- Use noncompetitive peer-oriented activities as a participation structure in classes with minority-group students, especially with Mexican- and Native-American students who often learn best in cooperative and one-on-one learning contexts (California State Department of Education, 1983; Kagan *et al.,* 1985).

- Provide support for language-minority students when they are in English-only learning contexts. One strategy is to use a buddy system in which students

Intelligence	End-States	Core Components
Logical/mathematical	Scientist, Mathematician	Sensitivity to, and capacity to discern, logical or numerical patterns; ability to handle long chains of reasoning.
Linguistic	Poet, Journalist	Sensitivity to the sounds, rhythms, and meanings of words; sensitivity to the different functions of language.
Musical	Composer, Violinist	Abilities to produce and appreciate rhythm, pitch, and timbre; appreciation of the forms of musical expressiveness.
Spatial	Navigator, Sculptor	Capacities to perceive the visual-spatial world accurately and to perform transformations on one's initial perceptions.
Bodily/kinesthetic	Dancer, Athlete	Abilities to control one's body movements and to handle objects skillfully.
Interpersonal	Therapist, Salesperson	Capacities to discern and respond appropriately to the moods, temperaments, motivations, and desires of other people.
Intrapersonal	Person with detailed, accurate self-knowledge	Access to one's own feelings and the ability to discriminate among them and draw upon them to guide behavior; knowledge of one's own strengths, weaknesses, desires, and intelligences.

TABLE 4.3   The Seven Intelligences

Connections

See Chapters 9 and 12 for teaching strategies that accommodate instruction to individual needs in diverse classrooms in which students may exhibit a variety of different abilities, disabilities, and learning styles.

determined by that of their parents and is set the day they are conceived. Others (such as Kamin, 1975; Humphreys, 1986) just as vehemently hold that intelligence is shaped by factors in a person's social environment, such as the amount a child is read to and talked to. Today, most investigators agree that both heredity and environment play an important part in intelligence (Schif *et al.*, 1982; Scarr and McCartney, 1983). It is clear that children of high-achieving parents are, on average, more likely to be high achievers themselves, but this is due as much to the home environment created by high-achieving parents as to genetics.

One important piece of evidence in favor of the environmental view is that schooling itself clearly affects intelligence. A recent review by Ceci (1991) found that the experience of being in school has a strong and systematic impact on intelligence. For example, studies of Dutch children who entered school late because of World War II show significant declines in IQ as a result. A study of the children of retarded mothers in inner-city Milwaukee (Garber, 1988) found that a program of infant stimulation and high-quality preschool could raise children's IQs substantially, and these gains were maintained at least through the end of elementary school. This and other evidence supports the idea that IQ is not a fixed, unchangeable attribute of individuals but can change as individuals respond to changes in their environment.

Intelligence, whether general or specific, is only one of many factors that influence the amount children are likely to learn in a given lesson or course. It is probably much less important than prior knowledge (the amount the student knew about the course beforehand), motivation, and the quality and nature of instruction. Intelligence does become important at the extremes, as it is a critical issue in identifying retarded and (in most cases) gifted students, but in the middle range where most students fall other factors are more important.

Many of the chapters in this book discuss issues of accommodating instruction to meet diverse needs. In particular, Chapter 9 presents strategies for adapting instruction to meet the needs of heterogeneous classes, and Chapter 12 discusses programs for **students at risk** and special education.

Self-Check

Define *intelligence*. Compare and contrast the general views of Binet, Spearman, Sternberg, Guilford, and Gardner about the nature of intelligence. Cite evidence supporting the claim that both heredity and environment play an important part in intelligence.

Define *learning styles* and describe the traits that define field dependence, field independence, impulsivity, and reflectivity. List five or more characteristics of learning environments or conditions that individuals may prefer. Give specific examples of effective strategies teachers might use to accommodate learning styles and culture-based differences in classroom behaviors.

Theories of Learning Styles. Just as students have different personalities, so do they have different ways of learning (see Messick, 1984). For example, think about how you learn the names of people you meet. Do you learn a name better if you see it written down? If so, you may be a *visual* learner, one who learns best by seeing or reading. If you learn better by hearing, you may be an *auditory* learner. Of course, we all learn in many ways, but some of us learn better in some ways than in others. Students with learning disabilities (see Chapter 12) may have great difficulty learning in one way even if they have no trouble learning in another.

There are several other differences in **learning styles** that educational psychologists have studied. One is **field dependence** versus **field independence** (Witkin *et al.*, 1977). Field-dependent individuals tend to see patterns as a whole, and have difficulty separating out specific aspects of a situation or pattern, while field-independent people

students at risk: students who are likely to be low-achieving or "at risk" for school failure.

learning styles: orientation for approaching learning tasks and processing information in certain ways.

field dependence: cognitive style in which patterns are perceived as whole.

field independence: cognitive style in which separate parts of a pattern are perceived and analyzed.

are more able to see the parts that make up a large pattern. Field-dependent people tend to be more oriented toward people and social relationships than are field-independent people; for example, they tend to be better at recalling such social information as conversations and relationships, to work best in groups, and to prefer such subjects as history and literature. Field-independent people are more likely to do well with numbers, science, and problem-solving tasks (Shuell, 1981; Witkin and Goodenough, 1981).

Another important cognitive style on which students differ is **impulsivity** versus **reflectivity** (Entwistle, 1981). Impulsive individuals tend to work and make decisions quickly, while reflective types are more likely to take a long time considering all alternatives. Impulsive students are the ones who always finish objective tests early, while reflective students are still chewing on their answers (and possibly their pencils as well) when time is called. Impulsive students tend to concentrate on speed, while reflective ones concentrate on accuracy. Impulsive students can be taught to be reflective by means of self-instructive training (Meichenbaum, 1977), in which they are trained to "talk to themselves" while they work to pace themselves appropriately and reinforce themselves for step-by-step progress. See Chapter 5 for more on this.

Students may also vary in preferences for different learning environments or conditions. For example, Dunn and Dunn (1987) have found that students differ in preferences regarding such things as the amount of lighting, hard or soft seating, quiet or noisy surroundings, for working alone or with peers, and so on.

Aptitude-Treatment Interactions. Given the well-documented differences in learning styles and preferences, it would seem logical that different styles of teaching would have different impacts on different learners, yet this common-sense proposition has been difficult to demonstrate conclusively. Studies that have attempted to match teaching styles to learning styles have only inconsistently found any benefits for learning (Corno and Snow, 1986; Pintrich *et al.,* 1985; Knight *et al.,* 1992; Snow, 1992). However, the search for such **aptitude-treatment interaction** goes on, and a few studies have found positive effects for programs that adapt instruction to an individual's learning style (Dunn *et al.,* 1989; Wilkerson and White, 1988).

---

impulsivity: cognitive style of responding quickly but often without regard for accuracy.

reflectivity: the act of analyzing oneself and one's own thoughts.

aptitude-treatment interaction: interaction of individual differences in learning with particular teaching methods.

Theory Into Practice

Finding Out about Culture-Based Classroom Behaviors

One area of difference in the classroom behaviors of multicultural populations of students that effective teachers must consider is diverse teacher–student interactions. Patricia Furey at the University of Pittsburgh (1986) and Pamela George at North Carolina Central University (1993) researched these differences in their efforts to train teachers in effective methods for multicultural teaching. A few areas of interaction are described here, and a broader scheme is provided in Figure 4.4.

Amount of Student Participation

Classroom norms for student participation vary considerably across cultures and are probably the most discussed attribute of diverse and multicultural

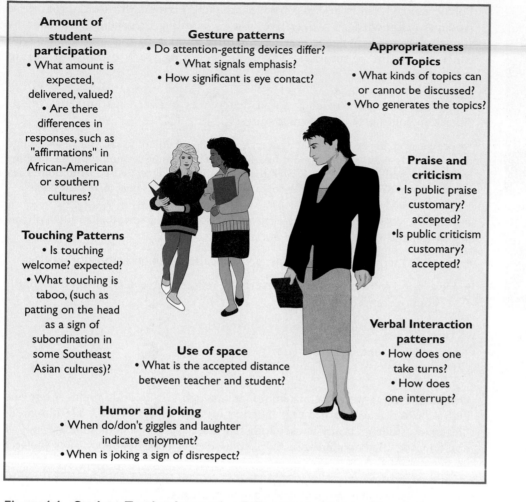

Amount of student participation
- What amount is expected, delivered, valued?
- Are there differences in responses, such as "affirmations" in African-American or southern cultures?

Gesture patterns
- Do attention-getting devices differ?
- What signals emphasis?
- How significant is eye contact?

Appropriateness of Topics
- What kinds of topics can or cannot be discussed?
- Who generates the topics?

Praise and criticism
- Is public praise customary? accepted?
- Is public criticism customary? accepted?

Touching Patterns
- Is touching welcome? expected?
- What touching is taboo, (such as patting on the head as a sign of subordination in some Southeast Asian cultures)?

Use of space
- What is the accepted distance between teacher and student?

Verbal Interaction patterns
- How does one take turns?
- How does one interrupt?

Humor and joking
- When do/don't giggles and laughter indicate enjoyment?
- When is joking a sign of disrespect?

Figure 4.4   Student–Teacher Interaction Differences in Diverse Classrooms

Furcy, P. (1986). A framework for cross-cultural analysis of teaching methods. In P. Byrd (ed.). *Teaching across cultures in the university ESL program.* Washington, DC: National Association for Foreign Student Affairs. George, P. (1993, March). Examining the culture of the classroom. Paper presented at the Comparative and International Education Society, Kingston, Jamaica.

classrooms. The amount of participation expected by teachers and by students may differ. The conditions for participation and silence and the means of soliciting student participation also differ. To think about your comfort with diversity in participation and its implication in your classroom ask yourself:

- If I ask a student a question and the student is slow to respond, how much time will I allow for an answer?

- If the time passes and the student still does not answer, what will I do?

Gesture Patterns

Cultural differences in the use of gestures are many, but the few mentioned here serve as illustrations. A third-grade teacher in Oakland had seven ethnic

According to some research, how may some Native-American students learn best? As a teacher, how might you accommodate culture-based differences in learning styles among your students?

Polynesian children in her class from Samoa and Hawaii. She noticed that these students acknowledged affirmative, not by nodding or saying "yes," but by silently lifting their eyebrows in a manner similar to the Anglo-European American gesture of surprise. "This expression took years to translate 'yes' to me," she reported.

A Chinese-American teacher noted differences between his and his Anglo-American colleagues' classroom gestures:

By comparison, my body motions are much restrained. I do not usually move all around the room. My colleagues are more like Phil Donahue going around with his probing mike. They prance around and wave their arms with exaggerated gesticulation. They motion to make main points on the board and their loud voices punctuate their points.

If you have a videotape of yourself teaching, you might review it in light of this discussion and think about these questions:

- How do I move my (hands, arms, body, location) demonstrably during class?

- How will I know if students nonverbally register agreement, readiness, confusion, or comprehension?

- How do I elicit student responses nonverbally?

Humor and Joking

One of the ways we recognize humor is through giggles and laughter, but one high school teacher warned that laughter is "not always joyful." He observed, "Hispanic students in my classes sometimes use giggles to communicate 'no,' 'I don't know,' 'I didn't prepare that,' 'please pass me,' or 'that makes me feel uncomfortable.' "

Another teacher in a multicultural classroom attests:

Prasong, the Thai student, handed me a note and bowed politely. I looked up and jokingly asked if it were a love letter. The young man's face blushed visibly. Laughter ricochetted around the room. The letter invited me to a drama club reception. The young man did not make eye contact with me for weeks. Joking with some students is risky business.

Touching Patterns

Another kind of interaction involves physical contact. Teachers sometimes exchange hugs and friendly slaps on the back with students. They may touch students to get their attention, to emphasize a point or a command, or to reward students. Questions about when, where, and under what conditions to touch students should be carefully considered.

- Do I touch (male, female) students (upon meeting, upon greeting, to get his or her attention, to emphasize a point, to give praise)?

- Was any student embarrassed, threatened, or made anxious by the touching? If so, how did I find out?

Teachers on Teaching

How do you foster social acceptance and multicultural awareness?

Wildcat! It was the Friday afternoon pep rally. Sometimes the students get a little over-enthusiastic. In the past they have thrown toilet paper—but this rally took a different turn. Our school is like any other school. We have our "in" crowd and our "out" crowd—all of whom stay within their own little groups. During the pep rally, the black students separated themselves by all sitting in one area of the gym. The problem started when some white students brought out a Confederate flag. A group of black students began to confront the students with the flag. Thanks to a quick-thinking assistant principal, the trouble was quickly averted. Needless to say, tension at the school was at an all-time high. In my English classes, I took advantage of an opportunity not only to teach literature but also to attempt to ease the racial tension that existed. We began reading *Roll of Thunder, Hear My Cry,* by Mildred Taylor. I felt it would be appropriate because racism of the thirties is shown through the segregation of the schools, stores, churches. Before we read, we had a discussion of discrimination. I tried to avoid focusing on black and white, but discussed other targets of discrimination, such as women, overweight people, shy people, short people, smart people, non–English-speaking people, and people with labels. I asked if students discriminated against people in these groups or were members of the groups themselves. Answers varied, but by the end of the discussion, the students agreed that any type of discrimination is wrong. As an educator, I feel a need to shape not only the minds of youth but also the character. Educators have a responsibility to help stop discrimination.

Ricardo C. Morris, Teacher, Grades 9–12
Hixson High School, Chattanooga, Tennessee

Nestled between three of the largest Ojibwe reservations in Minnesota, my high school has come full circle in recognizing its cultural diversity. We have a Multicultural Awareness Club, a Native American Club, and other groups in the school that promote diversity. But what pulls us together? Classroom teachers still handle history and literature with kid gloves. How does one introduce a Native American story? When this question was posed to Jim Bedeau, a White Earth Ojibwe, he said, "Why do you have to say, 'This is an Indian story'? Why not say, 'This is a story about a little girl who . . .'? Don't teach separation. If nothing in the story connects for you, you don't need it." Searching for unity in diversity is my goal in an assignment I designed for one of my English classes. After a lesson on aspects of culture all humans share, the class forms two groups to generate hypothetical cultures that include these universal elements. Each group creates artifacts that represent or illustrate the culture and buries these artifacts somewhere in the country. Then each group goes on an archaeological dig to recover the other group's artifacts and use them to interpret that fantasy culture. This requires creative cooperation and bridges cultural barriers in the classroom since all students must think about constructing new cultures. Jim Bedeau and other Ojibwes believe that everyone is born in balance. It is only as people face decisons that this delicate balance is continually maintained or destroyed. "We are born with love," Bedeau says, "and we learn to hate." With this culture project, students learn the fragility of this balance, and I can only hope they will carry that understanding with them when they walk out of the classroom.

Vicki Olsen, English Instructor
Bemidji High School, Bemidji, Minnesota

What Is Multicultural Education?

In recent years, "multicultural education" has become a much-discussed topic in American education. Definitions of **multicultural education** vary broadly. The simplest definitions emphasize the inclusion of non-European perspectives in the curriculum, such as including the works of African-, Hispanic-, and Native-American authors in English curricula, teaching about Columbus from the point of view of Native Americans, and teaching more about the cultures and contributions of non-Western societies (Hilliard, 1991/92). Banks (1993) defines multicultural education more broadly. He sees the term as encompassing all policies and practices schools might use to improve educational outcomes not only for students of different ethnic, social class, and religious backgrounds, but also of different genders and exceptionalities (*e.g.,* children who are retarded, deaf, blind, or gifted). He summarizes this definition as follows:

> Multicultural education is an idea stating that all students, regardless of the groups to which they belong, such as those related to gender, ethnicity, race, culture, social class, religion, or exceptionality, should experience educational equality in the schools. (Banks, 1993, p. 25)

In additon to recommendations about broadening the curriculum, this definition recommends such practices as reducing tracking, using a wide range of teaching methods (including cooperative learning, which is held to be more consistent with the learning styles of many non-European cultures), directly confronting racism and sexism, using bilingual education, and effectively mainstreaming students with disabilities.

The first step in multicultural education is for teachers, administrators, and other school staff to learn about the cultures from which their children come and to carefully examine all the policies, practices, and curricula used in the school to identify any areas of possible bias, exclusively **"eurocentric"** teaching, and so on. Books by Banks (1988; Banks and Banks, 1993) Baruth and Manning (1992), and Hernandez (1990) are good places to start. These and other books identify some of the characteristics of various cultures and teaching strategies and materials appropriate to each.

Multicultural education should pervade all aspects of school life. The following sections explore a few specific areas.

Multicultural Curriculum.   Multicultural education requires a multicultural curriculum. Sleeter and Grant (1988, pp. 153–155) make the following recommendations for implementation of a multicultural curriculum.

1. The curriculum should be reformed in such a way that it regularly presents diverse perspectives, experiences, and contributions. Similarly, concepts should be presented and taught that represent diverse cultural groups and both sexes.

2. The curriculum should include materials and visual displays that are free of race, gender, and disability stereotypes, and which include members of all cultural groups in a positive manner.

3. The curriculum should provide as much emphasis on contemporary culture as on historical culture, and groups should be represented as active and dynamic, *e.g.,* while the women's suffrage movement should be addressed, more contemporary problems confronting women also should be addressed.

4. The curriculum should ensure the use of nonsexist language.

---

multicultural education: education that teaches the value of cultural diversity.

eurocentric: based exclusively on European culture history, traditions, and values.

Women Who Made a Difference in New Mexico

How does this teacher's lesson suggest an integrated multicultural curriculum? What are the likely aims of this lesson? How does the lesson model multicultural awareness?

5. The curriculum and the teaching/learning methods should draw on children's experiential background, and curricular concepts should be based on children's daily life and experiences.

6. The curriculum should allow equal access for all students, *i.e.*, all students should be allowed to enroll in college preparatory courses or other special curricular areas.

Multicultural Classroom Activities.   Multicultural education will become a reality to the degree that children participate in a variety of activities that reinforce the idea that cultural differences are valued. A list of such activities, adapted from a Florida State Department of Education guide (1990), appears below.

- Make newcomers feel welcome through a formal program.
- Be sure that assignments are not offensive or frustrating to students of cultural minorities. For example, asking students to discuss or write about their Christmas experiences is inappropriate for non-Christian students. Let students discuss their similar holidays.
- Form a schoolwide planning committee to address the implementation of multicultural education.
- Let faculty knowledgeable about multicultural topics be guest teachers in your class.
- Take a cultural census of the class or school to find out what cultures are represented; let students be the ethnographers.
- Form a multicultural club.
- Select a theme to tie various multicultural activities together; hold school programs with art, music, and dramatic presentations; hold a multicultural fair or

festival featuring music, art, dance, dress, and so on; adopt a multicultural theme for existing activities.

- Hold a school cross-cultural food festival.
- Have multicultural celebrations and teach-ins with schoolwide activities in all classes.
- Decorate classrooms, hallways, and the library media center with murals, bulletin boards, posters, artifacts, and other materials representative of the students in the class or school, or other cultures being studied. Posters and other information are available from foreign government travel bureaus and education agencies, private travel agencies, consulates, the United Nations, and ethnic and cultural news and displays.
- Supplement textbooks with authentic material from different cultures taken from newspapers, magazines, and other media of the culture.
- Use community resources: representatives of various cultures talking to classes; actors portraying characters or events; and musicians and dance groups, such as salsa bands or bagpipe units performing.
- Feature stories in the local newspaper on multicultural topics.
- Make reminders during daily announcements about multicultural activities.
- Develop a radio or television program on multicultural themes for the educational or local community access channel.
- Study works in science, art, music, and literature of various cultures, focusing on the contributions of minority-group individuals.
- Have students write short stories or essays on multicultural topics.
- Have student debates, speeches, or skits on multicultural topics, and present them to classes, PTOs, nursing homes, and other community groups.
- Discuss the relevance of the Constitution and government in dealing with today's problems relating to minorities and cultural diversity.
- Have children of other cultures or their parents share native songs with classmates; have students share instruments or recordings of their native cultures.
- Take field trips to local multicultural sites, such as a neighborhood, ethnic recreation/social center, workplace, historical site, museum, restaurant, grocery.
- Establish pen-pal or video exchange programs with students from other cultures.
- Focus on the everyday artifacts of cultures that differentiate the way people behave in different cultures, such as greeting, friendly exchanges, farewells, expressing respect, verbal taboos, body language and gestures, gender roles, folklore, childhood literature , discipline, festivals, holidays, religious practices, games, music, pets, personal possessions, keeping warm and cool, fashions, competitions, dating and courtship, hobbies, and foods.
- Discuss what it means to be a responsible American citizen.

Assessing Effectiveness in Achieving Multicultural Goals.   How can teachers know if their classrooms are fair and positive toward all cultures? Baruth and Manning (1992, pp. 202–203) provide a self-evaluation guide, as follows.

1. Have there been efforts to understand and respect cultural diversity among learners, not as a problem to be reckoned with, but as a challenging opportunity and a rich gift?

2. Have there been efforts to provide a classroom in which learners feel free to speak and express diverse opinions? Are students free to express opinions contrary to middle-class Anglo-American beliefs? Did the teacher repress them or allow other students to stifle diverse opinion?

Teacher-Learner Conflict in a Culturally Diverse Classroom

While Millbrook, an urban multicultural high school, has for a decade been about half white/half African American, the demography has been changing. Amanda Gilbert is in her fifth year of teaching social studies at Millbrook. She now works in a school which, this year, is 42 percent African American, 38 percent Euro-American, and 20 percent Asian American and international students (predominantly of Chinese and Southeast Asian origin). Gilbert's classes roughly reflect this demographic blend.

Gilbert began this school year using a new questioning technique she had hoped would encourage homework assignment completion and preparation for class. Because she wanted to give each student an equal opportunity for participation in the question-and-answer (Q&A) sessions ("equal air time," the students dubbed it), she put each student's name on an index card and drew a respondent's name at random. Today the Q&A session went this way:

Ms. GILBERT: Your text identifies two different policies held by the U.S. and Canada. Name one. [Ms. Gilbert pause s about 10 seconds. She draws Susan James' name from the deck. Susan is a Euro-American student who has high marks for homework completion and accuracy.] Susan.

SUSAN: Canada's was the one called the "Montreal Accord."

Ms. GILBERT: That's right, the "Montreal Accord." Now, what was the name of the *U.S.* policy? [Ms. Gilbert a gain pauses. She draws An-Ji's name from the deck. An-Ji is a Chinese-American student who also has high marks for homework completion and accuracy.] An-Ji. [An-Ji looks down at her book but does not respond. Ms. Gilbert waits another 10 seconds; then, seeing one boy's eagerness among the hands going up all around the room] Albert.

Later in the week, Gilbert overheard a conversation among other teachers encountering difficulties in getting students of Asian origin to participate in class. These veteran teachers were describing these students as "reluctant," "passive," "shy," "reserved," "diffident," and "bashful." The tone of the conversation ranged from dismay to exasperation. Ms. Gilbert, remembering her experience with An-Ji, added the following example to the discussion.

Ms. GILBERT: I say, 'What about this?' And then I call on An-Ji, then I wait. And I stand there. Nothing. Then she looks down at her book. There is this silence . . . silence . . . silence. I have no experience with this—calling on a student and having the student outwait me.

Problem Solving

1. Note from the case, "An-Ji looks down at her book, but does not respond." What are some possible reasons An-Ji might behave in this manner in this context?

2. How much of this "reluctance" to participate do you think is inherent in An-Ji's cultural or personal learning style and how much is a result of Ms. Gilbert's methods?

3. Imagine that you were a part of these teachers' discussion on the difficulties of including "reluctant, passive, shy, reserved, diffident, or bashful" students in classroom activities. Extend the dialogue to show what techniques might encourage these students to participate.

3. Have there been efforts to have the classroom reflect cultural diversity? Do the walls, bulletin boards, and artwork of the classroom demonstrate respect for cultural diversity, or do the contents of the classroom indicate an appreciation or valuing of only one culture?

4. Have there been efforts to provide organizational patterns that do not result in segregation of some learners according to race, culture, ethnicity, or social class?

5. Have there been efforts to understand language differences and differing learning styles? Have organizational patterns and instructional methodologies been developed that might be helpful to culturally diverse learners?

6. Have there been efforts to understand culturally different learners' perspectives toward motivation, excelling among one's peers, competition, group welfare, and sharing?

7. Have there been efforts to understand culturally diverse parents and extended families and efforts to ensure their participation in learners' academic and social life at school?

8. Have there been efforts to treat each learner with respect, to consider each learner as equal to other students, and treat each learner as a valued and worthwhile member of the class? Are all learners accorded similar academic assistance? Do all learners receive help from the school's special service personnel?

9. Have there been efforts to allow (and indeed encourage) all students to work in cross-cultural groups, to carry on conversation and meaningful dialogue, and to feel a valued member of the group?

10. Have there been efforts to instill multiculturalism as a genuine part of the teaching/learning process and overall school environment?

Self-Check

Define multicultural education and describe its goals from both a narrow and a broad perspective. Reread the scenario at the beginning of this chapter. How, specifically, should Marva and John proceed? How might multicultural education help them resolve the issues they have about the Thanksgiving pageant?

Summary

What Is the Impact of Culture on Learning?
Culture profoundly affects learning. Many aspects of culture contribute to the learner's identity and self-concept and affect the learner's beliefs and values, attitudes and expectations, social relations, language use, and other behaviors.

How Does SES Affect Student Achievement?
Socioeconomic status—based on income, occupation, education, and social prestige—can profoundly influence the learner's attitudes toward school, background knowledge, school readiness, and academic achievement. Poverty places families under stress that contributes to child-rearing practices, communication patterns, and lowered expectations that handicap children when they enter school. Low-SES students often learn a normative culture that is different from the middle-class culture of the school, which demands independence, competitive-

ness, and goal-setting. Low achievement is not, however, the inevitable result of low socioeconomic status.

How Do Ethnicity and Race Affect Students' School Experiences?
Minority-group populations are growing dramatically as diversity in the United States increases. Students who are members of minority groups—self-defined by race, religion, ethnicity, origins, history, language, and culture, such as African Americans, Native Americans, and Latinos or Hispanics—tend to have lower scores than Anglo-European Americans on standardized tests of academic achievement. The lower scores correlate with lower socioeconomic status and reflect in part a legacy of discrimination against minority groups and consequent poverty. School desegregation, long intended as a solution to educational inequities due to race and social class, has

had mixed benefits. Continuing issues include delivering fairness and equal opportunity, fostering racial harmony, and preventing resegregation.

How Do Language Differences and Bilingual Programs Affect School Achievement?

Bilingual education addresses problems of students with limited proficiency in English and for whom English is a second language. Bilingual-bicultural programs may help students become proficient in both English and the home language while preserving self-esteem and cultural pride. Research suggests that bilingual education for all students has clear benefits. Difficulties include the shortage of bilingual teachers and adequate transition programs for students entering all-English classes.

How Do Gender and Gender Bias Affect Students' School Experiences?

Many observed differences between males and females are clearly linked to differences in early socialization when children learn sex-role behaviors regarded as appropriate. Gender bias in the classroom, including subtle teacher cueing and curriculum materials containing sex-role stereotypes, has clearly affected student choices and achievement. One outcome is a gender gap in mathematics and science, for example, though this gap has decreased steadily. The question of actual gender differences in thinking and abilities, however, is still a subject of research.

How Are Students Different in Intelligence and Learning Styles?

Students differ in their ability to deal with abstractions, to solve problems, and to learn. They also differ in any number of specific intelligences, so that accurate estimations of intelligence should probably rely on broader performances than traditional IQ tests allow. As a consequence, teachers generally should not base their expectations of students on IQ test scores. Binet, Spearman, Sternberg, Guilford, and Gardner and Hatch have contributed to theories and measures of intelligence. Both heredity and environment determine intelligence. Research shows that home environments, schooling, and life experiences can profoundly influence IQ.

Students differ in their prior learning and cognitive learning styles. Field-dependent learners, for example, learn best holistically and in social contexts rather than analytically and alone. Documented culture-based learning styles include, for example, a preference for learning by observation and cooperation rather than by performance and competition. Individual preferences in learning environments and conditions also affect student achievement.

What Is Multicultural Education?

Multicultural education is no single program but a philosophy—with instructional and curriculum recommendations—calling for the celebration of cultural diversity and the promotion of educational equity and social harmony in the schools.

Key Terms

aptitude-treatment interaction, 138
bilingual-bicultural program, 128
bilingual education, 127
culture, 114
English as a second language (ESL), 128
ethnicity, 116
ethnic group, 119
eurocentric, 142
field dependence, 137
field independence, 137
gender bias, 132
impulsivity, 138
intelligence, 134

intelligence quotient (IQ), 134
language minority, 127
learning styles, 137
limited English proficiency (LEP), 127
minority group, 119
multicultural education, 142
multiple intelligences, 135
race, 116
reflectivity, 138
sex-role behavior, 131
socioeconomic status (SES), 115
students at risk, 137

Self-Assessment

1. In a short essay, explain how multicultural education might have been implemented to address the goals of educational and social equality in your own school experience.

2. All of the following are defined as indicators of socioeconomic status (SES) *except*

   a. occupation

   b. race

   c. income

   d. education

3. In teaching simple tasks to their children, lower-class mothers are more likely than middle-class mothers to

   a. explain why the task needs to be done.

   b. give clear directions.

   c. take the child's perspective.

   d. demand that the task be done.

4. Multicultural education should be part of (a) the curriculum, (b) daily activities in the classroom and school, and (c) teachers' self-assessments. Give an example of each type of application.

5. The socioeconomic status of various racial/ethnic groups and the groups' scores on standardized tests appear to be

   a. positively correlated.

   b. negatively correlated.

   c. uncorrelated.

6. All of the following are disadvantages or limitations of bilingual programs *except*

   a. Such programs generally interfere with performance in either the native language or English.

   b. The transition from a bilingual program to an all-English program may be difficult for many students.

   c. There are insufficient bilingual teachers to support such programs.

   d. The class groupings that result may conflict with the goals of desegregation.

7. Studies report all of the following findings *except*

   a. Males score higher than females on tests of general knowledge.

   b. Females score higher than males on language measures.

   c. Females show more variability in performance than males.

   d. SAT math scores for females have been improving.

8. Through definitions and examples, distinguish among the concepts listed in (a) and (b) below.

   a. intelligence, intelligence quotient, multiple intelligences

   b. learning preferences; cognitive learning styles, cultural learning styles

5

Behavioral Theories of Learning

Chapter Outline	Chapter Objectives
What Is Learning?	▲ Define learning.
What Behavioral Learning Theories Have Evolved? I. Pavlov: Classical Conditioning E. L. Thorndike: The Law of Effect B. F. Skinner: Operant Conditioning	▲ Describe experiments that led to the theories of classical and operant condition and distinguish among these theories.
What Are Some Principles of Behavioral Learning? The Role of Consequences Reinforcers Punishers Immediacy of Consequences Shaping Extinction Schedules of Reinforcement Maintenance The Role of Antecedents	▲ Define and illustrate several principles of behavioral learning, including reinforcement and punishment, and discuss their applications to teaching.
How Has Social Learning Theory Contributed to Our Understanding of Human Learning? A. Bandura: Modeling and Observational Learning D. Meichenbaum: Cognitive Behavior Modification	▲ Describe social learning theories, such as observational learning and cognitive behavior modification, explain how they contribute to our understanding of the way people learn, and discuss their applications to teaching.
What Are the Implications of Behavioral Learning Approaches for Education?	▲ Evaluate the significance and limitations of behavioral learning theories in education.

J ulia Esteban, first-grade teacher at Tanner Elementary School, was trying to teach her students appropriate classroom behavior. "Children," she said one day, "we are having a problem in this class that I'd like to discuss with you. Whenever I ask a question, many of you shout out your answers instead of raising your hand and waiting to be called on. Can anyone tell me what you should do when I ask the class a question?" Rebecca's hand shot into the air. "I know, I know!" she said, "raise your hand and wait quietly!" Ms. Esteban sighed to herself. She tried to ignore Rebecca, who was doing exactly what she had just been told not to do, but Rebecca was the only student with her hand up, and the longer she delayed the more frantically Rebecca waved her hand and shouted her answer.

"All right, Rebecca. What are you supposed to do?"

"We're supposed to raise our hands and wait *quietly* for you to call on us."

"If you know the rule, why were you shouting out your answer before I called on you?"

"I guess I forgot."

"All right. Can anyone remind the class of our rule about talking out of turn?"

Four children raised their hands and shouted together.

"One at a time!"

"Take turns!"

"Don't talk when someone else is talking!"

Ms. Esteban called for order. "You kids are going to drive me crazy!" she said. "Didn't we just talk about how to raise your hands and wait for me to call on you?"

"But Ms. Esteban," said Stephen without even raising his hand. "You called on Rebecca and she wasn't quiet!"

Children are excellent learners. What they learn, however, may not always be what we intend to teach. Ms. Esteban is trying to teach students how to behave in class, but she is actually teaching them the opposite of what she intends by paying attention to Rebecca's outburst. Rebecca craves her teacher's attention, so being called on (even in an exasperated tone of voice) rewards her for calling out her answer. Not only does Ms. Esteban's response increase the chances that Rebecca will call out answers again, but Rebecca now serves as a model for her classmates' own calling out. What Ms. Esteban *says* is less important than her actual response to her students' behaviors.

The purpose of this chapter is to define learning and then to present **behavioral learning theories,** explanations for learning that emphasize observable behaviors. Behavioral theories emphasize the ways in which pleasurable or painful consequences of behavior change individuals' behavior over time and ways in which individuals model their behavior on that of others. Later chapters present **cognitive learning theories,** which emphasize unobservable mental processes that people use to learn and remember new information or skills. Behavioral learning theorists try to discover principles of behavior that apply to all living beings, while cognitive theorists are exclusively concerned with human learning. Actually, the boundaries between behavioral and cognitive learning theories have become increasingly indistinct in recent years as each school of thought has incorporated the findings of the other.

What Is Learning?

What is learning? This seems like a simple question until you begin to think about it. Consider the following examples. Are they instances of learning?

1. A young child takes her first steps.
2. An adolescent male feels a strong attraction to certain females.
3. A child feels anxious when he sees the doctor coming with a needle.
4. Long after learning how to multiply, a girl realizes on her own that another way to multiply by 5 is to divide by 2 and multiply by 10 (for example, 428 x 5 can be figured as follows: 428/2 = 214 x 10 = 2140).

Learning is usually defined as a change in an individual caused by experience (see Mazur, 1990; Rocklin, 1987). Changes caused by development (such as growing taller) are not instances of learning. Neither are characteristics of individuals that are present at birth (such as reflexes and responses to hunger or pain). However, human beings do so much learning from the day of their birth (and some say earlier) that learning and development are inseparably linked. Learning to walk (Example 1) is mostly a developmental progression, but also depends on experience

behavioral learning theory: explanation of learning that emphasizes observable changes in behavior.

cognitive learning theory: explanation of learning that focuses on mental processes.

learning: a change in an individual that results from experience.

with crawling and other activities. The adolescent sex drive (Example 2) is not learned, but learning shapes individuals' choices in desirable partners.

A child's anxiety on seeing a doctor with a needle (Example 3) is definitely learned behavior. The child has learned to associate the needle with pain, and his body reacts emotionally when he sees the needle. This reaction may be unconscious or involuntary, but it is learned nonetheless.

The fourth example, the girl's insight into the multiplication shortcut, is an instance of internally generated learning, better known as "thinking." Some theorists would not call this learning because it was not caused by the environment. But it might be considered a case of delayed learning, in which deliberate instruction in multiplication plus years of experience with numbers plus mental effort on the part of the girl produced an insight.

Learning takes place in many ways. Sometimes it is intentional, as when students acquire information presented in a classroom or when they look something up in the encyclopedia. Sometimes it is unintentional, as in the case of the child's reaction to the needle. All sorts of learning are going on all the time. As you (the reader) are reading this chapter, you are learning something about learning. However, you are also learning that educational psychology is interesting or dull, useful or useless. Without knowing it, you are probably learning about where on the page certain pieces of information are to be found. You may be learning to associate the content of this chapter with unimportant aspects of your surroundings as you read it, such as the musty smell of books in a library or the temperature of the room you are reading in. The content of this chapter, the placement of words on the page, and the smells, sounds, and temperature of your surroundings are all **stimuli**. Your senses are usually wide open to all sorts of stimuli, but you are consciously aware of only a fraction of them at any one time.

The problem faced by educators is not how to get students to learn; students are already engaged in learning every waking moment. Rather, it is to help them learn particular information, skills, and concepts that will be useful in adult life. How do we present students with the right stimuli on which to focus their attention and mental effort so that they will acquire important skills? That is the central problem of instruction.

Self-Check

List examples of "learning." As you read, identify your examples in terms of the kind of learning that is taking place, and add new examples.

What Behavioral Learning Theories Have Evolved?

The systematic study of learning is relatively new. It was not until the late nineteenth century that learning was studied in a scientific manner. Using techniques borrowed from the physical sciences, researchers began conducting experiments to understand how people and animals learned. Two of the most important early researchers were Ivan Pavlov and Edward Thorndike. Among later researchers, B. F. Skinner is important for his studies of the relationship between behavior and consequences.

> **stimuli:** environmental conditions that activate the senses.

Figure 5.1 Classical Conditioning

In classical conditioning, a neutral stimulus (such as a bell) that at first prompts no response becomes paired with an unconditioned stimulus (such as meat) and gains the power of that stimulus to cause a response (such as salivation).

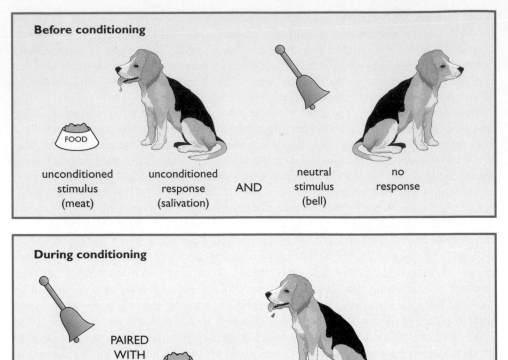

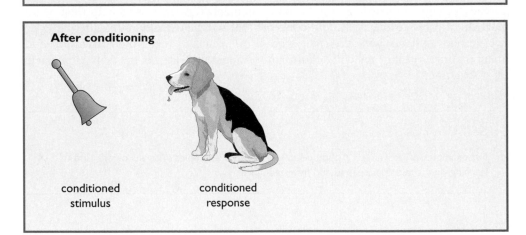

I. Pavlov: Classical Conditioning

In the late 1800s and early 1900s Pavlov and his colleagues studied the digestive process in dogs. During the research the scientists noticed changes in the timing and rate of salivation of these animals.

Pavlov observed that if meat powder was placed in or near the mouth of a hungry dog, the dog would salivate. Because the meat powder provoked this response automatically, without any prior training or conditioning, the meat powder is referred to as an **unconditioned stimulus.** Similarly, because salivation occurred automatically in the presence of meat, also without the need for any training or experience, this response of salivating is referred to as an **unconditioned response.**

While the meat will produce salivation without any previous experience or training, other stimuli, such as a bell, will not produce salivation. Because these stimuli have no effect on the response in question, they are referred to as **neutral stimuli.** Pavlov's experiments showed that if a previously neutral stimulus is paired with an unconditioned stimulus, the neutral stimulus becomes a conditioned stimulus and gains the power to prompt a response similar to that produced by the unconditioned stimulus. That is, the ringing of the bell alone causes the dog to salivate. This process is referred to as **classical conditioning.** A diagram of Pavlov's theory is shown in Figure 5.1.

1. Prior to training: Presenting unconditioned stimulus (meat) produces unconditioned response (salivation); presenting neutral stimulus (bell) does not produce any salivation.
2. During training: The bell is rung when the meat is presented. The formerly neutral stimulus (the bell) becomes a conditioned stimulus.
3. After training: Presenting conditioned stimulus (ringing the bell) produces conditioned response (salivation).

In experiments such as these, Pavlov and his colleagues showed how learning could affect what were once thought to be involuntary, reflexive behaviors, such as salivating.

The importance of Pavlov's work lies as much in the method as in the results. A look at the apparatus pictured in Figure 5.2 shows how Pavlov and his associates were able to carefully observe and measure their subjects' responses to various experiments. Pavlov's emphasis on observation and careful measurement,

Figure 5.2 Apparatus Used in Classical Conditioning Experiments

The apparatus that Pavlov used in his classical conditioning experiments included a harness to hold a dog quiet and a tube attached to the dog's salivary gland to measure salivation.

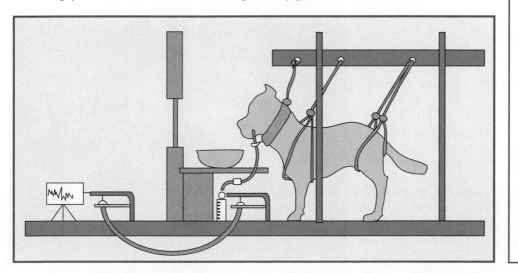

unconditioned stimulus (US): a stimulus that naturally evokes a particular response.

unconditioned response (UR): a behavior prompted automatically by stimuli.

neutral stimuli: stimuli that do not naturally prompt a particular response.

classical conditioning: associating a previously neutral stimulus with an unconditioned stimulus to evoke a conditioned response.

and his systematic exploration of a number of aspects of learning, helped advance the scientific study of learning. He also left other behavioral theorists with significant mysteries, such as the process by which "neutral" stimuli take on meaning. Also, what does his work tell teachers? Although his findings have few applications to classroom instruction, they can help a teacher understand such situations as when a child's anxiety about being among strangers gradually develops into a debilitating fear of coming to school.

E. L. Thorndike: The Law of Effect

Pavlov's work inspired researchers in the United States such as E. L. Thorndike (Hilgard and Bower, 1966). Thorndike, like many of the early behavioral learning theorists, linked behavior to physical reflexes. In his early work he also viewed most behavior as a response to stimuli in the environment. This view that stimuli can prompt responses was the forerunner of what became known as stimulus-response or S-R theory. Early learning theorists noted that certain reflexes, such as the knee jerking upward when it is tapped, occur without processing by the brain. They hypothesized that other behavior was also determined in a reflexive way by stimuli present in the environment rather than by conscious or unconscious thoughts.

Thorndike went beyond Pavlov by showing that stimuli that occurred *after* a behavior had an influence on future behaviors. In many of his experiments Thorndike placed cats in boxes from which they had to escape to get food. He observed that over time the cats learned how to get out of the box more and more quickly by repeating the behaviors that led to escape and by not repeating those behaviors that were ineffective. From these experiments, Thorndike developed his Law of Effect.

Thorndike's **Law of Effect** stated that if an act is followed by a satisfying change in the environment, the likelihood that the act will be repeated in similar situations increases. However, if a behavior is followed by an unsatisfying change in the environment, the chances that the behavior will be repeated decrease. Thus the consequences of one's present behavior were shown to play a crucial role in determining one's future behavior.

Law of Effect: an act followed by a favorable effect is more likely to be repeated in similar situations; an act followed by an unfavorable effect is less likely to be repeated.

How does this Skinner box work? What type of conditioning is the rat undergoing? How does that type of conditioning take place, and how is it different from the type of conditioning Pavlov studied?

B. F. Skinner: Operant Conditioning

It is clear that some human behaviors are prompted by specific stimuli. Just like Pavlov's dogs, we, too, salivate when we are hungry and see appetizing food. And we, too, lend credence to Thorndike's early emphasis on reflexive behavior when we learn things so well, such as how to ride a bicycle, that the brain seems to respond reflexively. However, B. F. Skinner proposed that such behavior accounts for only a small proportion of all actions. He proposed another class of behavior, which he labeled *operant* behaviors because they *operated* on the environment in the apparent absence of any unconditioned stimuli, such as food. Like Thorndike, Skinner's work focused on the relation between behavior and its consequences. For example, if an individual's behavior is immediately followed by pleasurable consequences, the individual will engage in that behavior more frequently. The use of pleasant and unpleasant consequences to change behavior is often referred to as **operant conditioning.**

Skinner's work focused on placing subjects in controlled situations and observing the changes in their behavior produced by systematically changing the consequences of their behavior (see Iversen, 1992). Skinner is famous for his development and use of an apparatus commonly referred to as the **Skinner box.** Skinner boxes contain a very simple apparatus for studying the behavior of animals, usually rats and pigeons. A Skinner box for rats would consist of a bar that is easy for the rat to press, a food dispenser that could give the rat a pellet of food, and a water dispenser. The rat cannot see or hear anything outside of the box, so all stimuli are controlled by the experimenter. In some of the earliest experiments involving Skinner boxes, the apparatus was first set up so that if the rat happened to press the bar, it would receive a food pellet.

After a few accidental bar presses, the rat would start pressing the bar frequently, receiving a pellet each time. The rat's behavior had been conditioned to strengthen bar pressing and weaken all other behaviors (such as wandering around the box). At this point, the experimenter might do any of several things. The electronics controlling the bar and food dispenser might be set up so that it now took several bar presses to obtain food, or so that some bar presses produced food but others did not, or so that bar presses no longer produced food. In each case, the rat's behavior would be automatically recorded. One important advantage of the Skinner box is that it allows for careful scientific study of behavior in a controlled environment. Skinner's contribution, like that of Pavlov, consists not only of what he discovered but also of the methods he used (Delprato and Midgley, 1992). Skinner's experiments can be repeated by anyone with the same equipment.

Self-Check

Develop a chart to compare and contrast the contributions of Pavlov, Thorndike, and Skinner to our understanding of learning. Chart headings might include, for example, name of theorist, name of theory, main concepts, and experiment (or research) conducted. Summarize the main research findings. What examples will you give of the application of these findings to human learning?

operant conditioning: using consequences to control the occurrence of behavior.

Skinner box: an apparatus developed by B. F. Skinner for observing animal behavior in experiments in operant conditioning.

What Are Some Principles of Behavioral Learning?

The Role of Consequences

Skinner's pioneering work with rats and pigeons established a set of principles of behavior that have been supported in hundreds of studies involving humans as well as animals. Perhaps the most important principle of behavioral learning theories is that behavior changes according to its immediate **consequences**. Pleasurable consequences "strengthen" behavior, while unpleasant consequences "weaken" it. That is, pleasurable consequences increase the frequency with which an individual engages in a behavior, while unpleasant consequences reduce the frequency of a behavior. If students enjoy reading books, they will probably read more often. If, instead, they find stories boring or are unable to concentrate, they may read less often, choosing other activities instead.

Pleasurable consequences are generally called *reinforcers,* while unpleasant consequences are called *punishers.*

Reinforcers

A **reinforcer** is defined as any consequence that strengthens (that is, increases the frequency of) behaviors. Note that the effectiveness of the reinforcer must be demonstrated. We cannot assume that a particular consequence is in fact a reinforcer until we have evidence that it strengthens behavior for a particular individual. For example, candy might generally be considered a reinforcer for young children, but after a big meal a child might not find candy pleasurable, and some children do not like candy at all. If teachers say, "I reinforced him with praise for staying in his seat during math time, but it didn't work," they may be misusing the term "reinforced," because they have no evidence that praise is in fact a reinforcer for this particular student. No reward can be assumed to be a reinforcer for everyone under all conditions.

Primary and Secondary Reinforcers.   Reinforcers fall into two broad categories: primary and secondary. **Primary reinforcers** satisfy basic human needs. Examples include food, water, security, warmth, and sex.

Secondary reinforcers are reinforcers that acquire their value by being associated with primary reinforcers or other well-established secondary reinforcers. For example, money has no value to a young child until the child learns that it can be used to buy things that are themselves primary or secondary reinforcers. Grades have little value to students unless their parents notice and value them, and parents' praise is of value because it is associated with love, warmth, security, and other reinforcers. Money and grades are examples of secondary reinforcers because they have no value in themselves but have been associated with primary reinforcers or with other well-established secondary reinforcers. There are three basic categories of secondary reinforcers: social reinforcers (such as praise, smiles, hugs, or attention), activity reinforcers (such as access to toys, games, or fun activities), and token (or symbolic) reinforcers (such as money, grades, stars, or points that individuals can exchange for other reinforcers).

consequence: a condition that follows a behavior and affects the frequency of future behavior.

reinforcer: a pleasurable consequence that maintains or increases a behavior.

primary reinforcer: food, water, or other consequence that satisfies basic needs.

secondary reinforcer: a consequence that people learn to value through its association with a primary reinforcer.

Strengthens Behavior	Discourages Behavior
Positive Reinforcement	**No Reinforcement**
Example: rewarding or praising	Example: ignoring
Negative Reinforcement	**Removal Punishment**
Example: excusing from an undesirable task or situation	Example: forbidding a desirable task or situation
	Presentation Punishment
	Example: imposing an undesirable task or situation

Table 5.1   Consequences in Behavioral Learning

When Ms. Esteban recognized Rebecca, she was inadvertently giving her a social reinforcer, her own attention.

Positive and Negative Reinforcers.   Most often, reinforcers used in schools are things given to students. These are called **positive reinforcers,** and include praise, grades, and stars. However, another way to strengthen a behavior is to have the behavior's consequence be an escape from an unpleasant situation or a way of preventing something unpleasant from occurring. For example, a parent might release a student from doing the dishes if the student completes his or her homework. If doing the dishes is seen as an unpleasant task, release from it will be reinforcing. Reinforcers that are escapes from unpleasant situations are called **negative reinforcers.**

This term is often misinterpreted to mean "punishment," as in "I negatively reinforced him for being late by having him stay in during recess." One way to avoid this error in terminology is to remember that reinforcers (whether positive or negative) *strengthen* behavior, while punishment weakens it. (See Table 5.1.)

The Premack Principle.   One important principle of behavior is that less desired ("low-strength") activities can be increased by linking them to more desired activities. In other words, access to something desirable is made contingent on doing something less desirable. For example, a teacher might say, "As soon as you finish your work, you may go outside," or "Clean up your art project and then I will read you a story." These are examples of the Premack Principle (Premack, 1965). The **Premack Principle** is sometimes called "Grandma's Rule" from the age-old statement, "Eat your vegetables and then you may play." Teachers can use the Premack Principle by alternating more enjoyable activities with less enjoyable ones, and making participation in the enjoyable activities depend on successful completion of the less enjoyable ones. (For example, it may be a good idea to schedule music, considered an enjoyable activity by most students, after completion of a difficult subject in elementary school, so that students will know that if they fool around in the difficult subject, they will be using up part of their desired music time.)

positive reinforcer: consequence given to strengthen behavior.

negative reinforcer: release from an unpleasant situation to strengthen behavior.

Premack Principle: using favored activities to reinforce participation in less desired activities.

Whenever she finishes her work early, this child gets to care for the class pet. What kind of consequence is she experiencing? What is being reinforced?

Theory Into Practice
Classroom Uses of Reinforcement

The most useful principle of behavioral learning theories for classroom practice is also the simplest: Reinforce behaviors you wish to see repeated. This principle seems obvious, but in practice it is not as easy as it appears. For example, some teachers take the attitude that reinforcement is unnecessary, on the grounds that, "Why should I reinforce them? They're just doing what they are supposed to do!"

The main principles of the use of reinforcement to increase desired behavior in the classroom are as follows:

1. Decide what behaviors you want from students, and reinforce them when they occur. For example, praise or reward good work. Do not praise or reward work that is not up to students' capabilities. (See the upcoming section on Shaping.)

2. Tell students what behaviors you want, and when they do them and you reinforce them, tell them why. (See the upcoming section on Discrimination.)

Many studies have shown that when reinforcement is given to students on the basis of their classroom behavior and schoolwork, their behavior improves. For example, Hall and colleagues (1968) described a highly disruptive third-grader, Robbie, who engaged in study behavior only 25 percent of the time. They then asked Robbie's teacher to praise him, smile at him, pat him on the back, or otherwise socially reinforce him from time to time when he was studying. Robbie's studying behavior increased to 71 percent of class time. When the teacher stopped reinforcing him, his study behavior dropped off, but when she resumed reinforcement, it increased. Later observations (postchecks) indicated that Robbie's improved study behavior remained several weeks after the reinforcement program was reinstated.

Several additional examples of the use of reinforcement to improve students' behaviors are presented in Chapter 11.

Punishers

Consequences that are not reinforcing—that is, that weaken behavior—are called punishers. Again, note the difference here between negative reinforcement (the *strengthening* of desirable behavior by withdrawing unpleasant consequences) and **punishment**, which is aimed at *reducing* behaviors by imposing unwanted consequences. Note also that there is the same catch in the definition of punishment as in the definition of reinforcement: If an apparently unpleasant consequence does not reduce the frequency of the behavior it follows, it is not necessarily a punisher. For example, some students *like* being sent to the principal's office or out to the hall because it releases them from what they see as an unpleasant situation, the classroom (Pfiffer *et al.,* 1985). Some students like to be scolded because it gains them the teacher's attention and perhaps enhances their status among their peers.

punishment: using unpleasant consequences to weaken a behavior.

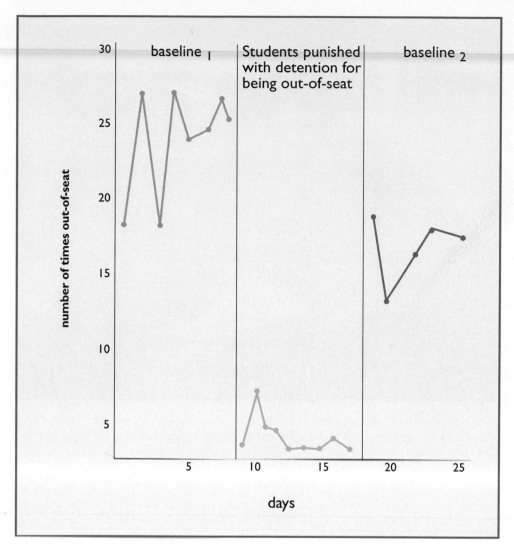

Figure 5.3   Punishment
The number of times that students were out of their seats without permission dropped sharply in this experiment when misbehavior led to after-school detention. Each instance of misbehavior recorded by the teacher cost the students five minutes of after-school detention. When misbehavior no longer prompted punishment (Baseline₂), students more often got out of their seats without permission.

Adapted from Hall et al., 1971, p. 25.

As with reinforcers, the effectiveness of a punisher cannot be assumed but must be demonstrated.

Presentation and Removal Punishment. Punishment can take two primary forms. **Presentation punishment** is the use of unpleasant consequences, or **aversive stimuli,** as when a student is asked to write "I will not talk in class" 100 times or is scolded or spanked. **Removal punishment** is the removal of reinforcers, as when a student must give up recess, stand in the hall, or lose a privilege.

In some cases, use of punishment can improve behavior. For example, one study (Hall *et al.,* 1971) used a simple punishment procedure to reduce the time that ten emotionally disturbed students spent out of their seats without permission. The researchers simply had the teacher carry a clipboard with students' names on it. Whenever students were out of their seats without permission, the teacher gave them a check mark worth five minutes of after-school detention. The results are illustrated in Figure 5.3.

presentation punishment: decreasing the chances that a behavior will occur again by presenting an aversive stimulus following the behavior.

aversive stimulus: a condition that a person tries to avoid or escape.

removal punishment: decreasing the chances that a behavior will occur again by removing a pleasant stimulus following the behavior.

What do you infer from this picture about the type of consequence the teacher is using? What is likely to be the effect of this consequence on the student's subsequent behavior? If this consequence proves ineffective, what other types might the teacher try?

Figure 5.3 clearly shows that the punishment program was effective in reducing the students' out-of-seat behaviors. However, note that when the punishment program was stopped (Baseline$_2$), the students' behavior worsened again.

Time Out. One frequently used form of punishment in classrooms is **time out**, having a student who misbehaves sit in the corner or the hall for several minutes. Time out is used in particular when teachers believe that the attention of other students is serving to reinforce misbehavior, so the student is deprived of this reinforcer, in which case time out would be considered removal punishment. However, being assigned to time out may also be embarrassing or shaming to the student and could therefore be considered presentation punishment. Either way, the use of time out as a consequence for misbehavior has generally been found to reduce the misbehavior (Skiba and Raison, 1990).

The topic of if, when, and how to punish has been a source of considerable controversy among behavioral learning theorists. Some have claimed that the effects of punishment are only temporary, that punishment produces aggression, and that punishment cau ses individuals to avoid settings in which it is used (Bates, 1987). However, even behavioral learning theorists who do support the use of punishment generally agree that it should be resorted to only when reinforcement for appropriate behavior has been tried and has failed, that when punishment is necessary it should take the mildest possible form, and that punishment should always be used

time out: removing a student from a situation in which misbehavior was reinforced.

as part of a careful plan, never inconsistently or out of frustration. Physical punishment in schools (such as spanking) is almost universally opposed by behavioral learning theorists on ethical as well as scientific grounds (see Jenson *et al.*, 1988; O'Leary and O'Leary, 1977).

Immediacy of Consequences

One very important principle of behavioral learning theories is that consequences that follow behaviors closely in time affect behavior far more than delayed consequences. If we waited a few minutes to give a rat in a Skinner box its food pellet after it pressed a bar, the rat would take a long time to learn the connection between bar pressing and food, because by the time the food arrived, it might be doing something other than bar pressing. A smaller reinforcer given immediately generally has a much larger effect than a large reinforcer given later (Kulik and Kulik, 1988). This concept explains much about human behavior. It suggests, for example, why people find it so difficult to give up smoking or overeating. Even though the benefits of giving up smoking or losing weight are substantial and well known, the small but immediate reinforcement of just one cigarette or one doughnut often overcomes the behavioral effect of the large but delayed reinforcers.

In the classroom the principle of immediacy of consequences is also very important. Particularly for younger students, praise for a job well done given immediately can be a stronger reinforcer than a grade given much later. A study by Leach and Graves (1973) demonstrated that immediate feedback can be a more effective reinforcer than delayed feedback. Two girls in a regular seventh-grade language arts class were having trouble completing their assignments. At first, the teacher asked the girls to write ten sentences using correct grammar and punctuation each day. The sentences were scored and returned the following day. Under these conditions, the girls averaged about 58 percent correct sentences. Then the teacher decided to grade and return the papers immediately. When the immediate correction procedure was introduced, the girls' correct sentence writing increased dramatically, to 90 percent for "Betty" and 93 percent for "Jane." When the immediate correction procedure was withdrawn, the girls' performances deteriorated but improved once more when it was reinstated.

Immediate feedback serves at least two purposes. First, it makes the connection between behavior and consequence clear. Second, it increases the informational value of the feedback. In the Leach and Graves (1973) study, immediate feedback not only increased the girls' motivation to write sentences but also probably made it easier for them to use the information on the correctness of their sentences to improve their sentence writing in the future. In practice, few classroom teachers can provide individual feedback immediately to all their students (although special education teachers with small classes can and must do so). However, the same results can be obtained by giving students answers right after they complete their work. In dealing with misbehavior, the principle of immediacy of consequences can be applied by responding immediately and positively when students are *not* misbehaving, catching them in the act of being good!

> **Connections**
>
> For applications of behavioral learning approaches to classroom management, see Chapter 11.

Shaping

Immediacy of reinforcement is important to teaching, but so is the decision of what to reinforce. Should a kindergarten teacher withhold reinforcement until a child can recite the entire alphabet? Certainly not. It would be better to praise children for saying one letter, then for saying several, and finally for learning all twenty-six letters. Also, should a music teacher withhold reinforcement until a young student has played a piano piece flawlessly? Or should the teacher praise the first halting run-through? Most students need reinforcement along the way. When teachers guide students toward goals by reinforcing the many steps that lead to success, they are using a technique called **shaping.**

The term *shaping* is used in behavioral learning theories to refer to the teaching of new skills or behaviors by reinforcing learners for approaching the desired final behavior. For example, in teaching children to tie their shoelaces, we would not simply show them how it is done and then wait to reinforce them until they do the whole job themselves. Rather, we would first reinforce them for tying the first knot, then for making the loops, and so on, until they can do the entire task. In this way, we would be shaping the children's behavior by reinforcing all those steps that lead toward the final goal.

Shaping is an important tool in classroom instruction. Let's say we want students to be able to write paragraphs with a topic sentence, three supporting details, and a concluding sentence. This task has many parts: being able to recognize and then produce topic sentences, supporting details, and concluding sentences; being able to write complete sentences, using capitalization, punctuation, and grammar correctly; and being able to spell. If a teacher taught a lesson on all these skills, asked students to write paragraphs, and then scored them on content, grammar, punctuation, and spelling, most students would fail, and might learn little from the exercise.

Instead, the teacher might teach the skills step by step, gradually shaping the final skill. Students might first be taught how to write topic sentences, then supporting details, then concluding sentences. Early on, they might be held responsible only for paragraph content. Later, the requirement for reinforcement might be increased to include grammar and punctuation. Finally, spelling might be added as a criterion for success. At each stage, students would have a good chance to be reinforced because the criterion for reiforcement would be within their grasp.

The principle here is that students should be reinforced for behaviors that are within their current capabilities but which also stretch them toward new skills. A student who can do ten math problems in 15 minutes should be reinforced for doing twelve, but not for doing eight. However, a classmate who can do twenty problems should be reinforced for doing twenty-four, not for doing fewer than twenty.

Chaining.   Shaping is being used effectively when students move rapidly from success to success. This requires breaking down tasks into small steps, a process called chaining, and then reinforcing students as they accomplish each step.

Here is a summary of the steps involved in shaping a new behavior:

Steps in Shaping

1. Choose your goal—make it as specific as possible.

2. Find out where the students are now. What do they already know?

3. Develop a series of steps that will serve as a stairway to take them from where they are now to your goal. For some students, the steps may be too big; for others, too small. Modify according to each student's ability.

4. Give feedback as the students go along. In some ways, learning is like driving a car. The more unfamiliar the area, the more feedback one needs—that is, the

shaping: using small steps combined with feedback to help learners reach goals.

more one will consult a map or look for street signs. Similarly, the newer the subject material, the more feedback students require.

Reverse Chaining.   One interesting form of shaping that has educational applications is called **reverse chaining**, a procedure in which a complex skill is taught "backwards." For example, in teaching the lesson on paragraph writing, we might first give students a paragraph missing only a concluding sentence and ask them to supply that one sentence. The final product of this exercise would be a complete paragraph. Next, students might be given another incomplete paragraph and asked to complete it by adding both one supporting detail *and* a concluding sentence. Then they might be given only a topic sentence and asked for several supporting details and a concluding sentence. The advantage of this teaching strategy is that the product of each exercise is a good paragraph. Students may be able to see the big picture better this way, and may take a shorter route to reinforcement.

Extinction

By definition, reinforcers strengthen behavior. But what happens when reinforcers are withdrawn? Eventually, the behavior will be weakened, and ultimately, it will disappear. This process is called **extinction** of a previously learned behavior.

Extinction is rarely a smooth process. When reinforcers are withdrawn, individuals often *increase* their rate of behavior for a while. For example, when you come to a door that is usually unlocked and find that it will not open, you might push even harder for a while, shake the door, turn the handle both ways, perhaps even kick the door. You are likely to feel frustrated and angry. However, after a short time you will realize that the door is locked and go away. If the door is permanently locked (without your knowing it), you might try it a few times over the next few days, then perhaps once after a month, and only eventually give up on it.

Your behavior when confronted by a locked door is a classic extinction pattern. Behavior intensifies when the reinforcer is first withdrawn and then rapidly weakens until it disappears. The behavior may return after much time has passed. For example, you might try the door again a year later to see if it is still locked. If it is, you will probably leave it alone for a longer time, but probably not forever.

Extinction is a key to managing the behavior of students. Undesirable behavior can often be extinguished if the reinforcer(s) maintaining the behavior are identified and removed. For example, in a study by Zimmerman and Zimmerman (1962) a teacher eliminated a student's tantrums by taking the child to an empty room and letting him scream and kick the floor to his heart's content. Because the child's tantrums no longer brought him the adult attention they once did, they soon ceased.

Note that in this case the behavior intensified before it diminished. If the teacher in the Zimmerman and Zimmerman (1962) study had given up after the boy's tantrums had gotten severe and released him from his solitary confinement, the results might have been disastrous. Giving in would have reinforced the undesirable behaviors—in fact, it would have strengthened them because the children would have learned that "if at first you don't succeed, try, try again." This was the case in the scenario presented at the beginning of this chapter. Ms. Esteban at first ignored Rebecca's calling out, so Rebecca called out even louder. Then she called on Rebecca, unintentionally communicating to her that only loud and persistent calling out would be reinforced!

reverse chaining: shaping process in which the final subskills of a complex task are learned before the first subskills.

extinction: eliminating or decreasing a behavior by removing reinforcement for it.

Extinction of a previously learned behavior can be hastened when some stimulus or cue informs the individual that behaviors that were once reinforced will no longer be reinforced. In the case of the locked door, a sign saying "Door permanently locked—use other entrance" would have greatly reduced the number of times we tried the door before giving up on it. Similarly, when a teacher says, "I will no longer accept papers handed in after the due date," the previously reinforced behavior (handing in late papers) is likely to diminish rapidly if the teacher sticks to the new rule.

Like behaviors, emotions can be extinguished. For example, a child might be fearful on the first day of school. If nothing happens to reinforce the child's fearfulness, the fear will ultimately extinguish. By the same token, students' interest in a subject or enthusiasm for learning may extinguish if they are never given reinforcement in the form of interesting lessons or engaging activities.

Schedules of Reinforcement

The effects of reinforcement on behavior depend on many factors, one of the most important of which is the **schedule of reinforcement**. This term refers to the frequency with which reinforcers are given, the amount of time that elapses between opportunities for reinforcement, and the predictability of reinforcement.

Fixed Ratio (FR).   One common schedule of reinforcement is the **fixed ratio** (FR), where a reinforcer is given after a fixed number of behaviors. For example, a teacher might say, "As soon as you finish ten problems, you may go outside." Regardless of the amount of time it takes, students are reinforced as soon as they finish ten problems. This is an example of an FR10 schedule (ten behaviors for one reinforcer). One common form of a fixed-ratio schedule is where each behavior is reinforced. This is called *continuous reinforcement,* or CRF, though it could just as well be called FR1 because one behavior is required for reinforcement. Putting money in a soda machine is (usually) an example of continuous reinforcement, because one behavior (inserting coins) results in one reinforcer (a soda). Giving correct answers in class is also usually continuously reinforced. The student gives a good answer and the teacher says "Right! Good answer!"

One important process in instruction is gradually increasing reinforcement ratios. Early in a sequence of lessons it may be necessary to reinforce students for every correct answer, such as a single math problem. However, this is inefficient in the long run. As soon as students are answering math problems correctly, it may be possible to reinforce every five problems (FR5), every ten (FR10), and so on. "Thinning out" the reinforcement schedule in this way makes the student more able to work independently without reinforcement and makes the behavior more resistant to extinction. Ultimately, students may be asked to do entire projects on their own, receiving no reinforcement until the project is completed. As adults, we often assume tasks that take years to complete and years to pay off. (Writing an educational psychology text is one such task!)

Fixed-ratio schedules are effective in motivating individuals to do a great deal of work, especially if the fixed ratio starts with continuous reinforcement (FR1) to get the individual going and moves to high requirements for reinforcement. One reason that high requirements for reinforcement produce higher levels of behavior than low requirements is that reinforcing too frequently can make the value of the reinforcer wear off. Older students who were praised for

schedule of reinforcement: the frequency and predictability of reinforcement.

fixed ratio: dispensing reinforcement for behavior emitted following a constant amount of time.

every math problem would soon grow tired of being praised, and the reinforcer might lose its value.

Variable-Ratio (VR). A **variable-ratio (VR) schedule** of reinforcement is one in which the number of behaviors required for reinforcement is unpredictable, although it is certain that the behaviors will eventually be reinforced. For example, a slot machine is a variable-ratio reinforcer. It might pay off after one pull one time, after 200 the next, and there is no way to predict which pull will win. In the classroom a variable-ratio schedule exists when students raise their hands to answer questions. They never know when they will be reinforced by being able to give the correct answer, but they may expect to be called upon about one time in thirty (in a class of thirty). This is called a VR30 schedule because, on average, thirty behaviors are required for one reinforcer. Variable-ratio schedules tend to produce high and stable rates of behavior. In fact, almost all gambling games involve VR schedules, and as such they can be quite literally addicting. Similarly, use of frequent random checks of student work can help "addict" students to high achievement.

Variable-ratio schedules are highly resistant to extinction. That is, even after behaviors are no longer being reinforced, people may not give up working for a long time. Because they have learned that it may take a lot of work to be rewarded, they keep on working in the mistaken belief that the *next* effort might just pay off.

Fixed Interval (FI). In **fixed-interval schedules** reinforcement is available only at certain periodic times. The final examination is a classic example of a fixed-interval schedule. Fixed-interval schedules create an interesting pattern of behavior. The individual may do very little until just before reinforcement is available, then put forth a burst of effort as the time for reinforcement approaches. This pattern can be demonstrated with rats and pigeons on fixed-interval schedules, but it is even more apparent in students who cram at the last minute before a test or who write their monthly book reports the night before they are due. These characteristics of fixed-interval schedules suggest that frequent short quizzes may be better than infrequent major exams for encouraging students to give their best effort all the time rather than putting in "all-nighters" before the exam (Crooks, 1988).

Variable Interval (VI). In a **variable-interval schedule** reinforcement is available at some times but not at others, and we have no idea when behavior will be reinforced. An example of this is a teacher making spot checks of students who are doing assignments in class. If the students are working well at the particular moment the teacher comes by, they are reinforced. Since they cannot predict when the teacher will check them, students must be doing good work all the time. People may obey traffic laws out of respect for the law and civic responsibility, but it also helps that the police randomly check drivers' compliance with the law. Troopers hide on overpasses or behind hills so they can get a random sampling of drivers' behavior. If they were always in plain sight, they would be a signal to drive carefully, so the necessity for driving carefully at other times would be reduced.

Like variable-ratio schedules, variable-interval schedules are very effective for maintaining a high rate of behavior and are highly resistant to extinction. For example, let's say a teacher has a policy of having students hand in their seatwork every day. Rather than checking every paper, the teacher pulls three at random, and gives these students extra credit if their seatwork was done well. This variable-

variable-ratio schedule (VR): dispensing reinforcement following an unpredictable number of correct behaviors.

fixed-interval schedule: dispensing reinforcement for a behavior emitted following a constant amount of time.

variable-interval schedule: dispensing reinforcement for behavior emitted following an unpredictable amount of time.

Schedule	Definition	Response Patterns	
		During Reinforcement	During Extinction
Fixed ratio	Constant number of behaviors required for reinforcement	Steady response rate; pause after reinforcement	Rapid drop in response rate after required number of responses passes without reinforcement
Variable ratio	Variable number of behaviors required for reinforcement	Steady, high response rate	Response rate stays high, then drops off
Fixed interval	Constant amount of time passes before reinforcement is available	Uneven rate, with rapid acceleration at the end of each interval	Rapid drop in response rate after interval passes with no reinforcement
Variable interval	Variable amount of time passes before reinforcement is available	Steady, high response rate	Slow decrease in response rate

Table 5.2   Schedules of Reinforcement

Specific response patterns during reinforcement and extinction characterize each of the four types of schedules.

interval schedule would probably motivate students to do their seatwork carefully. If the teacher secretly stopped spot-checking halfway through the year, the students might never know it, figuring that their own paper just hadn't been pulled to be checked rather than realizing that reinforcement was no longer available for anyone.

Tables 5.2 and 5.3 define and give additional examples of the schedules of reinforcement.

Theory Into Practice

Establishing Reinforcement Schedules

Classroom teachers offer practical tips such as the following for using reinforcement schedules:

1. Treat ratio schedules as good behavior games.

EXAMPLE: For younger elementary students, teachers may use cut-outs of letters to spell a word, such as T-R-E-A-T, on a bulletin board, one letter at a time next to children's names, for good behavior on a daily basis. When a child collects all the letters and spells out the word, he or she gets to choose a treat from the class treat bag. This is an example of a fixed-ratio reinforcement schedule.

EXAMPLE: For older elementary students, teachers may establish a secret weekly "magic" number, say between 20 and 40. The teacher places "good behavior" marks on the board for the class collectively, at the same time

Continuous reinforcement (reinforcement every time the response is made)	• Using a token to ride the subway.	• Kissing your boyfriend or girlfriend.	• Putting coins in a vending machine to get candy or soda.
Fixed-ratio schedule (reinforcement after a fixed number of responses)	• Being paid on a piecework basis—in the garment industry workers may be paid so much per 100 dresses sewn.	• Taking a multi-item test. This is an example of negative reinforcement—as soon as you finish those items on the test, you can leave!	
Variable-ratio schedule (reinforcement after a varying number of responses)	• Playing a slot machine — the machine is programmed to pay off after a certain number of responses have been made, but that number keeps changing. This type of schedule creates a steady rate of responding, because players know if they play long enough, they will win.	• Sales commissions—you have to talk to many customers before you make a sale, and you never know whether the next one will buy. Again, the number of sales calls you make, not how much time passes, will determine when you are reinforced by a sale. And the number of sales calls will vary.	
Fixed-interval schedule (reinforcement of first response after a fixed amount of time has passed)	• You have an exam coming up and don't study as the days go by, so you have to make up for it all by a certain time, which means cramming.	• Picking up a salary check, which occurs every week or every two weeks.	
Variable-interval schedule (reinforcement of first response after varying amounts of time)	• Surprise quizzes in a course cause a steady rate of studying because you never know when they'll occur, so you have to be prepared all the time.	• Dialing a friend on the phone and getting a busy signal. This means that you have to keep dialing every few minutes because you don't know when your friend will hang up. Reinforcement doesn't depend on how many times you dial; it depends on dialing *after* the other person has hung up.	• Watching a football game, waiting for a touchdown. It could happen any time— if you leave the room to fix a sandwich, you may miss it, so you have to keep watching continuously.

Table 5.3   Examples of Reinforcement in Everyday Life
Source: Adapted from Landy, 1984, p. 219

erasing marks whenever something bad happens. At the end of the week, students tally the marks and check them against the teacher's secret number. If the number is the same or larger, the teacher treats the class to a special event or privilege.

2. Use interval schedules as rewards for the development of study and self-management skills.

This team can't be sure that the next play will lead to a yard gain. Only by trying do they have a chance of success. What type of reinforcement schedule does this situation exemplify? What is the the reason for your answer?

> EXAMPLE: Middle-school students benefit from weekly quizzes, especially in subjects that require a good deal of factual knowledge. Weekly quizzes, an example of fixed-interval reinforcement, gives students a chance to see what the teacher considers important and to predict what will be on the test.

> EXAMPLE: High school teachers may encourage students to prepare for tests or start long-term projects early by making performance assessments unpredictable. Announcing that students will be taking a test "in the next few days" or "sometime this week" forces students to prepare and is an example of variable-interval reinforcement.

Maintenance

The principle of extinction holds that when reinforcement for a previously learned behavior is withdrawn, the behavior fades away. Does this mean that teachers must reinforce students' behaviors indefinitely or they will disappear?

Not necessarily. For rats in a Skinner box, the withdrawal of reinforcement for bar pressing will inevitably lead to extinction of bar pressing. However, humans live in a much more complex world. Our world is full of *natural* reinforcers for most of the skills and behaviors learned in school. For example, students may require constant reinforcement for behaviors that lead to reading. However, once they can read, they have a skill that unlocks the entire world of books, a world that is highly reinforcing to most students. After a certain point, reinforcement for reading may no longer be necessary because the content of the books themselves maintains the behavior. Similarly, poorly behaved students may need careful, systematic reinforcement for doing schoolwork. After a while, however, they will find out that doing schoolwork pays off in grades, in parental approval, in ability to understand what is going on in class, and in knowledge. These natural reinforcers for doing schoolwork were always available, but the students could not experience them until their schoolwork was improved by more systematic means.

Maintenance also occurs with behaviors that do not need to be reinforced because they are *intrinsically reinforcing*, which is to say that engaging in these behaviors is pleasurable in itself. For example, many children love to draw, to figure out problems, or to learn about things even if they are never reinforced for doing so. Many of us even pay good money for books of crossword puzzles or other problem-solving activities, even though after we have completed them no one will ever check our work!

The concept of resistance to extinction, discussed earlier in Schedules of Reinforcement, is very important for understanding maintenance of learned behavior. As noted earlier, when new behaviors are being introduced, reinforcement for correct responses should be frequent and predictable. However, once the behaviors are established, reinforcement for correct responses should become less frequent and less predictable. The reason for this is that variable schedules of reinforcement, and schedules of reinforcement that require many behaviors before reinforcement is given, are much more resistant to extinction than are fixed schedules or "easy" ones. For example, if a teacher praises a student every time the student does a math problem, but then stops praising, the student may stop doing math problems. In contrast, if the teacher gradually increases the number of math problems a student must do to get praised, and praises the student at random intervals (a variable-ratio schedule), then the student is likely to continue to do math problems for a long time with little or no reinforcement from the teacher.

The Role of Antecedents

We have seen that the consequences of behavior strongly influence behavior. Yet it is not only what follows a behavior that has influence. The stimuli that precede a behavior—the antecedents to behavior—also play an important role.

Cueing. **Antecedent stimuli** are also known as **cues** because they inform us what behavior will be reinforced and/or what behavior will be punished. Cues come in many forms and give us hints as to when we should change our behavior and when we should not. For example, during a math session most teachers will reinforce students who are working on problems and punish those who are doing nothing. However, after the teacher has announced that math is over and it is time for lunch, the consequences change. The ability to behave one way in the presence of one stimulus—"It's math time"—and a different way in the presence of another stimulus—"It's time for lunch"—is known as *stimulus discrimination*.

maintenance: continuation of behavior.

antecedent stimulus: event that comes before a behavior.

cue: signal as to what behavior(s) will be reinforced or punished.

Focus On

Reinforcers in Classroom Interaction

The value of using reinforcers to increase the incidence or frequency of desired behavior is well known to teachers and parents. What may not be so well known, however, is how subtle reinforcers can be. Simple behaviors, such as mere eye contact, signalling attention, may be reinforcing on a quantum scale. In fact, five seconds of undivided silent attention may be more reinforcing than five minutes of verbal praise.

Almost by necessity, teachers with very large classes tend to develop an interaction style that treats students collectively much of the time. It is mainly in the fishbowl of very small classes or one-room schoolhouses that observers can see how teachers interact with students as individuals. Of interest are how teachers learn to tailor reinforcers to help each individual maximize her or his achievement or performance and how teachers shape interaction among students themselves.

Reinforcers may be so subtle that teachers sometimes apply them unawares, for instance, by training students in the art of evoking an amusing habit the teacher displays when annoyed. Nowhere is the subtlety of reinforcement more revealing, however, than in unintentional teacher interaction with students as members of particular groups, such as girls.

Researchers' televised videotapes of classroom female teachers in action show a common pattern of interaction in which reinforcers are unintentionally lavished on boys and/or withheld from girls. Measurable indicators other than eye contact include the time spent in discourse; the number of students called on; the teacher's physical proximity to students or time spent at students' desks during seatwork; the number of corrections or amount of feedback given; the number of questions asked; the use of praise, rewards, or other incentives; and the number of minor misbehaviors ignored. Beginning in the upper elementary grades, boys typically fare better than girls on all measures.

Critical Thinking

Are you aware of having been treated differently in school because of your gender? What are some causes and consequences of such differences? What reinforcers proved especially effective for you as a student? What would you include on a list of guiding principles for teachers on using reinforcers in the classroom?

Source: Alberto, P., and Troutman, A. C., *Applied Behavioral Analysis for Teachers.* Merrill, 1990; L. Berk, *Child Development.* Allyn & Bacon, 1992; M. Sadker, D. Sadker, and S. Klein, The issue of gender in elementary and secondary education, *Review of Research in Education,* 1991.

Discrimination.   When is the best time to ask your boss for a raise? When the company is doing well, the boss looks happy, and you've just done something especially good? Or when the company has just gotten a poor earnings report, the boss is glowering, and you've just made a costly error? Obviously, the first situation is more likely to lead to success. You know this because you have learned to *discriminate* between good and bad times to ask your boss to do something for you.

Discrimination is the use of cues, signals, or information to know when behavior is likely to be reinforced. The company's financial condition, the boss's mood, and your recent performance are discriminative stimuli with regard to the chances that your request for a raise will be successful. A pigeon can be trained to peck a disk if it sees a triangle but refrain from pecking if it sees a square or even to correctly discriminate between the printed words "peck" and "don't peck."

For students to learn discriminations they must have feedback on the correctness or incorrectness of their responses. Laboratory studies of discrimination learning

discrimination: perception of and response to differences in stimuli.

have generally found that students most need to know when their responses are incorrect. Praising students for correct answers but not giving them feedback on incorrect answers is not an effective feedback strategy (Barringer and Gholson, 1979; Getsie *et al.*, 1985).

Learning is largely a matter of mastering more and more complex discriminations. For example, all letters, numbers, words, and mathematical symbols are discriminative stimuli. A young child learns to discriminate between the letters "b" and "d." An older student learns the distinction between the words "effective" and "efficient." An educational psychology student learns to discriminate "negative reinforcement" from "punishment." A teacher learns to discriminate facial and verbal cues indicating that students are bored or interested by a lecture.

Applying the concept of discriminative stimuli to classroom instruction and management is easy: Teachers should tell students what behaviors will be reinforced. In theory, a teacher could wait until students did something worthwhile and then reinforce it, but this would be incredibly inefficient. Rather, teachers should give students messages that say, in effect, "To be reinforced (with praise, grades, or stars, for example), these are the things you must do." In this way teachers can avoid having students spend time and effort on the wrong activities. If students know that what they are doing will pay off, they will usually work hard.

Generalization. If students learn to stay in their seats and do careful work in math class, will their behavior also improve in science class? If students can subtract three apples from seven apples, can they also subtract three oranges from seven oranges? If students can interpret symbolism used by Shakespeare, can they also interpret symbolism used by Molière?

These are all questions of **generalization** of behaviors learned under one set of conditions to other situations. Generalization cannot be taken for granted. Usually, when a behavior management program is successfully introduced in one setting, students' behaviors do not automatically improve in other settings. Instead, students learn to discriminate among settings. Even young children readily learn what is encouraged and what is forbidden in kindergarten, what goes at home, and what goes at various friends' houses. Their behavior may be quite different in each setting, according to the different rules and expectations.

For generalization to occur, it usually must be planned for. A successful behavior management program used in social studies class may be transferred to English class to ensure generalization to that setting. Students may need to study the use of symbolism by many playwrights before they acquire the skill to interpret symbolism in playwrights in general.

Obviously, generalization is most likely to occur across similar settings or across similar concepts. A new behavior is more likely to generalize from reading class to social studies class than to recess or home settings. However, even in the most similar-appearing settings, generalizations may not occur. For example, many students will demonstrate complete mastery of spelling or language mechanics and then fail to apply this knowledge to their own compositions. Teachers should not assume that because students can do something under one set of circumstances, they can also do it under a different set of circumstances. Maybe the students don't pick up cues that signal the similarity between the two situations. Or maybe they do pick up the signal but are not motivated to respond.

Such situations demonstrate that the behavioral theories focusing on observable behavior fall short of completely explaining human actions. A behavioral theory that gives us some more answers is called social learning theory.

generalization: carryover of behaviors, skills, or concepts from one setting or task to another.

How Has Social Learning Theory Contributed to Our Understanding of Human Learning?

Social learning theory is a major outgrowth of the behavioral learning theory tradition. Developed by Albert Bandura (1969), **social learning theory** accepts most of the principles of behavioral theories, but focuses to a much greater degree on the effects of cues on behavior and on internal mental processes, emphasizing the effects of thought on action and action on thought (Bandura, 1986).

A. Bandura: Modeling and Observational Learning

Bandura noted that the Skinnerian emphasis on the effects of the consequences of behavior largely ignored the phenomena of **modeling**—the imitation of others' behavior—and vicarious experience—learning from others' successes or failures. He felt that much of human learning is not shaped by its consequences, but is more efficiently learned directly from a model (Bandura, 1986). The physical education teacher demonstrates a jumping jack and students imitate. Bandura calls this "no-trial learning" because students do not have to go through a shaping process but can reproduce the correct response immediately.

Bandura's (1977) analysis of **observational learning** involves four phases: attentional, retention, reproduction, and motivational.

1. Attentional Phase: The first phase in observational learning is paying attention to a model. In general, students pay attention to models who are attractive, successful, interesting, and popular. This is why so many students copy the dress, hairstyle, and mannerisms of pop culture stars. In the classroom the teacher gains the attention of the students by presenting clear and interesting cues, by using novelty or surprise, and by motivating students to pay attention (for example, by saying, "Listen closely, this will be on your quiz tomorrow").

2. Retention Phase: Once teachers have students' attention, it is time to model the behavior they want students to imitate and then to give students a chance to practice or rehearse. For example, a teacher might show how to write a script "A." Then students would imitate the teacher's model by trying to write "A's" themselves.

3. Reproduction: During the reproduction phase students try to match their behavior to the model's. In the classro om this takes the form of an assessment of student learning. For example, after seeing the script "A" modeled and practicing it several times, can the student reproduce the letter so that it looks like the teacher's model?

social learning theory: theory that emphasizes learning through observation of others.

modeling: learning by observing others' behavior.

observational learning: learning by observation and imitation of others.

4. Motivational Phase: The final stage in the observational learning process is motivation. Students will imitate a model because they feel that doing so will increase their own chances to be reinforced. For example, they may imitate a rock star because they see that he is successful and popular, and they hope to capture some of the same popularity for themselves. In fact, it is peer support for imitating popular stars that maintains the imitation. No matter how popular the rock star is, few students would imitate him if their friends did not value imitating him.

In the classroom, the motivational phase of observational learning more often consists of praise or grades given for matching the teacher's model. Students pay attention to the model, practice it, and reproduce it because they have learned that this is what the teacher likes and that pleasing the teacher pays off.

Effective use of Bandura's principles of modeling can increase achievement. In one study teachers who were taught these principles (ensuring attentiveness, describing each action while doing it, teaching memory aids, and helping students evaluate their own performance) were much more successful in teaching a concept to five-year-olds than were teachers who were not taught the principles (Zimmerman and Kleefeld, 1977).

Vicarious Learning.   While most observational learning is motivated by an expectation that correctly imitating the model will lead to reinforcement, it is also important to note that people learn by seeing others reinforced or punished for engaging in certain behaviors. This is why magazine distributors always include happy winners in their advertisments to induce people to enter promotional contests. We may consciously know that our chances of winning are one in several million, but seeing others so handsomely reinforced makes us want to imitate their contest-entering behavior.

Classroom teachers use the principle of **vicarious learning** all the time. When one student is fooling around, teachers often single out others who are working well and reinforce them for doing a good job. The misbehaving student sees that working is reinforced and (it is hoped) gets back to work.

This technique was systematically studied by Broden *et al.* (1970a). Two disruptive second-graders, "Edwin" and "Greg," sat next to each other. After a baseline period, the teacher began to notice and praise Edwin whenever he was paying attention and doing his classwork. Edwin's behavior improved markedly under this condition. Of greater interest, however, is that Greg's behavior also improved, even though no specific reinforcement for appropriate behavior was directed toward him. Apparently, Greg learned from Edwin's experience. In the case of Ms. Esteban and Rebecca, the opposite occurred; other students saw Rebecca get Ms. Esteban's attention by calling out answers, so they modeled their behavior on hers.

One of the classic experiments in social learning theory is a study done by Bandura (1965). Children were shown one of three films. In all three an adult modeled aggressive behavior. In one film the model was severely punished. In another the model was praised and given treats. In a third the model was given no consequences. After viewing one of the films, the children were observed playing with toys. The children who had seen the model punished engaged in significantly fewer aggressive acts in their own play than did the children who had seen the model rewarded or had viewed the no-consequences film.

vicarious learning: learning from observation the consequences of others' behavior.

How does the action in this picture relate to Bandura's social learning theory? What four learning phases will the children experience before they acquire the new behavior? How could you use Meichenbaum's cognitive behavior modification strategy to help these students master the new behavior quickly and effectively?

Self-Regulation.   Another important concept in social learning theory is **self-regulation.** Bandura (1977) hypothesized that people observe their own behavior, judge it against their own standards, and reinforce or punish themselves. We have all had the experience of knowing we've done a job well and mentally patted ourselves on the back, regardless of what others have said. Similarly, we all know when we've done less than our best. To make these judgments, we have to have expectations for our own performance. One student might be delighted to get 90 percent correct on a test, while another might be quite disappointed.

D. Meichenbaum: Cognitive Behavior Modification

Students can be taught to monitor and regulate their own behavior. Strategies of this kind are often called **cognitive behavior modification** (see Manning, 1991; Harris, 1990). For example, Meichenbaum and Goodman (1971) developed a strategy in which emotionally disturbed students are trained to say to themselves, "What is my problem? What is my plan? Am I using my plan? How did I do?" (see Meichenbaum, 1977). This strategy has also been used to reduce disruptive behavior of students at many grade levels (Wilson, 1984). For example, Manning (1988) taught disruptive third-graders self-statements to help them remember appropriate behavior and to reinforce it for themselves. As one example, for appropriate hand-raising, students were taught to say to themselves while raising their hands, "If I scream out the answer, others will be disturbed. I will raise my hand and wait my turn. Good for me. See, I can wait!" (Manning, 1988, p. 197). Similar strategies have been successfully applied to helping students monitor their own achievement. For example, poor readers have been taught to ask themselves questions as they read and to summarize paragraphs to help them comprehend text (Kendall, 1981; Bornstein, 1985).

The steps involved in self-instruction are described by Meichenbaum (1977, p. 32) as follows.

1. An adult model performs a task while talking to self out loud (cognitive modeling).
2. The child performs the same task under the direction of the model's instructions (overt, external guidance).
3. The child performs the task while instructing self aloud (overt, self-guidance).
4. The child whispers the instructions to self as he or she goes through the task (faded, overt self-guidance).
5. The child performs the task while guiding his or her performance via private speech (covert self-instruction).

self-regulation: rewarding or punishing one's own behavior.

cognitive behavior modification: procedures based on both behavioral and cognitive learning principles for changing your own behavior by using self-talk and self-instruction.

Note the similarity of Meichenbaum's cognitive behavior modification strategy to the Vygotskian approach to scaffolded instruction described in Chapter 2. Both approaches emphasize modeling private speech and gradually moving from teacher-controlled to student-controlled behaviors, with the students using private speech to talk themselves through their tasks. Cognitive behavior modification and self-regulation are both examples of teaching students to think about their own thinking, or metacognitive strategies (see Chapter 7 for more on this). Cognitive behavior modification strategies have not only been found to improve performance on the task students were taught but have also generalized to other tasks (Harris, 1990; Harris and Pressley, 1992).

Self-Reinforcement. Drabman *et al.* (1973) designed and evaluated a procedure to teach students to regulate their own behavior. They asked teachers to rate student behaviors each day and reinforce students when they earned high ratings. Then they changed the program and asked students to guess what rating the teacher had given them. The students were reinforced for guessing correctly. Finally, the reinforcers were gradually removed. The students' behavior improved under the reinforcement and guessing conditions, and it remained at its improved level long after the program was ended. The authors explained that students taught to match the teacher's ratings developed their own standards for appropriate behavior and reinforced themselves for meeting those standards. Information about one's own behavior has often been found to change behavior (Rosenbaum and Drabman, 1982), even when that information is self-provided. For example, Broden *et al.* (1971) improved the on-task behavior of an eighth-grader by having her mark down every few minutes whether or not she had been studying in the last few minutes. When coupled with self-reinforcement, self-observation often has important effects on student behavior (Jenson *et al.*, 1988). Many of us use this principle in studying, saying to ourselves that we will not take a break for lunch until we have finished reading a certain amount of material.

Some reviewers have questioned whether self-reinforcement is really necessary, or whether monitoring one's own progress is equally effective (Hayes *et al.*, 1985). The answer is that it probably depends on the task and on other factors. For most school tasks, it may well be enough for students to record or otherwise monitor their own behavior and to mentally congratulate themselves when they make progress toward some important goal.

Research on Cognitive Behavior Modification. A lesson from research on cognitive behavior modification is that, when assigned a long or complex task, students should be provided with a form for monitoring their progress. For example, a teacher might assign students to write a report on the life of Martin Luther King, Jr. Students might be given the following self-monitoring form:

Task Completion Form

_____ Located material on Martin Luther King, Jr., in the library.
_____ Read and took notes on material.
_____ Wrote first draft of report.
_____ Checked draft for sense.
_____ Checked draft for mechanics:

        _____ Spelling
        _____ Grammar
        _____ Punctuation

_____ Composed final draft typed or neatly handwritten.

The idea behind this form is that breaking down a complex task into smaller pieces encourages students to feel that they are making progress toward their larger goal. Checking off each step allows them to give themselves a mental "pat on the back" that reinforces their efforts (see Jenson *et al.*, 1988).

Self-Check

Extend the comparison chart you began earlier by adding the contributions of social learning theorists as represented by Bandura and Meichenbaum.

Connections

Developments in social learning theory relate to Vygotskian and neo-Piagetian views of development, discussed in Chapter 2, which emphasize the importance of social interaction and environmental influences. Social learning theory also relates to the cognitive theories of learning discussed in Chapters 6 and 7 because of the emphasis on the social construction of meaning. See, for example, the section on reciprocal teaching in Chapter 7.

Teachers on Teaching

How have you applied behavioral and social learning theories in your teaching?

I have used behavioral and social learning theories with mainstreamed special-needs students. My experience with many children suffering the pain of family dysfunction has led me to see the school as a reenacted family setting. For students whose early years are marked by abuse, alcohol, and neglect, development and behavior are anything but normal. In recently working with one such child I saw immediately that this ten-year-old, new to my school, had had little or no exposure to language models, social skills, experiential stimulation, or appropriate work habits. Surprisingly, this fifth-grader did not qualify for remedial services in any academic areas and so would remain in the regular classroom throughout the day. To begin the work of filling the blatant gaps in this child's development, an informal teacher-assistance team was created, made up of the guidance counselor, pupil personnel worker, special education teacher, and an administrator, to design a learning and behavior management plan. Three broad goals were identified as desirable outcomes: cooperating in a group, working independently for at least 15 minutes, and following directions. We decided that an efficient way to shape appropriate behavior would be to use some primary needs not sufficiently met for this child in the past. Food, for example, was an extremely effective behavior modifier. His involvement in his management program was established by having him draw up a list of favorite foods, which he could "purchase" from a snack box with points he earned by following his plan.

Gemma Staub Hoskins, Teacher, Grade 5
Jarrettsville Elementary School, Jarrettsville, Maryland
1992 Maryland Teacher of the Year

Identifying reinforcers can be tricky. For instance, I had one nine-year-old boy in my class who was extremely disruptive on a daily basis. He would shove and hit other children, poke them with scissors and pencils, throw food. He was continually speaking out and out of seat. Separating him from other children didn't help because the minute I turned my attention from him, he would slam down a book, or tear up a classmate's paper. Initially, I set up a behavior modification program that rewarded Artie at five-minute intervals for proper school behavior. A pattern quickly emerged in which he would have a good day, followed by two days when I could not find a way to reward him. During good days, Artie was a totally different child. He would be helpful toward classmates. He'd raise his hand and answer appropriately. He also showed his true academic ability on these days. Soon, however, I noticed Artie having more bad days. After receiving a one-day suspension, his mother returned him to school, and that's when I learned for the first time how Artie's older brother, who had by then dropped out of school, was the only consistent male figure in his life, and Artie looked up to him. Whenever Artie brought home a good report, his brother would ridicule him. When his brother found out about the suspension, he praised Artie and spent more time with him as a reward, taking him out to lunch. At school, those of us who had daily contact with Artie decided to spend more time talking with him about setting positive goals for himself. Repeatedly, we stressed pride and trust. It took a while, and there were setbacks, but Artie's behavior and academic performance began to improve. By the end of the year, everyone noticed his improved behavior and he earned his way onto the Good Citizens Wall.

Benetta M. Skrundz, Learning Disabilities Teacher
Franklin Elementary School, East Chicago, Indiana

What Are the Implications of Behavioral Learning Approaches for Education?

Behavioral learning theories are so central to educational psychology (see Kratochwill and Bijou, 1987) that they are discussed in many parts of this book. The most direct application of these theories is to classroom management and discipline (Chapter 11). This chapter also contains a section on the ethics of behavior modification. Behavioral objectives and task analysis, which show how principles of discrimination and shaping are applied in the classroom, are detailed in Chapter 13. Bandura's four phases of observational learning are translated into practical methods in Chapter 8. Discussed there are means of gaining student attention and motivation, modeling information and skills, having students practice and then demonstrate new skills, and providing feedback and reinforcement to students. Finally, specific instructional methods based on behavioral learning theories, including programmed instruction, mastery learning, and the Keller Plan, are included in Chapter 9.

Strengths and Limitations of Behavioral Learning Theories. The basic principles of behavioral learning theories are as firmly established as any in psychology and have been demonstrated under many different conditions. These principles are useful for explaining much of human behavior, and they are even more useful in changing behavior.

It is important to recognize, however, that behavioral learning theories are limited in scope. With the exception of social learning theorists, behavioral learning theorists focus almost exclusively on observable behavior. This is one reason that so many of the examples presented in this chapter (and in Chapter 11) involve the management of behavior.

Behavioral, Social, and Cognitive Learning. Less visible learning processes, such as concept formation, learning from text, problem solving, and thinking, are difficult to observe directly and have therefore been less often studied by behavioral learning theorists. These processes fall more into the domain of cognitive learning, discussed in Chapters 6 and 7 (see Schwartz and Reisberg, 1991). Social learning theory, which is a direct outgrowth of behavioral learning theories, helps bridge the gap between these two perspectives. Behavioral and cognitive theories of learning are often posed as competing, opposite models. There are indeed specific areas in which these theories take contradictory positions. However, it is more accurate to see them as complementary rather than competitive—that is, as tackling different problems.

Self-Check

Use the concepts presented in this chapter to briefly explain what happened in Ms. Esteban's class in the scenario at the beginning of the chapter. Then use the principles presented in this chapter to propose specific alternative solutions to the problem. Conclude by writing a one-sentence definition of learning that would encompass both the problem and the solutions you proposed.

➡ Case to Consider

Self-Regulated Learning

Allyson Mizuno, a sixth-grade teacher at Langley Middle School, feels frustrated in her efforts to get her students to work more independently and to monitor and regulate their own learning. At the end of the first quarter, many students are still depending too much on her for help.

CLARENCE: Ms. Mizuno, am I doing this right?

ALLYSON: What do you think, Clarence?

CLARENCE: I don't know.

ALLYSON: Well, explain the task to me in your own words.

CLARENCE: I'm supposed to figure out what my family is going to eat for supper all next week. I have to make the menus, decide how much of everything we will need, find out about the nutritional value of each meal, and find out how much each meal will cost.

ALLYSON: Yes, that's it! You've got it, okay?

CLARENCE: But I'm not sure what you want.

ALLYSON: I know how I would do this assignment, but I'm much more interested in how you think about it, Clarence. There are several ways to complete this assignment. Why don't you make a plan listing the steps you think you will take to do it.

CLARENCE: Well, I'll try.

ALLYSON: Jesse, how are you doing?

JESSE: Okay I guess. This is fun!

ALLYSON: What have you done so far?

JESSE: Well, I got confused at first, thinking about all the food we could eat and not being sure what goes together. Mr. Green told us about USDA daily minimums and stuff like that, so I got sidetracked.

ALLYSON: How did you get back on track?

JESSE: I made a plan. I listed steps for what I would do, and I started a chart, see? It has a box for each day. And I divided each box into four sections for the four food groups. Now I'm thinking about what foods we all like in my family, so that everyone gets to eat something they really like. When my chart is filled in, I can make my grocery list from it.

ALLYSON: Great going, Jesse! I like the way you made a plan, and I think your chart will be a big help.

CHRISTINE: Ms. Allyson, I need help.

ALLYSON: What is it, Christine?

CHRISTINE: I don't know where to start! There's too much to do, and it's hard. Besides, how can I find out how much food costs in the supermarket if I'm sitting here? I don't see how I can do this.

Critical Thinking

1. How are social learning theories on self-regulated learning relevant to Allyson's situation?

2. What could Allyson do to help Clarence and Christine? What metacognitive skills could she teach? How could she encourage her students' self-observation? What might she say to model self-reinforcing talk, and what other kinds of self-reinforcement might she suggest?

3. Apply your solutions to Allyson's dilemma by extending the dialogue in writing or in role play.

Summary

What Is Learning?
Learning involves the acquisition of abilities that are not innate. It depends on experience, including feedback from the environment.

What Behavioral Learning Theories Have Evolved?
Early research into learning studied the effects of stimuli on reflexive behaviors. Ivan Pavlov contributed the idea of classical conditioning in which neutral stimuli can acquire the capacity to evoke behavioral responses through their association with unconditioned stimuli that trigger reflexes. E.L. Thorndike developed the law of effect, emphasizing the role of the consequences of present behavior in determining future behavior. B.F. Skinner continued the study of the relationship between behavior and consequences. He described operant conditioning, in which reinforcers and punishers shape behavior.

What Are Some Principles of Behavioral Learning?
Reinforcers increase the likelihood of a behavior, while punishers decrease its likelihood. Reinforcement can be positive or negative, primary or secondary. Punishment involves weakening behavior by either introducing aversive consequences or removing reinforcers.

Schedules of reinforcement are used to increase the probability, frequency, or persistence of desired behavior. Reinforcement schedules may be based on ratios or intervals and may be fixed or variable. Each type of schedule has its benefits in particular classroom contexts.

Antecedent stimuli serve as cues indicating which behaviors will be reinforced or punished. Discrimination involves using cues to detect differences between stimulus situations, whereas generalization involves responding to similarities between stimuli. Extinction is the weakening and gradual disappearance of behavior as reinforcement is withdrawn. Shaping through timely feedback on each step of a task is an effective teaching practice based on behavioral learning theory.

How Has Social Learning Theory Contributed to Our Understanding of Human Learning?
Social learning theory is based on a recognition of the importance of observational learning and self-regulated learning. Bandura noted that learning through modeling—directly or vicariously—involves four phases: paying attention, retaining the modeled behavior, reproducing the behavior, and being motivated to repeat the behavior. Bandura proposed that students should be taught to have expectations for their own performances and to reinforce themselves. D. Meichenbaum proposed steps for self-regulated learning based on the concept of cognitive behavior modification.

What Are the Implications of Behavioral Learning Approaches for Education?
Behavioral learning theories are central to applying educational psychology in the classroom in classroom management, discipline, motivation, instructional models, individualized instruction, and other areas. Behavioral learning theories are limited in scope in that they describe only observable behavior that can be directly measured.

Key Terms

antecedent stimuli, 171
aversive stimuli, 161
behavioral learning theory, 152
classical conditioning, 155
cognitive behavior modification, 176
cognitive learning theory, 152
consequences, 158
cues, 171
discrimination, 172
extinction, 165
fixed-interval (FI) schedule, 167
fixed ratio (FR), 166
generalization, 173
Law of Effect, 156
learning, 152
maintenance, 171
modeling, 174
negative reinforcers, 159

neutral stimuli, 155
observational learning, 174
operant conditioning, 157
positive reinforcers, 159
Premack Principle, 159
presentation punishment, 161
primary reinforcer, 158
punishment, 160
reinforcer, 158
removal punishment, 161
reverse chaining, 165
schedule of reinforcement, 166
secondary reinforcer, 158
self-regulation, 176
shaping, 164
Skinner box, 157
social learning theory, 174
stimuli (*sing.* stimulus), 153

Self-Assessment

1. Which of the following most clearly represents an example of *learning?*

   a. moving one's hand away from a hot object

   b. being startled by a loud noise

   c. feeling thirsty after exercising

   d. feeling anxious when a teacher announces a pop quiz

   e. all of the above are valid examples

2. Match the following theories or laws of learning with a related experiment (a situation may be used more than once or not at all):

   ___ classical conditioning

   ___ the Law of Effect

   ___ operant conditioning

   ___ social learning theory

   a. Animals learned to press a lever to get food.

   b. The behavior of children was observed after they had seen films in which adults acted aggressively.

   c. Before reading a passage about Buddhism, students reviewed the concepts of Christianity.

   d. Animals used trial-and-error to learn to escape from a box.

   e. Animals exhibited conditioned responses when they heard a tone.

3. An example of a primary reinforcer is

   a. safety or security.

   b. good grades in school.

   c. money.

   d. praise.

   e. access to toys.

4. What is the Premack Principle? Give two examples of classroom practices that clearly illustrate the Premack Principle.

5. Match these types of consequences with the most probable example of each.

   ___ positive reinforcement

   ___ negative reinforcement

   ___ punishment

   a. "Write 'I will not talk' 500 times."

   b. "Students who finish this work will not be assigned extra homework tonight."

   c. "Good job, class! I'm proud of you!"

6. Match the following types of reinforcement schedules with the appropriate description.

   ___ fixed ratio

   ___ variable ratio

   ___ fixed interval

   ___ variable interval

   a. taking a pop quiz

   b. being paid for every ten magazine subscriptions sold

   c. dialing a phone number and having the person you want to talk to answer

   d. taking a weekly quiz

7. In social learning theory, attention, retention, reproduction, and motivation are four phases in

   a. observational learning.

   b. reverse chaining.

   c. self-regulation.

   d. scaffolding.

8. Meichenbaum's model for cognitive behavior modification involves *all* of the following concepts *except*

   a. self-regulated learning.

   b. private speech.

   c. vicarious learning.

   d. modeling.

6

Cognitive Theories of Learning: Basic Concepts

Chapter Outline	Chapter Objectives
What Is an Information Processing Model? Sensory Register Short-Term Memory Long-Term Memory Levels of Processing and Other Information Processing Models	▲ Explain how the information processing model works, and illustrate its processes in a diagram.
What Causes People to Remember or Forget? Forgetting and Remembering Does Practice Make Perfect?	▲ Identify factors that lead to forgetting and to the retention of information.
How Can Memory Strategies Be Taught? Verbal Learning Paired-Associate Learning Serial and Free-Recall Learning	▲ Describe several ways in which memory strategies can be directly taught.
What Makes Information Meaningful? Rote versus Meaningful Learning Schema Theory	▲ Define "meaningful learning," and explain how schema theory aids in our understanding of how learning becomes meaningful.

Verona Bishop's biology class was doing a unit on human learning. At the start of one lesson she did an experiment with her students. For three seconds, using an overhead projector, she flashed a diagram of a model of information processing identical to the one in Figure 6.1. Then she asked students to recall what they noticed. Some mentioned that they saw green boxes and blue arrows. Some saw the words "memory" and "forgotten" and inferred that the figure had something to do with learning. One student even "saw" the word *learning* even though it wasn't in the figure.

"Come now," said Ms. Bishop. "You noticed a lot more than that! You just may not have noticed what you noticed. For example, what did you smell?"

The whole class laughed; they all recalled smelling the broccoli cooking in the cafeteria. The students caught on to the idea and began to recall all the other details they noticed that had nothing to do with the diagram: the sounds of a truck going by, details of the classroom and the people in it, and so on.

After this discussion, Ms. Bishop continued as follows.

"Isn't the brain amazing? In only three seconds you received an enormous amount of information. You didn't even know you were noticing the smell of the broccoli until I reminded you about it, but it was in your mind just the same. Also, in only three seconds your mind was already starting to make sense of the information in the figure. Cheryl thought she saw the word *learning,* which wasn't there at all. But her mind leaped to that word because she saw words like "memory" that relate to learning.

"Now imagine that you could keep in your mind *forever* everything that occurred in the three seconds you looked at the diagram: the arrows, the boxes, the words, the truck, the broccoli, everything. In fact, imagine that you could keep everything that ever entered your mind. What would that be like?"

"You'd be a genius!" ventured Samphan.

"You'd go crazy!" countered Jamal.

"I think Jamal is closer to the truth," said Ms. Bishop. "If your mind filled up with all this useless junk, you'd be a blithering idiot! One of the most important things we're going to learn about learning is that learning is an active process of focusing in on important information, screening out unimportant information, and using what is already in our minds to decide which is which."

Ms. Bishop turned on the overhead projector again.

"When we study this diagram in more detail, you'll use what you already know about learning, memory, forgetting, and diagrams to make sense of it, and I hope you'll always remember the main ideas it's trying to show you. You'll soon forget that the arrows are blue and the boxes are green, and even the smell of the broccoli will fade from your memory, but the parts of this diagram that make sense to you and answer questions you care about may stay in your memory your whole life!"

The human mind is a meaning maker. From the first microsecond you see, hear, taste, or feel something, you start a process of deciding what it is, how it relates to what you already know, whether it is important to keep or should be discarded. This whole process may take place consciously or unconsciously, or both. This chapter describes how information is received and processed in the mind, how memory and forgetting work, and how teachers can help students understand and remember critical information, skills, and ideas. Along with Chapter 7, it presents *cognitive* theories of learning, theories that relate to processes that go on within the minds of learners, and means of helping students use their minds more effectively to learn, remember, and use knowledge.

What Is an Information Processing Model?

Information constantly enters our minds through our senses. Most of this information is almost immediately discarded, and much of it we may never even be aware of. Some is held in our memories for a short time and then forgotten. For example, we may remember the seat number on a baseball ticket until we find our seats, at which point we will forget it. However, some information is retained much longer, perhaps for the rest of our lives. What is the process by which information is absorbed, and how can teachers take advantage of this process to help students retain critical information and skills? These are questions that have been addressed by cognitive learning theorists and that have led to **information-processing theory,** the dominant theory of learning and memory for the past twenty years.

information-processing theory: cognitive theory of learning that describes the processing, storage, and retrieval of knowledge from the mind.

Research on human memory (see, for example, Atkinson and Shiffrin, 1968; Bransford *et al.,* 1986a; Case, 1985; Siegler, 1986) has helped learning theorists describe the process by which information is remembered (or forgotten). This process is illustrated in Figure 6.1.

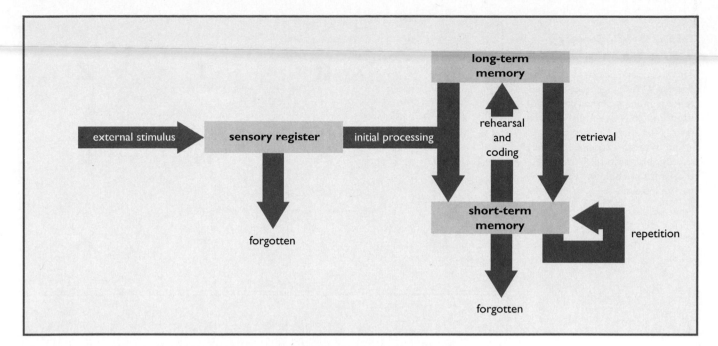

Figure 6.1   The Sequence of Information Processing

Information that is to be remembered must first reach a person's senses, then be attended to and transferred from the sensory register to the short-term memory, then be processed again for transfer to long-term memory.

From Morris, 1993, p. 233.

Sensory Register

The first component of the memory system that incoming information meets is the **sensory register.** Sensory registers receive large amounts of information from the senses (sight, hearing, touch, smell, taste) and hold it for a very short time, no more than a couple of seconds. If nothing happens to information held in the sensory registers, it is rapidly lost.

Ingenious experiments have been used to detect the sensory registers. A person might be shown a display like that in Figure 6.2 for a very short period of time, say 50 milliseconds. The person is usually able to report seeing three, four, or five of the letters, but not all twelve of them. Sperling (1960) presented a display like Figure 6.2 to people. After the display disappeared, he signaled viewers to try to recall the top, middle, or bottom row. He found that people could recall any one row almost perfectly. Therefore they must have seen all the letters in the 50 milliseconds and retained them for a short period of time. However, when people tried to recall all twelve letters, the time it took them to do so apparently exceeded the amount of time the letters lasted in their sensory registers, so they lost some of the letters.

The existence of sensory registers has two important educational implications. First, people must pay attention to information if they are to retain it. And second, it takes time to bring all the information seen in a moment into consciousness.

sensory register: component of the memory system where information is received and held for very short periods of time.

Figure 6.2

Display Used in Sensory Register Experiments

This is a typical display used by Sperling (1960) to detect the existence and limits of the sensory register. People who were shown the display for an instant and then asked to recall a specific row were usually able to do so. However, they were not able to recall all twelve letters.

From Sperling, 1960.

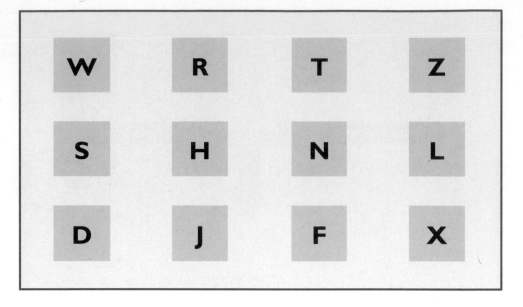

For example, if students are bombarded with too much information at once and are not told which aspects of the information they should pay attention to, they may have difficulty learning any of the information at all.

Perception.   As soon as stimuli are received by the senses, the mind immediately begins working on some of them. Therefore the sensory images that we are conscious of are not exactly the same as what we saw, heard, or felt; they are what our senses perceived. **Perception** of stimuli is not as straightforward as reception of stimuli; rather, it is influenced by our mental state, past experience, knowledge, motivations, and many other factors.

First, we attend to different stimuli according to rules that have nothing to do with the inherent characteristics of the stimuli. If you are sitting in a building, for example, you may not pay much attention to or even hear a fire engine's siren. If you are driving a car, you pay a great deal more attention. If you are standing outside a burning building waiting for the fire company to arrive, you pay even more attention. Second, we do not record the stimuli we perceive as we see or sense them but as we know (or assume) they really are. From across a room, a book on a bookshelf looks like a thin strip of paper, but we infer that it is a rectangular form with many pages. You may see the edge of a table and mentally infer the entire table.

Gestalt Psychology.   Questions of sensation, perception, and memory occupied the early Greeks and Romans, but in modern times the scientific study of how we receive and process information from the environment largely began with the **Gestalt psychology** movement in Germany (and later the United States and elsewhere) around World War I. *Gestalt* is a German word meaning "form" or "configuration." Gestalt psychologists, such as Max Wertheimer, Kurt Koffka, and Wolfgang Köhler, suggested that we perceive whole units rather than pieces of sensation, that the whole of a sensation is more than its parts. For example, in Figure 6.3a we readily see a circle and a square, even though parts of the figures are left out. This illustrates the principle of **closure,** which states that people organize their perceptions so that they are as simple and logical as possible, filling in gaps in

---

perception: a person's interpretation of stimuli.

Gestalt psychology: a psychological movement, started in Germany, that advanced the understanding of perception.

closure: the mental tendency to organize perceptions so they make sense.

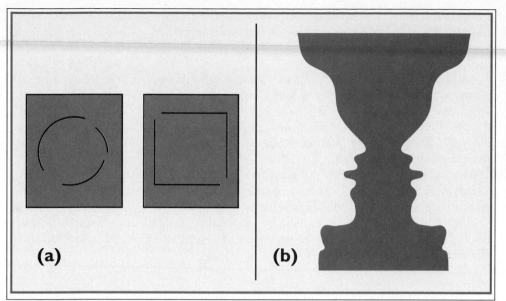

Figure 6.3

Examples of Closure and Figure-Ground Relationships

Even though the figures in (a) are incomplete, they are perceived as a circle and a square, illustrating the mind's tendency to seek closure. Is (b) a picture of a vase? or of two faces in profile? Which part of the picture is the figure and which the ground? What you see can depend on what you are looking for.

perceptions if necessary. This principle also applies when we try to remember an event from the past. We may add details to the memory of the event to make it more comprehensible. For example, in recalling an automobile accident in which one driver was clearly at fault, we might mentally add details that were not actually present to buttress our impression, such as that the innocent driver was wearing a seat belt or had signaled a turn.

Another important principle of Gestalt psychology is that we try to separate figure (that which we focus on) and ground (background). For example, when meeting a friend in a crowded airport, you'd probably focus only on the friend's face and generally ignore all other faces. In this circumstance you might miss seeing another friend in the crowd because all faces other than the one you are searching for are relegated to "ground" rather than "figure." A classic case of a **figure-ground relationship** is illustrated in Figure 6.3b. Do you see a vase or two faces? If you were told to look for a vase, you might never see the faces (which would be perceived as background), and if you were told to look for faces, you might not see the vase.

Attention. When teachers ask students to "pay attention" or "lend me your ears," they are using the words "pay" and "lend" appropriately. Like money, **attention** is a limited resource. When teachers ask students to spend their limited attention capacity on whatever they are saying, students must give up actively attending to other stimuli, they must shift their priorities so that other stimuli are screened out. For example, when people listen intently to an interesting speaker, they are unaware of minor body sensations (such as itches or hunger) and other sounds or sights. An experienced speaker knows that when the audience looks restless, its attention is no longer focused on the lecture, but may be turning toward considerations of lunch or other activities, and it is time to recapture the attention of the listeners.

Gaining Attention. How can teachers focus students' attention on the lesson at hand, in particular on the most important aspects of what is being taught?

There are several ways to gain students' attention, all of which go under the general heading of "arousing student interest." One is to use cues that indicate "this is

figure-ground relationship: perceiving selected parts of a stimulus to stand out (figure) from other parts (background).

attention: the process of focusing on certain stimuli while screening out others.

important." Some teachers raise or lower their voices to signal they are about to impart critical information. Others use gestures, repetition, or position to communicate the same message. Textbook publishers use different colors or typefaces to indicate important points.

Another way to gain attention is to increase the emotional content of material. Some publications accomplish this by choosing very emotional words. This can be why newspaper headlines say "Senate *Kills* Mass Transit Proposal" rather than "Senate *Votes Against* Mass Transit Proposal." Olson and Pau (1966) found that use of such emotionally charged words helped students retain information better than more neutral synonyms.

Attention is also attracted by unusual, inconsistent, or surprising stimuli. For example, science teachers often introduce lessons with a demonstration or magic trick to engage student curiosity (see Berlyne, 1965).

Finally, attention can be gained by informing students that what follows is important to them. For example, teachers can assure attention by telling students, "This will be on tomorrow's test!"

Short-Term Memory

Information that a person perceives and pays attention to is transferred to the second component of the memory system, the **short-term memory** (Glanzer, 1982). Short-term memory is a storage system that can hold a limited amount of information for a few seconds. It is the part of memory where information currently being

> **Connections**
>
> Recall David Meichenbaum's work on cognitive behavior modification, discussed in Chapter 5, which included identifying the internal messages children use to call themselves to attention.

In terms of information-processing theory, why are these children likely to remember the story they are being told? Which type of memory is involved?

> **short-term memory:**
> component of memory where limited amounts of information can be stored for a few seconds.

thought about is stored. The thoughts we are conscious of having at any given moment are being held in our short-term memory. When we stop thinking about something, it disappears from our short-term memory.

Information may enter short-term memory from sensory registers or from the third basic component of the memory system, **long-term memory**. Often both things happen at the same time. When we see a robin, our sensory register transfers the image of the robin to our short-term memory. Meanwhile, we may (unconsciously) search our long-term memory for information about birds so we can identify this particular one as a robin. Along with that recognition may come a lot of other information about robins, memories of past experiences with robins, or feelings about robins—all of which were stored in long-term memory but are brought into consciousness (short-term memory) by our mental processing of the sight of the robin.

One way to hold information in short-term memory is to think about it or say it over and over. You have probably remembered a phone number for a short time this way. This process of maintaining an item in short-term memory by repetition is called **rehearsal.** Rehearsal is important in learning because the longer an item remains in short-term memory, the greater the chance that it will be transferred to long-term memory. Without rehearsal, items probably will not stay in short-term memory for more than about thirty seconds. Because short-term memory has a limited capacity, information can also be lost from it by being forced out by other information. You have probably had the experience of looking up a telephone number, being interrupted briefly, and finding that you had forgotten the number.

Teachers must allocate time for rehearsal during classroom lessons. Teaching too much information too rapidly is likely to be ineffective because unless students are given time to mentally rehearse each new piece of information, later information is likely to drive it out of their short-term memories. When teachers stop a lesson to ask students if they have any questions, they are also giving students a few moments to think over and mentally rehearse what they have just learned. This helps students process information in short-term memory and thereby to establish it in long-term memory. This mental work is critical when students are learning new, difficult material.

Short-Term Memory Capacity.   Short-term memory is believed to have a capacity of five to nine "bits" of information (Miller, 1956). That is, we can think about only five to nine distinct things at a time. However, any particular "bit" may itself contain a great deal of information. For example, think how difficult it would be to memorize the following shopping list:

Flour	Orange juice	Pepper	Mustard
Soda pop	Parsley	Cake	Butter
Relish	Mayonnaise	Oregano	Canned tomatoes
Potatoes	Milk	Lettuce	Syrup
Hamburger	Hot dogs	Eggs	Onions
Tomato paste	Apples	Spaghetti	Buns

This list has too many "bits" of information to remember easily. All twenty-four food items would not fit into short-term memory in random order. However, you could easily memorize the list by organizing it according to familiar patterns. As shown in Table 6.1, you might mentally create three separate "memory files," breakfast, lunch, and dinner. Under each, you expect to find food and beverages,

long-term memory: components of memory where large amounts of information can be stored for long periods of time.

rehearsal: mental repetition of information, which can improve its retention.

Breakfast Food	Beverage	Dessert
Pancakes: —Flour —Milk —Eggs —Butter —Syrup	Orange Juice	

Lunch Food	Beverage	Dessert
Hot Dogs: —Hot dogs —Buns —Relish —Mustard Potato Salad: —Potatoes —Mayonnaise —Parsley	Soda Pop	Apple

Dinner Food	Beverage	Dessert
Spaghetti: —Spaghetti —Onions —Hamburger —Canned tomatoes —Tomato paste —Oregano —Pepper Salad: —Lettuce	Milk	Cake

Table 6.1   Example of Organization of Information to Facilitate Memory
A twenty-four-item shopping list that would be very hard to remember in a random order can be organized into a smaller number of familiar categories, making the list easier to recall.

Connections

This shopping list is reiterated in Chapter 7, where it is presented in connection with the importance of organizing information in the process of learning and remembering.

and under lunch and dinner you expect dessert as well. You can then think through the recipes for each item on the menus. In this way, you can recall what you have to buy and need maintain only a few bits of information in your short-term memory. When you enter the store, you are thinking, "I need food for breakfast, lunch, and dinner." First, you bring "breakfast" out of your long term memory. It contains food (pancakes) and beverage (orange juice). You might think through how you make pancakes step-by-step and buy each ingredient, plus orange juice as a beverage. When you have done this, you can discard "breakfast" from your short-term memory and replace it with "lunch," and then "dinner," going through the same processes. Note that all you did was to replace twenty-four little bits of information with three big bits that you could then separate into their components.

Short-term memory can be thought of as a bottleneck through which information from the environment reaches long-term memory. The limited capacity of short-term memory is one aspect of information processing that has important implications for the design and practice of instruction. For example, its limited capacity means that you cannot present students with too many ideas at once unless the ideas are so well organized and well connected to information already in the students' long-term memories that their short-term memories (with assistance from their long-term memories) can accommodate them, as in the case of the shopping list just discussed. Other instructional implications of the nature of short-term memory appear throughout this and the following chapters.

Individual Differences in Short-Term Memory. Individuals differ, of course, in the capacity of their short-term memories to accomplish a given learning task. One of the main factors in enhancing this capacity is background knowledge; the more a person knows about something, the better able the person is to organize and absorb new information (Chi and Ceci, 1987; Engle *et al.*, 1990; Kuhara-Kojima and Hatano, 1991). However, prior knowledge is not the only factor. Individuals also differ in their abilities to organize information and can be taught to consciously use strategies for making more efficient use of their short-term memory capacity (Peverly, 1991; Levin and Levin, 1990; Pressley and Harris, 1990). Strategies of this kind are discussed in Chapter 7.

Long-Term Memory

Long-term memory is that part of our memory system where we keep information for long periods of time. Long-term memory is thought to be a very large capacity, very long-term memory store. In fact, many theorists believe that we may never forget information in long-term memory; rather, we may just lose the ability to find the information within our memory.

Just as information can be stored in long-term memory a long time, so, too, the capacity of long-term memory seems to be very large. We do not live long enough to fill up our long-term memory.

The differences among sensory registers, short-term memory, and long-term memory are summarized in Table 6.2.

Theorists divide long-term memory into at least three parts: **episodic memory, semantic memory,** and **procedural memory** (Tulving, 1972, 1985). Episodic memory is our memory of personal experiences, a mental movie of things we saw or heard. When you remember what you had for dinner last night or what happened at your high school prom, you are recalling information stored in your long-term episodic memory. Long-term semantic memory contains the facts and generalized information that we know; concepts, principles, or rules and how to use them; and our problem-solving skills and learning strategies. Most things learned in class lessons are retained in semantic memory. Procedural memory refers to "knowing how" as opposed to "knowing that" (Sylwester, 1985). The abilities to drive, type, or ride a bicycle are examples of skills retained in procedural memory. Figure 6.4 illustrates the differences between episodic, semantic, and procedural memory.

episodic memory: a part of long-term memory that stores images of our personal experiences.

semantic memory: a part of long-term memory that stores facts and general knowledge.

procedural memory: a part of long-term memory that stores information about how to do things.

Focus On

Memory

The ability to remember is a feature of intelligence and a key predictor of academic achievement or success in other activities that depend on intellect. Having a good memory involves being able to readily recall and correctly reuse information. Because of the important role of memory in cognitive development and learning, scientists begin research on subjects as young as infants in hopes of predicting future learning problems.

One study, for example, uses eighty laboratories across the nation to test the memories of infants at risk. At-risk infants include premature babies and those with early severe illnesses. As the babies are shown paired pictures, researchers record the babies' eye movements indicating the recognition and comparison of images. Recognizing like pairs of images later indicates the ability to remember. Researchers hope to diagnose potential memory deficiencies in time for appropriate remediation, which can affect a child's measured IQ.

The role that memory plays in reading is the subject of research at Carnegie-Mellon in Pittsburgh. Using college students as subjects and special cameras and computers, researchers try to determine how the brain processes the printed word. So far, tests reveal that unfamiliar and complex words take a longer time to process as the reader searches for meaning and that readers give greater than expected attention to sentences' last words. Researchers hope to find out how printed texts can be written to flow more directly into the mind, making reading comprehension more automatic.

The selectivity of the memory and the role of attention in memory are also subjects of investigation. Why might you clearly remember an event that took place many years ago, for instance, but forget what you ate for lunch yesterday? What mechanisms might cause you to more readily forget the name of someone you dislike? While much about memory remains a mystery, research shows it's a good idea to try to remember. Regularly exercising one's memory appears to confer similar benefits as regular physical workouts.

Critical Thinking

What did you have for dinner last night? What did you have for dinner exactly one week ago? In answering these questions, what techniques did you use to jog your memory? Could those techniques help you improve your overall ability to remember?

Source: M. Conway, "In Defense of Everyday Memory," *American Psychologist*, 1991; Elizabeth Schulz, "When Memory Fails," *Teacher*, February 1991.

---

not important things that happened yesterday? Most forgetting occurs because information in short-term memory was never transferred to long-term memory. However, it can also occur because we lost our ability to recall information that is in long-term memory.

Interference.   One important reason people forget is **interference** (Postman and Underwood, 1973). Interference happens when information gets mixed up with or pushed aside by other information. One form of interference is when people are prevented from mentally rehearsing newly learned information. For example, Peterson and Peterson (1959) gave subjects a simple task, the memorization of sets of three nonsense letters (such as FQB). The subjects were then immediately asked to count backward by threes from a three-digit number (for example, 287, 284, 281, etc.) for up to eighteen seconds. At the end of that time the subjects were asked to recall the letters. They had forgotten far more of them than had subjects who had learned the letters and then simply waited for eighteen seconds to repeat them. The reason for this is that the subjects told to count backward were deprived of the opportunity to mentally rehearse the letters to establish them in their short-term memories.

interference: a process that occurs when recall of certain information is inhibited by the presence of other information in memory.

As noted earlier in this chapter, teachers must take into account the limited capacity of short-term memory by allowing students time to absorb or practice (that is, to mentally rehearse) new information before giving them additional instruction.

Inhibition and Facilitation. Another form of interference is called **retroactive inhibition.** This occurs when previously learned information is lost because it is mixed up with new and somewhat similar information. For example, young students might have no trouble recognizing the letter *b* until they are taught the letter *d.* Because these letters are similar, students often confuse them. Learning the letter *d* thus interferes with the previously learned recognition of *b.* In the same way, a traveler may know how to get around in a particular airport, but then lose that skill to some extent after visiting many similar airports.

Proactive inhibition occurs when learning one set of information interferes with learning of later information. A classic case is an American learning to drive on the left side of the road in England. It may be easier for an American nondriver to learn to drive in England than for an experienced American driver because the latter has so thoroughly learned to stay to the right, a potentially fatal error in England.

It should also be noted that learning one thing can often help a person learn similar information. For example, learning Spanish first may help an English-speaking student learn Italian, a similar language. This would be a case of **proactive facilitation.** On the other hand, learning a second language can help with an already established language. It is often the case, for example, that English-speaking students find the study of Latin helps them better understand their native language. This would be **retroactive facilitation.**

For another example, consider teaching. We often have the experience that learning to teach a subject helps us understand the subject better. Since later learning (for example, learning to teach addition of fractions) increases the understanding of previously learned information (addition of fractions), this is a prime example of retroactive facilitation. Table 6.3 summarizes the relationships among retroactive and proactive inhibition and facilitation.

Of all the reasons for forgetting, retroactive inhibition is probably the most important. This phenomenon explains, for example, why we have trouble remembering frequently repeated episodes, such as what we had for dinner a week ago.

retroactive inhibition: decreased ability to recall previously learned information caused by learning of new information.

proactive inhibition: decreased ability to learn new information because of interference of present knowledge.

proactive facilitation: increased ability to learn new information due to previously acquired information.

retroactive facilitation: increased comprehension of previously learned information due to the acquisition of new information.

Table 6.3 Retroactive and Proactive Inhibition and Facilitation

Summary of the effects on memory of retroactive and proactive inhibition and facilitation.

| | Effect on Memory | |
	Negative (Inhibiting)	Positive (Facilitating)
Later learning affects earlier learning	Retroactive inhibition (Example: Learning "d" interferes with learning "b"	Retroactive facilitation (Example: Learning to teach math helps with previously learned math skills)
Earlier learning affects later learning	Proactive inhibition (Example: Learning to drive in the U.S. interferes with learning to drive in the U.K.)	Proactive facilitation (Example: Learning Spanish helps with later learning of Italian)

What kind of memory strategy does this picture illustrate? According to research on memory and forgetting, what factors will determine how well this student remembers the information?

Theory Into Practice

Reducing Retroactive Inhibition

One implication of retroactive inhibition is that confusing, similar concepts should not be taught too closely in time. Each concept should be taught thoroughly before the next is introduced. For example, students should be completely able to recognize the letter *b* before the letter *d* is introduced. If these letters were introduced at close to the same time, learning of one would inhibit learning of the other. When introduced, the differences between *b* and *d* must be carefully pointed out and discrimination between the two drilled until students can unerringly say which is which. If you were teaching the words *etymology* (the study of words) and *entomology* (the study of insects), you would want to make sure that students readily understood and were able to use one of these terms before you introduced the other.

Another way to reduce retroactive inhibition is to use different methods to teach similar concepts or to vary other aspects of instruction for each concept. For example, Andre (1973) had students study two descriptions of African tribes. For some students, the two passages were organized and printed in the same way. For others, the second passage was organized differently from the first and printed on different-colored paper. Students given the second procedure showed less confusion between the two passages on a later test. Researchers also found that when students were asked to memorize two lists, those who used the same memorization strategy for both forgot more than those who used a different strategy for each (Andre *et al.*, 1976). This and other research implies that teachers can help students retain information and avoid confusion if they vary their presentation strategies for different material. For example, a teacher might teach about Spain using lectures and discussion, about France using group projects, and about Italy using films. This would help students avoid confusing information about one country with information about the others. Most things that are forgotten were never firmly learned in the first place. The best way to ensure long-term retention of material taught in school is to make certain that students have mastered the essential features of the material. This requires frequent assessment of students' understanding and reteaching if it turns out that students have not achieved adequate levels of mastery.

primacy effect: the tendency for items that appear at the beginning of a list to be more easily recalled than other items.

recency effect: the tendency for items that appear at the end of a list to be more easily recalled than other items.

Primacy and Recency Effects.   One of the oldest findings in educational psychology is that when people are given a list of words to learn and then tested immediately afterward, they tend to learn the first few and last few items much better than those in the middle of the list (Stigler, 1978). The tendency to learn the first things presented is called the **primacy effect;** the tendency to learn the last things, the **recency effect.** The most common explanation for the primacy effect is that we pay more attention and devote more mental effort to items presented first. As noted earlier in this chapter, mental rehearsal is important in establishing new information in long-term memory. Usually, much more mental rehearsal is devoted to the first items presented than to later items (Rundus and Atkinson, 1970). Recency effects, on the other hand, are due in large part to the fact that little or no other information intervenes between the final items and the test (Greene, 1986).

Primacy and recency effects should be considered by teachers. They imply that information taught at the beginning or the end of the period is more likely to be retained than other information. To take advantage of this, teachers might organize their lessons to put the most essential new concepts early in the lesson, and then to summarize at the end. Many teachers take roll, collect lunch money, check homework, and do other noninstructional activities at the beginning of the period. However, it is probably a better idea to postpone these activities, to start the period right away with important concepts and only toward the end of the period deal with necessary administrative tasks.

Does Practice Make Perfect?

The most common method for committing information to memory is also the most mundane—practice. Does practice make perfect ?

Practice is important at several stages of learning. As noted earlier in this chapter, information received in short-term memory must be mentally rehearsed if it is to be retained for more than a few seconds. The information in short-term memory must usually be practiced until it is established in long-term memory.

Massed and Distributed Practice.   Is it better to practice newly learned information intensively until it is thoroughly learned (**massed practice**) or to practice a little each day over a period of time (**distributed practice**)? Massed practice allows for faster initial learning, but for most kinds of learning, distributed practice is better for retention, even over short time periods. This is especially true of factual learning (Dempster, 1989); "cramming" factual information the night before a test may get you through that test, but the information probably won't be well integrated into your long-term memory. Long-term retention of all kinds of information and skills is greatly enhanced by distributed practice. This is the primary purpose of homework: to provide practice on newly learned skills over an extended period of time in order to increase the chances that the skills will be retained.

Part and Whole Learning.   It is very difficult for most people to learn a long list all at once. Rather, it is easier to break the list down into smaller lists. This is called **part learning**. Its effectiveness explains why teachers teaching multiplication facts, for example, first have students master the twos table, then the threes, and so on. Note that this strategy helps reduce retroactive inhibition, as the earlier partial lists are thoroughly learned before the next partial list is introduced.

Automaticity.   Not everything requires conscious attention. For instance, your brain monitors breathing and heart rate without your attention. Tasks that require higher-level thinking can also be done without much attention if they have been learned very thoroughly. Think back to elementary school when you learned cursive handwriting. At first you had to make conscious decisions about forming every letter. Your teacher may have told you to watch the slant of the letters and their neatness. Before long, however, you gained experience and could devote much less attention to the act of writing. This process in which tasks require less attention as they become well learned has been called **automaticity** by Shiffrin and Schneider (1977). Automaticity is important because we want the skills we teach children to become second nature to them to free their short-term memories for more complex tasks.

For example, students' knowledge of the sounds each letter makes and how to decode (read) simple words must become automatic. Students who must put

---

massed practice: technique in which facts or skills to be learned are repeated many times over a concentrated period of time

distributed practice: technique in which items to be learned are repeated at intervals over a period of time.

part learning: mastering new material by learning it one part or subskill at a time.

automaticity: process by which thoroughly learned tasks can be performed with little mental effort.

mental effort into sounding out each word in a sentence cannot adequately attend to what the sentence is saying because all their attention (short-term memory) is taken up with the decoding task (Samuels, 1981). Automaticity is primarily gained through drill and practice. Just as coaches drill athletes in essential physical skills until they become second nature, so must teachers drill students in certain facts and skills until they are second nature, to free their mental capacities for more complex and important tasks. Gaining automaticity on lower-level processes has enormous consequences for higher-level learning; Bloom (1986), who has studied the role of automaticity in the performances of gifted pianists, mathematicians, athletes, and others, calls automaticity the "hands and feet of genius."

Overlearning.   As noted earlier, one of the most important indicators of long-term retention of information or skills is how well they were learned in the first place. If students practice just long enough to learn something and then do no more, they are likely to forget much of what they have learned. However, if they continue to practice beyond the point where they can recall the answers, retention will increase. This strategy is called **overlearning.** For example, Krueger (1929) had students learn a list of words until they could recite the list with no errors. Then some students were asked to engage in overlearning, to keep practicing the list for an amount of time equal to what it took them to learn the list originally. Four days after the experiment these students retained six times as many words as were retained by the students who did not engage in overlearning. By the twenty-eighth day, the nonoverlearning group had forgotten all the words, while the overlearning group still had a few.

Overlearning has only a few important applications in instructional practice. It is useful for drilling information that must be accurately recalled for a long time but has little meaning. The prime example of a learning task suitable for overlearning is memorization of multiplication facts, which students should be able to recall automatically and without error. Overlearning of multiplication facts is often accomplished by the regular use of speed drills, mental arithmetic (for example, "Class: What is four times seven minus three divided by five times nine?"), or games. Spelling lists may also be overlearned, particularly for frequently missed words that do not follow regular spelling rules.

Enactment.   Everyone knows that we learn by doing. It turns out that research on **enactment** supports this common sense conclusion. In learning how to perform tasks of many kinds, individuals learn much better if they are asked to enact the tasks (to physically carry them out) than if they simply read the instructions or watch a teacher enact the task (Cohen, 1989). For example, students would learn much more from a lesson on drawing geometric solids (such as cubes and spheres) if they had an opportunity to draw some rather than just watching the teacher do so.

overlearning: method of improving retention by practicing new knowledge or behaviors after mastery is achieved.

enactment: learning process in which individuals physically carry out tasks.

Self-Check

Reread the scenario at the beginning of this chapter on Ms. Bishop's memory experiment. Using concepts from this section, offer two or more possible explanations for the instances of forgetting described in the case. Now suggest two or more possible explanations for the instances of remembering. How might the different kinds of "practice" enhance the students' learning in this case?

How Can Memory Strategies Be Taught?

Many of the things that students learn in school are facts that must be remembered. These form the framework on which more complex concepts depend. Factual material must be learned as efficiently and effectively as possible to leave time and mental energy for meaningful learning, such as problem-solving, conceptual, and creative activities. If students can memorize the routine things more efficiently, they can "free their minds to spend more time on tasks that involve understanding and reasoning. . . . Even tasks that involve reasoning and understanding require that you remember the facts in order to reason with them and understand them" (Higbee, 1978, p. 150).

Some learning involves memorization of facts or of arbitrary associations between terms. For example, *pomme,* the French word for "apple," is an arbitrary term associated with an object. The capital of Iowa could just as well have been called "Iowapolis" as "Des Moines." Similarly, the figure "2" is an arbitrary representation of the concept "two." Students often learn things as facts before they understand them as concepts or skills. For instance, students may learn the formula for the volume of a cylinder as an arbitrary fact long before they understand *why* the formula is what it is.

Verbal Learning

In many studies psychologists have examined **verbal learning,** or how students learn verbal materials in laboratory settings. For example, students might be asked to learn lists of words or nonsense syllables. Three types of verbal learning tasks typically seen in the classroom have been identified and studied extensively: the paired-associate task, the serial learning task, and the free-recall learning task.

1. **Paired-associate learning** tasks involve learning to respond with one member of a pair when given the other member of the pair. Usually there is a list of pairs to be memorized. In typical experiments the pairs are arbitrary. Educational examples of paired-associate tasks include learning the states' capitals, the names and dates of Civil War battles, the addition and multiplication tables, the atomic weights of the elements, and the spelling of words.

2. **Serial learning** involves learning a list of terms in a particular order. Memorization of the notes on the musical staff, the Pledge of Allegiance, the elements in atomic weight order, and poetry and songs are serial learning tasks. Serial learning tasks occur less often in classroom instruction than paired-associate tasks.

3. **Free-recall learning** tasks also involve memorizing a list, but not in a special order. Recalling the names of the fifty states, types of reinforcement, kinds of poetic feet, and the organ systems in the body are examples of free-recall tasks.

Paired-Associate Learning

In paired-associate learning the student must associate a response with each stimulus. For example, the student is given a picture of a bone (the stimulus) and must respond "tibia," or is given the symbol "Au" and must respond "gold." One important aspect of the learning of paired associates is the degree of familiarity the

Connections

Memory strategies are metacognitive skills because they focus learners' attention on the processes and products of their own thinking. The concept of metacognition, introduced in Chapters 1 and 2, is developed further in Chapter 7.

verbal learning: learning of words or facts under various conditions.

paired-associate learning: a task involving the linkage of two items in a pair so that when one is presented the other can be recalled.

serial learning: a task requiring recall of a list of items.

free-recall learning: a task requiring recall of a list of items in any order.

student already has with the stimuli and the responses. For example, it would be far easier to learn to associate foreign words with English words, such as dog—*chien* (French) or dog—*perro* (Spanish) than to learn to associate two foreign words, such as *chien—perro*. By the same token, a student who knew Latin could learn medical or legal terms that are Latin or derived from Latin more easily than could someone who was not familiar with Latin.

The first step in learning paired associates is stimulus discrimination. That is, the learner must be able to discriminate among the various stimuli. For example, consider the following lists of Spanish and English words.

A	B
llevar—to carry	*perro*—dog
llorar—to cry	*gato*—cat
llamar—to call	*caballo*—horse

List B is much easier to learn. The similarities among the Spanish words in List A (they are all verbs, all start with "ll," end with "ar," and have the same number of letters and syllables) make them very difficult to tell apart. The English words in List A are also somewhat difficult to discriminate because all are verbs that start with a "c." In contrast, the stimulus-and-response words in List B are easy to discriminate from one another. Because of the problem of retroactive inhibition discussed earlier, presenting the word pairs in List A in the same lesson would be a terrible instructional strategy. Students would be likely to confuse the three Spanish words because of their similar spellings. Rather, students should be completely familiar with one word pair before the next is introduced.

Imagery. Many powerful memory techniques are based on forming mental images to help remember associations. For example, the French word for fencing is *l'escrime,* pronounced "le scream." It is easy to remember this association (fencing—*l'escrime*) by forming a mental picture of a fencer screaming while being skewered by an opponent, as illustrated in Figure 6.6 .

Mental **imagery** can be a very effective aid to memory. For example, Anderson and Hidde (1971) asked students to study a list of sentences that were all of the form "The (*occupation*—noun) (*did*—an action)," such as "The doctor opened the closet." Half the students were told to rate the sentences according to how easily they could form a mental image of them. The other half of the group rated the sentences according to how easy it was to pronounce them. The students who had to form mental images recalled three times as many sentences as the other group.

One ancient method of enhancing memory by use of imagery is the creation of stories to weave together information (Egan, 1989). For example, Greek myths about the stars have long been used to help recall the constellations.

Stimulus Selection and Coding.   **Stimulus selection** is a process by which students learning paired associates choose a particular aspect of the stimulus to pay attention to. For example, students may principally pay attention to the first letters of words or to their order on the list. These shortcuts may help them learn a list of paired associates, but will be of little use when the words are presented out of order or in different contexts. Stimulus selection has been demonstrated in pigeons, who were taught to peck when they were shown blue triangles and not peck when they saw red circles. Some pigeons focused on the color and would peck in response to any blue shape. Others focused on the shape and pecked in response to any triangle. None, however, focused on both attributes of the blue triangle.

imagery: use of mental images to improve memory.

stimulus selection: choosing aspects of stimuli on which to focus attention.

Figure 6.6   Example of the Use of Images to Aid Recall

An English-speaking student learning French can easily remember that the French word for fencing is *l'escrime* by linking it to the English word "scream" and picturing a fencer screaming.

Stimulus coding is a related process in which students may connect a particular image or other association with a stimulus. For example, a student might remember *caballo* means "horse" by thinking of a horse pulling a cab. Stimulus coding is used in many strategies for remembering paired associates.

Finally, students learn the associations between the various stimuli. Methods for enhancing paired-associate learning are the most extensively studied of all memory strategies. Several methods of learning such material have been developed and researched. These are called **mnemonics,** a Greek word meaning "aiding the memory" (Higbee, 1979).

Keyword Mnemonics.   One of the most extensively studied methods of using imagery and mnemonics to help paired-associate learning is the **keyword method,** originally developed for teaching foreign language vocabulary but later applied to many other areas (Atkinson, 1975; Hall, 1991; Pressley, 1991). The example used earlier of employing vivid imagery to recall the French word *l'escrime* is an illustration of the keyword method. In that case, the keyword was "scream." It is called a keyword because it evokes the connection between the word *l'escrime* and the mental picture. Another illustration given by Atkinson (1975) is learning the Spanish word for duck, *pato.* Since this is pronounced something like "pot-o," the learner is instructed to imagine a duck swimming on a lake with a little pot on its head. In this case, "pot" is the keyword linking the image to the new word. The Russian word for building, *zdanie,* pronounced "zdawn'-yeh," might be recalled using the keyword "dawn" by imagining the sun coming up behind a building with an onion dome on top. Atkinson and Raugh (1975) used this method to teach students a list of 120 Russian words over a three-day period. Other students were given English translations of the Russian words and allowed to study as they

stimulus coding: using aspects of stimuli and mental images to promote recall.

mnemonics: methods for aiding the memory.

keyword method: strategy for improving memory by using images to link pairs of items.

wished. At the end of the experiment the students who used the keyword method recalled 72 percent of the words, while the other students recalled only 46 percent. This result has been repeated dozens of times, using a wide variety of languages (Pressley *et al.,* 1982), with students from preschoolers to adults. However, young children seem to require pictures of the mental images they are meant to form while older children (starting in upper elementary school) learn equally well making their own mental images (Pressley and Levin, 1978).

The images used in the keyword method work best if they are vivid and active (Delin, 1969), preferably involving interaction. For example, the German word for room, *zimmer* (pronounced "tsimmer"), might be associated with the keyword "simmer." The German word would probably be better recalled using an image of a distressed person in a bed immersed in a huge, steaming cauldron of water in a large bedroom than using an image of a small pot of water simmering in the corner of a bedroom. The drama, action, and bizarreness of the first image make it memorable, while the second is too commonplace to be easily recalled.

While most research on mnemonic learning strategies has focused on learning foreign language vocabulary, several studies have demonstrated that the same methods can be used for other information, including names of state capitals and English vocabulary words (Levin *et al.,* 1980; Miller *et al.,* 1980). More recent studies applied mnemonics to reading comprehension (Peters *et al.,* 1985), biographical information (McCormick and Levin, 1984), and science facts (Levin *et al.,* 1986). However, it should be noted that most of the research done on use of mnemonic strategies has taken place under rather artificial, laboratorylike conditions, using materials thought to be especially appropriate for these strategies. Evaluations of actual classroom applications of these strategies show more mixed results (Pressley and Levin, 1983). Although the strategies have been relatively successful for teaching foreign language vocabulary (especially nouns) to elementary school students, they have yet to show success in helping students actually speak foreign languages better. However, research is under way on the practical applications of paired-associate learning strategies to a broader range of skills, and it is likely the strategies will prove useful in helping students learn certain kinds of information (see Pressley *et al.,* 1989).

According to research, how does the ability to form mental images of verbal information affect learning? In what memory aids does mental imagery play a key role?

Serial and Free-Recall Learning

Serial learning is learning facts in a particular order. Learning events on a time-line, the order of operations in long division, or the relative hardnesses of minerals are examples of serial learning. Free-recall learning is learning a list of items that need not be remembered in order, such as the names of the nine Supreme Court justices or the six major exports of New Zealand.

One important thing about learning lists, as in serial and free-recall learning, is that items near the beginning and end of the list are more easily remembered than those in the middle. If, for example, we wished to teach the names of various parts of the body, it would be important to go over the list several times, varying the order of presentation, so that each body part appeared in a different place on the list each time.

For much serial and free-recall learning, the best memory strategy is to organize the list to be learned into meaningful, easily remembered categories. This was demonstrated earlier in the example of the grocery list that could be organized into breakfast, lunch, and dinner, and then further broken down into recipes for particular foods.

The Loci Method.   A mnemonic device for serial learning, used by the ancient Greeks, employs imagery associated with a list of locations (see Anderson, 1980). In the **loci method** the student thinks of a very familiar set of locations, such as rooms in his or her own house, and then imagines each item on the list to be remembered in one specific location. Vivid or bizarre imagery is used to place the object in the location. Once the connections between room or other location and object are established, the learner can recall each place and its contents in order.

The same locations can be mentally "cleared" and used to memorize a different list. However, they would always be used in the same order to ensure that all items on the list were remembered.

The Pegword Method.   Another imagery method useful for ordered lists is called the **pegword method** (see Paivio, 1971). To use this mnemonic, the student might memorize a list of "pegwords" that rhyme with the numbers one to ten.

To use this method, the student creates mental images relating to items on the list to be learned with particular pegwords. For example, in learning the order of the first ten U.S. presidents, you might picture George Washington eating a bun (one) with his wooden teeth, John Adams tying his shoe (two), Thomas Jefferson hanging by his knees from a branch of a tree (three), and so on.

Theory Into Practice
Teaching Rhyming Pegwords

A very old and quite effective technique for enhancing memory is rhyming. Most of us depend on rhymes such as:

- Thirty days hath September . . .

- "i" before "e" except after "c" . . .

- When two vowels go walking, the first one does the talking.

loci method: strategy for remembering lists by picturing items in familiar locations.

pegword method: strategy for memorization in which images are used to link lists of facts to a familiar set of words or numbers.

- In fourteen hundred ninety-two Columbus sailed the ocean blue.

- A B C D E F G H I J K L M N O P . . ,

Rhymes, songs, and catchy phrases are so effective that you often remember them long after you have forgotten what they refer to. For example, most of you would recognize some of the following sayings:

- Tippecanoe and Tyler too!

- It's a long way to Tipperary . . .

- Fifty-four forty or fight!

- We are marching to Pretoria . . .

- Damn the torpedoes, full speed ahead!

- Remember the *Maine!*

However, do you know who or what Tippecanoe was? (William Henry Harrison, hero of the Battle of Tippecanoe and ninth president of the United States.) Where is Tipperary? (Ireland.) Your ability to remember expressions without remembering what they refer to illustrates the power of rhymes and sayings to stay with us beyond any reasonable use.

When teaching in any content area, look for opportunities to create rhyming pegwords, and instruct students directly in their use. Your students will also enjoy assignments in which they create rhyming pegwords and other mnemonic devices and teach them to their classmates.

Initial-Letter Strategies.   One memory strategy involving a reorganization of information is taking initial letters of a list to be memorized and making a more easily remembered word or phrase. For example, many trigonometry classes have learned about the imaginary SOH CAH TOA tribe, whose letters help recall: sine = opposite/hypotenuse; cosine = adjacent/hypotenuse; tangent = opposite/adjacent. Many **initial-letter strategies** exist for remembering the order of the planets from the sun. The planets, in order, are Mercury, Venus, Earth, Mars, Jupiter, Saturn, Uranus, Neptune, and Pluto. Students are taught a sentence in which the first letters of the words are the first letters of the planets in order: *My very educated monkey just served us nine pizzas.*

In a similar fashion, acronyms help in remembering the names of organizations. Initial-letter strategies may also be used to help students remember procedural knowledge, such as steps in a process.

> **initial-letter strategy:**
> strategy for memorization in which initial letters of a list to be memorized are taken to make a word or phrase that is more easily remembered.

Theory Into Practice
Teaching "MURDER"

Initial-letter strategies to teach study strategies have been developed for college students who have difficulty with metacognitive strategies (Dansereau *et al.*,

Teachers on Teaching

What strategies have you used to help students process and retain new learning?

I used semantic mapping with third-graders who had been studying the food chain and dissecting owl pellets in science. In reading class, I asked them to brainstorm everything they knew about owls. We filled the chalkboard. I was purposely accessing their prior knowledge to help them understand a new piece of reading I planned to give them later. Then we categorized the information on the board using semantic mapping. The students mapped with me, and we talked about how we were organizing all the information. My next aim was to get the students to want to find out more ideas. We developed a list of questions that we thought our reading might answer. Then when they had a purpose for reading, I gave them the new piece of reading. After reading, I asked them what they had learned, and we added that information to the appropriate categories on their maps. They found they had to create some new categories to accommodate new ideas. They also learned that some of their original brainstorming ideas were incorrect and had to be eliminated. Recognizing these things for themselves helped them learn responsibility for their own learning. I asked each student to use the information on their maps to write a report on barn owls. I showed them how each category could be turned into a topic sentence and how the details in each category could then be turned into supporting sentences. The most important part for me is seeing them use these learning strategies when they go on to other themes in science. The students see how easy it is to map an expository piece of writing to organize and remember what they read.

Audrey E. Seguin, Teacher, Grades 3–4
Hinks Elementary School, Alpena, Michigan

Retention improves if the concept lesson itself is memorable. Geography concepts were particularly challenging to my third-graders. I gave what I thought was a good lesson. The results of the first short quiz, however, showed me that I had not been successful. During recess duty the next day, I noticed groups of children playing four-square, and I suddenly got the idea of using those squares to teach the concepts of north, south, east, and west. After recess, my class was thrilled with the idea of returning to the playground. With a piece of chalk, I had a child draw a large compass rose next to the four-square. This analogy worked perfectly. We were able to establish that the horizontal center line of the four-square was equivalent to the equator on the compass rose, and that the vertical center line was equivalent to the prime meridian. We marked each quadrant (NE, NW, SE, and SW) and then the children took turns standing in various quadrants while the other children called out the location. After every child had demonstrated competence, I drew lines subdividing the quadrants, representing degrees of latitude and longitude. I had the children number the horizontal lines and give a letter value to the vertical lines. Then each child chose a spot to stand on where two lines intersected and had to describe the geographical coordinates. Evaluating the students' understanding was easy. Each child took a turn directing another child to a particular spot and was the judge as to whether or not that child was successful. This activity gave each child a lot of experience using geography concepts. They also used their bodies as well as their minds to learn, and they were learning in a memorable context.

Gail C. Hartman, Kindergarten Teacher
Edison Elementary School, Hobbs, New Mexico

1979). The program's developers used the acronym MURDER to help students remember the strategy. The components of the MURDER strategy are:

- *Mood*—get in the mood for learning.

- *Understand* the goals and conditions of the task. To do this, you must identify what you do not understand.

- *Recall* information relevant to the task. Use such strategies as paraphrasing, imagery, and analyzing key concepts to develop the ability to recall the material.

- *Detect* omissions, errors, and ways of organizing the information. Use resources to clear up any misunderstandings and omissions identified in the *U* step.

- *Elaborate* the information into a proper response. Expand upon information and relate it to material in memory by asking your self questions such as: What questions would I ask the author if I could? How can the material be applied?

- *Review* the material and focus on information you have not learned well.

These descriptions are based on Dansereau *et al.,* 1979; and Dansereau, 1985. Dansereau also discusses several other support strategies, including goal setting and scheduling, concentrating, and monitoring difficulties. Several studies have shown that training programs based on these procedures can enhance the "individual's capacity for acquiring and using information" (Dansereau, 1985, p. 1).

Try developing initial-letter strategies for your students to help with subject area content, procedural knowledge, or metacognitive and study skills.

Self-Check

Sketch a concept map or diagram with MEMORY STRATEGIES at the center and spokes or arrows to three subgroups: PAIRED-ASSOCIATE, SERIAL, and FREE-RECALL. Then try to correctly categorize the specific strategies described in this section, listed below. Note that some strategies may appear more than once. Check the section for accuracy.

loci method	pegword method
rhyming pegwords	initial-letter strategies
imagery	stimulus selection
keyword method	stimulus coding

What Makes Information Meaningful?

Consider the following sentences:

1. Enso flrs hmen matn snoi teha erso iakt siae otin tnes esna nrae.
2. Easier that nonsense information to makes then sense is learn.
3. Information that makes sense is easier to learn than nonsense.

Which sentence is easiest to learn and remember? Obviously, Sentence 3. All three sentences have the same letters, and Sentences 2 and 3 have the same words. Yet to learn Sentence 1, we would have to memorize fifty-two separate letters, and to learn Sentence 2, we would have to learn ten separate words. Sentence 3 is easiest because to learn it, we need only learn one concept, a concept that readily fits our common sense and prior knowledge about how learning takes place. We know the individual words, we know the grammar that connects them, and we already have in our minds a vast store of information, experiences, and thoughts about the same topic. For these reasons, Sentence 3 slides smoothly into our understanding.

The message in Sentence 3 is what this chapter is all about. Most human learning, particularly school learning, involves making sense out of information, sorting it in our minds until it fits in a neat and orderly way, and using old information to help assimilate new learning. We have limited ability to recall rote information—how many telephone numbers can you remember for a month? However, we can retain meaningful information far more easily. Recall that most of the mnemonic strategies discussed in the previous section involve adding artificial "meaning" to arbitrary associations in order to take advantage of the much greater ease of learning meaningful information.

The message in Sentence 3 has profound implications for instruction. One of the teacher's most important tasks is to make information meaningful to students, by presenting it in a clear, organized way, by relating it to information already in students' minds, and by making sure that students have truly understood the concepts being taught and can apply them to new situations.

Rote versus Meaningful Learning

Ausubel (1963) discussed the distinction between rote learning and meaningful learning. **Rote learning** refers to the memorization of facts or associations, such as the multiplication tables, the chemical symbols for the elements, words in foreign languages, or the names of bones and muscles in the human body. Much of rote learning involves associations that are essentially arbitrary. For example, the chemical symbol for gold (Au) could just as well have been Go or Gd. In contrast, **meaningful learning** is not arbitrary, and it relates to information or concepts learners already have. For example, if we learn that silver is an excellent conductor of electricity, this information relates to our existing information about silver and about electrical conductivity. Further, the association between "silver" and "electrical conductivity" is not arbitrary. Silver really is an excellent conductor, and while we could state the same principle in many ways or in any language, the *meaning* of the statement "Silver is an excellent conductor of electricity" could not be arbitrarily changed.

Uses of Rote Learning.   We sometimes get the impression that rote learning is "bad," meaningful learning "good." This is not necessarily true. For example, when the doctor tells us we have a fractured tibia, we hope the doctor has mastered the rote association between the word "tibia" and the leg bone it names. Foreign language vocabulary is an important case of rote learning. However, rote learning has gotten a bad name in education because it is overused; we can all remember being taught to parrot facts that were supposed to be meaningful, but that we were forced to learn as rote, meaningless information. William James, in a

rote learning: memorization of facts or associations.

meaningful learning: mental processing of new information leading to its linkage with previously learned knowledge.

book called *Talks to Teachers on Psychology* (1912), gave an excellent example of this kind of false learning:

> A friend of mine, visiting a school, was asked to examine a young class in geography. Glancing at the book, she said: "Suppose you should dig a hole in the ground, hundreds of feet deep, how should you find it at the bottom—warmer or colder than on top?" None of the class replying, the teacher said: "I'm sure they know, but I think you don't ask the question quite rightly. Let me try." So, taking the book, she asked: "In what condition is the interior of the globe?" and received the immediate answer from half the class at once. "The interior of the globe is in a condition of igneous fusion." (James, 1912, p. 150)

Clearly, the students had memorized the information without learning its meaning. The information was useless to them because it did not tie in with other information they had.

Inert Knowledge.   The "igneous fusion" information that students had memorized in the class James's friend visited is an example of what Bransford *et al.* (1986a) call **inert knowledge.** This is knowledge that could and should be applicable to a wide range of situations but is only applied to a restricted set of circumstances. Usually, inert knowledge is information or skills learned in school that we cannot apply in life. For example, you may know people who could pass an advanced French test but would be unable to communicate in Paris or who can solve volume problems in math class but have no idea how much sand to order to fill a sandbox. Many problems in life arise not from a lack of knowledge but from an inability to use the knowledge we already have.

An interesting experiment by Perfetto *et al.* (1983) illustrates the concept of inert knowledge. In the experiment, college students were given problems such as the following:

> Uriah Fuller, the famous Israeli superpsychic, can tell you the score of any baseball game *before* the game starts. What is his secret?

Before seeing the problems, some of the students were given a list of sentences to memorize that were clearly useful in solving the problems; among the sentences were "Before it starts, the score of any game is 0 to 0." Students who were told to use the sentence in their memories as clues performed much better on the problem-solving task than did other students, but students who memorized the clues *but were not told to use them* did no better than students who never saw the clues! What this experiment tells us is that having information in your memory does not at all guarantee that you can bring it out and use it when appropriate. Rather, you need to know how and when to use the information you have.

Teachers can help students learn information in a way that will make it useful as well as meaningful to them. Effective teaching requires an understanding of how to make information *accessible* to students so that they can connect it to other information and apply it outside of the classroom.

---

inert knowledge: learned information that can be applied to only a restricted, often artificial set of circumstances.

Schema Theory

As noted earlier, meaningful information is stored in long-term memory in networks of connected facts or concepts called schemata. Recall the representation of the concept "bison" presented in Figure 6.5, showing how this one concept was linked to a wide range of other concepts.

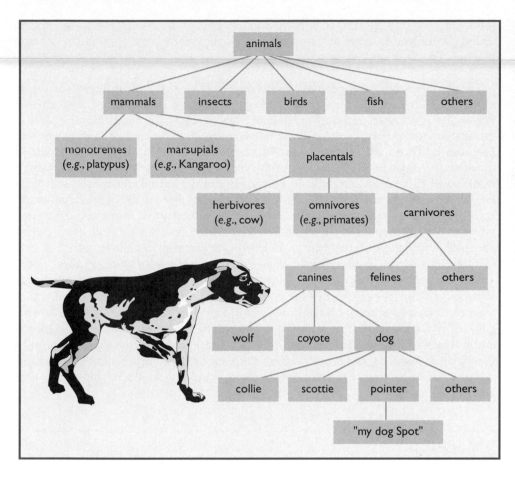

Figure 6.7

Example of a Knowledge Structure Arranged as a Hierarchy

A person who understands the place of a particular animal ("Spot") within the animal kingdom might have that information arranged in memory as shown here.

From Royer and Feldman, 1984, p. 225

The most important principle of **schema theory** is that information that fits into an existing schema is more easily understood, learned, and retained than information that does not fit into an existing schema (Ausubel, 1968; Anderson and Bower, 1983; Rumelhart and Ortony, 1977). The sentence "Bison calves can run soon after they are born" is an example of information that would be easily incorporated into your "bison" schema because you know that (1) bison rely on speed to escape from predators, and (2) more familiar animals (such as horses) that also rely on speed have babies that can run very early. Without all this prior knowledge, "Bison calves can run soon after they are born" would be more difficult to mentally assimilate and easily forgotten.

Hierarchies of Knowledge.   It is thought that most well-developed schemata are organized in hierarchies similar to outlines, with specific information grouped under general categories, which are grouped under still more general categories. This is illustrated in Figure 6.7. Note that in moving from the top to the bottom of the figure, you are going from general (animals) to specific (my dog Spot). The concepts in Figure 6.7 are well "anchored" in the schema (Ausubel, 1963). Any new information relating to this schema will probably be learned and incorporated into the schema much more readily than would information relating to less established schemata or rote learning that does not attach to any schema.

One important insight of schema theory is that meaningful learning requires the active involvement of the learner, who has a host of prior experiences and

schema theory: theory that information is stored in long-term memory in networks of connected facts and concepts that provide a structure for making sense of new information.

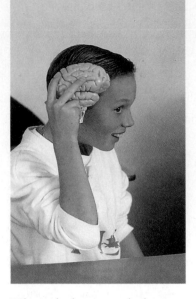

Why is the lesson on the human brain meaningful to this student? What background knowledge and schema is he likely to have to make sense of the new information the teacher is presenting? How might you diagram this student's possible schema for the "brain"?

knowledge to bring to understanding and incorporating new information (Andre, 1984). What you learn from any experience depends in large part on the schema you apply to the experience.

The Importance of Background Knowledge.   One of the most important determinants of how much you can learn about something is how much you already know about it. A recent study in Japan by Kuhara-Kojima and Hatano (1991) illustrated this clearly. College students were taught information about baseball and music. Those who knew a great deal about baseball but not music learned much more about baseball; the opposite was true of those who knew much about music and little about baseball. In fact, background knowledge was much more important than general learning ability in predicting how much the students would learn. Learners who know a great deal about a subject have more well-developed schemata for incorporating new knowledge. However, learners will often fail to use their prior knowledge to help them learn new material. Teachers must link new learning to students' existing background knowledge (Pressley *et al.*, 1992).

This chapter has discussed how learners receive, make sense of, and remember knowledge. This is only half of the cognitive story. Chapter 7 presents ways that teachers can help students learn how to build bridges from their existing knowledge to new knowledge, to discover new information and solve complex problems, and to transfer knowledge from one subject to another and from the classroom to life. It also discusses means of helping students become aware of and then consciously use their own strategies for learning, studying, and applying knowledge and skills.

Connections

Recall the discussion of the importance of background knowledge earlier in this chapter in which research confirms the observation that how much you can learn about something depends largely on how much you already know about it.

Self-Check

Explain the difference between rote and meaningful learning, the role of schema in learning, and the importance of prior knowledge in learning. Contrast rote learning and meaningful learning by giving three examples of each one. Then develop a model of a schema for one of your examples of meaningful learning. What aspects of your schema highlight the importance of background knowledge in learning?

Knowledge and Learning How to Learn

Two eleventh-grade U.S. history teachers, Helen Baker and George Kowalski, are talking in George's classroom after school. Helen has taught seven years and George twenty-one years at Garfield High School, home of the current state high school basketball champions. Both teachers are members of the Social Studies Department's curriculum committee, which is in the process of revising the U.S. history course.

HELEN: It really is wonderful, the kind of school spirit we have here at G.H.S.

GEORGE: Well, having won the state basketball championship twice in the last five years hasn't hurt any! Do you realize we were among the top four teams each of the last ten years except 1988 and 1991?

HELEN (smiling): You're very good with facts like that, George. And speaking of facts, I wanted to talk to you about our disagreement about the curriculum revision. I thought that if you and I can work out our differences, maybe the committee will get out of the stalemate we're in.

GEORGE: Well, Helen, as I see it, you contend that students first need to master the facts of U.S. history before they can move on to higher-order thinking like problem solving and working with abstract concepts. My view is just the reverse. For generations we've taught students facts, and they forget them right after the test is over. That's because we don't ask them to use the facts in higher-order thought. To me, that's the only way you can learn to think abstractly and solve problems.

HELEN: But, George, trying to think abstractly and solve problems must be based on knowledge. Otherwise, problem solving is a pointless exercise—it amounts to a sharing of ignorance among the uninformed.

GEORGE: But I don't think that's as pointless as the other extreme—sticking to lecture and discussion and objective tests on key names, dates, terms, and events!

HELEN: I know you use a lot of small-group and independent study work and give essay-type tests. I heard some students talking about how your questions really "blew their minds." I think one was, "What would the United States be like today if the South had won the Civil War?"

GEORGE (chuckling): Yes, that stirred them up a bit!

HELEN: But, George, believe it or not, I've asked my students to write on that question from time to time when we're on the Civil War, and their answers were terrible—totally devoid of facts. The kids just wrote their opinions.

GEORGE: That's my point, Helen! Students have to learn *how* to use facts—and practice organizing and incorporating them into answers. Basketball players look terrible the first time they try a slam-dunk. But after they learn the technique, it's easy!

HELEN: I think where we really disagree is on strategy. I maintain that learning the facts is the first step and higher-order thinking follows. You begin by posing problems and questions and hope that the kids will learn the facts to answer the questions. That seems like throwing kids into a lake and asking them to swim.

GEORGE: Sure, the facts and fundamentals are important, but in my experience, kids just forget them. But if you compel kids to determine and then use the facts, they'll remember them long after the test. I'll bet some of the things they learn in my course are still with them when they're adults.

HELEN: Well, George, I just don't see how we can reconcile our two positions. Can you?

Critical Thinking

1. How do Helen's and George's positions differ on the nature of information processing, memory, and forgetting? What are the merits and drawbacks of each approach?

2. If you were settling the argument between Helen and George, what advice would you give them on the basis of information in this chapter?

3. Extend the dialogue with a third character who brings a problem-solving approach to the impasse.

Summary

How Does the Information Processing Model Work?

The three major components of memory are the sensory register, short-term memory, and long-term memory. The sensory registers are very-short-term memories linked to the senses. Information received by the senses but not attended to will be quickly forgotten. Once information is received, it is processed by the mind in accord with our experiences and mental states. This activity is called perception.

Short-term memory is a storage system that holds five to nine bits of information at any one time. Information enters short-term memory from both the sensory register and the long-term memory. Rehearsal is the process of repeating information in order to hold it in short-term memory.

Long-term memory is the part of the memory system in which a large amount of information is stored for an indefinite time period. Cognitive theories of learning stress the importance of helping students relate information being learned to existing information in long-term memory.

The three parts of long-term memory are episodic memory, which stores our memories of personal experiences; semantic memory, which stores facts and generalized knowledge in the form of schemata; and procedural memory, which stores knowledge of how to do things. Schemata are networks of related ideas that guide our understanding and action. Information that fits into a well-developed schema is easier to learn than information that cannot be so accommodated. Levels-of-processing theory suggests that learners will remember those things that they process. Students are processing information when they manipulate it, look at it from different perspectives, and analyze it. Dual code theory further suggests the importance of using both visual and verbal coding to learn bits of information. Other elaborations of the information processing model are transfer-appropriate processing and parallel distributed processing.

What Causes People to Remember or Forget?

Interference theory helps explain why people forget. It suggests that students can be confused by—and forget—pieces of similar information. Interference theory states that two situations cause forgetting: proactive inhibition, when learning one task interferes with the retention of tasks learned later; and retroactive inhibition, when learning a second task makes a person forget something learned previously. The primacy and recency effects state that people remember best information that is presented first and last in a series. Practice strengthens associations of newly learned information in memory. Distributed practice, which involves practicing parts of a task over a period of time, is usually more effective than massed practice. Part learning, automaticity, overlearning, and enactment also help students remember information.

How Can Memory Strategies Be Taught?

Teachers can help students remember facts by presenting lessons in an organized way and by teaching students to use memory strategies called mnemonics. Three types of verbal learning are paired-associate learning, serial learning, and free-recall learning.

Paired-associate learning is learning to respond with one member of a pair when given the other member. It involves stimulus discrimination, stimulus selection, and stimulus coding. Students can improve their learning of paired associates by using imagery techniques such as the keyword method.

Serial learning involves recalling a list of items in a specified order, whereas free-recall learning involves recalling the list in any order. Helpful strategies are organization, the loci method, the pegword method, rhyming, and stimulus selection.

What Makes Information Meaningful?

Information that makes sense and has significance to students is more meaningful than inert knowledge and information learned by rote. In schema theory, individuals' meaningful knowledge is constructed of networks and hierarchies of schemata.

Key Terms

attention, 189
automaticity, 203
closure, 188
distributed practice, 203
dual code theory of memory, 198
enactment, 204
episodic memory, 193

figure-ground relationship, 189
free-recall learning, 205
Gestalt psychology, 188
imagery, 206
inert knowledge, 214
information-processing theory, 186
initial-letter strategy, 210

Self-Assessment

1. Sperling's study involving the recall of very briefly displayed letters illustrated the limitations of

   a. long-term memory.

   b. short-term memory.

   c. rehearsal and coding.

   d. retrieval processes.

   e. the sensory register.

2. Match the following memory components with the characteristics that describe each:

   ___ episodic memory

   ___ semantic memory

   ___ short-term memory

   ___ sensory register

   a. the memory component from which information is most easily lost

   b. component in which enormous amounts of general information can be stored in networks of related schemata

   c. component that processes new information and also old information that has been brought to consciousness

   d. storage system in which memories of experiences can be stored for a lifetime

3. All of the following teaching strategies would be recommended for reducing retroactive inhibition, *except:*

   a. Be consistent in the methods used when teaching similar concepts.

   b. Teach one concept thoroughly before introducing the next one.

   c. Use mnemonic devices to point out differences between the concepts.

   d. Teach the concepts at different times, such as in separate class periods.

4. A student who has trouble remembering the location of the African countries Ghana and Guinea after learning about the South American country of Guyana has fallen prey to

   _____ inhibition. Conversely, a student who has trouble learning how to spell "guerrilla" after having earlier learned to spell "gorilla" is being hindered by _____ inhibition.

5. Using concepts in this chapter, write a well-reasoned argument supporting or refuting the claim that "practice makes perfect."

6. Match the following types of learning tasks with a correct example of each.

   ___ paired-associate

   ___ serial

   ___ free recall

   a. memorizing the names of the world's continents in order by size

   b. paraphrasing each of a series of sentences

   c. memorizing the names, functions, and locations of the major organs in the human body

   d. learning that a group of geese is a gaggle, a group of lions is a pride, a group of birds is a flight, and a group of quails is a bevy

7. Match the following learning tasks with the most appropriate memory strategy:

   ___ paired-associate

   ___ serial

   ___ free recall

   a. loci or pegword method

   b. keyword method

   c. rhyming method

8. Interconnected networks and hierarchies of knowledge are represented in a model of

   a. rote learning.

   b. inert knowledge.

   c. disequilibration.

   d. schema theory.

7

Cognitive Theories: Constructivist Approaches

"You'll all recall," started Mr. Dunbar, "how last week we figured out how to compute the area of a circle and the volume of a cube. Today you're going to have a chance to discover how to compute the volume of a *cylinder*. This time, you're really going to be on your own. At each of your lab stations you have five unmarked cylinders of different sizes. You also have a metric ruler and a calculator, and you may use water from your sink. The most important resources you'll have to use, however, are your *minds* and your *partners*. Remember, at the end of this activity everyone in every group must be able to explain not only the formula for volume of a cylinder, but also precisely how you derived it. Any questions? You may begin!" The students in Mr. Dunbar's middle school math/science class got right to work. They were seated around lab tables in groups of four. One of the groups, the Master Minds, started off by filling up all its cylinders with water.

"OK," said Miguel, "we've filled up all of our cylinders. What do we do next?"

"Let's measure them," suggested Margarite. She took the ruler and asked Dave to write down her measurements.

"The water in this little one is 36 millimeters high and . . . just a sec . . . 42 millimeters across the bottom."

"So what?" asked Yolanda. "We can't figure out the volume this way. Let's do a little thinking before we start measuring everything."

"Yolanda's right," said Dave. "We'd better work out a plan."

"I know," said Miguel, "let's make a hypo, hypotha, what's it called?"

"Hypothesis," said Yolanda. "Yeah! Let's guess what we think the solution is."

"Remember how Mr. Dunbar reminded us about the area of a circle and the volume of a cube? I'll bet that's an important clue."

"You're right, Miguel," said Mr. Dunbar, who happened to be passing by. "But what are you guys going to do with that information?"

The Master Minds were quiet for a few moments. "Let's try figuring out the area of the bottom of one of these cylinders," ventured Dave. "Remember that Margarite said the bottom of the little one was 42 millimeters? Give me the calculator . . . now how do we get the area?"

Yolanda said, "I think it was pi times the radius squared."

"That sounds right. So 42 squared . . ."

"Not 42, 21 squared," interrupted Margarite. "If the diameter is 42, the radius is 21."

"OK, OK, I would have remembered. Now, 21 squared is . . . 441, and pi is about 3.14, so my handy dandy calculator says . . . 13, 847."

"Can't be," said Miguel. "Four hundred times three is twelve *hundred*, so 441 times 3.14 can't be thirteen *thousand*. I think you did something wrong."

"Let me do it again. 441 times 3.14 . . . you're right. Now it's about 1384."

"So what?" said Yolanda.

"That doesn't tell us how to figure the volume!"

Margarite jumped in excitedly. "Just hang on for a minute, Yolanda. Now, I think we should multiply the area of the bottom by the height of the water."

"But why?" asked Miguel.

"Well," said Margarite, "when we did the volume of a cube we multiplied length times width times height. Length times width is the area of the bottom. I'll bet we could do the same with a cylinder!"

"The girl's brilliant!" said Miguel. "Sounds good to me. But how could we prove it?"

"I've got an idea," said Yolanda. She emptied the water out of all the cylinders and filled the smallest one to the top. "This is my idea. We don't know what the volume of this cylinder is, but we do know that it's always the same. If we pour the same amounts of water into all four cylinders and use our formula, it should always come out to the same amount!"

"Let's try it!" said Miguel. He poured the water from the small cylinder into a larger one, refilled it, and poured it into another of a different shape. The Master Minds measured the bases and the heights of the water in their cylinders, wrote down the measurements, and tried out their formula. Sure enough, their formula always gave the same answer for the same volume of water. In great excitement they called Mr. Dunbar to come see what they were doing. Mr. Dunbar asked each of the students to explain what they did. "Terrific!" he said. "You not only figured out a solution, but everyone in the group participated and understood what you did. Now I'd like you to help me out. I've got a couple of groups that are really stumped. Do you suppose you could help them? Don't give them the answer, but help them get on track. How about Yolanda and Miguel helping with the Brainiacs, and Dave and Margarite help with the Dream Team. OK? Thanks!"

Learning is much more than memory. For students to really understand and be able to apply knowledge, they must work to solve problems, to discover things for

constructivist theories of learning: state that learners must individually discover and transform complex information, checking new information against old rules and revising them when they no longer work.

top-down processing: students begin with complex problems to solve and then work out or discover (with guidance) the basic skills required.

themselves, to wrestle with ideas. Mr. Dunbar could have told his students that the formula for the volume of a cylinder is $\pi r^2 h$. With practice the students would have been able to feed numbers into this formula and grind out correct answers. But how much would it mean to them, and how well could they apply the *ideas* behind the formula to other problems? The task of education is not to pour information into the heads of students, but to engage students' minds with powerful and useful concepts. The focus of this chapter is on ways of doing this.

What Is the Constructivist View of Learning?

One of the most important principles of educational psychology is that teachers cannot simply give students knowledge. Students must construct knowledge in their own minds. The teacher can facilitate this process, by teaching in ways that make information meaningful and relevant to students, by giving students opportunities to discover or apply ideas themselves, and by teaching students to be aware of and consciously use their own strategies for learning. They can give students ladders that lead to higher understandings, yet the students themselves must climb these ladders.

A revolution is taking place in educational psychology. This revolution goes by many names, but the name most frequently used is **constructivist theories of learning.** The essence of constructivist theory is the idea that learners must individually discover and transform complex information if they are to make it their own (Brooks, 1990; Leinhardt, 1992; Brown *et al.*,1989). Constructivist theory sees learners as constantly checking new information against old rules and then revising the rules when they no longer work. This view has profound implications for teaching, as it suggests a far more active role for students in their own learning than is typical in the great majority of classrooms.

Historical Roots of Constructivism. The constructivist revolution has deep roots in the history of education. It draws heavily on the work of Piaget and Vygotsky (recall Chapter 2), both of whom emphasized that cognitive change only takes place when previous conceptions go through a process of disequilibration in light of new information. Piaget and Vygotsky also emphasized the social nature of learning and both suggested the use of mixed-ability learning groups to promote conceptual change. Later, Bruner (1966) advocated discovery learning, the use of instructional approaches in which students learn from their own active explorations of concepts and principles. Bruner put it this way:

> We teach a subject not to produce little living libraries on that subject, but rather to get a student to think . . . for himself, to consider matters as an historian does, to take part in the process of knowledge-getting. Knowing is a process, not a product. (1966, p. 72)

Top-Down Processing. Constructivist approaches to teaching emphasize top-down rather than bottom-up instruction. "Top-down" means that students begin with complex problems to solve and then work out or discover (with the teacher's guidance) the basic skills required. For example, students might be asked to write compositions and only later learn about spelling, grammar, and punctuation. This **top-down processing** approach is contrasted with the traditional bottom-up strategy in which basic skills are gradually built into more complex skills. In top-down teaching, the tasks students begin with are complex, complete, and "authentic,"

According to the constructivist view, how could this special education teacher present and follow up this cucumber preparation lesson in a way that stimulates top-down processing?

Connections

Constructivism has been defined previously in connection with constructivist views of development (Chapter 2), and constructivist views in relation to behavioral and social learning theories (Chapter 5).

In practical terms, scaffolding may include giving students more structure at the beginning of a set of lessons and gradually turning responsibility over to them to operate on their own (Palincsar, 1986a; Rosenshine and Meister, 1992). For example, students can be taught to generate their own questions about material they are reading. Early on, the teacher might suggest the questions, modeling the kinds of questions students might ask, but later students take over the question-generating task. The next section describes questioning strategies that can be directly taught to students.

Self-Check

Develop a three-column chart comparing and contrasting discovery learning, reception learning, and assisted learning in terms of the following categories of information: Major Theorist; Main Goals; Role of Students; Role of Teacher; Chief Methods. How will you use your chart to defend the idea that the three instructional models represent different approaches to the same constructivist ends?

How Do Metacognitive Skills Help Students Learn?

The term **metacognition** means knowledge about one's own learning (Flavell, 1985; Garner and Alexander, 1989), or knowing how to learn. Thinking skills and study skills are examples of **metacognitive skills.** Students can be taught strategies for assessing their own understanding, figuring out how much time they will need to study something, and choosing an effective plan of attack to study or solve problems. For example, in reading this book, you are bound to come across a paragraph that on first reading you don't understand. What do you do? Perhaps you reread the paragraph more slowly. Perhaps you look for other clues, such as pictures, graphs, or glossary terms to help you understand. Perhaps you read further back in the chapter to see if your difficulty arose because you did not fully understand something that came earlier. These are all examples of metacognitive strategies; you have learned how to know when you are not understanding and how to correct yourself (Zimmerman and Schunk, 1989). Another metacognitive strategy is the ability to predict what is likely to happen or to tell what is sensible and what is not. For example, when you first read the word "reinforcer" in Chapter 5, you knew right away that this did not refer to the little gummed circles of the same name because you knew that meaning would not fit in the context of this book.

Questioning Strategies

While most students do gradually develop adequate metacognitive skills, others do not. Teaching metacognitive strategies to students can lead to a marked improvement in their achievement. Students can learn to think about their own thinking processes and apply specific learning strategies to think themselves through difficult tasks (Pressley *et al.*, 1990, 1992). Often, this involves teaching students to look for common elements in a given type of task and to ask themselves questions about these elements. For example, many researchers (*e.g.,* Dimino *et al.,*

metacognition: knowledge about one's own learning, or knowing how to learn and monitoring one's own learning behaviors to determine the degree of progress and strategies needed for accomplishing instructional goals.

metacognitive skills: student's knowledge of how much time will be needed to study something and how to study or problem-solve; for example, thinking skills and study skills.

1990; Stevens *et al.*, 1987) have taught students to look for characters, settings, problems, and problem solutions in stories, starting with specific questions and then letting students find these critical elements on their own. Paris *et al.* (1984) and King (1992a) found that students comprehended better if they were taught to ask themselves *who, what, where,* and *how* questions as they read. Englert *et al.* (1991) gave students planning sheets to help them plan creative writing. Among the questions students were taught to ask themselves were "For whom am I writing? What is being explained? What are the steps?" Essentially, students are taught to talk themselves through the activities they are engaged in, asking themselves or each other the questions a teacher would ask. Students have been successfully taught to talk themselves through mathematics problem solving (Cardelle-Elawar, 1990), spelling (Block and Peskowitz, 1990), creative writing (Zellermayer *et al.*, 1991), and many other subjects (see Chan *et al.*, 1992; Guthrie *et al.*, 1991).

Reciprocal Teaching

One well-researched example of a constructivist approach based on principles of question-generation is **reciprocal teaching** (Palincsar and Brown, 1984). This approach, designed primarily to help low achievers learn reading comprehension, involves the teacher working with small groups of students. Initially the teacher models questions students might ask as they read, but soon students are appointed to act as "teacher" to generate questions for each other. Figure 7.2 presents an example of reciprocal teaching in use. Note in the example how the teacher directs the conversation about crows at first, but then turns the responsibility over to Jim (who is about to turn it over to another student as the example ends). The teacher is modeling the behaviors she wants the students to be able to do on their own and then changes her role to that of facilitator and organizer as the students begin to generate the actual questions. Research on reciprocal teaching has generally found this strategy to increase the achievement of low achievers (Palincsar and Brown, 1984; Palincsar, 1987; Lysynchuk *et al.*, 1990; Rosenshine and Meister, 1991).

Theory Into Practice

Introducing Reciprocal Teaching

In introducing reciprocal teaching to students, you might begin as follows: "For the coming weeks we will be working together to improve your ability to understand what you read. Sometimes we are so busy figuring out what the words are that we fail to pay much attention to what the words and sentences mean. We will be learning a way to pay more attention to what we are reading. I will teach you to do the following activities as you read:

1. To think of important questions that might be asked about what is being read and to be sure that you can answer those questions.

2. To summarize the most important information that you have read.

3. To predict what the author might discuss next in the passage.

4. To point out when something is unclear in the passage or doesn't make sense and then to see if we can make sense of it.

> **reciprocal teaching:** based on the principles of question generation, teaches metacognitive skills through instruction and teacher modeling to improve the reading performance of students who have poor comprehension.

in the following way _____

_____."

- "From the title of the passage, I would predict that the author will discuss

_____."

- If *appropriate,* "When I read this part, I found the following to be unclear

_____."

5. Invite the students to make comments regarding your teaching and the passage. For example:

- "Was there more important information?"

- "Does anyone have more to add to my prediction?"

- "Did anyone find something else confusing?"

6. Assign the next segment to be read silently. Choose a student to act as teacher for this segment. Begin with students who are more verbal and who you suspect will have less difficulty with the activities.

7. Coach the student "teacher" through the activities as necessary. Encourage the other students to participate in the dialogue, but always give the student "teacher" for that segment the opportunity to go first and lead the dialogue. Be sure to give the student "teacher" plenty of feedback and praise for his or her participation.

8. As the training days go by, try to remove yourself more and more from the dialogue so that the student "teacher" initiates the activities himself or herself and other students provide feedback. Your role will continue to be monitoring, keeping students on track, helping them over obstacles. Throughout the training, however, continue to take your turn as teacher, modeling at least once a session.

Self-Check

Define metacognition, then explain how each of the following student behaviors is an example of the effective use of metacognitive abilities to promote learning.

using context clues	self-talking
predicting	generating questions
problem solving	using study strategies
reciprocal teaching	

How Do Cognitive Teaching Strategies Help Students Learn?

In *Alice in Wonderland* the white rabbit is unsure how to tell his story in the trial of the Knave of Hearts. The King of Hearts gives him a bit of advice: "Begin at the beginning . . . and go on until you come to the end: then stop."

The "King of Hearts method" is a common means of delivering lectures, especially at the secondary and college levels. However, teachers can do more to help their students understand lessons. They can prepare students to learn new material by reminding them of what they already know, they can use questions, and they can help students link and recall new information. Many aspects of effective lesson presentation are covered in Chapter 8, but the following sections discuss practices derived from cognitive psychology that can help students understand, recall, and apply essential information, concepts, and skills.

Making Learning Relevant/Activating Prior Knowledge

Read the following passage.

> With the hocked gems financing him our hero bravely defied all scornful laughter that tried to prevent his scheme. Your eyes deceive he had said. An egg, not a table, correctly typifies this unexplored planet. Now three sturdy sisters sought proof. Forging along, sometimes through calm vastness, yet more often through turbulent peaks and valleys, days became weeks as many doubters spread fearful rumors about the edge. At last, from nowhere, welcome winged creatures appeared signifying momentous success. (Dooling and Lachman, 1971, p. 217)

Now read the paragraph again with the following information: The passage is about Christopher Columbus. Before you knew what the passage was about, it probably made little sense to you. You could understand the words and grammar and could probably infer that the story involved a voyage of discovery. However, once you learned that the story was about Columbus, you could bring all your prior knowledge about Columbus to bear on comprehending the paragraph, so that seemingly obscure references made sense. The "hocked gems" (Queen Isabella's jewelry), the egg (the shape of the earth), the three sturdy sisters (*Niña, Pinta, Santa Maria*), and the winged creatures (birds) become comprehensible when you know what the story is about.

In terms of schema theory, advance information that the story concerns Columbus activates your schema relating to Columbus. You are ready to receive and incorporate information relating to Columbus, to Isabella and Ferdinand, and to the ships. It is as though you had a filing cabinet with a drawer labeled "Columbus." When you know you are about to hear about Columbus, you mentally open the drawer, which contains files marked "Isabella," "ships," and "scoffers and doubters." You are now ready to file new information in the proper places. If you learned that the Santa Maria was wrecked in a storm, you would mentally file that information under "ships." If you learned that most of the educated world agreed with Columbus that the earth was round, you would file that information under "scoffers and doubters." The file drawer analogy is not completely appropriate, however, because the "files" of a schema are all logically connected with one another. Also, you are actively using the information in your "files" to interpret and organize the new information.

Advance Organizers. David Ausubel (1960, 1963) developed a means called **advance organizers** to orient students to material they were about to learn and to help them recall related information that could be used to assist in incorporating the new information. As outlined earlier in this chapter, an advance organizer is an initial statement about a subject to be learned that provides a structure for the new information and relates it to information students already possess. For example, in one study (Ausubel and Youssef, 1963) college students were assigned to read a passage on Buddhism. Before reading the passage, some students were given an

Connections
Giving effective lessons includes making learning relevant, activating prior knowledge, elaborating and organizing information, and using questioning techniques. Steps in giving an effective lesson are elaborated in Chapter 8.

advance organizers: general statements given before instruction that relate new information to existing knowledge.

advance organizer comparing Buddhism to Christianity, while others read an unrelated passage. The students who were given the advance organizer retained much more of the material than did the other students. Ausubel and Youssef maintained that the reason for this was that the advance organizer activated most students' knowledge of Christianity, and the students were able to use that knowledge to incorporate information about a less familiar religion.

Many studies have established that advance organizers increase students' understanding of certain kinds of material (see, for example, Corkill, 1992; Glover *et al.,* 1990; Mayer, 1984). Advance organizers seem to be most useful for teaching content that has a well-organized structure that may not be immediately apparent to students. However, they have not generally been found to help students learn factual information that does not lend itself to a clear organization or subjects that consist of a large number of separate topics (Corkill, 1992; Mayer, 1984; Ausubel, 1978). In addition, methods that activate prior knowledge (such as advance organizers) can be counterproductive if the prior knowledge is weak or lacking (Alvermann *et al.,*1985). If students know little about Christianity, relating Buddhism to Christianity might confuse rather than help them. Here is a classic example of a helpful advance organizer:

> A docent (teacher-guide) beginning a tour of an art museum with a group of high school students says, "I want to give you an idea that will help you understand the paintings and sculpture we are about to see. The idea is simply that art, although it is a personal expression, reflects in many ways the culture and times in which it was produced. This may seem obvious to you at first when you look at the differences between Oriental and Western art. However, it is also true that, within each culture, as the culture changes, so the art will change—and that is why we can speak of *periods* of art. The changes are often reflected in the artists' techniques, subject matter, colors, and style. Major changes are often reflected in the forms of art that are produced." The guide then points out examples of one or two changes in these characteristics. She also asks the students to recall their elementary school days and the differences in their drawings when they were five and six and when they were older. She likens the different periods of growing up to different cultures.
>
> In the tour that follows, as the students look at paintings and sculpture, the docent points out to them the differences that result from changing times. "Do you see here," she says, "how in this painting the body of the person is almost completely covered by his robes, and there is no hint of a human inside his clothes? In medieval times, the church taught that the body was unimportant and that the soul was everything." Later she remarks, "You see in this painting how the muscularity of the man stands out through his clothing and how he stands firmly on the earth. This represents the Renaissance view that man was at the center of the universe and that his body, mind, and his power were very important indeed." (Joyce and Weil, 1986, p. 70).

Note that the guide first gave her students an organizing framework for understanding the paintings they were about to see: Art reflects aspects of the culture and times in which it was produced. She also related the concept of periods in art history to the students' own experiences by reminding them of how their own artwork changed over time. Thus the guide activated prior knowledge and provided an organizational schema into which information on the paintings themselves would fit. Finally, when the students actually saw some paintings and sculpture, the guide pointed out particulars that related to the schema she had presented earlier.

While the use of advance organizers is a valuable strategy in its own right, research on advance organizers illustrates a broader principle that is extremely important: Activating prior knowledge enhances understanding and retention (Pressley *et al.*,1992b). Strategies other than advance organizers draw on this same principle. For example, having students discuss what they already know about a topic before they learn it (Pressley *et al.*, 1990) and making predictions about material to be learned (Fielding *et al.*, 1990) are additional instances of means of getting students to make conscious use of prior knowledge. In the scenario at the beginning of this chapter, for example, Mr. Dunbar asked students to recall what they had learned about the areas of circles and the volumes of cubes as a way to get students to use background knowledge to help solve their problem.

Analogies. Like advance organizers, use of explanatory **analogies** can contribute to an understanding of the lessons or the text. For example, a teacher could introduce a lesson on the human body's disease-fighting mechanism by telling students to imagine a battle and to consider it as an analogy for the body's fight against infection. Similarly, a teacher could preface a lesson on termite societies by asking students to think of the hierarchy of citizens within a kingdom, using that as an analogy for such insect societies. Analogies can help students learn new information by relating it to concepts they already have (Vosniadou and Schommer, 1988; Genter, 1989; Zook, 1991).

One interesting study (Halpern *et al.*,1990) found that analogies work best when they are most different from the process being explained. For example, college students' learning about the lymph system was aided more by an analogy of the movement of water through a sponge than by one involving the movement of blood through veins. What this probably illustrates is that it is more important that analogies be thoroughly familiar to the learner than that they relate in any direct way to the concepts being taught.

Elaborations. Cognitive psychologists use the term **elaboration** to refer to the process of thinking about material to be learned in a way that connects the material to information or ideas already in the learner's mind (Reigeluth, 1983). As an example of the importance of elaboration, Stein *et al.* (1984) conducted a series of experiments in which students were given lists of phrases to learn, such as "The gray-haired man carried the bottle." Some students were given the same phrases embedded in a more elaborated sentence: "The gray-haired man carried the bottle *of hair dye.*" These students recalled the phrases much better than did those who did not receive the elaboration because the additional words tied the phrase to a well-developed schema already in the students' minds. The connection between "gray-haired man" and "bottle" is arbitrary until we give it meaning by linking these words with the "hair dye" idea.

The principle that elaborated information is easier to understand and remember can be applied to helping students comprehend lessons. Students may be asked to think of connections between ideas or to relate new concepts to their own lives. For example, it might help students to understand the U.S. annexation of Texas and California if they consider these events from the perspective of Mexicans or if they compare them to a situation in which a friend borrows a seldom used bicycle and then decides not to give it back. In discussing a story or novel, students might be asked from time to time to stop and visualize what is happening or what's about to happen as a means of helping them elaborate their understanding of the material. Elaboration can be taught as a skill to help students comprehend what they read (Weinstein *et al.*, 1988/89).

analogies: pointing out the similarities between things that are otherwise unlike, to help students learn new information by relating it to concepts they already have.

elaboration: the process of thinking about new material in a way that helps to connect it with existing knowledge.

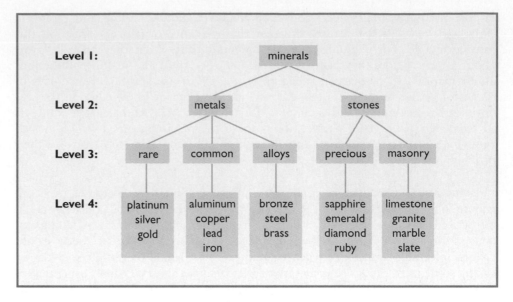

Figure 7.3   The Hierarchical Structure for Minerals
From Bower *et al.,* 1969.

Organizing Information

Recall the shopping list presented in Chapter 6. When the list was presented in random order, it was very difficult to memorize, partly because it contained too many items to be held in short-term memory all at once. However, when the list was organized in a logical way, it was meaningful and therefore easy to learn and remember. The specific foods were grouped in familiar recipes (for example, flour, eggs, and milk were grouped under "pancakes"), the recipes and other foods were grouped under "food," "beverage," or "dessert," and these were in turn grouped under "breakfast," "lunch," and "dinner."

Material that is well organized is much easier to learn and remember than material that is poorly organized (Durso and Coggins, 1991). Hierarchical organization, in which specific issues are grouped under more general topics, seems particularly helpful for student understanding (Van Patten *et al.,*1986). For example, in a study by Bower *et al.* (1969), one group of students was taught 112 words relating to minerals in random order. Another group was taught the same words, but in a definite order. Figure 7.3 shows some of the words organized in a hierarchy. The students were taught the words at levels 1 and 2 in the first of four sessions; those at levels 1, 2, and 3 in the second session; and levels 1 to 4 in the third and fourth sessions. The students in this second group recalled an average of 100 words, in comparison to only 65 for the group receiving the random presentation, demonstrating the effectiveness of a coherent, organized presentation.

In teaching complex concepts, it is not only necessary that material be well organized; it is also important that the organizing framework itself be made clear to students (Shimmerlik, 1978; Kallison, 1986). For example, in teaching about the minerals shown in Figure 7.3 the teacher might refer frequently to the framework and mark transitions from one part of it to another, as follows:

"Recall that *alloys* are combinations of two or more *metals*."

"Now that we've covered *rare* and *common metals* and *alloys*, let's move on to the second category of minerals: *stones*."

Using Questioning Techniques.   One strategy that helps students learn from written texts, lectures, and other sources of information is the insertion of questions, so that students must stop from time to time to assess their own understanding of what the text or teacher is saying (Pressley *et al.,* 1990; Rickards, 1979; Crooks, 1988). However, questions presented *before* the introduction of the instructional material can help students learn material related to the questions but hinder them in learning material that is not related to the questions (Hamilton, 1985; Hamaker, 1986). The solution is to ask questions about *all* important information. In addition, factual questions that paraphrase, rather than repeat, the instructional text help students learn the meaning of the text instead of simply memorizing it (Andre and Sola, 1976; Andre and Womack, 1978).

Using Conceptual Models.   Another means that teachers can use to help students comprehend complex topics is the introduction of diagrams showing how elements of a process relate to one another. Figure 6.1, which illustrates information processing, is a classic example of a conceptual model. Use of such models organizes and integrates information. Examples of topics that lend themselves to use of conceptual models include the study of electricity, mechanics, computer programming, and the processes by which laws are passed. When models are part of a lesson, students not only learn more, but they are also better able to apply their learning to creatively solve problems (see Mayer, 1989; Mayer and Gallini, 1990; Winn, 1991; Hiebert *et al.,*1991).

What study strategy is this student using? What will determine the extent to which the student will use this strategy effectively?

Self-Check

Identify the general purpose of each set below of cognitive teaching strategies, and then give a classroom example illustrating the use of each strategy. How could you illustrate all the strategies in the context of one particular lesson you might teach?

1. advance organizer, analogy, elaboration
2. questioning, conceptual model

What Study Stategies Help Students Learn?

How are you reading this book? Are you underlining or highlighting key sentences? Are you taking notes or summarizing? Are you discussing the main ideas with a classmate? Are you putting the book under your pillow at night and hoping the information will somehow seep into your mind? These and many other strategies have been used by students since the invention of reading and have been studied almost as long; even Aristotle wrote on the topic. Yet educational psychologists are still debating which study strategies are most effective.

Research on effective study strategies is confusing at best. Few forms of studying are *always* found to be effective, and fewer still are *never* effective. Clearly, the

Connections

The guidelines for study skills apply to everyone who wishes to become an expert learner. They involve the metacognitive abilities and executive control processes discussed in this chapter and in Chapter 6.

value of study strategies depends on their specifics and on the uses to which they are put. Thomas and Rohwer (1986) have proposed a set of principles of effective studying that apply across particular study methods. These are as follows:

1. Specificity: Study strategies must be appropriate to the learning objectives and the types of students with whom they are used. For example, research has found that the same strategies work differently with older and younger students or with high and low achievers. Writing summaries for others to read may be an effective study method, but it is probably too difficult for young children (Hidi and Anderson, 1986).

2. Generativity: One of the most important principles of effective study strategies is that they should involve reworking the material studied, generating something new. This activity forces students to engage in a high level of mental processing, which probably must occur for any study strategy to be effective. Examples of strategies that use a high degree of generativity are writing summaries and generating questions for others, organizing notes into outlines, diagramming relationships among main ideas, and teaching partners about text contents. Strategies low in generativity, such as indiscriminate underlining, taking notes without having to identify main ideas, or writing extensive summaries without having to focus on what is important, have been less successful in helping students learn.

3. Effective Monitoring: The principle of effective monitoring simply means that students should know how and when to apply their study strategies and how to tell if they are working for them (Nist *et al.,* 1991).

4. Personal Efficacy: Students must have a clear sense that studying will pay off for them if they are to work hard at it. Teachers can create a sense that studying will pay off by giving frequent quizzes and tests based directly on the material students have studied and by making performance on these assessments a major portion of students' grades.

Note Taking

A common study strategy used both in reading and in learning from lectures is note taking. This can be effective for certain types of material because it can require mental processing of main ideas; as in the case of underlining only one sentence per paragraph, note taking requires decisions about what to write. However, the effects of note taking have been found to be inconsistent. Positive effects are most likely when note taking is used with complex, conceptual material in which the critical task is to identify the main ideas (Anderson and Armbruster, 1984). Also, note taking that requires some mental processing is more effective than simply writing down what was read (Kiewra *et al.,*1991; Kiewra, 1991). For example, Bretzing and Kulhavy (1981) found that writing paraphrase notes (stating the main ideas in different words) and taking notes in preparation to teach others the material were effective note-taking strategies because they required a high degree of mental processing of the information.

One apparently effective means of increasing the value of students' note taking is for the teacher to provide "skeletal" notes before a lecture or reading, giving students categories to direct their own note taking. Several studies have found that this practice, combined with student note taking and review, increases student learning (Kiewra, 1991).

Underlining. Perhaps the most common study strategy is underlining or highlighting. Yet despite the widespread use of this method, research on it generally finds few benefits (Anderson and Armbruster, 1984; Snowman, 1984). The problem is that most students fail to make decisions about what material is most critical and simply underline too much. When students are asked to underline the *one* sentence in each paragraph that is most important, they do retain more, probably because deciding which is the most important sentence requires a higher level of processing (Snowman, 1984).

Summarizing. Summarization involves writing brief statements that represent the main idea of the information being read. The effectiveness of this strategy depends on how it is used (Hidi and Anderson, 1986; King, 1991). One effective way is to have students write one-sentence summaries after reading each paragraph (Wittrock, 1991). Another is to have students prepare summaries intended to help others learn the material, partly because this activity forces the summarizer to be brief and to seriously consider what is important and what is not (Brown *et al.*, 1983). However, it is important to note that several studies have found no effects of summarization, and the conditions under which this strategy increases comprehension or retention of written material are not well understood (Anderson and Armbruster, 1984; Snowman, 1984; Wittrock, 1991; Wittrock and Alesandrini, 1990).

Outlining and Mapping. A related family of study strategies requires the student to represent the material studied in skeletal form. These strategies include outlining, networking, and mapping. Outlining presents the main points of the material in a hierarchical format, with each detail organized under a higher-level category, as in Figure 7.3 on minerals. In networking and mapping, students identify main ideas and then diagram connections between them. For example, the schematic representation of the concept "bison" shown in Figure 6.5 might have been produced by students themselves as a network to summarize factual material about bison and their importance to Native Americans of the Plains (see Clarke, 1990; Rafoth *et al.*,1993).

Research on outlining, networking, and mapping is limited and inconsistent, but generally finds that these methods are helpful as study aids (Anderson and Armbruster, 1984; Van Patten *et al.*,1986).

Cooperative Scripting

Many students find it helpful to get together with classmates to discuss material they have read or heard in class. A formalization of this age-old practice has been researched by Dansereau and his colleagues (1985). In it, students work in pairs and take turns summarizing sections of the material for one another. While one student summarizes, the other listens and corrects any errors or omissions. Then the two students switch roles, continuing in this way until they have covered all the material to be learned. A series of studies of this **cooperative scripts** method has consistently found that students who study this way learn and retain far more than students who summarize on their own or who simply read the material (for example, McDonald *et al.*, 1985). It is interesting that while both participants in the cooperative pairs gain from the activity, the larger gains are for the sections students taught to their partners rather than those for which they served as listeners (Spurlin *et al.*,1984).

cooperative scripts: a study method in which students work in pairs and take turns orally summarizing sections of material to be learned.

Theory Into Practice

Using Cooperative Scripting

In the study strategy called cooperative scripting, students work in pairs and take turns playing roles as "recaller" and "listener." The specific instructions given to college students using the cooperative scripts method are as follows (adapted from Spurlin *et al.*, 1984):

1. Decide by coin flip who will serve first as *recaller* and who will serve as *listener*.

2. At the end of each major section (500 to 600 words), stop reading.

3. The *recaller* summarizes aloud what has been read as completely as possible *without looking at the passage*. The recaller should try to include all of the important ideas and facts in the summary.

4. After the recaller has completed the summary, the *listener* should do the following while looking at the passage:

   a. To improve your own and your partner's understanding of the passage, correct your partner's summary by discussing the important information he or she did not include, and point out any ideas or facts that were summarized incorrectly.

   b. Help yourself and your partner to remember the material better by coming up with *clever* ways of memorizing the important ideas or facts. One way to do this is to relate the information to earlier material and to other things you know. You can also use drawings and mental pictures to aid memory.

5. The recaller can help the listener in correcting and memorizing the summary.

6. After completing and discussing the summary, switch roles as recaller and listener, read the next major section, and then follow the same procedures. Keep switching roles, summarizing, and discussing summaries until you have completed the material.

In assigning students to use cooperative scripts, teachers should establish in advance how much material is to be read before students stop to summarize. With younger students or with difficult material, the passage lengths should be kept short. Note that research establishing the effectiveness of cooperative scripts has taken place entirely at the college level, and therefore applies most directly to college students and perhaps to secondary students. However, related cooperative learning methods that involve partner reading and discussion have been successfully used at the elementary level (Stevens *et al.*, 1987).

The PQ4R Method

PQ4R: a method for studying text that involves six steps: Preview, Question, Read, Reflect, Recite, Review.

One of the best known study techniques for helping students understand and remember what they read is a procedure called the **PQ4R Method** (Thomas and Robinson, 1972), which is based on an earlier version known as SQ3R, developed by F. P. Robinson (1961). The acronym means Preview, Question, Read, Reflect, Recite, and Review.

Research has shown the effectiveness of the PQ4R method for older children (Adams *et al.*,1982), and the reasons seem clear. Following the PQ4R procedure focuses students on the meaningful organization of information and involves students in other effective strategies, such as question generation, elaboration, and "distributed practice," opportunities to review information over a period of time (Anderson, 1990).

Theory Into Practice

Teaching the PQ4R Method

Explain and model the steps of the PQ4R method for your older students, using the following guidelines.

1. Preview: *Survey* or *scan* the material quickly to get an idea of the general organization and major topics and subtopics. Pay attention to headings and subheadings, and identify what you will be reading about and studying.

2. Question: Ask yourself questions about the material as you read it. Use headings to invent questions using the "wh" words: who, what, why, where.

3. Read: Read the material. Do not take extensive written notes. Try to answer the questions you posed while reading.

4. Reflect on the Material: Try to understand and make meaningful the presented information by (1) relating it to things you already know; (2) relating the subtopics in the text to primary concepts or principles; (3) trying to resolve contradictions within the presented information; and (4) trying to use the material to solve simulated problems suggested by the material.

5. Recite: Practice remembering the information by stating points out loud and asking and answering questions. You may use headings, highlighted words, and notes on major ideas to generate those questions.

6. Review: In the final step actively review the material, focusing on asking yourself questions and rereading the material only when you are not sure of the answers.

Self-Check

Brainstorm and list six study strategies that are effective in promoting learning; then review to make sure you have included all the ones this section treats as important. Develop a plan with steps you would use for directly teaching to your students each study strategy in your list.

How Do Students Learn and Transfer Concepts?

Much meaningful learning involves the learning of **concepts**. A concept is a category under which specific elements may be grouped. For example, a red

concepts: categories into which objects, ideas, and experiences may be grouped.

ball, a red pencil, and a red chair are all instances of the simple concept "red." A green book is a non instance of the concept "red." If you were shown the red ball, pencil, and chair and asked to say what they have in common, you would produce the concept "red objects." If the green book were also included, you would have to fall back on the much broader concept "objects."

Of course, many concepts are far more complex and less well defined than the concept "red." For example, the concept "justice" is one that people may spend a lifetime trying to understand. This book is engaged primarily in teaching concepts; in fact, at this very moment you are reading about the concept "concept"!

Concept Learning and Teaching

Concepts are generally learned in one of two ways. Most concepts that we learn outside of school we learn by observation. For example, a child learns the concept "car" by hearing certain vehicles referred to as a "car." Initially, the child might include pickup trucks or motorcycles under the concept "car," but as time goes on, the concept is refined until the child can clearly differentiate "car" from "noncar." Similarly, the child learns the more difficult concepts "naughty," "clean," or "fun" by observation and experience.

Other concepts are typically learned by definition. For example, it is very difficult to learn the concepts "aunt" or "uncle" by observation alone. One could observe hundreds of "aunts" and "nonaunts" without deriving a clear concept of "aunt." In this case, the concept is best learned by definition: To be an aunt, one must be a female whose brother or sister (or brother- or sister-in-law) has children. With this definition, instances and noninstances of "aunt" can be readily differentiated.

Definitions.   Just as concepts can be learned in two ways, so can they be taught in two ways. Students may be given instances and noninstances of a concept and later asked to derive or infer a definition. Or students may be given a definition and then asked to identify instances and noninstances. Some concepts lend themselves to the example-definition approach. For most concepts taught in school, it makes most sense to state a definition, present several instances (and noninstances, if appropriate), and then restate the definition, showing how the instances typify the definition. Use of this pattern, called **rule-example-rule,** has been found to be characteristic of instructionally effective teachers (see Chapter 8). For example, the concept "learning" might be defined as "a change in an individual caused by experience." Instances might include learning of skills, of information, of behaviors, and of emotions. Noninstances might include maturational changes, such as changes in behaviors or emotions caused by the onset of puberty. Finally, the definition might be restated and discussed in light of the instances and noninstances.

Examples.   Teaching concepts involves extensive and skillful use of examples. Tennyson and Park (1980, p. 59) suggest that teachers follow three rules when presenting examples of concepts:

1. Order the examples from easy to difficult.
2. Select examples that differ from one another.
3. Compare and contrast examples and nonexamples.

Consider the concept "mammal." Easy examples are dogs, cats, and humans, and nonexamples are insects, reptiles, and fish. No problem so far. But what about

rule-example-rule: pattern of teaching concepts by presenting a rule or definition, giving examples, and then showing how examples illustrate the rule.

dolphins? Bats? Snakes that bear live young? Kangaroos? Each of these is a more difficult example or nonexample of the concept "mammal" because it challenges the simplistic belief, based on experience, that terrestrial animals that bear live young are mammals, while fish, birds, and other eggs layers are not. The easy examples (dogs versus fish) establish the concept in general, but the more difficult examples (snakes versus whales) test the true boundaries of the concept. Students should thoroughly understand simple examples before tackling the odd cases.

Teaching for Transfer of Learning

Students often get so wrapped up in preparing for tests, and teachers in preparing students to take tests, that both forget what the primary purpose of school is: to give students the skills and knowledge necessary for them to function effectively as adults. If a student can fill in blanks on a language arts test but cannot write a clear letter to a friend or a prospective employer, or can multiply with decimals and percents on a math test but cannot figure sales tax, then that student's education has been sadly misdirected. Yet all too frequently students who do very well in school or on tests are unable to transfer their knowledge or skills to real-life situations.

"Real-Life" Learning. Some principles of **transfer of learning** were discussed in Chapter 5 in relation to *generalization*. Essentially, transfer of learning from one situation to another depends on the degree to which the information or skills were learned in the original situation, and on the degree of similarity between the situation in which the skill or concept was learned and the situation to which it is to be applied. These rather obvious principles, known since the beginning of the twentieth century (Thorndike and Woodworth, 1901), have important implications for teaching. We cannot simply assume that students will be able to transfer their school learning to practical situations, so we must teach them to use skills in situations like those they are likely to encounter in real life or in other situations to which we expect learning to transfer. Students must be given specific instruction in how to use their skills and information to solve problems and be exposed to a variety of problem-solving experiences if they are to be able to apply much of what they learned in school.

The most important thing to know about transfer of learning is that it cannot be assumed. Just because a student has mastered a skill or concept in one setting or circumstance, there is no guarantee whatsoever that the student will be able to apply this skill or concept to a new setting, even if the setting seems (at least to the teacher) to be very similar (Butterfield, 1988). For example, Lave (1988) describes a man in a weight loss program who was faced with the problem of measuring out a serving of cottage cheese that was three quarters of the usual two-thirds cup allowance. The man, who had passed college calculus, measured out two-thirds of a cup of cottage cheese, dumped it out in a circle on a cutting board, marked a cross on it, and scooped away one quadrant. It never occurred to him to multiply $2/3 \times 3/4 = 1/2$, an operation any sixth grader could do on paper (but few could apply in a practical situation).

Learning in Context. If transfer of learning depends in large part on similarity between the situation in which information is learned and that in which it is applied, then how can we teach in the school setting so that students will be able to apply their knowledge in the very different setting of real life?

As a teacher, what steps would you take to teach this child the concept "five"? What examples and nonexamples might you use as part of your lesson? How would you determine if the student knew the concept well enough to transfer her learning?

Connections

Recall the discussion of generalization in Chapter 5. Through generalization, transfer of learning also enlarges the knowledge base on which future learning relies.

transfer of learning: the application of knowledge acquired in one situation to new situations.

Concept to be taught: *Minge*
Definition: To gang up on a person or thing.

Same-Context Examples	Varied-Context Examples
• The three riders decided to converge on the cow.	• The band of sailors angrily denounced the captain and threatened a mutiny.
• Four people took part in branding the horse.	• A group in the audience booed the inept magician's act.
• They circled the wolf so it would not escape.	• The junk dealer was helpless to defend himself from the three thieves.
• All six cowboys fought against the rustler.	• All six cowboys fought against the rustler.

Table 7.1   Teaching of Concepts

Research demonstrates that to teach new concepts, teachers should first present examples of the concept used in similar contexts and then offer examples in widely different contexts. This approach promotes the students' abilities to transfer the concept to new situations. The following example comes from a classic study in which students learned new concepts from the traditional culture of cowboys.

Source: Adapted from Nitsch, 1977.

One important principle of transfer is that the ability to apply knowledge in new circumstances depends in part on the variety of circumstances in which we have learned or practiced the information or skill (Salomon and Perkins, 1989). For example, a few weeks' experience as a parking attendant, driving all sorts of cars, would probably be better than years of experience driving one kind of car for enabling a person to drive a completely new and different car (at least in a parking lot!).

In teaching concepts, one way to increase the chance that the concepts will be appropriately applied to new situations is to give examples from a range of situations. A set of classic experiments by Nitsch (1977) illustrated this principle. Students were given definitions of words and were then presented with examples to illustrate the concepts. Some were given several examples in the same context, while others received examples from mixed contexts. For example, "minge" is a cowboy word meaning "to gang up on." The examples are shown in Table 7.1.

Students given only the same-context examples were able to identify additional examples in the same context, but were less successful in applying the concepts to new contexts. On the other hand, the students who learned with the varied-context examples had some difficulties in learning the concept at first, but once they did, they were able to apply it to new situations. The best strategy was a hybrid in which students were given the same-context examples first and then the varied-context examples.

Transfer versus Initial Learning.   The tricky aspect of teaching for transfer is that the procedures for enhancing transfer are exactly the opposite of those for initial learning. As the Nitsch (1977) study illustrated, teaching a concept in many different contexts was confusing to students if it was done at the beginning of a sequence of instruction, but it enhanced transfer if done after students understood the concept in one setting. The implications of this principle for teaching are

What strategies have you used to encourage creative problem solving among your students?

As a student teacher, I had been teaching a sixth-grade science unit on light, and my supervisor was observing as I demonstrated how the students could fashion a homemade prism using three microscope slides taped together to form a triangle. The prism could be filled with water by working it on both ends with modeling clay. With one end of my model already sealed, I showed the class how to pour in the water. To my absolute horror, the walls of the prism burst apart, releasing water everywhere. "I don't believe this!" I moaned. Then, determined to turn this disaster into a worthwhile lesson, I turned to the students. "How can I solve this problem?" The students responded enthusiastically. "Let's try masking tape!" "Glue?" "Use clay!" We tried all the suggestions. None worked, but the group attacked this problem with creativity and ingenuity. This made a significant impression on me. The students were actually more stimulated by this problem than by the straightforward activity I had planned. I realized that by wondering aloud what I could do to salvage the situation, I had invited suggestions rather than abandoning the activity and gave the students a chance to test out their ideas. I had validated creative thinking and underlined the importance of problem solving. This experience convinced me that children are challenged and motivated by problems that (1) invite multiple solutions; (2) have solutions that are not obvious but are perceived as possible; (3) involve strategies and thought processes that people use in nonschool situations and environments; and (4) are also intriguing and thought-provoking to teachers and adults. Now in my teaching I strive to intentionally create experiences that meet these criteria in all the content areas I teach.

Jodi Libretti, Teacher, Grades 5–6
Escondido Elementary School, Palo Alto, California

Three teaching professionals, forty-seven excited juniors, an "anywhere" classroom, and a three-hour time block—and that's APE (Algebra II, Physics I, and English III). In APE, students are involved in an integrated study to connect up what they are learning in different content areas and in the real world. From the start, students knew they would have to keep an open mind, learn about learning, get along well with others, and become successful contributing members of a small learning community. The year began with a Puritan literature research project. The students worked in groups and presented their research to the class. The one requirement was that the presentation had to inform us and capture our interest. The presentations included a "convention" (featuring slides, food, and gifts) aimed at persuading Europeans to come to the New World, commercials aimed at persuading Europeans *not* to come to America, television games, a debate, and even a Puritan assembly. The entire school was talking about what the APEs were doing. As teachers, we had permitted creativity in the expression of knowledge. This meant we had to let go of teacher-centered control and let the students think for themselves. At the same time we collaborated to develop an integrated curriculum in English, algebra, and physics. Students found out how to drop eggs from a tower without having them break, how to make human parabolas in the parking lot, and how to illustrate vocabulary words so that no one would ever forget their meaning. APE has made a significant mark on each child's attitude toward learning. Creative problem solving is now relevant for them in everyday life, and they have come to understand how they must "own" and be responsible for their own knowledge and skills.

Melissa C. Scott, Melissa I. Smith, and Sandra Taylor
Greenwood High School, Bowling Green, Kentucky

extremely important. When introducing a new concept, it is important to use *similar* examples until the concept is well understood and only then to use diverse examples that still demonstrate the essential aspects of the concept.

As one example of this, consider a series of lessons on evolution. In introducing the concept it would first be important to use clear examples of how animals evolved in ways that increased their chances of survival in their environments, using such examples as the evolution of flippers in seals or the evolution of humps in camels. Then evolution in plants (for example, evolution of a waxy skin on desert plants) might be presented, somewhat broadening the concept. The evolution of social behaviors (such as cooperation in lions, baboons, and humans) might then be discussed, and, finally, phenomena that resemble the evolutionary process (such as the modification of businesses in response to selective pressures of free-market economies) might be explored. The idea here is to first establish the idea of evolution in one clear context (animals) and to gradually broaden the concept until students can see how processes in quite different contexts demonstrate the principles of selective adaptation. If the lessons had begun with discussion of animals, plants, societies, and businesses, it would have been too confusing. If it had never moved beyond the evolution of animals, however, the concept would not have had much chance of transferring to different contexts. After learning about the concept of evolution in many different contexts, students are much more likely to be able to distinguish scientific and metaphorical uses and apply the concept to a completely new context, such as the "evolution" of art in response to changes in society.

It is important in teaching for transfer not only to provide many examples, but also to point out in each example how the essential features of the concept are reflected. In the evolution example, the central process might be explained as it applied to each particular case. The development of cooperation among lions, for example, shows how a social trait evolved because groups of lions who cooperated were better able to catch game, to survive, and to ensure that their offspring would survive. Pointing out the essential elements in each example provides a feature analysis that helps students "bridge" a concept to new instances they have never encountered (Perkins and Salomon, 1988).

Self-Check

Construct an example showing how you would use the following approaches to teach your students a particular concept: rule-example-rule; examples and nonexamples. Now explain how you would use feature analysis, generalization, and real-life applications to help students transfer their learning of that concept.

How Are Problem Solving and Thinking Skills Taught?

One indication of transfer of learning is the ability to use information and skills to solve problems. For example, a student might be quite good at adding, subtracting, and multiplying but have little idea of how to solve this problem: Sylvia bought four hamburgers at $1.25 each, two orders of french fries at 65 cents and three large sodas at 75 cents. How much change did she get from a ten-dollar bill?

Sylvia's situation is not an unusual one in real life, and the computations involved are not difficult. However, many students (and even some otherwise competent adults) would have difficulty solving this problem. The difficulty of most applications problems in mathematics lies not in the computations, but rather in knowing how to set the problem up so it can be solved. **Problem solving** is a skill that can be taught and learned (Polya, 1957; Silver, 1985).

Steps in the Problem-Solving Process

The first step in solving a problem is to identify the goal of the problem and figure out how to proceed. Newell and Simon (1972) suggest that the problem solver repeatedly ask, "What is the difference between where I am now and where I want to be? What can I do to reduce that difference?" For example, in solving Sylvia's problem, the goal is to find out how much change she will receive from a ten-dollar bill after buying food and drinks. We might then break the problem into substeps, each with its own subgoal.

1. Figure how much Sylvia spent on hamburgers.
2. Figure how much Sylvia spent on french fries.
3. Figure how much Sylvia spent on sodas.
4. Figure how much Sylvia spent in total.
5. Figure how much change Sylvia gets from $10.00.

Means-Ends Analysis.   Deciding what the problem is and what needs to be done involves a **means-ends analysis.** Learning to solve problems requires a great deal of practice with different kinds of problems that demand thought. All too often textbooks in mathematics and other subjects that include many problems fail to present problems that will make students think. For example, they might give students a set of word problems whose solutions require the multiplication of two numbers. Students soon learn that they can solve such problems by looking for any two numbers and multiplying them.

In real life, however, problems do not neatly line themselves up in categories. We may hear, "Joe Smith got a 5 percent raise last week, which amounted to $1200." If we want to figure out how much Joe was making before his raise, the hard part is not doing the calculation, but knowing what calculation is called for. In real life this problem would not be on a page titled "Dividing by Percents"!

The more different kinds of problems students learn to solve, and the more they have to think to solve them, the greater the chance that when faced with real-life problems, they will be able to transfer their skills or knowledge to the new situation.

Extracting Relevant Information.   Realistic problems are rarely neat and tidy. Imagine that Sylvia's problem had been as follows:

> Sylvia walked into the fast-food restaurant at 6:18 with three friends. Between them, they bought four hamburgers at $1.25 each, two orders of french fries at 65 cents, and three large sodas at 75 cents. Onion rings were on sale for 55 cents. Sylvia's mother told her to be in by 9:00, but she was already twenty-five minutes late by the time she and her friends left the restaurant. Sylvia drove the three miles home at an average of 30 miles per hour. How long was Sylvia in the restaurant?

The first part of this task is to clear away all the extra information to get to the important facts. The means-ends analysis suggests that only time information is

problem solving: the application of knowledge and skills to achieve certain goals.

means-ends analysis: problem-solving technique that encourages identifying the goal (ends) of a problem, the current situation, and what needs to be done (means) to reduce the difference between the two conditions.

relevant, so all the money transactions and the speed of Sylvia's car can be ignored. Careful reading of the problem reveals that Sylvia left the restaurant at 9:25. This (plus her arrival time of 6:18) is all that matters for solving the problem. Once we know what is relevant and what is not, the solution is easy.

Representing the Problem.   For many kinds of problems, graphic representation may be an effective means of finding a solution. Adams (1974) provides a story that illustrates this. A Buddhist monk has to make a pilgrimage and stay overnight in a temple that is at the top of a high mountain. The road spirals around and around the mountain. The monk begins walking up the mountain at sunrise. He walks all day long and finally reaches the top at about sunset. He stays all night in the temple and performs his devotions. At sunrise the next day the monk begins walking down the mountain. It takes him much less time than walking up and he is at the bottom shortly after noon. The question is: Is there a point on the road when he was coming down that he passed at the same time of day when he was coming up the mountain?

This can seem a difficult problem because people begin to reason in a variety of ways as they think about the man going up and down. Adams points out one representation that makes the problem easy. Suppose there were two monks, one leaving the top at sunrise and one starting up at sunrise. Would they meet? Of course they would.

Obstacles to Problem Solving

Sometimes we fail to see the answer to a problem because we cannot free ourselves from familiar knowledge and assumptions. For example, Maier (1930) gave students the following problem:

> Two strings are hanging from the ceiling. The strings are of such a length and distance apart that you cannot reach one string while holding onto the other. You have a scissors, a paper clip, a pencil, and a piece of chewing gum in your pocket. Your task is, using just those materials, to tie the strings together.

Many of Maier's students were stumped because they did not consider that the scissors could be used for something besides cutting. To solve the problem, they had to use the scissors as a weight with which to make a pendulum swing one of the strings toward the other. The problem would have been easier to solve if the word "scissors" had been replaced by "fishing weight," as that object's function is more like that of a pendulum weight. This blocking of a new use of an object by its common use is called **functional fixedness.** For example, Duncker (1945) gave students three boxes, candles, tacks, and matches. In some cases, the candles, tacks, and matches were in the box; in others, they weren't. The task was to attach a candle to the wall in such a way that it could be lighted. The solution is to tack to the wall a box on which the candle can stand. Duncker found that when the other objects were in the box—which emphasized the box's container function—students were less likely to use the box as a candle stand. Other researchers found that when the instructions mentioned the box among the materials to be used, the subjects were more likely to solve the problem. This finding suggests that people erect a mental boundary against using objects not mentioned in the instructions to a problem.

Emotional factors can also contribute to blocks in problem solving. Teachers and parents teach us that it is good to be "right" and bad to be "wrong." Therefore,

functional fixedness: block to solving problems caused by an inability to see new uses for familiar objects or ideas.

Using a map, these students have to find and follow a particular trail. What steps should they take to successfully solve the problem? How does the problem's real-life context contribute to creative problem solving?

when faced with problems, we may impose boundaries that don't really exist. People who do well on tests of creative problem solving seem to be less afraid of making mistakes and appearing foolish than those who do poorly. They also seem to treat problem-solving situations more playfully (Getzels and Jackson, 1962). This implies a relaxed, fun atmosphere may be important when teaching problem solving. Students should certainly be encouraged to try different solutions and not be criticized for taking a wrong turn.

Teaching Creative Problem Solving

Most of the problems students encounter in school may require careful reading and some thought, but no creativity.

However, many of the problems we face in life are not so cut-and-dried. The scissors-and-string problem discussed earlier is of this type. Life is full of situations that call for creative problem solving, as in figuring out how to change or end a relationship without hurt feelings, or how to repair a machine with a bent paper clip.

The following sections describe a strategy for teaching creative problem solving, based on a review of research proposed by Fredericksen (1984a).

Incubation. Creative problem solving is quite different from the analytical, step-by-step process used to solve Sylvia's problems. In creative problem solving, one important principle is to avoid rushing to a solution, but rather to pause and reflect on the problem and think through several alternative solutions before choosing a course of action. Consider the following simple problem: Roger baked an apple pie in his oven in three-quarters of an hour. How long would it take him to bake three apple pies?

Many students would rush to multiply forty-five minutes by three. However, if they took some time to reflect, most would realize that baking three pies in the same oven would actually take about the same amount of time as one pie! In teaching this process, teachers must avoid putting time pressures on students. Instead of speed, they should value ingenuity and careful thought.

Suspension of Judgment.   In creative problem solving, students should be encouraged to suspend judgment, to consider all possibilities before trying out a solution. One specific method based on this principle is called "brainstorming" (Osborn, 1963), where two or more individuals suggest as many solutions to a problem as they can think of, no matter how seemingly ridiculous. Only after all ideas are out is any evaluated as a possible solution. The idea of brainstorming is to avoid focusing on one solution too early and perhaps ignoring better ways to proceed.

Appropriate Climates.   Creative problem solving is enhanced by a relaxed, even playful environment (Wallach and Kogan, 1965). Perhaps even more importantly, students engaging in creative problem solving must feel that their ideas will be accepted. Establishing appropriate climates is an important step.

Analysis.   One method of creative problem solving often suggested is to analyze and juxtapose major characteristics or specific elements of a problem (Lesgold, 1988). For example, the scissors-and-string problem mentioned earlier might have been solved by listing characteristics of the strings (one of which might have been that they are too light to be swung together) and of the scissors (one of which is that they have weight). Careful analysis of the situation might help solve the following problem:

> A tennis tournament was set up with a series of rounds. The winner of each match advanced to the next round. If there were an odd number of players in a round, one player (chosen at random) would advance automatically to the next round. In a tournament with 147 players, how many matches would take place before a single winner would be declared?

We might solve this problem the hard way, making diagrams of the various matches. However, careful analysis of the situation would reveal that each match would produce exactly one loser. Therefore it would take 146 matches to produce 146 losers (and one winner).

Thinking Skills.   Teach the underlying cognitive abilities. Students can be taught specific strategies for approaching creative problem solving, such as (see Beyer, 1988):

- thinking of unusual ideas
- generating many ideas
- planning
- mapping the possibilities
- assembling the facts
- getting the problem clearly in mind

Feedback.   Provide practice with feedback. Perhaps the most effective way to teach problem solving is to provide students with a great deal of practice on a wide variety of problem types, giving feedback not only on the correctness of their solutions but also on the process by which they arrived at the solutions (Swanson, 1990). The role of practice with feedback in solving complex problems cannot be overemphasized. Mr. Dunbar's students, in the scenario presented at the beginning of this chapter, could never have arrived at the solution to their problem if they had not had months of practice and feedback on simpler problems.

Theory Into Practice
Problem Solving through Real-Life Applications

Students often have difficulty applying the skills they have learned in school to real-life situations because those skills were presented in a *school* context, rather than a *real-life* context. School tasks are often *decontextualized* and, thus, are not meaningful to many students because students cannot relate the tasks to what they already know. Teachers can help students to learn problem solving by placing tasks in a real-life context. Three examples of real-life applications are provided below.

- Elementary: Your family is planning a vacation and has asked you to decide where your family will go, how you will get there, how long you will be gone, and how much money will be needed. Present a travel and activity schedule, map, and an estimated budget for all expenses.

- Junior High: Imagine that you are an investigative reporter for a local newspaper. Three supermarkets in your community have been running TV commercials in which they claim to have the lowest prices. How can each store claim to have the lowest prices? Your task is to investigate these claims by designing a way to determine which store actually has the lowest prices. Collect data at each store and present your findings in an article to be published in your class newspaper.

- High School: As an expert on sleep, you have been hired by a law enforcement agency to write a sleep manual. Law enforcement officers often must work for long periods of time with little or no sleep. When suffering from sleep deprivation, an officer's performance may be compromised, sometimes resulting in a risk of loss of life. The agency needs a clear, concise, but comprehensive manual that will give officers the knowledge of sleep they need to maintain a high level of performance on the job.

Although these problems require more time than most school tasks, they are rich in academic content and skills that are placed in real-life contexts. To solve the problems, students must identify the problem, identify possible solutions, choose a solution, carry out the solution, and analyze and report their findings. But just as importantly, students will learn to *apply* academic skills such as information gathering, computing, writing, and speaking in a real-life context.

Teaching Thinking Skills

One of the oldest dreams in education is that there might be some way to make students *smarter*—not just more knowledgeable or skillful but actually more able

Figure 7.4

Examples from Analytic Perception

Look at the figure at the right. For each drawing in the left column, there is a drawing in the right column that completes it. Write the number and the letter of the two forms you combined to make the completion. The child must select the appropriate drawing from the left to complete the one on the right so as to obtain a figure identical to the model at the top of the page. The task requires representation, internalization and labeling of the model, definition of the missing parts, systematic work, and comparison to the model for self-criticism.

From Feuerstein and Jensen, 1980.

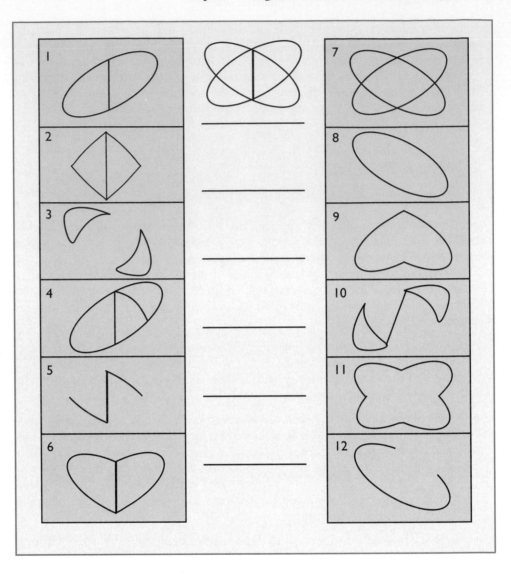

Instrumental Enrichment: a thinking-skills program in which students work through a series of paper-and-pencil exercises designed to develop various intellectual abilities.

to learn new information of all kinds. Perhaps someday someone will come up with a "smart pill" that will have this effect, but in the meantime, several groups of researchers have been developing and evaluating instructional programs designed to increase students' general thinking skills.

The most widely known and extensively researched of several thinking-skills programs currently in use was developed by an Israeli educator, Reuven Feuerstein (1980). In this program, called **Instrumental Enrichment,** students work through a series of paper-and-pencil exercises intended to build such intellectual skills as categorization, comparison, orientation in space, and numerical progressions. Figure 7.4 (from Feuerstein and Jensen, 1980) shows one example of an activity designed to increase "analytic perception." The Instrumental Enrichment treatment is meant to be administered for three to five hours per week over a period of at least two years, usually to underachieving or learning-disabled adolescents. Studies of this

A Vygotskian Approach to Instruction

Teachers participating in an inservice workshop on scaffolding were just finishing their last session. They wanted to review the information and discuss classroom applications with the instructor, Elena.

ELENA: What did Vygotsky mean by higher mental functions?

NANCY: "Mediated behaviors"—like directing memory, directing attention, thinking in symbols . . .

TYRONE: And our job is to help kids transform lower mental functions into higher ones.

ELENA: How?

TYRONE: By giving them the tools, like teaching measurement and number or categorization and mnemonics. . . .

ELENA: How do tools like those help kids build on lower mental functions?

NANCY: Well, for instance, mnemonics and categorization help them remember information better, and you can get them to pay better attention to a task by helping them concentrate on small parts of it.

ELENA: Let's look at a concrete example. What tools could you use to teach addition?

NANCY: Manipulation—fingers or blocks—or pencil marks, until kids can add mentally.

JULES: And once they can add mentally, the concept of "number" becomes a tool they can use in lots of situations besides addition.

TYRONE: Who was that other theorist? I didn't quite follow that research experiment about colors.

ELENA: That was Leont'ev, one of Vygotsky's colleagues. He had children of different ages play a question and answer color-card game with particular rules they had to follow. For instance, "white" was a forbidden name, but they could say a card was "the same color as snow." Also, each permitted color name could only be used once, so if they got a red card, they could say "red" but the next time they were shown a red card, they would have to say "like an apple" or "crimson" or something like that. They had to remember the forbidden color names and the number of times a color was drawn, and they had to be able to think of alternative names for colors. Very young children didn't get it at all. They couldn't follow the first rule.

The teachers analyzed the following sample dialogues, which illustrate the types of answers given by each age group in Leont'ev's experiment (Vygotsky, 1981):

Preschool-Age Child
MARIA: "This is a green card. I have a green dress at home. I like pink too," as she lays all of the cards on the table.

EXPERIMENTER: "What is the color of snow?"

MARIA: "White."

Elementary School-Age Child
TOMMY: "I'm going to make two piles. This pile is for colors I can't say, like black and white. This pile is for colors I can say." Tommy divides the cards into two groups.

EXPERIMENTER: "What is the color of snow?"

TOMMY: "It can be brown when it is dirty," as he looks at the brown card in the "useable" pile. He then puts the brown card in the "forbidden" pile.

EXPERIMENTER: "What color is flour?" Tommy: "Red. Oops, it isn't red," as he looks at the last card left in the "useable" pile.

Middle School-Age Child
MEILI: "I'm going to make two piles. This is for the ones I can say and this is for the ones I can't say."

EXPERIMENTER: "What color is snow?"

MEILI: "Gray when it melts," as she moves gray into the "forbidden" pile.

EXPERIMENTER: "What color is flour?"

MEILI: "The same color as clean snow," as she notices that there are no appropriate colors left in the "useable" pile —only red and green.

Problem Solving

1. How do Maria, Tommy, and Meili use the cards in different ways? What "tools" did each possess?

2. How might Vygotsky have explained the differences between the children's performances?

3. Extend each dialogue to show how a teacher might serve as mediator in helping Maria, Tommy, and Meili acquire the tools that would enable them to better perform the task.

1. Distinguishing between verifiable facts and value claims

2. Distinguishing relevant from irrelevant information, claims, or reasons

3. Determining the factual accuracy of a statement

4. Determining the credibility of a source

5. Identifying ambiguous claims or arguments

6. Identifying unstated assumptions

7. Detecting bias

8. Identifying logical fallacies

9. Recognizing logical inconsistencies in a line of reasoning

10. Determining the strength of an argument or claim

Table 7.2

Critical Thinking Skills

Source: Adapted from Beyer, 1988

---

duration have found that the program has positive effects on tests of aptitude, such as IQ tests, but generally not on achievement (Savell, Twohig, and Rachford, 1986; Sternberg and Bhana, 1986). Less intensive interventions, particularly those involving fewer than eighty hours of instruction, have rarely been successful. In one study done in Israel (Feuerstein *et al.*, 1981) and one in Venezuela (Ruiz, 1985), positive effects of Instrumental Enrichment on aptitude test scores were still found two years after the program ended.

Many reviewers of the research on Instrumental Enrichment have suggested that this method is simply teaching students how to take IQ tests rather than teaching them anything of real value (Sternberg and Bhana, 1986). Many of the exercises, such as the one reproduced in Figure 7.4, are, in fact, quite similar to items used in nonverbal IQ tests. A similar pattern of results has been found for many other thinking-skills programs (Adams, 1989). In fact, researchers have now begun to question whether there are broadly applicable "thinking skills"; the evidence points more toward the existence of teachable thinking skills in specific domains, such as math problem solving or reading comprehension (Perkins and Salomon, 1989).

Until thinking-skills programs can demonstrate effects not only on IQ tests but also on school achievement, their use in schools will probably remain limited (Bransford *et al.*, 1986b). However, in recent years researchers have begun to combine teaching of thinking skills with instruction in specific content areas, and results of these combined models are more encouraging (Adams, 1989; Prawat, 1991; Brainin, 1985; Derry and Murphy, 1986).

Critical Thinking

One key objective of schooling is enhancing students' abilities to think critically, to make rational decisions about what to do or what to believe (Hitchcock, 1983; Ennis, 1989). Examples of **critical thinking** include identifying misleading advertisements, weighing competing evidence, and identifying assumptions or fallacies in arguments. As with any other objective, learning to think critically requires practice—students can be given many dilemmas, logical and illogical arguments, valid and misleading advertisements, and so on (Norris, 1985). Effective teaching of critical thinking depends on setting a classroom tone that encourages the acceptance of divergent perspectives and free discussion. There should be an emphasis on giving reasons for opinions rather than only giving correct answers. Skills in critical thinking are best acquired in relationship to topics with which students are familiar. For example, students will learn more from a unit evaluating Nazi propaganda if they know a great deal about the history of Nazi Germany and the culture of the 1930s and 1940s. Perhaps most important, the goal of teaching critical thinking is to create a critical spirit, which encourages students to question what they hear and to examine their own thinking for logical inconsistencies or fallacies (Norris, 1985).

Beyer (1988, p. 57) identified ten critical thinking skills that students might use in judging the validity of claims, or arguments, understanding advertisements, and so on, shown in Table 7.2. He notes that this is not a sequence of steps but rather a list of possible ways a student might approach information to evaluate whether or not it is true or sensible. The key task in teaching critical thinking to students is to help them learn not only how to use each of these strategies but also how to tell when each is appropriate.

---

critical thinking: ability to make rational decisions about what to do or what to believe.

Self-Check

Explain how you would apply the techniques below to solve the following problem:
Two buses at stations 100 miles apart leave their respective stations at precisely 2:00 P.M. and drive toward each other at an average speed of 50 miles per hour. At the same moment, a small plane at Station A takes flight and flies at a hundred miles an hour back and forth two times between the two oncoming buses. How many miles will the plane have flown by the time the two buses meet?

performing a means-ends analysis   extracting relevant information
identifying misleading information   overcoming functional fixedness
identifying assumptions   thinking divergently
representing the problem

How would you teach these techniques to students as mediated behaviors, using a Vygotskian approach?

Summary

What Is the Constructivist View of Learning?
Constructivists believe that knowing is a process and that learners must individually and actively discover, transform, and "own" complex information. Constructivist approaches use top-down processing in which students begin with complex problems or tasks and discover the basic knowledge and skills needed to solve the problems or perform the tasks. Constructivist approaches also emphasize generative learning, questioning or inquiry strategies, and other metacognitive skills.

What Are Some Instructional Models Based on Constructivist Principles?
Discovery learning, reception learning, and scaffolding can be seen as different approaches based on cognitive learning theories. Bruner's discovery learning highlights students' active self-learning, curiosity, and creative problem solving. Scaffolding, based on Vygotsky's and Piaget's views, calls for teacher assistance to students at critical points in their learning. Ausubel's reception learning calls for expository teaching, in which teachers structure lessons.

How Do Cognitive Teaching Strategies Help Students Learn?
Advance organizers help students process new information by activating background knowledge, suggesting relevance, and encouraging accommodation. Analogies, organizational schemes, conceptual models, and information elaboration are other examples of teaching strategies based on cognitive learning theories.

How Do Metacognitive Skills Help Students Learn?
Metacognition helps students learn by thinking about, controlling, and effectively using their own thinking processes.

Reciprocal teaching and the PQ4R method are examples of strategies to teach metacognitive skills.

What Study Strategies Help Students Learn?
Note taking, underlining, outlining, summarizing, questioning, concept mapping, and cooperative scripting can effectively promote learning.

How Do Students Learn and Transfer Concepts?
Students learn concepts through observation and definition. Concepts are taught through examples and nonexamples and through the rule-example-rule approach in which teachers first state a definition, then give examples, and finally restate the definition. Easy examples should be given before hard ones, and teachers should compare and contrast examples given. Students transfer their learning to similar situations and must be taught to transfer concepts to different contexts and real-life situations.

How Are Problem Solving and Thinking Skills Taught?
Problem-solving skills are taught through a series of steps, including, for example, means-ends analysis and problem representation. Creative problem solving requires incubation time, suspension of judgment, conducive climates, problem analysis, the application of thinking skills, and feedback. Thinking skills include, for example, planning, classifying, divergent thinking, identifying assumptions, identifying misleading information, and question generation.

8

Effective Instruction

Chapter Outline	Chapter Objectives
What Is Direct Instruction?	▲ Define direct instruction, and list the parts of a direct instruction lesson.
How Is a Direct Instruction Lesson Taught? State Learning Objectives Orient Students to the Lesson Review Prerequisites Present New Material Conduct Learning Probes Provide Independent Practice Assess Performance and Provide Feedback Provide Distributed Practice and Review	▲ Describe and illustrate the steps and strategies used in presenting a direct instruction lesson.
What Does Research on Direct Instruction Methods Suggest? The Missouri Mathematics Program Madeline Hunter's Mastery Teaching "Systematic Instruction" Models Advantages and Limitations of Direct Instruction	▲ Describe variants of the direct instruction model, including "master teacher" programs and "systematic instruction," and assess their advantages and limitations.
How Is Cooperative Learning Used in Instruction? Student Teams Achievement Divisions (STAD) Research on Cooperative Learning	▲ Identify some benefits of cooperative learning, and describe the use of Student Teams Achievement Divisions in the classroom.
How Are Discussions Used in Instruction? Whole-Class Discussion Small-Group Discussions	▲ Compare and contrast whole-class and small-group discussions in terms of appropriate contexts, prerequisites, advantages, and limitations.
How Do Humanistic Approaches Differ from Direct Instruction? Open Schools Constructivist Approaches to Humanistic Education Humanistic Education versus Direct Instruction	▲ Compare and contrast direct instruction with humanistic and constructivist instructional models.

Ms. Logan's physical science class is a happy mess. Students are working in small groups at lab stations filling all sorts of bottles with water and then tapping them to see how various factors affect the sound. One group has set up a line of identical bottles and put different amounts of water in each so that tapping the bottles in sequence makes a crude musical scale. "The amount of water in the bottle is all that matters," one group member tells Ms. Logan, and her groupmates nod in agreement. Another group has an odd assortment of bottles and has carefully measured the same amount of water into each. "It's the shape and thickness of the bottles that makes the difference," says one group member. Other groups are working more chaotically, filling and tapping large and small, narrow and wide, and thick and thin bottles with different amounts of water. Their theories are wild and varied. After a half hour of experimentation, Ms. Logan calls the class together and asks group members to describe what they did and what they concluded. Students loudly uphold their group's point of view. "It's the amount of water!" "It's the height of the bottles!" "It's the thickness of the bottles!" "No, it's their shape!" "It's how hard you tap the bottles!" Ms. Logan moderates the conversation but lets students confront each other's ideas and give their own arguments.

The next day, Ms. Logan teaches a lesson on sound. She explains how sound causes waves in the air, and how the waves cause the eardrum to vibrate, transmitting sound information to the brain. She has two students come to the front of the class with a Slinky and uses the Slinky to illustrate how sound waves travel. She asks many questions of students, both to see if they are understanding and to get them to take the next mental step. She then explains how sound waves in a tube become lower in pitch the longer the tube. To illustrate this she plays a flute and a piccolo. Light bulbs are starting to click on in the students' minds, and Ms. Logan can tell from the responses to her questions that the students are starting to get the idea. At the end of the period, Ms. Logan lets the students get back into their groups to discuss what they have learned and to try to apply their new knowledge to the bottle problem.

When the students come into class on the third day of the sound lesson they are buzzing with excitement. They rush to their lab stations and start madly filling and tapping bottles to test out the theories they came up with the day before. Ms. Logan walks among the groups listening in on their conversations. "It's not the amount of *water,* it's the amount of *air,*" she hears one student say. "It's not the *bottle;* it's the *air,*" says a student in another group. She helps one group that is still floundering get on track. Finally, Ms. Logan calls the class together to discuss their findings and conclusions. Representatives of some of the groups demonstrate the experiments they used to show how it was the amount of air in each bottle that determined the sound.

"How could we make one elegant demonstration that it's *only* the amount of air that controls the sound?" asks Ms. Logan . The students buzz among themselves, and then assemble all their bottles into one experiment. They make one line of identical bottles with different amounts of water. Then to show that it is the air, not the water, that matters, they put the same amount of water in bottles of different sizes. Sure enough, in either case the more air space left in the bottle, the lower the sound.

Ms. Logan ends the period with a homework assignment, to read a chapter on sound in a textbook. She tells the students they will have an opportunity to work in their groups to make certain that every group member understands everything in the sound lesson, and then there will be a quiz in which students will have to individually show that they can apply their new knowledge. She reminds them that their groups can be "superteams" only if everyone knows the material.

The bell rings, and students pour into the hallway, still talking excitedly about what they have learned. Some groupmates promise to call each other that evening to prepare for the group study the next day. Ms. Logan watches them file out. She's exhausted, but she knows that this group of students will never forget the lessons they've learned about sound, about experiments, and most importantly, about their ability to use their minds to figure out difficult concepts!

The lesson is where education takes place. All other aspects of schooling, from buildings to buses to administration, are designed to support teachers in delivering effective lessons. They do not educate in themselves. Most teachers spend most of their time teaching lessons. The typical elementary or secondary school teacher may teach 800 to 1000 class lessons each year!

Conducting effective lessons is at the heart of the teacher's craft. Some aspects of lesson presentation have to be learned on the job; good teachers get better at it every year. Yet educational psychologists have studied the elements that go into effective lessons, and we know a great deal that is useful in day-to-day teaching at every grade level and in every subject (Good and Brophy, 1989; Porter and

Brophy, 1988). This chapter and the three that follow it present the principal findings of this research and translates them into ways of thinking about the practical demands of everyday teaching.

As Ms. Logan's lesson illustrates, effective lessons use many teaching methods. In four periods on one topic, she used discovery, direct instruction, discussion, cooperative learning, and other techniques. These methods are often posed as different philosophies, and the ideological wars over which is best go on incessantly (see, for example, Berg and Clough, 1990/91; Hunter, 1990/91). Yet few experienced teachers would deny that teachers must be able to use all of them and to know when to use each. Traditionally, teachers have used too much direct instruction and not enough discovery or cooperative learning. Yet there are times when discovery learning is inefficient, or when students are not likely to discover the right principles. I once visited a teacher using an exciting, inquiry-oriented approach to science that tried to teach entirely through discovery. "What do you do if students discover the wrong principles?" I asked the teacher. She looked around carefully and then beckoned me over to a quiet corner. "I *teach* them," she whispered in a conspiratorial tone.

What Is Direct Instruction?

There are times when the most effective and efficient way to teach students is for the teacher to present information, skills, or concepts in a direct fashion. The term **direct instruction** is used to describe lessons in which the teacher transmits information directly to students, structuring class time to reach a clearly defined set of objectives as efficiently as possible. Direct instruction is particularly appropriate when teaching a well-defined body of information or skills that all students must master. It is less appropriate when deep conceptual change is an objective or when exploration, discovery, and open-ended objectives are the object of instruction.

An enormous amount of research was done in the 1970s and early 1980s to discover the elements of effective direct instruction lessons. Different authors describe these elements differently (see, for example, Gagné and Briggs, 1979; Hunter, 1982; Good *et al.,* 1983; Evertson *et al.,* 1984; Rosenshine and Stevens, 1986). For example, Robert Gagné (1974, 1977, Gagné and Briggs, 1979) proposed a model based on information-processing theory in which essential **events of instruction** correspond with key events in the learning process. Gagné's model is presented in Figure 8.1. There is general agreement among researchers and teachers as to the sequence of events that characterize effective direct instruction lessons. First, students are brought up-to-date on any skills they might need for today's lesson (for example, the teacher might briefly review yesterday's lesson if today's is a continuation) and are told what they are going to learn. Then most of the lesson time is devoted to the teacher teaching the skills or information, giving students opportunities to practice the skills or express the information, and questioning or quizzing students to see whether or not they are learning the objectives.

A brief description of the parts of a direct instruction lesson follows:

1. *State Learning Objectives and Orient Students to Lesson:* Tell students what they will be learning and what performance will be expected of them. Whet students' appetites for the lesson by informing them how interesting, important, or personally relevant it will be to them.

Connections

Gagné's theory uses the information processing model by matching steps in instruction with phases in the processing of information during learning. Information processing and memory are the subjects of Chapter 6.

direct instruction: approach to teaching in which lessons are goal-oriented and structured by the teacher.

events of instruction: a model of instruction developed by Gagné that matches instructional strategies with the cognitive processes involved in learning.

Figure 8.1

Events of Learning and Instruction

According to Gagné, an act of learning includes eight phases. The phases (shown outside the boxes on the left) are external events that can be structured by the learner or teacher. Each is paired with a process that takes place within the learner's mind (shown inside the boxes). Gagné's strategy for lesson presentation, listed on the right, suggests that teachers lead students through a series of events that have been identified as necessary for learning.

From Gagné, 1974, pp. 28, 119.

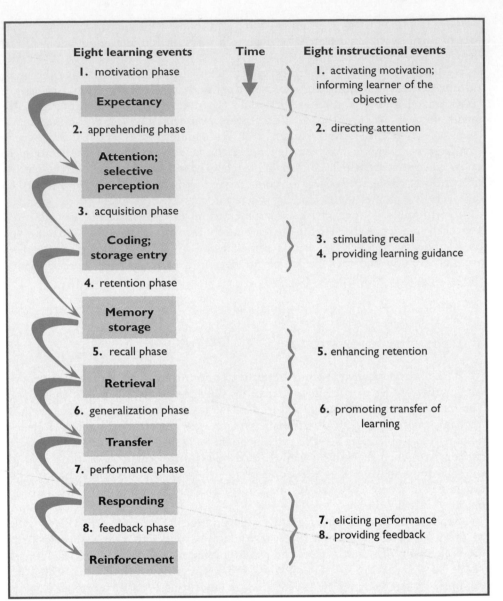

Eight learning events	Time	Eight instructional events
1. motivation phase		1. activating motivation; informing learner of the objective
Expectancy		
2. apprehending phase		2. directing attention
Attention; selective perception		
3. acquisition phase		3. stimulating recall
Coding; storage entry		4. providing learning guidance
4. retention phase		
Memory storage		
5. recall phase		5. enhancing retention
Retrieval		
6. generalization phase		6. promoting transfer of learning
Transfer		
7. performance phase		
Responding		
8. feedback phase		7. eliciting performance
Reinforcement		8. providing feedback

2. *Review Prerequisites:* Go over any skills or concepts needed to understand today's lesson.

3. *Present New Material:* Teach the lesson, presenting information, giving examples, demonstrating concepts, and so on.

4. *Conduct Learning Probes:* Pose questions to students to assess their level of understanding and correct their misconceptions.

5. *Provide Independent Practice:* Give students an opportunity to practice new skills or use new information on their own.

6. *Assess Performance and Provide Feedback:* Review independent practice work or give quiz. Give feedback on correct answers, and reteach skills if necessary.

7. *Provide Distributed Practice and Review:* Assign homework to provide distributed practice on the new material. Review material in later lessons and provide practice opportunities to increase the chances that students will remember what they learned and will be able to apply it in different circumstances.

How Is a Direct Instruction Lesson Taught?

The general lesson structure would take vastly different forms in different subject areas and at different grade levels. Teachers of older students might take several days for each step of the process, ending with a formal test or quiz; teachers of younger students might go through the entire cycle in a class period, using informal assessments at the end. Two quite different lessons are presented in Tables 8.1 and 8.2 to illustrate how the seven-step lesson structure would be applied to different subjects and grade levels. The first lesson, "Subtraction with Renaming," is an example of the first of a series of lessons directed at a basic math skill. In contrast, the second lesson, "The Origins of World War II," is an example of a lesson directed at higher-order understanding of critical events in history and their causes and interrelationships. Note that the first lesson (see Table 8.1) proceeds step-by-step and emphasizes frequent learning probes and independent practice to help students thoroughly learn the concepts being taught, while the second (see Table 8.2) is characterized by an alternation between new information, discussion, and questions to assess comprehension of major concepts.

The sequence of activities outlined in these two lessons flows along a logical path, from arousing student interest to presenting new information to allowing students to practice their new knowledge or skills to assessment. This orderly progression is essential to effective lessons at any grade level and in any subject, although the various components and how they are implemented would, of course, look different for different subjects and grades.

State Learning Objectives

The first step in presenting a lesson is planning it in such a way that the reasons for teaching and learning the lesson are clear. What do you want students to know or be able to do at the end of the lesson? Setting out objectives at the beginning of the lesson is an essential step in providing a framework into which information, instructional materials, and learning activities will fit.

Various approaches to setting objectives exist, which are taken up in greater detail in Chapter 13. In general, objectives may specify changes in behavior, skill level, performance level, attitude, or learning outcome. The objectives listed at the beginning of each chapter in this text are examples.

Theory Into Practice

Planning a Lesson

The first step of a lesson, stating learning objectives or outcomes, represents a condensation of much advance **lesson planning.** As a teacher planning a lesson, you will need at the least to answer the following questions:

Connections

Chapter 13 discusses the planning of courses, units, and lessons in relation to objectives and assessment by a process of "backward planning."

lesson planning: involves stating learning objectives; thinking through what the students will know or be able to do after the lesson; what information, activities, and experiences the teacher will provide; the time needed to reach the objective; what books, materials, and media support will be provided by the teacher; and the method(s) of instruction.

Lesson Part	Teacher Presentation
1. State learning objective and orient students to lesson.	"There are 32 students in this class. Let's say we were going to have a party, and I was going to get one cupcake for each student in the class. But 5 of you said you didn't like cupcakes. How many cupcakes would I need to get for the students who do like cupcakes? Let's set up the problem on the chalkboard the way we have before, and mark the tens and ones . . ."

tens	ones	
3	2	Students
−	5	Don't like cupcakes

	"All right, let's subtract: 2 take away 5 is . . . *hey!* We can't do that! 5 is more than 2, so how can we take 5 away from 2? We can't! "In this lesson we are going to learn how to subtract when we don't have enough ones. By the end of this lesson, you will be able to show how to rename tens as ones so that you can subtract.
2. Review prerequisites.	"Let's review subtraction when we have enough ones." Put on the chalkboard and have students solve:

47	56	89
− 3	− 23	− 8

	How many tens are in 23? _____ How many ones are in 30? _____ Give answers, discuss all items missed by many students.
3A. Present new material (first subskill).	Hand out 5 bundles of 10 popsicle sticks each and 10 individual sticks to each student. Using an overhead projector, explain how to use sticks to show 13, 27, 30. Have students show each number at their own desks. Walk around to check.

Table 8.1   Sample Lesson for Basic Math: Subtraction with Renaming

This teacher is planning a lesson. What is her first step? What decisions will she make as part of the first step in lesson planning?

Lesson Part	Teacher Presentation
4A. Conduct learning probes (first subskill).	Have students show 23 using their sticks. Check desks. Then have students show 40. Check desks. Continue until all students have the idea.
3B. Present new material (second subskill).	Using an overhead projector, explain how to use sticks to show 6 minus 2 and 8 minus 5. Then show 13 and try to take away 5. Ask for suggestions on how this could be done. Show that by removing the rubber band from the tens bundle, we have a total of 13 ones and can remove 5. Have students show this at their desks.
4B. Conduct learning probes (second subskill).	Have students show 12 (check), and then take away 4 by breaking apart the ten bundle. Then have students show 17 and take away 9. Continue until all students have the idea.
3C. Present new material (third subskill).	Give students worksheets showing tens bundles and single units. Explain how to show renaming by crossing out a bundle of ten and rewriting it as 10 units, and then subtracting by crossing out units.
4C. Conduct learning probes (third subskill).	Have students do the first items on the worksheet one at a time, until all students have the idea.
5. Provide independent practice.	Have students continue, completing the worksheet on their own.
6. Assess performance and provide feedback.	Show correct answers to worksheet items on overhead projector. Have students mark their own papers. Ask how many got item no. 1, no. 2, etc., and discuss all items missed by more than a few students. Have students hand in papers.
7. Provide distributed practice and review.	Hand out homework and explain how it is to be done. Review lesson content at start of following lesson and in later lessons.

1. What will students know or be able to do after the lesson? What will be the outcomes of their learning? How will you know when and how well students have achieved the learning outcomes or objectives?

2. What information, activities, and experiences will you provide to help students acquire the knowledge and skills needed to demonstrate the learning outcomes? How much time will be needed? How will you use in-class and out-of-class time? How will seatwork and homework assignments help students achieve the learning objectives?

3. What books and materials will you use to present the lesson, and what is their availability? When will you preview or test all the materials and create guidelines for students' responses to them? Are all materials accurate, pedagogically sound, and appropriate in content and grade level?

4. How many different methods of teaching will you incorporate; for example, will you combine reading, lecture, role playing, videotape viewing, a demonstration, and a writing assignment?

5. What "participation structures" will you use: whole-group or small-group discussions, cooperative learning groups, ability groups, individual assignments? What learning tasks will groups and individuals perform? How will you organize, monitor, and evaluate groups?

Connections

The relationships between objectives and assessment are taken up in detail in Chapter 13.

Lesson Part	Teacher Presentation
1. State learning objective and orient students to lesson.	"Today we will begin to discuss the origins and causes of World War II—perhaps the most important event in the twentieth century. The political situation of the world today—the map of Europe, the political predominance of the United States, the problems of the Eastern European countries formerly under Soviet domination, even the problems of the Middle East—all can be traced to the rise of Hitler and the bloody struggle that followed. I'm sure many of you have relatives who fought in the war or whose lives were deeply affected by it. Raise your hand if a relative or someone you know well fought in World War II. • "Germany today is peaceful and prosperous. How could a man like Hitler have come to power? To understand this, we must first understand what Germany was like in the years following its defeat in World War I and why an unemployed Austrian painter could come to lead one of the largest countries in Europe. • "By the end of this lesson you will understand the conditions in Germany that led up to the rise of Hitler, the reasons he was successful, and the major events of his rise to power."

2. Review prerequisites.	Have students recall from the previous lesson:
	 • The humiliating provisions of the Treaty of Versailles
	    —reparations
	    —demilitarization of the Ruhr
	    —loss of territory and colonies
	
	 • The lack of experience with democracy in Germany

3. Present new material.	Discuss with students:
	 • Conditions in Germany before the rise of Hitler
	    —failure of the Weimar Republic
	    —economic problems, inflation, and severe impact of the U.S. Depression
	    —belief that Germany lost World War I because of betrayal by politicians
	    —fear of communism
	 • Events in Hitler's rise to power
	    —organization of National Socialist (Nazi) party
	    —Beer-Hall Putsch and Hitler's imprisonment
	    —*Mein Kampf*
	    —organization of Brown Shirts (S.A.)
	    —election and appointment as chancellor

4. Conduct learning probes.	Questions to students throughout lesson should assess student comprehension of the main points.
5. Provide independent practice.	Have students independently write three reasons why the situation in Germany in the 1920s and early 1930s might have been favorable to Hitler's rise, and have students be prepared to defend their answers.
6. Assess performance and provide feedback.	Call on randomly selected students to read and justify their reasons for Hitler's success. Discuss well-justified and poorly justified reasons. Have students hand in papers.
7. Provide distributed practice and review.	Review lesson content at start of next lesson and in later lessons.

Table 8.2   Sample Lesson for History: The Origins of World War II

Orient Students to the Lesson

The principal task at the beginning of a lesson is to establish an attitude (or **mental set**) in students that "I'm ready to get down to work; I'm eager to learn the important information or skills the teacher is about to present, and I have a rough idea of what we will be learning."

This "set" can be established in many ways. First, it is important to expect students to be on time to class and to start the lesson immediately when the period begins (Evertson *et al.*, 1984). This establishes a sense of seriousness of purpose that is lost in a ragged start.

Second, it is important to arouse students' curiosity or interest in the lesson they are about to learn (Gregory, 1975). This was done in the first sample lesson by introducing subtraction with renaming as a skill that would be necessary to decide how many cupcakes the class would need for a party, a situation of some reality and interest to young students. In the second sample lesson the importance of the lesson was "advertised" on the basis that understanding the origins and events of World War II would help students understand events today and was made personally relevant to students by having them think of a relative who fought in World War II or was deeply affected by it. In the chapter opening scenario Ms. Logan whetted students' curiosity about sound by giving them an opportunity to experiment with it before the formal lesson.

A lesson on genetics might be introduced as follows:

> Did you ever wonder why tall parents have taller-than-average children, and red-haired children usually have at least one red-haired parent? Think of your own family—if your father and mother are both taller than average, then you will probably be taller than average. Well, today we are going to have a lesson on the science called *genetics,* in which we will learn how characteristics of parents are passed on to their children.

This introduction might be expected to grab students' interest because it makes the subject personally relevant.

Humor or drama can also establish a positive mental set. One teacher occasionally used a top hat and a wand to capture student interest by "magically" transforming adjectives into adverbs ("sad" into "sadly," for example). Popular and instructionally effective children's television programs use this kind of device constantly to get the attention and hold the interest of young children in basic skills (Ball and Bogatz, 1970, 1972).

Finally, it is important in starting a lesson to give students a road map of where the lesson is going and what they will know at the end. Stating lesson objectives clearly has generally been found to enhance student achievement of those objectives (Melton, 1978). Giving students an outline of the lesson may also help them to incorporate new information (Kiewra, 1985). Telling students that the material you are about to teach will be tested can be another effective means of increasing attention to the lesson.

Theory Into Practice
Communicating Objectives to Students

Teacher education programs include training in creating lesson plans, beginning with a consideration of instructional objectives and learning outcomes. Sharing

mental set: students' readiness to begin a lesson.

Connections

Cognitive learning theories and research, discussed in Chapters 6 and 7, support the practice of orienting students to the lesson, communicating the lesson objectives, and reviewing prerequisites.

lesson plans with students is a good idea, because research suggests that knowledge of objectives can lead to improvements in student achievement. Practical suggestions follow for sharing lesson objectives with students.

1. The objectives you communicate to students should be broad enough to encompass everything the lesson will teach. Research suggests that giving students too narrow a set of objectives may lead them to devalue or ignore other meaningful aspects of a lesson. In addition, broad objectives provide greater flexibility for adapting instruction as needed once the lesson is underway.

2. The objectives you communicate should be specific enough in content to make clear to students what the outcomes of their learning will be—what they will know and be able to do and how they will use their new knowledge and skills. In Chapter 13 you will find information on writing clear objectives and planning learning outcomes in conjunction with assessment criteria.

3. Consider stating objectives both orally and in writing and repeating them during the lesson to remind students why they are learning. Teachers use verbal and written outlines or summaries of objectives. Providing demonstrations or models of learning products or outcomes is also effective. Examples of outcomes, along with the steps or skills involved, help students see the organization of the lesson and what it will take to complete the lesson objectives.

4. Consider using questioning techniques to elicit from students their own statements of objectives or outcomes. Their input will likely reflect and inform your lesson plan. Some teachers ask students to express their ideas for meeting objectives or demonstrating outcomes, because research suggests that students who have a stake in the lesson plan and a sense of control over their learning will be more motivated to learn.

Review Prerequisites

The next major task in a lesson is to be sure that students have mastered prerequisite skills and to link information already in their minds to the information you are about to present. If today's lesson is a continuation of yesterday's, and you are reasonably sure that students understood yesterday's lesson, then the review may just remind them about the earlier lesson and ask a few quick questions before beginning the new one. For instance: "Yesterday we learned how to add the suffix 'ed' to a word ending in 'y.' Who will tell us how this is done?"

Since today's lesson—adding other suffixes to words ending in "y"—is a direct continuation of yesterday's, this brief reminder is adequate. However, if a new skill or concept is being introduced, and it depends on skills learned much earlier, then more elaborate discussion and assessment of prerequisite skills might be needed.

Sometimes it is necessary to assess students on prerequisite skills before starting a lesson. In the first sample lesson (see Table 8.1) students were briefly quizzed on subtraction without renaming and numeration skills in preparation for a lesson on subtraction with renaming. If students had shown poor understanding of either prerequisite skill, the teacher would have reviewed those skills before going on to the new lesson.

Another reason to review prerequisites is to provide advance organizers. As defined in Chapter 7, advance organizers are introductory statements by the teacher that remind students of what they already know and give them a framework for

Connections

The importance of activating a student's prior knowledge was discussed in Chapter 7.

understanding the new material to be presented. In the second sample lesson (Table 8.2) the teacher set the stage for the new content (Hitler's rise to power) by reviewing the economic, political, and social conditions in Germany that made Hitler's success possible.

Present New Material

Here begins the main body of the lesson—the point at which the teacher presents new information or skills.

Lesson Structure.   Lessons should be logically organized. Recall from Chapters 6 and 7 that information that has a clear, well-organized structure is retained better than less clearly presented information. A lesson on the legislative branch of government might be presented as follows:

The Legislative Branch of the Federal Government (First Lesson)

I. Functions and Nature of the Legislative Branch
    A. Passes laws
    B. Approves money for executive branch
    C. Has two houses—House of Representatives and Senate

II. House of Representatives
    A. Designed to be closest to the people—representatives elected to two-year terms—proportional representation
    B. Responsible for originating money bills

III. Senate
    A. Designed to give greater continuity to legislative branch—senators elected to six-year terms—each state has two senators
    B. Approves appointments and treaties made by executive branch

This would be a beginning lesson on the legislative branch of the U.S. government (subsequent lessons would present how laws are introduced and passed, checks and balances on legislative power, and so on). It has a clear organization that should be pointed out to students. For example, you might pause at the beginning of the second topic and say, "Now we are going to learn about the lower house of Congress, the House of Representatives." The purpose of this is to help students form a mental outline that will help them remember the material. Clearly laid out structure and transitional statements about the structure of the lesson have been found to increase student understanding (Kallison, 1986).

The better organized students believe a lesson to be, the more they learn from it (Belgard *et al.,* 1971). Further, teachers who make smooth, orderly transitions from topic to topic in a lesson have been found to be more instructionally effective than teachers who change topics abruptly or stray from their main points (Smith and Cotten, 1980).

Lesson Emphasis.   In addition to making clear the organization of a lesson by noting when the next subtopic is being introduced, several researchers (Petrie, 1963; Maddox and Hoole, 1975) have found that instructionally effective teachers give clear indications about the most important elements of the lesson, by saying, for example, "It is particularly important to note that . . ." Important points should be repeated and brought back into the lesson whenever appropriate. For example, in teaching about the presidential veto in the lesson on the legislative branch of government, it might be good to say:

> Here again, we see the operation of the system of checks and balances we discussed earli-er. The executive can veto legislation passed by the Congress, which in turn can withhold funds for actions of the executive. Remember, understanding how this system of checks and balances works is critical to an understanding of how the U.S. government works.

The idea here is to emphasize one of the central concepts of the U.S. govern-ment—the system of checks and balances among the executive, legislative, and judi-cial branches—by bringing it up whenever possible and by labeling it as important.

One carefully controlled experiment found that teachers who used the lesson pre-sentation strategies outlined in this section were more successful than other teachers in increasing student achievement (Clark *et al.,* 1979). The researchers studied the effectiveness of teachers who reviewed main ideas, stated objectives at the beginning of the lesson, outlined lesson content, signaled transitions between parts of the lesson, indicated important points in the lesson, and summarized the parts of the lesson as the lesson proceeded. These teachers' students scored significantly better on the lesson content and learned more than students whose teachers did not do these things.

Lesson Clarity.   One consistent feature of effective lessons is clarity, the use of direct, simple, and well-organized language to present concepts (McCaleb and White, 1980; Smith and Land, 1981; Land, 1987). Clear presentations avoid the use of vague terms that do not add to the meaning of the lesson, such as the itali-cized words in the following sentence (from Smith and Land, 1981):

> *Maybe* before we get to *probably* the main idea of the lesson, you should review a *few* prerequisite concepts.

Even more destructive to clarity are "mazes," or false starts, as in:

> This mathematics lesson *will enab* . . . will get you to understand *number, uh,* . . . number patterns (Smith and Land, 1981).

Wandering off into digressions or irrelevant topics or otherwise interrupting the flow of the lesson also detract from clarity. One physics teacher loved to interrupt his own lessons with stories about his experiences in the navy. This was a lot of fun for the students but added little to their knowledge of physics!

Explanations.   Effective teachers have also been found to use many explana-tions and explanatory words (such as "because," "in order to," "consequently") and to frequently use a pattern of rule-example-rule when presenting new concepts (Rosenshine, 1971; Van Patten *et al.,* 1986). For example:

> Matter may change forms, but it is never destroyed. If I were to burn a piece of paper, it would appear that the paper is gone, but in fact it has been combined with oxygen atoms from the air and changed to a gas (mostly carbon dioxide) and ash. If I could count the atoms in the paper plus the atoms from the air before and after I burned the paper, we could see that the matter involved did not disappear, but merely changed forms.

Note that the rule was stated ("matter . . . is never destroyed"), an example was given, and the rule was restated in explaining how the example illustrates the rule.

Also note that a rule-example-rule sequence was used in this book to illustrate the rule-example-rule pattern!

Demonstrations, Models, and Illustrations. Cognitive theorists emphasize the importance of seeing and, when appropriate, having hands-on experience with concepts and skills. Visual representations are maintained in long-term memory far more readily than information that is only heard (see Gagné and Briggs, 1979; Hiebert *et al.*, 1991; Mayer and Gallini, 1990). Recall how Ms. Logan gave her students both hands-on experience (filling and tapping bottles) and a visual analogue (the Slinky representing sound waves) to give the students clear and lasting images of the main principles of sound. Visual media (*e.g.*, video, film, and slides) can be especially effective in providing visual information (Kozma, 1991).

Maintaining Attention. Straight, dry lectures can be boring, and bored students quickly stop paying attention to even the most carefully crafted lesson. For this reason, it is important to introduce variety, activity, or humor to enliven the lecture and maintain student attention. For example, use of humor has been found to increase student achievement (Kaplan and Pascoe, 1977; Ziv, 1988), and illustrating the lecture with easily understood graphics can help hold students' attention. On the other hand, too much variation in mode of presentation can hurt achievement if it distracts students from the lesson content (Wyckoff, 1973).

Several studies have established that students learn more from lessons that are presented with enthusiasm and expressiveness than from dry lectures (Coats and Smidchens, 1966; Abrami *et al.*, 1982; Crocker and Brooker, 1986). It is apparently helpful for student interest and achievement to vary types of questions, lengths of lessons, and presentation modes (Rosenshine, 1971). In one sense, teaching is performing, and it appears that some of the qualities we'd seek in a performer are also those that increase the effectiveness of teachers (see Timpson and Tobin, 1982).

Content Coverage and Pacing. One of the most important factors in effective teaching is the amount of content covered. Students of teachers who cover more material learn more than other students (*e.g.*, Barr and Dreeben, 1983; Barr, 1987).

This does not necessarily mean that teachers should teach faster; obviously, there is such a thing as going too fast and leaving students behind, yet research on instructional pace does imply that most teachers could increase their pace of instruction (Good *et al.*, 1983), as long as degree of mastery is not sacrificed. In addition to increasing content coverage, a relatively rapid pace of instruction can help with classroom management (see Chapter 11).

Conduct Learning Probes

Imagine an archer who shoots arrows at a target but never finds out how close to the bull's eye the arrows fall. The archer wouldn't be very accurate to begin with and would certainly never improve in accuracy.

Similarly, effective teaching requires that teachers be constantly aware of the effects of their instruction. All too often, teachers mistakenly believe that if they have covered a topic well and students appear to be paying attention, then their instruction has been successful. Even students often believe that if they have listened

> **Connections**
>
> Recall the discussion in Chapter 6 on the importance of attention in learning.

This teacher is presenting new material in a lesson. What measures will she take to ensure that the lesson is effective?

intently to an interesting lecture, they know the material presented. Yet this may not be true. If teachers do not regularly probe students' understanding of the material being presented, students may be left with serious misunderstandings or gaps in knowledge.

The term **learning probe** refers to a variety of ways of asking for brief student responses to lesson content. Learning probes give the teacher feedback on students' levels of understanding and permit students to try out their understanding of a new idea to see if they have it right. Learning probes can take the form of questions to the class, as in the sample lesson on World War II presented in Table 8.2, or brief written or physical demonstrations of understanding, as in the sample subtraction lesson in Table 8.1.

Checks for Understanding.   Regardless of whether the response to the learning probe is written, physical, or oral, the purpose of the probe is what Hunter (1982) and Rosenshine and Stevens (1986) call "checking for understanding." That is, the learning probe is used not so much to teach or provide practice as to find out whether students have understood what they just heard. Teachers use the probes to set their pace of instruction. If students are having trouble, teachers must slow down and repeat explanations. If all students show understanding, the teacher can move on to new topics. The following interchange shows how a teacher might use learning probes to uncover student strengths and misunderstandings, and then adjust instruction accordingly. The teacher, Mr. Swift, has written several sentences containing conversation on an overhead projector transparency, and students are learning the correct use of commas and quotation marks:

learning probe: methods, such as questions, that help teachers find out if students understand a lesson.

MR. SWIFT: Now we are ready to punctuate some conversation. Everyone get out a sheet of paper and copy this sentence, adding punctuation where needed: Take the criminal downstairs Tom said condescendingly. Is everyone ready? Carl, how did you punctuate the sentence?

CARL: Quote take the criminal downstairs quote comma Tom said condescendingly period.

MR. SWIFT: Close, but you made the most common error people make with quotation marks. Maria, what did you write?

MARIA: I think I made the same mistake Carl did, but I understand now. It should be: Quote take the criminal downstairs comma quote Tom said condescendingly period.

MR. SWIFT: Good. How many got this right the first time? (Half of class raises hands.) Okay, I see we still have some problems with this one. Remember, commas and periods go inside the quotation mark. I know that sometimes this doesn't make much sense, but if English always made sense, a lot of English teachers would be out of work! Think of quotation marks as wrappers for conversation, and the conversation, punctuation and all, goes inside the wrapper. Let's try another. Drive carefully Tom said recklessly. Dave?

DAVE: Quote drive carefully comma quote Tom said recklessly period.

MR. SWIFT: Great! How many got it? (All but one or two raise hands.) Wonderful, I think you're all with me. The quotation marks "wrap up" the conversation, including its punctuation. Now let's try one that's a little harder: I wonder Tom said quizzically whether quotation marks will be on the test.

There are several features worth noting in this interchange. First, Mr. Swift had all students work out the punctuation, called on individuals for answers, and then asked all students whether they got the right answers. This is preferable to asking only one or two students to work (say, on the chalkboard) while the others watch, thus wasting the time of most of the class. When all students have to figure out the punctuation and no one knows on whom Mr. Swift will call, all students actively participate and test their own knowledge, and Mr. Swift gets a quick reading on the level of understanding of the class as a whole.

Note also that when Mr. Swift found that half the class missed the first item, he took time to reteach the skill students were having trouble with, using a different explanation from the one he had used in his first presentation. By giving students the mental image of "quotation marks as wrappers," he helped them remember the order of punctuation in conversation. (Recall that the use of vivid imagery was one of the memory strategies discussed in Chapter 6.) When almost all students got the second item, he moved to the next step, because the class had apparently mastered the first one.

Finally, note that Mr. Swift had plenty of sentences prepared on the overhead projector, so he did not have to use class time to write out sentences. Learning probes should always be brief and should not be allowed to destroy the tempo of the lesson. By being prepared with sentences for learning probes, Mr. Swift was able to maintain student involvement and interest. In fact, he might have done even better to give students photocopies with sentences on them to reduce the time used in copying the sentences.

Questions.   Questions to students in the course of the lesson serve many purposes (Carlsen, 1991). Questions may be used as Socrates used them, to prompt students to take the next mental step (for example, "Now that we've learned that heating a gas makes it expand, what do you suppose would happen if we cool a gas?"). They may be used to encourage students to think further about information they learned previously or to get a discussion started (for example, "We've learned that if we boil water, it becomes water vapor. Now, water vapor is a colorless, odorless, invisible gas. In that case, why do you suppose we can see steam coming out of a tea kettle?"). With guidance, a class discussion would eventually arrive at the answer, which is that the water vapor recondenses when it hits the relatively cool air—and that what is visible in steam is water droplets, not vapor. It is often helpful to have students generate their own questions, either for themselves or for each other (King, 1992a).

Finally, questions can be used as learning probes. In fact, any question is to some degree a learning probe, in that the quality of response will indicate to the teacher how well students are learning the lesson. Research on the frequency of questions indicates that teachers who ask more academically relevant questions are more instructionally effective than those who ask relatively few questions related to the lesson at hand (Dunkin and Biddle, 1974; Stallings and Kaskowitz, 1974; Gall *et al.*, 1978). This corresponds with cognitive research on questions (discussed in Chapter 7), which also finds that posing questions in the course of instruction increases learning (Andre, 1979; Hamaker, 1986). With elementary-age students, a large number of relatively easy questions on facts or skills seems to be most effective for increasing student achievement, while thought-provoking questions become increasingly effective in secondary schools (Winne, 1979; Samson *et al.*, 1987). However, at all levels of schooling it is probable that factual questions will help with factual skills (Clark *et al.*, 1979) and questions that encourage students to think about concepts will help with conceptual skills (Fagan *et al.*, 1981; Redfield and Rousseau, 1981; Gall, 1984).

Teachers typically ask a lot of questions. One study found that teachers asked about 150 questions per hour in elementary science and social studies (Gall, 1970). It seems logical, then, that the way in which teachers ask questions should be an important part of their instructional effectiveness.

Wait Time.   One issue regarding questioning that has received much research attention is **wait time,** the length of time the teacher waits for a student to answer a question before giving up. Research has found that teachers tend to give up too rapidly on students they perceive to be low achievers, which tells those students that the teacher expects little from them (Rowe, 1974; Tobin and Capie, 1982).

Teachers who wait approximately three seconds after asking a student a question obtain better learning results than those who give up more rapidly (Tobin, 1986). Further, following up with students who do not respond has been associated with higher achievement (Brophy and Evertson, 1974; Anderson *et al.*, 1979; Larrivee, 1985). Waiting for students to respond, or staying with them when they do not, communicates positive expectations for them (Brophy and Good, 1974).

Calling Order.   In asking questions, **calling order** is a concern. Anderson *et al.* (1979) found that in reading groups it was better to call on students in a prescribed order (such as around the circle) than to call on them at random, at least in part because this method ensures that all students will be called on. However, the authors expressed doubt that ordered turns would work as well in lessons to the whole class because when students know they will not be called on for some time, they often fail to pay attention. Calling on volunteers is perhaps the most common method, but this allows some students to avoid participating in the lesson by keeping their hands down (Brophy and Evertson, 1974).

Thus research is unclear concerning how students should be called on. Common sense would suggest that when the question is a problem to be worked (as in math), all students should work the problem before any individual is called on. When questions are not problems to be worked, it is probably best to pose the question to the class as a whole and then ask a randomly chosen student (not necessarily a volunteer)

wait time: length of time that a teacher allows a student to take to answer a question.

calling order: the order in which students are called by the teacher to answer questions asked during the course of a lesson.

What choral response technique is the teacher using in this class? How might it help the teacher? Why might it have a positive effect on student learning?

to answer. Some teachers even carry around a class list on a clipboard and check off the students called upon to make sure that all get frequent chances to respond. One teacher put her students' names on cards, shuffled them before class, and used the cards to decide on whom to call. This system worked well until one student found the cards after class and removed his name from the deck!

Choral Response.   In conducting learning probes it may be especially important to ask questions of students who usually perform above, at, and below the class average to be sure that all students understand the lesson. Also, many researchers favor the frequent use of **choral responses** when there is only one possible correct answer (Becker and Carnine, 1980; Hunter, 1982; Rosenshine and Stevens, 1986). For example, the teacher might say, "Class: In the words listed on the board (*write, wring, wrong*), what sound does the 'wr' make?" to which the class responds together, "Rrrr!" Similarly, when appropriate, all students can be asked to use hand signals to indicate true or false, to hold up a certain number of fingers to indicate an answer in math, or to write a short answer on a small chalkboard and hold it up on cue (Hunter, 1982). This type of all-pupil response has been found to have a positive effect on student learning (McKenzie, 1979; McKenzie and Henry, 1979). In the subtraction with renaming example used earlier in this chapter, recall that all students worked with popsicle sticks at their desks, and the teacher walked around to check their work. The purpose of these all-student responses is to give students many opportunities to respond and to give the teacher information on the entire class's level of knowledge and confidence.

choral response: a response to a question made by an entire class in unison.

Provide Independent Practice

The term **independent practice** refers to work students do in class on their own to practice or express newly learned skills or knowledge. For example, after hearing a lesson on solving equations in algebra, students need an opportunity to work several equations on their own without interruptions, both to crystallize their new knowledge and to help the teacher assess their knowledge. Practice is an essential step in the process of transferring new information in short-term memory to long-term memory (see Chapter 6).

Independent practice is most critical when students are learning skills, such as mathematics, reading, grammar, composition, map interpretation, or a foreign language. Students can no more learn arithmetic, writing, or Spanish without practicing them than they could learn to ride a bicycle from lectures alone! On the other hand, independent practice is less necessary for certain concept lessons, such as the lesson on the rise of Hitler described earlier or a science lesson on the concept of magnetic attraction. In lessons of this kind independent practice can be used to let students rehearse knowledge or concepts on their own, as was done in the World War II lesson, but rehearsal is not as central to this type of lesson as practice of skills is to a subtraction lesson.

Seatwork.   Research on **seatwork,** or in-class independent practice, suggests that it is typically both overused and misused (Good and Grouws, 1977; Brophy and Good, 1986; Anderson, 1985). Several researchers have found that student time spent receiving instruction directly from the teacher is more productive than time spent in seatwork (Brophy and Evertson, 1974; Good and Grouws, 1977; Evertson *et al.,* 1980). For example, Evertson *et al.* (1980) found that the most effective seventh- and eighth-grade math teachers in their study spent about sixteen minutes on lecture-demonstration and nineteen minutes on seatwork, while the least effective teachers spent less than seven minutes on lecture-demonstration and about twenty-five minutes on seatwork. Yet studies of elementary mathematics and reading find students spending 50 to 70 percent of their class time doing seatwork (Fisher *et al.,* 1978; Rosenshine, 1980). Anderson *et al.* (1985) have noted that time spent on seatwork is often wasted for students who lack the motivation, reading skills, or self-organization skills to work well on their own. Many students simply give up when they run into difficulties, while others fill out worksheets with little care for correctness. They apparently interpret the task as finishing the paper rather than learning the material.

Effective Use of Independent Practice Time.   A set of recommendations for effective use of independent practice time, derived from the work of Anderson (1985), Good *et al.* (1983), and Evertson *et al.* (1984), follows.

1. *Do Not Assign Independent Practice Until You Are Sure Students Can Do It:* This is probably the most important principle. Independent practice is *practice,* not instruction, and the students should be able to do most of the items they are assigned to do on their own (Brophy and Good, 1986). In cognitive terms, practice serves as rehearsal for transferring information from short-term memory to long-term memory. For this to work, the information must first of all be established in students' short-term memories.

A high success rate on independent practice work can be accomplished in two ways. First, worksheets should be clear and self-explanatory and should cover

independent practice: component of instruction in which students work by themselves to demonstrate and rehearse new knowledge.

seatwork: work that students are assigned to do independently during class.

content on which all students can succeed. Second, students should rarely be given independent practice worksheets until they have indicated in learning probes that they can handle the material. For example, a teacher might use the first items of a worksheet as learning probes, assigning them one at a time and discussing each one after students have attempted it, until it is clear that all or almost all students have the right idea.

2. *Keep Independent Practice Assignments Short:* There is rarely a justification for long independent practice assignments. About ten minutes of work is adequate for most objectives, but this is far less than what most teachers assign (Rosenshine, 1980). Massed practice (for example, many items at one sitting) has a limited effect on retention; students are more likely to profit from relatively brief independent practice in class supplemented by distributed practice in the form of homework (Dempster, 1989; Krug *et al.,* 1990).

3. *Give Clear Instructions:* In the lower grades it may be necessary to ask students to read or paraphrase the instructions to be sure that they have understood them.

4. *Get Students Started, and Then Avoid Interruptions:* When students start on their independent practice work, circulate among them to be sure that everyone is under way before attending to the problems of individual students or other tasks. Once students have begun, avoid interrupting them.

5. *Monitor Independent Work:* It is important to monitor independent work (see Medley, 1979)—for example, by walking around the class while students are doing their assignment. This helps keep students working and makes the teacher easily available for questions.

6. *Collect Independent Work and Include It in Student Grades:* A major problem with seatwork as it is often used is that students see no reason to do their best on it because it has little or no bearing on their grades. Students should usually know that their seatwork will be collected and will count toward their grade. To this end, it is a good idea to save a few minutes at the end of each class period to briefly read answers to worksheet questions and allow students to check their own papers or exchange worksheets with partners. Then students may pass in their papers for spot checking and recording. This procedure gives students immediate feedback on their seatwork and relieves the teacher of having to check all papers every day.

Assess Performance and Provide Feedback

Every lesson should contain an assessment of the degree to which students have mastered the objectives set for the lesson. This assessment may be done informally by questioning students, may use independent work as an assessment, or may involve a separate quiz. One way or another, however, the effectiveness of the lesson must be assessed, and the results of the assessment should be given to students as soon as possible (Brophy and Evertson, 1976; Gage, 1978; Rosenshine, 1979). Students need to know when they are right and when they are wrong if they are to use feedback to improve their performance (see Barringer and Gholson, 1979; Meyer, 1987).

In addition to assessing the results of each lesson, teachers need to test students from time to time on their learning of larger units of information. In general, more frequent testing results in greater achievement than less frequent testing, but any testing is much more effective than none at all (Bangert-Drowns *et al.,* 1986). Feedback to students is important, but feedback to teachers on student performance

This teacher is monitoring students' independent practice. What principles should she observe to ensure a meaningful and efficient use of seatwork time?

is probably even more important. If students are learning everything they are taught, it may be possible to pick up the pace of instruction. On the other hand, if assessment reveals serious misunderstandings, the lesson can be retaught or other steps taken to get students back on track. If some students mastered the lesson and some did not, it may be appropriate to give more instruction just to the students who need it.

Provide Distributed Practice and Review

Retention of many kinds of knowledge is increased by practice or review spaced out over time (Dempster, 1989). This has several implications for teaching. First, it implies that reviewing and recapitulating important information from earlier lessons enhances learning (Nuthall, 1987). Reviews of important material at long intervals (*e.g.*, monthly) is particularly important to maintain previous skills. In addition, it is important to assign homework in most subjects and grade levels. Homework gives students a chance to practice skills learned in one setting and at one time (school) in another setting at a different time (home). Research on homework finds that it generally does increase achievement, particularly if it is checked and comments on it are given to students (Marshall, 1982; Keith *et al.*, 1986; Elawar and Corno, 1985). However, the effects of homework are not as clear in elementary schools as they are at the secondary level (Cooper, 1989; Epstein, 1988).

Self-Check

Continue the list you began in the previous section by adding information about each step, or part, of a direct instruction lesson. Add information for each of the following categories: Purpose, Strategies, Example.

What Does Research on Direct Instruction Methods Suggest?

Direct instruction methods fall into two distinct categories. One might be called "master teacher" models (following Rosenshine, 1982) because they are based on the practices of the most effective teachers. This category includes Madeline Hunter's Mastery Teaching model, the Missouri Mathematics Program, and several others.

The other category of direct instruction methods might be called "systematic instruction" models. These are based on principles similar to those behind the master teacher models, but are far more structured. Typically, they provide specific instructional materials and highly organized, systematic methods of teaching, motivating students, managing the classroom, and assessing student progress (see Rosenshine, 1986).

The Missouri Mathematics Program

The **Missouri Mathematics Program** (MMP) is based on principles of instruction discovered in research that compared the teaching strategies of teachers who consistently obtained outstanding achievement from their students with those of teach-

or exceptions (for example, "In the sentence 'I went on a walk,' what part of speech is the word 'walk'?").

3. *Checking Understanding and Guided Practice:* Check that all students understood the information just presented. For example, give students a multiple-choice question and have them answer using hand signals. For example:

How many half-steps are there in an octave?

a. 8

b. 12

c. 14

d. 16

Students might indicate their choices all at the same time by holding up one finger for "a," two for "b," and so on; or by writing their choice on a small chalkboard and holding it up. This permits the teacher to immediately see how many students are grasping the main ideas of the lesson. Teachers can accomplish the same goal by using choral responses or by calling on individual students.

Guided practice refers to methods of giving students problems or questions one or two at a time and checking their answers immediately. The purpose of guided practice is to let students try out their new information and receive immediate feedback on their levels of understanding. The same types of response formats used in checking understanding are also used to check students' work in guided practice. For example, you might have students work a math problem at their desks and then walk around to look at their papers to see that they have the right idea.

4. *Independent Practice:* After students indicate they understand the main points of the lesson, give them independent practice. For example, ask them to work several math problems, to fill in country names on an outline map, to write main ideas for a series of paragraphs, or to make adjectives and nouns agree in number and gender in a foreign language. Hunter emphasizes that independent practice should be relatively brief and that practice exercises should be checked as soon as possible so students can find out how they did.

Despite its widespread popularity, evaluations of Madeline Hunter's Mastery Teaching program have not generally found that the students of teachers trained in the model have learned more than other students (Stallings and Krasavage, 1986; Donovan et al., 1987; Mandeville and Rivers, 1991; Slavin, 1986a). A somewhat similar program was found by Stallings (1979) to improve the reading skills of high school students in remedial reading classes, but a second evaluation was less encouraging (Thieme-Busch and Prom, 1983). More successful have been direct instruction models that place a greater emphasis on building teachers' classroom management skills (e.g., Evertson et al., 1985), and models that improve teachers' use of reading groups (Anderson et al., 1979).

While the research on applications of "master teacher" models is mixed, most researchers agree that the main elements of these models are essential *minimum* skills that all teachers should have (for example, Gage and Needels, 1989). When studies find no differences between teachers trained in the models and other

guided practice: component of instruction in which students work with teacher guidance to demonstrate and rehearse new knowledge.

ers who were less instructionally successful (Good and Grouws, 1977, 1979). The program primarily applies the prescriptions for lesson components specified by Gagné and Briggs (1979), Rosenshine and Stevens (1986), and others in the direct instruction tradition to the teaching of mathematics at the elementary and middle school levels. The principal features of MMP lessons are summarized in Table 8.3 (adapted from Good et al., 1983).

In the first study of MMP (Good and Grouws, 1979), fourth-graders whose teachers used the MMP methods learned considerably more than did students whose teachers were not trained in MMP. Later evaluations of the Missouri Mathematics Program found smaller positive effects. In three studies MMP students gained somewhat more in mathematics achievement than did control students (Good et al., 1983; Gall et al., 1984; Slavin and Karweit, 1985).

Most of the principles of direct instruction discussed in this chapter have been derived from **process-product studies,** in which observers recorded the teaching practices of teachers whose students consistently achieved at a high level. These principles have been assembled into specific direct instruction programs, such as MMP, and evaluated in field experiments. That is, other teachers have been trained in the methods used by successful teachers, and their students' achievement has been compared to that of students whose teachers did not receive the training. Madeline Hunter's **Mastery Teaching Program** is another example of this approach.

Madeline Hunter's Mastery Teaching

Madeline Hunter's (1982) Mastery Teaching Program provides a general guide to effective lessons in any subject area or grade level. Mastery Teaching lessons proceed in four principal steps: (1) getting students set to learn, (2) input and modeling, (3) checking understanding and guided practice, and (4) independent practice.

Theory Into Practice
Using the Hunter Method

1. *Getting Students Set to Learn:* In the first few minutes of class, complete the following three activities:

•*Review:* Ask students either to answer a few review questions orally or in writing or to summarize the previous day's lesson. This may go on while the teacher attends to taking roll or other "class-keeping" activities.

•*Anticipatory Set:* An **anticipatory set** is created in students by focusing their attention on the material to be presented, reminding them of what they already know, and stimulating their interest in the lesson. This step parallels the suggestion made earlier in this chapter to help students get into the proper mental set before starting a lesson.

•*Objective:* State the learning objective (see Chapter 13).

2. *Input and Modeling:* Present information to students in a logical, well-organized sequence, using clear language and models and demonstrations.

Missouri Mathematics Program: a method of teaching math using direct instruction.

process-product studies: research approach in which the teaching practices of effective teachers are recorded through classroom observation.

Mastery Teaching Program: a program using direct instruction in any subject area or grade level. Mastery Teaching lessons proceed in four principal steps: (1) getting students set to learn, (2) input and modeling, (3) checking understanding and guided practice, and (4) independent practice.

anticipatory set: students focus their attention on the material to be presented, being reminded of what they already know, and stimulating their interest in the lesson.

Opening (First 8 minutes except Mondays)			
A. Briefly review the concepts and skills associated with the homework.	B. Collect and deal with homework assignments.	C. Ask several mental computation exercises (for example: "Compute in your head 3 x 4 - 5 + 3 = ").	

Development (About 20 minutes)			
A. Briefly focus on prerequisite skills and concepts.	B. Focus on meaning and promoting student understanding by using lively explanations, demonstrations, and illustrations. Keep the pace rapid and lively.	C. Assess student comprehension • frequent, rapid short-answer questions (but give students enough time to respond) • single practice items	D. Repeat and elaborate on the meaning portion as necessary.

Seatwork (About 15 minutes)			
A. Provide uninterrupted successful practice. Most students should be getting at least 80 percent of their items correct	B. Momentum: Keep the ball rolling—get everyone involved, then sustain involvement.	C. Alerting: Let students know their work will be checked at end of period.	D. Accountability: Check the students' work.

Homework Assignment			
A. Assign homework on a regular basis at the end of each math class.	B. Require about 15 minutes of work to be done at home.	C. Include one or two review problems in homework assignments.	

Special Reviews			
A. Weekly review/maintenance: • Conduct during the first 20 minutes each Monday. • Focus on skills and concepts covered during the previous week.	B. Monthly review/maintenance: • Conduct every fourth Monday. • Focus on skills and concepts covered since the last monthly review		

TABLE 8.3 Missouri Mathematics Program

The Missouri Mathematics Program applies the principles of direct instruction to the teaching of mathematics at the elementary and middle school level. A summary of the key instructional behaviors for MMP is shown here.

SOURCE: Adapted from Good et al., 1983.

Hunter suggests "teaching to both halves of the brain" by first presenting information verbally and then summarizing it on the chalkboard, using simple diagrams, models, and mnemonics. She also emphasizes "modeling what you mean" by giving frequent examples of concepts to make their meanings clear, moving from clear and easily understood examples (for example, " 'book' is a noun," " 'read' is a verb") to more thought-provoking examples

---

Connections

The method of computing Individual Learning Expectation (ILE) base scores and improvement points, which is explained in Chapter 10, is appropriate for a variety of cooperative learning strategies, including STAD.

Connections

Recall the benefits of cooperative learning methods in promoting harmony in culturally diverse classrooms, discussed in Chapter 4. The benefits of cooperative learning methods in the social integration of mainstreamed students with special education needs are discussed in Chapter 12.

6. Recognize team accomplishments. As soon as you have calculated points for each student and figured team scores, you should provide some sort of recognition to any teams that averaged two improvement points or more. You might write a newsletter to recognize successful teams, give certificates to team members, or prepare a bulletin board display. It is important to help students value team success. Your own enthusiasm about team scores will help. If you give more than one quiz in a week, combine the quiz results into a single weekly score. After five or six weeks of STAD, reassign students to new teams. This gives students who were on low-scoring teams a new chance, allows students to work with other classmates, and keeps the program fresh.

Research on Cooperative Learning

Research has focused primarily on group study methods, such as Student Teams Achievement Divisions, or STAD (Slavin, 1986b). The research finds that students learn substantially more in cooperative learning than in traditional instruction if two conditions are met. First, there must be some reward or recognition provided to students, such as certificates or small privileges for groups that do well. Second, the success of the group must depend on the *individual* learning of each group member, not on a single group product. That is, groups must ultimately be working to make certain that all their members are learning, not just the highest achievers or the loudest members. When these conditions are fulfilled, cooperative learning has been effective in grades 2 through 12, in every subject, and in many types of schools (see Slavin, 1990b, 1991). Cooperative learning methods built around discussion (Johnson and Johnson, 1979) and around group projects (Sharan and Schachar, 1988) have also been effective. In addition to achievement, cooperative learning methods have had positive effects on such outcomes as race relations (Slavin, 1985a,b,c), self-esteem, attitudes toward school, and acceptance of mainstreamed children with special education needs (Slavin, 1990b).

Self-Check

List at least three specific benefits of cooperative learning that research findings confirm and explain how you would go about introducing STAD in your classroom.

How Are Discussions Used in Instruction?

This chapter has so far focused primarily on teaching methods for transmitting knowledge or skills from teacher to students. However, while every subject has a certain body of information, concepts, and skills that must be mastered by students as firmly and as efficiently as possible, there are three kinds of learning objectives that do not fall into this mold (see Gall, 1987). First, in many subjects there are questions that do not have simple answers. There may be one right answer to an algebra problem or one right way to conjugate a German verb, but is there one right set of factors that led up to the Civil War? How were Shakespeare's writings influenced by the politics of his day? Should genetic engineering be banned as a danger to world health? These and many other questions are open to interpretation, so it is important for students to discuss and understand these issues instead of simply receiving and rehearsing information or skills.

Subjective and Controversial Subjects. Such subjects as history, government, economics, literature, art, and music contain many issues that lend themselves to discussion because there are no single right answers. Discussing controversial issues has been found to increase knowledge about the issues as well as to encourage deeper understanding of the various sides of an issue (Johnson and Johnson, 1979).

Difficult and Novel Concepts. The second category that lends itself to discussion are objectives that do contain single right answers but involve difficult concepts that force students to see something in a different way. For example, a science teacher could simply give a lesson on buoyancy and specific gravity. However, since this lesson would challenge a simplistic view of why things float ("Things float because they are light"), students might understand buoyancy and specific gravity better if given an opportunity to make and defend their own theories about why things float, and if they were confronted with such questions as " If things float because they are light, then why does a battleship float?" and "If you threw some things in a lake, they would sink part way but not to the bottom—why would they stop sinking?" In searching together for theories to explain these phenomena, students might gain an appreciation for the meaning of buoyancy and specific gravity that a lecture could not provide. Ms. Logan, in the example presented at the beginning of this chapter, used discussions in just this way to teach about sound. Science and social studies include many concepts that lend themselves to discussion.

Affective Objectives. The third situation calling for use of discussions is where affective objectives are of particular importance. For example, in a course on civics or government there is much information to be taught about how our government works, but there are also important values to be transmitted, such as civic duty and patriotism. A teacher could teach "six reasons why it is important to vote," but the real objective here is not to teach reasons for voting, but rather to instill respect for the democratic process and a commitment to register and vote when the time comes. Similarly, a discussion of peer pressure might be directed at giving students the skills and the willingness to say "no" when classmates pressure them to engage in illegal, unhealthy, or undesirable behaviors. A long tradition of research in social psychology has established that group discussion, particularly when group members must publicly commit themselves, is far more effective at changing individuals' attitudes and behaviors than even the most persuasive lecture (see Lewin, 1947).

Whole-Class Discussion

Discussions take two principal forms. In one the entire class discusses an issue, with the teacher as moderator. In the other students form small groups (usually with four or five students in each group) to discuss a topic, and the teacher moves from group to group, aiding the discussion.

What differentiates a **whole-class discussion** from a usual lesson is that in discussions the teacher plays a less dominant role. Teachers may guide the discussion and help the class avoid dead ends, but the ideas should be drawn from the students.

Connections

Relate the sections on whole-group and small-group discussions to information in Chapter 7 on the role of questioning in learning. The instructional use of questioning for conducting learning probes is discussed earlier in this chapter.

whole-class discussion: a discussion among all the students in a class with the teacher as moderator.

The following vignette (from Joyce and Weil, 1986, pp. 55–56) illustrates an inquiry-oriented discussion led (but not dominated) by a teacher:

> One morning, as Mrs. Harrison's fourth-grade students are settling down to their arithmetic workbooks, she calls their attention. As they raise their eyes toward her, a light bulb directly over Mrs. Harrison's desk blows out, and the room darkens.
>
> "What happened?" asks one child.
>
> "Can't you see, dopey?" remarks another. "The light bulb blew out."
>
> "Yeah," inquires another, "but what does that mean?"
>
> "Just that. We have all seen a lot of light bulbs blow out, but what does that really mean? What happens?" their teacher prods.
>
> Mrs. Harrison unscrews the light bulb and holds it up. The children gather around and she passes it among them. After she receives it back, she says, "Well, why don't you see if you can develop a hypothesis about what happened?"
>
> "What's inside the glass?" asks one of the children.
>
> "I'm afraid I can't answer that," she replies. "Can you put it another way?"
>
> "Is there a gas inside?" asks another.
>
> "No," says Mrs. Harrison. The children look at one another in puzzlement. Finally, one asks, "Is it a vacuum?"
>
> "Yes," nods Mrs. Harrison.
>
> "Is it a complete vacuum?" someone inquires.
>
> "Almost," replies Mrs. Harrison.
>
> "Is the little wire made of metal?"
>
> "Yes," she agrees.

In asking questions such as these, the children gradually identify the materials that make up the light bulb and the process that caused it to burn out. Finally, they begin to venture hypotheses about what happened. After they have thought up four or five of these, they search through reference books in an effort to verify them.

Inquiry Training.   In the example the teacher used an unplanned event (the bulb burning out) to start a discussion on light bulbs, but the principles she used apply just as well to the more typical case where the teacher introduces a discussion into a lesson planned in advance. The teacher knows the answers to the question at hand ("How does a light bulb work?"), but wants the students to find out for themselves. The lesson is less on light bulbs as such than on how to use scientific methods and other resources to answer questions. The teacher is using a particular strategy called **inquiry training,** in which students are presented with a puzzling event or experiment and must try out theories to explain what happened. The teacher only answers yes-or-no questions, and provides information only when students ask the right questions. This simulates the situation faced by scientists, for whom asking the right questions is the most important step toward finding answers.

The light bulb example is unique in some ways, but it has many characteristics common to most whole-class discussions. First, the teacher took a nondirective role, leaving the primary responsibility for bringing up and exploring ideas to the

inquiry training: teaching practice aimed at helping students to develop skills in asking questions and drawing conclusions.

students. The teacher served as a source of information and as a moderator, but otherwise did not direct the lesson. The teacher encouraged all students to participate and did not discourage them from making educated guesses or trying out their own theories.

Exploring Points of View.   In contrast to the light bulb example, the following vignette describes a situation in which a teacher does not have a specific principle or concept in mind, but rather wants students to explore and develop their own ideas about a topic, using information they have recently learned:

Ms. WILSON: In the past few weeks we've been learning about the events leading up to the American Revolution. Of course, since we are all Americans, we tend to take the side of the revolutionaries. We use the term "Patriots" to describe them; King George probably used a less favorable term. Yet many of the colonists were Loyalists, and at times, the Loyalists outnumbered the Patriots. Let's think about how Loyalists would have argued against the idea of independence from Britain.

BETH: I think they'd say King George was a good king.

Vinnie: But what about all the things he did to the colonists?

Ms: WILSON: Give some examples.

Vinnie: Like the Intolerable Acts. The colonists had to put up British soldiers in their own houses, and they closed Boston Harbor.

TANYA: But those were to punish the colonists for the Boston Tea Party. The Loyalists would say that the Patriots caused all the trouble in the first place.

Ms. WILSON: Good point.

FRANK: I think the Loyalists would say, "You may not like everything he does, but King George is still our king."

RICHARD: The Loyalists probably thought the Sons of Liberty were a bunch of hoods.

Ms. WILSON: Well, I wouldn't put it quite that way, but I think you're right. What did they do that makes you think that?

RAMON: They destroyed things and harassed the Loyalists and the British troops. Like they called them names and threw things at them.

Ms. WILSON: How do you think Loyalists would feel about the Boston Massacre?

BETH: They'd say those creeps got what they deserved. They'd think that it was Sam Adams's fault for getting everyone all stirred up.

Ms. WILSON: Let's think about it another way. We live in California. Our nation's capital, Washington, is 3000 miles away. We have to pay all kinds of taxes, and a lot of those taxes go to help people in Boston or Baltimore rather than people here. Many of the things our government does make people in California mad. We've got plenty of food, and we can make just about anything we want to right here. Why don't we have a California Revolution and have our own country?

SARA: But we're part of America!

TANYA: We can't do that! The army would come and put down the revolution!

Ms. WILSON: Don't you think that the Loyalists thought some of the same things?

VINNIE: But we can vote and they couldn't.

RAMON: Right. Taxation without representation!

BETH: I'll bet a lot of Loyalists thought the British would win the war and it would be better to stay on the side of the winners.

In this discussion the teacher was not looking for any particular facts about the American Revolution, but rather was trying to get students to use the information they had learned previously to discuss issues from a different perspective. Ms. Wilson let the students determine the direction of the discussion to a substantial degree. Her main tasks were to keep the discussion rolling, to get students to use specifics to defend their positions, to ensure that many students participated, and to help the students avoid dead ends or unproductive avenues.

Information Before Discussion.   Before beginning a discussion it is important to make sure that students have an adequate knowledge base. There is nothing so dreary as a discussion in which the participants don't know much about the topic. The light bulb discussion would have been less fruitful if students had not already had a concept of a vacuum and of air as a gas. The American Revolution discussion depended on students' knowledge of the main events preceding the Revolution. Sometimes a discussion can be used before instruction as a means of generating interest in a topic, but at some point students must be given information. For example, Ms. Logan let students discuss and experiment not only before presenting a formal lesson but also after the lesson when they had more information.

Small-Group Discussions

In a **small-group discussion** students work in four- to six-member groups to discuss a particular topic. Because small-group discussions require that students work independently of the teacher most of the time, young or poorly organized students need a great deal of preparation and, in fact, may not be able to benefit from them at all. However, most students at or above the fourth grade can profit from small-group discussions.

As with any discussions, most small-group discussions should follow the presentation of information through teacher-directed lessons, books, or films. When students know something about a subject, they may start to work in their groups, pulling desks together if necessary to talk and hear one another more easily.

Each group should have a leader appointed by the teacher. Leaders should be responsible, well-organized students, but should not always be the highest-achieving students. Groups may all discuss the same topic, or they may each discuss a different subtopic of a larger topic that the whole class is studying. For example, in a unit on the Great Depression one group might focus on causes of the Depression, another on the collapse of the banking system, a third on the social consequences of the Depression, and a fourth on the New Deal. Each group should be given a series of questions to be answered on the topic to be discussed. For example, if the topic were the collapse of the banking system the questions might be:

1. What was the connection between the stock market crash of 1929 and the failures of so many banks?
2. What caused savers to lose confidence in the banks?
3. Why did the banks not have enough funds to pay savers who wished to withdraw their money?
4. Why is a widespread run on banks unlikely today?

small-group discussion: a discussion among four to six students in a group working independently of a teacher.

The leader's role in each discussion group is to make sure that the group stays on the topic and questions assigned to it, and to ensure that all group members participate. A group secretary may be appointed to write down the group's ideas. At the

Teachers on Teaching

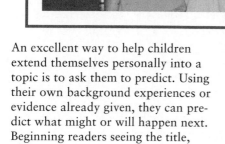

What strategies have you used to involve students meaningfully in learning?

An excellent way to help children extend themselves personally into a topic is to ask them to predict. Using their own background experiences or evidence already given, they can predict what might or will happen next. Beginning readers seeing the title, *Peter and the Penny Tree,* might be encouraged to write and illustrate their own stories about having a penny tree even before they read Thomas James's book. Every story offers possibilities, times when the teacher can halt the reading or the discussion to ask *who? what? whom? where? why?* and *how?* questions. And, when a child or a group seems to be losing interest, a request for a personal reaction or prediction will help refocus attention. It can be difficult at first to get children to risk predicting and developing prediction skills. Initially, therefore, predicting should be done with topics or questions with no right or wrong answers. Ground rules for any predicting activities are that no prediction based on rational or logical thinking is wrong. Children should understand that they are not allowed to laugh at or change or add on to anyone else's prediction. Both teacher and students should listen to and respect all ideas. If there are errors of thought in a prediction, the child can usually be led to correct his or her ideas through simple questioning, such as "Do you think that would work?" or "Is that what you would do?" In addition to developing better thinking and reasoning skills and group discussion skills, predicting brings the children's attention to the task, arouses interest and curiosity, and gives them a sense of ownership in their learning.

Dorothy A. Paulsen, Chapter I Teacher
Grant Elementary School, Wausau, Wisconsin

I have often thought of redesigning menus in foreign countries to accommodate students of traditional language courses in this country. Instead of asking for a wine list, students could demand the house "verb list" and order food and drink based on the complexity of a choice of verbs and tenses. Some of my early attempts to motivate students to learn verb forms met with as much success as would my attempt to have the menus changed. Success at rote memory of isolated words or groups of words was marginal at best, since there was little connection in the student's mind to anything approaching reality. I began giving students the opportunity to actually use skills and knowledge—whether it is verbs, other vocabulary, or culture insights in a reality-based setting. My students, for instance, using the target language, have corresponded with friends in a foreign country via the school fax machine. Students and teachers in my state today are involved in one of the most comprehensive school reform efforts imaginable. Changes in the second-language curriculum reflect ideas ranging from multi-age learning in new primary programs to the development of programs to ensure that every child in the state will be able to communicate in both English and a second language by graduation. Gone is the need to redesign the world to fit outdated education techniques and goals. Instead we have a combination of outcomes-based learning and the use of such concepts as cooperative learning, cross-disciplinary teaching, and multiple-intelligence learning opportunities.

Thomas E. Welch, State Foreign Language Consultant
Department of Education, Frankfort, Kentucky
1992 Kentucky Teacher of the Year
Jessamine County High School, Nicholasville, Kentucky

end of the discussion the group members may prepare a report on their activities or conclusions to be presented to the rest of the class.

Research on small-group discussions indicates that these activities can increase student achievement more than traditional lessons if the students are well prepared to work in small groups and the group task is well organized (Sharan *et al.*, 1984; Sharan and Shachar, 1988). Also, some research suggests that small-group discussions have greater effects on student achievement if students are encouraged to engage in controversy rather than to seek a consensus (Johnson and Johnson, 1979).

Self-Check

Create a two-column chart comparing and contrasting whole-group and small-group discussion in terms of the following categories: Appropriate uses, Prerequisites, Benefits, Limitations.

How Do Humanistic Approaches Differ from Direct Instruction?

Educational psychology has always had two principal schools of thought. One focuses primarily on the role of education in increasing students' knowledge and skills. This movement currently goes under the name of "direct instruction." The other is more focused on the affective outcomes of schooling, learning how to learn, and enhancing creativity and human potential. This is called the **humanistic education** movement, and it was a dominant force in American education in the 1960s and 1970s, and is making a substantial resurgence in the 1990s.

Self-Regulated Learning.   One of the most important ideas behind humanistic education is that students should have a substantial hand in directing their own education, in choosing what they will study and, to some degree, when and how they will study it. The idea is to make students self-directed, self-motivated learners rather than passive recipients of information. The motivational benefits of students' abilities to choose their own activities have been demonstrated (Campbell, 1964; Wang and Stiles, 1976); students will do more work with greater motivation if they have some choice in what they will study.

Affective Education.   Humanistic educators usually put as much value on affective goals of education as on cognitive learning goals, arguing that it is more important that students become responsible, caring, feeling adults than that we squeeze a few more points on a standardized test out of them (Combs, 1967; Jones, 1968; Glasser, 1969; Rogers, 1969). Glasser (1969) and Lefkowitz (1975) developed specific methods for holding "class meetings" to discuss interpersonal problems, values, and feelings. More typically, humanistic educators recommend that teachers emphasize such values as consideration, cooperativeness, mutual respect, and honesty, both by setting an example and by discussing and reinforcing these values when appropriate.

"Authentic" Assessment.   Another characteristic of humanistic education is the avoidance of grades, standardized testing, and most other formal methods of

---

Connections

Recall the discussion of self-regulated learning in Chapter 5. Authentic assessment is reintroduced in Chapter 13 and discussed in detail in Chapter 14.

---

humanistic education: an educational philosophy that focuses on developing students' attitudes, feelings, and independent learning.

▣▶ Focus On

Curriculum Issues

The curriculum of American schools has always served as a philosophical testing arena and battleground for educational theories, instructional methods, and course content. Two current curriculum issues have to do with the best way to teach reading and the desirability and goals of multicultural education. The two main camps in the debate over the best way to teach reading are the phonics and the whole-language advocates. Those who champion the whole-language approach stress keeping language whole by beginning with whole words rather than sounds and by including listening, speaking, and writing with reading instruction. Children in a teacher-designed whole-language unit might, for example, compose, recite, write, and read stories, respond to stories in daily journals, and work cooperatively on story-related projects. The whole-language approach also emphasizes treating language in "real" contexts, with children using language in ways that relate to their own knowledge and experiences.

The whole-language movement began as a reaction against a perceived overemphasis in traditional instruction on decoding sound systems, taking vocabulary worksheet drills, and working with basal readers that are constructed with an eye more to teaching basic skills than to authenticity for learners. Critics of whole-language express concern that teachers will produce a generation of learners who can't pronounce, spell, and use words properly. They urge teachers to teach phonics first or at least to keep a sensible balance between phonics and whole-language instruction.

The debate over multicultural curricula is, if anything, more complex because of differing notions of multiculturalism. What is it? What is it supposed to do? And what's the best way to do it? In some eyes it's a step backward toward racial and ethnic separatism as the status quo. Others see it as simply a more open celebration of diversity across the curriculum and at all grade levels—for example, classroom activities in recognition of Kwanzaa or Tet, multicultural sensitivity training, or analyses of American policies toward Central America from Central American points of view.

Most agree that the curriculum and the textbooks that support it should fairly reflect both American cultural diversity— the "great American mosaic"—and the contributions of non-European civilizations to history and the world. Nowhere is this need more evident than in social studies and history curricula, as California discovered during its trend-setting curriculum reforms. The state adopted a new K–12 "History-Social Sciences Framework" in 1987 that proclaims the value of cultural differences and minority-group achievements as well as the national and democratic values that are supposed to belong to all Americans equally. California also mandates the study of world history over a three-year period so that all civilizations' histories, not just Europe's, can be explored to some depth. For some minority-group parents and educators, however, such curriculum reform is too little too late. Amid controversy, cultural pride programs and private schools of, by, and for particular minority groups have sprung up across the country.

Critical Thinking

What curriculum issues, if any, came to your attention during your school years? To your knowledge, how were they decided? How would you resolve the controversy over reading instruction? What is your answer to the riddle of choosing a sound multicultural curriculum?

Susan Harman, "The Basal Conspiracy," *Teacher,* March 1992; Lynn Olsen, "Whole Language," *Teacher,* May-June 1992; Diane Ravitch, "Multiculturalism in the Curriculum," *Network News and Views,* March 1990; Robert Rothman, "Balance Between Phonics and Whole Language Urged," *Education Week,* January 10, 1990; Debra Viadero, "Multicultural Debate Rages," *Teacher,* 1991.

evaluation. Humanistic educators often recommend using written evaluations, "authentic" evaluations (such as solving real problems or conducting experiments), or no evaluations at all (Kirschenbaum *et al.,* 1971). Although research on graded versus ungraded ("pass-fail") courses indicates that the use of some sort of grading increases student achievement at the college level (see Gold *et al.,* 1971), there is little evidence either way on the effects of grading in elementary or secondary schools and equally little research comparing written evaluations to letter grades (see Chapter 13 for more on innovative assessment methods).

Self-Motivation.   Another principle of humanistic education is that education should teach students how to learn and to value learning for its own sake. All educators hope that students will develop positive attitudes toward learning and will be able to use various resources to obtain information, but humanistic educators especially emphasize these goals and strongly recommend designing instruction to give students many opportunities to locate information on their own or with minimal teacher guidance. Humanistic programs therefore generally include frequent use of open-ended activities in which students must find information, make decisions, solve problems, and create their own products. For example, teachers might have students write a history of their school, with students taking responsibility for searching school archives, old yearbooks, and other records, for interviewing older teachers and former students, and for searching the local newspaper's archives for information about the school. To help learn math, students might set up a simulated (or real) store or bank, or pretend to invest in the stock market. Most humanistic educators would recommend frequent field trips and explorations in the world outside school. One teacher took students to visit an old graveyard next to the school. The students' task was to find ways to use the information on headstones to learn about the history of the area and about how people lived many years ago. The teacher had two kinds of objectives in mind for students. One was the content itself—the history of an area—and the other was to give students an experience of finding out something for themselves, of using their brains and their imaginations to learn, of learning how rich the world is in information if only we know how to get at it, of finding out how much fun it is to learn.

Open Schools

The instructional programs most closely associated with the humanistic education movement of the early 1970s are called **open schools** or "open classrooms." Often the classrooms have no walls.

Open schools vary considerably in their particulars and philosophies, but they do have several features in common, shown in Table 8.5. Some researchers doubt that *all* the features of open education were ever widely used, even when the open school movement was at its height in the 1970s (Epstein and McPartland, 1975; Marshall, 1981). However, there is no question that many open schools have given students a wide variety of instructional opportunities and a wide range of choices as to what and how they will learn.

Open classrooms typically use **learning stations,** areas located around the room that contain projects, individualized workbooks or units, or other activities. Students choose the order in which they will pursue individual activities, but they typically must accomplish some set of objectives by some time. The particular objectives vary from student to student and may be negotiated with the teacher. In open classrooms the teacher rarely delivers a lesson to the entire class but more often spends time with individuals and small groups working on a common activity.

Reviews of studies of open versus traditional education have uniformly concluded that the effects of open-education programs did not support the early enthusiasm for them (for example, Horwitz, 1979; Peterson, 1979; Marshall, 1981; Giaconia and Hedges, 1982; Rothenberg, 1989). Students in open schools generally learn

open schools: schools in which students are actively involved in deciding what and how they will study.

learning stations: areas where students work on individualized units or other independent activities.

Roles of Children and Teachers

• Children are active in guiding their own learning.	• Children actively choose materials, methods, and pace of learning.	• Teachers serve as resource persons rather than as directors of classroom activities.

Diagnostic Evaluation

• Observation, written histories, and samples of student work (rather than conventional tests or grades) are used to evaluate progress.	• Purpose of evaluation is to guide instruction, not to grade or rank students.

Materials to Manipulate

• Diverse materials are used to stimulate student exploration and learning.	• Emphasis is on use of materials students can touch and explore; real-world natural materials are preferred to worksheets and books alone.

Individualized Instruction

• Instruction is based on individual needs and abilities. Students proceed at their own rates.	• Materials are adapted to provide for differences in students' preferred modes of learning.	• Instruction is given to individuals and small groups, rarely to large groups. • Students set individual goals for learning.

Multi-age Grouping

• Students of different ages may work in the same classroom without age distinction.	• Grade levels may not be used to categorize students.

Open Space

• Physical environment of the classroom involves flexible use of space and furnishings.	• Classrooms lack interior walls; many classrooms may share resources and personnel.	• Seating arrangements are flexible.

Team Teaching

• Two or more teachers plan together, share resources, mix students.	• Two or more teachers may completely combine classes in a large area.	• Parents are often used as volunteer aides.

Table 8.5   **Features of Open Education**

Source: Adapted from Giaconia and Hedges, 1982, pp. 593–594.

slightly less than do students in traditional programs. On affective outcomes, such as attitudes toward school, cooperativeness, social adjustment, and self-concept, students in open classrooms have scored only slightly better than traditionally

Choosing Instructional Approaches

John Harrison, a fourth-grade teacher in his second year of teaching, and Barbara Monteiro, a third-grade teacher with seven years' experience, are both members of their school's curriculum committee. They are conferring before attending a committee meeting.

BARBARA: What is the situation you said you were concerned about, John?

JOHN: Well, somehow I haven't been able to hit my stride with this year's group of kids. I seem to have a handful of academic superstars and also a small group that's having real trouble with math and reading. And then there's the fifteen or so kids right in the middle. It just seems like I have two or three classes in one. What would you do with a class like that?

BARBARA: I don't think there's any magic solution, but it's a very common problem. All of us face it to some extent.

JOHN: I know. The principal suggested that I group the kids for some subjects, but I'm not sure that feels right to me. Last year my students were so similar in their abilities that I was able to be much more flexible with them. Boy, did we do some great projects! We always had time to cover the curriculum, and then some.

BARBARA: Well, different groups of students do demand different approaches. Have you thought about direct instruction? Sometimes that can be very effective for work with low math achievers on their basic skills, for instance. It could also be good for your whole-class lessons on social studies and the like.

JOHN: Yeah, I tried a form of direct instruction during one of my stints of student teaching. But I never got comfortable with it. It seemed too artificial and structured and subject-matter oriented.

BARBARA: Pretty negative reaction!

JOHN: Well, I felt that I never had time to talk with the kids and see what *they* were thinking and what *they* wanted to learn. They have some pretty good ideas sometimes, you know.

BARBARA: Yes, they do. Let's see. What teaching strategy have you enjoyed using the most?

JOHN: I guess I like the humanistic approach. I've found I'm interested in the whole child, not just the subject matter the child has learned. One science sequence I used last year encouraged the students to think up and solve problems on their own. Those kids took the projects in directions I never would have dreamed of! But I was afraid to do that kind of thing too often, because I know t his district puts a lot of emphasis on covering the curriculum in science—and in other subjects—and preparing children for standardized tests.

BARBARA: Well, we *do* have to prepare kids for those tests.

JOHN: True, but I just don't think the test scores say much about the whole child. And when we pay too much attention to scores, we forget about feelings and motivations and creativity. Those belong in the curriculum too.

BARBARA: I agree with you, John. Still, I'm hearing you say that you've got some students who need help with basic math and reading skills. The question is, will a humanistic approach help those kids catch up in your class?

JOHN: When you put it like that, maybe not. Maybe direct instruction would be better—for certain well-defined applications, at least. I could be won over if I saw my students make real gains.

BARBARA: I have an idea. Let's bring this up at the committee meeting. Maybe we can work out a mix of approaches that we could all use for our various students in reading and math.

Problem Solving

1. What advice would you give John about choosing instructional strategies? Would humanistic teaching procedures help the students in his classroom who are behind in math and reading?

2. What are the goals and practices of humanistic education? Of direct instruction? What are the differences, strengths, and weaknesses of the two?

3. In writing or role play, extend the dialogue between John and Barbara to develop an actual plan for "a mix of approaches."

Summary

What Is Direct Instruction?

Direct instruction is a teaching approach that emphasizes teacher control of all classroom events and the presentation of highly structured lessons. Direct instruction programs call for active teaching; clear lesson organization; step-by-step progression between subtopics; and the use of many examples, demonstrations, and visual prompts.

What Are the Parts of a Lesson in Direct Instruction?

The first part of a lesson is stating learning objectives and orienting students to the lesson. The principal task is to establish both a "mental set" so that students are ready to work and learn and a "road map" so students know where the lesson is going.

Part two of a lesson is to review prerequisites or pretest to ensure students have previously mastered required knowledge and skills. The review may serve the function of an "advance organizer" for the lesson.

Part three involves presenting the new material in an organized way, providing explanations and demonstrations and maintaining attention.

Part four, conducting learning probes, elicits students' responses to lesson content. This practice gives teachers feedback and lets students test their ideas. Questioning techniques are important, including the uses of calling order and wait time.

Part five of a lesson is independent practice or seatwork in which students apply their new skill. Research shows independent practice should be given as short assignments with clear instructions and no interruptions, only when students can do them. Teachers should monitor work, collect it, and include it in assessments.

Part six is to assess performance and provide feedback. Every lesson includes an assessment of student mastery of the lesson objectives.

Part seven is to provide distributed practice, or homework, and review. Information is retained better when practice is spaced out over a period of time.

What Does Research on Direct Instruction Methods Suggest?

"Master teaching" and "systematic instruction" models are two generally effective variants of the direct instruction approach. Teachers using the master-teaching Missouri Mathematics Program had comparatively greater success, measured by student achievement. Research does not support any clear superiority of Madeline Hunter's Mastery Teaching Program over other direct instruction methods. Mastery Teaching involves four broad steps: getting students set to learn, providing input and modeling, checking understanding and providing guided practice, and providing independent practice.

"Systematic" programs, including Behavior Analysis and DISTAR, were proven successful for reading and mathematics achievement among low achievers and students at risk.

How Is Cooperative Learning Used in Classroom Instruction?

In cooperative learning, small groups of students work together to help one another learn. Research suggests that four-member mixed-ability groupings work best and that group skills should be directly taught. Cooperative learning groups are used in discovery learning, discussion, and study for assessment. Cooperative learning programs such as Student Teams Achievement Divisions (STAD) are successful because they reward both group and individual effort and improvement and groups are responsible for the individual learning of each group member.

How Are Discussions Used in Classroom Instruction?

In whole-group discussion the teacher plays a less dominant role than in a regular lesson. When using an inquiry training strategy, the teacher answers only yes-or-no questions and provides information only when students ask the right questions. Students need an adequate knowledge base before beginning a discussion. In small-group discussion each group should have a leader and a specific focus.

How Do Humanistic Education Approaches Differ from Direct Instruction?

Humanistic approaches focus on learning how to learn, being creative, and meeting human potential. It is based on the idea that students should help direct their own education. Affective goals are as important as cognitive goals, and informal evaluations of progress are preferred to formal assessments such as letter grades and standardized tests. Open classrooms stress individualized instruction, team teaching, inquiry approaches, and the development of independent learning skills.

Key Terms

anticipatory set, 283
authentic learning, 300

calling order, 278
choral response, 279

9

Accommodating Instruction to Individual Needs

Chapter Outline	Chapter Objectives
What Is Effective Instruction? Carroll's Model of School Learning The QAIT Model of Effective Instruction	▲ Give several reasons that effective instruction involves more than giving good lectures, and explain how the QAIT model of effective instruction provides opportunities for accommodating differences in student ability.
How Are Students Grouped by Ability? Between-Class Ability Grouping Within-Class Ability Grouping	▲ Compare between-class ability grouping and within-class ability grouping in terms of advantages, disadvantages, and appropriate use in relation to five general principles of ability grouping.
What Are Some Effective Programs to Use with Ability Groups? Ability-Grouped Active Teaching Cooperative Integrated Reading and Composition	▲ Describe at least two effective instructional programs for use with ability groups.
What Is Mastery Learning? What Forms Does Mastery Learning Take? How Does Mastery Learning Work? Outcomes-Based Education	▲ Identify the principles on which mastery learning is based, describe some forms mastery learning takes, and plan steps for teaching a unit using mastery learning.
What Are Some Ways of Individualizing Instruction? Tutoring Programmed Instruction Team Assisted Individualization Informal Remediation and Enrichment Computer-Assisted Instruction	▲ Evaluate several methods for individualizing instruction, incorporating computer-assisted instruction in the classroom, and providing appropriate levels of instruction.

Mr. Arbuthnot is in fine form. He is presenting a lesson on long division to his fourth-grade class and feels that he's never been so clear, so interesting, and so well organized. When he asks questions, several students raise their hands, and when he calls on them, they always know the answers. "Arbuthnot, old boy," he says to himself, "I think you're really getting to these kids!"

At the end of the period he passes out a short quiz to see how well his students have learned the long-division lesson. When the papers are scored, he finds to his shock and disappointment that while about a third of the class got every problem right, another third missed every problem. The remaining students fell somewhere in between. "What went wrong?" he thinks. "Well, no matter, I'll set the situation aright in tomorrow's lesson."

The next day Mr. Arbuthnot is even better prepared, uses vivid examples and diagrams to show how to do long division, and gives an active, exciting lesson. Even more hands than before go up when he asks questions, and the answers are usually correct. However, some of the students are beginning to look bored, particularly those who got perfect papers on the quiz and those who got none right.

Toward the end of the period he gives another brief quiz. The scores are better this time, but there is still a group of students who got none of the problems correct. He is crestfallen. "I had them in the palm of my hand," he thinks. "How could they fail to learn?"

To try to find out what went wrong, he goes over the quiz papers of the students who missed all the problems. He immediately sees a pattern. By the second lesson, almost all students were proceeding correctly in setting up the long-division problems. However, some were making consistent errors in subtraction. Others had apparently forgotten their multiplication facts. Their problems were not with division at all; they simply lacked the prerequisite skills.

"Well," thinks Mr. Arbuthnot, "at least I was doing great with some of the kids." It occurs to him that one of the students who got a perfect paper after the first lesson might be able to give him an idea about how to teach the others better. He asks Teresa how she grasped long division so quickly. "It was easy," she says. "We learned long division last year!"

What Is Effective Instruction?

As Mr. Arbuthnot learned to his chagrin, effective instruction takes a lot more than effective lectures. He gave a great lesson on long division, yet it was only appropriate for some of his students, those who had the needed prerequisites but had not already learned long division. To make his lesson effective for *all* of his students, he needed to adapt it to meet their diverse needs. Further, the best lesson in the world won't work if students are unmotivated to learn it, or if there is inadequate time allotted to allow all students to learn.

If the quality of lectures were all that mattered in effective instruction, we could probably find the best lecturers in the world, make videotapes of their lessons, and show the tapes to students. If you think about why videotaped lessons wouldn't work very well, you will realize how much more is involved in effective instruction than simply giving good lectures. First, the video teacher would have no idea of what students already knew. A particular lesson might be too advanced or too easy for a particular group of students. Second, some students might be learning the lesson quite well, while others were missing key concepts and falling behind. The video teacher would have no way of knowing which students needed additional help and, in any case, would have no way of providing it. There would be no way to question students to find out if they were getting the main points and then to reteach any concept they had missed. Third, the video teacher would have no way of motivating students to pay attention to the lesson or to really try to learn it. If students failed to pay attention or misbehaved, the video teacher couldn't do anything about it. Finally, the video teacher would never know at the end of a lesson whether students had actually learned the main concepts or skills. This analysis of video teaching illustrates why teachers must be concerned with many elements of instruction in addition to the presentation of information. Teachers must know how to adapt their instruction to the students' levels of knowledge. They must motivate students to learn, manage student behavior, group students for instruction, and assess the students' learning. To help make sense of all these elements of effective instruction, educational psychologists have proposed models of effective instruction. These models explain the critical features of high-quality lessons and how they relate to one another to enhance learning.

Carroll's Model of School Learning

One of the most influential articles ever published in the field of educational psychology was a paper by John Carroll entitled "A Model of School Learning" (1963). In it he describes teaching in terms of the management of time, resources, and activities to ensure student learning. The model presented by Carroll proposes five elements that contribute to the effectiveness of instruction:

1. *Aptitude:* Students' general abilities to learn.
2. *Ability to Understand Instruction:* Students' readiness to learn a particular lesson. This is related to abilities, but also to knowledge of prerequisite skills or information needed to understand the next lesson. For example, no matter how able students are, they cannot learn to do long division if they do not know how to multiply and subtract.
3. *Perseverance:* The amount of time students are willing to actively spend learning. Perseverance is mostly a product of students' motivation to learn.
4. *Opportunity:* The amount of time allowed for learning. Opportunity relates to the amount of time teachers spend teaching a particular skill or concept.
5. *Quality of Instruction:* The effectiveness with which a lesson is actually delivered. Quality of instruction is high if students learn the material presented in the lesson as rapidly as their abilities and levels of prior knowledge and skills allow.

Carroll discussed these elements in terms of (1) time actually spent on learning and (2) time needed to learn, proposing the following relationship:

Degree of Learning = *f* (Time Spent/Time Needed)

That is, learning is greater the more time students spend on it in relation to the amount of time they need to learn. "Time needed" is a product of aptitude and ability to learn, whereas time actually spent depends on opportunity, quality of instruction, and student perseverance.

What is important about Carroll's model is that it puts the major elements of effective instruction into relationship with one another and discusses them in terms of one variable, time (see Clark, 1987; Carroll, 1989). Many researchers have assumed that degree of learning is primarily a product of student aptitude or intelligence, but what Carroll was implying is that differences in aptitude need not be seen as restricting the *amount* that can be learned, but only as determining the time it takes. In other words, just about anyone can learn just about anything if the quality of instruction is high and if enough time is spent in learning. Carroll's model led directly to Bloom's (1968) theory of mastery learning, discussed later in this chapter.

Carroll's model mixes two kinds of elements: those that are directly under the control of the teacher and those that are characteristic of individual students. Aptitude is mostly a characteristic of students over which an individual teacher can have little control. Ability to understand instruction and perseverance are partly controlled by the teacher but are also partly characteristics of each student. For example, the ability to understand instruction partly depends on the student's ability but also depends on the teacher's ability to ensure that students have the necessary prerequisites to learn a new lesson. Perseverance results from both the motivation to learn that a student brings to school and from specific strategies a teacher or school might use to encourage students to do their best. Opportunity (time) and quality of instruction are directly under the control of the teacher or the school.

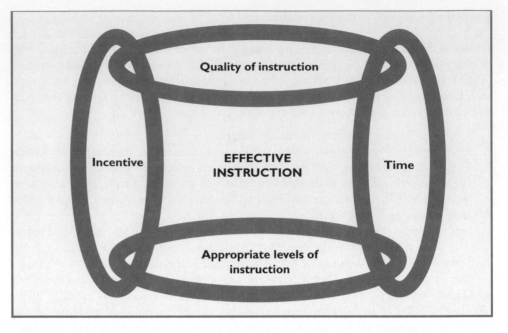

Figure 9.1

The QAIT Model

Each of the elements of the QAIT model is like a link in a chain, and the chain is only as strong as the weakest link.

The QAIT Model of Effective Instruction

Slavin (1987d) described a model focusing on the *alterable* elements of Carroll's model, those that the teacher or school can directly change. It is called the QAIT (quality, appropriateness, incentive, time) model of effective instruction.

1. *Quality of Instruction:* The degree to which information or skills are presented so that students can easily learn them. Quality of instruction is largely a product of the quality of the curriculum and of the lesson presentation itself.
2. *Appropriate Levels of Instruction:* The degree to which the teacher makes sure that students are ready to learn a new lesson (that is, have the necessary skills and knowledge to learn it) but have not already learned the lesson. In other words, the level of instruction is appropriate when a lesson is neither too difficult nor too easy for students.
3. *Incentive:* The degree to which the teacher makes sure that students are motivated to work on instructional tasks and to learn the material being presented.
4. *Time:* The degree to which students are given enough time to learn the material being taught.

The shared feature of the four elements in the **QAIT model** is that all must be adequate for instruction to be effective. No matter how high the quality of instruction, students will not learn a lesson if they lack the necessary prior skills or information, if they lack the motivation, or if they lack the time they need to learn the lesson. On the other hand, if the quality of instruction is low, then it makes no difference how

These students are applying what they have learned in science about electricity. According to the QAIT model of effective instruction, what four aspects of this activity would you most directly and importantly influence as their teacher?

much students already know, how motivated they are, or how much time they have. Figure 9.1 illustrates the relationship among the elements in the QAIT model.

Quality of Instruction.   Quality of instruction refers to the set of activities most people first think of when they think of teaching: lecturing, calling on students, discussing, helping students with seatwork, and so on. When instruction is high in quality, the information presented makes sense to students, is interesting to them, and is easy to remember and apply.

The most important aspect of quality of instruction is the degree to which the lesson makes sense to students. To make lessons make sense, teachers must present material in an orderly, organized way. They need to relate new information to what students already know. They need to use examples, demonstrations, pictures, and diagrams to make ideas vivid for students. They may use such cognitive strategies as advance organizers and memory strategies. Sometimes a concept will not make sense to students until they discover it or experience it themselves, or until they discuss it with others.

Another important aspect of quality of instruction is the degree to which the teacher monitors how well students are learning and adapts the pace of instruction so that it is neither too fast nor too slow. For example, teachers should frequently ask questions to see how much students have grasped. If the answers show that students are keeping up with the lesson, the teacher might move along a little more rapidly. But if students' answers show they are having trouble keeping up, the teacher might review parts of the lesson and slow down the pace.

QAIT model: a model of effective instruction that focuses on elements that teachers can directly control.

Appropriate Levels of Instruction.   Perhaps the most difficult problem of classroom organization is dealing with the fact that students come into class with different levels of knowledge, skills, learning rate, and motivation. This was Mr. Arbuthnot's main dilemma. Student diversity requires teachers to provide appropriate levels of instruction. Teaching a class of thirty students (or even a class of ten) is fundamentally different from one-to-one tutoring because of the inevitability of student-to-student differences that affect the success of instruction. Teachers can always be sure that if they teach one lesson to the whole class, some students will learn the material much more quickly than others. In fact, some students may not learn the lesson at all because they lack important prerequisite skills or are not given adequate time (because to give them enough time would waste too much of the time of students who learn rapidly). Recognition of these instructionally important differences leads many teachers to search for ways of individualizing instruction, adapting instruction to meet students' different needs, or grouping students according to their abilities. However, some of these solutions create problems of their own that may be more serious than the ones they are meant to solve!

For example, a teacher might give all students materials appropriate to their individual needs and allow them to work at their own rates. This solves the problem of providing appropriate levels of instruction but creates serious new problems of managing the activities of twenty or thirty students doing twenty or thirty different things. A teacher might group students by ability (for example, Redbirds, Bluebirds, and Yellowbirds) so that each group would have a relatively narrow range of abilities. However, this creates problems, too, because when the teacher is working with the Redbirds, the Bluebirds and Yellowbirds must work without supervision or help.

There are effective ways of adapting instruction to meet student needs. These are discussed later in this chapter.

Connections

Individual and group incentive systems for student learning are described in Chapter 10. Individual and group incentive systems for student conduct are described in Chapter 11.

Incentive.   Thomas Edison once wrote that "genius is one per cent inspiration and ninety-nine per cent perspiration." The same could probably be said for learning. Learning is work. This is not to say that learning isn't or can't be fun or stimulating, that it has to be a dreary chore—far from it. But it is true that students must exert themselves to pay attention, to conscientiously perform the tasks required of them, and to study, and they must somehow be motivated to do these things. This incentive, or motivation, may come from characteristics of the tasks themselves (for example, the interest value of the material being learned), from characteristics of students (such as their curiosity or positive orientation toward learning), or from rewards provided by the teacher or the school (such as grades and certificates).

If students want to know something, they will be more likely to exert the necessary effort to learn it. This is why there are students who can rattle off the names, batting averages, number of home runs, and all sorts of other information about every player on the Chicago Cubs, but can't name the fifty states or the basic multiplication facts. To such students, baseball facts have great interest value, so they are willing to invest a great deal of effort to master them. Some information is naturally interesting to some or all students, but teachers can do much to *create* interest in a topic by arousing students' curiosity or by showing how knowledge gained in school can be useful outside of school. For example, a baseball fan might be much more interested in learning about computing proportions if told that this information is necessary for computing batting averages.

However, not every subject can be made fascinating to all students at all times. Most students need some kind of recognition or reward if they are to exert maximum effort to learn skills or concepts that may seem unimportant at the moment but will be critical for later learning. For this reason, schools use praise, feedback, grades, certificates, stars, prizes, and other rewards to increase student motivation. These rewards, and general principles of motivation, are discussed in Chapter 10.

Time.   The final element of the QAIT model is time. Instruction takes time. More time spent teaching something does not necessarily mean more learning, but if instructional quality, appropriateness of instruction, and incentive are all high, then more time on instruction *will* pay off in greater learning.

The amount of time available for learning depends largely on two factors. The first is the amount of time that the teacher (1) schedules for instruction and (2) actually uses to teach. The other is the amount of time students pay attention to the lesson. Both kinds of time are affected by classroom management and discipline strategies. If students are well behaved, well motivated, and have a sense of purpose and direction, and if teachers are well prepared and well organized, then there is plenty of time for students to learn whatever teachers want to teach. However, many factors, such as interruptions, behavior problems, and poor transitions between activities eat away at the time available for learning (see Karweit, 1989).

Principles of classroom management and discipline are discussed in Chapter 11.

Self-Check

Draw a diagram or concept map showing the significance of and interrelationships among the following terms:

strong incentive	high quality of lesson presentation
appropriate levels of instruction	effective instruction
high quality of curriculum	optimal use of time

How Are Students Grouped by Ability?

From the day they walk into school, students differ in their knowledge, skills, motivations, and predispositions toward what is about to be taught. Some students are already reading when they enter kindergarten, while others need much time and support to learn to read well. A teacher starting a new lesson can usually assume that some students already know a great deal about the lesson's content, some know less but will master the content early on, and some may not be able to master the content at all within the time provided. Some have the prerequisite skills and knowledge needed to learn the lesson, while others do not. This was Mr. Arbuthnot's problem; some of his students were not ready to learn long division, while others had already learned it before he began. Some of his students lacked basic multiplication and subtraction skills that are crucial for long division. Others already knew long division before he began his lesson, and many probably learned it during the first lesson and did not need the second. If Mr. Arbuthnot stopped to review multiplication and division, he would be wasting the time of the better-

Connections

Students differ in general intelligence, specific aptitudes and abilities, and learning styles, discussed in Chapter 4. Characteristics of exceptional learners are discussed in Chapter 12.

prepared students. If he set his pace of instruction according to the needs of his more able students, those with learning problems would never catch up. How can Mr. Arbuthnot teach a lesson that will work for *all* of his students: students who are performing within the normal range but differ in prior knowledge, skills, and learning rates?

Accommodating instruction to student differences is one of the most fundamental problems of education and often leads to politically and emotionally charged policies. For example, most countries outside of North America attempt to deal with the problem of student differences, or student "heterogeneity," by testing children at around ten to twelve years of age and assigning them to different types of schools, only one of which is meant to prepare students for higher education. These systems have long been under attack and are changing in some countries (such as the United Kingdom), but remain in others (such as Germany). In the United States a similar function is carried out by assignment of students to "college preparatory," "general," and "vocational" **tracks** in high school, and by grouping students in classes according to ability level in junior/middle schools and often in elementary schools as well. This practice is called **between-class ability grouping.** Another common means of accommodating instruction to student differences in elementary schools is **within-class ability grouping,** as in the use of reading groups (Bluebirds, Redbirds, Yellowbirds) that divide students according to their reading performance. The problem of accommodating student differences is so important that many educators have suggested that instruction be completely individualized so that students can work independently at their own rates. In the past twenty-five years this point of view has led to the creation of individualized instructional programs and computer-assisted instruction. ·

Each of the many ways of accommodating students' differences has its own benefits, but each introduces its own problems, which sometimes outweigh the benefits. This chapter discusses the research on various means of accommodating classroom instruction to student differences. Some student differences can be easily accommodated. For example, different learning styles can often be accommodated by, for example, augmenting verbal presentations with visual cues such as writing on the chalkboard or showing pictures and diagrams to emphasize important concepts. Other differences in learning style can be accommodated by varying classroom activities, such as alternating active and quiet tasks or individual and group work. Teachers can sometimes work with students on an individual basis and adapt instruction to their learning styles—for example, by reminding impulsive students to take their time or by teaching overly reflective students strategies for skipping over items they are having problems with so they can complete tests on time.

Differences in prior knowledge and learning rate are more difficult to deal with. Sometimes the best way to deal with these differences is to ignore them, to teach the whole class at a single pace, perhaps offering additional help to low-achieving students and giving extra enrichment activities to students who tend to finish assignments rapidly. For example, it is probably less important to accommodate student achievement differences in social studies, science, and English than in mathematics, reading, and foreign languages. This is because in the latter subjects skills build directly on one another, so teaching at one pace to a heterogeneous class may be a disservice to both low and high achievers; low achievers may fail because they lack prerequisite skills, while high achievers may become bored at what is for them a slow pace of instruction. This was the case in Mr. Arbuthnot's mathematics class.

The remainder of this chapter discusses strategies for accommodating student achievement differences.

tracks: classes or curricula targeted for students of a specified achievement or ability level.

between-class ability grouping: the practice of grouping students by ability level in separate classes.

within-class ability grouping: system of accommodating student differences by dividing a class of students into two or more ability groups for instruction in certain subjects.

Between-Class Ability Grouping

Probably the most common means of dealing with instructionally important differences is to assign students to classes according to their abilities. This between-class ability grouping may take many forms. In high schools there may be "college preparatory " and "general" tracks that divide students on the basis of measured ability. In some junior high and middle schools students are assigned to one class by general ability, and they then stay with that class, moving from teacher to teacher. For example, the highest-performing seventh-graders might be assigned to class 7-1, middle-performing students to 7-5, and low-performing students to 7-12. In other junior high/middle schools (and many high schools) students are grouped separately by ability for each subject, so that a student might be in a high-performing math class and an average-performing science class. In high schools this is accomplished by course placements. For example, some ninth-graders take Algebra I, while others who do not qualify for Algebra I take general mathematics. Elementary schools use a wide range of strategies for grouping students, including many of the patterns used in secondary schools. Often students in elementary schools will be assigned to a mixed-ability class for homeroom, social studies, and science , but regrouped by ability for reading and math. Elementary schools are less likely than secondary schools to use ability grouping *between* classes, but more likely to use ability grouping *within* classes, especially in reading (McPartland *et al.,* 1987). At any level, however, provision of separate special education programs for students with serious learning problems is one form of between-class ability grouping, as is provision of separate programs for the academically gifted and talented. Special education and gifted programs are discussed in Chapter 12.

Research on Between-Class Ability Grouping.   Despite the widespread use of between-class ability grouping, research on this strategy does not support its use. Researchers have found that while ability grouping may have slight benefits for students assigned to high-track classes, these benefits are balanced by losses for

Some of these students are reading well above grade level, while others are still only learning to read. As a teacher, how might you group these students to accommodate instruction to their different abilities?

students assigned to low-track classes (for example, Good and Marshall, 1984; Oakes, 1985; Slavin, 1987b, 1990a).

Why is between-class ability grouping so ineffective? Several researchers have explored this question. The primary purpose of ability grouping is to reduce the range of student performance levels teachers must deal with so they can adapt instruction to the needs of a well-defined group. However, grouping is often done on the basis of standardized test scores or other measures of general ability rather than performance in a particular subject. As a result, the reduction in the range of differences that are actually important for a specific class may be too small to make much difference. Further, concentrating low-achieving students in low-track classes seems to be harmful because it exposes them to too few positive role models (Rosenbaum, 1980). Then, too, many teachers do not like to teach such classes and may subtly (or not so subtly) communicate low expectations for students in them. (Good and Marshall, 1984).

Several studies have found that the quality of instruction is lower in low-track classes than in middle- or high-track classes. For example, teachers of low-track classes are less enthusiastic, less organized, and teach more facts and fewer concepts than do teachers of high-track classes. Instruction in mixed-ability, untracked classes more closely resembles that in high- and middle -track classes than that in low-track classes (Goodlad, 1983; Oakes, 1985). Perhaps the most damaging effect of tracking is its stigmatizing effect on students assigned to the low tracks, its message to these students that academic success is not within their capabilities. Schafer and Olexa (1971) interviewed one non–college-prep girl who said that she carried her general-track books upside down to avoid being humiliated walking down the hall. A former delinquent described in an interview how he felt when he went to junior high school and found out he was in the basic track:

> . . . I felt good when I was with my [elementary] class, but when they went and separated us—that changed us. That changed our ideas, our thinking, the way we thought about each other, and turned us to enemies toward each other—because they said I was dumb and they were smart.

> When you first go to junior high school you do feel something inside—it's like a ego. You have been from elementary to junior high, you feel great inside . . . you get this shirt that says Brown Junior High . . . and you are proud of that shirt. But then you go up there and the teacher says—"Well, so and so, you're in the basic section, you can't go with the other kids." The devil with the whole thing—you lose—something in you—like it goes out of you. (Schafer and Olexa, 1971, pp. 62–63)

Students in lower-track classes are far more likely than other students to become delinquent and truant and drop out of school (Schafer and Olexa, 1971; Rosenbaum, 1980; Goodlad, 1983; Oakes, 1985). These problems are certainly due in part to the fact that students in low-track classes are low in academic performance to begin with. However, this is probably not the whole story. For example, students assigned to the low track in junior high school experience a rapid loss of self-esteem (Goodlad, 1983), as the preceding interview illustrates. Slavin and Karweit (1982a) found that fifth- and sixth-graders in urban elementary schools were absent about 8 percent of the time. When these same students entered the tracked junior high school, absenteeism rose almost immediately to 26 percent, with the truancy concentrated among students assigned to the bottom-track classes. The change happened too rapidly to be attributed entirely to characteristics of students; something about the organization of the junior high school apparently convinced a substantial number of students that school was no longer a rewarding place to be.

While individual teachers can rarely set policies on between-class ability group-ing, it is useful for all educators to know that research does not support this prac-tice at any grade level, and tracking should be avoided whenever possible. This does not mean that *all* forms of between-class grouping should be abandoned, however. For example, there is probably some justification for acceleration pro-grams, such as offering Algebra I to mathematically talented seventh-graders or offering advanced placement classes in high school. Also, some between-class grouping is bound to occur in secondary schools because some students choose to take advanced courses while others do not. However, the idea that having high, middle, and low sections of the same course can help student achievement has not been supported by research. Mixed-ability classes can be successful at all grade lev-els, particularly if other more effective means of accommodating student differ-ences are used (see Slavin *et al.,* 1989). These include within-class ability grouping, tutoring for low achievers, and certain individualized instruction programs described in this chapter, as well as cooperative learning strategies presented in Chapter 8.

Regrouping for Reading and Mathematics.   Another form of ability grouping often used in the elementary grades is called **regrouping.** In regrouping plans stu-dents are in mixed-ability classes most of the day but are assigned to reading and/or math classes on the basis of their performance in these subjects. For exam-ple, at 9:30A.M. the fourth-graders in a school may move to a different teacher so that they can receive reading instruction appropriate to their reading levels. One form of regrouping for reading, the **Joplin Plan,** regroups students across grade lines. For example, a reading class at the fourth-grade, first-semester reading level may contain third-, fourth-, and fifth-graders.

One major advantage of regrouping over all-day ability grouping is that in regrouping plans the students spend most of the day in a mixed-ability class. Thus low achievers are not separated out as a class and stigmatized. In the Joplin Plan even the ability-grouped reading class has students of all ability levels (but different ages). Perhaps for these reasons, regrouping plans, especially the Joplin Plan, have generally been found to increase student achievement (Slavin, 1987b).

Within-Class Ability Grouping

Another means of adapting instruction to differences in student performance levels is to group students *within* classes, as is typical in elementary school reading classes. For example, a third-grade teacher might have the "Rockets" group using a 3-1 (third-grade, first semester) text, the "Stars" using a 3-2 (third-grade, sec-ond-semester) text, and the "Planets" using a 4-1 (fourth-grade, first-semester) text.

Within-class ability grouping is far more common in elementary schools than in secondary schools (Goodlad, 1983; McPartland *et al.,* 1987). It is almost univer-sal in elementary reading classes and frequent in math classes but rarely used in other subjects. In reading, teachers typically have each group working at a differ-ent point in a series of reading texts and allow each group to proceed at its own pace. Teachers who group in math may use different texts with the different groups or, more often , allow groups to proceed at their own rates in the same book, so that the higher-performing group will cover more material than the lower-performing group. In many math classes the teacher teaches one lesson to

regrouping: a method of ability grouping in which stu-dents in mixed-ability classes are assigned to reading or math classes on the basis of their performance levels.

Joplin Plan: a regrouping method in which students are assigned to groups for reading instruction across grade lines.

the whole class and then meets with two or more ability groups during times when students are doing seatwork to reinforce skills or provide enrichment as needed.

Research on Within-Class Ability Grouping.

Research on the achievement effects of within-class ability grouping has taken place almost exclusively in elementary mathematics classes. This is because researchers want to look at teaching situations in which some teachers use within-class ability grouping and others do not, and only in elementary math is this typically true. Until recently, almost all elementary reading teachers have used reading groups, while in elementary subjects other than math and in secondary classes, very few teachers do. Most studies that have evaluated within-class ability grouping methods in math (where the different groups proceed at different paces on different materials) have found that students in the ability-grouped classes learned more than those in classes that did not use grouping (Slavin, 1987b). Students of high, average, and low achievement levels seem to benefit equally from within-class ability grouping.

The research suggests that small numbers of ability groups are better than large numbers (Slavin and Karweit, 1984a). Smaller numbers of groups have the advantage of allowing more direct instruction from the teacher and using less seatwork time and transition time. For example, in a class with two ability groups students must spend at least half of their class time doing seatwork without direct supervision. With three groups this rises to two-thirds of class time.

Teachers who try to teach more than three reading or math groups also may have problems with classroom management. Dividing the class into more than three groups does not decrease the size or range of differences within each group enough to offset these problems (see Hiebert, 1983).

It is important to note that the research finding benefits of within-class grouping in elementary mathematics was mostly done many years ago with traditional teaching methods primarily intended to teach computations rather than problem solving. As mathematics moves toward use of constructivist approaches more directed at problem solving, discovery, and cooperative learning, within-class grouping may become unnecessary. The main point to be drawn from research on within-class ability grouping is not that it is desirable, but that if some form of grouping is felt to be necessary, grouping within the class is preferable to grouping between classes. Beyond its more favorable achievement outcomes, within-class grouping can be more flexible, less stigmatizing, and occupies a much smaller portion of the school day than between-class grouping (Rowan and Miracle, 1983; Weinstein, 1976).

Effective Use of Reading Groups.

Among some educators, there has been a movement away from the use of reading groups (see Slavin *et al.,* 1989; Barr, 1990), but there is little research to indicate whether this is a good idea. On one hand, it seems important to give students reading material on their reading level. On the other, the use of reading groups leads to considerable amounts of seatwork, which, unlike the situation in mathematics, is often of questionable value (Anderson *et al.,* 1985). Within-class ability grouping is practiced most widely in elementary reading classes, where "Bluebirds," "Yellowbirds," and "Redbirds" have been in use for generations in American schools. However, only recently has educational research begun to explore the problem of how best to organize and manage reading groups (see Hiebert, 1983). Table 9.1 summarizes one set of principles of reading group instruction found to be effective in a study of first-grade reading (Anderson *et al.,* 1982).

The students in this cooperative learning team work in pairs and then as a group. As a teacher, in what contexts might you use cooperative learning in your classroom as a means of accommodating instruction?

Self-Check

Name and define the two broad types of ability grouping. Then give examples of their appropriate use. What is their comparative effectiveness in light of education research? What are some grouping practices that increase the effectiveness of reading instruction?

What Are Some Effective Programs to Use with Ability Groups?

Specific programs for using ability groupings observe the general principles outlined in Table 9.2 on page 322. Next, two examples of successful specific programs are given.

Ability-Grouped Active Teaching

Ability-Grouped Active Teaching (AGAT) was developed by Slavin and Karweit (1982b) for use in upper elementary and middle school mathematics classes. AGAT was designed as an ability-grouped version of the Missouri Mathematics Program (MMP), described in Chapter 8. It uses two ability groups rather than the more typical three to increase the amount of time the teacher can spend with each group and to minimize time lost in transitions. Two studies of the effectiveness of AGAT found that students in AGAT classes gained substantially more than students in traditionally taught classes in mathematics computations (Slavin and Karweit, 1985). Table 9.3 on page 323 summarizes the main elements of this approach.

> **Ability-Grouped Active Teaching (AGAT):** a method of teaching upper elementary and middle school math that uses within-class ability grouping.

Table 9.1

Principles Of Reading Group Instruction

General Principles	
Length	Instruction should last 25–30 minutes on average.
Academic focus	Teacher must effectively manage reading groups *and* students doing independent work.
Pace	Use small steps to allow high success rates and a brisk pace.
Error rate	Steps are appropriately small if students can correctly answer about 80 percent of the questions.
Organization	
Seating	Teacher must be able to see most other students while working with a reading group.
Transitions	Students should move to their reading group from other activities quickly.
Instruction	
Lesson start	Start lessons promptly. Prepare needed materials beforehand.
Overviews	Help students establish a mental set by previewing lesson content.
New words	Say new words, show their spelling, and offer phonetic clues.
Independent work	Ensure that students understand seatwork directions by having them demonstrate skills to be practiced.
Group participation	Ensure participation of all by asking students to read aloud, asking questions about words and concepts, calling on students in a systematic way, discouraging call-outs, and checking student progress—especially that of low-achievers.

(continued)

Cooperative Integrated Reading and Composition

A serious drawback to the use of reading groups is the need for follow-up activities—work students can do at their desks while the teacher is occupied with a reading group. Students do not usually use this time very well, and many teachers believe that follow-up activities are largely intended to keep students busy rather than to teach them.

One approach to the problem of follow-up time in the upper elementary grades is a program called **Cooperative Integrated Reading and Composition,** or **CIRC** (Madden *et al.,* 1986; Stevens *et al.,* 1987). In this program students work in four-member cooperative learning teams. The teams contain two pairs of students from two different reading groups. Rather than working on workbooks

---

Cooperative Integrated Reading and Composition (CIRC): a program that supplements reading-group activities by having students practice related skills in mixed-ability teams.

Questions	
Emphasis	Focus on sentence and story comprehension, word recognition, and identifying sounds within words.
Wait time	Wait for an answer as long as student seems to be thinking about the question and may respond.
Help	Simplify or rephrase questions or give feedback if it will help student find an answer.
Answers	Ensure that all students hear correct answers, either from the teacher or another student.
Explanations	Explain reasoning behind an answer if logic or problem-solving skills are involved.
Acknowledgment of correctness	Note correctness of answers, unless the correctness is obvious.
Praise and Criticism	
Praise	Give specific, informative praise.
Corrections	Focus on academic content when correcting student responses.

Table 9.1 Principles Of Reading Group Instruction (Continued)

Specific methods of organizing and teaching elementary school reading groups have been shown to increase student achievement.

SOURCE: Adapted from Anderson et al., 1982, pp. 2–9.

during follow-up time, students engage in a series of activities with one another. They take turns reading stories to one another; answer questions about the characters, setting, and plot of each story; practice together on new vocabulary words, reading comprehension skills, and spelling; and write about the stories they have read. Three studies of the CIRC program have found positive effects on students' reading skills, including scores on standardized reading and language tests (Stevens *et al.,* 1987; Stevens and Slavin, 1991). These findings suggest that many of the problems inherent in the practice of grouping for reading can be solved by combining the use of mixed-ability, cooperative learning groups with the use of homogeneous reading groups.

Connections

Distinguish "mastery learning" from Hunter's Mastery Teaching model that was discussed in Chapter 8 as a method of direct instruction. Mastery learning, while it incorporates the principles of direct instruction, is a method of adapting instruction to individual needs.

Self-Check

What cooperative learning strategies enhance the effectiveness of within-class ability groupings, and how do those strategies work?

1. Students should remain in heterogeneous (mixed-ability) classes at most times and be regrouped by ability only in subjects, such as reading and mathematics, in which reducing heterogeneity is particularly important. Students' primary identification should be with a heterogeneous class.

2. Group assignment should be based on performance in a specific skill, not on IQ or general achievement level.

3. Grouping plans should frequently reassess student placements and should be flexible enough to allow for easy reassignment if student performance warrants it.

4. Teachers should vary their level and pace of instruction in regrouped classes to adapt to students' needs.

5. In within-class ability grouping the number of groups should be kept small (two to three groups) so the teacher can provide enough direct instruction to each group.

Table 9.2

General Principles of Ability Grouping

Source: Slavin (1987b).

---

mastery learning: system of instruction that emphasizes the achievement of instructional objectives by all students by allowing learning time to vary.

mastery criterion: a standard students must meet to be considered proficient in a skill.

What Is Mastery Learning?

One means of adapting instruction to the needs of diverse students is called **mastery learning** (Block and Anderson, 1975; Block and Burns, 1976; Bloom, 1976). The basic idea behind mastery learning is to make sure that all or almost all students have learned a particular skill to a preestablished level of mastery before moving on to the next skill.

Mastery learning was first proposed as a solution to the problem of individual differences by Benjamin Bloom (1976), who based his recommendations in part on the earlier work of John Carroll (1963). As discussed earlier in this chapter, Carroll had suggested that school learning was related to the amount of time needed to learn what was being taught and the amount of time spent on instruction.

One implication of Carroll's model is that if "time spent" is the same for all students and all students receive the same kind of instruction, then differences in student achievement will primarily reflect differences in student aptitude. However, in 1968 Bloom proposed that rather than providing all students with the same amount of instructional time and allowing *learning* to differ, perhaps we should require that all or almost all students reach a certain level of achievement by allowing *time* to differ. That is, Bloom suggests that we give students as much time and instruction as necessary to bring them all to a reasonable level of learning. If some students appear to be in danger of not learning, then they should be given additional instruction until they do learn.

Bloom (1976) hypothesizes that given additional instructional time, students who do not master their lessons in the time usually allowed should be able to reach achievement levels typically attained by only the most able students. In fact, he proposes that 80 percent of all students should be able to achieve at a level usually attained by only 20 percent of students, and that under these circumstances aptitude or ability should be nearly unrelated to achievement. In a hospital we would not give the same amount of treatment to a patient with a cold as to one with double pneumonia; we treat both patients until they are healthy, giving them as much treatment as they need to reach that goal. Similarly, Bloom argues, we should "treat" students until they reach a preestablished level of mastery. Figure 9.2a shows how, under traditional instructional methods, students start out with a certain distribution of skills. As instruction goes on, "the rich get richer and the poor get poorer"; that is, high-achieving students gain more than low achievers. In contrast, in Figure 9.2b additional instruction is given to low achievers until their performance comes to resemble that of the high-achieving students.

The assumption underlying mastery learning is that almost every student can learn the essential skills in a curriculum. This assumption is both communicated to the students and acted upon by the teacher, whose job it is to provide the instruction necessary to make the expectation come true.

What Forms Does Mastery Learning Take?

The problem inherent in any mastery learning strategy is how to provide the additional instructional time to students who need it. In some of the research on mastery learning, this additional instruction is given outside of regular class time, such as after school or during recess. Students who failed to meet a preestablished **mastery criterion** (such as 90 percent correct on a quiz) following a lesson were given this extra **corrective instruction** until they could earn a 90

Opening (2–4 min.)	1. Students hand in homework.	2. Students in Teaching Group 1 go immediately to their teaching group area and begin work on starter problems. Students in Teaching Group 2 go to their desks and continue to work on seatwork relating to the previous day's lesson. The teacher helps Teaching Group 2 get started on their seatwork.	
Teaching Group Lessons (15–17 min.)	1. Give answers to starter problems. Briefly go over any problems attempted but missed by more than one-quarter of students.	2. Give answers to seatwork. Briefly go over any problems attempted but missed by more than one-quarter of students. Collect seatwork and starter problems.	3. Briefly review any prerequisite skills for new lesson (if necessary).
	4. Actively demonstrate new concept or skill, emphasizing the meaning and importance of the skill (8–12 min.)	5. Assess student comprehension with short answers and supervised practice (1–2 problems at a time).	6. When success rate is high, move students to seatwork.
Seatwork (15–17 min.)	1. Assign seatwork, start Teaching Group 2 on starter problems, and get Teaching Group 1 started on their seatwork.	2. Monitor one teaching group's seatwork while you are working with the other group. Recognize students who are working well.	
Facts Test (5–7 min.)	1. If students have not all mastered addition, subtraction, multiplication, and division facts, give the class appropriate facts tests twice each week.		
Homework Assignment (2 min.)	1. Assign homework every day except Friday.		
Quizzes and Tests	1. Give quizzes at logical points in the curriculum, averaging once a week. Before each quiz, review the material to be covered in the quiz.	2. Use quiz score information to adjust pace of instruction.	3. Give tests at logical points in the curriculum, averaging once a month. Before each test, review the material to be tested.

Table 9.3 Outline of Activities for Ability-Grouped Active Teaching (AGAT)

Teachers who use Ability-Grouped Active Teaching should provide a specific set of instructional activities during each segment of a class period.

Figure 9.2

Theoretical Achievement Distributions during Traditional Instruction and Mastery Learning

When teachers present a series of learning tasks using traditional instruction, they may find that students who do not learn the first task will also fail at the second and that those students, plus others, will fail at the third (as shown in (a) on top). However, when teachers make sure that most students thoroughly learn one task before tackling similar but more advanced tasks, they may find that the number of high achievers in their class will increase (as shown in (b) at bottom).

From Bloom, 1982.

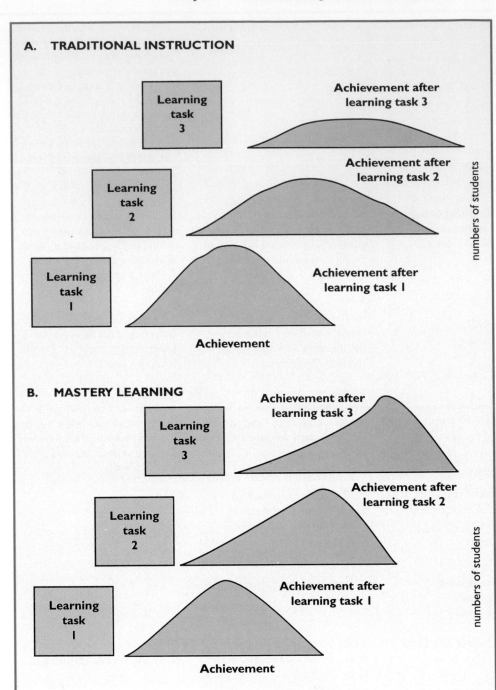

corrective instruction: educational activities given to students who initially fail to master an objective; designed to increase the number of students who master educational objectives.

Keller Plan: a form of mastery learning in which students advance through the curriculum by passing mastery tests.

percent score on a similar quiz. Research on mastery learning programs that provide corrective instruction in addition to regular class time has generally found achievement gains, particularly for low achievers (Bloom, 1984; Kulik *et al.*, 1990; Slavin, 1987c).

Another form of mastery learning, called the **Keller Plan** (Keller, 1968), has students take tests following a series of lessons. Any students who fail to achieve at a preestablished level of mastery (80–90 percent correct) continue to study or work with fellow students who did achieve mastery until they can pass the tests. In this method students who pass the tests the first time spend much less time on those lessons than students who require several tries. The Keller Plan has been found to be very effective in increasing the academic achievement of students at the college level (Kulik *et al.*, 1979).

Neither the Keller Plan nor forms of mastery learning that require additional instructional time are easily applicable to elementary or secondary education, where amounts of time available are relatively fixed. For example, it is possible to have students stay after school to receive corrective instruction for an experiment lasting a few weeks (see, for example, Tenenbaum, 1982), but this would be difficult to arrange over the long haul. Also, there is some question whether the additional time required for corrective instruction in mastery learning might not be better spent in covering more material. For example, Arlin and Webster (1983) taught an experimental unit on sailing consisting of four chapters. Students in a mastery learning condition received corrective instruction if they missed more than one item on chapter tests, while students in the traditionally taught condition were allowed to go on. Although mastery students scored much better than nonmastery students on a final test, it took them twice as long to complete the unit. Bloom (1976) hypothesizes that as time goes on, students in mastery learning should need less and less corrective instruction, but in a four-year study of a school using mastery learning, Arlin (1984b) found no such trend; in fact, as time went on, the students needed more time for corrective instruction.

How Does Mastery Learning Work?

Because of the impracticality of providing corrective instruction outside of regular class time, most elementary and secondary schools that use mastery learning use a form developed by Block and Anderson (1975) in which corrective instruction is given during class. This form of mastery learning follows a regular cycle of activities, which is repeated for each major skill or concept taught. Each cycle lasts an average of one to two weeks and its principal activities are:

1. Orient students to mastery.
2. Teach the lesson.
3. Give the formative quiz.
4. Give students either corrective instruction—for those who did not achieve mastery on the formative quiz—or enrichment activities—for those who did achieve mastery.
5. Give the summative quiz to students.

Planning for Corrective Instruction. Orienting students to the mastery learning strategy involves conveying the message that they are going to learn by a method of instruction designed to help all of them learn well and that they will be graded solely on the basis of their performance on the **summative quiz**. Students will need to know that they will be graded against a predetermined performance standard and not in relation to the performance of their classmates. For example, the teacher might indicate that the standard of A work will be a score of 90 percent, or eighteen correct answers on a twenty-item quiz. The teacher emphasizes that every student can achieve mastery, that mastery, not grades, is the most important goal, and that each student who attains the standard will receive an A.

Lessons for mastery learning are planned according to the lesson presentation guidelines described in Chapter 8. These guidelines include clearly specifying objectives for each lesson and gathering teaching materials and practice materials for those objec-

summative quiz: final test of an objective.

tives. Presentation of the lesson itself in mastery learning may be accomplished using any whole-class instructional method (such as those described in Chapter 8). Students take a **formative quiz** when you have completed your planned sequence of lessons. The provision of corrective instruction to students who do not achieve the mastery criterion on the formative quiz is the most important feature of mastery learning, as it is the means by which the strategy addresses the problem of providing appropriate levels of instruction to students with instructionally important differences. Therefore the quality of your corrective instruction is critical to the success of a mastery learning strategy.

Theory Into Practice

Using Formative and Summative Quizzes in Mastery Learning

At the end of each set of lessons (usually one to two weeks of work), you will need to have prepared two parallel quizzes assessing students' understanding of the lessons just presented. The first of these quizzes is called a formative quiz, or a "no-fault" quiz. The second is a summative quiz, in other words, a final quiz. "Parallel" means that the quizzes should cover the same content and be equally difficult, but should typically use different items. For example

Formative Quiz

1. 1/3 + 1/4 =

2. The ___ were all broken.

    a. toy's

    b. toys

    c. toys'

3. The formula for calcium carbonate is ___.

4. The capital of Canada is ___.

Summative Quiz

1. 1/2 + 1/5 =

2. Whose ___ are these?

    a. books

    b. book's

    c. books'

3. The formula for potassium nitrate is ___.

4. The capital of Canada is ___.

Note that the fourth item ("The capital of Canada is ___") is identical in the formative and summative quizzes. The reason is that this is a specific piece of information the teacher wants the class to know, rather than a general skill to be applied to different problems (as in questions 1–3).

formative quiz: evaluation designed to determine whether additional instruction is needed.

The number and types of questions on the quizzes may vary, but quizzes should require no more than fifteen to twenty minutes for students to complete. The quizzes should focus precisely on assessing students' understanding of the lessons just presented.

You will need to establish what score indicates mastery of a given quiz. Mastery criteria are typically set somewhere between 80 and 90 percent correct, although for material that is essential for all students to know (such as multiplication facts), the mastery criterion should be 100 percent. Set the criterion for mastery at the percent correct usually regarded as A work, which in most schools is 90 percent (Block and Anderson, 1975).

The students' scores on the formative quiz are the basis for assigning enrichment activities or providing corrective instruction. When you feel that you have given sufficient corrective instruction, have students take the summative quiz. Students who achieved mastery on the formative quiz need not take the summative quiz.

Score the summative quizzes as soon as possible after class (you can have students check their own papers or exchange papers for correction in class if you wish). Return graded papers to students. By the time of the summative quiz, at least three-quarters of your students should have achieved the mastery criterion (or close to it). If this is not the case, you may repeat the corrective instruction–summative test cycle until at least three-quarters of your students have achieved mastery.

This form of mastery learning varies the instructional time given to students with different needs by providing corrective instruction to students who need it, while allowing those who do not to do enrichment work. For example, a high-school earth science teacher might teach a lesson on volcanoes and earthquakes. At the end of the lesson students are quizzed. Those who score less than 80 percent receive corrective instruction on concepts they had problems with, while the remaining students do **enrichment activities,** such as finding out about the San Francisco earthquake or the Mount Vesuvius eruption that buried Pompeii.

Enrichment activities should be educationally worthwhile (not busywork) but should not cover upcoming lessons, because all students will receive those lessons anyway. Rather, enrichment activities should broaden students' understanding of the material they have been studying. Applications of skills (such as word problems in math, short essays in language arts, practical science problems in science) are excellent enrichment activities because they allow students to use the information they have just gained. Academic games or brainteasers can be good if, again, they are not just busywork.

Theory Into Practice

Providing Corrective Instruction and Enrichment Activities

For every formative quiz you prepare, you will also need to prepare an alternative method of presenting the material for use as corrective instruction. For example, if you initially teach a lesson using lecture-discussion, you might prepare corrective instruction using demonstration with pictures or charts. Or you

enrichment activities: assignments or activities designed to broaden or deepen the knowledge of students who master classroom lessons quickly.

These students are running a program for enrichment in math. Their teacher is using a mastery learning model of instruction. What events in the mastery learning process were likely to precede their participation in this enrichment activity?

might choose a different textbook, peer tutoring (that is, a student who achieved mastery on the formative quiz might tutor a classmate who did not), adult tutoring, computer-assisted instruction, or programmed instruction to provide the corrective instruction.

If you are giving corrective instruction during regular class time, you will need to divide your class into two groups: students who achieved the mastery criterion on the formative test and those who did not. If the "masters" group is small, you might send these students to a separate area of the room to work on their enrichment materials while you work with the "nonmasters" at their own desks. If the nonmasters group is small, you might gather them in a special area for additional instruction.

Keep masters usefully occupied while you are providing corrective instruction to other students (unless you decide to have these students tutor classmates who did not achieve mastery).

Make sure that the students doing enrichment activities have plenty to do so that you do not have to interrupt your corrective lessons to answer their questions or otherwise become involved with them. Keep in mind that the most effective form of mastery learning involves giving corrective instruction outside of regular class time, either during the school day or after school. Aides, special education teachers, peers, parent volunteers, or computers may be used. However, in most cases, practical considerations dictate that corrective instruction be given during regular class time.

Research on Mastery Learning.   Research on the form of mastery learning that Block and Anderson developed is much less clear than that on other forms of mastery learning (see Slavin, 1987c). Studies of at least four weeks' duration in which instructional time was the same for mastery and nonmastery classes generally found either no differences in effectiveness or small and short-lived differences favoring the mastery groups. Some of the most promising forms of mastery learning are ones that combine this approach with cooperative learning, where students work together to help each other learn in the first place and then help their groupmates who need corrective instruction (Guskey, 1990; Mevarech, 1985).

The practical implications of research on mastery learning are only partially clear. First, if the staff time is available to provide corrective instruction in addition to regular classroom instruction, the effects of mastery learning on achievement can be quite positive. Second, any form of mastery learning can help teachers become more clear about their objectives, routinely assess student progress, and modify their instruction according to how well students are learning—all elements of effective instruction. Third, when high levels of mastery are needed to form a basis for later learning, mastery learning appears particularly appropriate. For example, many mathematics skills are fundamental for later learning, and these skills might profitably be taught using a mastery approach. Similarly, basic reading skills, map or chart interpretation, essential vocabulary and grammar in foreign languages, and elements of the periodic table lend themselves to mastery learning.

However, the central problem of mastery learning is that it involves a tradeoff between the amount of content that can be covered and the degree to which stu-

Teachers on Teaching

What kinds of ability groupings work best for you and your students?

Teachers make informal observations and administer diagnostic tests, which are compared to achievement test scores from the three previous years. This provides a basis for heterogeneous groupings. We hold class meetings to discuss the "groups of four"—both a physical arrangement of desks and a method of teaching that facilitates cooperative learning. In groups of four, students are allowed to help one another and to talk quietly so long as they stay on task. If no one in the group understands a problem, one member raises his or her hand. This is a great time saver and allows for even the most timid child to speak. The groups of four are "designer" groups, mixing together students with special needs; students who are gifted or talented; and students who would not normally socialize. Having groups eliminates arguing, encourages cooperation, and allows the teacher more time to circulate and to instruct. Groups change monthly. The students choose their groups randomly by picking from a deck of cards. The four "sixes" become a group, for instance. A new group and location offers a fresh start. Within the groups, students are also engaged in peer tutoring, individualized instruction, whole-class instruction, and cross-grade tutoring. Peer tutoring takes place within the group, while students working much above or much below grade level are placed in individualized programs. Cross-grade tutoring occurs once a month with our first-grade partners.

Joyce Flaxbeard, Teacher, Sixth Grade
Gentilly Terrace Creative Arts Magnet School,
New Orleans, Louisiana

I feel that within-class ability grouping is essential to a good learning environment. To group my students for language arts, initially I use an informal reading assessment from a published whole-language series I use. I also examine each student's performance within the instructional setting. I then group each child, starting out with one group for "average" and one for "above average" and subdividing further as necessary. My day usually includes thirty minutes of whole-class instruction in spelling and grammar and then a longer period of small-group literature instruction. Moving to small groups is a little tricky. While one group is reading a new chapter or working on a project, I read, reteach grammar and spelling skills, and so on, with the other group. The average/low average group always receives more time because those students need more reinforcement and have greater difficulty working independently. Within my two large groups, I regroup the students every day into dyads, triads, girls and boys, all students wearing tennis shoes, all not wearing tennis shoes—anything clever. The kids love it and it helps keep the same kids from being together all the time. In addition, I love to use cooperative learning groups, especially for report writing and group projects.

Cooperative learning groups work best when the responsibility for cooperating is placed on the students themselves. They realize that they are a team, and that if one person does not do their job the rest of their team suffers. The children learn so much more from each other and from discovering things together that I feel cooperative learning should be a part of the day in every classroom.

Karen Kusayanagi, Fourth-Grade Teacher
Jean Hayman Elementary School,
Lake Elsinore, California

dents master each concept (Arlin, 1984a; Slavin, 1987c). The time needed to bring all or almost all students to a preestablished level of mastery must come from somewhere. If corrective instruction is provided during regular class time, it must reduce content coverage. And, as noted in Chapter 8, content coverage is one of the most important predictors of achievement gain (Cooley and Leinhardt, 1980). This is not at all to say that mastery learning should be used only when additional time for corrective instruction is available but merely to emphasize that teachers should be aware of the tradeoff involved and make decisions accordingly. Mastery learning should be part of every teacher's skills, for use on material that all students must master, but it is not necessary or effective in every situation.

Outcomes-Based Education

> ### Connections
>
> Outcomes-based education is discussed again in Chapters 13 and 14 in connection with outcomes-based assessments of student learning.

Outcomes-based education is an approach to instruction and school organization that emphasizes clear specification of what students should know and be able to do at the end of a course of study and then directs time and resources to see that all students meet this goal. As in mastery learning, outcomes-based education proposes that outcomes be held constant and time and other resources should be allowed to vary. For example, students in outcomes-based education might redo assignments or retake alternate versions of tests until they can achieve a high minimum standard. Spady (1988) recommends that teachers "grade in pencil rather than ink," so that students can do additional work or study to improve their grades. Rather than emphasizing coverage of large amounts of material, teachers using outcomes-based education emphasize mastery of a well-defined, well-justified core of knowledge and skills.

> ### Self-Check
>
> Be able to (a) define mastery learning; (b) explain its underlying philosophy and assumptions; (c) describe the different forms it can take; (d) describe how the form developed by Block and Anderson works; and (e) identify appropriate contexts for using mastery learning. Specifically, be able to explain formative assessment, summative assessment, corrective instruction, and enrichment. Also, relate mastery learning to outcomes-based education.

What Are Some Ways of Individualizing Instruction?

The problem of providing all students with appropriate levels of instruction could be completely solved by simply assigning all students their own teacher. Not surprisingly, studies of one adult–one student tutoring find substantial positive effects of tutoring on student achievement (Bloom, 1984; Polloway *et al.*, 1986; Wasik and Slavin, 1993). One major reason for the effectiveness of tutoring is that the tutor can provide **individualized instruction**, can tailor instruction precisely to a student's needs. If the student learns quickly, the tutor can move to other tasks; if not, the tutor can figure out what the problem is, try another explanation, or just spend more time on the task.

> **individualized instruction:** teaching approach in which each student works at his or her own level and rate.

What type of tutoring is taking place in this picture? What other means of individualizing instruction are available to you as a teacher?

Tutoring

There are situations in which tutoring by adults is feasible and necessary, and peer tutors (usually older students working with younger ones) can also be very effective. In addition, educational innovators have long tried to simulate the one-to-one teaching situation by individualizing instruction with programmed instruction or computer-assisted instruction. All of these strategies are discussed in the following sections.

Peer Tutoring.   Students can help one another learn. When one student teaches another, this is called **peer tutoring.** There are two principal types of peer tutoring: cross-age tutoring, where the tutor is several years older than the student being taught, and same-age peer tutoring, where one student tutors a classmate. **Cross-age tutoring** is more often recommended by researchers than same-age tutoring (Devin-Sheehan *et al.,* 1976), partly because of the obvious fact that older students are more likely to know the material and partly because students may accept an older student as a tutor but resent having a classmate appointed to tutor them.

Most often, it is recommended that tutors and tutees (the person being taught) be separated by two to three grade levels. Sometimes cross-age tutoring is used with students in need of special assistance, in which case a few older students may work with a few younger students. Other tutoring schemes have involved, for example, entire fifth-grade classes tutoring entire second-grade classes. In these cases, half of the younger students might be sent to the older students' classroom, while half of the older students are sent to the younger students' classroom. Otherwise peer tutoring may take place in the cafeteria, library, or another school facility. Same-sex pairs are often used in cross-age tutoring, although research does not indicate any advantage of same- or cross-sex pairing for tutoring (Devin-Sheehan *et al.,* 1976). Adequate training and monitoring of tutors is essential (Jenkins and Jenkins, 1987).

Research on Peer Tutoring.   Research evaluating the effects of peer tutoring on student achievement has generally found that this strategy increases the achievement of both tutees and tutors (Devin-Sheehan *et al.,* 1976; Palincsar *et al.,* 1987; Ehly and Larsen, 1980; Rekrut, 1992). In fact, many studies have found greater achievement gains for tutors than for tutees (Cloward, 1967), and peer tutoring is

peer tutoring: one student teaching another.

cross-age tutoring: peer tutoring between an older and a younger student.

often used as much to improve the achievement of low-achieving older students as to improve that of the students being tutored (Osguthorpe, 1984; Top and Osguthorpe, 1987). As many teachers have noted, the best way to learn something thoroughly is to teach it to someone else!

One caution about the research on peer tutoring: Almost all studies of peer tutoring use tutoring *in addition* to regular instruction and compare results to those for regular instruction alone. For this reason, at least part of the effectiveness of peer tutoring could be attributed to the extra instruction time rather than to the value of peer tutoring itself. However, viewed as an addition to regular class instruction, peer tutoring does seem to be an effective way to provide appropriate levels of instruction to students.

Adult Tutoring.   One-to-one adult-to-child tutoring is one of the most effective instructional strategies known, and it essentially solves the problem of appropriate levels of instruction. The principal drawback to this method is its cost.

However, it is often possible, on a small scale, to provide adult tutors for students having problems learning in the regular class setting. For example, adult volunteers such as parents, college students, or senior citizens may be willing to tutor students (Morris *et al.*, 1990). Tutoring is an excellent use of school aides; some school districts hire large numbers of paraprofessional aides precisely for this purpose. In fact, classroom aides often have little impact on student achievement unless they are doing one-to-one tutoring (see Slavin, 1994).

There are some circumstances in which the high costs of one-to-one tutoring can be justified. One of these is for first-graders who are having difficulties learning to read. Failing to learn to read in the lower grades of elementary school is so detrimental to later school achievement that an investment in tutors who can prevent reading failure is worthwhile. A one-to-one tutoring program, Reading Recovery, uses highly trained, certified teachers to work with first-graders who are at risk for failing to learn to read. Research on this strategy has found that students who received tutoring in first grade were still reading significantly better than comparable students at the end of third grade (Pinnell, 1989). Other one-to-one tutoring programs for at-risk first-graders have also found substantial positive effects (see Wasik and Slavin, 1993).

Theory Into Practice

Instructing Tutors

Tutors in any subject area and at any grade level might follow the guidelines presented below.

1. Identify the exercise or assignment and tell the student exactly in what way it will help him or her in learning. For example, perhaps the exercise will help in correctly using a part of speech or finding the square root of a number.

2. Praise correct answers as the student completes items in the exercise. If the student is unable to do an item or responds incorrectly, prompt, model, or demonstrate a correct approach by breaking down the problem into parts or steps and working toward an overall solution. For example, if a child is unable to read a word, a tutor might sound out the letters individually, have

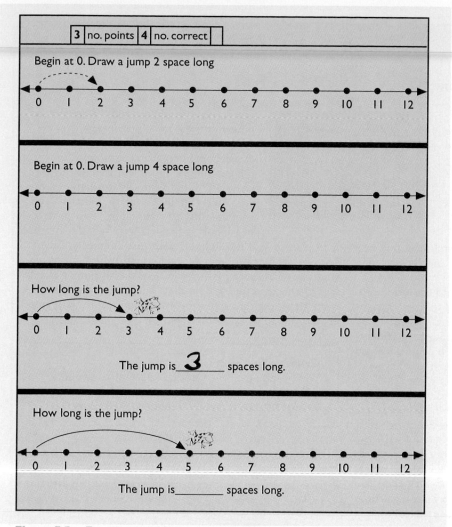

Figure 9.3 Programmed Instruction Skillsheet

Programmed instructional materials are designed to lead a student step-by-step from simple skills to more complex ones.

From IPI ® Mathematics, 1972.

the student repeat them, then pronounce the sounds to show how they blend to make the word, and then have the student pronounce the word.

3. Avoid moving to the next item or step before the student has met the objective or performance criterion for each preceding one. Acceptable performance in reading words, for example, is reading each word with no pause or break between the sounds. Skipping items that seem too hard or otherwise lowering standards of performance does not help the student academically and also conveys the wrong message. Students need to know that they can succeed. Consult with the student's teacher or counselor if you find that the student seems unable or unwilling to succeed.

4. At the end of the session, review accomplishments and praise the student. Record the results of the session in a tutor log.

Computers in the Classroom

Technology has the potential to dramatically change the way people learn. In the 1930s, experts thought that film would revolutionize instruction, while in the 1950s, television took the spotlight. While film and television are used in schools, they have not changed instruction or challenged the role of textbooks the way computers will. Computer-based technologies, such as interactive laser disks and communications networks, could easily have a greater impact on teaching than any other media.

This impact cannot be felt, however, until education professionals get acquainted with all the capabilities of computer technologies. One study shows that presently only about a third of teachers in the United States in kindergarten through grade twelve have had even as much as ten hours of computer training. In addition, training has tended to focus on learning about computers rather than on using them effectively for classroom instruction. Teachers who do use computers spend on average little more than one hour a week on them, a mere four percent of instructional time.

Another reason for delay in the impact of computer technologies is the lack of computers in the classroom. School districts have not acquired enough machines to allow the kind of access needed to include them as a basic element in instruction. Their lack is especially evident in schools in low-income neighborhoods. Where computers do exist in sufficient numbers, they tend to be stockpiled in labs for specialized classes, not in regular classrooms.

Signs suggest times will change, however. In 1990, the Kentucky legislature created a five-year plan "for the efficient and equitable use of technology" and pledged to support it financially. When the system is in place it will link schools with one another and with state government computers, and it will help mainstream students with special education needs. Computers allied with the modem and fax machine allow students in a district, state, region, or nation to communicate with one another and to work cooperatively on a variety of projects.

Critical Thinking

Why would you be or not be reluctant to use computers instructionally? Are you receiving the training you need to use computer technologies effectively?

Larry Bushmen, "Katie's Computer," *Instructor,* February 1992; Donald A. Cook, "Prometheus in the Classroom: Education and the Computer Today," *Future Choices,* Winter 1989; Lynn Olsen, "Profiles in Technology" and "State of the Art," *Teacher,* January 1992; Elizabeth Schulz, "Back to the Future," *Teacher,* January 1992.

Programmed Instruction

The term **programmed instruction** refers to individualized instruction methods in which students work on self-instructional materials at their own levels and rates (see Fletcher, 1992). For example, one math class might contain some students working on division, others on fractions, others on decimals, and still others on measurement or geometry, all at the same time. The materials students use are meant to be self-instructional, which is to say the students are expected to learn (at least in large part) from the materials, rather than principally from the teacher. For this reason, programmed instruction materials typically break skills down into small subskills, so that students may go step-by-step with little chance of making an error at each step. Figure 9.3 shows an example of a lesson from Individually Prescribed Instruction (IPI), probably the most widely used programmed instruction method when this approach was at its peak of popularity in the mid-1970s.

programmed instruction: structured lessons that students can work on individually, at their own pace.

Studies on the first generation of programmed instruction models have been one of the great disappointments of educational research (see Rothrock, 1982). Despite great expectations and considerable investments, the programmed instruction techniques developed in the 1960s and 1970s generally failed to show any achievement benefits. The results vary somewhat by subject, but with few exceptions reviewers have concluded that these programmed instruction methods have not lived up to expectations (Miller, 1976; Schoen , 1976; Bangert *et al.*, 1983).

Partly as a result of these disappointing finds and partly because of the expense and difficulty of using programmed instruction, this strategy is seldom employed today as a primary approach to instruction. However, programmed instruction materials are still frequently used in special education (see Chapter 12) and as supplements to more traditional methods. They can help meet the needs of students who perform either above or below the level of the rest of the class, though this function is increasingly being taken over by computer-assisted instruction (Fletcher, 1992).

Team Assisted Individualization

Programmed instruction may have failed to increase student levels of achievement as expected because the benefits of providing appropriate levels of instruction may have been offset by losses in quality of instruction, student motivation, and instructional time (Slavin, 1987a). For example, quality of instruction may have suffered if teachers had to spend too much time checking materials and managing rather than teaching; student motivation may have suffered because programmed instruction day after day can be boring.

To test this analysis, researchers developed a mathematics instruction program designed to solve the problems of individualized instruction (Slavin, 1985a,b) In this program, called **Team Assisted Individualization (TAI)**, students work on individualized self-instructional materials at their own levels and rates, just as in earlier programmed instruction methods. However, students do their individualized work in four-member, mixed-ability learning teams. Teammates help each other, check each other's work against answer sheets, and encourage each other to work rapidly and accurately, since the team is rewarded (with certificates and recognition) on the basis of the number and accuracy of assignments completed by all team members. The partners' helping frees the teac her to teach groups of students (drawn from the various teams) working at the same point in the individualized program, as in within-class ability grouping. The division of students into three teaching groups solves the problem of quality of instruction by having instruction come from the teacher rather than from written materials alone, and the team reward system solves the problem of incentive by motivating students to work rapidly and accurately and to encourage their teammates to do so. The team reward and student checking systems solve the time problem by motivating students to stay on-task and reducing the time spent waiting for the teacher to check work.

In contrast to research on earlier programmed instruction methods, TAI has been found to be very effective in increasing student mathematics achievement. In six studies involving students in grades 3–6, students in TAI classes gained substantially more, especially on measures of computation, than did students in traditional classes (Slavin, 1985a,b; Slavin and Karweit, 1985; Stevens and Slavin, 1991, 1992).

Team Assisted Individualization (TAI): teaching program in which students work on individualized instruction materials in four-member mixed-ability groups.

Informal Remediation and Enrichment

Perhaps the most common means of attempting to provide appropriate levels of instruction is to make informal adjustments within whole-class instruction. For example, many teachers teach a lesson, assign seatwork, and while students are doing the seatwork, try to work with students they feel are likely to have problems. Other teachers find time outside of regular class to work with students who need extra help. This extra help is called **remediation.** For students who work very rapidly, teachers will often provide enrichment activities to broaden these students' knowledge or skills in the area being studied. For example, advanced students in an English class might be asked to write a special report on the life of the Brontë sisters. Many schools now have special "gifted and talented" classes for the most able students, but even in schools that have such classes there will always be some rapid learners remaining in the regular classes.

There is little research on informal means of providing remediation or enrichment; both are usually seen as just standard parts of teaching. A recent study by MacIver (1992) found that low-performing middle school students gained from participating in remedial "extra period" programs. However, there is one principle that teachers should be aware of: Do not allow remediation and enrichment activities to interfere with the main course of instruction. One consistent research finding is that time spent with one pupil while the rest of the class has nothing important to do is detrimental to the learning of the class as a whole (see, for example, Stallings and Kaskowitz, 1974).

Computer-Assisted Instruction

One means of individualizing instruction that has been receiving a great deal of attention in recent years is **computer-assisted instruction,** or **CAI.** The decreasing cost and increasing availability of microcomputers in schools have led researchers as well as teachers to become more interested in CAI. Most U.S. schools have at least one microcomputer (Becker, 1990a,b), and the number of computers per school is rapidly growing.

The idea behind computer-assisted instruction is to use the computer as a tutor to present information, give students practice, assess their level of understanding, and provide additional instruction if needed. In theory, a well-designed CAI program is nearly perfect at providing appropriate levels of instruction, as it can analyze student responses immediately to determine whether to spend more time on a particular topic or skill. The computer can be quite effective in presenting ideas, using pictures or diagrams to reinforce concepts. For many students, the computer seems to have a motivating quality of its own, so that they work longer and harder when using it than they would on comparable paper-pencil tasks. Many CAI programs stress drill and practice exercises; others teach students facts and concepts, while others engage students in complex problem-solving or discovery learning. Whatever their differences, CAI programs generally share the following characteristics: (1) use of a structured curriculum; (2) letting students work at their own pace; (3) giving students controlled, frequent feedback and reinforcement; and (4) measuring performance quickly and giving students information on their performance.

History of CAI.   The early work in CAI consisted mostly of drill and practice in mathematics and language arts for elementary school students, especially those who were disadvantaged. Atkinson (1968) developed a reading program that students

remediation: instruction given to students having difficulty learning.

computer-assisted instruction: individualized instruction administered by a computer.

could use without help from the classroom teacher. First-grade children sat at a computer terminal that had a typewriter keyboard, a television screen, a high-speed filmstrip, and a computer-controlled tape player. They answered questions by touching the screen with a light pen. The computer determined where they were pointing, evaluated their answers, and determined what material should be given next. The reading program taught students letters of the alphabet, basic vocabulary, and other reading skills.

Despite early successes (*e.g.*, Atkinson and Fletcher, 1972), researchers in the mid-1970s felt that the effects of CAI did not justify its costs, and few systems were being used. Then, in 1977, small low-cost microcomputers became available and revolutionized the use of computers in education. A national survey done in 1989 found that over 95 percent of schools have at least one computer, with the average elementary school having seventeen and the average high school having thirty-four. These numbers represent nearly a tenfold increase since the early 1980s (Becker, 1990a).

Unfortunately, not all schools have used their new computers wisely. One problem has been a lack of knowledge about *software* (the programs that run the computer), and the fact that not all software on the market is good. To solve this problem, several groups have been organized to develop CAI materials. For example, the Minnesota Educational Computer Consortium (MECC) has distributed materials for elementary and secondary schools. At present many more programs are being written for educational uses of microcomputers in all subjects, especially mathematics and science.

Most recently, integrated learning systems have been developed. An **integrated learning system** is a comprehensive set of computer-assisted instruction software marketed by one company, intended to provide instruction in many subjects and capable of being used over an extended period of time. Examples include CCC and Jostens. In these systems, software is maintained in a central server linked to 15 to 30 student computers. The computer keeps records of students' progress and learning needs (see Becker, 1992; EPIE Institute, 1990). The advantage of these integrated systems over the more typical use of a variety of software from many companies is that the integrated systems are more comprehensive, are designed to adapt the level and pace of instruction to student needs, and do a good job of record keeping for each student. Research on the effectiveness of integrated learning systems has generally found small and mixed but positive achievement outcomes (Becker, 1992). More traditional applications of computer technology, including **tutorials** and **simulations,** are listed in the Theory Into Practice titled "Choosing CAI Programs for Appropriate Use."

Theory Into Practice

Choosing CAI Programs for Appropriate Use
Characteristics of the various types of CAI programs help you to choose the best ones for your students and for your curriculum.

Drill and Practice Programs
- the most widely used:
  - resemble other teaching techniques such as flashcards and programmed instruction
  - provide practice on skills and knowledge so students can remember and use what they have been taught

integrated learning system: a comprehensive, multipurpose set of instructional software developed by one company.

tutorials: computer programs that teach lessons by varying their content and pace according to student responses.

simulations: computer programs that model real-life phenomena to promote problem solving and motivate interest in the areas concerned.

- involve repetition of a format in which the computer presents an exercise, the student types in a response, and the computer informs the student if the answer is correct
- usually address lower-level skills and have a narrow range of teaching strategies

Tutorials
- put the computer into the role of a teacher instructing an individual student
- actively involve the student in self-paced instruction, sometimes through actual dialogue
- guide learning by a sequenced series of leading questions, though ability to respond in a helpful manner may be limited

Simulations
- provide models of some part of the world in some state or at some point in time
- aim to teach facts, promote problem solving, foster understanding of a particular situation, and motivate interest in a subject
- present events that would otherwise be inaccessible because of expense, danger, or realities of time and place
- enhance student learning through realism (Woodward *et al.*, 1988), but seldom check if students are "on the right track"

Educational Games
- should not be low-level drill and practice exercises transplanted to exotic environments
- should have clear goals and structure and content that matches your curriculum and instructional objectives as well as students' ability levels
- develop problem-solving skills, reinforce skills and knowledge, and motivate interest in learning

Utility Programs
- turn the computer into a general-purpose tool for solving many problems most widely used are word-processing or text-editing programs
- allow students to understand composition as a flexible, creative process
- writing can be published
- can automatically check the spelling of every word in a composition
- can check punctuation and capitalization, inform the author about ungrammatical constructions, average sentence length, overuse of c ertain words or phrases, and phrases that appear sexist
- can analyze how closely a composition matches standard literary forms, such as an operational manual, a research article, or an eighteenth-century novel

Connections

The use of computers with students with disabilities is discussed in Chapter 12.

Research indicates that writers using computers write more, are less worried about making mistakes, take increased pride in their writing, have fewer motor control problems, give more attention to finding errors, and revise more (Cochran-Smith, 1991; Russell, 1991). These characteristics are valued by teachers who are guided by modern research, which argues that composition should be viewed as a *process* rather than as a *product*.

But can computers teach? Several extensive reviews of the research concerning the effectiveness of computer-assisted instruction have been conducted (Atkinson, 1984; Kulik *et al.*, 1984; Niemiec and Walberg, 1985; Roblyer *et al.*, 1988). These reviews generally agree that CAI can be effective in increasing student achievement, but not always. CAI is often effective when it is used *in addition* to regular classroom instruction but has smaller and less consistent achievement effects when it entirely replaces classroom instruction. Some reviewers have argued that when the *content* of instruction is carefully controlled, computers are no more effective than other instructional methods (Clark, 1985). For example, one study, which randomly assigned students to use CAI or traditional methods to learn mathematics, found that some CAI methods enhanced learning, whereas some were *less* effective than the traditional teaching methods (Becker, 1990). Researchers today generally agree that there is nothing magic in the computer itself, that what matters is the curriculum, instruction, and social context surrounding the use of the computer (Cochran-Smith, 1991; Hawkins and Sheingold, 1986; Salomon and Gardner, 1986; Salomon *et al.,* 1991). Asking whether computers enhance learning is like asking whether chalkboards enhance learning. In either case, it depends how they are used.

Leaving aside issues of effectiveness, it is clear that students do not all have the same access to computers. Middle-class children are considerably more likely than lower-class children to have access to computers, and within schools boys tend to spend much more time on computers than girls (Laboratory of Comparative Human Cognition, 1989; Sutton, 1991). To the extent that computers become increasingly effective and important in providing state-of-the-art instruction, these inequities must be addressed.

Use of computers and research on CAI are developing so rapidly that it is difficult to anticipate what the future will bring. However, at this time computers are rarely being used to provide basic instruction. In secondary schools they are primarily used to teach programming and word processing, and in elementary schools they are chiefly used for enrichment (Becker, 1986). Many schools that originally bought computers for CAI have ended up using them to teach computer programming or "computer literacy"—giving students hands-on experience with the computer, but not depending on it to carry a major instructional load (Becker, 1990).

Computer Programming.   A popular notion is that learning computer programming (learning to "teach the computer" rather than being taught by it) will increase children's achievement and ability to solve problems. Programming has also been promoted as a virtual synonym for the term "computer literacy." Much of the research on teaching computer programming to elementary students has focused on the computer language Logo, which was designed to be accessible to young children. Children draw on the computer's display screen by directing the movements of a graphic "turtle," a small triangular point that can move around the screen in response to messages sent it by the programmer. Seymour Papert (1980), one of the creators of Logo and a leading supporter of the use of computer programming to expand children's intellectual power, has argued that students who learn Logo will gain in general thinking skills, and others have made similar arguments for the teaching of other computer languages. Research is unclear on the degree to which this is true. Two studies did find a positive effect of extensive experience with Logo on cognitive skills, though not on academic achievement (Clements and Gullo, 1984; Clements, 1986). However, in these studies there was one teacher for every two to three students in the Logo group. Studies with more realistic teacher-student ratios found few effects (duBoulay and Howe, 1984; Pea and Kurland, 1984). When learning of computer programming has effects on thinking skills or other cognitive skills (such as mathematics), the effects are generally restricted to problem-solving skills most similar to those involved in the programming itself (Blume, 1985; Palumbo, 1990).

Computer programming is a useful skill in its own right, particularly for high school students interested in technical studies or careers. However, it is doubtful that teaching programming to young students is an efficient way to teach general problem-solving skills, in comparison to direct instruction in problem solving.

Self-Check

Be able to describe, compare, and identify the most appropriate uses of the methods of individualizing instruction, including tutoring, programmed instruction, TAI, remediation and enrichment, and CAI. Also be able to recognize the following statements as summaries of research-based general principles for choosing appropriate levels of instruction for students in mixed-ability classes:

• Balance the needs of individuals against the needs of a class as a whole.
• Use whole-class instruction when student differences in ability are not instructionally important.
• Use individualization appropriately for subjects requiring progressive skill building.
• If ability grouping is necessary, prefer forms of within-class ability grouping, such as mastery learning, cooperative learning, individualized instruction, or computer-assisted instruction.

Ability Grouping and Cooperative Learning

Sherry Lawrence and Clare Sims, two fourth-grade teachers at the Stonebridge Elementary School, are discussing their classes and the merits of different approaches to grouping students for instruction.

SHERRY: I had to regroup the whole class after the second week of school. I shouldn't have tried to use IQ scores to place the kids. I thought I was being so smart finding a shortcut.

CLARE: So, now you know. How is it working out now?

SHERRY: It's better, I think. I have three main reading groups, high, average, and low, based more on actual performance. I work most with the lower group while my assistant works with the average group. The high group is on their own a lot.

CLARE: What do they do while you and your assistant are busy?

SHERRY: They read silently or do worksheets or individualized activities. I do run out of things for them to do from time to time. They work on compositions on the computer, but there's always too much competition for the computer. I wish I had one for every kid. What do you do with your computer?

CLARE: I'm experimenting with cooperative learning groups, so each group gets a turn at the computer whenever they're ready to draft a composition.

SHERRY: Tell me more! Why are you doing cooperative learning groups? Not all the time I hope.

CLARE: Part of most days, yes! See, I didn't like the way my reading groups were going. It took too much time and trouble to make sure everyone had something to do for follow-up and to make sure everyone was working quietly and independently while I moved on to another group. I thought, why should my groups get interrupted so much? And why should kids spend so much time with worksheets? Even enrichment worksheets only go so far. So I started a cooperative learning program.

SHERRY: Oh, is it the one where they work in groups of four? I heard it's supposed to be really good, but isn't it kind of chaotic? I let my kids do group projects when we finish a unit, but I can only take it so long. Too unstructured.

CLARE: Oh, it's not like that at all. Come to my class, and you'll see. When I'm working with a reading group, all my other kids are in mixed-ability teams, and they're actually helping one another learn.

SHERRY: In your dreams. . . . C'mon, Clare, you can't be serious. In groups all the kids really want to do is talk or tease each other. There's too much noise and nothing gets done. That makes groups even less useful for follow-up than individual seatwork. Collecting workbooks seems a lot easier, and workbooks actually let you see where each kid is really at.

CLARE: I tell you, this cooperative learning program is working for me, and the kids love it. What can I say?

Problem Solving

1. Brainstorm a list of specific activities Clare's students could be doing in their cooperative learning teams while Clare is working with a particular reading group. What advantages over workbooks or worksheets might these activities have that Clare could point out?

2. How might Clare address Sherry's concerns about cooperative learning activity structures, classroom order, the quality of student interaction, and assessment feedback? How might Sherry address Clare's concerns about worksheets and individualized instruction?

3. Apply your examples and solutions by extending the dialogue between Sherry and Clare in writing or role play.

Summary

What Is Effective Instruction?
According to Carroll's model of school learning, effectiveness of instruction depends on student aptitude, ability to understand instruction, perseverance, opportunity to learn, and the quality of instruction. The model includes both student qualities and teacher qualities and relates these elements to learning in terms of time—the time spent in relation to the time needed to learn.

Slavin's QAIT model of effective instruction identifies four elements subject to the teacher's direct control: quality of instruction, appropriate level of instruction, incentive, and amount of time. The model proposes that instruction deficient in any of these elements will be ineffective. Improvements in more than one element are needed to significantly improve achievement.

How Are Students Grouped by Ability?
Schools manage student differences in ability and academic achievement through between-class ability grouping, or tracking, and regrouping into separate classes for particular subjects during part of a school day. However, research shows that within-class groupings are more effective, especially in reading and math, and are clearly preferable to groupings that segregate or stigmatize low achievers.

In providing appropriate levels of instruction, the needs of individual students must be balanced against the needs of the class as a whole and must be met without sacrificing quality of instruction. Individualizing instruction is most appropriate in subject areas that stress progressive skill building.

What Are Some Effective Programs to Use with Ability Groups?
Well-established principles exist for effective reading instruction using within-class ability grouping. Ability-Grouped Active Teaching (AGAT) is an effective within-class grouping system for teaching upper elementary-school and middle-school mathematics. Cooperative Integrated Reading and Composition (CIRC) is a flexible reading and writing program based on cooperative learning that also uses within-class ability grouping.

What Is Mastery Learning?
Mastery learning is based on the idea that amounts of instructional time should vary so all students have as much time as they need to attain the targeted knowledge and skills. Mastery learning takes a variety of forms, but all involve teacher planning of formative and summative tests, corrective instruction, and enrichment activities. Mastery learning is most effective with low achievers, when teaching basic skills, and when corrective instruction is supported outside of the classroom.

What Are Some Ways of Individualizing Instruction?
Peer and adult tutoring, programmed instruction, Team Assisted Individualization (TAI), informal remediation and enrichment, and computer-assisted instruction (CAI) are all methods for individualizing instruction. Research shows clear benefits of cross-age peer tutoring and of the self-managed learning that computer-assisted instruction and integrated learning systems make possible.

Key Terms

Ability-Grouped Active Teaching (AGAT), 319
between-class ability grouping, 314
computer-assisted instruction (CAI), 336
Cooperative Integrated Reading and Composition (CIRC), 320
corrective instruction, 322
cross-age tutoring, 331
enrichment activities, 327
formative quiz, 326
individualized instruction, 330
integrated learning systems, 337
Joplin Plan, 317
Keller Plan, 324
mastery criterion, 322

mastery learning, 322
peer tutoring, 331
programmed instruction, 334
QAIT model, 311
regrouping, 317
remediation, 336
simulations, 337
summative quiz, 325
Team Assisted Individualization (TAI), 335
tracks, 314
tutorials, 337
within-class ability grouping, 314

Self-Assessment

1. Which component of the QAIT model is considered an "alterable" element that is necessary for instruction to be effective?

   a. quality of instruction

   b. appropriate levels of instruction

   c. incentive

   d. time

   e. all of the above

2. Match the following elements from Carroll's model of instruction with the related description of a hypothetical classroom situation.

   ___ aptitude

   ___ ability to understand instruction

   ___ perseverance

   ___ opportunity

   ___ quality of instruction

   a. Students have the prerequisite skills needed for all the tasks that will be taught. .

   b. The teacher has set aside extra class time to present this lesson.

   c. Students are eager to study until the skills are mastered.

   d. Students have shown great ability to learn.

   e. The lesson is presented in such a way that students learn it as fast as their knowledge and abilities allow.

3. Match the following types of grouping strategies with the correct description of each.

   ___ Joplin Plan

   ___ Ability-Grouped Active Teaching

   ___ "College Preparatory" and "General" tracks

   ___ Team Assisted Individualization

   a. a within-class ability grouping method

   b. a regrouping method that extends across grade levels

   c. a cooperative learning method using mixed-ability groups

   d. a between-class ability grouping method

4. Briefly explain why within-class ability grouping may be preferable to between-class ability grouping.

5. Which of the following statements reflects the major philosophy of mastery learning regarding student differences?

   a. allows level of achievement to vary while holding learning time consistent

   b. allows both achievement and learning time to vary as much as possible

   c. keeps both level of achievement and learning time consistent

   d. allows learning time to vary while keeping level of achievement consistent

6. All of the following are central features of mastery learning *except:*

   a. norm-referenced tests that compare students to each other.

   b. formative quizzes that provide feedback on the student's progress while learning.

   c. summative quizzes that assess performance at the end of a lesson.

   d. corrective instruction given when mastery is not achieved.

   e. enrichment activities given when mastery is achieved.

7. Cross-age tutoring often leads to increased levels of achievement for both the student being taught and the tutor. True or false?

8. A student receives a CAI lesson about the Persian Gulf War. She proceeds at her own pace, reading the information provided and answering questions presented intermittently. Based on her responses, either a review or new material is presented in the following segments. This program illustrates the type of CAI called:

   a. tutorial.

   b. simulation.

   c. utility.

   d. drill-and-practice.

10

Motivating Students to Learn

The students in Cal Lewis's tenth-grade U.S. history class were all in their seats before the bell rang, eagerly awaiting the start of the period. But Mr. Lewis himself was nowhere to be seen. Two minutes after the bell, in he walked wearing an eighteenth century costume, including a powdered wig, and carrying a gavel. He gravely took his seat and rapped the gavel. "I now call to order this meeting of the Constitutional Convention." The students had been preparing for this day for weeks. Each of them represented one of the thirteen original states. They had been studying all about their states, the colonial era, the American Revolution, and the U.S. under the Articles of Confederation in groups of two and three. Two days earlier, Mr. Lewis had given each group secret instructions from their "governor" on the key interests of their state. For example, the Rhode Island and Delaware delegations were to make certain that small states were adequately represented in the government, while New York and Virginia wanted strict representation by population.

In preparing for the debate, each delegation had to make certain that any member of the delegation could represent the delegation's views. To ensure this, Mr. Lewis had assigned each student a number between one and three at random. When a delegation asked to be recognized, he would call out a number, and the student with that number would respond for the group.

Mr. Lewis, staying in character as George Washington, gave a speech on the importance of the task they were undertaking and then opened the floor for debate. First, he recognized the delegation from Georgia, represented by student number 2, Beth Andrews. Beth was a shy girl, but she had been well prepared by her fellow delegates and knew they were rooting for her.

"The great state of Georgia wishes to raise the question of a Bill of Rights. We have experienced the tyranny of government, and we demand that the people have a guarantee of their liberties!"

Beth went on to propose elements of the Bill of Rights drawn up by her delegation. While she was talking, Mr. Lewis was rating her presentation on historical accuracy, appropriateness to the real interests of her state, organization, and delivery. These ratings would be used in evaluating each delegation at the end of each class period. The debate went on. The North Carolina delegates argued in favor of the right of states to expand to the West, while the New Jersey delegation wanted western territories made into new states. Wealthy Massachusetts wanted taxes to remain in the states where they were collected, while poor Delaware wanted national taxes. Between debates the delegates had an opportunity to do some "horse trading," promising to vote for proposals important to other states in exchange for votes on issues important to them. At the end of the week, the class voted on ten key issues. After the votes were taken and the bell rang, the students poured into the hall still arguing about issues of taxation, representation, powers of the executive, and so on.

After school, Rick Ingram, another social studies teacher, dropped into Mr. Lewis' class. "I see you're doing your Constitutional Convention again this year. It looks great, but how can you cover all of U.S. history if you spend a month just on the Constitution?"

Cal smiled. "Don't you remember how boring high school social studies was?" he said. "It sure was for me. I know I'm sacrificing some coverage to do this unit, but look how motivated these kids are!" He picked up a huge sheaf of notes and position papers written by the South Carolina delegation. "These kids are working their tails off, and they're learning that history is fun and useful. They'll remember this material for the rest of their lives!"

Motivation is one of the most important ingredients of effective instruction. Students who want to learn can learn just about anything. But how can teachers ensure that every student wants to learn and will put in the effort needed to learn complex material?

Mr. Lewis knows the value of motivation, so he has structured a unit that taps many aspects of motivation. By having students work in groups and be evaluated based on presentations made by randomly selected group members he has created a situation in which students are encouraging each other to excel. Social motivation of this kind is very powerful, especially for adolescents. He is rating students' presentations on clear, comprehensive standards and giving them feedback each day. He is tying an important period in history to students' daily lives by having them take an active role in debating and trading votes. All of these strategies are designed not just to make history fun but to give students many sources of motivation to want to learn and remember the history they have studied. Mr. Lewis is right. The students will probably never forget their experience in his class and are likely to approach new information about revolutionary history and the Constitution with enthusiasm throughout their lives.

This chapter presents the many ways teachers can motivate students to want to learn academic material and the theories and research behind each.

What Is Motivation?

Motivation is one of the most important components of learning and one of the most difficult to measure. What makes a student want to learn? The willingness to put effort into learning is a product of many factors, ranging from the student's personality and abilities to characteristics of particular learning tasks, incentives for learning, settings, and teacher behaviors.

The term "motivation" has little practical meaning by itself; the question is, "motivation to do *what*?" All students are motivated. The problem is that some are more motivated to socialize, watch television, or do anything other than schoolwork. The educator's job is not to increase motivation per se but to discover, initiate, and sustain students' motivations to learn, and to engage in activities that lead to learning. Imagine that Cal Lewis had come to class in eighteenth-century costume but had not structured tasks and evaluations to induce students to study American history. The students might be amused and interested, but we cannot assume that they would be motivated to do the work necessary to learn the material.

Psychologists define motivation as an internal process that activates, guides, and maintains behavior over time (Baron, 1992; Schunk, 1990). In plain language, it's what gets you going, keeps you going, and determines where you're trying to go.

Motivation may vary in both *intensity* and *direction*. Two students may be motivated to play video games, but one of them may be more strongly motivated to do so than the other. Or one student may be strongly motivated to play video games and the other equally strongly motivated to play football. Gage and Berliner (1984) liken motivation to the engine (intensity) and steering wheel (direction) of a car. Actually, though, the intensity and direction of motivations are often difficult to separate. The intensity of a motivation to engage in one activity may depend in large part on the intensity and direction of motivations to engage in alternative activities (see Thibaut and Kelly, 1959). If someone has only enough time and money to go to the movies or to play video games, motivation to engage in one of these activities is strongly influenced by the intensity of motivation to engage in the other. Motivation is not only important in getting students to engage in academic activities. It is also important in determining how much students will learn from the activities they perform or the information to which they are exposed. Students who are motivated to learn something use higher cognitive processes in learning about it and absorb and retain more from it (Garner *et al.*, 1991; Graham and Golan, 1991). An important task for teachers is planning how they will support student motivation.

Motivation to do something can come about in many ways. Motivation can be a personality characteristic; individuals may have lasting, stable interests in participating in such broad categories of activities as academics, sports, or social activities. Motivation may come from *intrinsic* characteristics of a task. By making U.S. history fun, social, active, and engaging, Cal Lewis has made students eager to learn it. Motivation may also come from sources *extrinsic* to the task, as when Cal Lewis rated students' performances in the Constitutional Convention simulation. This chapter reviews theories of motivation and then presents methods teachers can use to increase students' motivations to learn.

Connections

Intrinsic and extrinsic motivation are discussed in more detail later in this chapter. Distinguish internal and external sources of motivation, which are characteristics of the learner, from intrinsic and extrinsic sources of motivational value to the learner, which are characteristics of tasks.

motivation: the influence of needs and desires on the intensity and direction of behavior.

Self-Check

Write a paragraph stating a definition of motivation, with an extended example illustrating the idea that there are different aims, kinds, intensities, and directions of motivation.

often difficult to determine students' motivations from their behavior because many different motivations can influence their behavior. Sometimes one type of motivation clearly determines behavior, at other times several motivations are influential. Because of the complexity of human motivations, behavioral theories have limited utility in explaining motivation.

Motivation and Human Needs

While behavioral learning theorists (for example, Skinner, 1953; Bandura, 1969) speak in terms of motivation to obtain reinforcers and avoid punishers, other theorists (for example, Maslow, 1954) prefer the concept of motivation to satisfy needs. Some basic needs that we all must satisfy are those for food, shelter, love, and maintenance of positive self-esteem. People differ in the degree of importance they attach to each of these needs. Some need constant reaffirmation that they are loved or appreciated, while others have greater needs for physical comfort and security. Also, the same person has different needs at different times; a drink of water would be much more appreciated after a four-mile run than after a four-course meal.

Figure 10.1   Maslow's Hierarchy of Needs

Maslow identifies two types of needs, deficiency needs and growth needs. People are motivated to satisfy needs at the bottom of the hierarchy before seeking those at the top.

Adapted from Maslow, 1954.

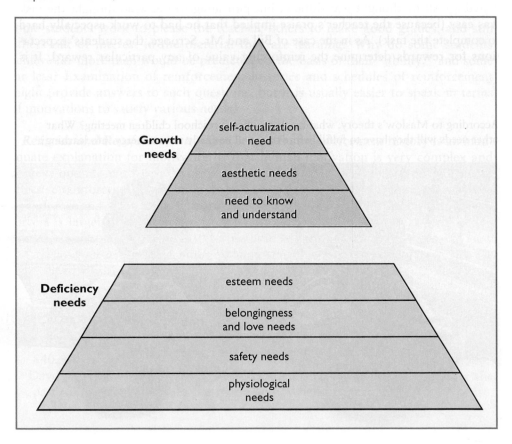

Maslow's Hierarchy of Needs.   Since people have many needs, which will they try to satisfy at any given moment? To predict this, Maslow (1954) proposed a hierarchy of needs, which is illustrated in Figure 10.1.

In Maslow's theory, needs lower in the hierarchy diagrammed in Figure 10.1 must be at least partially satisfied before a person will try to satisfy higher needs. For example, a hungry person or one in physical danger will be less concerned about maintaining a positive self-image than about obtaining food or safety, but once that person is no longer hungry or afraid, self-esteem needs may become paramount. One critical concept introduced by Maslow is the distinction between deficiency needs and growth needs. **Deficiency needs** (physiological, safety, love, and esteem) are those that are critical to physical and psychological well-being; these needs must be satisfied, but once they are, a person's motivation to satisfy them diminishes. In contrast, **growth needs,** such as the need to know and understand things, to appreciate beauty, or to grow and develop in appreciation of others, can never be satisfied completely. In fact, the more people are able to meet their need to know and understand the world around them, the *greater* their motivation may become to learn still more.

Self-Actualization.   Maslow's theory also includes the concept of **self-actualization,** which he defines as "the desire to become everything that one is capable of becoming" (Maslow, 1954, p. 92). Self-actualization is characterized by acceptance of self and others, spontaneity, openness, relatively deep but "democratic" relationships with others, creativity, humor, and independence—in essence, psychological health. Maslow places striving for self-actualization at the top of his hierarchy of needs, implying that achievement of this most important need depends on the satisfaction of all other needs. The difficulty of accomplishing this is recognized by Maslow (1968), who estimated that fewer than 1 percent of adults achieve self-actualization.

Implications of Maslow's Theory for Education.   The importance of Maslow's theory for education is in the relationship between deficiency needs and growth needs. Obviously, students who are very hungry or in physical danger will have little psychological energy to put into learning. Schools and governmental agencies recognize that if the basic needs of students are not met, learning will suffer, and have responded by providing free breakfast and lunch programs. In schools the most important deficiency needs ma y be those for love and self-esteem. If students do not feel that they are loved and that they are capable, they are unlikely to have a strong motivation to achieve the higher growth objectives, such as the search for knowledge and understanding for their own sake or the creativity and openness to new ideas characteristic of the self-actualizing person. A student who is unsure of his or her "lovableness" or capability will tend to make the "safe" choice: Go with the crowd, study for the test without interest in learning the ideas, write a predictable but uncreative essay, and so on. A teacher who is able to put students at ease, to make them feel accepted and respected as individuals, is more likely (in Maslow's view) to help them become eager to learn for the sake of learning and willing to risk being creative and open to new ideas. If they are to become self-directed learners, students must feel that the teacher will respond fairly and consistently to them, and that they will not be ridiculed or punished for honest errors.

Motivation and Dissonance Theory

The need to maintain a positive self-image is a powerful motivator (Covington, 1984). Much of our behavior is directed toward satisfying our own personal stan-

deficiency needs: basic requirements for physical and psychological well-being as identified by Maslow.

growth needs: needs for knowing, appreciating, and understanding, which people try to satisfy after their basic needs are met.

self-actualization: a person's desire to develop to his or her full potential.

dards; for example, if we believe that we are good and honest people, we are likely to engage in good and honest behavior even when no one is watching, because we want to maintain a positive self-image. If we believe that we are capable and intelligent, we will try to satisfy ourselves in achievement situations that we have behaved capably and intelligently.

However, sometimes the realities of life force us into situations where our behavior or beliefs contradict our positive self-image, or conflict with other behaviors or beliefs. For example, a student who is caught cheating on a test might justify his behavior by stating (and even believing) that "everyone does it," or "the teacher gives unfairly tricky tests, so I felt justified in cheating," or denying (and really believing his denial) that he cheated, despite overwhelming evidence to the contrary.

One psychological theory that deals with behaviors, explanations, and excuses used to maintain a positive self-image is called **cognitive dissonance theory** (Festinger, 1957). This theory holds that people experience tension or discomfort when a deeply held value or belief is challenged by a psychologically inconsistent belief or behavior. To resolve this discomfort, they may change their behaviors or beliefs, or they may develop justifications or excuses that resolve the inconsistency. For example, highly competitive athletes who are otherwise careful about their health might justify taking muscle-enhancing anabolic steroids by rationalizing that the drug will strengthen them and, thereby, help bring victory to their team. This rationalization is potentially very damaging but underscores the lengths to which people will go to justify their behavior.

Festinger's Experiment.   In the classic experiment illustrating cognitive dissonance, Festinger (1957) had some college students do a very boring task. Some were paid $20 for doing the task, and some were paid only $1. When asked how much they enjoyed the task and how interesting they thought it was, the subjects who were paid $1 reported that the task was interesting and enjoyable, while those paid $20 said that it was boring. Festinger explained this paradoxical finding by noting that the students paid only $1 were faced with a dilemma. They had done a lot of boring work for very little reward. If they perceived the task as boring, then they must be fools for doing it for only a dollar. To avoid this unpleasant conclusion, they could change their perception of the task, viewing it as interesting and the experience as enjoyable and worthwhile. This kind of change in attitude is often unconscious, but real nonetheless. In contrast, the subjects paid $20 did not have to engage in any attitudinal gymnastics to explain why they did the task. They could honestly judge it as boring because they knew why they did it—for the money. People want reassurance that they made the right choice and did the right thing. Other research (Ehrlick *et al.*, 1957) has found that before buying a car people read advertisements for all sorts of cars, but after buying it they mostly read those for the car they bought, seeking reassurance that they had made the right choice and avoiding the dissonance-producing advertisements for the cars that they did not buy.

Implications of Cognitive Dissonance for Education.   In educational settings cognitive dissonance theory often applies when students receive unpleasant feedback on their academic performance. For example, Teresa usually gets good grades, but receives a D on a quiz. The mark is inconsistent with her self-image, and causes her discomfort. To resolve this discomfort, Teresa may decide to work harder to make certain that she never gets such a low grade again. On the other hand, she may try to rationalize her low grade: "The questions were tricky, I wasn't feeling well, the teacher didn't tell us the quiz was coming. I wasn't really trying, it was too hot."

Connections

Distinguish the concept of cognitive dissonance from Piaget's related concept of disequilibrium, discussed in Chapter 2.

---

cognitive dissonance theory: an explanation of the discomfort people feel when new perceptions or behaviors clash with long-held beliefs.

These excuses would help Teresa account for one D, but suppose she gets several poor grades in a row. Now she might decide that she never did like this subject anyway ("sour grapes") or that the teacher shows favoritism to the boys in the class or is a hard grader. All of these changes in opinions and excuses are directed at avoiding an unpleasant pairing of inconsistent ideas: "I am a good student" and "I am doing poorly in this class, and it is my own fault."

Motivation and Personality Theory

The word "motivation" is used to describe a drive, need, or desire to do something. People can be motivated to eat if they haven't eaten in sixteen hours, to go to the movies today, to get better grades in English this year, or to improve the world around them. In other words, the word "motivation" can be applied to behavior in a wide variety of situations.

One use of the concept of motivation is to describe a general tendency to strive toward certain types of goals. In this sense, motivation is often seen as a relatively stable personality characteristic. Some people are motivated to achieve, some to socialize with others—and they express these motivations in many different ways. Motivation as a stable characteristic is a somewhat different concept from motivation to do something specific in a particular situation. For example, anyone may be motivated to eat by being deprived of food long enough (a situational motivation), but some people are more generally interested in food than others (motivation as a personality characteristic). This is not to say that situational and personality motivation are unrelated; motivation as a personality characteristic is largely a product of a person's history.

For example, if children are praised by their parents and teachers for showing interest in the world around them, are successful in school, read well enough to enjoy reading, and are reinforced for reading (both by parents and teachers and by the content of the books themselves), then they will develop a "love of learning" as a general personality trait, and will read and learn even when no one is encouraging them. However, this personality trait is the result of a long history of *situational* motivations to learn (McCombs, 1991). What this implies is that if, owing to a history quite different from that just described, a child fails to develop a love of learning as a personality characteristic, love of learning can still be instilled in the child and later become part of the child's personality. For example, many children from homes in which learning is not highly valued and in which little reading is done by adults do not develop as much of a "love of learning" as children in more achievement- and reading-oriented families. Yet positive school experiences and encouragement for learning, curiosity, and reading by teachers can, in time, overcome the lack of encouragement or models at home and develop love of learning in just about any child. Thus when we speak of motivation as a personality characteristic, it is important to keep in mind that this does not imply that stable, generalized motivations are unalterable, only that they tend to remain constant across a variety of settings and are difficult to change in the short run.

Motivation and Attribution Theory

Teresa is struggling to find a reason for her poor grades that does not require her to change her perception of herself as a good student. She attributes her poor performance to her teacher, to the subject matter, or to other students—external factors over which she has no control. Or, if she acknowledges that her poor performance is her own fault, she decides it must be a short-term lapse, due to a momentary (but reversible) lack of motivation or attention regarding this unit of instruction.

Attribution theory (see, for example, Weiner, 1986, 1989; Graham, 1991; Hunter and Barker, 1989) seeks to understand just such explanations and excuses, particularly when applied to success or failure (wherein lies the theory's greatest importance for education, where success or failure are recurrent themes). Weiner suggests that most explanations for success or failure have three characteristics. The first is whether the cause is seen as internal (within the person) or external. The second is whether it is seen as stable or unstable. The third is whether it is perceived as controllable or not. As in cognitive dissonance theory, a central assumption of attribution theory is that people will attempt to maintain a positive self-image (Covington, 1984). Therefore when anything good happens, they are likely to attribute it to their own efforts or abilities, but when anything bad happens, they will believe that it is due to factors over which they had no control. It has been demonstrated many times that if groups of people are given a task and then told that they either "failed" or "succeeded" (even though all, in fact, were equally successful), those who were told they failed will say that their failure was due to bad luck, while those who were told they succeeded will attribute their success to skill and intelligence (Forsyth, 1986).

Attributions for Success and Failure.   Attribution theory deals primarily with four explanations for success and failure in achievement situations: ability, effort, task difficulty, and luck. Ability and effort attributions are internal to the individual; task difficulty and luck attributions are external. Ability is taken to be a relatively stable, unalterable state; effort can be altered. Similarly, task difficulty is essentially a stable characteristic, while luck is unstable and unpredictable. These four attributions and representative explanations for success and failure are presented in Table 10.1.

Table 10.1 shows how students might seek to explain success and failure differently. When students succeed, they would like to believe that it was because they are smart (an internal, stable attribution), not because they were lucky or because

The winners of this intramural high school wrestling match may attribute their success to effort, hard training, and a positive attitude. Losers may attribute failure to bad luck, bad judging, a head cold, or (secretly) to personal inferiority. How would attribution theory and the concept of locus of control explain this situation, and what does that have to do with you as a teacher?

attribution theory: an explanation of motivation that focuses on how people explain the causes of their own successes and failures.

Attribution	Stability	
	Stable	Unstable
Internal	**Ability**	**Effort**
Success:	"I'm smart"	"I tried hard"
Failure:	"I'm dumb"	"I didn't really try"
External	**Task Difficulty**	**Luck**
Success:	"It was easy"	"I lucked out"
Failure:	"It was too hard"	"I had bad luck"

Table 10.1 Attributions for Success and Failure

Attribution theory describes and suggests the implications of people's explanations of their successes and failures.

SOURCE: Adapted from Weiner, 1986.

the task was easy, or even because they tried hard (because "trying hard" says little about their likelihood of success in the future). In contrast, students who fail would like to believe that they had bad luck (an external, unstable attribution), which allows for the possibility of succeeding next time (Whitley and Frieze, 1985; Marsh, 1986). Of course, over time these attributions may be difficult to maintain. As illustrated in the case of Teresa, a student who gets one bad grade is likely to blame it on bad luck or some other external, unstable cause. After several bad grades, though, an unstable attribution becomes difficult to maintain; no one can be unlucky on tests week after week. Therefore a student like Teresa may switch to a stable but still external attribution. For example, she might decide that the course is too difficult or make some other stable, external attribution that lets her avoid making a stable, internal attribution that would shatter her self-esteem: "I failed because I don't have the ability." She might even reduce her level of effort so that she could maintain the idea that she could succeed if she really wanted to (Jagacinski and Nicholls, 1990).

Locus of Control.   One concept central to attribution theory is **locus of control** (Rotter, 1954). The word "locus" means "location." A person with an "internal locus of control" is one who believes that success or failure is due to his or her own efforts or abilities. Someone with an "external locus of control" is more likely to believe that other factors, such as luck, task difficulty, or other people's actions, cause success or failure. Locus of control can be very important in explaining a student's school performance. For example, several researchers have found that students high in internal locus of control have better grades and test scores than do students of the same intelligence who are low in internal locus of control (Lefcourt, 1976; Nowicki *et al.*, 1978; Wilhite, 1990). Brookover *et al.* (1979) found that except for ability locus of control was the most important predictor of a student's academic achievement (see also Zimmerman *et al.*, 1992). The reason is easy to see. Students who believe that success in school is due to luck, the teacher's whims, or other external factors are unlikely to work hard. In contrast, students who believe that success and failure are due primarily to their own efforts can be expected to work hard (provided, of course, they *want* to succeed). In reality, success in a particular class is a product of both students' efforts and abilities (internal

Connections

Attributions for success or failure relate to the socioemotional factors of self-esteem and peer relations, discussed in Chapter 3.

locus of control: a personality trait that concerns whether people attribute responsibility for their own failure or success to internal factors or to external factors.

Connections

Robert Slavin's work with cooperative learning (1990) has shown that students' internal locus of control is positively influenced by cooperative learning methods. See Chapters 8 and 9 for more information on cooperative learning.

factors) and luck, task difficulty, and teacher behaviors (external factors). But the most successful students will tend to *overestimate* the degree to which their own behavior produces success and failure; some experiments have shown that even in situations in which success and failure are completely due to luck, students high in internal locus of control will believe that it was their efforts that made them succeed or fail (see Weiner, 1986).

It is important to note that locus of control can change, and depends somewhat on the specific activity or situation. One difficulty in studying the effects of locus of control on achievement is that achievement has a strong effect on it (Weiner, 1989). For example, the same student might have an internal locus of control in academics (because of high academic ability) but an external locus of control in sports (because of low athletic ability). If this student discovered some unsuspected skill in a new sport, he or she might develop an internal locus of control in that sport (but still not in other sports).

Implications of Attributions and Locus of Control for Education. In the classroom students receive constant information concerning their level of performance on academic tasks, either relative to others or relative to some norm of acceptability. This feedback ultimately influences students' self-perceptions (Pintrich and Blumenfeld, 1985). Attribution theory is important in under standing how students might interpret and use feedback on their academic performance, and in suggesting to teachers how they might give feedback that has the greatest motivational value (see Ames, 1992; Blumenfeld, 1992).

Students who believe that their past failures on tasks were due to lack of ability are unlikely to expect to succeed in similar tasks, and are therefore unlikely to exert much effort (Bar-Tal, 1979; Ethington, 1991). Obviously, the belief that you will fail can be self-fulfilling; if students believe they will fail, they may be poorly motivated to do academic work, and this may in turn cause them to fail. Therefore the most damaging idea a teacher can communicate to a student is that the student is hopelessly dumb. Few teachers would say such a thing directly to a student, but the idea can be just as effectively communicated in several other ways. One is to use a competitive grading system (for example, "grading on the curve") and to make grades public and relative student rankings important. This practice may make small differences in achievement level seem large, so that students who receive the poorest grades may decide that they can never learn. Alternatively, a teacher who deemphasizes grades and relative rankings, but expresses the (almost always correct) expectation that all students in the class can learn, is likely to help students see that their chances of success depend on their *efforts*—an internal but alterable attribution that lets students anticipate success in the future if they do their best (Ames and Ames, 1984). A stable, internal attribution for success ("I succeed because I am smart") is also a poor attribution for academic success; able students also need to feel that it is their *effort,* not their ability, that leads to academic success. Teachers who emphasize amount of effort as the cause of success as well as failure and reward effort rather than ability are more likely to motivate all their students to do their best than teachers who emphasize ability alone (Hunter and Barker, 1989; Raffini, 1986).

Some formal means of rewarding students for effort rather than ability are the use of individualized instruction (see Chapter 9), where the basis of success is progress at the student's own level; the inclusion of "effort" as a component of grading or as a separate grade (see Chapter 13); or the use of rewards for improvement (described later in this chapter).

Motivation and Expectancy Theory

Edwards (1954) and later Atkinson (1964) developed theories of motivation based on the following formula:

Motivation (M) = Perceived probability of success (P_S) x Incentive value of success (I_S)

The formula is called an expectancy model, or **expectancy-valence model**, because it largely depends on the person's expectations of reward (see Feather, 1982; Locke and Lathan, 1990). What this theory implies is that people's motivation to achieve something depends on the product of their estimation of their chance of success (perceived probability of success, or P_S) and the value they place on success (incentive value of success, or I_S). For example, if Mark says, "I think I can make the honor roll if I try, and it is very important to me to make the honor roll," then he will probably work hard to make the honor roll. However, one very important aspect of the $M = P_S \times I_S$ formula is that it is *multiplicative,* meaning that if people believe that their probability of success is zero *or* if they do not value success, then their motivation will be zero. If Mark would like very much to make the honor roll but feels that he hasn't a prayer of doing so, he will be unmotivated. On the other hand, if his chances are actually good but he doesn't care about making the honor roll, he will also be unmotivated.

Atkinson (1964) added an important aspect to **expectancy theory** in pointing out that under certain circumstances an overly high probability of success can be detrimental to motivation. If Mark is very able, it may be so easy for him to make the honor roll that he need not do his best. Atkinson (1958) explained this by arguing that there is a relationship between probability of success and incentive value of success such that success in an easy task is not as valued as success in a difficult one. Therefore motivation should be at a maximum at *moderate* levels of probability of success. For example, two evenly matched tennis players will probably play their hardest. Unevenly matched players will not play as hard; the poor player may want very much to win but will have too low a probability of success to try very hard, while the better player will not value winning enough to exert his or her best effort.

Also, people will exert maximum effort to the degree that this increases their probability of success over and above what they could expect with a minimum effort. In the case of the unevenly matched tennis players, the better player is not motivated to do his or her best because winning is extremely likely even with minimal effort; and the poorer player is unmotivated because even with maximum effort, a win is unlikely (see Slavin, 1977a).

Atkinson's Experiment. In Atkinson's (1958) classic study, college sophomores were given a task and told either that (1) the highest scorer among twenty subjects would be rewarded (Probability of success [P_S] = one in twenty [1/20]; (2) the highest five scorers in twenty would be rewarded ($P_S = 5/20 = 1/4$); (3) the highest ten scorers would be rewarded ($P_S = 10/20 = 1/2$); or (4) the highest fifteen scorers would be rewarded ($P_S = 15/20 = 3/4$). The results are depicted in Figure 10.2.

As can be seen in Figure 10.2, the students who achieved the most were those who had moderate levels of probability of success (P_S). When the probability of success was too high or too low, achievement fell off. Only students who considered themselves high achievers, and thus thought they had a chance to be the first out of twenty, were likely to be motivated by a one-in-twenty chance to earn the reward if they exerted maximum effort. In contrast, effort made no difference to

expectancy-valence model: a theory that relates the probability and incentive of success to motivation.

expectancy theory: theory of motivation based on the belief that people's efforts to achieve depend on their expectations of reward.

Figure 10.2

Expectancy Theory and Motivation

Motivation was found to be highest among college sophomores when the probability of success was neither very high nor very low. Note on the graph that performance peaked when students believed they had a one in two, or fifty-fifty, chance of succeeding.

Adapted from Atkinson, 1958, p. 91.

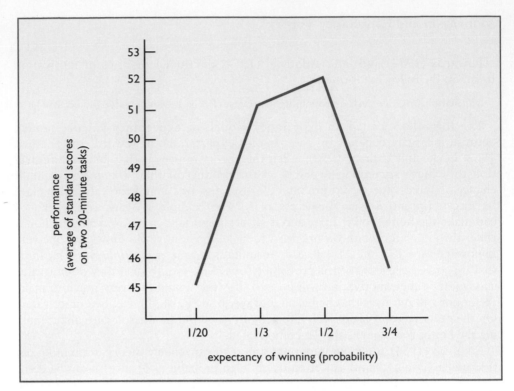

low achievers in the P_s = 1/20 condition, because even with maximum effort they had little hope of success. Similarly, the P_s = 3/4 condition was unmotivating for *high* achievers because they knew they would almost certainly be in the top fifteen even if they put out minimal effort. The best probability of success was found to be P_s = 1/2, where most students could see that they had a good chance to succeed if they exerted maximum effort, but also a good chance to fail if they did not (see Kukla, 1972b; Slavin, 1977a).

Implications of Expectancy Theory for Education.   As Atkinson's study shows, the most important implication of expectancy theory is the common-sense proposition that tasks for students should be neither too easy nor too difficult. However, expectancy theory does not suggest that questions asked in class or worksheet items should all be moderately difficult or should be answered correctly by only half of all students. An individual question or worksheet item does not usually call for effort but rather for knowledge gained by previous effort. Expectancy theory bears more on the criteria for success, as in grading. If some students feel that they are likely to get an A no matter what they do, then their motivation will not be at a maximum. Similarly, if some students feel certain to fail no matter what they do, their motivation will be minimal. Thus grading systems must be set up so that earning an A is difficult (but possible) for as many students as feasible, and earning a low grade is possible for students who exert little effort. Success must be within the reach, but not the easy reach, of all students.

Self-Check

Organize the information in this section into five schematic representations (for example, concept maps), one for each general theory about the sources of motivation: Behavioral Learning Theory, Human Needs Theory, Cognitive Dissonance Theory, Attribution Theory, and Expectancy Theory. For each one, define the underlying concept; identify any key theories, experiment, or classic study; and briefly describe and illustrate how the model works. Identify features that will enable you to recognize examples of applications and implications of each theory for classroom teachers.

How Can Achievement Motivation Be Enhanced?

One of the most important types of motivation for educational psychology is **achievement motivation** (McClelland and Atkinson, 1948), the generalized tendency to strive for success and to choose goal-oriented, success/failure activities. For example, French (1956) found that given a choice of work partners for a complex task, achievement-motivated students tend to choose a partner who is good at the task, while affiliation-motivated students (who express needs for love and acceptance) are more likely to choose a friendly partner. Achievement-motivated students will persist longer at a task than students less high in achievement motivation, even after they experience failure, and will attribute their failures to lack of effort (an internal but alterable condition) rather than to external factors such as task difficulty or luck. In short, achievement-motivated students want and expect to succeed, and when they fail, they redouble their efforts until they do succeed (see Weiner, 1989).

Not surprisingly, students high in achievement motivation tend to succeed on school tasks (Stipek, 1993). However, it is unclear which causes which: Does high achievement motivation lead to success in school, or does success in school (due to ability or other factors) lead to high achievement motivation? Actually, each contributes to the other; success breeds the desire for more success, which in turn breeds success (Gottfried, 1985). On the other hand, students who do not experience success in achievement settings will tend to lose the motivation to succeed in such settings and will turn their interest elsewhere (perhaps to social, sports, or even delinquent activities in which they may succeed).

Motivation and Goal Orientations

Dweck (1986; Dweck and Elliott, 1983) and Nicholls (1984) have found that some students are motivationally oriented toward **learning goals** (or **mastery goals**), while others are oriented toward **performance goals.** Students with learning goals see the purpose of schooling as gaining competence in the skills being taught, while those with performance goals primarily seek to gain positive judgments of their competence (and avoid negative judgments). Students striving toward learning goals are likely to take difficult courses and to seek challenges, while those with performance goals focus on getting good grades, take easy courses, and avoid challenging situations.

achievement motivation: the desire to experience success and to participate in activities in which success is dependent on personal effort and abilities.

learning goals: a motivational orientation of students who place primary emphasis on knowledge acquisition and self-improvement.

mastery goals: the goals students must reach to be considered proficient in a skill.

performance goals: a motivational orientation of students who place primary emphasis on gaining recognition from others and earning good grades.

Climate Dimensions	Mastery Goal	Performance Goal
Success defined as . . .	Improvement, progress	High grades, high normative performance
Value placed on . . .	Effort/learning	Normatively high ability
Reasons for satisfaction . . .	Working hard, challenge	Doing better than others
Teacher oriented toward . . .	How students are learning	How students are performing
View of errors/mistakes . . .	Part of learning	Anxiety eliciting
Focus of attention . . .	Process of learning	Own performance relative to others'
Reasons for effort . . .	Learning something new	High grades, performing better than others
Evaluation criteria . . .	Absolute, progress	Normative

TABLE 10.2   Achievement Goal Analysis of Classroom Climate

Source: From Ames and Archer, 1988, p. 261.

Learning versus Performance Goals.   Students with learning as opposed to performance goals do not differ in overall intelligence, but their performance in the classroom can differ markedly (McClelland, 1985). When they run into obstacles, performance-oriented students tend to become discouraged, and their performance is seriously hampered. In contrast, when learning-oriented students encounter obstacles, they tend to keep trying, and their motivation and performance may actually increase (Dweck, 1986). In particular, performance-oriented students who perceive their abilities to be low are likely to fall into a pattern of helplessness, since they feel they have little chance of earning good grades. Learning-oriented students who perceive their ability to be low do not feel this way, since they are concerned with how much they themselves can learn, without regard for the performance of others (Nicholls, 1984). The most important implication of research on learning versus performance goals is that teachers should try to convince students that learning rather than grades is the purpose of academic work. This can be done by emphasizing the interest value and practical importance of material students are studying and by deemphasizing grades and other rewards. For example, a teacher might say "Today we're going to learn about events deep in the earth that cause the fiery eruptions of volcanoes!" rather than "Today we're going to learn about volcanoes so that you can do well on tomorrow's test." In particular, use of highly competitive grading or incentive systems should be avoided (Ames *et al.,* 1977). When students perceive that there is only one standard of success in the classroom and that only a few people can achieve it, those who perceive their ability to be low will be likely to give up in advance (see Rosenholtz and Wilson, 1980; Gamoran, 1984; Cohen, 1986). Table 10.2 (from Ames and Archer, 1988) summarizes the differences in the achievement goals of students with mastery (learning) goals as opposed to those with performance goals.

Seeking Success versus Avoiding Failure.   Atkinson (1964), extending McClelland's work on achievement motivation, noted that individuals may be motivated to achieve in either of two ways: to seek success or to avoid failure. He found that some people were more motivated to avoid failure than to seek success ("failure avoiders"), while others were more motivated to seek success than to avoid failure ("success seekers"). Weiner and Rosenbaum (1965) found that given a choice between doing a puzzle (which had one right answer) or judging pictures (where there was no one answer), success seekers would choose the puzzle and failure avoiders the judgment task. Success seekers' motivation is increased following failure, as they intensify their efforts to succeed. Failure avoiders decrease their efforts following failure (Weiner, 1986).

One very important characteristic of failure avoiders is that they tend to choose either very easy or very difficult tasks. For example, Atkinson and Litwin (1960) found that in a ring toss game, failure avoiders would choose to stand very near the target or very far away, while success seekers would choose an intermediate distance. They hypothesized that failure avoiders preferred either easy tasks (on which failure was unlikely) or such difficult tasks that no one would blame them if they failed. Confirming this idea, Mahone (1960) found that failure avoiders made more unrealistic career choices (given their grades and test scores) than did success seekers, and Isaacson (1964) reported that failure avoiders chose easier and harder college courses than success seekers, who more often signed up for courses of moderate difficulty.

Understanding that it is common for failure avoiders to choose impossibly difficult or ridiculously easy tasks for themselves is very important for the teacher. For example, a poor reader might choose to write a book report on *War and Peace* and, when told that was too difficult, might choose a simple children's book. Such students are not being devious but are simply doing their best to maintain a positive self-image in a situation that is difficult for them.

Learned Helplessness and Attribution Training

An extreme form of the motive to avoid failure is called **learned helplessness,** which is a perception that no matter what one does, one is doomed to failure or ineffectuality: "Nothing I do matters" (Maier *et al.,* 1969). In academic settings learned helplessness can be related to an internal, stable explanation for failure: "I fail because I'm dumb, and that means I will always fail." (Dweck, 1975; Deiner and Dweck, 1978).

Learned helplessness can arise from inconsistent, unpredictable use of rewards and punishments by teachers, so that students feel that there is little they can do to be successful. It can be avoided or alleviated by giving students opportunities for success in small steps, immediate feedback, and, most important, consistent expectations and follow-through (see Seligman, 1981). Also, Dweck (1986) has found that focusing on learning goals as opposed to performance goals (see the previous section) can reduce helplessness, since learning goals can be attained to one degree or another by all students.

Changes in Achievement Motivation.   Motivation-related personality characteristics can be altered. They are altered in the natural course of things when

> **learned helplessness:** the expectation, based on experience, that one's actions will ultimately lead to failure.

This student is not learning. Why? If the broader reason is lack of achievement motivation or learned helplessness, what can you, as the teacher, do?

something happens to change a student's environment, as when students who have vocational but not academic skills move from a comprehensive high school in which they were doing poorly to a vocational school in which they find success. Such students may break out of a long-standing pattern of external locus of control and low achievement motivation because of their newfound success experience. "Late bloomers," students who have difficulty in their earlier school years but take off in their later years, may also experience lasting changes in motivation-related personality characteristics, as may students who are initially successful in school but who later experience difficulty keeping up. However, achievement motivation and attributions can also be changed directly by special programs designed for this purpose.

DeCharms's Classic Study in Attribution Training. DeCharms (1984) worked with black children in inner-city elementary schools to improve their achievement motivation. The DeCharms program emphasized treating students as "origins" rather than "pawns," and teaching them to think of themselves as "origins"—that is to say, masters of their own fates. Students were taught to take personal responsibility for their actions, to choose realistic objectives and plan how to achieve those objectives. The children trained under the DeCharms program showed substantial increases in achievement as compared to an untrained control group. Trained students also attended school more regularly, and a follow-up study found that they were more likely than untrained students to graduate from high school.

Several studies have found that learned helplessness in the face of repeated failure can be modified by an attribution training program that emphasizes lack of effort, rather than lack of ability, as the cause of poor performance (McCombs, 1984; Fösterling, 1985). For example, Schunk (1982, 1983) found that students who received statements attributing their past successes and failures to effort performed better than did students who received no feedback. Dweck (1975) used a similar procedure and found that it reduced the tendency for failure avoiders to give up after experiencing failure.

Theory Into Practice

Helping Students Overcome Learned Helplessness

The concept of learned helplessness derives from the theory that students may become academic failures through a conditioning process based on negative feedback from teachers, school experiences, peers, and students themselves. Numerous studies show that when goal achievement is systematically hindered, students eventually give up in their attempts to achieve those goals. They become conditioned to helplessness (Seligman, 1975).

Teachers can help counter this syndrome in a variety of ways at both the elementary and the secondary levels, including attribution training, goal restructuring, self-esteem programs, success-guaranteed approaches, and positive feedback systems. The following general principles are helpful to all students but especially to students who have shown a tendency to accept failure.

1. *Accentuate the positive:* Get to know the student's strengths and then use them as building blocks. All students have something they do well. Be careful that the strength is authentic. Don't make up a strength. For example, a student may like to talk a lot but writes poorly. Have the student complete assignments by talking rather than writing. As confidence is restored, then slowly introduce writing.

2. *Eliminate the negative:* Don't play down a student's weaknesses. Deal with them directly but tactfully. As in the above example, talk to the student about problems with writing. Then have the student develop a plan to improve on the writing. Discuss the plan and together make up a contract about how the plan will be completed.

3. *Go from the familiar to the new, using advance organizers or guided discovery:* Some students have difficulties with concepts, skills, or ideas with which they are not familiar. Also, students relate better to lessons that are linked to their own experiences. For example, a high-school math teacher might begin a lesson with a math problem students may think of facing, such as calculating the interest that accrues on a charge card when a CD player is purchased. Further, the teacher can ask students to bring to class math problems they have faced outside of school. The whole class can become involved in solving a student's math problem.

4. *Create challenges in which students actively create problems and solve them using their own knowledge and skills.*

Connections

Motivational factors affecting the academic performance of students at risk of school failure are discussed again in Chapter 12.

Teacher Expectations and Achievement

On the first day of class Mr. Erhard called roll. Soon he got to a name that looked familiar.

"Wayne Clements?"

"Here!"

"Do you have a brother named Victor?"

"Yes."

"I remember Victor. He was a terror. I'm going to keep my eye on you!" As he neared the end of the roll, Mr. Erhard saw that several boys were starting to whisper to one another in the back of the room. "Wayne! I asked the class to remain silent while I read the roll. Didn't you hear me? I knew I'd have to watch out for you!"

This dialogue illustrates how teachers can establish expectations for their students, and how these expectations can be self-fulfilling. Mr. Erhard doesn't know it, but Wayne is generally a well-behaved, conscientious student, quite unlike his older brother, Victor. However, because of his experience with Victor, Mr. Erhard has expressed an expectation that he will have trouble with Wayne. When he saw several boys whispering, it was Wayne he singled out for blame, confirming for himself that Wayne was a troublemaker. After a few periods of this treatment, we might expect Wayne to actually begin playing the role Mr. Erhard has assigned to him.

Research on teachers' expectations for their students has generally found that students do (to some degree) live up to the expectations that their teachers express (directly or indirectly) for them (Good, 1987). In one study Rosenthal and Jacobson (1968) tested elementary school students and then picked out a few in each class that they told the teachers were "late bloomers" who should do well this year. In fact, these students were chosen at random and were of the same ability as their classmates. At the end of the year, when the students were tested again, those who had (falsely) been identified as "late bloomers" were found to have learned more than their classmates in the first and second grades, though this effect was not seen in grades 3–6. The teachers expected more from them and transmitted those expectations. The Rosenthal and Jacobson study has been severely criticized (see Elashoff and Snow, 1971), but later evidence has generally supported the idea that teachers' expectations can affect students' behaviors (Cooper and Good, 1983), particularly in the younger grades and when teachers know relatively little about their students' actual achievement levels (Raudenbush, 1984).

How Teacher Expectations Affect Student Performance.   What is the process by which teachers' expectations affect student performance? Good and Brophy have described a five-step process (Good and Brophy, 1973, p. 75):

1. The teacher expects specific behavior and achievement from particular students.
2. Because of these expectations, the teacher behaves differently toward different students.
3. This treatment by the teacher tells each student what behavior and achievement the teacher expects from him or her and affects the student's self-concept, achievement, motivation, and level of aspiration.
4. If this teacher treatment is consistent over time, and if the student does not actively resist or change it in some way, it will shape his or her achievement and behavior. High-expectation students will be led to achieve at high levels, but the achievement of low-expectation students will decline.
5. With time, the student's achievement and behavior will conform more and more closely to what was originally expected of him or her.

How Teachers Communicate Positive Expectations.   It is important for teachers to communicate to their students the expectation that they can learn (see Cooper and Tom, 1984). Obviously it is a bad idea to state the contrary, that a particular student cannot learn, and few teachers would explicitly do so. There are several implicit ways teachers can communicate positive expectations of their students (or avoid negative ones).

1. *Wait for Students to Respond:* Rowe (1974) and others have noted that teachers wait longer for answers from students for whom they have high expectations

than from other students. Longer wait times may communicate high expectations and increase student achievement (Tobin, 1986, 1987).

2. *Avoid Unnecessary Achievement Distinctions among Students:* Grading should be a private matter between students and their teacher, not public information. Reading and math groups may be instructionally necessary in many classrooms (see Chapter 9), but teachers should avoid establishing a rigid hierarchy of groups, should treat the groups equally and respectfully, and should allow for moving a student out of one group and into another when appropriate (see Gamoran, 1984; Rosenholtz and Simpson, 1984). Students usually know who is good in school and who is not, but teachers can still successfully communicate the expectation that all students, not just the most able ones, are capable of learning.

3. *Treat All Students Equally:* Call on students at all achievement levels equally often and spend equal amounts of time with them. In particular, guard against bias. Research finds that teachers often unwittingly hold lower expectations for certain categories of students, such as minority-group students (Baron *et al.,* 1985) or females (Good and Findley, 1985; Sadker and Sadker, 1985).

> **Connections**
>
> Recall the discussions of the effects of teacher expectations on the academic performance of males and females (in Chapter 4) and of high and low achievers (in Chapter 9).

Anxiety and Achievement

Anxiety is a constant companion of education. Every student feels some anxiety at some time while in school, but for certain students anxiety seriously inhibits learning or performance, particularly on tests (see King and Ollendick, 1989).

The main source of anxiety in school is the fear of failure, and with it, loss of self-esteem (Hill and Wigfield, 1984). Low achievers are particularly likely to feel anxious in school, but they are by no means the only ones; we all know very able, high-achieving students who are also very anxious, terrified to be less than perfect on any school task.

Anxiety can block school performance in several ways (Tobias, 1985; Naveh-Benjamin, 1991). Anxious students may have difficulty learning in the first place; they may have difficulty using or transferring knowledge they do have, and they may have difficulty demonstrating their knowledge on tests. Anxious students are likely to be overly self-conscious in performance settings, which distracts attention from the task at hand (Wine, 1980).

One particularly common form of debilitating anxiety is "math phobia." Many students (and adults) simply freeze up when given math problems, particularly word problems. Girls are especially likely to suffer from serious math anxiety (Richardson and Woolfolk, 1980), at least in part because girls, particularly in adolescence, feel less able in math than boys (Parsons *et al.,* 1982).

There are many strategies teachers can apply to reduce the negative impact of anxiety on learning and performance. Clearly, creating a classroom climate that is accepting, comfortable, and noncompetitive helps. Giving students opportunities to correct errors or improve their work before handing it in also helps anxious children, as does providing clear, unambiguous instructions (Wigfield and Eccles, 1989). In testing situations, teachers can do many things to help anxious students to do their best. One is to avoid time pressure, to give students plenty of time to complete a test and check their work. Tests that begin with easy problems and only gradually introduce more difficult ones are better for anxious students, and tests with standard, simple answer formats help such students (Phillips *et al.,* 1980). Test-anxious children can be trained in test-taking skills, and this can have a positive impact on their test performance (Hill and Horton, 1985). Table 10.3 shows some of the key test-taking skills taught in the Hill and Horton study.

1. General test skills and knowledge:

    a. Be comfortable and sit where you can write easily.
    b. Pay attention when the teacher talks.
    c. The teacher can help you understand how to work on the test but can't tell you the answer to a problem on the test.
    d. Taking tests is something we learn to do in school.

2. Positive motivation—doing your best:

    a. All I ask is that you do your best. I will be really pleased if you try to do your best.
    b. If you finish a section before time is up, go back and check your answers. Don't disturb others; instead, work quietly at your desk.
    c. Before we begin, remember to carefully listen to me, be quiet, take a deep breath, and feel relaxed.

3. Positive motivation—expectancy reassurance:

    a. Some tests have some very hard problems. Don't worry if you can't do some problems.
    b. It's OK if you aren't sure what the right answer is. Choose the answer you think is best. It's OK to guess.
    c. If you work hard but don't finish a test, don't worry about it! The most important thing to me is that you try hard and do as well as you can. I know you'll do a good job if you try!

4. Test strategy and problem-solving skills:

    a. There is only *one* best answer.
    b. Do what you know first. If you can't answer a problem or it's taking a lot of time move on to the next one. You can come back later if you have time.
    c. Don't rush. If you work *too fast,* you can make careless errors. You have to work carefully.
    d. Don't work too slowly. Do the problems at a moderate rate.
    e. Pay close attention to your work.
    f. Keep track of where you are working on the page by keeping one hand on this spot.

Table 10.3   Examples of Test-Taking Skills and Motivational Dispositions
Source: Adapted from Hill and Wigfield, 1984, p. 123.

Self-Check

Define achievement motivation and contrast the motivational characteristics of students in terms of their approaches to academic success or failure and their goals in attending school. How can attribution training and changes in teacher expectations affect students' motivation and performance?

How Can Teachers Increase Students' Motivation to Learn?

Learning takes work. Euclid, the ancient Greek mathematician who wrote the first geometry textbook, was asked by his king if there were any shortcuts he could use to learn geometry, since he was a very busy man. "I'm sorry," Euclid replied, "but there is no royal road to geometry." The same is true of every other subject: Students get out of any course of study only what they put into it.

The remainder of this chapter discusses the means by which students can be motivated to exert the efforts needed to learn. First, the issue of intrinsic motivation—the motivational value of the content itself—is presented. Extrinsic motivation—the use of praise, feedback, and incentives to motivate students to do their best—is then discussed.

Also in this section are specific strategies for enhancing student motivation and suggestions for solving motivational problems common in classrooms, including reward-for-improvement incentive systems and cooperative learning methods.

Intrinsic and Extrinsic Motivation

Sometimes a course of study is so fascinating and useful to students that they are willing to do the work required to learn the material with no incentive other than the interest level of the material itself. For example, many students would gladly take auto mechanics or photography courses and work hard in them, even if they offered no credit or grades. For these students, the favorite subject itself has enough **intrinsic incentive** value to motivate them to learn. Other students love to learn about insects or dinosaurs or famous people in history, and need little encouragement or reward to do the work necessary to become knowledgeable about their favorite topics (Gottfried, 1990).

However, much of what must be learned in school is not inherently interesting or useful to most students in the short run. Students receive about 900 hours of instruction every year, and it is unrealistic to expect that intrinsic interest alone will keep them enthusiastically working day in and day out. For this reason, schools apply a variety of **extrinsic incentives**, reinforcers for learning that are not inherent in the material being learned. Extrinsic reinforcers may range from praise to grades to recognition to prizes or other rewards.

In the scenario presented at the beginning of this chapter, Cal Lewis tried to enhance both intrinsic and extrinsic motivation. His simulation of the Constitutional Convention was intended to arouse students' intrinsic interest in the subject, while his ratings of students' presentations and his feedback at the end of each period were intended to provide extrinsic motivation.

Lepper's Experiment on the Impact of Rewards on Motivation.   An important question in research on motivation concerns whether or not the providing of extrinsic rewards diminishes intrinsic interest in an activity. In a classic experiment exploring this topic, Lepper *et al.* (1973) gave preschoolers an opportunity to draw with felt-tipped markers, which many of them did quite enthusiastically. Then the researchers randomly divided the children into three groups: one was told they would receive a reward for drawing a picture for a visitor (a "Good Player Award"); one was given the same reward as a surprise (not dependent on their drawing); and one received no reward. Over the next four days observers recorded the free-play activities of the children. Those who had received a reward for drawing spent about half as much time drawing with felt-tipped markers as those who had received the "surprise" reward and those who had gotten no reward. The authors suggested that promising extrinsic rewards for an activity that is intrinsically interesting may undermine intrinsic interest by inducing children to expect a

This student is performing a task that has intrinsic value to her. How is her motivation affected? As a teacher, how could you maintain or extend her motivation? How would you present the same task to another student for whom the task does *not* have intrinsic value?

---

intrinsic incentive: an aspect of an activity that people enjoy and, therefore, find motivating.

extrinsic incentive: a reward that is external to the activity, such as recognition or a good grade.

reward for doing what they had previously done for nothing. In a later study (Greene and Lepper, 1974) it was found that just telling children they would be watched (through a one-way mirror) had an "undermining" effect similar to that found for a promised reward. This study has been repeated many times with similar results (Morgan, 1984; Deci and Ryan, 1985).

Do Rewards Destroy Intrinsic Motivation?   In understanding the results of these studies it is important to recall the conditions of the research. The students chosen for the studies were ones who showed an intrinsic interest in using marking pens; those who did not were excluded from the experiments. Also, drawing with felt-tip pens does not resemble most school tasks. Many children love to draw at home, but few, even those most interested in school subjects, would independently study grammar and punctuation, work math problems, or learn the valences of chemical elements. Further, our most creative and self-motivated scientists, for example, were heavily reinforced as students with grades, science fair prizes, and scholarships for doing science, and virtually all successful artists have been reinforced at some point for engaging in artistic activities. This reinforcement certainly did not undermine their intrinsic interest. Research on older students doing more school-like tasks has generally failed to replicate the results of the Lepper *et al.* (1973) experiment (Pittman *et al.* 1983). In fact, the use of rewards sometimes *increases* intrinsic motivation, especially when rewards are contingent on the quali-

Figure 10.3   Some Factors Affecting Individual Motivation

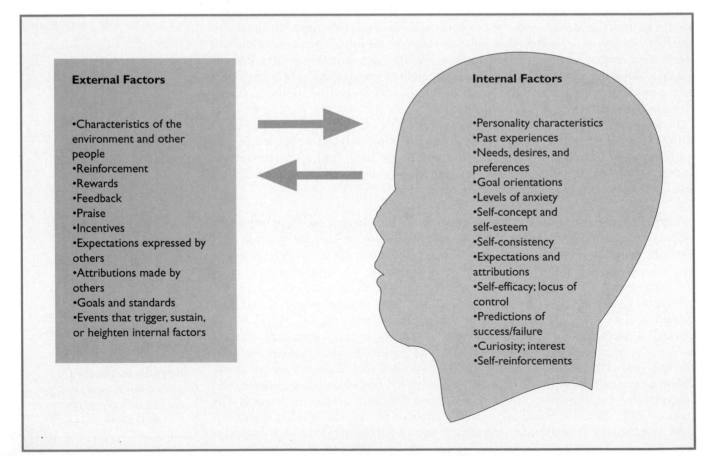

ty of performance rather than on mere participation in an activity (Deci and Ryan, 1985, 1987; Lepper, 1983), when the rewards are seen as recognition of competence (Rosenfield *et al.*, 1980), when the task in question is not very interesting (Morgan, 1984) or when the rewards are social (for example, praise) rather than material (Ryan and Stiller, 1991; Miller and Hom, 1990).

The research on the effects of extrinsic rewards on intrinsic motivation does counsel caution in the use of material rewards for intrinsically interesting tasks. Teachers should attempt to make everything they teach as intrinsically interesting as possible and should avoid handing out material rewards when they are unnecessary, but they should not refrain from using extrinsic rewards when they *are* needed (Lepper, 1983). Often, extrinsic rewards may be necessary to get students started in a learning activity, but may then be phased out as students come to enjoy and succeed at the activity (Stipek, 1993). Figure 10.3 shows the many factors involved in individual motivation.

How Can Teachers Enhance Intrinsic Motivation?

Classroom instruction should enhance intrinsic motivation as much as possible. This means that teachers must try to get their students interested in the material they are presenting and then present it in an appealing way that both satisfies and increases students' curiosity about the material itself. A discussion of some means of doing this follows (also see Brophy, 1987; Malone and Lepper, 1988; Corno and Rohrkemper, 1985).

Arousing Interest. It is important to convince students of the importance and interest level of material about to be presented. This is the idea behind the use of an instructional set to begin a lesson. The instructional set relates the lesson about to be presented to students' interests, and if possible shows how the knowledge to be gained will be useful to students. For example, intrinsic motivation to learn a lesson on percents might be increased by introducing the lesson as follows:

> Today we will begin a lesson on percents. Percents are important in our daily lives. For example, when you buy something at the store and a salesperson figures the sales tax, he or she is using percents. When we leave a tip for a waiter or waitress, we use percents. We often hear in the news things like, "Prices rose seven percent last year." In a few years many of you will have summer jobs, and if they involve handling money, you'll probably be using percents all the time.

Similarly, a lesson on microorganisms might begin with a statement about the billions of microorganisms that live in and on the human body. A lesson on the settlement of the American Southwest might begin:

> Do you ever wonder why so many cities and towns in California, Arizona, New Mexico, and Texas have Spanish names? San Francisco means "St. Francis," Los Angeles means "The Angels," and San Antonio means "St. Anthony." The literal meaning of Sierra Nevada is "Snowy Saws," from the sawtooth shape of the mountains. These place names tell us that the American Southwest was settled by people from Spain. This week we will be learning about the Spanish discovery and settlement of this region of our country.

The purpose of these instructional sets is to arouse student curiosity about the lesson to come, thereby enhancing intrinsic motivation to learn the material. Another way to enhance students' intrinsic interest is to give them some choice over what they will study or how they will study it (Stipek, 1993).

Connections

Recall the discussion in Chapter 7 of the importance of student interest in creative problem solving and other constructivist approaches. The importance of student interest in lesson content and presentation are also discussed in Chapters 8 and 11.

Maintaining Curiosity.   A skillful teacher uses a variety of means to further arouse or maintain curiosity in the course of the lesson. Science teachers, for instance, often use demonstrations that surprise or baffle students and induce them to want to understand why. A floating dime makes students curious about the surface tension of liquids. "Burning" a dollar bill covered with an alcohol-water solution (without harming the dollar bill) certainly increases curiosity about the heat of combustion. Less dramatically, the "subtraction with renaming" lesson described in Chapter 8 got students comfortable with subtracting such numbers as $47 - 3$ and $56 - 23$, but then stumped them with $13 - 5$. Students were shocked out of a comfortable routine and forced to look at the problem in a new way.

Berlyne (1965) discussed the concept of "epistemic curiosity," behavior aimed at acquiring knowledge to master and understand the environment. He hypothesized that epistemic curiosity results from conceptual conflict, as when new information appears to contradict earlier understandings. Berlyne suggests the deliberate use of surprise, doubt, perplexity, bafflement, and contradiction as means of arousing epistemic curiosity. Two examples he gives are teaching about how plants use chlorophyll to carry out photosynthesis, and then introducing the problem of fungi, which do not need sunlight; and teaching about latitude and longitude, and then asking students how they would estimate their location in the middle of the desert.

Theory Into Practice:

Keeping Curiosity Alive

Curiosity is fostered by the ability to ask "why" and the freedom to pursue an answer. Therefore, curiosity is aroused and maintained by activities and questions that:

- are open-ended.

- are baffling or surprising.

- lead to further inquiry.

- cause discussion or debate.

- provide contradictory points of view or evidence.

- allow discovery.

Most curiosity-fostering activities are not age-specific and can be utilized at many grade levels. Among these are:

- laboratory experiments in science done either individually or in groups.

- student collaborative teams where groups of students research a topic or question in depth over an extended period of time.

- discussion groups.

- simulations and games.

- "hands-on" or experiential activities ranging from field trips to cooperative work-study programs with community businesses.

Teaching practices that can enhance curiosity include:

- taking a multidisciplinary approach by integrating material across subject matter and content areas.

- utilizing multiple teaching methods and media.

Young children are concrete thinkers. They like to touch, see, hear, and experience things. For preschool and elementary school ages, therefore, the following activities are especially appropriate:

- "live" demonstrations and models that allow students to have direct sensory contact.

- doing activities that allow students to participate physically such as performing a play.

- field trips.

- experiential or "hands-on" activities such as raising plants or animals or building models.

Also for younger students:

- peer teaching activities will keep more advanced students curious as they try to explain material to others.

- computer games can enhance drill and practice activities.

Adolescents are more abstract thinkers. They like to explore possibilities. They also are more concerned that material is relevant to the "real world." For middle school and high school, therefore, the following activities are especially appropriate:

- debates and discussions that allow multiple views and perspectives on the material.

- field work or internships such as becoming involved in local service groups or working part-time in an internship with a business.

- role play activities such as running a business or governing a country.

- research activities both in formal labs and in activities such as science fairs.

- using computer simulation programs to test and examine hypotheses.

Using a Variety of Interesting Presentation Modes.　The intrinsic motivation to learn something is enhanced by the use of interesting materials (Shirey and Reynolds, 1988), as well as by variety in mode of presentation. For example, student interest in a subject may be maintained by alternating use of films, guest speakers, demonstrations, and so on, although use of each resource must be carefully planned to be sure it focuses on the course objectives and complements the other activities. Use of computers can enhance the intrinsic motivation of most students to learn (Lepper, 1985).

One excellent means of increasing interest in a subject is to use games or simulations. A simulation, or role-play, is an exercise in which students take on roles and engage in activities appropriate to those roles. Cal Lewis used simulation to teach students about the Constitutional Convention. Programs exist that simulate many aspects of government, such as having students take roles as legislators who must negotiate and trade votes to satisfy their constituents' interests or as economic actors (farmers, producers, consumers) who run a minieconomy. However, creative teachers have long used simulations they designed themselves. For example, teachers can have students write their own newspaper; design, manufacture, and market a product; or set up and run a bank.

The advantage of simulations is that they allow students to learn about a subject from the inside. Although research on use of simulations (see Greenblat, 1982; VanSickle, 1986) finds that they are generally little or no more effective than traditional instruction for teaching facts and concepts, studies do consistently find that simulations increase students' interest, motivation, and affective learning (Dukes and Seidner, 1978). They certainly impart a different affective knowledge of a subject.

Nonsimulation games can also increase motivation to learn a given subject. The "spelling bee" is a popular example of a nonsimulation game. Teams-Games-Tournament, or TGT (DeVries and Slavin, 1978), uses games that can be adapted to any subject. Team games are usually better than individual games; they provide an opportunity for teammates to help one another and avoid one problem of individual games, which is that more able students may consistently win. If all students are put on mixed-ability teams, all have a good chance of success (see Slavin, 1990b).

Helping Students Set Their Own Goals.   One fundamental principle of motivation is that people work harder for goals they themselves set than for goals set for them by others. Klausmeier *et al.* (1975) developed and evaluated a program that capitalizes on this principle. The program, called **Individually Guided Motivation,** or **IGM,** involves having students meet on a regular basis with their teachers to set specific, measurable goals for the week. For example, students might set a minimum number of books they expect to read at home, or a score they expect to attain on an upcoming quiz. At the next goal-setting conference the teacher would discuss student attainment of (or failure to attain) goals, and set new goals for the following week. During these meetings the teacher would help students learn to set ambitious but not unrealistic goals and would praise them for setting and then achieving their goals.

Research on IGM has found that this method can be effective in increasing student achievement in areas in which goals were set (see Klausmeier *et al.*, 1975).

Principles for Providing Incentives to Learn

While teachers must always try to enhance students' intrinsic motivation to learn academic materials, they must at the same time be concerned about incentives for learning (Brophy, 1987). Not every subject is intrinsically interesting to all students, and students must be motivated to do the hard work necessary to master difficult subjects. The following sections discuss a variety of incentives that can be applied to motivate students to learn academic materials.

Expressing Clear Expectations.   Students need to know exactly what they are supposed to do, how they will be evaluated, and what the consequences of success will be. Often student failures on particular tasks stem from confusion about what they are being asked to do (see Brophy, 1982; L. Anderson *et al.*, 1985). Communicating clear expectations is important when introducing assignments. For example, a teacher might introduce a writing assignment as follows:

> Today, I'd like you all to write a composition about what Thomas Jefferson would think of government in the United States today. I expect your compositions to be about two

Individually Guided Motivation (IGM): an instructional program based on the idea that people are more motivated to achieve goals they have set for themselves than goals set by others.

pages long, and to compare and contrast the plan of government laid out by the nation's founders with the way government actually operates today. Your compositions will be graded on the basis of your ability to describe similarities and differences between the structure and function of the U.S. government in Thomas Jefferson's time and today, as well as on the originality and clarity of your writing. This will be an important part of your six weeks' grade, so I expect you to do your best!

Note that the teacher is clear about what students are to write, how much material is expected, how the work will be evaluated, and how important the work will be for the students' grades. This clarity assures students that efforts directed at writing a good composition will pay off—in this case, in terms of grades. If the teacher had just said, "I'd like you all to write a composition about what Thomas Jefferson would think about government in the United States today," students might write the wrong thing, write too much or too little, or perhaps emphasize the if-Jefferson-were-alive-today aspect of the assignment rather than the comparative-government aspect. Further, they would be unsure how much importance the teacher intended to place on the mechanics of the composition as compared to its content. Finally, they would have no way of knowing how their efforts would pay off, since the teacher gave no indication of how much emphasis would be given to the compositions in computing grades.

Providing Clear Feedback.   The word **feedback** means information on the results of one's efforts. The term has been used throughout this book to refer both to information students receive on their performance and to information teachers obtain on the effects of their instruction (see Chapter 8).

Feedback can serve as an incentive. Research on feedback has found that provision of information on the results of one's actions can be an adequate reward in some circumstances (Locke *et al.,* 1968; Waller and Gaa, 1974). However, feedback must be clear and specific and given close in time to performance to be an effective motivator (Bandura, 1969; Kulik and Kulik, 1988). This is important for all students, but especially for young ones. For example, praise for a job well done should specify what the student did well:

- "Good work! I like the way you used the guide words in the dictionary to find the words on your worksheet."
- "I like that answer. It shows you've been thinking about what I've been saying."
- "This is an excellent essay. It started with a statement of the argument you were going to make and then supported the argument with relevant information. I also like the care you took with punctuation and word usage."

Specific feedback is both informative and motivational (Kulhavy and Stock, 1989). It tells students what they did right, so that they will know what to do in the future, and helps give them an effort-based attribution for success ("You succeeded because you worked hard"). In contrast, if students are praised or receive a good grade without any explanation, they are unlikely to learn from the feedback what to do next time to be successful and may form an ability attribution ("I succeeded because I'm smart") or an external attribution ("I must have succeeded because the teacher likes me, the task was easy, or I lucked out"). As noted earlier in this chapter, effort attributions are most conducive to continuing motivation. Similarly, feedback about mistakes or failures can add to motivation if it focuses only on the performance itself (not on students' general abilities) and if it is alternated with success feedback (see Clifford, 1984, 1990).

> **Connections**
>
> Kinds and uses of feedback are discussed again in Chapter 14 in connection with assessment and standardized test scores.

> **feedback:** information on the results of one's efforts.

These children have earned the opportunity to work independently at activity centers. What incentives to learn has the teacher probably provided? As a teacher, what guidelines would you follow to ensure that you use extrinsic motivators ethically and effectively?

Providing Immediate Feedback.   Immediacy of feedback is also very important (Kulik and Kulik, 1988). If students take a quiz on Monday and don't receive any feedback on it until Friday, the informational and motivational value of the feedback will be diminished. First, if they made errors on the quiz, they may continue making similar errors all week that might have been averted by feedback on the quiz performance. Second, a long delay between behavior and consequence confuses the relationship between them. Young students, especially, may have little idea why they received a particular grade if the performance on which the grade is based took place several days earlier.

Providing Frequent Feedback.   Feedback and rewards must be delivered frequently to students to maintain their best efforts. For example, it is unrealistic to expect most students to work hard for six or nine weeks in hope of improving their grade unless they receive frequent feedback. Research in the behavioral learning theory tradition (for example, Bandura, 1969) has established that no matter how powerful a reward is, it may have little impact on behavior if it is given infrequently; small frequent rewards are more effective incentives than large infrequent ones. Research on frequency of testing has generally found that it is a good idea to give frequent brief quizzes to assess student progress rather than infrequent long tests (Peckham and Roe, 1977; Dempster, 1991). It also points up the importance of asking many questions in class, so that students can gain information about their own level of understanding and can receive reinforcement (praise, recognition) for paying attention to lessons.

Determining the Value and Availability of Extrinsic Motivators.   Expectancy theories of motivation, discussed earlier in this chapter, hold that motivation is a product of the value an individual attaches to success and the individual's estimate of the likelihood of success (see Atkinson and Birch, 1978). One implication of this is that incentives used with students must be valued by them. Some students are not particularly interested in teacher praise or grades but may value notes home to their parents, a little extra recess time, or a special privilege in the classroom.

Another implication of expectancy theory is that all students must have a chance to be rewarded if they do their best, but no student should have an easy time achieving the maximum reward. This principle is violated by traditional grading practices because some students find it easy to earn A's and B's, while others feel they have little chance of academic success no matter what they do. In this circumstance neither high achievers nor low achievers are likely to exert their best efforts. This is one reason that it is important to reward students for effort, for doing better than they have done in the past, or for making progress, rather than only for getting a high score. Not all students are equally capable of achieving a high score, but all *are* equally capable of exerting effort, exceeding their own past record, or making progress, so these are often better, more equally available criteria for reward.

Self-Check

Divide a sheet of paper into two equal columns headed "Intrinsic Motivation" and "Extrinsic Motivation." Then, brainstorm information to enter in each column, including characteristic examples of motivators and specific strategies teachers can use to enhance motivation in the classroom. When you have finished, review the section to see if you need to add any important details. Then reread the chapter opening scenario. Identify each event in Mr. Lewis's lesson in terms of the strategies you have listed in your chart.

Teachers on Teaching

How have you dealt with motivational challenges in your classroom?

A motivational challenge I was concerned with was the lower levels of participation and achievement of my middle-school female students. I had observed that the female students in my classes were more silent than the males, raised their hands less often, and shunned competitive situations. I assumed that socialized sex role stereotypes played an important role in silencing girls' voices, but at the same time I considered the possibility that I was a source of the problem. Did I really treat boys and girls equally in my classes? At the same time, was I sensitive to the possibility that boys and girls might learn differently?

Using information from educational research and books, such as *Women's Ways of Knowing*, by Belenky, Clinchy, Goldberger, and Tarule, I developed a series of weekly Socratic Seminars in which I altered my role as a teacher in a way that invited greater participation. I became a facilitator whose task was to ask questions rather than to tell information. During the debriefing sessions that followed, the girls were quick to explain how they felt freer to disagree with their friends. They heard a variety of opinions with no right or wrong answers so long as each premise can be supported. They were talking about serious ideas, and this made them feel that their opinions matter. Mutual respect among all the participants, who represented diversity in ethnicity as well as gender, pointed to the value of finding learning models that let all students choose to speak and be heard.

Nancy Letts, Gifted and Talented Teacher
Post Road School, White Plains, New York

Violet was an academically unmotivated seventh-grader. She was not "ready to learn." I followed the expected protocol. Each stage began with great expectations and promises but resulted in few sustained positive changes in behavior or work habits. I knew that I had to use strategies that would let Violet buy into the plan. I decided to try an Adopt-A-Student approach. Violet was delighted that I wanted to be her In-School Mom. I invited her to meet with me after school. This setting provided the groundwork for establishing positive rapport. I was able to use the strategies that had failed earlier, because we were developing a trust that had not been there before. I readministered a learning styles inventory and found that Violet would benefit most from active, hands-on, real-life learning. I also conducted a life-space interview and discovered how frightened Violet had been about entering junior high school and the negative perception she had of herself. Violet seemed to suffer from learned helplessness and had low self-esteem. In our after-school informal sessions, Violet gained confidence in her ability to successfully complete tasks, have positive interactions, and reflect on her classroom responsibilities and roles. She was finally ready to learn. This readiness transferred to her classwork, where she was provided with resources that matched her learning style preferences. As her confidence grew, Violet blossomed. I have used the Adopt-A-Student approach with students through the years and have found it works toward discovering motivating factors for low achievers, students with low self-esteem, and students who resist school structures and distrust authority figures.

Gloria H. Thompson, Science Teacher
Taft Junior High School, Washington, DC
1992 Washington, DC, Teacher of the Year

How Can Teachers Reward Performance, Effort, and Improvement?

As noted many times in this chapter, incentive systems used in the classroom should focus on student effort, not ability. A principal means of rewarding students for putting forth their best efforts is to reward effort directly, by praising students for their efforts or, as is done in many schools, giving a separate effort grade or rating along with the usual performance grade or including effort as an important part of students' grades.

Using Praise Effectively.   Praise serves many purposes in classroom instruction but is primarily used to reinforce appropriate behaviors and to give feedback to students on what they are doing right. Overall, it is a good idea to use praise frequently, especially with young children and in classrooms with many low-achieving students (Brophy, 1981). However, what is more important than the *amount* of praise given is the *way* it is given (Nafpaktitis *et al.*, 1985). O'Leary and O'Leary (1977) hold that praise is effective as a classroom motivator to the extent that it is contingent,, specific, and credible. **Contingent praise** depends on student performance of well-defined behaviors. For example, if a teacher says, "I'd like you all to open your books to page 279 and work problems 1–10," then praise would be given only to those students who follow directions. Praise should be given only for right answers and appropriate behaviors.

By specificity is meant that the teacher praises students for specific behaviors, not for general "goodness." For example, a teacher might say, "Susan, I'm glad you followed my directions to start work on your composition," rather than "Susan, you're doing great!"

When praise is credible, it is given sincerely for good work. Brophy (1981) notes that when teachers praise low-achieving or disruptive students for good work, they often contradict their words with tone, posture, or other nonverbal cues.

Madsen *et al.,* (1968) present a good summary of the use of contingent, specific, credible praise:

> Give praise and attention to behaviors which facilitate learning. Tell the child what he is being praised for. Try to reinforce behaviors incompatible with those you wish to decrease.

The last part of this statement is important: "Try to reinforce behaviors incompatible with those you wish to decrease." It means, for example, that if you want students to stop getting out of their seats without permission, you should praise them for staying in their seats (which is, of course, incompatible with wandering around). Brophy (1981) lists characteristics of effective and ineffective praise; this list appears in Table 10.4.

In addition to contingency, specificity, and credibility, Brophy's list includes several particularly important principles that reinforce topics discussed earlier in this chapter. For example, Guidelines 7 and 8 emphasize that praise should be given for good performance relative to a student's usual level of performance. That is, students who usually do well should not be praised for a merely average performance, but students who usually do less well should be praised when they do better. This relates to the principle of accessibility of reward discussed earlier in this chapter; rewards should be neither too easy nor too difficult for students to obtain.

Using Grades as Incentives.   The grading systems used in most schools serve

---

Connections

Recall the discussion in Chapter 5 on the use of praise as a reinforcer. The use of reinforcers and consequences in classroom discipline is discussed in Chapter 11.

---

contingent praise: praise that is effective because it refers directly to specific task performances.

Effective Praise	Ineffective Praise
1. Is delivered contingently.	1. Is delivered randomly or unsystematically.
2. Specifies the particulars of the accomplishment.	2. Is restricted to global positive reactions.
3. Shows spontaneity, variety, and other signs of credibility, suggests clear attention to the student's accomplishment.	3. Shows a bland uniformity, which suggests a conditioned response made with minimal attention.
4. Rewards attainment of specified performance criteria (which can include effort criteria, however).	4. Rewards mere participation, without consideration of performance processes or outcomes.
5. Provides information to students about their competence or the value of their accomplishments.	5. Provides no information at all or gives students information about their status.
6. Orients students towards better appreciation of their own task-related behavior and thinking about problem solving.	6. Orients students toward comparing themselves with others and thinking about competing.
7. Uses students' own prior accomplishments as the context for describing present accomplishments.	7. Uses the accomplishments of peers as the context for describing students' present accomplishments.
8. Is given in recognition of noteworthy effort or success at difficult tasks (for *this* student).	8. Is given without regard to the effort expended or the meaning of the accomplishment (for *this* student).
9. Attributes success to effort and ability, implying that similar successes can be expected in the future.	9. Attributes success to ability alone or to external factors such as luck or easy task.
10. Focuses students' attention on their own task-relevant behavior.	10. Focuses students' attention on the teacher as an external authority figure who is manipulating them.
11. Fosters appreciation of and desirable attributions about task-relevant behavior after the process is completed.	11. Intrudes into the ongoing process, distracting attention from task-relevant behavior.

Table 10.4   Guidelines for Effective Praise

If used properly, praise can be an effective motivator in classroom situations.

Source: Adapted from Brophy, 1981, p. 26.

three quite different functions at the same time: evaluation, feedback, and incentive (see Slavin, 1978a). This mix of functions makes grades less than ideal for each function . For example, because grades are based largely on ability rather than on effort, they are less than ideal for motivating students to exert maximum effort, as noted earlier in this chapter. Also, grades are given too infrequently to be very useful as either feedback or incentives for young children unable to see the connection

↪ **Focus On**

Motivating Students to Learn

Educators know the key to success is motivation. As the well-known high-school mathematics teacher Jaime Escalante said, "All you need is *ganas*" (desire). But how do students acquire that desire? One way is through the inspiration of excellent teachers such as Escalante, or the state and national Teachers of the Year award-winners, or the many others working quietly in most schools to turn students on to learning. Another way is through incentives, and a third way is through programs that boost self-esteem.

Innovative community-based incentive systems are the latest thing. In Ypsilanti, Michigan, for instance, high-performing students receive graded photo-ID cards each semester that qualify them for tangible rewards. For example, superior academic performance merits a prime spot in the school parking lot as well as discounts in stores and restaurants throughout the community. Despite some educators' concerns that learning should be its own reward, this incentive system is working its magic with both student achievement and school morale.

Opportunities to enhance self-esteem can also serve as incentives. Even very resistant students, such as those who have failed time and again, do respond in well-planned self-esteem enhancement programs. At the same time, results may not be dramatic in the short term. In a San Jose,

California, school district, for example, a six-year self-esteem program is credited with boosting achievement scores by ten percent. But attendance has increased to almost 98 percent, and 89 percent of students go on to post-secondary schools, considerably more than the 65 percent who did so before. In college preparatory programs for minority-group students, such as Native Americans, self-esteem and self-efficacy awareness are part of the curriculum.

> ### Critical Thinking
>
> Which of your teachers especially motivated you in a subject? What specifically did the teacher do that inspired you? What do you think of offering students perks and privileges for academic progress? How are incentives employed in the world outside of the classroom? What would you include on a list for teachers suggesting dos and don'ts for helping students develop greater self-esteem?

Jaime Escalante, "Hold to a Dream," *Network News and Views,* February 1990; Jonathan Weisman, "The Apostles of Self-Esteem," *Education Week,* March 1991.

Connections

Principles and procedures for grading are discussed in detail in Chapter 13.

between today's work and a grade to be received in six weeks. Grades are effective as incentives for older students, however. Experiments comparing graded and ungraded college classes (for example, Gold *et al.,* 1971) find substantially higher performance in the graded classes. Grades work as incentives in part because they increase the value of other rewards given closer in time to the behaviors they reinforce. For example, when students get stars on their papers, they may value them in part because they are an indication that their grades in that subject may also be good. The "accessibility" problem of grades—the fact that good grades are too easy for some students but too difficult for others—may be partially diminished by the use of grading systems with many levels. For example, low-performing students may feel rewarded if they simply pass or if they get a C, while their high-performing classmates may not be satisfied unless they get an A. Also, one major reason that students value grades is that their parents value them, and parents are particularly likely to praise their children for *improvements* in their grades. Even though good grades are not equally attainable by all students, improved grades certainly are, except by straight A students.

Individual Learning Expectations (ILE)

Another way of providing incentives to learn is to recognize students' *improvement* over their own past record. The advantage of an improvement score is that it is quantifiable and does not rely as heavily on teachers' subjective judgments as an "effort" rating does. All but the highest-performing students are equally capable of improvement, and high-performing students can be rewarded for perfect papers, which should be well within their reach.

Slavin (1980; Beady *et al.*, 1981) developed and evaluated a method of rewarding students for improvement called **Individual Learning Expectations, or ILE.** It was found that use of ILE significantly increased student achievement in comparison with classes using traditional grading systems.

The idea behind ILE is to recognize students for doing better than they have done in the past, for steadily increasing in performance until they are producing excellent work all the time. In this way, all students have an opportunity to earn recognition for academic work simply by doing their best.

Theory Into Practice
Computing ILE Base Scores and Improvement Points

Students should take at least one short quiz per week in any subject(s) in which ILE is being used. Ten items are usually sufficient. Quizzes should be scored in class immediately after being given by having students exchange papers and then having the teacher read the answers. Let students see their own papers, discuss any frequently missed items, and then pass their papers in.

Initial Base Scores
Base scores represent students' average scores on past quizzes. If you are starting ILE at the beginning of the year, assign initial base scores according to students' grades in the same subjects last year.

Computing Initial Base Scores

Last Year's Grade	Initial Base Score
A	90
A- or B+	85
B	80
B- or C+	75
C	70
C- or D+	65
F	60

If your school uses percentages rather than grades, you may use last year's average as this year's base score. If you are starting to use ILE after you have given some quizzes in your class, use the average percent correct on those quizzes to compute an initial base score.

Improvement Points
Every time you give a quiz, compare students' quiz scores with their base scores, and give students improvement points as shown in the chart.

Individual Learning Expectation (ILE): a teaching method that includes evaluation of students' improvement relative to past achievement.

Case to Consider

Motivating a Reluctant Student

Carl Stevenson, a fourth-grade teacher with ten years' experience, talks in his classroom after school to Ruth Duncan about Ruth's son, Jeremy.

CARL: I appreciate your taking time to come down today.

RUTH: Oh, I was glad to come. I must say, though, it's tricky—my husband and I run a store, and it's a twenty-four-hour-a-day job. Anyway, how is Jeremy doing?

CARL: Well, I'm sure you've noticed from his report cards that Jeremy has not been reaching our minimum goals for him in several areas, especially math. He seems to have trouble applying himself in class. His attention wanders. Also, he doesn't always turn in his homework. What happens to the work I send home with him?

RUTH: Well, he certainly doesn't seem to sit down and dig into it on his own. I see some books come home, but when I ask him about what he's supposed to do, he says it's nothing.

CARL: Hmm. I'd like to see that attitude change. Good work motivation develops early, and Jeremy needs to get a good start.

In math period the next day, the class is working on adding two-digit numbers with renaming. Carl sets up a "store" activity with Peter and a reluctant Jeremy.

CARL: OK, my desk is the counter, and these empty pencil boxes are new Lego kits, right? Each one has a price label. And you each have plenty of Monopoly money. So—may I help you, sir?

PETE:: Well, I'll take these two. $17 and $26.

CARL: Fine. Now, unfortunately, my cash register is broken, sir, so I need you to add up what you owe me. Here, use the blackboard.

PETE: (working): Seven and six makes thirteen, put down the three . . . $33? No, wait. I think I forgot something. We did this yesterday on that worksheet, right? Don't tell me, let me try again. $43!

CARL: Correct. And a good job of sticking with the problem, Pete. Here you are, sir, enjoy your purchases. Now, sir, what can I do for you?

JEREMY: Nothing. I don't want to do this.

CARL: Hey, Jeremy, this isn't hard. You made a good start on these kinds of problems when I worked with you yesterday, remember?

JEREMY: Maybe, but I still don't get it. It's not my fault, Mr. Stevenson. I just can't do it. I hate math.

CARL: Well, let me ask you, what do you like?

JEREMY: Like? I like riding my bike. I like helping my dad in his store.

CARL: You help in the store? That's excellent. What do you do to help?

JEREMY: I don't know. Sometimes I just hang around. Or I arrange the displays. Sometimes I tell Dad if we're out of something, or I show people where things are.

CARL: How about helping out with money? Do you put on price tags or work the cash register?

JEREMY: No, Mr. Stevenson! I couldn't do any of that! I can't do math.

CARL: Well, you just put your finger on the whole point. You need to learn to add and subtract here in school. Then you'll be able to have a lot more responsibility and do a lot of interesting things that you like to do.

JEREMY: I don't care. I'll learn math soon enough, I guess. Anyway, my mom and dad wouldn't ever let me use the cash register. They don't care about me doing math. Anyway, I could do most of those problems if I tried, I bet.

CARL: You might just be right about that. So how about trying?

JEREMY: Yeah, maybe sometime, Mr. Stevenson.

Problem Solving

1. How can Carl help motivate Jeremy to learn? Is it possible for one person to motivate another, or is motivation something inside a person? How can Carl encourage intrinsic motivation while using extrinsic motivation?

2. Drawing upon what you know about the situation, develop a problem-solving approach for getting Jeremy motivated. How will you involve Jeremy's parents?

3. Model your problem-solving approach by extending the dialogue in writing or role play to the next day.

Summary

What Is Motivation?

Motivation is an internal process that activates, guides, and maintains behavior over time. There are different kinds, intensities, aims, and directions of motivation. Motivation to learn is critically important to students and teachers.

What Are Some Theories of Motivation?

In behavioral learning theory (Skinner and others), motivation is a consequence of reinforcement. However, the reinforcement value of a reinforcer depends on many factors and the strength of motivation may be different in different students.

In Maslow's human needs theory, based on a hierarchy of needs, people must satisfy their "lower" (deficiency) needs before they will be motivated to try to satisfy their "higher" (growth) needs. Maslow's concept of self-actualization, the highest need, is defined as the desire to become everything one is capable of becoming. In cognitive dissonance theory (Festinger and others), people experience tension or discomfort when one of their deeply held beliefs is challenged by some inconsistent belief or behavior. Then they develop justifications to resolve the inconsistency. A classroom example is a student experiencing cognitive dissonance after receiving negative feedback about a performance.

Attribution theory seeks to understand people's explanations for their success or failure. A central assumption is that people will attempt to maintain a positive self-image, so that when good things happen, they attribute them to their own abilities, while they attribute negative events to factors beyond their control. Locus of control may be internal (success or failure due to personal effort or ability) or external (success or failure due to luck or task difficulty). Expectancy theory holds that a person's motivation to achieve something depends on the product of that person's estimation of his or her chance of success and the value he or she places on success. Motivation should be at a maximum at moderate levels of probability of success. An important educational implication is that learning tasks should be neither too easy nor too difficult.

How Can Achievement Motivation Be Enhanced?

Teachers can emphasize "learning" goals and positive or empowering attributions. Students with learning goals see the purpose of school as gaining knowledge and competence and have higher motivation to learn than students with "performance" goals of positive judgments and good grades. Teachers can use special programs such as attribution training to help students out of learned helplessness, in which students feel they are doomed to fail despite their actions. Teachers' expectations significantly affect students' motivation and achievement. Teachers can communicate positive expectations that students can learn and can take steps to reduce anxiety.

How Can Teachers Increase Students' Motivation to Learn?

An incentive is a reinforcer that people can expect to receive if they perform a specific behavior. Teachers can enhance intrinsic motivation by arousing students' interest; maintaining curiosity; using a variety of presentation modes; letting students set their own goals; stating clear expectations; giving clear, immediate, and frequent feedback; and determining the value and availability of rewards.

How Can Teachers Reward Performance, Effort, and Improvement?

Classroom rewards include praise, which is most effective when it is contingent, specific, and credible. Feedback and grades can serve as incentives. A general method of rewarding effort is to recognize students' improvement over their own past records. The Individual Learning Expectations (ILE) program, for example, is based on the principle of recognizing individual students who show improvement over their own past performance. The ILE program uses quizzes, initial base scores, improvement points, feedback, certificates, recomputations of base scores, and improvement points in addition to grades. Teachers can also use cooperative learning methods that emphasize cooperative goal structures over competitive goal structures and reward effort and improvement.

Key Terms

achievement motivation, 359
attribution theory, 354
cognitive dissonance theory, 352
contingent praise, 376
deficiency needs, 351
expectancy theory, 357
expectancy-valence model, 357
extrinsic incentives, 367
feedback, 373
goal structure, 381
growth needs, 351

Individual Learning Expectations (ILE), 379
Individually Guided Motivation (IGM), 372
intrinsic incentive, 367
learned helplessness, 361
learning goals, 359
locus of control, 355
mastery goals, 359
motivation, 347
performance goals, 359
self-actualization, 351

Self-Assessment

1. The following needs from Maslow's hierarchy are listed in alphabetical order. Sequence them in the correct order of the hierarchy, starting with the most basic.

   a. aesthetic

   b. belongingness and love

   c. self-esteem

   d. need to know and understand

   e. physiological

   f. safety

   g. self-actualization

2. Match each theory of motivation with the correct descriptive characteristic.

   ___ cognitive dissonance

   ___ attribution

   ___ expectancy

   a. Motivation hinges on whether success is linked to internal or external factors.

   b. Motivation is triggered by the need to resolve inconsistent perceptions.

   c. Motivational levels depend on value and perceived chance of success.

3. A student with an internal locus of control is likely to attribute a high test grade to

   a. the test being easy.

   b. favored treatment from the teacher.

   c. careful studying.

   d. good luck.

4. Teachers who want their students to try harder regardless of ability level or task difficulty are trying to develop attributions that fall in the _____ category.

   a. internal-stable

   b. internal-unstable

   c. external-stable

   d. external-unstable

5. A student who tends to choose either very easy or very hard tasks would most likely be

   a. seeking success.

   b. avoiding failure.

   c. risking learned helplessness.

   d. choosing an internal locus of control.

6. Which behavior is characteristic of students who are motivationally oriented toward *learning goals?*

   a. taking a challenging course

   b. trying to make the honor roll

   c. trying to obtain positive recognition from the teacher

   d. becoming discouraged in the face of obstacles

7. The main idea underlying the Individual Learning Expectations (ILE) model is

   a. a pass-fail grading system.

   b. an ungraded evaluation.

   c. grading on the basis of improvement.

   d. grading on the basis of comparison with other students.

   e. criterion-referenced grading.

8. Match the following goal structures with the correct description of each.

   ___ competitive

   ___ cooperative

   ___ individualized

   a. All succeed or all fail.

   b. One person's success or failure has no influence on another's fate.

   c. Some will succeed and others will fail.

"No."

"I was just looking at you," the teacher responds.

"I didn't cough," the girl maintains. "I sneezed."

"Well, for goodness' sake," the teacher says, "Go to my desk and get a tissue." The girl does not get up.

It is 11:11. The group finally begins the lesson. The teacher tells the students to circle the word "like." One boy is not writing. He does not have a pencil.

"Where's your pencil?" the teacher asks. "You didn't listen." He says he has lost his pencil. She sends him to his desk to look for it, then tells him to use a crayon.

Meanwhile, the students who are not in the group at the back of the room are sitting at their desks with workbooks open. No one is working. Three are pointing pencils at each other; two others watch in apparent fascination. At 11:20 the group completes a few words. The teacher tells the students to get ready for lunch.

She says, "Now, let's see who's ready to go to the cafeteria." She calls the students one at a time, by name, to line up. At 11:25 the lunch bell rings, and the class goes to the cafeteria.

At the end of the twenty-five minute period the class had spent less than nine minutes on actual learning. (Adapted from Salganik, 1980)

Learning takes time. One of the teacher's most critical tasks is to organize the classroom so as to provide enough time on instructionally important tasks for all

Figure 11.1   Resources for Effective Classroom Management

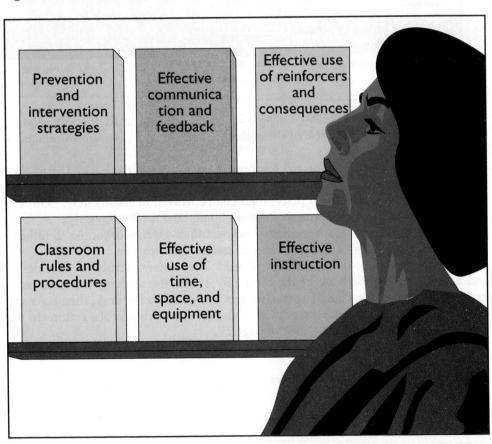

students to learn. In Ms. Green's class students learned little reading because much of the reading period was taken up with noninstructional activities. The description of Ms. Green's class was taken from observations made by a reporter for the *Baltimore Sun;* it really happened, though "Ms. Green" is not the real name of the teacher observed. Of course, her class was not typical, but the example does illustrate some ways in which time scheduled for instruction is lost. We will return to discuss Ms. Green's class several times.

This chapter focuses on the means available to teachers of managing instructional time effectively, of preventing disruptions that reduce time for instruction, and, when necessary, of taking action to deal with discipline problems. The chapter takes an approach to **classroom management** and **discipline** that emphasizes *prevention* of misbehavior, on the theory that effective instruction itself is the best means of avoiding discipline problems. In the past, classroom management has often been seen as an issue of dealing with individual student misbehaviors. Current thinking emphasizes management of the class as a whole in such a way as to make individual misbehaviors rare (Doyle, 1986). Teachers who present interesting, well-organized lessons, who use incentives for learning effectively, who accommodate their instruction to students' levels of preparation, and who plan and manage their own time effectively will have few discipline problems to deal with. Still, every teacher, no matter how effective, will encounter discipline problems sometimes, and this chapter also presents means of handling these problems when they arise. Figure 11.1 shows the resources teachers have for effective classroom management.

What Is the Impact of Time on Learning?

Obviously, if no time is spent teaching a subject, the subject will not be learned. However, within the usual range of time allocated to instruction, how much difference does time make? This has been a focus of considerable research. While it is clear that more time spent in instruction has a positive impact on student achievement, the effects of additional time are often modest or inconsistent (Karweit, 1989c). In particular, the typical differences in lengths of school days and school years among different districts have only a minor impact on student achievement (see Karweit, 1981; Walberg, 1988). What seems to be more important is how time is used in class. **Engaged time,** or **time on-task,** the number of minutes actually spent learning, is the time measure most frequently found to contribute to learning (for example, Marliave *et al.,* 1978; Anderson *et al.,* 1979; Karweit and Slavin, 1981). In other words, the most important aspect of time is the one under the direct control of the teacher—the organization and use of time in the classroom.

Where Does the Time Go?

Time is a limited resource in schools. A typical school is in session for about 6 hours a day for 180 days. While time for educational activities can be expanded by means of homework assignments or (for some students) summer school, the total time available for instruction is essentially set. Out of this six hours (or so) must come time for teaching a variety of subjects, plus time for lunch, recess or physical

---

classroom management: methods used to organize classroom activities, instruction, physical structure, and other features to make effective use of time, to create a happy and productive learning environment, and to minimize behavior problems and other disruptions.

discipline: methods used to prevent behavior problems from occurring or to respond to behavior problems so as to reduce their occurrence in the future.

engaged time: time students spend actually learning; same as time on-task.

time on-task: time spent actively engaged in learning the task at hand.

Figure 11.2

Where Does the Time Go?

Observations of elementary school mathematics classes showed that the time students actually spend learning in class is only about 60 percent of the time allocated for instruction.

Based on data from Karweit and Slavin, 1981.

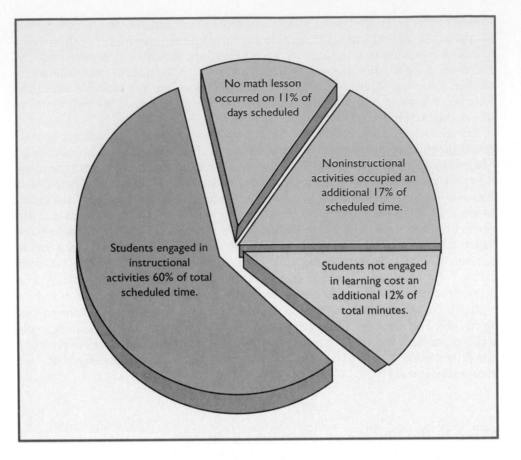

education, transitions between classes, announcements, and so on. In a forty- to sixty-minute period in a particular subject, many quite different factors reduce the time available for instruction. Figure 11.2 illustrates how time scheduled for mathematics instruction in twelve grade 2–5 classes observed by Karweit and Slavin (1981) was whittled away.

The classes Karweit and Slavin (1981) observed were in schools in and around a rural Maryland town. Overall, the classes were well organized and businesslike, with dedicated and hardworking teachers. Students were generally well behaved and respectful of authority. However, even in these very good schools the average student spent only 60 percent of the time scheduled for mathematics instruction actually learning mathematics. First of all, about twenty class days were lost to such activities as standardized testing, school events, field trips, and teacher absences. On days when instruction was given, class time was lost because of late starts and noninstructional activities such as discussions of upcoming events, announcements, passing out of materials, and disciplining students. Finally, even when math was being taught, many students were not actually engaged in the instructional activity. Some were daydreaming during lecture or seatwork times, goofing off, or sharpening pencils; others had nothing to do, either because they were finished with their assigned work or had not yet been assigned a task. The 60 percent figure estimated by Karweit and Slavin is, if anything, an overestimate. In a much larger study Weinstein and Mignano (1993) found that only about a third of elementary school time was spent engaged in meaningful tasks.

Using Allocated Time for Instruction

A principal of an outstanding elementary school in Houston often tells his teachers, "If you don't have a lesson plan for your students, they will have a lesson plan for you." What he means, of course, is that if teachers are not well organized and prepared for class, they may lose control of the class to the students, who are probably more interested in fun and games than in working. This was one major problem experienced by poor Ms. Green. Her students were not bad or lazy, but her lack of organization and preparedness created unnecessary losses of instructional time. She had not established routines so that students would know that at reading group time they had to have a pencil and a green book. Just when she had her students assembled and ready to go, she left them to get her teacher's edition of the workbook, which she should have had ready. She wasted prime instructional time dealing unnecessarily with a student's coughing (or sneezing). She did not give the students in other reading groups a clear assignment and did not monitor them, so they did nothing while she was trying to get her one reading group together. In short, Ms. Green didn't have a clearly laid out lesson plan for her students, so they carried out their own "lesson plan," goofing off instead of reading.

Another term for instructional time is **allocated time,** which is the time during which students have an opportunity to learn. When the teacher is lecturing, students can learn by paying attention. When students have seatwork or other tasks, they can learn by doing them. A discussion of some common ways allocated time can be maximized follows.

Avoiding Lost Time.   One way in which much instructional time is lost is through losses of entire days or periods. Many of these losses are inevitable—because of such things as standardized testing days and snow days—and we certainly would not want to abolish important field trips or school assemblies just to get in a few more periods of instruction. However, frequent losses of instructional periods interrupt the flow of instruction and can ultimately deprive students of sufficient time to master the curriculum.

Another source of lost days, and one that is much more controllable, is teachers' failures to teach a lesson because "today isn't a good day." For example, a teacher might end a unit on a Thursday and not want to begin a new unit until the following Monday. Another teacher might avoid giving a lesson just before or after a holiday.

Making good use of all classroom time is less a matter of squeezing out a few more minutes or hours of instruction each year than of communicating to students that learning is an important business that is worth their time and effort. If a teacher finds excuses not to teach, students may learn that learning is not a serious enterprise. In studying an outstandingly effective inner-city Baltimore elementary school, Salganik (1980) described a third-grade teacher who took her class to the library, which she found locked. She sent a student for the key, and while the class waited, she whispered to her students, "Let's work on our doubles. Nine plus nine? Six plus six?" The class whispered the answers back in unison. Now, did a couple of minutes working on addition facts increase the students' achievement? Of course not. But it probably did help develop a perception that school is for learning, not for marking time.

Avoiding Late Starts, Early Finishes.   A surprising amount of allocated instructional time is lost because the teacher does not start teaching at the beginning of the period. This can be a particular problem in self-contained elementary classes,

Connections

Recall the discussions in Chapters 8 and 9 of the importance of time use and time management in effective teaching. Time is a major factor in Carroll's model and the QAIT model of effective instruction.

allocated time: time during which students have the opportunity to learn.

This class is out of hand. According to research, what probably went wrong? As a teacher, what would you do to restore order, and what would you do to help prevent this kind of situation from happening again?

where there are no bells or fixed schedules to structure the period, but it is also a problem in departmentalized secondary schools, where teachers may spend a long time dealing with late students or other problems before starting the lesson.

A crisp, on-time start to a lesson is important for setting a purposive tone to instruction. If students know that a teacher does not start on time, they may be lackadaisical about getting to class on time, which makes future on-time starts increasingly difficult.

Teachers can also shortchange students if they stop teaching before the end of the period. This is less damaging than a ragged or late start, but is still worth avoiding by planning more instruction than you think you'll need against the possibility that you will finish the lesson early (Evertson, 1982).

Avoiding Interruptions.   One important source of lost allocated time for instruction is interruptions. Interruptions may be externally imposed, as with announcements or the need to sign forms sent from the principal's office, or they may be caused by teachers or students themselves (Behnke, 1979). Interruptions not only directly cut into the time for instruction, they also break the *momentum* of the lesson, which reduces students' attention to the task at hand.

Avoiding interruptions takes planning. For example, some teachers put a "Do not disturb—learning in progress!" sign on the doors to inform would-be interrupters to come back later. One teacher wore a special hat during small-group lessons to remind her other second-graders not to interrupt her during that time. Rather than signing forms or dealing with other "administrivia" at once, some teachers keep a box where students and others can put any forms and then deal with them after the lesson is over.

Anything the teacher can delay doing until after a lesson should be delayed. For example, if the teacher has started a lesson and a student walks in late, the teacher should go on with the lesson and deal with the tardiness issue later.

Handling Routine Procedures Smoothly and Quickly.   Some teachers spend too much time on simple classroom routines. For example, Ms. Green spent many minutes getting students ready for lunch because she called them by name, one at a time. This was unnecessary. She could have saved time for instruction by having the students line up for lunch by tables or rows. Early in the school year she could have established a routine that only when the entire table (or row) was quiet and ready to go would they be called to line up. Lining up for lunch would then take seconds, not minutes.

Other procedures must also become routine for students. Early in the school year they must learn classroom rules and procedures. They must know, for example, when they may go to the washroom or sharpen a pencil and not to ask to do these things at other times. Papers may be collected by having students pass them to the front or to the left, or by having table monitors collect the table's papers. Distribution of materials must also be planned for. It is less important exactly how these tasks are done than that students know clearly what they are to do. Many teachers assign regular classroom helpers to take care of distribution and collection of papers, taking messages to the office, erasing the blackboard, and other routine tasks that are annoying interruptions for teachers but that students love to do. Teachers should use "student power" as much as possible.

The wise teacher also notes in a daily lesson plan what he or she will need and what students will need for a lesson, and then makes sure that these needs are provided for (see Doyle, 1984).

Minimizing Time Spent on Discipline.   Methods of disciplining students are discussed at length later in this chapter. However, one aspect of disciplining should be mentioned at this point. Whenever possible—which is almost always—disciplinary statements or actions should not interrupt the flow of the lesson. A sharp glance, silently moving close to an offending student, or a hand signal, such as putting finger to lips to remind a student to be silent, are usually effective for the kind of minor behavior problems that teachers must constantly deal with, and they allow the lesson to proceed without interruption. For example, Ms. Green had no need to get involved with the girl who sneezed. If students need talking to about discipline problems, the time to do it is after the lesson or after school, not in the middle of a lesson. If Diana and Martin are talking during seatwork instead of working, it would be better to say, "Diana and Martin, see me at three o'clock," than to launch into an on-the-spot speech about the importance of being on-task during seatwork times.

Using Engaged Time Effectively

Engaged time (or time on-task) is the time individual students actually spend doing assigned work. Allocated time and engaged time differ in that while allocated time refers to the opportunity for the entire class to engage in learning activities, engaged time may be different for each student, depending on a student's attentiveness and willingness to work. Strategies for maximizing student time on-task are discussed in the following sections. Teacher training programs based on principles presented in the following sections have been found in several studies to increase student engagement (for example, Emmer *et al.*, 1982; Evertson *et al.*, 1983) and in some cases, learning (Evertson *et al.*, 1985; Evertson, 1989).

Teaching Engaging Lessons.   The best way to increase students' time on-task is to teach lessons that are so interesting, engaging, and relevant to students' interests that they will pay attention and eagerly do what is asked of them. Part of this is to emphasize active, rapidly paced instruction with varied modes of presentation and frequent opportunities for students to participate and to de-emphasize independent seatwork, especially unsupervised seatwork (as in followup time in elementary reading classes). Research has consistently shown that student engagement is much higher when the teacher is teaching than during seatwork (Anderson, 1984; Evertson and Harris, 1992). Giving students many opportunities to actively participate in lessons is also associated with greater learning (Finn and Cox, 1992), and engaged time is much higher in well-structured cooperative learning programs than in independent seatwork (Slavin, 1990b).

Maintaining Momentum.   Maintaining momentum during a lesson is a key to keeping task engagement high. Momentum refers to the avoidance of interruptions or slowdowns (Kounin, 1970). In a class that maintains good momentum, students always have something to do and once started working are not interrupted. Anyone who has, for example, tried to write a term paper, only to be interrupted by telephone calls, knocks on the door, and other disturbances, knows that these interruptions cause much more damage to concentration and progress than the amount of time they take.

Kounin (1970) gives the following example of teacher-caused slowdowns and interruptions.

> The teacher is just starting a reading group at the reading circle while the rest of the children are engaged in seatwork with workbooks. She sat in front of the reading group and asked, "All right, who can tell me the name of our next chapter?" Before a child was called on to answer, she looked toward the children at seatwork, saying: "Let's wait until the people in Group Two are settled and working." (Actually most are writing in their workbooks.) She then looked at John who was in the seatwork group, naggingly asking, "Did you find your pencil?" John answered something which was inaudible. The teacher got up from her seat, saying, "I'd like to know what you did with it." Pause for about two seconds. "Did you eat it?" Another pause. "What happened to it? What color was it? You can't do your work without it." The teacher then went to her desk to get a pencil to give to John, saying, "I'll get you a pencil. Make sure the pencil is here tomorrow morning. And don't tell me you lost that one too. And make it a new one, and see that it's sharpened." The teacher then returned to the reading circle. This pencil transaction lasted 1.4 minutes. (p. 104)

This teacher destroyed the momentum of a reading lesson by spending more than a minute dealing with a child in the seatwork group who did not have a pencil. Of course, during this interchange the entire class—both the reading group and the seatwork group—were off-task, but what is worse, they required much more time to get resettled and back to work after the incident. Just as a lesson was getting under way and students were ready to listen, the teacher broke this chain of activities with a completely unnecessary reprimand for a behavior that could easily have been ignored.

Kounin found momentum to be strongly related to total time on-task, and Brophy and Evertson (1976) and Anderson *et al.* (1979) found momentum to be related to student achievement. It is significant that some of the features of effective lessons described in Chapter 8 are largely directed at maintaining momentum. For example, in the Missouri Mathematics Program (MMP; Good

---

Connections

The elements discussed under "Using Time Effectively" relate to the characteristics of effective lessons discussed in Chapter 8.

et al., 1983), the teacher has students try a few problems under his or her watchful eye ("controlled practice") before letting them start their seatwork, to make sure that the flow from lesson to seatwork is not interrupted by student questions and problems.

Maintaining Smoothness of Instruction. "Smoothness" is another term used by Kounin (1970) to refer to continued focus on a meaningful sequence of instruction. Smooth instruction avoids jumping without transitions from topic to topic, or from the lesson to other activities, which produces "jarring breaks in the activity flow" (Kounin, 1970, p. 97). For example:

> The teacher was conducting a recitation with a subgroup. She was walking towards a child who was reciting when she passed by the fish bowl. She suddenly stopped walking toward the boy, and stopped at the fish bowl, saying: "Oh my, I forgot to feed the fish!" She then got some fish food from a nearby shelf and started to feed the fish, saying: "My, see how hungry it is." She then turned to a girl, saying: "See, Margaret, you forgot to feed the fish. You can see how hungry it is. See how quickly it comes up to eat." (Kounin, 1970, pp. 98–99)

This example illustrates how smoothness and momentum are related. The teacher jumped from her lesson to housekeeping to (unnecessary) disciplining, interrupting one student's recitation and making it virtually impossible for the other students to focus on the lesson. As with momentum, smoothness was found to be strongly associated with student time on-task (Kounin, 1970) and achievement (Brophy and Evertson, 1976; Anderson *et al.*, 1979).

Managing Transitions. Transitions are changes from one activity to another, as from lecture to seatwork, subject to subject, or lesson to lunch. Elementary classes have been found to have an average of thirty-one major transitions a day, occupying 15 percent of class time (Burns, 1984). Transitions are the "seams" of class management at which classroom order is most likely to come apart; Anderson *et al.* (1979) and Evertson *et al.* (1980) found that teachers' efficiency at managing transitions between activities was positively related to their students' achievement.

Following are three rules for the management of transitions:

1. When making a transition, the teacher should give a clear signal to which the students have been taught to respond (Arlin, 1979; Doyle, 1984).

For example, in the elementary grades some teachers use a bell to indicate to students that they should immediately be quiet and listen to instructions.

2. Before the transition is made, students must be absolutely certain about what they are to do when the signal is given (Arlin, 1979).

For example, a teacher might say, "When I say 'Go,' I want you all to put your books away and get out the compositions you started yesterday. Is everyone ready? All right, go!" When giving instructions to students to begin independent seatwork, the teacher can help them get started with the activity before letting them work independently, as in the following example:

TEACHER: "Today we are going to find guide words for different pages in the dictionary. Everyone should have a ditto sheet with the words on it and a dictionary. Class, hold up your ditto sheet. [They do.] Now hold up your dictionary. [They do.] Good. Now turn to page 102. [The teacher walks around to see that everyone does so.] Look at the top of the page and put your finger on the first guide word. [The teacher walks around to check on this.] Class, what is the first guide word?"

CLASS: "Carrot!"

TEACHER: "Good. The first guide word is carrot. Now look to the right on the same page. Class, what word do you see there?"

CLASS: "Carve!"

TEACHER: "Right. The guide words are carrot and carve. Now turn to page 555 and find the guide words. [Students do this.] Class, what is the first guide word on page 555?"

CLASS: "Scheme!"

TEACHER: "Class, what is the second guide word?"

CLASS: "Scissors!"

TEACHER: "Great! Now do the first problem on your ditto sheet by yourselves, and then stop."

The teacher would then check whether all or almost all students have the first item correct before telling them to complete the worksheet. The idea, of course, is to make sure that students know exactly what they are to do before they start doing it.

3. Make transitions all at once.

Students should be trained to make transitions all at once, rather than one student at a time (Charles, 1989). The teacher should usually give directions to the class as a whole or to well-defined groups: "Class, I want you all to put away your laboratory materials and prepare for dismissal as quickly and quietly as you can. . . . I see that Table 3 is quiet and ready. Table 3, please line up quietly. Table 6, line up. Table 1 . . . Table 4. Everyone else may line up quietly. Let's go!"

Maintaining Group Focus During Lessons.   "Maintaining group focus" refers to the use of classroom organization strategies and questioning techniques that ensure that all students in the class stay involved in the lesson, even when only one student is called on by the teacher. Two principal components of Kounin's "maintaining group focus" were found to be significantly related to students' on-task behavior: accountability and group alerting.

Kounin (1970) uses the term **accountability** to mean "the degree to which the teacher holds the children accountable and responsible for their task performances during recitation sessions" (p. 119). Examples of strategies for increasing accountability are the use of choral responses, having all students hold up their work so the teacher can see it, circulating among the students to see what they are doing, and drawing other children into the performance of one child (for example, "I want you all to watch what Suzanne is doing so you can tell me whether you agree or disagree with her answer").

The idea behind these strategies is to maintain the involvement of all students in all parts of the lesson. A study of third- and fourth-graders found that students raised their hands an average of once every six minutes and gave an answer only once every fifteen minutes, with some students hardly ever participating (Potter, 1977). This is not enough participation to ensure student attention. Teachers

---

Connections

Arousing student interest and focusing student attention, discussed in Chapters 7 and 8, relate to this discussion on using instructional time efficiently and effectively.

---

accountability: the degree to which people are held responsible for their task performances or decision outcomes.

should be concerned not only about drawing all students into class activities but also about avoiding activities that relegate most students to the role of spectator for long periods. For example, a very common teaching error is to have one or two students work out a lengthy problem on the chalkboard or read an extended passage while the rest of the class has nothing to do. Such strategies waste the time of much of the class, break the momentum of the lesson, and leave the door open for misbehavior (Gump, 1982).

Group alerting refers to questioning strategies designed to keep all students on their toes during a lecture or discussion. One example of group alerting is creating suspense before calling on a student by saying, "Given triangle *ABC,* if we know the measures of sides *A* and *B* and of angle *AB,* what else can we find out about the triangle? . . . (Pause) . . . Maria?" Note that this keeps the whole class thinking until Maria's name is called. The opposite effect would have been created by saying, "Maria, given triangle *ABC* . . . ," because only Maria would have been alerted. Calling on students in a random order is another example of group alerting, as is letting students know that they may be asked questions about the last reciter's answers. For example, the teacher might follow up Maria's answer with, "What is the name of the postulate that Maria used? . . . Ralph?"

Maintaining Group Focus During Seatwork. During times when students are doing seatwork and the teacher is available to work with them, it is important to monitor the seatwork activities and to informally check individual students' work. That is, the teacher should circulate among the students' desks to see how they are doing. This allows the teacher to identify any problems students are having before they waste seatwork time practicing errors or giving up in frustration.

While seatwork times provide excellent opportunities for providing individual help to students who are struggling to keep up with the class, teachers should resist the temptation to work too long with an individual student. Interactions with students during seatwork should be as brief as possible (Brophy and Evertson, 1976; Anderson *et al.,* 1979), because if the teacher gets tied down with any one student, the rest of the class may drift off-task or run into problems of their own (Doyle, 1984).

Withitness. **Withitness** is another term coined by Kounin (1970). It describes teachers' actions that indicate awareness of students' behavior at all times. Kounin calls this awareness "having eyes in the back of one's head." Teachers who are "with it" can respond immediately to student misbehavior and know who started what. Teachers who lack withitness can make the error of scolding the wrong student, as in the following instance:

> Lucy and John, who were sitting at the same table as Jane, started to whisper. Robert watched this and he too got into the act. Then Jane giggled and said something to John. Then Mary leaned over and whispered to Jane. At this point, the teacher said, "Mary and Jane, stop that!" (Adapted from Kounin, 1970, p. 80).

By responding only to Mary and Jane, who were late to get involved in the whispering and giggling incident, the teacher indicated that she did not know what was going on. A single incident of this kind may make little difference, but after many such incidents students recognize the teacher's tendency to respond inappropriately to their behavior.

Another example of a lack of withitness is responding too late to a sequence of misbehavior. Lucy and John's whispering could have been easily nipped in the bud,

group alerting: methods of questioning that encourage students to pay attention during lectures and discussions.

withitness: the degree to which the teacher is aware of and responsive to student performance.

perhaps with just a glance or a finger to the lips. By the time the whispering had escalated to giggling and spread to several students, it took a full stop in the lesson to rectify the situation. Kounin (1970) found the withitness of teachers to be strongly related to their effectiveness as class managers, and Brophy and Evertson (1976) and Anderson *et al.* (1979) found that withit teachers also produced better student achievement.

A major component of withitness is scanning the class frequently and establishing eye contact with individual students. Several studies have found that more effective managers frequently scan the classroom visually, to monitor the pace of activity as well as individual students' behaviors (Emmer *et al.*, 1980; Evertson and Emmer, 1982; Brooks, 1985). Effective classroom managers have the ability to interpret and act on the mood of the class as a whole. They notice when students are beginning to fidget or are otherwise showing signs of flagging attention, and they act on this information to change activities to recapture student engagement (Carter *et al.*, 1988).

Overlapping. **Overlapping** refers to the teacher's ability to attend to interruptions or behavior problems while continuing a lesson or other instructional activity. For example, one teacher was teaching a lesson on reading comprehension when he saw a student looking at a book unrelated to the lesson. Without interrupting his lesson, he walked over to the student, took her book, closed it, and put it on her desk, all while continuing to speak to the class. This took care of the student's misbehavior without slowing the momentum of the lesson; the rest of the class hardly noticed that the event occurred.

Another example of a teacher doing a good job of overlapping is as follows:

> The teacher is at the reading circle and Lucy is reading aloud while standing. Johnny, who was doing seatwork at his desk, walks up toward the teacher, holding his workbook. The teacher glances at Johnny, then looks back at Lucy, nodding at Lucy, as Lucy continues to read aloud. The teacher remains seated and takes Johnny's workbook. She turns to Lucy, saying, "That was a hard word, Lucy, and you pronounced it right." She checks about three more answers to Johnny's book saying, "That's fine, you can go ahead and do the next page now," and resumes looking at the reading book as Lucy continues reading. (Kounin, 1970, p. 84)

Now, Johnny's interruption of the reading group might have been avoided altogether by a good classroom manager, who would have assigned enough work to keep all students productively busy during reading circle time and given clear instructions on what they were to do when they finished their seatwork. However, interruptions are sometimes unavoidable, and the ability to keep the main activity going while handling them is strongly related to overall classroom order (Kounin, 1970; Copeland, 1983) and to achievement (Brophy and Evertson, 1976; Anderson *et al.*, 1979).

Avoiding "Mock Participation"

overlapping:
a teacher's ability to respond to behavior problems without interrupting a classroom lesson.

This chapter began with the example of poor Ms. Green, whose class management problems were greatly interfering with her ability to teach. Her example is certainly not one to emulate. However, it is possible to go too far in the other direction, emphasizing time on-task to the exclusion of all other considerations (Weade and Evertson, 1988). For example, in a study of time on-task in elementary mathematics, one teacher's class was found to be engaged essentially 100 percent of the time. The teacher accomplished this by walking up and down the rows of desks looking for the slightest flicker of inattention. This class learned very little math over the course of the year. An overemphasis on engaged time rather than engaging instruction can produce what Bloome *et al.*, (1989) call **mock participation.**

Several studies have found that increasing time on-task in classes in which students were already reasonably well behaved did not increase student achievement (Blackadar and Nachtigal, 1986; Slavin, 1986a; Stallings and Krasavage, 1986). An overemphasis on time on-task can be detrimental to learning in several ways. For example, complex tasks involving creativity and uncertainty tend to produce lower levels of time on-task than simple cut-and-dried tasks (Atwood, 1983; Doyle and Carter, 1984). Yet it would clearly be a poor instructional strategy to avoid complex or uncertain tasks in order to keep time on-task high. Maintaining classroom order is an important goal of teaching, but it is only one of many (see Doyle, 1983, 1986; Slavin, 1987a).

Self-Check

Review the scenario at the beginning of the chapter, and identify all the ways that time was used in Ms. Green's class. Then describe the distribution and use of school time, and differentiate between allocated time and engaged time. What are four ways that allocated time can be maximized? What are six strategies for increasing students' time on-task? Use specific examples to show how a teacher might exhibit withitness and overlapping.

What information has this teacher posted on the bulletin board? According to research, what effect will this strategy have on his ability to manage his class?

mock participation:
overemphasis on time on-task, which can be detrimental to learning.

What Practices Contribute to Effective Classroom Management?

Research has consistently shown that basic commonsense planning and ground-work go a long way to preventing discipline problems from ever developing. Simple measures include starting the year properly, arranging the classroom for effective instruction, setting class rules and procedures, and making expectations of conduct clear to students.

Different grade levels and student groups present different management concerns. For instance, with younger students teachers need to be concerned with socializing students to the norms and behaviors expected in school. Misbehavior in children is often out of misunderstanding of what is required of them.

Another management concern in elementary school relates to the widespread use of ability groups, in that other students are expected to work independently while the teacher works with a particular group. The teacher must balance giving attention to the group and ensuring that the class has enough to do and knows how to do it (Anderson *et al.*, 1979; Morine-Dershimer, 1983).

In middle school and high school, students can grasp the principles that underlie rules and procedures and can rationally consent to observe them. At the same time, some adolescents resist authority and place greater importance on peer norms. Aggressive behavior, truancy, and delinquency also increase as students enter adolescence. In the upper grades, departmentalization, tracking, and class promotion may become management issues, especially with students who have histories of learned helplessness or academic failure. Teachers of older students need to be more concerned with motivating them toward more self-regulation in observing rules and procedures and learning the material being presented. In addition, teachers must be particularly concerned with the interest level and relevance of their lessons (Allen, 1986).

Starting Out the Year Right.   Emmer *et al.* (1980) and Evertson and Emmer (1982) studied teachers' actions at the beginning of the school year and correlated them with students' behaviors later in the year. They found that the first days of school were critical in establishing classroom order. They compared teachers whose classes were mostly on-task over the course of the school year with teachers whose classes were less consistently on-task and found that the better classroom managers engaged in certain activities during the first days of school significantly more often than did the less effective managers. A list of six characteristics of effective classroom managers follows.

1. More effective managers had a clear, specific plan for introducing students to classroom rules and procedures and spent as many days as necessary carrying out their plan until students knew how to line up, ask for help, and so on.
2. More effective managers worked with the whole class initially (even if they planned to group students later). They were involved with the whole class at all times, rarely leaving any students without something to do or without supervision. For example, more effective managers seldom worked with an individual student unless the rest of the class was productively occupied (Sanford and Evertson, 1981; Doyle, 1984).
3. More effective managers spent much of the first days of school introducing procedures and discussing class rules (often encouraging students to suggest rules themselves). These teachers usually reminded students of class rules every day for at least the first week of school (Weinstein and Mignano, 1993).

4. More effective managers taught students specific procedures. For example, some had students practice lining up quickly and quietly; others taught students to respond to a signal, such as a bell, a flick of the light switch, or a call for attention.

5. As first activities, more effective managers used simple, enjoyable tasks. Materials for the first lessons were well prepared, clearly presented, and varied. Students were asked to get right to work on the first day of school and were then given instructions on procedures gradually, to avoid overloading them with too much information at a time.

6. More effective managers responded immediately to stop any misbehavior.

Theory Into Practice

Arranging the Classroom for Effective Instruction

One important aspect of planning for effective instruction is the physical arrangement of the classroom (see Weinstein, 1979, 1987). Suggestions for

Figure 11.3   Elementary Classroom Seating Arrangement

Teachers should arrange classrooms so that disruptions are minimized and all students can see and be seen by the teacher.

From Evertson *et al.*, 1984.

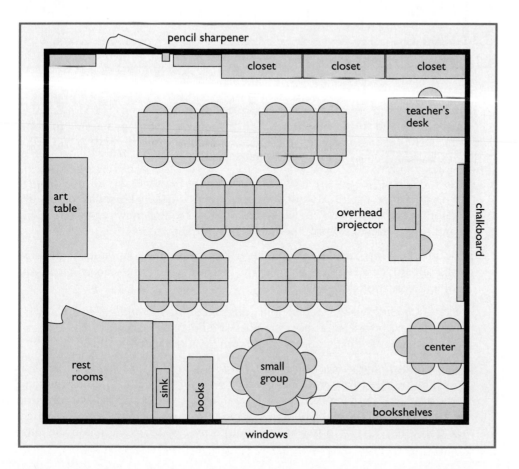

Figure 11.4

Secondary School Classroom Seating Arrangement

A traditional row-and-column seating arrangement is appropriate in many junior high school and high school classes.

From Emmer *et al.,* 1984.

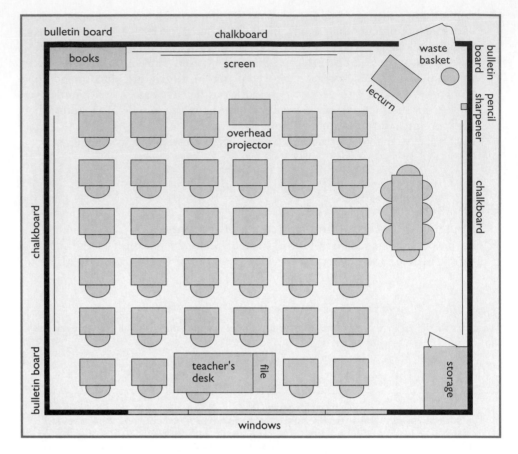

room arrangement for elementary and secondary classrooms are presented in Figures 11.3 and 11.4. Researchers have identified four principles of room arrangement for minimizing disturbances and disruptions (Emmer *et al.,* 1984; Evertson *et al.,* 1984). They are as follows:

1. *Keep high-traffic areas free of congestion:* For example, do not put the pencil sharpener where a student using it will block a doorway or disturb another student. Keep students' desks away from doorways, bookshelves, and supply areas to which the class needs frequent access.

2. *Be sure students can be easily seen by the teacher:* Set up student desks so that all students can be seen from the teacher's desk, chalkboard areas, and other instructional areas.

3. *Keep frequently used teaching materials and student supplies readily accessible:* Paper, books, and other supplies should be in easily available, clearly marked areas so that students can find them without teacher help.

4. *Be certain students can see instructional presentations and displays:* Students should be able to see the chalkboard, overhead projector, and instructional areas without moving their desks or craning their necks. If students are seated far from the action or in places where they can't easily see or hear presentations, they may stop paying attention to the lesson. Research on the inter-

What routine misbehavior is shown in this picture? Would changing the seating arrangement help? As a teacher, how would you use the principle of least intervention to manage routine misbehavior?

actions of teachers with students seated in various parts of the classroom indicates that students who are seated far from the teacher or away from the main activity rarely participate in class discussions or other instructional activities as much as students who are seated closer to the teacher (Woolfolk and Brooks, 1982; Weinstein, 1987; Good, 1983a).

Setting Class Rules. One of the first management-related tasks at the start of the year is setting class rules. Three principles govern this process. First, class rules should be few in number. Second, they should make sense and be seen as fair by students. Third, they should be clearly explained and deliberately taught to students (Emmer *et al.,* 1980; Brooks, 1985). A major purpose of clearly explaining general class rules is to give a moral authority for specific procedures. For example, all students will understand and support a rule such as "respect others' property." This simple rule can be invoked to cover such obvious misbehaviors as stealing or destroying materials, but also gives a reason for putting materials away, cleaning up litter, and refraining from marking up textbooks. Students may be asked to help set the rules, or they may be given a set of rules and asked to give examples of these rules. Class discussions give students a feeling of participation in setting rational rules that everyone can live by. When the class as a whole has agreed on a set of rules, offenders know that they are transgressing community norms, not the teacher's arbitrary regulations.

One all-purpose set of class rules follows:

1. *Be Courteous to Others:* This rule forbids interrupting others or speaking out of turn, teasing or laughing at others, fighting, and so on.
2. *Respect Others' Property.*
3. *Be On-task:* This includes listening when the teacher or other students are talking, working on seatwork, continuing to work during any interruptions, staying in one's seat, being at one's seat and ready to work when the bell rings, and following directions.
4. *Raise Hands to Be Recognized:* This is a rule against calling out or getting out of one's seat for assistance.

Self-Check

For the grade level you plan to teach, construct a classroom layout and a "To Do" list for starting the year in a way that will minimize behavior problems. Annotate your layout and list to identify the principles of problem prevention that you are applying.

What Are Some Strategies for Managing Routine Misbehavior?

The preceding sections of this chapter discussed means of organizing classroom activities to maximize time for instruction and minimize time for such minor disturbances as students talking out of turn, getting out of their seats without permission, and not paying attention. Provision of interesting lessons, efficient use of class time, and careful structuring of instructional activities will prevent most such minor behavior problems, and many more serious ones as well. For example, Kounin (1970) found that teacher behaviors associated with high time on-task were also associated with fewer serious behavior problems. Time off-task can lead to more serious problems; many behavior problems arise because students are frustrated or bored in school. Instructional programs that actively involve students and provide all of them with opportunities for success may prevent such problems.

However, effective lessons and good classkeeping are not the only means of preventing or dealing with inappropriate behavior. Besides structuring classes so as to reduce the frequency of behavior problems, teachers must have strategies for dealing with behavior problems when they do occur (see Cairns, 1987).

The great majority of behavior problems with which a teacher must deal are relatively minor disruptions—behaviors that would be appropriate on the playing field but not in the classroom. These include talking out of turn, getting up without permission, failing to follow class rules or procedures, and inattention—nothing really serious, but behaviors that must be minimized for learning to occur. Before considering disciplinary strategies, it is important to reflect on their purpose. Students should learn much more in school than the "3 R's." Hopefully, they learn that they are competent learners, and that learning is enjoyable and satisfying. A classroom environment that is warm, supportive, and accepting is critical in developing these attitudes.

A healthy classroom environment cannot be created if students do not respect teachers or teachers do not respect students. The teacher is the leader of the classroom and is responsible for the welfare of the entire class. Though teachers should involve students in setting class rules and take student needs or input into account when organizing the classroom, ultimately teachers are the leaders who establish and enforce rules that students must live by. These class rules and procedures should become second nature to students. Teachers who have not established their authority in the classroom are likely to spend much too much time dealing with behavior problems or yelling at students to be instructionally effective. Furthermore, the clearer the structure and routine procedures in the classroom, the more freedom the teacher can allow students. The following sections discuss strategies for dealing with typical discipline problems.

The Principle of Least Intervention.   In dealing with routine classroom behavior problems, the most important principle is that misbehaviors should be corrected using the simplest intervention that will work. Many studies have found that the amount of time spent disciplining students is negatively related to student achievement (for example, Stallings and Kaskowitz, 1974; Evertson *et al.,* 1980; Crocker and Brooker, 1986). The teacher's main goal in dealing with routine misbehavior is to do so in a way that both is effective and avoids unnecessarily disrupting the lesson (Emmer, 1987; Evertson and Harris, 1992). If at all possible, the show must go on while any behavior problems are dealt with. A continuum of strategies for dealing with minor misbehaviors, from least disruptive to most, is discussed in the following sections. These strategies are to employ (1) prevention, (2) nonverbal cues, (3) praise of incompatible, correct behavior, (4) praise for other students, (5) verbal reminders, (6) repeated reminders, and (7) consequences.

Prevention.   The easiest behavior problems to deal with are those that never occur in the first place. As illustrated earlier in this chapter, behavior problems can be prevented by presenting interesting and lively lessons, making class rules and procedures clear, keeping students busy on meaningful tasks, and using other effective techniques of basic classroom management (Doyle, 1983, 1986).

Varying the content of lessons, using a variety of materials and approaches, displaying humor and enthusiasm, can all reduce boredom-caused behavior problems (Kounin, 1970). Frustration caused by material that is too difficult or assignments that are unrealistically long can be avoided by breaking down assignments into smaller steps and doing a better job of preparing students to work on their own. Fatigue can be reduced by allowing short breaks, by varying activities, and by scheduling difficult subjects in the morning, when students are fresh.

Nonverbal Cues.   Much routine classroom misbehavior can be eliminated without breaking the momentum of the lesson by the use of simple **nonverbal cues** (Woolfolk and Brooks, 1985). Making eye contact with a misbehaving student may be enough to stop misbehavior. For example, if two students are whispering, the teacher might simply catch the eye of one or both of them. Moving close to a student who is misbehaving also usually alerts the student to shape up. If these fail, a light hand on the student's shoulder is likely to be effective (although touch should be used cautiously with adolescents, who may be touchy about touching). These nonverbal strategies all clearly convey the same message: "I see what you are doing and don't like it. Please get back to work." The advantage of communicating this message nonverbally is that the lesson need not be interrupted. In contrast, verbal reprimands can cause a ripple effect; many students stop working while one is being reprimanded (Kounin, 1970). Instead of interrupting the flow of concentration for many to deal with the behavior of one, nonverbal cues usually have an effect only on the student who is misbehaving, as was illustrated earlier in this chapter by the teacher who continued his lesson while silently closing and putting away a book one student was reading. That student was the only one in the class who paid much attention to the whole episode.

Praising Behavior that Is Incompatible with Misbehavior.   Praise can be a powerful motivator for many students. One strategy for reducing misbehavior in class is to make sure to praise students for behaviors that are incompatible with the misbehavior you want to reduce. That is, catch students in the act of doing *right*. If

nonverbal cues: eye contact, gestures, physical proximity, or touching used to communicate without interrupting verbal discourse.

students often get out of their seats without permission, praise them on the occasions when they do get to work right away.

Praising Other Students.　It is often possible to get one student to behave by praising others for behaving. For example, if Polly is goofing off, the teacher might say, "I'm glad to see so many students working so well—Jake is doing a good job, Carol is doing well, José and Michelle are working nicely . . ." When Polly finally does get to work, the teacher should praise her too, without dwelling on her past inattention, as follows: "I see James and Walter and Polly doing a good job."

Verbal Reminders.　If a nonverbal cue is impossible or ineffective, a simple verbal reminder may help bring a student into line. The reminder should be given immediately after students misbehave; delayed reminders are usually ineffective (Aronfreed and Reber, 1965). If possible, the reminder should state what students are supposed to be doing rather than dwelling on what they are doing wrong. For example, it is better to say, "John, please attend to your own work," than "John, stop copying off of Alfredo's paper." Stating the reminder positively communicates more positive expectations for future behavior than does a negative statement (see Good and Brophy, 1984). Also, the reminder should focus on the behavior, not on the student. While a particular student *behavior* may be intolerable, the student himself or herself is always accepted and welcome in the classroom (see Ginott, 1972).

Repeated Reminders.　Most often a nonverbal cue, reinforcement of other students, or a simple reminder will be enough to end minor misbehavior. However, sometimes students test the teacher's resolve by failing to do what has been asked of them or by arguing or giving excuses. This testing will diminish over time if students learn that teachers mean what they say and will use appropriate measures to enforce an orderly, productive classroom environment.

When a student refuses to comply with a simple reminder, one strategy to attempt first is a repetition of the reminder, ignoring any irrelevant excuse or argument. Canter and Canter (1976), in a program called **Assertive Discipline,** call this strategy the "broken record." Teachers should decide what they want the student to do, state this clearly to the student ("statement of want"), and then repeat it until the student complies. An example of the "broken record" from Canter and Canter (1976, p. 80) follows:

TEACHER:　"Craig, I want you to start your project now." (Statement of want)

CRAIG:　"I will as soon as I finish my game. Just a few more minutes."

TEACHER (firmly):　"Craig, I understand, but I want you to start your project now." (Broken record)

CRAIG:　"You never give me enough time with the games."

TEACHER (calmly, firmly):　"That's not the point, I want you to start your project now."

CRAIG:　"I don't like doing my project."

TEACHER (firmly):　"I understand, but I want you to start your project."

CRAIG:　"Wow, you really mean it. I'll get to work."

Assertive Discipline:
clear, firm, unhostile response to student misbehavior.

This teacher avoided a lengthy argument with a student by simply repeating the request. When Craig said, "You never give me enough time with the games," and "I don't like doing my project," he was not inviting a serious discussion but was simply procrastinating and testing the teacher's resolve. Rather than going off on a tangent with him, the teacher calmly restated the request, turning aside his excuses with "That's not the point . . ." and "I understand, but . . ." Of course, if Craig had a legitimate issue to discuss or a valid complaint, the teacher would have dealt with it, but all too often students' arguments or excuses are nothing more than a means of drawing out an interaction with the teacher to avoid getting down to work.

Applying Consequences.　In the (hopefully) rare case when all previous steps have been ineffective in getting the student to comply with a clearly stated and reasonable request, the final step is to pose a choice to the student: Either comply or suffer the consequences. Examples of consequences are sending the student out of class, making the student miss a few minutes of recess or some other privilege, having the student stay after school, and calling the student's parents. A consequence for not complying with the teacher's request should be mildly unpleasant, short in duration, and applied as soon as possible after the behavior occurs. Certainty is far more important than severity; students must know that consequences follow misbehavior as night follows day. One disadvantage of using severe or long-lasting punishment (for example, no recess for a week) is that it can create resentment in the student and a defiant attitude. Also, it may be difficult to follow through on severe or long-lasting consequences. Mild but certain consequences communicate, "I cannot tolerate that sort of *behavior,* but I care about *you* and want you to rejoin the class as soon as you are ready."

Before presenting a student with a consequence for noncompliance, teachers must be absolutely certain they can and will follow through if necessary. When teachers say, "You may choose to get to work right away or you may choose to spend five minutes of your recess doing your work here," they must be certain that someone will be available to monitor the student in the classroom during recess. Empty or vague threats ("You stop that or I'll make you wish you had!" or "You get to work or I'll have you suspended for a month!") are worse than useless. If teachers are not prepared to follow through with consequences, students will learn to shrug them off.

After a consequence has been applied, the teacher should avoid referring to the incident. For example, when the student returns from a ten-minute exclusion from class, the teacher should accept him or her back without any sarcasm or recriminations. The student now deserves a fresh start.

Self-Check

List the sequence of strategies in the principle of least intervention that are used for managing routine misbehavior. In each case how does the strategy work? How would you identify examples of these strategies in student–teacher dialogues? Reread the scenario at the beginning of this chapter. How could Ms. Green have managed her students' misbehavior?

Connections

Certain, though not necessarily severe, consequences for misbehavior can be incentives for students who are motivated to avoid failure or negative outcomes. See Chapter 10, "Motivating Students to Learn," for further discussion of consequences as motivators.

How Is Applied Behavior Analysis Used to Manage More Serious Behavior Problems?

The previous section discussed how to deal with behaviors that might be appropriate on the playing field but are out of line in the classroom. There are other behaviors that are not appropriate anywhere. These include fighting, stealing, destruction of property, and gross disrespect for teachers or other school staff. These are far less common than routine classroom misbehavior but far more serious.

For serious misbehaviors, swift and certain consequences must be applied. Any delay in punishment, or any uncertainty that the punishment will be applied, may make the consequences ineffective (Aronfreed and Reber, 1965; Solomon *et al.,* 1968). For most students, the most effective consequence for serious misbehavior is a call to the student's parent by the teacher, principal, or vice principal. If the behavior is repeated, the parents should be called in for a conference to help work out a plan for solving the problem. Behavior modification programs can also be effectively used to reduce serious behavior problems.

Behavioral learning theories, described in Chapter 5, have direct application to classroom management. Simply put, behavioral learning theories hold that behaviors that are not reinforced or are punished will diminish in frequency. The strategies for dealing with misbehavior discussed in the previous sections were based directly on behavioral learning theories: Appropriate behaviors are strengthened by praise, and inappropriate ones are diminished by ignoring them or by mild but certain punishment. The following section presents **applied behavior analysis,** an analysis of classroom behavior in terms of behavioral concepts, and gives specific behavior modification strategies for preventing and dealing with misbehavior (see Martin and Pear, 1992).

How Student Misbehavior Is Maintained

A basic principle of behavioral learning theories is that if any behavior persists over time, it must be maintained by some reinforcer. To reduce misbehavior in the classroom, we must understand which reinforcers maintain misbehavior in the first place.

The most common reinforcer for classroom misbehavior is attention—from the teacher, the peer group, or both. Students receiving one-to-one tutoring rarely misbehave, both because they already have the undivided attention of an adult and because no classmates are present to attend to any negative behavior. However, in the typical classroom students have to go out of their way to get the teacher's personal attention, and they have an audience of peers who may encourage or applaud their misdeeds.

Teacher's Attention.   Sometimes students misbehave because they want the teacher's attention, even if it is negative. This is a more common reason for misbehavior than many teachers think. A puzzled teacher might say, "I don't know what is wrong with Nathan. I have to stay with him all day to keep him working! Sometimes I get exasperated and yell at him. My words fall off him like water off a duck's back. He even smiles when I'm scolding him!"

When students appear to misbehave to gain the teacher's attention, the solution is relatively easy: pay attention to those students when they are doing well, and ignore them (as much as possible) when they misbehave. When ignoring their actions is impossible, time-out (for example, sending these students to a quiet corner or to the principal's office) will be more effective than scolding—in fact, scolding acts as a reinforcer for some students.

Peers' Attention.   Another very common reason that students misbehave is to get the attention and approval of their peers. The classic instance of this is the class

Connections

Distinguish the role of attention in maintaining misbehavior from the roles of attention in learning (Chapters 6 and 7) and in teaching (Chapters 8 and 9)

clown, who is obviously performing for the amusement of his or her classmates. However, many other forms of misbehavior are motivated primarily by peer attention and approval—in fact, few students completely disregard the potential impact of their behavior on their classmates. For example, students who refuse to do what the teacher has asked are consciously or unconsciously weighing the effect of their defiance on their standing among their classmates.

Even preschoolers and early elementary students may misbehave to gain peer attention, but beginning around the third grade (and especially during the middle/junior high school years), it is particularly likely that student misbehavior is linked to peer attention and support. As students enter adolescence, the peer group takes on extreme importance, and peer norms begin to favor independence from authority. When older children and teenagers engage in serious delinquent acts (such as vandalism, theft, and assault), they are usually supported by a delinquent peer group (Cloward and Ohlin, 1960).

Strategies for reducing peer-supported misbehavior are quite different from those for dealing with misbehavior meant to capture the teacher's attention. Ignoring misbehavior will be ineffective if the misbehavior is reinforced by peers. For example, if a student is balancing a book on his or her head and the class is laughing, the behavior can hardly be ignored, because it will continue as long as the class is interested (and will encourage others to behave likewise). Further, scolding may only attract more attention from classmates, or worse, enhance the student's standing among peers. Similarly, if two students are whispering or talking to each other, they are reinforcing each other for misbehaving, and ignoring their behavior will only encourage more of it.

There are two primary responses to peer-supported misbehavior. One is to remove the offender from the classroom to deprive him or her of peer attention. Another is to use **group contingencies,** strategies in which the entire class (or groups of students within the class) is rewarded on the basis of everyone's behavior. Under group contingencies, all students benefit from their classmates' good behavior, so peer support for misbehavior is removed. Group contingencies and other behavior management strategies for peer-supported misbehavior are described in more detail in the following sections.

Release from Unpleasant States or Activities.   A third important reinforcer for misbehavior is release from boredom, frustration, fatigue, or unpleasant activities. As explained in Chapter 5, escaping or avoiding an unpleasant stimulus is a reinforcer. Some students see much of what happens in school as unpleasant, boring, frustrating, or tiring. This is particularly true of students who experience repeated failure in school; for them, the classroom may be an endless psychological torture. But even the most able and motivated students feel bored or frustrated at times. Students often misbehave just to escape from unpleasant activities. This can be clearly seen with students who frequently ask permission to get a drink of water, go to the washroom, or sharpen their pencils. Such students are more likely to make these requests during seatwork than during lecture, because seatwork can be frustrating or anxiety-provoking for students who have little confidence in their academic abilities.

More serious misbehaviors can also be partially or completely motivated by a desire for release from boredom, frustration, or fatigue. A student may misbehave just to stir things up. Sometimes students misbehave precisely so that they will sent out of the classroom. Obviously, then, sending such a student to the hall or the principal's office can be counterproductive.

applied behavior analysis: the application of behavioral learning principles to understand and change behavior.

group contingencies: class rewards that depend on the behavior of all students.

The best solution for misbehaviors arising from boredom, frustration, or fatigue is prevention. Students rarely misbehave during interesting, varied, engaging lessons. Actively involving students in lessons can head off misbehaviors due to boredom or fatigue. Use of cooperative learning methods or other means of involving students in an active way can be helpful. Frustration may be avoided by the use of materials that ensure a high success rate for all, by making sure that all students are challenged but none are overwhelmed. Changing instruction and assessments to help students succeed can be an effective means of resolving frustration-related behavior problems. For example, Becker *et al.* (1967) used a combination of praise and small rewards to increase the on-task behavior of first- and second-graders with serious behavior problems. Either praise alone or praise plus reward were effective with most students, but not with one low-achieving student. However, when he was given a special reading tutor, his misbehavior virtually disappeared (even when he was not with the tutor). The experience of success at his own level was apparently enough to remove the need to escape from frustration and failure by misbehaving.

Principles of Behavior Modification

The behavior management strategies outlined in the previous sections (for example, nonverbal cues, reminders, mild but certain punishment) might be described as informal applications of behavioral learning theories. These practices, plus the prevention of misbehavior by the use of efficient class management and engaging lessons, will be sufficient to create a good learning environment in most classrooms.

However, in some classrooms more systematic **behavior modification** methods are needed. In classrooms in which most students are well-behaved but a few have persistent behavior problems, individual behavior modification strategies can be effective. In classrooms in which many students have behavior problems, particularly when there is peer support for misbehavior, whole-class behavior modification strategies or group contingencies may be needed. Such strategies are most often required when many low-achieving or poorly motivated students are put in one class, as often happens in special education classes and in schools that use tracking or other between-class ability grouping methods.

Setting up and using any behavior modification program requires following a series of steps that proceeds from the observation of the behavior through program implementation to program evaluation (see Medland and Vitale, 1984). The steps listed here are, to a greater or lesser extent, part of all behavior modification programs:

1. Identify target behavior(s) and reinforcer(s).
2. Establish a baseline for the target behavior.
3. Choose a reinforcer and criteria for reinforcement.
4. If necessary, choose a punisher and criteria for punishment.
5. Observe behavior during program implementation and compare it to baseline.
6. When the behavior modification program is working, reduce the frequency of reinforcement.

Individual behavior modification strategies are useful for coping with individual students who have persistent behavior problems in school. Strategies for dealing with this sort of chronic behavior problem follow (see Sulzer-Azaroff and Mayer, 1986).

Connections

Applied behavior analysis relates to information in Chapter 5 about reinforcers, consequences, behavior modification, and cognitive behavior modification.

---

behavior modification: systematic application of antecedents and consequences to change behavior.

Identify Target Behaviors and Reinforcers.   The first step in implementing a behavior modification program is to observe the misbehaving student to identify one or a small number of behaviors to target first and to see what reinforcers maintain the behavior(s). Another purpose of this observation is to establish a baseline against which to compare improvements. A structured individual behavior modification program should aim to change only one behavior or a small set of closely related behaviors. Tackling too many behaviors at a time risks failing with all of them because the student may not clearly see what he or she must do to be reinforced.

The first behavior targeted should be one that is serious, easy to observe, and, most importantly, occurs frequently. For example, if a child gets into fights in the playground every few days but gets out of his or her seat without permission several times per hour, you would start with the out-of-seat behavior and deal with the fighting later. Ironically, the more frequent and persistent a behavior, the easier it is to extinguish. This is because positive or negative consequences can be applied frequently, making the connection between behavior and consequence clear to the student.

As noted earlier, three reinforcers maintain most classroom misbehavior: teacher's attention; peers' attention; and release from boredom, frustration, or fatigue. In observing a student, try to determine which reinforcer(s) are maintaining the target behavior. If a student misbehaves in league with others (for example, talks without permission, swears, teases, fights) or if a student's misbehavior usually attracts the attention of others (for example, clowning, sassing the teacher), then you might conclude that the behavior is peer-supported. If the behavior does not attract much peer attention but always requires teacher attention (for example, getting out of seat without permission, constantly asking for help when help is not needed, refusing to work without constant prodding), then you might conclude that the behavior is supported by your own attention.

Establish Baseline Behavior.   On several successive days (at least three) observe the student to see how often the target behavior occurs. Before you do this, you will need to clearly define exactly what constitutes the behavior. For example, if the target behavior is "bothering classmates," you will have to decide what specific behaviors constitute "bothering" (perhaps teasing, poking, interrupting, taking materials).

Baseline measurements may be taken in terms of frequency (for example, how many times Charles got out of his seat without permission) or time (how many minutes Charles was out of his seat). Frequency records are usually easier to keep; you can simply make a tally on a sheet of paper on your desk.

Select Reinforcers and Criteria for Reinforcement.   Behavioral learning theories and behavior modification practice strongly favor the use of reinforcers for appropriate behavior rather than punishers for inappropriate behavior. The reasons for this are practical as well as ethical. Punishment often creates resentment, so that even if it solves one problem, it may create others (see Skinner, 1968). Also, punishment must be consistently applied. In contrast, successful reinforcement programs are supposed to be faded out over time. While reinforcers must be consistently given for appropriate behavior at the beginning of a behavior modification program, they should be given less and less consistently as behavior improves. Finally, an ethical note. Even where punishment would work as well as reinforcement, it should be avoided because it is not conducive to the creation of a happy, healthy classroom environment. Punishment of one kind or another is necessary in some circumstances, and it should be used without qualms when reinforcement strategies are impossible or ineffective. However, a program of punishment for misbehavior should always be the last option considered, never the first.

Typical classroom reinforcers include praise, privileges, and tangible rewards. In a carefully structured behavior modification program, praise can be extremely effective in improving student behavior. For example, Kirby and Shields (1972) had a teacher praise an underachieving seventh-grader immediately when he did his math work and ignore him when he was not on-task. The boy's rate of correct answers per minute tripled during the time when feedback and praise were given. Eventually the teacher praised him after every two problems, then every four, and later after every eight problems, and his problem-solving behavior remained at a high level. These results are illustrated in Figure 11.5. During Baseline 1 and Baseline 2 the teacher did not praise the boy for his math work; the difference made by the "praise and immediate feedback" treatment is apparent in the figure.

Praise is especially effective for students who misbehave to get the teacher's attention. It is often a good idea to start a behavior modification program using praise for appropriate behavior to see if this is sufficient but to be prepared to use stronger reinforcers if praise is not enough (see Becker *et al.*, 1967).

Ignoring inappropriate behavior is often the counterpart of praising appropriate behavior. However, this strategy is effective only if misbehavior is maintained by the teacher's attention. Zimmerman and Zimmerman (1962) give two examples of this. One emotionally disturbed eleven-year-old, David, when asked to spell words, would mumble letters completely unconnected with the words. The teacher would

Figure 11.5   Effects of Praise

The number of math problems a seventh-grade boy answered correctly per minute tripled when he was immediately praised for doing his work. The boy's work was not praised immediately during the baseline period.

From Kirby and Shields, 1972, p. 82.

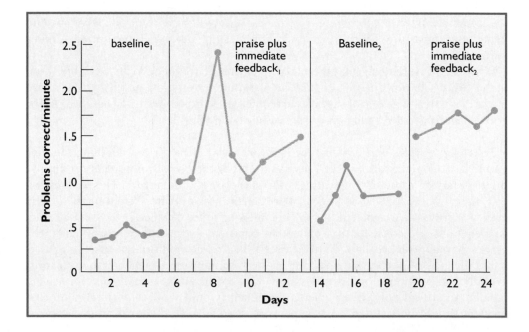

coax him for some time, giving the first letter and other clues and encouraging him to get started. This went on for weeks. Then the teacher decided to ignore David until he wrote a word correctly. She gave him an easy word and asked him to write it. He said, "I can't spell it," and hemmed and hawed for several minutes, during which time the teacher paid no attention to him. Finally he wrote the word correctly. The teacher looked up and said, "Good, now we can go on." This procedure was repeated for ten words, each of which took less and less time. At the end the teacher praised David, wrote an A on the paper, and asked him to help her color some Easter baskets, which he did gladly. Over the next week David's bizarre spelling and other inappropriate work behaviors disappeared entirely.

Another eleven-year-old emotionally disturbed boy, Sam, had terrific temper tantrums. Several adults and other children would routinely gather around to watch him lie on the floor, kicking and screaming.

After many such tantrums the teacher tried a different approach. One day Sam had a tantrum in the classroom before the other students arrived. The teacher ignored him completely, continuing to work at her desk. After about three minutes of screaming and crying, Sam looked up at the teacher. She said that she would be glad to work with him when he was ready. Sam cried and screamed with diminishing loudness for another five minutes, then lifted his head and said he was ready. The teacher smiled, said, "Good, now let's get to work," and worked with Sam for the rest of the period. A similar approach was used for a few later incidents of tantrums. If the tantrums occurred when other students were in the classroom, the teacher took Sam into an empty room to have his tantrum, but otherwise ignored him until he was calm. At all other times she made a point of giving Sam a lot of personal attention.

Soon the tantrums disappeared. Interestingly, many other inappropriate behaviors disappeared along with the tantrums. Positive spillover effects of this kind are common outcomes of successful behavior modification programs.

In the cases of David and Sam, the teacher's well-meaning efforts to help were in fact reinforcing the misbehavior. For example, David's bizarre spellings gained him a lot of attention, which he thrived on. When the attention was withdrawn, and he received attention only for spelling correctly, he was glad to comply, because his needs were as well satisfied by praise as by the coaxing he had received for his misspellings.

In addition to praise, many teachers find it useful to give students stars, "smilies," or other small rewards when they behave appropriately. Some teachers use a rubber stamp to mark students' papers with a symbol indicating good work. These small rewards make the teacher's praise more concrete and visible and also let students take their work home and receive praise from their parents.

Select Punishers and Criteria for Punishment, if Necessary. When a serious behavior problem does not respond to a well-designed reinforcement program, punishment may be necessary. A punisher is any unpleasant stimulus that an individual will try to avoid. Common punishers used in schools are reprimands, being sent out of class or to the principal's office, and detention or missed recess. Corporal punishment (for example, spanking), is illegal in some states and districts (see Sulzer-Azaroff and Mayer, 1986) and highly restricted in others, though the practice is still often seen (Rose, 1984). However, corporal punishment is neither a necessary nor an effective response to misbehavior in school.

O'Leary and O'Leary (1972, p. 152) list seven principles for the effective and humane use of punishment:

This student is in time out. In what contexts can time out be an appropriate and effective punisher? What ethical guidelines would you need to follow when considering behavior modification strategies?

1. Use punishment sparingly.
2. Make it clear to the child why he or she is being punished.
3. Provide the child with an alternative means of obtaining some positive reinforcement.
4. Reinforce the child for behaviors incompatible with those you wish to weaken (for example, if you punish for being off-task, also reinforce for being on-task).
5. Avoid physical punishment.
6. Avoid punishing while you are in a very angry or emotional state.
7. Punish when a behavior starts rather than when it ends (see Walters *et al.*, 1965).

Many studies have demonstrated the effectiveness of certain, mild punishment for reducing inappropriate behavior. For example, Hall *et al.* (1971) evaluated a program in which each of ten emotionally disturbed boys received check marks next to their names every time they got out of their seats without permission. Each check mark equaled five minutes after school. This procedure reduced out-of-seat behaviors for the boys from an average of 23 per session to 2.2 per session. O'Leary *et al.* (1970) found that softly delivered, firm reprimands for misbehaviors were much more effective than yelling.

One effective punisher is called **time out.** The teacher tells a misbehaving student to go to a separate part of the classroom, the hall, the principal's or vice principal's office, or another teacher's class. The place where the student is sent should be uninteresting and out of view of classmates. An empty room may be best, although Canter and Canter (1976) suggest that pairs of teachers agree in advance that if one teacher's students need time out, they can be sent to the other's classroom.

One advantage of time-out procedures is that they remove the student from the attention of his or her classmates. Therefore time out may be especially effective for students whose misbehavior is primarily motivated by peer attention.

Teachers should assign time outs infrequently, but when they do assign them, they should do so calmly and surely: The student is to go straight to the time-out area and stay there until the prescribed time is up. Time-out assignments should be brief; about five minutes is usually adequate. However, timing should begin only after the student settles down; if the student yells or argues, that time should not count. During time out no one should speak to the student. Teachers should not scold that student during time out. Students should be told why they are being given time out, but not otherwise lectured. If the principal's office is used, the principal should be asked not to speak to the student.

Observe and Compare Behavior to Baseline.   It is important to assess the effectiveness of your program. A behavior modification program usually works within a few days. If behavior is not improving after a week, try a different system or different reinforcers.

Reduce the Frequency of Reinforcement.   Once a behavior modification program has been in operation for a while and the student's behavior has improved and stabilized at a new level, the frequency of reinforcement can be reduced. Initially, reinforcers might be applied to every instance of appropriate behavior; as time goes on, every other instance, then every several instances, might be reinforced. Reducing the frequency of reinforcement helps maintain the new behaviors over the long run, and aids in extending the behaviors to other settings.

time out: removing a student from a situation in which misbehavior was reinforced.

Issues in School Discipline

Research suggests that maintaining classroom discipline is one of the most pressing concerns of preservice teachers. Teachers do learn and successfully apply techniques for getting students to change their disruptive or inappropriate behavior, but they soon discover that classroom management is part of the larger matters of schoolwide discipline policies and community expectations. Consider nationally publicized issues, such as the use of forms of punishment in the schools and the impact of school violence on students and school life.

School punishment in traditional stereotypes meant rapped knuckles, dunce caps, pulled ears, and paddled seats. Although in legal challenges to school authority the courts routinely rule against corporal punishment as cruel and unusual or discriminatory treatment, twenty-eight states still permit teachers to punish students by inflicting physical pain with public humiliation. Corporal punishment is vigorously opposed by the American Bar Association, the American Medical Association, the National Education Association, and, according to a 1988 Gallup Poll, by a slight majority of teachers.

Time out, after-school detention, in-school suspension, and like measures are more commonly used. These measures serve to punish behavior, although some individuals—students in school "resistance cultures" for instance—may actually feel reinforced. Used with elementary-school students, time out represents the removal of all reinforcement by isolating the student to some degree—from a desk in the corner of the classroom to a padded cell. Occasional lawsuits nationally have involved abuses of time out principles and procedures, such as locking frightened young children in closets, leaving students alone and unsupervised for too long a time, or denying bathroom privileges. Critics of punitive approaches to school discipline point out that some punishments, such as permanently expelling students or denying driving licenses to truants and dropouts, may in the long run heap even greater punishment on society at large.

Student violence, including racial conflict, sexual harassment, and gang-related armed assault, has also become a focus of national concern. Some big-city schools use metal detectors, security police, and streetworkers or gang outreach workers. Some districts have implemented effective prevention or intervention programs in an effort to make schools safe places to learn. Other districts employ innovative peer counseling, cooperative learning, mediation, and conflict-resolution programs, including courses designed to help students control their anger without resorting to violence. One midwestern city operates a conflict-resolution program that reaches more than 14,000 students throughout the system, using trained student mediators to identify and defuse potentially explosive situations. Because of their impact, district- and school-wide approaches to issues of conduct and discipline are as much a concern to teachers as classroom management.

Critical Thinking

In what contexts, if any, do you think corporal punishment in school would be justified? How, if at all, would you carry out a time-out policy in your class? What are some causes and consequences of increased violence among children and youths? How would you respond to an act of violence between your students?

"Florida Bars Licenses to Reduce Dropout Toll," *New York Times*, October 4, 1989, p. 89. Daniel Gursky, "Spare the Child," *Teacher*, February 1992; Millicent Lawton, "Fatal Attraction: American Youth Have Developed a Deadly Fascination with Firearms," *Teacher*, January 1992; Sharon K. Williams, "We Can Work It Out: Schools Are Turning to Conflict Resolution to Help Stop the Violence," *Teacher*, October 1991; "Teaching Tolerance," *Teacher*, February 1991.

Four Applied Behavior Analysis Programs

Home-based reinforcement strategies and daily report card programs are examples of applied behavioral analysis in the service of individual students. Token rein-

Figure 11.6

Example of a Daily Report Card

Teachers who use a home-based reinforcement program must set up a daily report card so that a student's work and behavior can be assessed and reported to the student's parents.

From Dougherty and Dougherty, 1972.

PERIOD	BEHAVIOR	SCHOOLWORK	TEACHER
STUDENT _Homer H._	DAILY REPORT CARD	DATE _March 21_	
Reading	1 2 ③ 4	1 ② 3 4	Ms. Casa
Math	1 2 3 ④	1 2 3 ④	Ms. Casa
Lunch	1 2 ③ 4		Mr. Mason
Recess	1 2 ③ 4		Ms. Hauser
Language	1 2 3 ④	1 2 3 ④	Ms. Casa
Science/Soc. Stud.	1 2 ③ 4	1 2 ③ 4	Ms. Casa

1 = Poor
2 = Fair
3 = Good
4 = Excellent

1 = Assignments not completed
2 = Assignments completed poorly.
3 = Assignments completed adequately.
4 = Assignments completed—excellent!

Total rating _33_   😊   Score needed: _30_

forcement and group contingency programs are examples of applied behavioral analysis in which the whole class is involved. In whole-class behavior modification, all the students are reinforced (or punished) for their behavior under the same rules (see Litow and Pumroy, 1975). For example, if the teacher says, "Any student who finishes the worksheet may go to recess," this is a simple whole-class behavior modification system; all students have the same opportunity to be rewarded according to the same standard.

Home-Based Reinforcement.   Some of the most practical and effective behavior modification–based classroom management methods are **home-based reinforcement strategies** (see Barth, 1979). Teachers give students a daily or weekly report card to take home, and parents are instructed to provide special privileges or rewards to students on the basis of these teacher reports. Home-based reinforcement is not exactly a new idea; a museum in Vermont displays weekly report cards from the 1860s.

Home-based reinforcement methods have been used to improve the behavior of individual disruptive children in classrooms (Sluyter and Hawkins, 1972) as well as that of entire disruptive classrooms (Ayllon *et al.*, 1975). Dougherty and Dougherty (1977) used home-based reinforcement to motivate students to hand in homework, complete their schoolwork, and refrain from talking without permission.

Home-based reinforcement has several advantages over other, equally effective behavior management strategies. First, parents can give much more potent rewards and privileges than schools can. For example, parents control access to such activities as television, trips to the store, and going out with friends. Parents also know what their own children like and therefore can provide more individual privileges than the school.

home-based reinforcement strategies: behavior modification strategies in which a student's school behavior is reported to parents, who supply rewards.

Second, home-based reinforcement gives parents frequent good news about their children. Parents of disruptive children usually hear from the school only when their child has done something wrong. This is bad for parent-school relations and leads to much blame and finger-pointing.

Third, home-based reinforcement is easy to administer. Any adults who deal with the child (other teachers, bus drivers, playground or lunch monitors) can be involved in the program by having a student carry a daily report card all day (Runge *et al.,* 1975).

Finally, over time daily report cards can be replaced by weekly report cards and then biweekly report cards without loss in effectiveness (Dougherty and Dougherty, 1977), until the school's usual six- or nine-week report cards can be used.

Individual Daily Report Cards. Figure 11.6 presents a **daily report card** for Homer Heath, an elementary school student. His teacher, Ms. Casa, rated his behavior and schoolwork at the end of each academic period, and she arranged to have the lunch monitor and the recess monitor rate his behavior when Homer was with them. Homer was responsible for carrying his report card with him at all times and for making sure that it was marked and initialed at the end of each period. Whenever he made at least 30 points, his parents agreed to give him a special privilege—his father was to read him an extra story before bedtime and let him stay up fifteen minutes longer than usual. Whenever he forgot to bring home his report card, his parents were to assume that he did not meet the criterion.

If Homer had been a junior or senior high school student, or if he had been in a departmentalized elementary school (where he changed classes for each subject), he would have carried his report card to every class, and each teacher would have marked it. Obviously, this would take some coordination among the teachers, but the effort would certainly be worthwhile if the daily report card dramatically reduced his misbehaviors and increased his academic output, as it has in dozens of studies evaluating this method (Barth, 1979).

Theory Into Practice:

Using a Daily Report Card System

Steps for setting up and implementing a daily report card system are as follows:

1. *Decide on Behaviors to Include in the Daily Report Card:* Choose a behavior or set of behaviors on which the daily report card is to be based. Devise a rating scheme for each behavior, and construct a standard report card form. Your daily report card might be more or less elaborate than the one in Figure 11.6. For example, you might break "behavior" down into more precise categories, such as "getting along with others," "staying on-task," and "following class rules." If a student's sole problem is fighting, then the card might only have a rating for "getting along with others."

   Students need not be rated every period; one rating at the end of the day may be enough. In fact, the easiest form of a home-based reinforcement program would be to give students whose behavior meets a high criterion a "good behavior certificate" to take home each day. However, for young children or those with serious behavior problems, one rating at the end of the whole day may be too long a wait and too vague a criterion to be effective.

daily report card: a behavior-management system requiring parent participation and reinforcing desirable conduct.

2. *Explain the Program to Parents:* Since home-based reinforcement programs depend on parent participation, it is critical to inform parents about the program and to obtain their cooperation. Ayllon *et al.* (1975), who worked in an inner-city school where most households were headed by single working women, asked parents to attend a two-hour meeting and called or visited those who could not attend. However, other researchers (Edlund, 1969; Dougherty and Dougherty, 1977; Lahey *et al.,* 1977) found that writing letters to parents worked quite well, and Karraker (1972) reported that home-based reinforcement programs involving one-hour parent conferences, fifteen-minute conferences, or one-page letters to parents were equally effective.

However they are notified and involved, parents should be told what the daily report card means, and asked to reward their children whenever they bring home a good report card. In presenting the program to parents, teachers should explain what parents might do to reward their children. Communications with parents should be brief, positive, and informal; they should generate a feeling that "we're going to solve this together." The program should focus on rewarding good behavior rather than punishing bad behavior (see Runge *et al.,* 1975). Examples of rewards parents might use at home (adapted from Walker and Shea, 1980) are:

- special activities with a parent (for example, reading, flying a kite, building a model, shopping, playing a game, going to the zoo).

- special foods.

- baking cookies or cooking.

- operating equipment usually reserved for adults (for example, the dishwasher or vacuum cleaner).

- access to special games, toys, equipment.

- small rewards (such as coloring books, paper, comic books, erasers, stickers).

- additional play time, television time, and the like.

- having a friend spend the night.

- later bedtime or curfew.

Parents should be encouraged to choose rewards they can give every day (that is, nothing too expensive or difficult).

The best rewards are ones that build closeness between parent and child, such as doing special activities together. Many children who have behavior problems in school also have them at home and may have less than ideal relationships with their parents. Home-based reinforcement programs provide an opportunity for parents to show their love for their child at a time when the child has something to be proud of. A special time with Dad can be especially valuable as a reward for good behavior in school and for building the father–son or father–daughter relationship.

3. *When Behavior Improves, Reduce the Frequency of the Report:* When home-based reinforcement works, it often works dramatically (Dickerson *et al.,* 1973). Once the behavior of students has improved and has stabilized, it is time to decrease the frequency of the reports to parents. Report cards

might then be issued only weekly (for larger but less frequent rewards). As noted in Chapter 5, the best way to ensure maintenance is to thin out the reinforcement schedule—that is, to increase the interval between reinforcers.

Whole-Class Token Reinforcement. As is the case with all the behavior modification–based classroom management programs discussed in this chapter, whole-class behavior modification strategies have been consistently found to have strong, often dramatic effects on student behavior. For example, O'Leary and Becker (1967) evaluated a program in which emotionally disturbed third-graders were given points according to a rating of their academic behaviors (in seat, facing front, raising hand, working, paying attention, desk clear). The points (or tokens) could be exchanged at the end of each day for items such as candy, pennants, comic books, perfume, or kites. Disruptive behavior among the students dropped from 76 percent of class time to 10 percent almost as soon as the program was introduced.

Similar results have been obtained in many studies in a wide variety of settings using a wide variety of point systems and reinforcers. Broden *et al.* (1970a) gave junior high school special education students points for being in seat and doing assignments quietly and charged them points for misbehavior. Students could exchange their points for privileges, such as a pass to go to lunch five minutes early, the opportunity to move their desks to a new location, or a five-minute quiet break during class time. This **token reinforcement system** increased students' on-task time from 39 percent of class time to 83 percent. Ayllon and Roberts (1974) gave students in a regular fifth-grade class who were experiencing serious discipline problems points each day for completing reading assignments at 80 percent correct, with extra points for perfect papers. Students could exchange these points for a variety of rewards, such as ten minutes of extra recess time, access to a movie, the privilege of changing their seat in the cafeteria, or the opportunity to have their lowest test grade removed. "Auctions" were held for such privileges as being hall captain or "assistant teacher" for a week. This program increased the accuracy of students' work from 48 to 70 percent and substantially reduced inappropriate behavior (even though the points were only for completing assignments accurately, not for behavior per se).

Because of their difficulty and expense, token reinforcement systems are rarely used today except in special education. In general, they have given way to more practical group contingencies and home-based reinforcement systems.

Group Contingency Programs. A **group contingency program** is a reinforcement system in which an entire group is rewarded on the basis of the behavior of the group members. Teachers have always used group contingencies, as "We'll go to lunch as soon as *all students* have put their work away and are quiet." When the teacher says this, any one student can cause the entire class to be late to lunch. Or the teacher might say, "If the class averages at least ninety on tomorrow's quiz, then you'll all be excused from homework for the rest of the week." This group contingency would depend on the average performance of all group members rather than on any single student.

One important advantage of group contingencies is that they are easier to administer than other behavior modification–based classroom management strategies. For one thing, record keeping for a group contingency is usually much easier. Also, most often the whole class is either rewarded or not rewarded, which avoids having to do one thing with some students and something else with others. For example, suppose

token reinforcement system: system where tokens earned for academic work and positive classroom behavior can be exchanged for some desired reward.

group contingency program: program in which rewards or punishments are given to a class as a whole for adhering to or violating rules of conduct.

Figure 11.7

Group Contingency Program

Rewarding teams of fourth-graders for good behavior caused a dramatic decrease in the percent of one-minute intervals during which students talked out of turn or got out of their seats. During the baseline and reversal periods, the teacher used routine classroom management strategies.

From Barrish et al., 1969, p. 122.

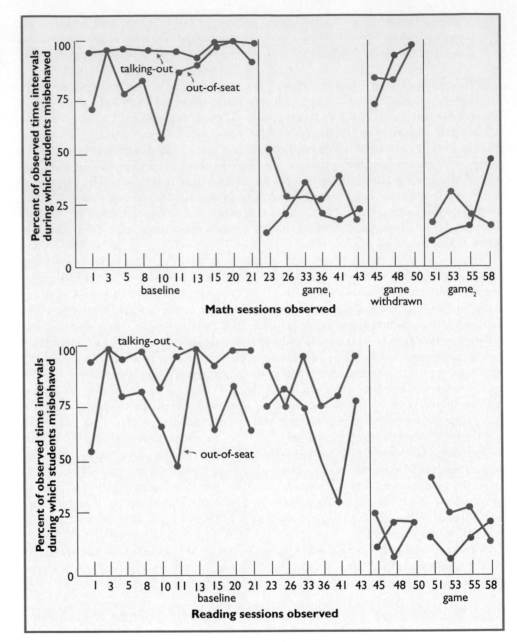

a teacher says, "If the whole class follows the class rules this morning, we will have five extra minutes of recess." If the class does earn the extra recess, they all get it together; the teacher need not arrange to have some students stay out longer while others are called inside.

The theory behind group contingencies is that when a group is rewarded on the basis of the behavior of its members, the group members will encourage one another to do whatever helps the group gain the reward (Hayes, 1976; Slavin, 1990b). Group contingencies can turn the same peer pressure that often *supports* misbehaviors to *opposing* misbehavior. When the class can earn extra recess only if all students are well behaved all morning, no one is liable to find it funny when Joan balances a book on her head or Quinn sasses the teacher.

Group contingencies have been successfully used in many forms and for many purposes. Barrish *et al.* (1969) divided a fourth-grade class into two teams during math period. When the teacher saw any member of a team disobeying class rules, the whole team received a check mark on the chalkboard. If a team had five or fewer check marks at the end of the period, all team members would take part in a free-time activity at the end of the day. If both teams got more than five check marks, the one that got fewer would receive the free time. A recent study found positive effects of the "good behavior game" on aggressive and shy behavior among first-graders (Dolan *et al.*, 1992). Figure 11.7 shows the results of the program.

Note that in math period talking without permission and out-of-seat behavior dropped dramatically during the "good behavior game," resumed when the game was removed, and dropped again when the game was reinstated. When the program was then extended to reading period, similar results were obtained.

Winett and Vachon (1974) evaluated a simple group contingency in an inner-city fifth-grade class. The teacher simply rated the class's behavior during an afternoon instruction period. The class was rated on such things as attention, noise level, work quality, and amount of work done. At the end of class the teacher totaled the ratings and explained them to students. This group feedback strategy alone (with no rewards) produced an increase in appropriate behavior from 62 percent of class time to 76 percent. When the class was given an opportunity to earn free time, games, or a chance to go outside if they got an "excellent" total rating, appropriate behavior rose to 84 percent of class time.

Theory Into Practice

Establishing a Group Contingency Program

As noted earlier, a group contingency behavior management program can be as simple as the statement, "Class, if you are all in your seat, on-task, and quiet this morning, you may have five extra minutes of recess." However, a little more structure than this can increase the effectiveness of the group contingency.

1. *Decide Which Behaviors Will Be Reinforced:* As in any whole-class behavior modification program, the first step in setting up a group contingency is to establish a set of class rules.

2. *Set up a Developmentally Appropriate Point System:* There are essentially three ways to implement a group contingency behavior management program. One is to simply rate class behavior each period or during each activity. That is, an elementary school class might receive 0–5 points during each individual instructional period such as reading, language arts, and math. A secondary class might receive one overall rating each period or separate ratings for behavior and completed assignments. Students would t hen be rewarded each day or week if they exceeded a preestablished number of points.

   Another way to set up a group contingency is to rate the class at various times during the day. For example, you might set a timer to ring on the average of once very ten minutes (but varying randomly from one to twenty minutes). If the whole class is conforming to class rules when the timer rings, then the class earns a point. The same program can be used without

Teachers on Teaching

What classroom management techniques work best for you and your students?

Classroom expectations and consequences must be clearly defined. The teacher has to know the students, how they learn, and how they are motivated. Teachers also have to be comfortable with their own philosophy of education. If they are not clear about their own beliefs, then their management systems will falter for lack of congruence. To provide a safe environment for my students to explore and grow in, I use nonverbal and verbal cues. The "look" is the first step. The second is moving closer to the student. The last is letting the student make a responsible choice. For example, Drew was leaning back in his chair during math class, an unacceptable behavior. We had established a rule about that on the first day of school and the consequence for breaking the rule was the loss of the chair. My first response to Drew was eye contact. He saw me looking and put his chair down. Shortly, however, Drew was rocking back in his chair again. I proceeded to walk in his direction and placed my hand on his desk. Again, he ended the misbehavior. When Drew leaned back in his chair again, I discussed the situation with Drew and reminded him of the rule. I told him he had two choices: to sit in the chair properly or to do without it. He chose to sit properly—for a while; but later during that hour, Drew had to relinquish his seat. Putting the responsibility in the hands of the student allows him to reflect upon the consequences and make his own decision. The problem becomes the student's problem, not the teacher's. A perfect classroom management system does not exist. However, a good management system includes a purpose, clearly defined expectations and consequences, and good rapport between the teacher and the students.

Julie A. Addison, Teacher, Grade 4
Roxborough Elementary School, Littleton, Colorado

As an Acting Assistant Principal, I have tried to transfer my experience with successful classroom discipline to the challenge of schoolwide discipline. I'm guided by a single simple principle: The time spent disciplining a child represents lost instructional time. Students who are sitting in my office are not engaged in academic learning—their most important role and, for some of these kids, their only hope. Students are referred to me when their behavior is disruptive to the degree that it prevents the teacher from teaching others. I know each student individually, so my first strategy is to appeal to his or her self-concept as an individual. I suggest that they are too intelligent, too worthwhile, too valued to conduct themselves in an inappropriate manner. I remind them of their qualities or accomplishments that they and others—their families, teachers, or peers—are proud of. I ask students to bring their grievances to me for mediation before getting to the point where they act on those grievances through name calling or physical aggression. With a large group of students—in the cafeteria, for instance—I might have to chew out the kids, target a couple of troublemakers to see me after school, and then leave before anyone has a chance to talk back. The worst thing you can do in the heat of a circumstance is to get sucked into a discussion about who did what to whom and why or who started what when. Parental cooperation in a discipline matter is important for getting kids to permanently change their inappropriate behavior. The parents understand my guiding principle: Discipline time is lost instructional time for learning, and lost learning time is more than time wasted; it can add up to lost kids.

James Williams, History Teacher; Acting Assistant Principal;
Frank V. Thompson Middle School, Dorchester, MA
1991 Golden Apple Award Winner

the timer if the teacher gives the class a point every ten minutes or so if all students are conforming to class rules. Canter and Canter (1976) suggest that teachers use a bag of marbles and a jar, putting a marble into the jar from time to time whenever the class is following rules. Each marble would be worth thirty seconds of extra recess. In secondary schools, where extra recess is not possible, each marble might represent thirty seconds of "break time" held at the end of the period on Friday.

3. *Consider Deducting Points for Serious Misbehavior:* The group contingency reward system by itself should help improve student behavior. However, it may still be necessary to react to occasional serious misbehavior. For example, you might deduct 10 points for any instance of fighting or of serious disrespect for the teacher. When points must be deducted, do not negotiate with students about it. Just deduct them, explaining why they must be deducted and reminding students that they may earn them back if they follow class rules.

4. *When Behavior Improves, Reduce the Frequency of the Points and Reinforcers:* Initially, the group contingency should be applied every day. When the class's behavior improves and stabilizes at a new level for about a week, you may change to giving rewards once a week. Ultimately, the class may graduate from the point-and-reward system entirely, though feedback and praise based on class behavior should continue.

5. *Combine Group and Individual Contingencies if Necessary:* The use of group contingencies need not rule out individual contingencies for students who need them. For example, students who continue to have problems in a class using a group contingency might still receive daily or weekly report cards to take home to their parents.

Ethics of Behavioral Methods

The behavior analysis strategies described in this chapter are powerful. Properly applied, they will usually bring the behavior of even the most disruptive students to manageable levels. However, there is a danger that teachers may use behavior modification techniques to overcontrol students. They may be so concerned about getting students to sit down, stay quiet, and look productive that they lose sight of the fact that school is for learning, not for social control. Winett and Winkler (1972) wrote an excellent article entitled "Current Behavior Modification in the Classroom: Be Still, Be Quiet, Be Docile," in which they warned that behavior modification–based classroom management systems are being misused if teachers mistakenly believe that a quiet class is a learning class. This point parallels the basic premise of the QAIT model of effective instruction presented in Chapter 9. Behavior management systems can increase time for learning, but unless quality of instruction, appropriate levels of instruction, and incentives for learning are also adequate, the additional time may be wasted (see Emmer and Aussiker, 1990; Canter, 1989).

Some people object to behavior modification on the basis that it is bribing students to do what they ought to do anyway or that it is mind control. However, it is important to remember that all classrooms use rewards and punishers (such as grades, praise, scolding, suspension). Behavior modification strategies simply use these rewards in a more systematic way and avoid punishers as much as possible.

Behavior modification methods should be used only when it is clear that preventative or informal methods of improving classroom management are not enough to create a positive environment for learning. It is unethical to overapply these methods, but it may be equally unethical to fail to do so when they could avert serious problems. For example, it might be unethical to refer a child to special education or to suspend, expel, or retain a child on the basis of a pattern of behavior problems before using positive behavior modification methods long enough to see if they can resolve the problem without more draconian measures.

Theory Into Practice
Making Ethical Use of Behavioral Methods

Teachers should use behavior modification strategies ethically by observing the following principles.

1. Encourage reliance on prevention and on intrinsic rewards and incentives first and whenever possible. Make sure extrinsic rewards are understood as symbols of task mastery and not as ends in themselves. Phase out reward systems as student motivation and success improve.

2. Use behavioral methods in appropriate contexts to reinforce positive academic and social learning behaviors, not merely to enforce rules of conduct.

3. Use reinforcement selectively, and only when needed. Try the simplest, most positive, least restrictive, and least intrusive procedures first. Leave as much responsibility for learning as possible in the hands of students.

On matters of law and order, school and community needs often coincide. What are steps you could take as a teacher to help prevent delinquency or serious discipline problems among your students?

4. Encourage student awareness of and cooperation in behavior change programs. So far as possible, make sure changes in behavior occur for reasons students themselves understand and accept.

5. Know your students. Fit behavioral strategies to the special needs of each one, carefully considering all possible consequences. This includes carefully selecting reinforcers and fitting rewards to the individual. Consult with parents and school professionals to ensure that a reinforcement program is appropriate for, and will not harm, the student. At the same time, consider the needs of other students and of the whole group when implementing reinforcement programs that target particular individuals.

Self-Check

Explain how applied behavior analysis is done. Then describe the appropriate and ethical use of each of the following applications of principles of behavior modification:

praise	punishment
home-based reinforcement	daily report cards
token reinforcement	group contingencies

How Can Serious Behavior Problems Be Prevented?

Everyone misbehaves. There is hardly a person on earth who has not at some time done something he or she knew to be wrong or even illegal. However, some people's misbehavior is far more frequent and/or serious than others', and students who fall into this category cause their teachers and school administrators (not to mention their parents and themselves) a disproportionate amount of trouble and concern.

Serious behavior problems are not evenly distributed among students or schools. Most students who are identified as having severe behavior problems are male; from three to eight times as many boys as girls are estimated to have serious conduct problems (Coleman, 1986; Kauffman, 1989). Serious delinquency is far more common among students from impoverished backgrounds, particularly in urban locations. Students with poor family relationships are also much more likely than other students to become involved in serious misbehavior and delinquency, as are students who are low in achievement and those who experience attendance problems (see Gottlieb et al., 1991; Kauffman, 1989).

The school has an important role to play in preventing or managing serious misbehavior and delinquency, but the student and the school are only one part of the story; delinquent behavior often involves the police, courts, social service agencies, as well as the student's parents and peers. However, there are some guidelines for prevention of delinquency and serious misbehaviors (see Wolfgang and Glickman, 1980; Weiss and Sederstrom, 1981).

Understanding Causes of Misbehavior. Even though some types of students are more prone to misbehavior than others, these characteristics do not *cause* misbehavior. Some students misbehave because they perceive that the rewards for misbehavior outweigh the rewards for good behavior. For example, students who do not experience success in school may perceive that the potential rewards for hard work and good behavior are small, so they turn to other sources of rewards. Some put their energies into sports, others into social activities. Some, particularly those who are failing in many different domains, find their niche in groups that hold norms against achievement and other prosocial behavior. This can all happen very early, as soon as some students realize that they are unlikely to do well in school or to receive much support at home, from peers, or from the school itself for their academic efforts. Over time, students who fail in school and get into minor behavior difficulties may fall in with a delinquent subgroup and begin to engage in serious delinquent or even criminal behavior. The role of the delinquent peer group in maintaining delinquent behavior cannot be overstated. Delinquent acts among adolescents and preadolescents are usually done in groups and are supported by antisocial peer norms (Kauffman, 1989).

Enforcing Rules and Practices. Expectations that students will conform to school rules must be consistently expressed (Gottfredson, 1984). For example, graffiti or other vandalism must be repaired at once, so that other students do not get the idea that misbehavior is common or sanctioned.

Enforcing School Attendance. Truancy and delinquency are strongly related (Gold, 1970); when students are out of school, they are often in the community making trouble. While there are few proven methods available to schools that are known to reduce delinquency in the community, there are effective means of reducing truancy. Brooks (1975) had high school teachers sign cards carried by students with serious attendance problems at the end of each period they attended. Students received a ticket for each period attended, plus bonus tickets for good behavior in class and for going five days without missing a class. The tickets were used in a drawing for a variety of prizes. Before the program began, the target students were absent 60 percent of all school days. During the program absences dropped to 19 percent of school days. Over the same period, truancy among students not in the program increased from 59 to 79 percent.

Barber and Kagey (1977) markedly increased attendance in an entire elementary school by making full participation in once-a-month parties depend on student attendance. Several activities were provided during the parties, and students could earn access to some or all of them according to the numbers of day they attended.

Fiordaliso *et al.* (1977) increased attendance among chronically truant junior high school students by having the school call their parents whenever the students were present several days in a row. The number of days before calling depended on how severe the student's truancy had been; parents of the most truant students, who had been absent six or more days per month, were called after the student attended for only three consecutive days. In these and other studies truancy was successfully reduced using behavior modification principles. Since truancy is one aspect of delinquency over which the school does have some control, reducing it should be an important part of any delinquency prevention program.

Accommodating Instruction. Tracking (between-class ability grouping) should be avoided if possible. Low-track classes are ideal breeding grounds for antisocial delinquent peer groups (Howard, 1978). Similarly, behavioral and academic problems should be dealt with in the context of the regular class as much as possible, rather than in separate special education classes (Safer, 1982; Madden and Slavin,

1983b). Individualization in the regular, heterogeneous classroom is the best means of dealing with most behavioral as well as academic deficits (Calhoun and Elliott, 1977). In addition, in secondary schools the curriculum should be differentiated to allow for instruction relevant to non–college-bound students. This means making available technical preparation courses, as well as other curricular offerings related to the life experiences and needs of students.

Practicing Intervention. Classroom management strategies should be used to reduce inappropriate behavior before it escalates into delinquency. Improving students' behavior and success in school can prevent delinquency. For example, Hawkins *et al.* (1988) used preventative classroom management methods such as those emphasized in this chapter along with interactive teaching and cooperative learning to help low-achieving seventh-graders. In comparison with control-group students, the students who were involved in the program were suspended and expelled less often, had better attitudes toward school, and were more likely to expect to complete high school. Use of behavior modification–based programs for misbehavior in class can also contribute to the prevention of delinquency. Group contingencies can be especially effective with predelinquent students because they can deprive students of peer support for misbehavior.

As noted earlier, peer support is central to the great majority of delinquent acts by older students. For example, Graubard (1969) used a group contingency with emotionally disturbed, delinquent preadolescents. Students earned points for following class rules, which they helped formulate. Every few minutes a bonus bell was rung. If all students were following class rules when the bell rang, they all received ten bonus points. All students in the class were rewarded if *every* student earned a certain minimum number of points. Under this system, students continually reminded their classmates that inappropriate behavior affected them all. As a result, inappropriate behavior dropped markedly and declined even further when individual contingencies were added to the group contingencies. Graubard (1969) contrasted the group contingency approach to the traditional "artichoke" method, in which "the teacher attempts to peel the child away from the [delinquent] group just as one peels artichoke leaves off the stem" (p. 268). Because of the power of peer pressure among delinquent students, Graubard argued, individual students cannot easily be peeled. A more promising strategy is to deal with the artichoke as a whole, to use group contingencies to change peer group norms.

Requesting Family Involvement. Involve the student's home in any response to serious misbehavior. When misbehavior occurs, parents should be notified. If it persists, they should be involved in establishing a program, such as a home-based reinforcement program, to coordinate home and school responses to misbehavior.

Judiciously Applying Consequences. Avoid the use of suspension (and expulsion) as punishment for all but the most serious misbehavior (see Chobot and Garibaldi, 1982; Moles, 1984, 1990). Suspension often exacerbates truancy problems, both because it makes students fall behind in their work and because it gives them experience in the use of time out of school. In-school suspension, detention, and other penalties are more effective.

When students misbehave, they should be punished, but when punishment is applied, it should be brief. Being sent to a time-out area or detention room is a common punishment and effective for most students. Loss of privileges may be used. However, whatever punishment is used should not last too long. It is better to make a student miss two days of football practice than to throw him off the team, in part because once the student is off the team, the school may have little else to offer or withhold.

When misbehavior occurs, punish it, but then reintegrate the student. Serious misbehavior must be consistently and firmly punished, but once the punishment is over, the student should be allowed to participate in educational programs without reminders or continuing penalties. Every child has within him or herself the capacity for good behavior as well as for misbehavior. The school must be the ally of the good in each child at the same time it is the enemy of misbehavior. Overly harsh penalties, or penalties that do not allow the student to reenter the classroom on an equal footing with others, risk pushing students into the antisocial, delinquent subculture. When a student has paid his or her debt by losing privileges, experiencing detention, or whatever, he or she must be fully reaccepted as a member of the class.

Self-Check

Evaluate and discuss with classmates the general strategies presented in this section for prevention and intervention against serious school discipline problems. Develop and defend a five-point plan for best preventing delinquency among your students.

An Ounce of Prevention

Althea Johnson, a third-grade teacher, is standing in front of her new class on the second day of school.

ALTHEA: OK, class. I want to spend a few minutes talking with you about class rules. Let's start by listing some on the board. Please raise your hands and wait until I call on you.

In a few minutes Althea has written the following on the board under the heading "Rules":

- Do not talk in class.
- Do not run in the hallways.
- Do not put gum under your desk.
- Do not throw spitballs (or paper airplanes).
- Do not draw on your desk.
- Do not fight.
- Do not come late without a note from home.
- Do not yell in class.
- Do raise your hand to be called on.
- Do not bring radios to school.
- Do not pass notes to your friends.
- Do not write in your books.

ALTHEA: Does everyone think these rules are fair? Hands? [Hands go up.] OK, that's a good start. But I see two problems. First, this is a long list to remember. And second, most of them start with "Do not." I'd like to try to group these as a *few* rules that tell us what we *should* do.

Her students offer ideas, and eventually the board shows the following rules, each with several examples underneath:

1. Respect the rights of others.
2. Respect other people's property.
3. Be courteous to others.
4. Be on-task.
5. Raise your hand to be called on.

ALTHEA: OK, we've all agreed that these rules are fair. But if somebody does forget and breaks a rule, what should happen? What should the consequence be? Clare?

CLARE: You go to the principal's office.

ALTHEA: Yes, that's one consequence. Let's list more.

As before, Althea lists the students' suggestions under the heading "Consequences":

- Go to the principal's office.
- Sit in the corner for half an hour.
- Miss recess.
- Stay after school.
- Get a letter sent home to your parents.

ALTHEA: Who has a suggestion for making people want to *keep* the rules in the first place, not break them? A kind of reward? Mimi? Clare?

MIMI: Getting gold stars?

CLARE: We could all get an extra recess if the whole class was good all day.

BILLY (interrupting):   We could all just stay home!

ALTHEA: Billy, we've all agreed to raise hands and to be courteous. So are you trying to give the class an example of how not to behave?

BILLY: Sorry, Mrs. Johnson.

ALTHEA: OK, now I want everyone to copy down our basic rules and think about them. We'll talk a little more about rewards and consequences tomorrow.

Problem Solving

1. Do you agree with Althea that third-graders should be involved in setting class rules? How might a teacher of younger or older children approach the same task?

2. For the grade level you plan to teach, develop a problem-prevention plan of action for the first week of school. Model your plan by extending the dialogue with another character; for example, have Althea talk with a novice teacher.

Summary

What Is the Impact of Time on Learning?

Methods of maximizing allocated time include avoiding late starts and early finishes, avoiding interruptions, handling routine procedures smoothly and quickly, anticipating needs, and minimizing time spent on discipline. Engaged time, or time on-task, is the time individual students spend actually doing assigned work, which can be maximized by proper arrangement of the classroom, starting the year properly, setting class rules, maintaining momentum, maintaining smoothness of instruction, managing transitions, maintaining group focus, withitness, and overlapping.

A major component of the teacher's task with early elementary students (K–2) is socialization to expected behavior. In the middle elementary grades (2–5) classroom management revolves around maintenance of momentum in lessons and enforcing compliance with rules that are reasonably well understood by students. In the middle/junior high school grades (5–9) students become more likely to resist authority and embrace peer norms. During the high school grades (9–12) teachers must be concerned with the interest level and relevance of their lessons and the use of incentives to motivate students to do academic work.

What Practices Contribute to Effective Classroom Management?

Starting the year properly involves planning engaging lessons, arranging the classroom for effective instruction, and developing rules and procedures. Class rules and procedures should be explicitly presented to students and applied promptly and fairly.

What Are Some Strategies for Managing Routine Misbehavior?

One principle of classroom discipline is good management of routine misbehavior. The principle of least intervention means using the simplest methods that will work. There is a continuum of strategies from least disruptive to most: prevention of misbehavior; nonverbal cues, such as eye contact, which can stop a minor misbehavior; praise of incompatible, correct behavior; praise of other students who are behaving; simple verbal reminders given immediately after students misbehave; repetition of verbal reminders; and application of consequences when students refuse to comply. For serious behavior problems, swift and certain consequences must be applied. A call to the student's parents can be effective.

How Is Applied Behavior Analysis Used to Manage More Serious Behavior Problems?

The most common reinforcer for both routine and serious misbehavior is attention from teacher or peers. When the student misbehaves to get the teacher's attention, one effective strategy is to pay attention to correct behavior while ignoring misbehavior as much as possible; scolding often acts as a reinforcer. Strategies for reducing peer-supported misbehavior include time out (removing the child from the classroom) and group contingencies (rewarding the class only when everyone's behavior is good).

Individual behavior modification strategies are useful for students with persistent behavior problems in school.

Home-based reinforcement strategies involve giving students daily or weekly report cards to take home, and instructing parents to provide rewards on the basis of these reports. The steps to setting up such a program include deciding on behaviors to use for the daily report card and explaining the program to parents.

Group contingency and token reinforcement systems are those in which an entire group is rewarded on the basis of the behavior of the group members.

The danger of behavior modification techniques is that they can be used to overcontrol students. Behavior modification strategies always emphasize praise and reinforcement, reserving punishment as a last resort.

How Can Serious Discipline Problems Be Prevented?

There are few sure methods of preventing delinquency, but some general principles are: clearly expressing and consistently enforcing classroom rules; reducing truancy however possible; avoiding the use of between-class ability grouping; using behavior modification classroom management strategies; involving parents in any response to serious misbehavior; avoiding the use of suspension; applying only brief punishment; and reintegrating students after punishment.

Key Terms

Students at Risk and Exceptional Learners

12

Chapter Outline	Chapter Objectives
Who Are "Students at Risk" and What Educational Programs Exist for Them? Compensatory Education Early Intervention Programs Prevention Programs	▲ Explain what is meant by "at-risk" students, and describe and evaluate three kinds of educational programs that serve students at risk.
Who Are "Exceptional" Learners? Types of Exceptionalities and the Numbers of Students Served Mental Exceptionalities Mental Retardation Learning Disabilities Communication Disorders Emotional and Behavioral Disorders Sensory, Physical, and Health Impairments Giftedness	▲ Explain what is meant by "exceptional" students; distinguish the terms *handicap* and *disability;* and describe the characteristics of students who are mentally retarded, have specific learning disabilities, are gifted and talented, or have emotional disorders, behavioral disorders, communication disorders, or sensory or physical impairments or disabilities.
What Is Special Education? Public Law 94–142 A Continuum of Special Education Services	▲ Explain what is meant by "special education," analyze the laws that govern student placement in special education programs, and describe the continuum of services for students with special needs.
What Is Mainstreaming? Research on Mainstreaming Computers and Students with Disabilities Buddy Systems and Peer Tutoring Special Education Teams Social Integration of Students with Disabilities	▲ Explain what is meant by "mainstreaming," and describe and illustrate four approaches to accommodating instruction for mainstreamed students with special needs.

Elaine Wagner, vice principal at Pleasantville Elementary School, came into work one day and was stopped by the school secretary. "Good morning," she said, "There's a new parent here to see you, waiting in your office. Looks nervous—I gave her some coffee and settled her down."

"Thanks Beth," said Ms. Wagner. She went into her office and introduced herself to Helen Ross, the new parent.

"I appreciate your seeing me," said Ms. Ross. "We're planning to move to Pleasantville next fall, and I wanted to look at the schools before we move. We have one child, Tommy, going into second grade, and Annie is going into kindergarten. I'm really concerned about Tommy. In the school he's in now he's not doing very well. It's spring, and he's hardly reading at all. His teacher says he might have a learning disability, and the school wants to put him in special education. I don't like that idea. He's a normal, happy kid at home, and it would crush him to find out he's 'different,' but I want to do what's best for him. I guess the main thing I want to see is what you do with kids like Tommy."

"Well," said Ms. Wagner, "the most important thing I can tell you about our school is that our philosophy is that every child can learn, and it is our job to find out how to reach each one. I can't tell you exactly what we'd do with Tommy, of course, since I don't know him, but I can assure you of a few things. First, we'll attend to his reading problem right away. We believe in prevention and early intervention. If Tommy is having serious reading problems, we'll probably arrange to give him one-to-one tutoring so that he can catch up quickly with the other second-graders. Second, we'll try to keep him in his regular classroom if we possibly can. If he needs special education services he'll get them, but in this school we try everything to solve a child's learning problems before we refer him or her for testing that might lead to special education placement. Even if Tommy does qualify for special education, we'll structure his program so that he is with his regular class as much as possible. We will develop an individualized education plan for him Finally, I want to assure you that you will be very much involved in all decisions that have to do with Tommy, and that we'll talk with you frequently about his progress and ask for your help at home to make sure that Tommy is doing well."

"Ms. Wagner, that all sounds great. But how can you give Tommy the help he needs and still let him stay in his regular class?"

"Why don't I take you to see some of our classes in operation right now?" said Ms. Wagner. "I think you'll see what I mean. "

Ms. Wagner led the way through the brightly lit corridors covered with student projects, art work, and compositions. She turned in at Mr. Esposito's second-grade class. There she and Ms. Ross were met by a happy and excited buzz of activity. The children were working in small groups measuring each others' heights and the lengths of fingers, feet, and other parts of each others' bodies, and were trying to figure out how to measure the distance around each others' heads. Another teacher, Ms. Park, was working with some of the groups.

Ms. Wagner and Ms. Ross stepped into the hall. "What I wanted to show you," said Ms. Wagner, "is how we integrate our special education students in the regular classroom. Could you tell which students they were?"

"No," admitted Ms. Ross.

"That's what we hope to create—a classroom in which children with special needs are so well integrated that you can't pick them out. Ms. Park is the special education teacher for the younger grades, and she teams with Mr. Esposito during math and reading periods to serve all of the second-graders who need special services. Ms. Park will help any child who is having difficulty, not just special education students, since a large part of her job is to prevent students from ever needing special education. Sometimes she'll work with individual kids or small groups that need help. For example, she often does pre-teaching with kids she thinks might need it. She might have gone over measurement with some of the kids before this lesson so that they'd have a leg up on the concept."

Ms. Wagner led the way to the music room. She pointed through a window at a teacher working with one child. "What you see there is a tutor working with a first-grader who is having difficulty in reading. If your Tommy were here, this is what we might be doing with him. This tutor is provided by our Chapter 1 program."

"What's that?"

"Chapter 1 is a federal program that provides money to schools like ours. We try to use our Chapter 1 dollars to keep kids from falling behind in the first place, so they can stay out of special education and progress along with their classmates."

Ms. Wagner showed Ms. Ross all over the school, where they saw children with disabilities integrated in classrooms in a variety of ways. Ms. Ross was fascinated.

"I had no idea a school could be like this. I'm so excited that we're moving to Pleasantville. This looks like the perfect school for both of my children. I only wish we could have moved here two years ago!"

Pleasantville Elementary School is a school organized around two key ideas: first, that all children can learn; and second, that it is the school's responsibility to find ways to meet each child's needs in the regular classroom to the maximum extent possible. Pleasantville Elementary is organized to identify children's strengths as well as problems and to provide the best program it can for each child. In every school there are children who are at risk for school failure because of disabilities, previous failures, poor preparation at home, or other factors. This chapter describes children who are at risk and programs designed to help them achieve their full potential.

Who Are "Students at Risk" and What Educational Programs Exist for Them?

The term **students at risk** is increasingly used in education to refer to children who are likely to fail to learn adequately in a typical school program. The term "at risk" is borrowed from medicine, where it has long been used to describe individuals who do not have a given disease but are more likely than average to develop it. For example, a person with high blood pressure may be considered at risk for heart attack, a heavy smoker for emphysema or lung cancer. In the same way it is possible to identify factors that place a child at risk for school failure.

Before children enter school, we can predict that those with poor language development or other delayed development, those from low-income homes, or those who exhibit aggressive or withdrawn behavior will be more likely than other students to experience problems in school (Spivak *et al.*, 1986; Kellam and Werthamer-Larson, 1986; Silver and Hagin, 1990). After children begin school, such risk factors as poor reading performance and failing a grade become more important in predicting dropout, delinquency, and other serious school problems (Ensminger and Slusarcick, 1992; Lloyd, 1978). Some risk factors, such as evidence of brain damage or such genetic abnormalities as Down syndrome, make a child certain to have problems meeting the usual school demands, while others only increase the likelihood. For example, many children from low-income backgrounds do very well in school. Many brilliant adults were late walkers or talkers or were poor readers at first. Just as many heavy smokers never develop cancer or emphysema, students who are at risk may turn out to do well in school, but as a group they are much less likely to do so than are other students.

While this chapter takes a broad view of the concept of students at risk, it is well to keep in mind that important differences divide this group. Chief among these differences is the source of the risk—the difference, say, between students who are placed at risk for dropping out of school because of social factors, such as family dysfunction, poverty, or homelessness, and students who are at risk for academic failure because of cognitive, sensory, or physical disabilities or handicaps.

Educational programs for students at risk fall into three major categories: compensatory education, early intervention programs, and special education. Compensatory education is designed to prevent or remediate learning problems among students who are from low-income families or who attend schools in low-income communities. Some intervention programs target at-risk infants and toddlers to prevent later potential needs for remediation. Other intervention programs are aimed at keeping kids in school. Special education is designed to serve children

students at risk: students with backgrounds, characteristics, or behaviors that threaten or diminish their ability to succeed academically in typical school programs.

Helping Students at Risk

Because of the belief that all Americans need an education that allows them to become self-sufficient, contributing members of a democratic society, schools have always given serious attention to students who are at risk of failure. Special programs for providing extra help in critical subjects and skills have been a feature of American schools for at least half a century.

Because serious deficiencies generally become apparent in grades 4 through 8, many remediation efforts are focused on the middle school. Virtually every middle school in the country offers extra-help programs in reading and math. Typically, students who are not performing successfully are removed from their regular classes and placed in special remedial classes. Some schools use peer tutoring or individualized adult tutoring, programs that often operate outside the regular school day.

A study conducted by the Center for Research for Disadvantaged Students at The Johns Hopkins University verifies what many teachers already know. These pull-out programs do not work very well. Results from more than 1000 middle schools indicate that reading achievement increased only slightly when students were placed into special classes, and math achievement did not increase at all.

The same study showed that some remedial programs not commonly used in schools do work. When at-risk students are given two periods of math or reading in place of other electives, they show significant gains in those subjects. Increasing the instructional time is the key, and findings such as these fuel the demands in some communities for year-round public schools.

Other successful programs for middle school students who are at risk use computers, dramatic techniques, dialogues between students and teachers, and thining-skill development. For at-risk high-school students more dramatic changes are often needed to keep students in school until graduation. Corporate–school partnerships focus on teaching job skills, sometimes providing on-the-job training or loaning out computers for home use.

An alternative high school in Boston holds classes in a wing of a community college. Students do volunteer work at local soup kitchens and nursing homes and participate in a work/study program at a local children's hospital. Teachers take time to know each student personally. More than 75 percent of the students graduate, and 70 percent of graduates go on to 2- or 4-year colleges.

Critical Thinking

What reasons can you suggest for the poor results of pull-out programs? Why do you think double-period programs are more successful? What are some benefits and potential drawbacks of corporate-sponsored alternative programs for students at risk?

Mary Kopke, "All in the Family," *Teacher*, March 1992; Elizabeth Schulz, "Two Classes Are Better Than One," October 1991; Douglas MacIver

with more serious learning problems as well as children with physical or psychological problems.

Compensatory Education

Programs designed to overcome the problems associated with being brought up in low-income communities are called **compensatory education.** Compensatory education programs supplement the education of students from disadvantaged backgrounds who are experiencing trouble in school or who are felt to be in danger of having school problems. Two such programs, Head Start and Follow Through, are designed to give disadvantaged preschool and primary school children the skills necessary for a good start in school. However, the largest compensatory education

compensatory education: programs designed to supplement the education of low-achieving disadvantaged students.

program, and the one most likely to affect regular classroom teachers, is called **Chapter 1** (formerly Title I), a federally funded program that gives schools money to provide extra services for students who are from low-income families and are having trouble in school. Title I was begun in 1965 as part of President Johnson's War on Poverty. During the Reagan administration, the legislation relating to Title I programs was changed in the Education Consolidation and Improvement Act of 1981. Compensatory education programs were included under Chapter 1 of this act, which is why Title I programs are now called Chapter 1. More than 90 percent of all school districts, 75 percent of elementary schools, and 34 percent of middle schools and high schools provide Chapter 1 services (Birman *et al.*, 1987). In addition, many states supplement Chapter 1 with their own compensatory education programs.

Chapter 1 is not merely a transfer of money from the federal government to local school districts. According to the federal guidelines, Chapter 1 funds must be used to "supplement, not supplant" local educational efforts. This means that most school districts cannot use the money to reduce class size for all students or increase teachers' salaries; it must go directly toward increasing the academic achievement of low achievers in schools serving many disadvantaged students. The exception is that schools serving very disadvantaged neighborhoods—in which at least 75 percent of the students receive a free lunch—can use Chapter 1 money to improve the school as a whole.

Chapter 1 Programs.   Chapter 1 programs can take many forms. Most often a special Chapter 1 teacher provides remedial help to disadvantaged students experiencing difficulties in reading and, in many cases, in other subjects as well (Birman *et al.,* 1987). Programs of this type are called **pull-out programs** because the students are pulled out of their regular classes.

Pull-out programs have come under increasing criticism. A large-scale study of Chapter 1 pull-out programs found that students left without Chapter 1 services in the regular classroom achieved just as well as, and sometimes better than, students pulled out for special assistance (Glass and Smith, 1977). One major problem with pull-out programs is that there is often little coordination between the regular teacher and the Chapter 1 teacher, so that students who need the most consistent and structured instruction often have to deal with two completely different approaches (Allington and McGill-Franzen, 1989; Meyers *et al.*, 1990; Johnston *et al.*, 1985). One study found that half of a group of Chapter 1 teachers could not even name the reading text *series* their students were using in regular class; two-thirds could not name the specific book (Johnston *et al.*, 1985). These researchers argue that Chapter 1 programs must be directed at ensuring the success of students in the regular classroom and should therefore be closely coordinated with the regular teacher's instructional activities. For example, if a student is having trouble in the regular class with finding the main ideas of paragraphs, the Chapter 1 teacher should be working on main ideas, perhaps using the same instructional materials the classroom teacher is using.

Increasingly, school districts are avoiding the problems of pull-out programs by having the Chapter 1 teacher or aide work as a team teacher in the regular reading classroom (see Harpring, 1985). This way, two teachers can give reading lessons to two groups of students at the same time, which avoids some of the problems of within-class ability grouping (see Chapter 9). Team teaching can also increase the levels of communication and collaboration between the regular classroom teacher and the Chapter 1 teacher. However, such in-class models of Chapter 1 services have not been found to be any more effective than pull-out programs (Archambault, 1989; Anderson and Pellicer, 1990).

Connections

Recall the discussion of compensatory education in Chapter 3 in the context of early childhood education and developmentally appropriate practice.

Chapter 1: A federal program that gives school districts money to improve educational services for schools with many disadvantaged students.

pull-out programs: compensatory education programs in which students are placed in separate classes for remediation.

Many other innovative programs have been found to accelerate the achievement gains of disadvantaged students. Among these are tutoring programs, "continuous progress" programs in which students are frequently assessed and regrouped as they proceed through a sequence of skills, and other structured instructional programs with clear objectives and frequent assessments of students' attainment of these objectives (see Slavin and Madden, 1987; Slavin *et al.*, 1989). The most effective approaches, however, are ones that *prevent* students from ever having academic difficulties in the first place (Hamburg, 1992; Slavin *et al.*, 1994). These include high-quality preschool and kindergarten programs (Berrueta-Clement *et al.*, 1984; Reynolds, 1991), and one-to-one tutoring for first-graders who are just beginning to have reading problems (Pinnell, 1990; Wasik and Slavin, 1993).

Research on Compensatory Education. Early research on Title I programs found few positive effects on students (Glass and Smith, 1977; National Institute of Education, 1978). However, later studies focusing on Title I/Chapter 1 programs that were well implemented found that these programs do help low achievers gain one grade equivalent each year; that is, although (on average) the programs do not

Figure 12.1   Effect of Title I (Chapter 1) Programs on Achievement

Low-income students who participated in these programs gained more in reading and math than low-income students not in special programs. However, the extra help did not close the gap in achievement between low-income and other students.

From Carter, 1984, p. 7.

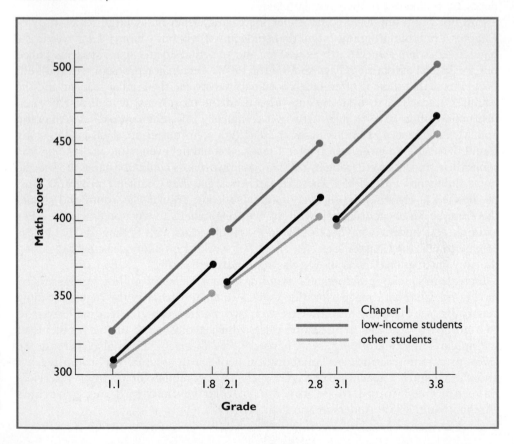

significantly accelerate these students, they keep them from falling further behind. Without compensatory programs, students eligible for Chapter 1 gain only about two-thirds of a grade equivalent each year, which means they fall further behind each year (Cooley and Leinhardt, 1980).

The largest and most carefully controlled study of compensatory education found consistent benefits of the program, particularly for students in the early grades (Carter, 1984). These results are illustrated in Figure 12.1. Note that in grades 1, 2, and 3, low-income students receiving Chapter 1 services started at the same achievement level as other low-income students not in Chapter 1. By the end of the year, the Chapter 1 students significantly exceeded the non–Chapter 1 low-income students. However, as in the early studies, Chapter 1 programs did not narrow the achievement gap between low-income and regular students, although it did keep the gap from widening (see also Kennedy *et al.*, 1986).

Research on Chapter 1 classes finds that, in general, effective practices that work well in regular classes also work well in Chapter 1 classes. For example, more instructional time, time on-task, and other indicators of effective classroom management are important predictors of achievement gain in Chapter 1 classes (Stein *et al.*, 1989; Cooley, 1981; Crawford, 1989), as are improved curricular approaches (Knapp *et al.*, 1990; Presseisen, 1988). Improving the quality of curriculum and instruction in the regular classroom can be as important or more important for the achievement of Chapter 1 students than the amount or quality of supplementary instruction (Knapp and Shields, 1990; Slavin *et al.*, 1989).

Early Intervention Programs

Traditionally, Chapter 1 and state and local compensatory education programs have overwhelmingly emphasized remediation. They typically provide services to children after they have already fallen behind. However, in recent years there has been an increasing emphasis on prevention and early intervention rather than remediation in serving children who are at risk for school failure (see Slavin *et al.*, 1994). For example, the findings of long-term benefits of preschool for disadvantaged children (Berrueta-Clement *et al.*, 1984) have led to a dramatic expansion of preschool programs for disadvantaged four-year-olds. Programs emphasizing

Connections

How might the principle of "scaffolding," discussed in Chapter 2, be applied to teaching students at risk? See Rosenshine, B. and Meister, C. (1993). The use of scaffolds for teaching higher-level cognitive strategies. In A. Woolfolk (ed.). *Readings and cases in educational psychology.* Boston: Allyn and Bacon.

These children attend an early intervention program in their community. How do such programs differ from traditional compensatory education programs?

infant stimulation, parent training, and other services for children from birth to age five also have been found to have long-term effects on at-risk students' school success (Garber, 1988; Ramey and Campbell, 1984; Wasik and Karweit, 1994). In addition to such preventive programs, there is evidence that early intervention can keep children from falling behind in the early grades. For example, a program called Reading Recovery (Pinnell *et al.*, 1988) provides one-to-one tutoring from specially trained teachers to first-graders who are not reading adequately. This program is able to bring nearly all at-risk children to adequate levels of performance and has long-lasting positive effects. Other structured tutoring programs have had similar effects (Wasik and Slavin, 1993).

Success for All (Slavin *et al.*, 1992) is a comprehensive approach to prevention and early intervention in elementary schools serving very disadvantaged students. This program provides research-based preschool, kindergarten, and grades 1–5 reading programs, one-to-one tutoring for first-graders who need it, family support services, and other changes in instruction, curriculum, and school organization designed to ensure that students do not fall behind in the early grades, no matter what! Longitudinal studies of Success for All have shown that students in this program read substantially better than do students in matched control schools throughout the elementary grades, and they are far less likely to be assigned to special education or to fail a grade (see Madden *et al.*, 1993).

Research on Success for All, Reading Recovery, and other preventive strategies shows that at-risk children can succeed if we are willing to provide them high-quality instruction and intensive services early in their school careers. At risk does not mean doomed to fail for any but the most seriously disabled children.

Prevention Programs

While early intervention programs, such as Success for All, are designed to prevent academic failure in children who are at risk because of their achievement problems or socioeconomic status, other intervention and prevention programs address specific social and behavioral problems of students that contribute to school failure or to dropping out of school. Prevention and intervention programs may target, for example, child abuse or neglect, drug or alcohol abuse, teen pregnancy, truancy, delinquency, and other problems that involve students' families and communities. The following sections address two of these problem areas.

Child Abuse Prevention.   The Child Abuse Prevention and Treatment Act (1974) defines child abuse and neglect as "physical or mental injury, sexual abuse, negligent treatment, or maltreatment of a child under the age of eighteen by a person who is responsible for the child's welfare under circumstances which indicate that the child's health or welfare is harmed or threatened thereby." Certain social and cultural factors seem to increase the chances of child abuse. These include parents' history of being abused, poverty and undereducation, and a physically violent environment (Kauffman, 1989). However, child abuse and neglect occur among all ethnic groups and all socioeconomic levels.

Teachers have both an ethical responsibility and (in most states) a legal one to report incidents of suspected child abuse or neglect (Rose, 1980). Although it is sometimes difficult to differentiate the characteristics of abuse and neglect from other sources of injury (such as accidents), it is better to be on the safe side so

---

Connections

Other problems of childhood and adolescence, such as those described in Chapter 3, may place students at risk of school failure. Recall factors relating to student diversity discussed in Chapter 4 that may place students at risk, such as poverty and limited English proficiency.

that the situation can be investigated. Most reporting laws protect teachers who report suspected child abuse in good faith (Beezer, 1985). All teachers should learn the procedures to follow if they suspect that a student has been abused or neglected (see Bear *et al.*, 1992/93). Table 12.1 presents several symptoms of abuse and neglect.

Drug and Alcohol Abuse Prevention.   Unfortunately, drug and alcohol abuse in many schools is an everyday occurrence. While drug abuse is diminishing, it is still at a high level (see U.S. Department of Health and Human Services, 1991). Figure 12.2 shows that 41 percent of all seniors reported using marijuana at some time, and about 14 percent of them had used marijuana within the past month. About 2 percent of the seniors reported *daily* use of marijuana, and 3.7 percent reported daily alcohol use. Alarmingly, there has been a trend toward students using drugs at earlier grades; almost 20 percent of eighth-graders have used some illicit drugs, usually marijuana.

One of the main factors in drug and alcohol use is peer pressure (Zucker, 1979). Another risk factor for alcohol abuse is parents drinking at home (Lawson *et al.*, 1983). Occasional drug and alcohol use are only slightly more common among boys than girls, but heavy drinking or daily marijuana use is twice as common among boys, and boys are more likely to use cocaine and heroin. Students planning to go to college are less likely to use marijuana and other drugs than those who do not have college plans (U.S . Department of Health and Human Services, 1991).

Table 12.1   Symptoms of Child Abuse and Neglect

Teachers have an ethical and legal responsibility to report suspected cases of child abuse and neglect. To meet this responsibility, they must know the symptoms of maltreatment.

SOURCE: Berdine and Blackhurst, 1981, pp. 44. Reprinted by permission of Scott Foresman and Company.

Abuse	Neglect
1. evidence of repeated injury	1. clothing inappropriate for the weather
2. new injuries before previous ones have healed	2. torn, tattered, unwashed clothing
3. frequent complaints about abdominal pain	3. poor skin hygiene
4. evidence of bruises	4. rejection by other children because of body odor
5. bruises of different ages	5. need for glasses, dental work, hearing aid, or other health services
6. welts	6. lack of proper nourishment
7. wounds, cuts, or bruises	7. consistent tiredness or sleepiness in class
8. scalding liquid burns with well-defined parameters	8. consistent very early school arrival
9. caustic burns	9. frequent absenteeism or chronic tardiness
10. frostbite	10. tendency to hang around school after dismissal
11. cigarette burns	

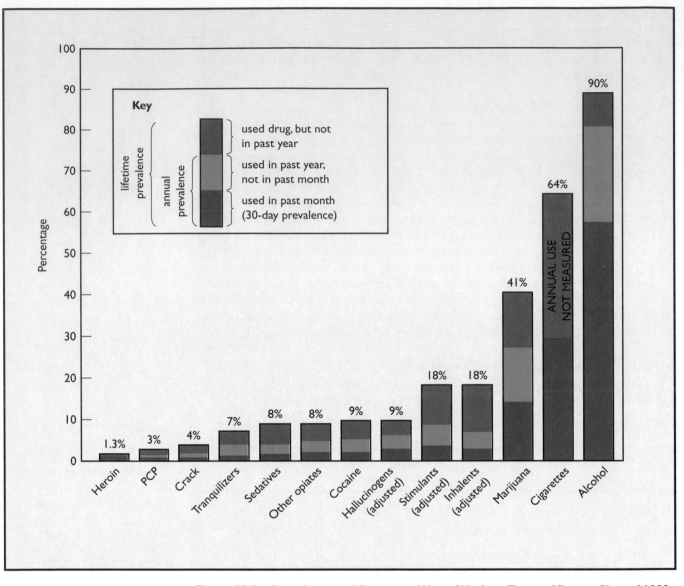

Figure 12.2   Prevalence and Recency of Use of Various Types of Drugs, Class of 1990
From U.S. Department of Health and Human Services, 1991.

Not surprisingly, heavy use of drugs and alcohol can seriously impair students' academic performance. The drug-use statistics cited for high school seniors probably understate the problem, because many drug and alcohol users never make it to the senior class.

If a teacher suspects that a student is using drugs or alcohol or has problems in the home that might lead to such behavior, it is a good idea to consult the school counselor or other appropriate school staff members. Also, there are now several drug- and alcohol-abuse prevention programs available (for example, Gern and Gern, 1986; Botvin, 1984; National Clearinghouse for Drug Abuse Information, 1986).

Self-Check

What do "at risk" and "placed at risk" mean in reference to students? List several examples of the kinds of conditions that may place students at risk. Begin a three-column chart to compare and contrast compensatory education programs, early intervention and prevention programs, and special education programs in terms of the student populations they serve, their aims, their general provisions, and their effectiveness.

Who Are "Exceptional" Learners?

Some students need special programs other than compensatory programs and early intervention and prevention programs that will help them to meet their full potential. These students are often called **exceptional learners** or are said to exhibit one or more exceptionalities in relation to their ability to learn.

In one sense, all children are exceptional. No two are exactly alike in their ways of learning and behaving, in their activities and preferences, skills and motivations. All students would benefit from programs uniquely tailored to their individual needs.

However, schools cannot practically meet the precise needs of every student. For the sake of efficiency, students are grouped into classes and given common instructional experiences designed to provide the greatest benefit to the largest number at a moderate cost. This system works reasonably well for the great majority of students. However, some students do not fit easily into this mold. Some have physical or sensory disabilities, such as hearing or vision impairment or orthopedic disabilities, that restrict their ability to participate in the regular classroom program without special assistance. Other students are mentally retarded or have emotional disorders or learning disabilities that make it difficult for them to learn in the regular classroom without special assistance. Finally, some students have such outstanding talents that the regular classroom teacher is unable to provide for their unique needs without help. **Exceptionality** is defined more by the challenges a student presents for the instructional program than by the characteristics of the student. For example, Mercer (1973) notes that most children are labeled "mentally retarded" only after they enter school, and that many children whose behavior at home is well within normal limits may still be labeled "exceptional" by the school system (Edgerton, 1984). She introduced the concept of "six-hour retardation" to describe students who are only "retarded" in school.

To receive special education services, a student must have one of a small number of categories of disabilities or disorders. These general labels, such as "learning disabled," "mentally retarded," or "orthopedically disabled," cover a wide diversity of problems. As experience and research produce a clearer understanding of **handicaps** and **disabilities,** categories evolve. For example, many students who would previously have been called mildly retarded are now identified as learning disabled. In fact, the practical distinctions among slow learners, students with learning disabilities, and students with mild retardation are difficult to make consistently and vary from district to district and from tester to tester (see Ysseldyke and Algozzine, 1982; Gerber and Semmel, 1984). In addition, labels

exceptional learners: students who have abilities or problems so significant that the students require special education or other services to reach their potential.

exceptionality: mental, emotional, or physical condition that creates special educational needs.

handicap: a condition imposed on a person with disabilities by society, the physical environment, or the person's attitude.

disability: the inability to do something specific such as walk or hear.

Type of Disability	Percent of Children Aged 3–21 Served		
	1976–1977	1982–1983	1988–1989
All conditions	8.33	10.73	11.30
Learning disabled	1.80	4.39	4.94
Mentally retarded	2.16	1.91	1.40
Emotionally disturbed	0.64	0.89	0.89
Speech impaired	2.94	2.85	2.41
Hard of hearing and deaf	0.20	0.18	0.14
Visually impaired	0.09	0.07	0.06
Orthopedically disabled	0.20	0.14	0.12
Other health impaired	0.32	0.13	0.11
Multidisabled	—	0.16	0.21
Deaf-blind	—	0.01	0.01

Table 12.2   Percent of Children Served in Special Education Programs

The largest segments of the school-age special needs population are people with speech impairments, learning disabilities, and mental retardation. The size of the different segments changes somewhat as definitions of the special needs change.

SOURCE: Adapted from National Center for Educational Statistics, 1988, 1991.

can be harmful to the students the special education system is designed to serve. Labels tend to stick, making change difficult, such that the labels themselves can become handicaps for the student. Education professionals must also avoid using labels in a way that unintentionally stigmatizes students, dehumanizes them, segregates them socially from their peers, or encourages discrimination against them in any form. Teachers of exceptional learners need to be sensitive to the political and social dimensions of being exceptional. Many students resent being called by the generic labels for disability groups, for example, such as "the retarded" or "the learning disabled."

The appropriateness of the terms *handicap* and *disability* have also been questioned. A *disability* is a functional limitation a person has that interferes with the person's physical or cognitive abilities. A *handicap,* on the other hand, is a condition imposed on a person with disabilities by society, the physical environment, or the person's attitude. For example, a student who uses a wheelchair is handicapped by a lack of access ramps. *Handicap* is therefore not a synonym for *disability*.

Even though labels are neither exact nor unchanging and may be harmful in some situations, they are a useful shorthand to indicate the type and severity of a student's disabilities, as long as you remember the limitations of the labels. The following sections discuss characteristics of students with the types of disabilities most commonly seen in schools.

Types of Exceptionalities and the Numbers of Students Served

Some exceptionalities, such as impairments of vision and hearing, are relatively easy to define and measure. Others, such as mental retardation, learning disabilities, and emotional disorders, are much harder to define, and their definitions have evolved over time. In fact, there has been a dramatic change over the past twenty years in these categories, with substantially increasing numbers of students receiving special education services for learning disabilities. Table 12.2 shows the percentages of all students in each category of exceptionality in 1976–1977, 1982–1983, and 1988–89. Note that while most of the easily defined physical impairments have remained fairly stable, the relative number of students categorized as learning disabled has steadily increased, and the use of the category "mentally retarded" has diminished. This trend continues today (see U.S. Department of Education, 1992).

Other than the changes over time among the categories, there are several pieces of information worthy of note in Table 12.2. First, notice that the overall percentage of students receiving special education in 1988–1989 was more than 11 percent; one out of every nine students aged three to twenty-one was categorized as exceptional. Second, serious physical disabilities, such as deafness, blindness, and orthopedic disabilities, are relatively rare. Learning problems, speech disorders, and emotional disorders are considerably more common, accounting for about 73 percent of all students receiving special education services. In a class of thirty a regular classroom teacher will, on average, have one student with learning disabilities and one with a speech impairment. In contrast, only about one class in forty is likely to have a student who is hard of hearing, visually impaired, or otherwise physically disabled.

Mental Exceptionalities

The Federal Rehabilitation Act of 1973 (Section 504) lists four categories of **mental disability**: retardation, learning disability, psychiatric disability, and head trauma. The term **cognitive impairment** is also used for mental disability. Giftedness in some of its forms is a mental or cognitive exceptionality not normally regarded as a disability. The following sections describe these and other exceptionalities in greater detail.

Mental Retardation

Approximately 13 percent of all students with disabilities are mentally retarded (U.S. Department of Education, 1991). There are several definitions of **mental retardation.** The 1992 American Association on Mental Retardation (AAMR) defined mental retardation as follows:

mental disability: cognitive impairment as a result of retardation, learning disability, psychiatric disability, or head trauma.

cognitive impairment: mental disability; impairment of the ability to think, process information, or reason.

mental retardation: condition, usually present at birth, that results in below-average intellectual skills and poor adaptive behavior.

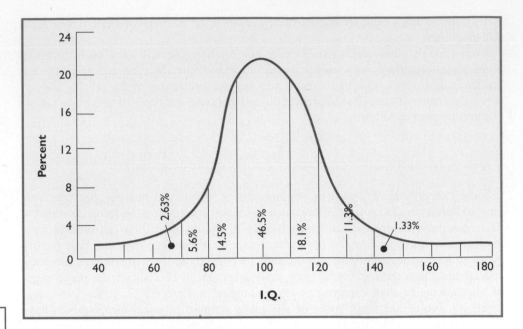

Figure 12.3

Distribution of Intelligence Test Scores

The distribution of intelligence test scores resembles a bell-shaped curve, called a normal curve. Scores from 80 to 120 are in the low-average to high-average range.

Adapted from Thorndike *et al.*, 1986, p. 29

Connections

The concept and origin of intelligence and its measurement are discussed more fully in Chapters 4 and 14.

Mental retardation refers to substantial limitations in present functioning. It is characterized by significantly subaverage intellectual function, existing concurrently with related limitations in two or more of the following applicable adaptive skill areas: communication, self-care, home living, social skills, community use, self-direction, health and safety, functional academics, leisure and work. Mental retardation manifests before age 18.

This means that people with mental retardation have low scores on tests of intelligence and also show difficulty in maintaining standards of personal independence and social responsibility expected for their age and cultural group (Luckasson *et al.,*1992). In addition, these impairments in intelligence and adaptive behavior become apparent sometime between conception and age eighteen.

One of the best responses to mental retardation is early intervention. Studies have shown that preschool programs providing cognitively stimulating environments and instruction in basic skills can improve chances of later school success (Casto and Mastropieri, 1986; Garber, 1988).

Causes of Mental Retardation.   Among the many causes of mental retardation are genetic inheritance; chromosomal abnormalities, such as Down syndrome; diseases passed between mother and fetus in utero, such as rubella (German measles) and syphilis; fetal chemical dependency syndromes caused by a mother's abuse of alcohol or cocaine during pregnancy; birth accidents that result in oxygen deprivation; childhood diseases and accidents, such as encephalitis and head trauma; and toxic contamination from the environment, such as lead poisoning. Mental retardation may be classified on the basis of the origin or cause of the condition or in terms of the severity of the impairment. For school systems, the severity of impairment is especially important.

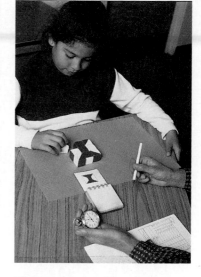

This student is taking the Weschler Intelligence Scale for Children–Revised, a widely used test for measuring children's IQ. If the test supports behavioral and social observations that she may be mentally retarded, how will you help her adapt to the school environment?

Intelligence Quotient (IQ).   To understand how severity of impairment in children with mental retardation is identified, it is first important to recall (from Chapter 4) the concept of IQ, or **intelligence quotient,** derived from scores on standardized tests. Figure 12.3 illustrates a theoretical distribution of IQs among all students on the Stanford-Binet Intelligence Scale, which has a mean of 100 and a standard deviation of 15 (see Chapter 1 for definition of standard deviation). Notice that the IQ scores form a bell-shaped curve, called a **normal curve.** The greatest number of scores fall near the mean, with fewer scores extending above and below the mean. Students with IQs above 70 are generally regarded as being in the normal range. Slightly more than 2 percent of students have IQs below this range.

Consistent with AAMR recommendations, education professionals do not use IQs alone to determine severity of cognitive impairment. They take into account a student's school and home performance, scores on other tests, and the student's cultural background. IQ tests have been criticized for cultural bias. Critics also claim that IQ scores have been misused to discriminate against certain groups or to group students inappropriately for instruction or special education services (Hilliard, 1992).

Classifications of Mental Retardation.   The AAMR lists four degrees of severity of mental retardation in terms of ranges of IQ, including mild retardation (IQs 50–55 to 70–75), moderate retardation (IQs 35–40 to 50–55), severe (IQs 20–25 to 35–40), and profound (IQs below 20–25) (Luckasson *et al.,* 1992). Mild retardation is often not diagnosed until children enter school because their behavior is within or near the normal range at home (Robinson and Robinson, 1976).

In another common classification, students with mild retardation, typically with IQs between 55 and 70, are regarded as "educable" (EMR)——able to learn basic academic skills up to a fifth-grade level. Students with moderate retardation (IQs 40–55) are classified as "trainable" (TMR), able to learn independent self-care and job skills for sheltered workshops (MacMillan and Forness, 1992). Children below IQ 50 are often termed "custodial" and usually receive out-of-school services. This classification system is challenged by some professionals who believe that the emphasis in present-day special education is that *all* people can learn and that education and training cannot be clearly differentiated (Smith and Luckasson, 1992). However, most school districts use this or a similar simplified system of classification (see Matson and Mulick, 1988).

The Theory Into Practice on "Teaching Adaptive Behavior Skills" suggests ways regular classroom teachers can help students who are mentally retarded to acquire such skills. Specific ways of modifying instruction for students with special needs are discussed later in this chapter.

Connections

The strategies for teaching adaptive behavior skills mirror the strategies for helping students in their socioemotional development, discussed in Chapter 3.

intelligence quotient: an intelligence test score that for people of average intelligence should be near 100.

normal curve: bell-shaped symmetrical distribution of scores in which most scores fall near the mean, with progressively fewer occurring as distance from the mean increases.

Theory Into Practice
Teaching Adaptive Behavior Skills

Instructional objectives for helping students who are mentally retarded acquire adaptive behavior skills are not very different from those that are valuable for all students. Every student needs to cope with the demands of school, develop interpersonal relationships, develop language skills, grow emotionally, and take care of personal needs. Teachers can help students by directly instructing or supporting students in the following areas (see Hardman *et al.*, 1993).

1. *Coping with the Demands of School:* attending to learning tasks, organizing work, following directions, managing time, and asking questions.

2. *Developing Interpersonal Relationships:* learning to work cooperatively with others, responding to social cues in the environment, using socially acceptable language, responding appropriately to teacher directions and cues, and enhancing social awareness.

3. *Developing Language Skills:* understanding directions, communicating needs and wants, expressing ideas, listening attentively, using appropriate voice modulation and inflection.

4. *Socioemotional Development:* seeking out social participation and interaction (decreasing social withdrawal) and being motivated to work (decreasing work avoidance, tardiness, and idleness).

5. *Personal Care:* practicing appropriate personal hygiene, dressing independently, taking care of personal property, moving from one location to another.

Learning Disabilities

Learning disabilities are not a single condition but a name for a wide variety of specific disabilities that are presumed to stem from some dysfunction of the brain or central nervous system. The following definition is adapted from the National Joint Committee on Learning Disabilities (1988, p. 1).

> Learning disabilities is a general term for a diverse group of disorders characterized by significant difficulties in the acquisition and use of listening, speaking, reading, writing, reasoning, or computing. These disorders stem from the individual and may occur across the life span. Problems in self-regulatory behaviors, social perception, and social interaction may exist with learning disabilities but do not by themselves constitute a learning disability. Learning disabilities may occur concomitantly with other handicapping conditions but are not the result of those conditions.

Older definitions of learning disability included specific reference to dyslexia, a severely impaired ability to read; dysgraphia, an impaired ability to write; and dyscalculia, an impaired ability to learn mathematics. The source of these conditions in brain dysfunction can seldom be proven, however, and these terms must be used with caution (Smith and Luckasson, 1993).

Identifying Learning Disabilities.   Different interpretations of the many definitions of learning disability have led state and local school districts to vary widely in their eligibility requirements and provisions for students with learning disabilities. The increasing numbers of students identified as having learning disabilities (recall Table 12.2) has contributed to the confusion. In 1988–89, for example, nearly 47 percent of all children with disabilities were identified as having specific learning disabilities (U.S. Department of Education, 1992).

Education professionals have the task of distinguishing learning-disabled students from low achievers and students with mild mental retardation. In some

learning disabilities (LD): disorders that impede academic progress of people who are not mentally retarded or emotionally disturbed.

school districts a student who falls more than two grade levels behind expectations and has an IQ in the normal range is likely to be called learning disabled. Some characteristics of students with learning disabilities are listed in Table 12.3.

Attention Deficit Disorder. Students with specific learning disabilities often also have behavioral problems. They may be unable to control their behavior, for example, and have difficulty remaining still and paying attention (Aleman, 1990; Swanson, 1980). Attention deficits become a particularly serious problem as students get beyond the second grade (McKinney and Speece, 1986). Such children may be labeled impulsive or hyperactive and are sometimes treated with behavior-control drugs. A new general classification has been proposed for children who have difficulty focusing their attention long enough or well enough to learn, called **attention deficit disorder (ADD).** Distinguishing attention deficit disorder from learning disabilities and from behavioral disorders or misbehavior is a continuing challenge, especially since students with learning disabilities often have attentional and emotional and behavioral problems as well.

Attention deficit hyperactivity disorder (ADHD) is a special designation for students who cannot concentrate attention because they cannot remain still for long. This differentiates them from students with learning disabilities who have attention deficits for other unknown reasons (American Psychiatric Association, 1987). Children with attention deficit disorders do not qualify for special education unless they also have some other disability condition that is defined in the law (Aleman, 1990).

Characteristics of Students with Learning Disabilities. On average, students with learning disabilities tend to have lower self-esteem than nondisabled students (Chapman, 1988; Bear *et al.*, 1991). However, as mentioned previously, on most social dimensions children with learning disabilities resemble other low achievers (Larrivee and Horne, 1991; Sater and French, 1989).

Boys are more likely than girls to be labeled learning disabled. Males, African Americans, and children from families in which the head of household has not attended college tend to be overrepresented in special education classes, while female students are underrepresented (U.S. Department of Education, 1991, pp. 52–53).

Communication Disorders

One of the most common exceptionalities is communication disorders—problems with speech and language. About one in every forty students has a communication disorder serious enough to warrant speech therapy or other special education services.

While the terms "speech" and "language" are often used interchangeably, they are not the same. Language is the communication of ideas using symbols and includes written language, sign language, gesture, and other modes of communication in addition to oral speech. Speech refers to the formation and sequencing of sounds. It is quite possible to have a speech disorder without a language disorder or a language disorder without a speech disorder.

Speech Disorders. There are many kinds of **speech disorders.** The most common are articulation (or phonological) disorders, such as omissions, distortions, or substitutions of sounds. For example, some students have difficulty pronouncing "r's," saying "sowee" for "sorry." Others have lisps, substituting "th" for "s," saying "thnake" for "snake."

- normal intelligence or even giftedness

- discrepancy between intelligence and performance

- delays in achievement

- attention deficit or high distractibility

- hyperactivity or impulsiveness

- poor motor coordination and spatial relation ability

- difficulty solving problems

- perceptual anomalies, such as reversing letters, words, or numbers

- difficulty with self-motivated, self-regulated activities

- overreliance on teacher and peers for assignments

- specific disorders of memory, thinking, or language

- immature social skills

- disorganized approach to learning

Table12.3

Characteristics of Students with Learning Disabilities

SOURCE: Adapted from Smith, D. S. and Luckasson, T. (1993). *Introduction to Special Education.* Boston: Allyn & Bacon, pp. 227–233.

attention deficit disorder: the inability to concentrate for long periods of time.

speech disorders: articulation problems occurring most frequently among children in the early elementary school grades.

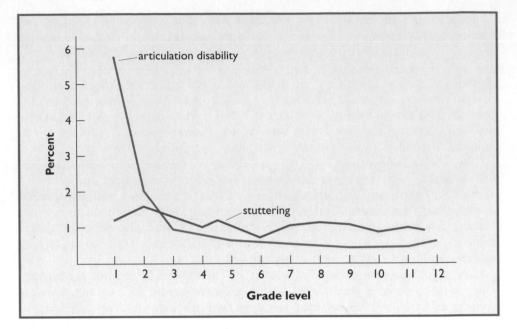

Figure 12.4

Prevalence of Speech Impairment by Grade Level

Articulation problems are most common among children in the early elementary grades. These problems, as well as stuttering, generally fall off with age.

From Hull and Hull, 1973, p. 200.

Misarticulated words are common and developmentally normal for many children in kindergarten and first grade but drop off rapidly through the school years. Figure 12.4 shows that moderate and extreme deviations in articulation diminish over the school years, with or without speech therapy (Shriberg, 1980). For this reason, speech therapists will often decide not to work with a child with a mild articulation problem. However, speech therapy is called for if a student cannot be understood or if the problem is causing the student psychological or social difficulties (such as teasing).

A less common but often more troublesome speech disorder is stuttering, the "abnormal timing of speech sound initiation" (Perkins, 1980). Everyone stutters sometimes, but children with a serious problem stutter to a degree that impairs their ability to communicate. Stutterers may prolong sounds ("wwwwwe wwwwwent to the store") or they may have difficulty making any sound at times. It is often particular sounds or words or situations that give stutterers difficulties. Unfortunately, anxiety increases stuttering, creating a vicious cycle: when stutterers are afraid of stuttering, their fear makes them stutter.

With or without therapy, stuttering usually disappears by early adolescence. However, as in the case of articulation problems, speech therapy is often prescribed for stuttering because of the psychological and social problems it causes youngsters.

Speech disorders of all kinds are diagnosed by and treated by speech pathologists or speech therapists. The classroom teacher's role is less important here than with the mental exceptionalities. However, the classroom teacher does have one crucial role to play: displaying acceptance of students with speech disorders. Recall (from Figure 12.4) that most speech disorders will eventually resolve themselves. The lasting damage is more often psychological than phonological; students with speech disorders often undergo a great deal of teasing and social rejection. Teachers can model acceptance of the child with speech disorders in several ways. First, they should be patient with students who are stuttering or have trouble producing words, never finishing a student's sentence or allowing others to do so. Second, they should avoid putting students with speech problems into high-pressure situations requiring quick verbal responses. Third, teachers should refrain from correcting students' articulation in class.

Language Disorders.   Language disorders are impairments of the ability to understand language or to express ideas in one's native language. Problems due to limited English-speaking ability for students whose first language is not English are not considered **language disorders** (these are discussed in Chapter 4).

Difficulties in understanding language (*receptive language disorders*) or in communicating (*expressive language disorders*) may result from such physical problems as hearing or speech impairment. If not, they are likely to indicate mental retardation or learning disabilities (Wallach and Miller, 1988). Many students from disadvantaged backgrounds come to school with what appear to be receptive or expressive language disorders, but that in fact result from a lack of experience with standard English. Preschool programs rich in verbal experience and direct instruction in the fundamentals of standard English have been found to be effective in overcoming language problems characteristic of children from disadvantaged homes (see Chapter 3).

Emotional and Behavioral Disorders

All students are likely to have emotional problems at some point in their school career, but about 1 percent have such serious, long lasting, and pervasive emotional or psychiatric disorders that they require special education. As in the case of learning disabilities, seriously emotionally disturbed students are far more likely to be boys than girls, by a ratio of more than three to one (U.S. Department of Education, 1992).

A student with an **emotional disorder** has been defined as one whose educational performance is adversely affected over a long period of time to a marked degree by any of the following conditions:

1. an inability to learn that cannot be explained by intellectual, sensory, or health factors
2. an inability to build or maintain satisfactory interpersonal relationships with peers and teachers
3. inappropriate types of behavior or feelings under normal circumstances
4. a general, pervasive mood of unhappiness or depression
5. a tendency to develop physical symptoms, pains, or fears associated with personal or school problems

Causes of Emotional Disturbance.   Serious and long-term emotional disorders may be the result of a number of causal factors in the makeup and development of an individual. Neurological functioning, psychological processes, a history of maladaptations, self-concept, and lack of social acceptance all play a role (Hardman *et al.,* 1993). Some of the same factors, including family dysfunction, also play a role in short-term disturbances that may temporarily affect a child's school performance.

language disorders: impairments in the ability to understand language or to express ideas in one's native language.

emotional disorders: category of exceptionality characterized by problems with learning, interpersonal relationships, and control of feelings and behavior.

Connections

Distinguish the emotional and conduct disorders discussed here from the resolution of psychosocial crises during child and adolescent development, described in Chapter 3 in connection with Erikson's work.

Many factors affecting families may disrupt a student's sense of security and self-worth for a period of time. Changes in the family structure, for example, may leave a child depressed, angry, insecure, defensive, and lonely, especially in the case of divorce, relocation to a new community, the addition of a younger sibling, the addition of a new step-parent, or the death or serious illness of a family member.

Researchers have investigated the effects of divorce on children. Longfellow (1979) summarized one such survey. At ages seven and eight children showed feelings of sadness, loss, fear, and insecurity. They felt abandoned and rejected. Children aged nine and ten reported that they were ashamed and outraged, yet also lonely and rejected. The children who were thirteen to eighteen years old reported anger, shame, sadness, and embarrassment. In a five-year follow-up study Wallerstein and Ketty (1980) reported that 34 percent of those surveyed were happy and 29 percent were doing reasonably well; 37 percent, however, still reported feelings of depression. Death or serious illness in a child's family is also likely to cause anxiety, depression, or behavior problems. Young children may not fully understand what death means. If a student experiences a death in his or her family, the teacher should at least acknowledge it and perhaps take the opportunity to discuss the topic of death, but then return the student to a regular routine as soon as possible.

One problem in identifying serious emotional disorders is that the term covers a wide range of behaviors, from aggression or hyperactivity to withdrawal or inability to make friends (Epstein and Cullinan, 1992) to anxiety and phobias (King and Ollendick, 1989). Also, children with emotional disorders quite frequently have other disabilities, such as learning disabilities or mental retardation, and it is often hard to tell whether an emotional problem is causing the diminished academic performance or school failure is causing the emotional problem.

Procedures used to identify children with serious emotional disturbances include observation, behavior rating scales and inventories, and psychological testing. Observation is the most direct method and requires the least amount of interference on the teacher's part (Taylor, 1984). However, although observation can help document the behavior under question, a trained professional's judgment is required in deciding the amount, frequency, or degree of behavior that must be present for a student to be characterized as "disturbed" or "disordered."

Behavior rating scales used by teachers provide a measure of behavior characteristics. For example, a behavior rating scale might include a number of items (descriptions such as "is hostile and aggressive toward peers") grouped according to various categories of behavior (such as withdrawn, immature, aggressive). This information compares the behavior of one student with that of others and profiles the student's behavioral difficulties (see Achenbach and McConaughy, 1987; Walker *et al.*, 1988).

Characteristics of Students with Emotional and Conduct Disorders.   Scores of characteristics are associated with emotional disturbance (Kneedler, 1984). The important issue is the *degree* of the behavior problem. Virtually any behavior that is exhibited excessively over a long period of time might be considered an indication of emotional disturbance.

However, most students identified as emotionally disturbed share some general characteristics. These include poor academic achievement, poor interpersonal relationships, and poor self-esteem (Kneedler, 1984). Quay and Werry (1986) noted four general categories: conduct disorder, anxiety-withdrawal, immaturity, and socialized-aggressive disorder. Children who fall into the "conduct disorder" category are characterized frequently as disobedient, distractible, selfish, jealous, destructive, impertinent, resistive, and disruptive. Quay and Werry noted that these factors represent behaviors that are maladaptive or sources of personal distress, except "socialized aggressive," which seems to be tied more to poor home conditions that model or reward aggressive behavior.

However, the inclusion of **conduct disorders** in classifications of emotional and behavioral disorders is controversial. By law, students with conduct disorders must have some other recognized disability or disorder to receive special education services.

Aggressive Behavior.   Most children engage in aggressive acting-out behavior from time to time. However, emotionally disturbed students with conduct disorders may frequently fight, steal, destroy property, and refuse to obey teachers. These students tend to be disliked by their peers, their teachers, and even (sometimes especially) their parents. They typically do not respond to punishment or threats, though they may be skilled at avoiding punishment. Aggressive children not only pose a threat to the school and to their peers, but they also put themselves in grave danger. Aggressive children, particularly boys, often develop serious emotional problems later in life, have difficulty holding jobs, and become involved in criminal behavior (Robins, 1974).

The most effective treatments for aggressive emotionally disturbed students are well-structured, consistently applied behavior modification programs, such as those described in Chapter 11 (see Brigham *et al.*, 1985), and teaching students alternative ways of responding to situations that usually lead to aggression (Knapczyk, 1988). Many times these programs can be used in the regular classroom and thus avoid segregating the student with a group of equally aggressive peers (Madden and Slavin, 1983a). Successful treatments for seriously emotionally disturbed students have also used special education resource rooms one or two hours a day for assistance (Glavin *et al.*, 1971).

Withdrawn and Immature Behavior.   While the aggressive child causes distressing problems to teachers and peers, children who are withdrawn, immature, low in self-esteem, or depressed can be just as disturbed. Typically, such students have few friends or may play with children much younger than themselves. They may have elaborate fantasies or daydreams and either very poor or grandiose self-images. Some may be overly anxious about their health and may feel genuinely ill when under stress. Some emotionally disturbed students exhibit school phobia, refusing to attend school or running away from school.

Unlike aggressive emotionally disturbed children, who may appear quite normal when they are not being aggressive, withdrawn and immature children often appear odd or awkward at all times. They almost always suffer from a lack of social skills. Some of the more successful therapies for these children involve teaching them the social skills that other students acquire without special instruction (see Gottlieb and Leyser, 1981; Gresham, 1981; Strain and Kerr, 1981).

Hyperactivity.   As mentioned previously in the discussion of learning disabilities, one very common emotional/behavioral problem is **hyperactivity,** an inability to sit still or to concentrate for any length of time. Hyperactive children exhibit excessive restlessness and short attention span. Hyperactivity is particularly common among students with learning disabilities and is much more frequently seen in boys than in girls. It is more prevalent among elementary school students (O'Leary, 1980).

If a student were removed from your class because her emotional outbursts were upsetting to other students, what might you say to that student afterwards and how would you follow up?

conduct disorders: socioemotional and behavioral disorders indicated in individuals who, for example, are chronically disobedient or disruptive.

hyperactivity: condition characterized by extreme restlessness and short attention spans relative to peers.

Hyperactive children are usually impulsive, acting before they think or without regard for the situation they are in, and they find it hard to sit still (Shaywitz and Shaywitz, 1988). Students who are diagnosed as hyperactive are often given a stimulant medication, such as Ritalin. More than a million children take Ritalin, and this number has been rising in recent years (Weiss, 1989). These drugs usually do make hyperactive children more manageable and sometimes improve their academic performance (Gadow, 1981; Ottenbacher and Cooper, 1983), but they can also have serious side effects, such as insomnia, weight loss, and blood pressure changes (Hersen, 1986). Further, students who receive drugs for hyperactivity during the elementary years often have more serious behavioral disorders in adolescence, perhaps because they have not really learned to control their behavior.

Severe Emotional Disturbances.   A very small number of children, about one in a thousand, suffer from severe emotional disturbances such as childhood schizophrenia or other psychotic disorders or autism (Kauffman, 1985). Psychotic children are likely to live in a fantasy world and to lack normal relationships with others. Autistic children are typically extremely withdrawn and have such severe difficulties with language that they may be entirely mute. They (and often psychotic children as well) may engage in self-stimulation, such as rocking, twirling objects, or flapping their hands. However, they may have normal or even outstanding abilities in certain areas.

Sensory, Physical, and Health Impairments

Sensory impairments refer to problems with the ability to see or hear or otherwise receive information through the body's senses. Physical disorders found among students include conditions such as cerebral palsy, spina bifida, spinal cord injury, and muscular dystrophy. Health disorders include, for example, acquired immune deficiency syndrome (AIDS), seizure disorders, diabetes, cystic fibrosis, sickle cell anemia (in African-American students), and bodily damage from chemical addictions, child abuse, or attempted suicide (Hardman *et al.*, 1993).

Visual Impairments.   Most visual problems exhibited by students are correctable by glasses or another type of corrective lens. A **visual impairment** is considered a visual disability only if it is not correctable. It is estimated that approximately one out of every 1000 children is visually impaired. Those with such disabilities are usually referred to as blind or partially sighted. According to the American Medical Association (1934), a legally blind child is one whose vision is judged to be 20/200 or less in the better eye even with correction or whose field of vision is significantly narrower than that of a person with normal vision. Partially sighted persons, according to this classification system, are those whose vision is between 20/70 and 20/200 in the better eye with correction (Rogow, 1988).

It is a misconception to assume that legally blind individuals have no sight. In one large study Willis (1976) found that only 18 percent of legally blind students were totally blind, and 52 percent of these students could read large- or regular-print books rather than Braille (an alphabet that uses raised dots to represent letters and is read by touch). This implies that many visually impaired students can be taught using a modification of usual teaching materials. Hallahan and Kauffman (1991) offered an educational definition of visual impairment that depends on the amount of adaptation required in the school setting. They suggested that "the

sensory impairments: problems with the ability to receive information through the body's senses.

visual impairment: degree of blindness; uncorrectable inability to see well.

blind are those who are so severely impaired that they must be taught to read by Braille, while the partially sighted can read print even though they need to use magnifying devices or books with large print."

Classroom teachers should be aware of the signs that indicate a child is having a vision problem. Undoubtedly, children who have difficulty seeing also have difficulty in many areas of learning because classroom lessons typically use a tremendous amount of visual material. The National Society for the Prevention of Blindness (1969) suggested several symptoms of visual problems. These include (1) holding one's head in an awkward position or holding material very close to the eyes; (2) tuning out when information is presented on the chalkboard; (3) constant questioning as to what is going on in the classroom; (4) being inordinately affected by glare; (5) a pronounced squint, excessive rubbing of the eyes, or pushing the eyeballs; and (6) physical eye problems such as redness, swelling, or crusting. If you notice any of these problems, you should refer the student for appropriate vision screening.

Hearing Impairments. Hearing impairments range from complete deafness to problems that can be alleviated with a hearing aid. The appropriate classification of an individual with **hearing impairments** depends on the measures required to compensate for the problem. Davis (1970) indicated the educational implications that correspond to the various degrees of hearing loss (see Table 12.4).

The amount of adaptation required for a teacher to communicate with a hearing-impaired student obviously depends on the degree of hearing loss. Simply having a student sit at the front of the classroom may be enough to compensate for a mild hearing loss. Many children can communicate adequately by listening to your voice and watching your lips. Others might need a hearing aid, while those with more severe problems will need to use a nonverbal form of communication such as sign language. Following are several suggestions that you should keep in mind (Blackhurst and Berdine, 1981):

1. Seat hard-of-hearing children in the front of the room, slightly off center toward the windows. This will allow them to see your face in the best light.
2. If the hearing problem is predominantly in one ear, students should sit in a front corner seat so that their better ear is toward you.
3. Speak at the student's eye level whenever possible.
4. Give important information and instructions while facing the class. Avoid talking to the chalkboard.
5. Do not use exaggerated lip movements when speaking.
6. Learn how to assist a child with a hearing aid.

Cerebral Palsy. **Cerebral palsy** is a motor impairment caused by brain damage. The damage can be produced by any number of factors that result in oxygen deprivation—poisoning, cerebral bleeding, or direct injury. The damage usually occurs before, during, or shortly after birth and causes some degree of paralysis, weakness, or incoordination (Eiben and Crocker, 1983). Cerebral palsy is not a disease that is contagious, nor does it get progressively worse. Not all cerebral-palsied individuals are retarded. The damage to the brain is in the motor area and may not be associated with damage to other areas of the brain. Children with cerebral palsy may have average intelligence.

The severity of cerebral palsy varies tremendously. Some people have virtually no voluntary control over any of their movements, while others have a motor problem that is barely discernible. In the more severe cases there is great difficulty in speaking.

hearing impairment: degree of deafness; uncorrectable inability to hear well.

cerebral palsy: disorder in ability to control movements caused by damage to the motor area of the brain

Levels of Loss	Sound Intensity for Perception (Decibels [dB])	Educational Implications
Mild	27–40 dB	May have difficulty with distant sounds. May need preferential seating and speech therapy.
Moderate	41–55 dB	Understands conversational speech. May miss class discussion. May require hearing aids and speech therapy.
Moderately severe	56–70 dB	Will require hearing aids, auditory training, speech and language training of an intensive nature.
Severe	71–90 dB	Can only hear loud sounds close up. Sometimes considered deaf. Needs intensive special education, hearing aids, speech and language training.
Profound	91 dB+	May be aware of loud sounds and vibrations. Relies on vision rather than hearing for information processing. Considered deaf.

Table 12.4   Educational Significance of Hearing Impairments

Students with mild hearing losses may need only to be seated in an advantageous location to understand a teacher's presentations. Greater accommodation must be made for students with more severe hearing impairments.

SOURCE: Davis and Silverman, 1970. Reprinted by permission of Holt, Rinehart, and Winston.

Obviously, the degree of severity affects the amount of adaptation that is necessary in the classroom. Increasingly sophisticated adaptive equipment, particularly in the area of communication, is now available to allow students with cerebral palsy to participate in regular as well as special education classes.

Seizure Disorders.   **Seizure disorders,** or epilepsy, are caused by an abnormal amount of electrical discharge in the brain. Witnessing a seizure can be a frightening experience for an unknowledgeable observer.

There are several types of seizures that a child might experience. One type, tonic, affects the whole brain and results in a major seizure characterized by loss of consciousness, rigidity, shaking, and jerking. Before a seizure a child may experience

seizure disorders: forms of epilepsy.

an "aura," a peculiar sensation in which certain sounds are heard, odors smelled, or images seen. Experiencing an identifiable aura often gives the child enough time to lie down. Immediately after the seizure, a deep sleep may follow. The most violent part of a tonic seizure lasts only about three to four minutes, but during it care must be taken that the children do not hurt themselves by biting their lips or tongues or involuntarily striking furniture or other objects.

Heward and Orlansky (1980, p. 249) offered the following suggestions for when a student has a seizure:

1. Ease the child to the floor and loosen his or her collar. You cannot stop the seizure. Let it run its course, and do not try to revive the child.
2. Remove hard, sharp, or hot objects that may injure the child, but do not interfere with his or her movements.
3. Do not force anything between the child's teeth. If the child's mouth is already open, you might place a soft object, like a handkerchief, between the side teeth. Be careful not to get your fingers caught between the teeth.
4. Turn the head to one side for release of saliva. Place something soft under the child's head.
5. When the child regains consciousness, allow time for the child to rest.
6. If the seizure lasts beyond a few minutes, or if the child seems to pass from one seizure to another without gaining consciousness, call the school nurse or doctor for instructions and notify the parents. This rarely happens, but should be treated immediately.

A few other suggestions are also helpful. If you know that a child in your class is prone to having seizures, discuss this with the class so they won't be surprised. The important thing is for everyone to remain calm. A clonic seizure is less severe but occurs more frequently. In this type of seizure the student experiences brief lapses of consciousness. During these short intervals (usually about five to fifteen seconds) the student might look blank, stare, and flutter the eye lids. Clonic seizures often go unnoticed or are misinterpreted as a short attention span or a behavior problem. Between seizures, epileptic children usually show no signs of disability, and new medications have allowed most seizure disorders to be partially or completely controlled.

Giftedness

Who are the gifted? Almost everyone, according to their parents, and in fact many students do have outstanding talents or skills in some area. **Giftedness** was once defined almost entirely in terms of superior IQ or demonstrated ability, such as outstanding performance in mathematics or chess, but the definition now encompasses students with superior abilities in a wide range of activities, including the arts. For this reason, the term "gifted and talented" is coming to be used more often than simply "gifted." High IQ is still considered part of the definition of "gifted and talented," and most students so categorized have IQs above 130. It is notable, however, that some groups are underidentified as gifted or talented, including females, students with disabilities, underachievers, and students who are members of racial or ethnic minority groups (Maker and Schiever, 1989; Smith and Luckasson, 1992).

The 1978 Gifted and Talented Act indicated that "the gifted and talented are children . . . who are identified . . . as possessing demonstrated or potential abilities

giftedness: category of exceptionality characterized by being very bright, creative, or talented.

that give evidence of high performance capabilities in areas such as intellectual, creative, specific academic or leadership ability or in the performing or visual arts and to by reason thereof require services or activities not ordinarily provided by the school" (Public Law 95–561, Section 902). This definition is meant to include students who possess extraordinary capabilities in any number of activities, not just those areas that are part of the school curriculum. According to these rather vague criteria (see Gallagher, 1992), somewhere between 3 and 5 percent of all students are "gifted and talented" (Mitchell and Erickson, 1980). However, the percentage of students identified as gifted and talented varies from less than one percent in North Dakota to almost 10 percent in New Jersey (National Center for Educational Statistics, 1988). This does not mean that New Jersey's students are especially talented; rather it indicates the vast differences found in defining and identifying the gifted and talented in different states.

Characteristics of Gifted and Talented Children.   Intellectually gifted children typically have strong motivation. They are also academically superior, usually learn to read early, and, in general, do excellent work in most school areas (Gallagher, 1992). One of the most important studies of the gifted, begun by Louis Terman in 1926, is following 1528 individuals who had IQs over 140 as children. Terman's research exploded the myth that high-IQ individuals were brainy but physically and socially inept. In fact, Terman found that children with outstanding IQs were larger, stronger, and better coordinated than other children and became better adjusted and more emotionally stable adults (Terman and Oden, 1959).

Education of the Gifted.   How to educate gifted students is a matter of debate (see Torrance, 1986). Some programs for gifted and talented children involve special secondary schools for students gifted in science or in the arts. Some programs are special classes for high achievers in regular schools. One debate in this area concerns *acceleration* versus *enrichment*. Advocates of acceleration (*e.g.,* Stanley, 1979; Van Tassel-Baska, 1989) argue that gifted students should be encouraged to move through the school curriculum rapidly, perhaps skipping grades and going to college at an early age. Others (for example, Gallagher, 1992; Renzulli, 1986; Feldhusen, 1989) maintain that rather than only moving students through school more rapidly, programs for the gifted should engage them in more problem-solving and creative activities.

Research on the gifted provides more support (in terms of student achievement gains) for acceleration than for enrichment (Kulik and Kulik, 1984; Swiatek and Benbow, 1991). However, as Fox (1979) points out, this may be because the outcomes of enrichment, such as creativity or problem-solving skills, are difficult to measure. **Acceleration programs** for the gifted often involve the teaching of advanced mathematics to students at early ages, as in Stanley's (1979) Study of Mathematically Precocious Youth (SMPY) program. This program had a stated goal of getting mathematically talented seventh- and eighth-graders from Algebra I through second-year college mathematics (Calculus III, linear algebra, and differential equations) in as short a time as possible (see Stanley and Benbow, 1986).

Enrichment programs take many forms. Many successful enrichment programs have involved self-directed or independent study (Parke, 1983; Reiss and Cellerino, 1983). Others have provided gifted students with adult mentors (Nash *et al.,* 1980). Renzulli (1986) suggests an emphasis on three types of activities: general exploratory activities, such as allowing students to find out about topics on their own; group training activities, such as games and simulations to promote

acceleration programs: rapid promotion through advanced studies for students who are gifted or talented.

enrichment programs: programs in which assignments or activities are designed to broaden or deepen the knowledge of students who master classroom lessons quickly.

creativity and problem-solving skills; and individual and small-group investigations of real problems, such as writing books or newspapers, interviewing elderly people to write oral histories of an area, and conducting geological or archaeological investigations.

The main problem with enrichment programs for the gifted is simply stated: There are few activities suggested for gifted students that would not be beneficial for *all* students. However, students who are gifted may be better able to take advantage of enrichment programs, because they are able to master the regular curriculum rapidly enough to allow them the time to engage in more exploratory activities.

Self-Check

Define "exceptionality" and distinguish between "disability" and "handicap." Give examples of each, and explain why labeling has limitations. Then define and describe the characteristics of each of the following categories of exceptionality. Work from memory first; then review the chapter to add important details.

mental retardation	learning disability
giftedness	emotional disorder
conduct disorder	communication disorder
physical disability	speech disorder
visual impairment	language disorder
hearing impairment	cerebral palsy
seizure disorder	attention deficit disorder

What Is Special Education?

Special education refers to any program provided for children with disabilities instead of, or in addition to, the regular classroom program. The practice of special education has changed dramatically in recent years and is still evolving. Federal legislation has been critical in setting standards for special education services administered by states and local districts.

Public Law 94–142

Thirty years ago education of exceptional children was quite different from what it is today. Many "handicapped" students received no special services at all. Those who did get special services usually attended separate schools or institutions for "the retarded," emotionally disturbed, deaf, or blind.

In the late 1960s the special education system came under attack (see, for example, Dunn, 1968; Christoplos and Renz, 1969). Critics argued that the seriously disabled were too often shut away in state institutions with inadequate educational services or left at home with no services at all, and that the mildly disabled (particularly those with mild mental retardation) were being isolated in special programs that failed to teach them the skills they needed to function in society. Four million of the eight million disabled students of school age were not in school.

special education:
programs that address the needs of students with mental, emotional, or physical disabilities.

According to Public Law 94-142
and related legislation, exactly
what entitlements do children
with disabilities have?

As a result, in 1975 Congress passed **Public Law 94–142,** the Education For All Handicapped Act. PL94–142, as it is commonly called, has profoundly affected both special and regular education throughout the United States. It prescribes the services that all disabled children must receive and gives them and their parents legal rights that they did not previously possess.

A basic component of PL94–142 is that every disabled child is entitled to special education appropriate to the child's needs at public expense. This means, for example, that school districts or states must provide special education to severely retarded and disabled children.

PL94–142 has been extended beyond its original focus in two major pieces of legislation. In 1986, **Public Law 99–457** extended the entitlement to free, appropriate education to children ages three to five. It also added programs for seriously disabled infants and toddlers. **Public Law 101–476,** passed in 1990, changed the name of the special education law to the Individuals with Disabilities Education Act (IDEA), required that schools plan for the transition of adolescents with disabilities into further education or employment starting at age 16, and replaced the term "handicapped children" with "children with disabilities."

Least Restrictive Environment.   The provision of PL94–142 of greatest importance to regular classroom teachers is that students with disabilities must be assigned to the "least restrictive placement" appropriate to their needs. This provision gives a legal basis for the practice of **mainstreaming,** or placing disabled students with nondisabled peers for as much of their instructional program as possible. This means that regular classroom teachers are likely to have in their classes students with mild disabilities (such as learning disabilities, mild mental retardation, physical disabilities, or speech problems) who may leave class for special instruction part of the day. It also means that classes for students with more serious disabilities are likely to be located in regular school facilities, and that these students will probably attend some activities with their nondisabled peers.

Individualized Education Program (IEP).   Another important requirement of PL94–142 is that every disabled student must have an **Individualized Education Program,** or **IEP,** that guides the services the student receives. The IEP describes a student's problems and delineates a specific course of action to address these problems. Generally, it is prepared by special education teachers and a special education supervisor or school psychologist in consultation with the principal, counselor, and

Public Law 94–142: 1975 federal law requiring provision of special education services to eligible students.

Public Law 99–457: 1986 federal law extending special education eligibility to children ages three to five and to seriously disabled infants and toddlers.

Public Law 101–476: 1990 federal law changing the name of PL94–142 to Individuals with Disabilities Act (IDEA) and broadening services to adolescents with disabilities.

mainstreaming: the placement, for all or part of the school day, of disabled children in regular classes.

Individualized Education Program (IEP): program tailored to the needs of an exceptional child.

the classroom teacher, and it must be consented to by the student's parent. The idea behind the use of IEPs is to give everyone concerned with the education of a child with a disability an opportunity to help formulate the child's instructional program. The requirement that a parent sign the IEP is designed to ensure parental awareness of and approval of what the school proposes to do with the child; a parent may hold the school accountable if the child does not receive the promised services.

The law requires that evaluations of students for possible placement in special education programs be done by qualified professionals. Although classroom and special education teachers will typically be involved in the evaluation process, teachers are not generally allowed to give the psychological tests (such as IQ tests) that are used for placement decisions.

PL94–142 gives children with disabilities and their parents legal safeguards with regard to special education placement and programs. For example, if parents feel that a child has been diagnosed incorrectly or assigned to the wrong program, or if they are unsatisfied with the services a child is receiving, they may bring a grievance against the school district. Also, the law specifies that parents be notified about all placement decisions, conferences, and changes in program.

A Continuum of Special Education Services

An important aspect of an IEP is a special education program appropriate to the student's needs. Every school district provides up to seven levels of special education services:

1. direct or indirect consultation, support for regular teacher
2. special education up to one hour per day
3. special education one to three hours per day; resource program
4. special education more than three hours per day; self-contained special education
5. special day school
6. special residential school
7. home/hospital

In general, students with more severe disabilities receive more restrictive services than those with less severe disabilities. For example, a severely retarded student is unlikely to be placed in a regular classroom during academic periods, while a student with a speech problem or a mild learning disability is likely to be in a regular classroom for most or all of the school day. However, severity of disability is not the sole criterion for placement; also considered is the appropriateness of the various settings for an individual student's needs. For example, a student in a wheelchair with a severe orthopedic disability can easily attend and profit from regular classes, while a student with a hearing deficit might not.

Table 12.5 shows the percentages of students with disabilities who receive special education services in various settings. Note that with the exception of students who have physical or sensory disabilities, few students received special education outside of a regular school building. The great majority of students who are learning disabled or have speech impairments attend regular classes part or most of the day, usually supplemented by one or more hours per day in a special education resource room. This is also true for the majority of physically disabled students and almost half of all students with emotional disorders. Most other special needs students attend special classes located in regular school buildings. The continuum of services available to students with disabilities, from least to most restrictive, is described in the following sections.

| Disability | Regular Class | Educational Environments | | | | |
		Resource Room	Separate Class	Separate School	Residential Facility	Homebound/ Hospital
Specific learning disabilities	20.7%	56.1%	21.7%	1.3%	0.1%	0.1%
Speech or language impairments	76.8	17.7	3.8	1.5	0.1	0.1
Mental retardation	6.7	20.1	61.1	10.3	1.4	0.4
Serious emotional disturbance	14.9	28.5	37.1	13.9	3.6	2.0
Hearing impairments	27.0	18.2	31.7	10.6	12.3	0.2
Multiple disabilities	5.9	14.3	43.7	29.5	3.9	2.7
Orthopedic impairments	29.6	18.9	34.7	9.9	1.0	5.9
Other health impairments	31.2	22.3	24.6	7.8	1.0	13.1
Visual impairments	39.3	23.7	21.1	4.5	10.8	0.6
Deaf-blindness	8.0	16.3	29.9	16.6	28.4	1.0
All disabilities	31.5	37.6	24.9	4.6	0.9	0.6

Table 12.5   Percentage of Students Aged 6–21 Served in Different Educational Environments by Disability: School Year 1989–90

Includes data from 50 states, the District of Columbia, and outlying areas. Educational placements for children aged 3–5 are not reported by disability.

Source: U.S. Department of Education, 1992.

Regular Classroom Placement.   The needs of many students with disabilities can be met in the regular classroom with little or no outside assistance. For example, students who have mild vision or hearing problems may simply be seated near the front of the room. Students with mild to moderate learning disabilities may have their needs met in the regular classroom if the teacher uses strategies (such as those described in Chapter 9) for accommodating instruction to student differences. For example, the use of instructional aides, tutors, or parent volunteers can allow exceptional students to remain in the regular classroom. Classroom teachers can often adapt their instruction to make it easier for students to succeed. For example, one teacher noticed that a student with perceptual problems was having difficulties with arithmetic because he could not line up his numbers. She solved the problem by giving him graph paper to work on.

Research generally shows that the most effective strategies for dealing with learning and behavior problems are those used in the regular classroom. Special education options should usually be explored only after serious efforts have been made to meet students' needs in the regular classroom (see Madden and Slavin, 1983a).

Consultation and Itinerant Services.   Many school districts provide classroom teachers with consultants to help them adapt their instruction to the needs of students with disabilities. Consulting teachers typically are trained in special as well as regular education. They may come into the classroom to observe the behavior of a student but most often suggest solutions to the regular teacher rather than working directly with students. Research finds that well-designed consulting models can be effective in assisting teachers to maintain students with mild disabilities, particularly those with learning disabilities, in the regular class (Cantrell and Cantrell, 1976; Graden *et al.*, 1985; Fuchs and Fuchs, 1989).

For some types of disabilities, itinerant (traveling) teachers may provide special services to students a few times a week. This pattern of service is typical of programs for students with speech and language disorders.

Resource Room Placement.   Many students with disabilities are assigned to regular classes for most of their school day but participate in resource programs at other times. Most often resource programs focus on teaching reading, language arts, mathematics, and occasionally other subjects. Resource room programs usually involve small numbers of students working with a special education teacher. Ideally, the resource teacher meets regularly with the classroom teacher to coordinate programs for students and to suggest ways the regular classroom teacher can adapt instruction when the students are in the regular class.

Sometimes resource teachers work in the regular classroom. For example, a resource teacher might work with one reading group while the regular classroom teacher works with another. This arrangement avoids pulling students out of class, which is both inefficient because of the transition time required and potentially demeaning because the students are excluded from class for some period of time. Team teaching involving regular and special teachers also enhances communication between the teachers.

Special Class Placement with Part-Time Mainstreaming.   Many students with disabilities are assigned to special classes taught by a special education teacher but are mainstreamed with nondisabled students part of the school day. Most often these students join other students for music, art, and physical education, and somewhat less often for social studies, science, mathematics, or (least often) reading. One important difference between this category of special services and the resource room model is that in the resource room, the student's primary placement is in the regular class; the classroom teacher is the homeroom teacher and generally takes responsibility for the student's program, with the resource teacher providing extra support. In the case of a student assigned to special education and mainstreamed part of the day, the situation is reversed. The special education teacher serves as the homeroom teacher and takes primary responsibility.

Self-Contained Special Education.   A self-contained special education program is a class located in a school separately from the regular instructional program. Until the mainstreaming movement began in the early 1970s, this (along with separate schools for retarded and disabled children) was the typical placement for students with disabilities. Self-contained programs are taught by special education teachers with relatively few contacts with the regular instructional program.

Some students attend separate, special day schools. These are typically students with severe disabilities, such as severe retardation or physical disabilities, or those whose presence might be disruptive to the regular school, such as students with serious emotional disturbances. In addition, small numbers of students with disabilities attend special residential schools for profoundly disabled students with disabilities that require special treatment.

Other Special Services.   In addition to the placements just described, other special services are often needed by exceptional students. For example, school psychologists are often involved in the process of diagnosing students with disabilities and sometimes participate in the preparation of Individualized Education Plans. In addition, they may counsel the student or consult with the teacher about behavioral and learning problems. Speech and language therapists generally work with students on a one-to-one basis, though some small-group instruction may be provided for students with similar problems. They also consult with teachers about ways to address student difficulties.

Physical and occupational therapists treat motor difficulties under the direction of a physician. Students who have physical disabilities may see a physical or occupational therapist whose treatment focuses on the development of large and small muscle skills.

School social workers and pupil personnel workers serve as a major link between the school and the family and are likely to become involved when problems at home are affecting students' school performance or behavior.

For students with disabilities who are unable to attend school because of a lengthy illness or complications related to a disability, instruction is often provided at home or in the hospital. Such instruction is designed to maintain and continue a student's academic progress. Homebound instruction is intended for short periods of time.

Classroom teachers have important roles in the education of children with disabilities. They are important in referring students to receive special services, in participating in the assessment of students, and in preparing and implementing IEPs. This section describes the process by which classroom teachers seek special education services for students (see Odle and Galtelli, 1980; Turnbull and Brantley, 1982).

In Figure 12.5 a flow chart shows how the IEP process operates, and an example of an IEP appears in Figure 12.6.

Theory Into Practice
Preparing IEPs

Initial Referral
Referrals for special education assessment can be made by parents, physicians, principals, or teachers. Classroom teachers most often initiate referrals for children with suspected learning disabilities, mental retardation, speech impairment,

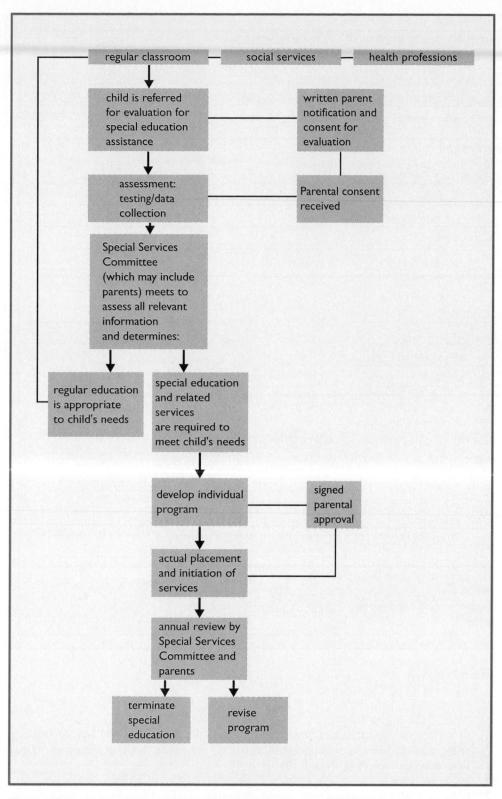

Figure 12.5 **Flow Chart for the Individualized Program Process**
Adapted from Smith, 1989, p. 28.

INDIVIDUALIZED EDUCATION PROGRAM

School Year _94-95_

Confidential Information

Name _Patrick Milton_ DOB _11/7/82_   School _Field_   Grade _6_

Handicapping condition _Learning Disability_   Date of IEP meeting _10/15/94_ Notification to parent _11/12/94_

Initiation and anticipated duration of services _11/94 11/95_ Eligibility/Triennial _10/12/94_ Plan to be reviewed no later than _3/95_
M-Y to MY   M-D-Y   M-Y

Educational/Vocational Program

Special Education Services

Work with LD resource teacher on reading and language arts; may be taught in group of up to five students; summer school (1995) recommended.

Total Amount   Times/Wk. _5_   Hrs./Day _____

Regular Education Services

Regular sixth grade

Total Amount   Times/Wk. _5_   Hrs./Day _5_

Related Services

Type   Amount

Speech-language sessions with speech-language therapist for 30 minutes 2 times/ week to work on lateral lisp and improve oral fluency.

Adapted Class   Amount _None_

Regular Class   Amount _As scheduled_

Transportation

Special _NA-walk to sch._ Regular _____

Current Level of Performance

Reading: Second grade, first semester; special difficulty with word-attack skills; knows 70 basic sight words.
Language Arts: Cursive writing mostly illegible; not able to construct sentences in composition; mostly phonetic spelling; poor ability to give verbal descriptions.
Math and other areas: Completes work with 80% or better accuracy at grade level.
Work Habits: Consistently completes about 20% of language arts assignments with about 50% accuracy.

Participants in Plan Development

Name	Title
Marie Milton	Mother
Melissa Borden	LD resource teacher
Tim Triumph	Sixth grade teacher
Evan Gorley	Principal
Kate Nona	Speech-language therapist
Ron Horsely	School psychologist

For High School Students ONLY (to be initially completed at 9th grade IEP meeting and reviewed annually).

This student is a candidate for: High School Diploma _____ : Special Ed. Certificate _____ : GED Equivalency Diploma _____ .

Is the Minimum Competency Test to be administered this school year? Yes _____ No _____ If yes, attach addendum.

White: Confidential Folder Yellow: Parent Copy

Figure 12.6   Individualized Education Program

From Hallahan and Kauffman, 1991.

or emotional disturbance; most other disabilities are diagnosed before students enter school. In most schools initial referrals are made to the building principal, who contacts relevant school district staff.

Screening and Assessment

As soon as the student is referred for assessment, an initial determination is made to accept or reject the referral. In practice, almost all referrals are

INDIVIDUALIZED EDUCATION PROGRAM

School Year _94-95_

ANNUAL GOAL: The student _Patrick Milton_ will _complete all assigned work in language arts and reading with 90% or better accuracy at Fifthgrade level by September 1985_ **PROGRESS REPORTS**

SHORT TERM OBJECTIVES	Grading Periods		COMMENTS
Objective: Given 200 sight words from his reader, Pat will read them with 90% accuracy.	1	✕	
	2	12/94	
Beginning Skill Level: 2² (Ginn); knows 70 Dolch words	3	3/95	P-Learning average of 2 new sight words/school day
Date Initiated: _11/21/94_	4		M-Now knows all Dolch words and all words in reader
Objective: Given a topic with which he is familiar, Pat will write at least 5 complete sentences on the topic within 30 minutes.	1	✕	
	2	12/94	P-will write 2 or 3 sentences before refusing to continue; tells sentence from nonsentence with 75% accuracy.
Beginning Skill Level: Does not know sentence from non sentence.	3	3/95	P-
Date Initiated: _11/21/94_	4		
Objective: Given instructions to copy 5 lines of printed material from a book, Pat will write the material on lined paper using cursive letters so that another teacher can	1	✕	
immediately decipher at least 90% of the material.	2	12/94	P-Most written work now 60% legible; 75% legible when copying.
Beginning Skill Level: Only letters legible 80% of thetime are e,p,w	3	3/95	M-Nearly all written work is legible
Date Initiated: _11/21/94_	4		
Objective: Given 50 sight words from his reading book and 50 CVCE words, Pat will read them with 100% accuracy; given the same words from dictation, he will spell them with 95% accuracy.	1	✕	
	2	12/94	P--Reads CVCE words with 95% accuracy and writes them with 80% accuracy.
Beginning Skill Level: Tested spelling grade level = 2'.	3	3/95	
Date Initiated: _11/21/94_	4		

Evaluation Procedures: Annual goals will be evaluated during the annual review. Short term objectives will be monitored at each nine week marking period. Beginning skill level indicates the sutdent's performance prior to instruction.

Progress Key: No mark-Objective not initiated **P**-Progressing on the Objective **D**-Having difficulty with the objective (comment to describe difficulty)

M-Objective mastered   **M/R**-Objective mastered, but needs review to maintain mastery

White: Confidential Folder   **Yellow:** Parent Progress Report   **Pink:** Teacher Working Copy   **Goldenrod:** Parent Original

accepted. The evaluation/placement team may look at the student's school records and interview classroom teachers and others who know the student. If the team members decide to accept the referral, they must obtain parental permission to do a comprehensive assessment.

Members of the evaluation/placement team include professionals designated by the school district plus the parents of the referred student and, if appropriate, the referred student. If the referral has to do with learning or emotional problems, a school psychologist or guidance counselor will usually be involved; if it has to do with speech or language problems, a speech pathologist or speech teacher will typically serve on the team. The building principal usually chairs the team but may designate a special education teacher or other professional to do so.

The referred student is then given a battery of tests to assess strengths and weaknesses. For learning and emotional problems, these tests are usually given by a school psychologist; specific achievement tests (such as reading or mathematics assessments) are often given by special education or reading teachers.

Writing the IEP

When the comprehensive assessment is complete, the evaluation/placement team members meet to consider the best placement for the student. If they determine that special education is necessary, they will prepare an IEP. Usually the special education teacher and/or the classroom teacher prepares the IEP. The student's parent(s) must sign a consent form regarding the placement decision, and in many school districts a parent must also sign the IEP. This means that parents can (and in some cases do) refuse to have their children placed in special education programs. At a minimum, the IEP must contain the following information (see Odle and Galtelli, 1980, p. 248):

1. *Statements indicating the child's present level of performance:* This typically includes the results of specific tests as well as descriptions of classroom functioning. Behavior rating checklists, work samples, or other observation forms may be used to clarify a student's strengths and weaknesses.

2. *Goals indicating anticipated progress during the year:* For example, a student might have goals of reading at a fourth-grade level as measured by a standardized test, of improving classroom behavior so that disciplinary referrals are reduced to zero, or of completing a bricklaying course in a vocational education program.

3. *Intermediate (shorter-term) instructional objectives:* A student having difficulties in reading might be given an intermediate objective to complete a certain number of individualized reading comprehension units per month, or an emotionally disturbed student might be expected to get along with peers better and avoid fights.

4. *A statement of the specific special education and related services to be provided as well as the extent to which the student will participate in regular education programs:* The IEP might specify that a student will receive two thirty-minute sessions with a speech therapist each week. An IEP for a learning-disabled student might specify forty-five minutes per day of instruction from a resource teacher in reading, plus consultation between the resource teacher and the classroom teacher on ways to adapt instruction in the regular classroom. A mentally retarded student might be assigned to a self-contained special education class, but the IEP might specify that the student participate in the regular physical education program. Any adaptations necessary to accommodate students in the regular class, such as wheelchair ramps, large-type books, or cassette tapes, would be specified in the IEP.

Teachers on Teaching

What rewarding experience have you had with a student with special needs?

As the Coordinator of Handicapped Services, I have assisted teachers in mainstreaming children with a variety of disabling conditions into the classroom setting. One child I remember very well is Roberta, an alert, bright-eyed little girl who had been diagnosed as apraxic (a condition in which receptive language is normal but there is little or no expressive language). When Roberta first entered the program, other children often initiated conversation with her and could not understand why she was unable to respond. Roberta's teacher and I explained that we all have things we do really well and things that are hard for us to do. The children gave examples of personal strengths and weaknesses, which included recognizing letters of the alphabet, riding two-wheelers, and tying shoes. The teacher explained that one thing Roberta could not do very well was talk. The children accepted this without difficulty. Roberta's teacher and I worked on deemphasizing Roberta's weaknesses and emphasizing her strengths. As a calendar helper, for example, Roberta naturally showed classmates how she communicated through the use of gestures. With a minimum of adult intervention, her classmates quickly accepted her as a regular member of the class. Roberta's teacher and I developed an Individualized Preschool Plan, along with staff from the local Intermediate Unit, Roberta's mother, and the consulting preschool special education teacher. Roberta's interaction skills developed nicely and she entered public school. Today, Roberta continues to be in a mainstreamed classroom. She relates well to both adults and children and continues to progress academically.

Lynne McKee, School Psychologist
Indiana University of Pennsylvania
Indiana, Pennsylvania

I teach a high school work experience class, a restaurant job station open to the school's staff and students. Our self-sufficient place is called The Breakfast Club, and we take orders, cook, deliver food, process checks, and do everything else a regular restaurant does. My challenge is to attract other students as customers while protecting my own pupils from the negative aspects of being special. I have dealt with the need for peer acceptance in several different ways. First, my class is part of the Work-Study department, which avoids negative labeling and involves all students. Customers are often unaware of the shared background of my workers. Then, when my enrollment is low, I recruit aides from our Future Teachers of America chapter, who work side by side with my students and me. In addition, my students' jobs help them toward social integration. Because The Breakfast Club is an escape from study-hall boredom, it is a rewarding environment and my students enjoy a measure of prestige in other students' eyes. We have had school personnel and parents as patrons on several occasions, and we've even had elementary classes visit on field trips. Several teachers at our schools use The Breakfast Club as a reward for their own students. My most important role is making sure my workers' training is effective and complete. I also emphasize high quality in all aspects of our service. Quality control helps my students gain pride with each successful day on the job, and this usually pays off in growing self-esteem, confidence, and the ability to handle other situations. My students learn social skills and teamwork in the process, which furthers social acceptance by others. Positive contact with other people in a variety of situations is what gives special students the chance to grow.

Terry Olive, Special Education Teacher
Elyria High School, Elyria, Ohio

This student with disabilities is in a full inclusion program. According to research, how effective are full inclusion and mainstreaming compared to other approaches? As a teacher, how might you foster this child's social acceptance by peers?

5. *The projected date for the initiation of services and the anticipated duration of services:* Once the IEP is written, students must receive services within a reasonable time period. They may not be put on a waiting list—the school district must provide or contract for the indicated services.

6. *Evaluation criteria and procedures for measuring progress toward goals on at least an annual basis.*

The IEP should specify a strategy for remediating students' deficits. In particular, the IEP should state what objectives the student is to achieve and how those objectives are to be attained and measured. It is critical to direct special education services toward a well-specified set of learning or behavior objectives rather than simply deciding that a student falls into some category and therefore should receive some service. Ideally, special education for students with mild disabilities should be a short-term, intensive treatment to give students the skills needed in a regular class. All too often a student assigned to special education remains there indefinitely, even after the problem for which the student was initially referred has been remediated.

Note that IEPs must be updated at least once a year. The updating provides an opportunity to change programs that are not working or to reduce or terminate special education services when the student no longer needs them.

Self-Check

Define "special education," and explain the main provisions of Public Law 94–142. How have PL99–457 and PL101–476 altered the original legislation? Describe the five main kinds of placement extended to students with special needs and list other special services that are made available. List the minimum information that an Individualized Education Plan must contain, then list the steps you would take to prepare an IEP.

What Is Mainstreaming?

The "least restrictive placement" clause of PL94–142 revolutionized the practice of special as well as regular education. As already noted, it requires that exceptional students be assigned to the least restrictive placement appropriate to their needs. The effect of this provision has been to greatly increase contacts between nondisabled and disabled students. In general, students with all types of disabilities have moved one or two notches up the continuum of special education services. Students who were once placed in special schools are now generally put in separate classrooms in regular schools. Students who were once placed in separate classrooms in regular schools, particularly students with mild retardation and learning disabilities, are now most often assigned to regular classes for most of their instruction. A growing movement, called **full inclusion,** calls for including all children in regular classes with appropriate assistance (see Gartner and Lipsky, 1987; Cole and Meyer, 1991; Sailor, 1991). Proponents of full inclusion argue that pull-out programs discourage effective partnerships between regular and special educators

full inclusion: policy or practice of placing all students in regular classes with appropriate assistance.

in implementing individualized plans and that students in pull-out programs are stigmatized when segregated from other students. Opponents of full inclusion argue that regular classroom teachers lack appropriate training and materials and are already over-burdened with large class sizes and inadequate support services.

Many (perhaps most) classroom teachers have students identified as disabled who are usually receiving some type of special educational services part of the day. Most of these mainstreamed students are categorized as having learning disabilities, speech impairments, mild retardation, or emotional disorders. High-quality mainstreaming can dramatically improve the achievement and self-confidence of these students. Mainstreaming also allows students with disabilities to interact with peers and to learn conventional behavior. However, mainstreaming also creates challenges. When mainstreamed students are performing below the level of the rest of the class, some teachers struggle to adapt instruction to the mainstreamed students' needs and to cope with the attitudes of the nondisabled students toward their disabled classmates, which are often negative (Gottleib and Leyser, 1981) and defeat attempts at social integration. Unfortunately, some classroom teachers are uncomfortable about having students with disabilities in their classes, and many feel poorly prepared to accommodate their needs (Alexander and Strain, 1978). It occasionally happens that a teacher will present a lesson to twenty-nine students while one supposedly mainstreamed child sits in the back of the room coloring a picture or doing nothing at all.

Figure 12.7

Achievement of Students in Regular and Special Education Classes

In a classic study, placement in regular rather than special education classes resulted in higher achievement levels over three years for "emotionally disturbed" (ED) and "educable mentally retarded" (EMR) students.

From Madden and Slavin, 1983a, p. 525. Based on data from Calhoun and Elliott, 1977.

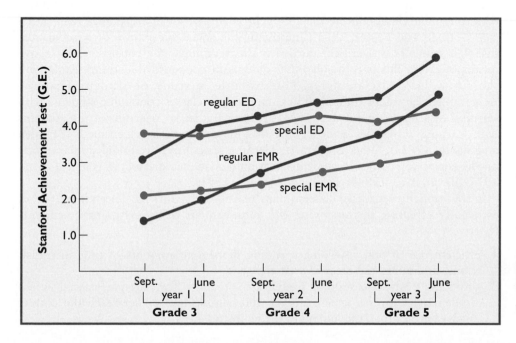

Research on Mainstreaming

Research on mainstreaming has focused on students with learning disabilities, mild retardation, and mild emotional disorders, whose deficits can be termed "mild academic disabilities" (Madden and Slavin, 1983b; MacMillan *et al.,* 1986). Several studies have compared students with mild academic disabilities in special education classes to those in regular classes. When the regular teacher uses an instructional method designed to accommodate a wide range of student abilities, students with mild disabilities generally learn much better in the regular classroom than in special education. One classic study on this topic was done by Calhoun and Elliott (1977), who compared "educable mentally retarded" (EMR) students and "emotionally disturbed" (ED) students in regular and special classes. Regular as well as special education classes used the same individualized materials, and teachers (trained in special education) were rotated across classes to ensure that the only difference between the regular and special programs was the presence of nondisabled classmates. The results of the Calhoun and Elliott (1977) study, depicted in Figure 12.7, suggest the superiority of regular class placement.

Research on programs for regular classrooms containing students with mild academic disabilities indicates that the most successful strategy is to use individualized instructional programs. For example, the Team Assisted Individualization (TAI) and Cooperative Integrated Reading and Composition (CIRC) programs described in Chapter 9 have both been found to improve the achievement of mainstreamed students with learning disabilities, in comparison to mainstreamed students in traditionally organized classes (Slavin *et al.,* 1984a,b; Madden *et al.,* 1986). Highly structured resource room programs that use programmed instruction and behavior modification techniques to supplement the regular teacher's reading and mathematics instruction have also been found to be effective (Glavin *et al.,* 1971).

One of the reasons for the growth in the 1950s of segregated classes for students with academic disabilities was the observation that these students were poorly accepted by their classmates (Johnson, 1950). When these students were reintegrated into regular classes during the 1970s, problems of social acceptance reappeared (see Gottlieb and Leyser, 1981). Improving the social acceptance of academically disabled students is a critical task of mainstreaming. One consistently effective means of doing this is to involve the students in cooperative learning teams with their nondisabled classmates. For example, a study of Student Teams—Achievement Divisions (described in Chapter 8) in classes containing students with learning disabilities found that STAD reduced the social rejection of the students with learning disabilities while significantly increasing their achievement (Madden and Slavin, 1983a). Other cooperative learning programs have found similar effects on the social acceptance of students with mild academic disabilities (Ballard *et al.,* 1977; Slavin *et al.,* 1984b; Slavin and Stevens, 1991).

In traditionally organized classes, many teacher behaviors have been identified as especially effective in improving the achievement of mainstreamed students (Larrivee, 1985):

1. efficient use of time, avoiding spending inordinate amounts of time in transitions, discipline, and unstructured activities
2. providing positive, sustaining feedback to students (for example, staying with a student who gives a wrong answer and helping him or her reach the correct answer rather than moving on to the next student)

Connections

The strategies for accommodating instruction to individual needs discussed in Chapter 9 are appropriate to mainstreaming, for example, the strategies for individualized instruction and cooperative learning.

3. responding supportively (rather than critically) to students
4. asking questions to which students are likely to be able to respond correctly
5. using classroom management strategies that maintain the continuity of the lesson and minimize discipline problems (see Chapter 11)

In other words, teacher behaviors associated with effective teaching for mainstreaming students are essentially the same as those that improve achievement for all students (Leinhardt and Bickel, 1987). While good classroom instruction for most students with learning disabilities is similar to good instruction for nondisabled students (Larrivee, 1985; Leinhardt and Bickel, 1987), some adaptations in instructional strategies will help you to better meet their needs. Whether you use individualized instruction, cooperative learning, or other means of accommodating student differences, you need to know how to adapt lessons to address the needs of students. When students have difficulty with instruction or materials in learning situations, the recommendation is frequently to adapt or modify the instruction or the materials (see Burnette, 1987). The particular adaptation required depends on the student's needs (Lambie, 1980) and could be anything from format adaptation to rewriting textbook materials to lower the reading level or designing materials to incorporate specific features (Allen *et al.,* 1982). The Theory Into Practice describes three common types of adaptations for accommodating mainstreamed students.

Theory Into Practice

Adapting Instruction for Students with Special Needs

Format Adaptations for Written Assignments

Teachers can change the format in which a task is presented without changing the actual task, for a variety of reasons: (1) an assignment is too long; (2) the spacing on the page is too close to allow the student to focus on individual items; (3) the directions for the task are insufficient or confusing; or (4) the models or examples for the task are either absent, misleading, or insufficient. The critical concept here is that while task and response remain the same, you make adaptations in the way the material is presented.

To adapt the length of an assignment, you might present only one portion of it at a time. For instance, the assignment might be twenty subtraction problems arranged in five rows of four problems each. You might have students complete five small assignments by cutting the paper into five strips and presenting one row at a time. Or you might teach children to divide the assignment into manageable chunks themselves, completing one chunk, then checking with you or taking a short break before continuing with the next chunk. Adaptations may be needed because the items on the page are too close together to allow students to concentrate attention on one item at a time or to write a complete response. You may need to cut the items apart and mount them on other paper. Again, the task has not changed, only the format.

Occasionally, the directions for a task or assignment must be simplified. For example, you might substitute in a set of directions the word "circle" for "draw a ring around." You could also teach students the words commonly found in directions (Cohen and deBettencourt, 1983). By teaching students how to understand such words, you will make them more independent learners. Models or examples presented with a task may also be changed to more closely resemble the task.

Adaptations in Content

In some instances, students may require an adaptation in the content being presented, such as when so much new information is presented that the student is unable to process it quickly or when the student lacks a prerequisite skill or concept necessary to complete a task.

Adaptations in the amount of content being presented may be made by isolating each concept (Bos and Vaughn, 1988) and requiring mastery of each concept as a separate unit before teaching the next concept. Although this type of adaptation involves smaller units of material, the same content will be covered in the end.

Adaptations required because students lack essential prerequisites may be as simple as explaining vocabulary or concepts prior to teaching a lesson. More complex adaptations are required when students lack prerequisite skills or concepts that cannot be explained easily or when they do not have a skill necessary to learn the lesson. For example, if the math lesson involves solving word problems that require the division of three-digit numerals, and the student has not yet learned how to divide three-digit numerals, this skill would have to be taught before the word problems could be addressed.

Adaptations in Modes of Communication

Some students require adaptations either in the way they receive information or the way they demonstrate their knowledge of specific information. Many students are unable to learn information when their only means of getting it is through reading. They can learn if the information is made available in other forms. Be creative in considering the possibilities. You might have students watch a demonstration, filmstrip, film, videotape, television program, computer program, or play. Or you might have them listen to an audiotape, lecture/discussion, or debate.

A different type of adaptation may be required if a student cannot respond as the task directs. If a student has a writing problem, for example, you might ask the student to tell you about the concept in a private conversation, record the student's response on a tape recorder, or ask the student to present an oral report to the class. Or you might let the student represent the knowledge by drawing a picture or diagram or by constructing a model or diorama.

Teaching Learning Strategies and Metacognitive Awareness

Many students do poorly in school because they have failed to "learn how to learn." Programs directed at helping students learn such strategies as note taking, summarization, and memorization methods have been very successful with adolescents who have learning disabilities (Deshler and Schumaker, 1986). Reciprocal teaching, a method for helping nondisabled students learn metacognitive strategies for reading, described in Chapter 7, has also been successful with adolescents with learning disabilities (Palincsar, 1987).

Computers and Students with Disabilities

Connections

Recall the discussion of computer-assisted instruction in Chapter 9.

Computers provide opportunities for individualized instruction to disabled students in regular as well as special education classes. There are four major advantages in using computers to help exceptional children learn. First, computers can help individualize instruction in terms of method of delivery, type and frequency of reinforcement, rate of presentation, and level of instruction. Second, computers can give immediate corrective feedback and emphasize the active role of children in learning. Third, they can hold the attention of children who are easily distractible. Fourth, computer instruction is motivating and patient. For physically disabled students, computers may permit greater ease in learning and communicating information.

Children in special education programs seem to like learning from computers. Poorly motivated students have become more enthusiastic about their studies. They feel more "in control" because they are being taught in a context that is positive, reinforcing and nonthreatening. However, actual learning benefits of computer-assisted instruction for students with disabilities have been inconsistent (Malouf *et al.,* 1990).

One valuable approach using computers is to provide academically disabled children with activities in which they can explore, construct, and communicate. Word processors serve this purpose, and other programs have been specifically designed for children with disabilities. For example, in CARIS (Computer Animated Reading Instruction System) children can select words for sentences by touching a computer screen with a light pen. The computer then generates a brief animated cartoon acting out the meaning of the sentence. Many combinations of words can be explored. Advantages of this program include the control that children have when using it and the immediate visual feedback it supplies.

Buddy Systems and Peer Tutoring

One way to help meet the needs of students with disabilities in the regular classroom is to provide these students with assistance from nondisabled classmates, using either a buddy system to help with noninstructional needs or peer tutoring to help with learning problems.

A student who volunteers to be a special education student's buddy can help that student cope with the routine tasks of classroom life. For example, a buddy can guide a visually impaired student, help an academically disabled student when directions are not understood, or deliver cues or prompts as needed in some classes. In middle and high school settings a buddy can take notes for a student with hearing impairments or learning disabilities by making carbons or photocopies of his or her own notes. The buddy can also ensure that the exceptional student has located the correct textbook page during a lesson and has the materials necessary for a class. The primary responsibility of the buddy is to help the special education student adjust to the regular classroom, to answer questions, and to provide direction for activities. Use of this resource allows the regular classroom teacher to address more important questions related to instructional activities.

Another way of helping students within the regular classroom is to use peer tutoring (Scruggs and Richter, 1986). Teachers who use peers to tutor in their classroom should ensure that these tutors are carefully trained. This means the peer tutor must be taught how to provide assistance by modeling and explaining, how to give specific positive and corrective feedback, and when to allow the student to work alone. Peer tutors and tutees may both benefit: the special education student by acquiring academic concepts and the tutor by gaining a better acceptance and understanding of students with disabilities. Sometimes older students with disabilities tutor younger ones, and this generally benefits both students (Osguthorpe and Scruggs, 1986; Top and Osguthorpe, 1987).

Special Education Teams

When a student with disabilities is integrated into the regular classroom, the classroom teacher often works with one or more special educators to ensure the student's successful integration (Turnbull and Schulz, 1979). The classroom teacher may participate in conferences with special education personnel, the special education personnel may at times be present in the regular classroom, or the classroom teacher may consult with a special educator at regular intervals. Whatever the arrangement, the classroom teacher and the special educator(s) must recognize that each has expertise crucial to the student's success. The regular classroom teacher is the expert on classroom organization and operation on a day-to-day basis, the curriculum of the classroom, and the expectations placed on students for performance. The special educator, on the other hand, is the expert on the characteristics of a particular group of students with disabilities, the learning and behavioral strengths and deficits of the mainstreamed student, and instructional techniques for a particular kind of disability. All this information is important to the successful integration of students, which is why communication between the regular and special education teachers is so necessary (Laurie *et al.*, 1978; Leinhardt and Bickel, 1989).

Communication should begin before students are placed in the regular classroom and should continue throughout the placement. Both teachers must have up-to-date information about the student's performance in each setting to plan and coordinate an effective program. Only then can instruction targeted to improving the student's performance in the regular classroom be designed and presented. In addition, generalization of skills and behaviors from one setting to the other will be enhanced (see Fuchs *et al.*, 1990).

Social Integration of Students with Disabilities

Placement of students in the regular classroom is only one part of their integration into that environment. These students must be integrated socially as well as instructionally. The classroom teacher plays a critical role in this process. Much has been written about the effects of teacher expectations on student achievement and behavior (see Chapter 10). When integrating students with disabilities, the teacher's attitude toward these students is important not only for teacher–student interactions but also as a model for the nondisabled students in the classroom. Simpson (1980) identified the attitudes of teachers as a factor in influencing the attitudes of other students.

The research on attitudes toward individuals with disabilities provides several strategies that might be useful to the regular classroom teacher who wants to influence the attitudes of nondisabled students. One strategy is to use cooperative learning methods (Margulis and Schwartz, 1989; Slavin and Stevens, 1991). Social-skills training has been found to improve the social acceptance of children with disabilities (Gresham, 1986). Another strategy is to provide information to the class about various disabilities, perhaps using specially designed materials (for examples see Barnes *et al.*, 1978; Bookbinder, 1978).

Theory Into Practice

Fostering Social Integration of Students with Special Needs

More and more, students with special needs are becoming an integral part of the regular classroom experience. Regardless of the age or grade level taught, teachers have many ways to foster positive social integration of students with regular and special needs. Several suggestions follow.

1. Model the attitude that all students belong in your classroom by being caring and accepting.

2. Explain to students that everyone is capable of learning, just in different ways.

3. Use the Individualized Education Plan (IEP) to guide instruction of students with special needs.

4. Have expectations of students that are developmentally appropriate and achievement oriented.

5. Use cooperative learning strategies where all students are given a chance to work together to solve common problems.

6. Use peer tutors or peer helpers when assistance is needed.

7. Provide opportunities for all students to participate in classroom routines and responsibilities.

8. Set aside time for students to communicate and develop relationships with each other.

9. Capitalize on students' academic and leisure interests to bring students together.

Self-Check

Define "mainstreaming," and discuss research findings on the effectiveness of mainstreaming approaches. Describe the most effective strategies for accommodating instruction for classes with mainstreamed students. How do computers, buddy systems, peer tutoring, team consultation, and social integration approaches help students with special needs to succeed? Finally, reinterpret the chapter opening scenario in terms of the information in this section by identifying in greater detail the strategies to which Ms. Wagner called attention.

Inclusion

Hallie Stone and Meg Rico are tenth-grade teachers at a large urban school that is facing budget cutbacks. In Hallie's classroom, the two women meet with James Jackson, a member of the special education teaching staff. They are discussing recent directives calling for the full inclusion of students with special needs into regular classrooms.

HALLIE: What do you think of full inclusion, James? With your background in special education, you probably have a clearer idea than we do.

JAMES: I support it, Hallie, and it's about time! I believe that *all* students should have every opportunity to be included in the classroom.

MEG: Is it really so critical that special needs kids have a chance to interact with the others? What about the kids who are multihandicapped? This probably sounds childish, but I'm a little afraid of them.

JAMES: You wouldn't be assigned anyone on a full-time basis who couldn't function unassisted in a regular classroom. But you'd be amazed at what can be worked out with a little assistance. It is definitely beneficial to put the kids together, and there's a body of research to back that up.

HALLIE: It's probably just as important for the nondisabled kids. Isn't helping them to accept differences and social responsibilities a part of the curriculum?

JAMES: Yes, indeed. But somehow you don't sound convinced, Meg.

MEG: Inclusion looks good on paper, but will I really get the support I'll need? Next semester I'm getting a student with psychological problems, one with a learning disability in reading, and one with cerebral palsy who has never been in a regular classroom.

JAMES: Our staff is being cut because of the budget, as you know, but you'll have a special education teacher in your classroom for at least one hour a day. Also we'll be available to consult with you on ways to adapt instruction on a case-by-case basis through out the term.

HALLIE: I heard we'll have physical assistance and volunteers. . . . I certainly hope there will be someone there for the new student with mental retardation I've been assigned. Actually, I'm not clear at all on what he's supposed to come away with from sophomore chemistry.

JAMES: There's more to that than you think, actually. Sounds to me like the teachers and the special education folks need to get together and work out a few things.

MEG: Well, I just wish I had taken a course on special education when I was working toward my teaching degree. How will I know what I am doing or if I am doing something wrong?

JAMES: You sound like the history department. Frank Greenberg was telling me that this morning. He says they're also concerned about doing right by the other students if they have to spend extra time and energy with the special-needs kids. "The squeaky wheel gets the grease," he says.

HALLIE: Well, that's a little extreme, but we do have to think about the curriculum. It wouldn't do to have to water things down or not be able to finish the course.

JAMES: What do you think we should do about all this before the program starts?

MEG: Is there anything we can do?

Problem Solving

1. Identify and list all the concerns that are stated or implied in the dialogue. For each concern, think of approaches or strategies the teachers could use to resolve it.

2. Suggest ways that the classroom teachers and the special education teachers could cooperate to successfully implement a full inclusion program.

3. Brainstorm ways the classroom teachers could assist fully included students with special needs when no outside support is available.

4. Express your solutions by extending the dialogue in writing or in role play, using your list of concerns from above, as an agenda for a school-wide meeting.

Summary

Who Are "Students at Risk" and What Educational Programs Exist for Them?

Defined here, students at risk are any students who are likely to fail academically for any reason stemming from the student or from the student's environment. Reasons are diverse and may include poverty, family dysfunction, pregnancy, delinquency, and truancy, for example, which contribute to school failure and dropout rates. Other reasons include personality characteristics, the presence of disabilities, and factors of physical, cognitive, language, and socioemotional development.

Educational programs for students at risk include compensatory education, prevention and early intervention programs, and special education. Federally funded compensatory education programs include, for example, Head Start, which aims to help preschool-age children from low-income backgrounds to achieve school readiness, and Chapter 1, which mandates extra services in school to low-achieving students in schools with many low-income students. Extra services may include remediation, tutoring, pull-out programs, counseling, and team teaching. Research supports the effectiveness of compensatory education programs.

Research also supports the effectiveness of many prevention and intervention programs, such as Reading Recovery and Success for All, which provide extra services before children at risk fall behind. Child abuse prevention and drug abuse prevention are examples of policies and programs that address students' socioemotional and physical needs. Special education programs serve students with learning disabilities as well as children with physical or psychological problems.

Who Are "Exceptional" Learners?

Exceptionalities refer to special educational needs certain students may have in relation to societal or school norms. An inability to perform appropriate academic tasks, for any reason inherent in the learner, makes that learner exceptional. Gifted and talented students are also regarded as exceptional and may be eligible for special accelerated or enrichment programs. Classification systems for exceptionalities are often arbitrary and debated, and the use of labels may lead to inappropriate treatment or damage to students' self concepts.

Examples of exceptional learners are students with mental retardation or specific learning disabilities, emotional disorders, behavioral disorders, speech or language disorders, visual impairments, hearing impairments, cerebral palsy, or seizure disorders. Clearly identifying exceptionalities and accommodating instruction to meet the needs of exceptional learners are continual challenges.

What Is Special Education?

Special education programs serve children with disabilities and children who are handicapped by some condition. A "handicap" is a condition or barrier imposed by the environment or the self, while a "disability" is a functional limitation that interferes with a person's mental, physical, or sensory abilities. An "impairment" is a loss or abnormality of a part of the body.

Public Law 94–142 (1975), which is now called the Individuals with Disabilities Education Act (IDEA) according to PL101–476 (1990) and was amended by PL99–457 (1986) to include preschool children and seriously disabled infants, mandates that every disabled child is entitled to free and appropriate special education. The "least restrictive environment" clause means that special needs students must be mainstreamed into regular classes as much as possible. The "individualized education program (IEP)" provision requires that parents, teachers, and other professionals must agree on a plan for the placement and education of special needs students. A continuum of special education services exists, ranging from consultation to resource rooms to home schooling. About 11 percent of students are served by some special education program.

What Is Mainstreaming?

Mainstreaming means placing special-needs students in regular classrooms for at least part of the time. Full inclusion of all children in regular classes with appropriate assistance is a widely held goal. Research has shown that mainstreaming is effective in raising many students' performance levels, especially when cooperative learning, buddy systems, peer tutoring, computer instruction, modifications in lesson presentation, and training in social skills are a regular part of classroom learning.

Key Terms

acceleration programs, 460
attention deficit disorder, 451
cerebral palsy, 457
Chapter 1, 439

cognitive impairment, 447
compensatory education, 438
conduct disorders, 455
disability, 445

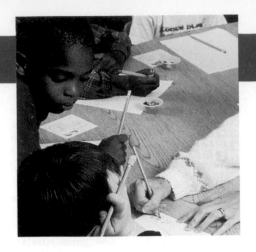

13

Assessing Student Learning

Chapter Outline	Chapter Objectives
What Are Instructional Objectives and How Are They Used? Planning Lesson Objectives Linking Objectives and Assessment Using Taxonomies of Instructional Objectives Research on Instructional Objectives	▲ Write appropriate, specific, and clear instructional objectives of various taxonomic types, and practice using backward planning to develop a unit of study.
Why Is Evaluation Important? Evaluation as Feedback Evaluation as Information Evaluation as Incentive	▲ Discuss six main reasons for the importance of evaluating student learning.
How Is Student Learning Evaluated? Formative and Summative Evaluations Norm-Referenced and Criterion-Referenced Evaluations Authentic Assessments Matching Evaluation Strategies with Goals	▲ Compare and contrast different kinds of classroom assessment and their appropriate use, including formative and summative tests and norm-referenced and criterion-referenced tests.
How Are Tests Constructed? Principles of Achievement Testing Using a Table of Specifications Writing Objective Test Items Writing and Evaluating Essay Tests	▲ Construct an appropriate objectives-based test with well-written multiple choice, true-false, completion, matching, essay, and problem-solving items.
How Are Grades Determined? Establishing Grading Criteria Assigning Letter Grades Assigning Report Card Grades	▲ Express an appropriate grading policy, defend it in relation to evaluation criteria or standards, and describe the conventions of reporting grades.

Mr. Sullivan was having a great time teaching about the Civil War, and his eleventh-grade U.S. History class was having fun too. Mr. Sullivan was relating all kinds of anecdotes about the war. He described a battle fought in the nude (a group of Confederates was caught fording a river), the time Stonewall Jackson lost a battle because he took a nap in the middle of it, and several stories about women who disguised their gender to fight as soldiers. He told the story of a Confederate raid (from Canada) on a Vermont bank. He passed around real Minié balls and grapeshot. In fact, Mr. Sullivan had gone on for weeks about the battles, the songs, the personalities and foibles of the generals. Finally, after an interesting math activity in which students had to figure out how much Confederate money they'd need to buy a loaf of bread, Mr. Sullivan had students put away all their materials to take a test.

The students were shocked. The only question was:

What were the main causes, events, and consequences of the Civil War?

Mr. Sullivan's lessons are fun. They are engaging. They use varied presentation modes. They integrate skills from other disciplines. They are clearly accomplishing one important objective of social studies: building enjoyment of the topic. However, as engaging as Mr. Sullivan's lessons are, there is little correspondence between what he is teaching and what he is testing. He and his students are on a happy trip, but where are they going?

This chapter discusses two important and closely linked topics: *objectives* and *evaluation*. The most important idea in the chapter is that teachers must have an objective, a plan for what students should know and be able to do at the end of a course of study; their lessons must be designed to accomplish these objectives; and their evaluation of students must tell them which objectives each student has actually mastered and can do by the end of the course. Put another way, every teacher should have a clear idea of where the class is going, how it will get there, and how to know if it has arrived.

What Are Instructional Objectives and How Are They Used?

What do you want your students to know or be able to do at the end of today's lesson? What should they know at the end of a series of lessons on a particular subject? What should they know at the end of the course? Knowing the answers to these questions is one of the most important prerequisites for quality instruction. A teacher is like a wilderness guide with a troop of tenderfeet. If the teacher does not have a map or a plan for getting the group where it needs to go, the whole group will surely be lost. Mr. Sullivan's students are having a lot of fun, but since their teacher has no plan for how his lessons will give them essential concepts relating to the Civil War, they will be unlikely to attain these concepts.

Setting out objectives at the beginning of a course is an essential step in providing a framework into which individual lessons will fit. Without such a framework it is easy to wander off the track, to spend too much time on topics that are not central to the course. One biology teacher spent most of the year teaching biochemistry; her students knew all about the chemical makeup of DNA, red blood cells, chlorophyll, and starch, but little about zoology, botany, anatomy, or other topics usually central to high school biology. Then in late May the teacher panicked because she realized that the class had to do a series of laboratory exercises before the end of the year. On successive days they dissected a frog, an eye, a brain, and a pig fetus! Needless to say, the students learned little from those hurried labs and little about biology in general. This teacher did not have a master plan but was deciding week to week (or perhaps day to day) what to teach, thereby losing sight of the big picture—the scope of knowledge that is generally agreed to be important for a high school student to learn in biology class. Few teachers rigidly follow a plan once they make it, but the process of making it is still very helpful (Clark and Peterson, 1986).

An **instructional objective**, sometimes called a behavioral objective, is a statement of skills or concepts students are expected to know at the end of some period of instruction. Typically, an instructional objective is stated in such a way as to make clear how the objective will be measured (see Mager, 1975). Some examples of instructional objectives are:

instructional objective: a statement of information or tasks that students should master after one or more lessons.

• Given 100 division facts (such as 27 divided by 3), students will give correct answers to all 100 in three minutes.

	Performance	Conditions	Criterion
	An objective always says what a learner is expected to do.	An objective always describes the conditions under which the performance is to occur.	Wherever possible, an objective describes the criterion of acceptable performance.
Question Answered:	What should the learner be able to do?	Under what conditions do you want the learner to be able to do it?	How well must it be done?
Example	Correctly use adjectives and adverbs.	Given ten sentences with missing modifiers . . .	. . . the student will correctly choose an adjective or adverb in at least nine of the ten sentences.

Table 13.1   Parts of a Behavioral Objectives Statement

- When asked, students will name at least five functions that characterize all living organisms (respiration, reproduction, etc.)
- In an essay, students will be able to compare and contrast the artistic styles of van Gogh and Gauguin.
- Given the statement, "Resolved: The United States should not have entered World War I," students will be able to argue persuasively either for or against the proposition.

> **Connections**
>
> Recall the discussion of lesson planning and lesson objectives as components of effective instruction in Chapter 8.

Note that even though these objectives vary enormously in the type of learning involved and the ability level they address, they have several things in common. Mager (1975), whose work began the behavioral objectives movement, described objectives as having three parts: performance, conditions, and criteria. Explanations and examples are given in Table 13.1.

Planning Lesson Objectives

In practice, the skeleton of a behavioral objective is condition-performance-criterion. First, state the conditions under which learning will be assessed, as in the following:

- Given a ten-item test . . .
- In an essay the student will be able to . . .
- Using a compass and protractor, the student will be able to . . .

The second part of an objective is usually an action verb that indicates what students will be able to do, for example (from Gronlund, 1978):

- writes
- distinguishes between
- identifies
- matches

Finally, a behavioral objective generally states a criterion for success, as:

- . . . all 100 multiplication facts in three minutes.
- . . . at least five of the nations that sent explorers to the New World.

Sometimes a criterion for success cannot be specified as "number correct." Even so, success should be specified as clearly as possible, as in the following:

- The student will write a two-page essay describing the social situation of women as portrayed in *A Doll's House*.
- The student will think of at least six possible creative uses for an eggbeater other than beating eggs.

Writing Specific Objectives.   Instructional objectives must be adapted to the subject matter being taught (Hamilton, 1985). When students must learn well-defined skills or information with a single right answer, specific instructional objectives should be written as follows:

- Given ten problems involving addition of two fractions with like denominators, students will solve at least nine correctly.
- Given ten sentences lacking verbs, students will correctly choose verbs that agree in number in at least eight sentences. Examples are: My cat and I _____ birthdays in May. (has, have) Each of us _____ to go to college. (want, wants)

Some material, of course, does not lend itself to such specific instructional objectives, and it would be a mistake in such cases to adhere to objectives that have numerical criteria (TenBrink, 1986). For example, it would be possible to have an objective as follows:

- The student will list at least five similarities and five differences between the situation of immigrants to the United States in the early 1900s and that of immigrants today.

However, this objective asks for lists, which may not demonstrate any real understanding of the topic. A less specific but more meaningful objective might be:

- In an essay the student will compare and contrast the situation of immigrants to the United States in the early 1900s and that of immigrants today.

This general instructional objective would allow students more flexibility in expressing their understanding of the topic and would promote comprehension rather than memorization of lists of similarities and differences.

Writing Clear Objectives.   Instructional objectives should be specific enough to be meaningful. For example, an objective concerning immigrants might be written as follows:

- Students will develop a full appreciation for the diversity of peoples who have contributed to the development of American society.

This sounds nice, but what does "full appreciation" mean? Such an objective neither helps the teacher prepare lessons nor helps students understand what is to be taught and how they will be assessed. Mager (1975, p. 20) lists more and less slippery words used to describe instructional objectives:

Words Open to Many Interpretations	*Words Open to Fewer Interpretations*
to know	to write
to understand	to recite
to appreciate	to identify
to fully appreciate	to sort
to grasp the significance	to solve
to enjoy	to construct

Performing a Task Analysis. In planning lessons, it is important to consider the skills required in the tasks to be taught or assigned. For example, a teacher might ask students to use the school library to write a brief report on a topic of interest. The task seems straightforward enough, but consider the separate skills involved:

- knowing alphabetical order
- using the card catalog to find books on a subject
- using a book index to find information on a topic
- getting the main idea from expository material
- planning or outlining a brief report
- writing expository paragraphs
- knowing language mechanic skills (such as capitalization, punctuation, and usage)

These skills could themselves be broken down into subskills, all the way back to letter recognition and handwriting. The teacher must be aware of the subskills involved in any learning task to be certain that students know what they need to know to succeed. Before assigning the library report task, the teacher would need to be sure that students knew, among other things, how to use the card catalog and book indexes and could comprehend and write expository material. The teacher might teach or review these skills before turning students loose in the library.

Similarly, in teaching a new skill, it is important to consider all the subskills that go into it. Think of all the separate steps involved in long division, in writing chemical formulas, or in identifying topic sentences and supporting details. For that matter, consider the skills that go into making a pizza, as illustrated in Figure 13.1.

This process of breaking tasks or objectives down into their simpler components is called **task analysis** (see Gagné, 1977; Gardner, 1985). In planning a lesson, a three-step process for task analysis may be used:

1. *Identify Prerequisite Skills:* What should students already know before you teach the lesson? For example, for a lesson on long division, students must know their subtraction, multiplication, and division facts, and must be able to subtract and multiply with renaming.
2. *Identify Component Skills:* In teaching the actual lesson, what subskills must students be taught before they can learn to achieve the larger objective? To return to the long-division example, students will need to learn estimating, dividing, multiplying, subtracting, checking, bringing down the next digit, and then repeating the process. Each of these steps must be planned for, taught, and assessed during the lesson.
3. *Plan How Component Skills Will Be Assembled into the Final Skill:* The final step in task analysis is to assemble the subskills back into the complete process being taught. For example, students may be able to estimate, to divide, and to

task analysis: breaking down tasks into fundamental subskills.

Figure 13.1   Example of a Task Analysis

Read the diagram this way: Before students can practice the main skill (making pizza), they must be able to use an oven, make dough, and make sauce. These skills must all be learned before the main skill can be mastered. They are independent of one another and can be learned in any order. Before making dough or making sauce, students must be able to read a recipe and measure ingredients. Finally, to read a recipe the learner first has to learn how to decode abbreviations.

Adapted from Mager, 1984, p. 100.

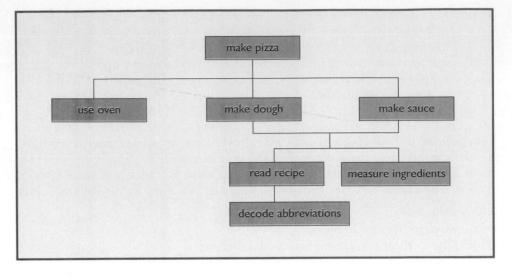

multiply, but this does not necessarily mean they can do long division. The subskills must be integrated into a complete process that students can understand and practice.

Backward Planning.   Just as lesson objectives are more than the sum of specific task objectives, the objectives of a course of study are more than the sum of specific lesson objectives. For this reason it makes sense to start by writing broad objectives for the course as a whole, then objectives for large units, and only then specific behavioral objectives (see Gronlund, 1991). For example, Mr. Sullivan would have done well to have identified the objective of his Civil War unit as follows:

> Students will understand the major causes, events, and consequences of the Civil War.

Then he might have written more detailed objectives relating to causes, events, and consequences. An elaborated example of this **backward planning** process is given in the next Theory Into Practice.

Theory Into Practice

Planning Courses, Units, and Lessons

Up to now, this chapter has focused on planning of instruction according to specific instructional objectives. But how does this fit into the larger task of planning an entire course?

In planning a course, it is important to set long-term, middle-term, and short-term objectives before starting to teach (Brown, 1988; Shavelson, 1987). Before the students arrive for the first day of class, a teacher needs to have a general plan of what will be covered all year, a more specific plan for what will be in the first unit, and a very specific plan for the content of the first lessons. This is illustrated in Table 13.2.

backward planning: planning instruction by first setting long-range goals, then setting unit objectives, and finally planning daily lessons.

If you wanted your students to be able to give an oral report, how might you use task analysis to plan your lesson objectives? How would you guide your students in assessing one another's performance?

Note that Table 13.2 implies a backward planning process. First the course objectives are established. Then unit objectives are designated. Finally, specific lessons are planned. The course objectives list all the topics to be covered during the year. The teacher might divide the number of weeks in the school year by the number of major topics to figure what each will require. More or less time could be reserved for any particular topic, as long as adequate time is allowed for the others. It would be possible to spend a whole semester on any one of the topics in Table 13.2, but in a survey course on life science this would be inappropriate. The teacher must make hard choices about how much time to spend on each topic before the first day of class to avoid spending too much time on early topics and not having enough time left to do a good job with later ones. Some history teachers always seem to find themselves still on World War I in mid-May, so they have to compress most of the twentieth century into a couple of weeks!

Table 13.2 shows approximate allocations of weeks to each of the topics to be covered. These are just rough estimates to be modified as time goes on.

Unit Objectives and Unit Tests

After laying out course objectives, the next task is to establish objectives for the first unit and to estimate the number of class periods to spend on each objective. It is a good idea to write a unit test as part of the planning process. Writing a test in advance helps you to focus on the important issues to be covered. For example, in a four-week unit on the Civil War, you might decide that the most important things students should learn are the causes of the war, a few major points about the military campaigns, the importance of the Emancipation

Course Objectives (Weeks Allocated)	Unit Objectives (Days Allocated)	Lessons
Scientific Method 3	Observation and measurement 4	Lesson 1:
Characteristics of living things 3		• Questions
		• Observations
Cells 3	Prediction and control 2	Lesson 2:
Photosynthesis 3	Data 3	• Checking observation with measurement
Respiration 3	Experiments 3	
Human systems 4	Problem solving 3	Lesson 3:
Reproduction 4		• Measurement of length
Environment 3		Lesson 4:
Adaptation 4		• Measurement of mass
Relationships 3		• Measurement of volume
Balance 3		

Table 13.2   Example of Objectives for a Course in Life Science

Teachers can allocate instructional time for a course by (1) deciding what topics to cover during the year or semester, (2) deciding how many weeks to spend on each topic, (3) choosing units within each topic, (4) deciding how many days to spend on each, and (5) deciding what each day's lesson should be.

SOURCE: Objectives adapted from Wong *et al.,* 1978.

Proclamation, Lincoln's assassination, and the history of the Reconstruction period. These topics would be central to the unit test on the Civil War. Writing this test would put into proper perspective the importance of the various issues that should be covered.

The test you prepare as part of your course planning may not be exactly what you give at the end of the unit. You may decide to change, add, or delete items to reflect the content you actually covered. But this does not diminish the importance of having decided in advance exactly what objectives you wanted to achieve and how you were going to assess them.

Many textbooks provide unit tests and objectives, making your task easier. However, even if you have ready-made objectives and tests, it is still important to review their content and change them as necessary to match what you expect to teach.

If you prepare unit tests from scratch, use the guide to test construction described later in this chapter. Be sure to have the test items cover the various objectives in proportion to their importance to the course as a whole (that is, the more important objectives are covered by more items), and include items that assess higher-level thinking as well as factual knowledge.

Lesson Plans and Lesson Assessments

The final step in backward planning is to plan daily lessons. Table 13.2 shows how unit objectives might be broken down into daily lessons. The next step is to plan the content of each lesson. A lesson plan consists of an objective, a plan for presenting information, a plan for giving students practice (if appropriate), a plan for assessing student understanding and, if necessary, a plan for reteaching students (or whole classes) if their understanding is inadequate.

Linking Objectives and Assessment

Because instructional objectives are stated in terms of how they will be measured, it is clear that objectives are closely linked to **assessment.** An assessment is any measure of the degree to which students have learned the objectives set out for them. Most assessments in schools are tests or quizzes, or informal verbal assessments such as questions in class. However, students can also show their learning by writing an essay, painting a picture, doing a car tune-up, or baking a pineapple upside-down cake.

One critical principle of assessment is that assessments and objectives must be clearly linked. Students learn some proportion of what they are taught; the greater the overlap between what was taught and what is tested, the better students will score on the test and the more accurately any need for additional instruction can be determined (Cooley and Leinhardt, 1980). Teaching should be closely linked to instructional objectives, and both should clearly relate to assessment. If any objective is worth teaching, it is worth testing, and vice versa. This idea was illustrated by Mager as follows:

> During class periods of a seventh grade algebra course, a teacher provided a good deal of skillful guidance in the solution of simple equations. . . . When it came time for an examination, however, the test items consisted mainly of word problems, and the students did rather poorly. The teacher's justification for this "sleight of test" was that the students didn't "really understand" algebra if they could not solve word problems. Perhaps the teacher was right. But the skill of solving equations is considerably different from the skill of solving word problems; if he wanted his students to learn how to solve word problems, he should have taught them how to do so. (1975, p. 82)

Mager's algebra teacher really had one objective in mind (solving word problems), but taught according to another (solving equations). If he had coordinated his objectives, his teaching, and his assessment, he and his students would have been a lot happier, and the students would have had a much better opportunity to learn to solve algebra word problems.

One way to specify objectives for a course is to actually prepare test questions before the course begins (see Gronlund, 1991). This allows the teacher to write general **teaching objectives** and then to clarify them with very specific **learning objectives,** as in the following examples:

Teaching Objective

A. Ability to subtract three-digit numbers renaming once or twice

Specific Learning Objective (Test Questions)

A1. 237   A2. 412   A3. 596
    − 184   − 298   − 448

---

assessment: a measure of the degree to which instructional objectives have been attained.

teaching objectives: clear statement of what students are intended to learn through instruction.

learning objectives: specific behaviors students are expected to exhibit at the end of a series of lessons.

B. Use of language to set mood in Edgar Allen Poe's "The Raven"

B1. How does Poe reinforce the mood of "The Raven" after setting it in the first stanza?

C. Identifying the chemical formulas for common substances

Write the chemical formulas for the following:
C1. Water _____
C2. Carbon dioxide _____
C3. Coal _____
C4. Table salt _____

Using Taxonomies of Instructional Objectives

In writing objectives and assessments it is important to consider different skills and different levels of understanding. For example, in a science lesson for second-graders on insects, you might want to impart both information (the names of various insects) and an attitude (the importance of insects to the ecosystem). In other subjects, you may try to convey facts and concepts that differ by type. For example, in teaching a lesson on topic sentences in reading, you might have students first repeat a definition of "topic sentence," then identify topic sentences in paragraphs, and finally write their own topic sentences for original paragraphs. Each of these activities demonstrates a different kind of understanding of the concept "topic sentence," and we could not consider this concept adequately taught if students could do only one of these activities. These various lesson goals can be classified by type and degree of complexity. A taxonomy, or system of classification, helps a teacher categorize instructional activities.

Bloom's Taxonomy.   In 1956 Benjamin Bloom and some fellow researchers published a **taxonomy of educational objectives** that has been extremely influential in the research and practice of education ever since. Bloom and his colleagues categorized objectives from simple to complex, or from factual to conceptual. The key elements of what is commonly called Bloom's taxonomy (Bloom *et al.,* 1956) for the cognitive domain are (from simple to complex):

What kinds of instructional objectives would be involved if you wanted students to be able to identify the distinguishing features of this human skeleton, explain the relationships among its parts, and hypothesize what the person would have looked like in the flesh?

taxonomy of educational objectives: Bloom's ordering of objectives from simple learning tasks to more complex ones.

1. *Knowledge* (recalling information): The lowest level of objectives in Bloom's hierarchy, knowledge refers to objectives such as memorizing math facts or formulas, scientific principles, or verb conjugations.
2. *Comprehension* (translating, interpreting, or extrapolating information): Comprehension objectives require that students show an understanding of information as well as the ability to use it. Examples are interpreting the meaning of a diagram, graph, or parable, inferring the principle underlying a science experiment, and predicting what might happen next in a story.
3. *Application* (using principles or abstractions to solve novel or real-life problems): Application objectives require students to use knowledge or principles to solve practical problems. Examples include using geometric principles to figure out how many gallons of water to put into a swimming pool of given dimensions and using knowledge of the relationship between temperature and pressure to explain why a balloon is larger on a hot day than on a cold day.
4. *Analysis* (breaking down complex information or ideas into simpler parts to understand how the parts relate or are organized): Analysis objectives involve having students see the underlying structure of complex information or ideas. Analysis objectives might be contrasting schooling in the United States with education in Japan, understanding how the functions of the carburetor and distributor are related in an automobile engine, or identifying the main idea of a short story.
5. *Synthesis* (creation of something that did not exist before): Synthesis objectives involve using skills to create completely new products. Examples would include writing a composition, deriving a mathematical rule, designing a science experiment to solve a problem, and making up a new sentence in a foreign language.
6. *Evaluation* (judging something against a given standard): Evaluation objectives require making value judgments against some criterion or standard. For example, students might be asked to compare the strengths and weaknesses of two home computers in terms of flexibility, power, and available software.

> **Connections**
> Recall the discussion of thinking skills and critical thinking skills in Chapter 7

Because Bloom's taxonomy is organized from simple to complex, some people interpret it as a ranking of objectives from trivial (knowledge) to important (synthesis, evaluation). However, this is not the intent of the taxonomy. Different levels of objectives are appropriate for different purposes and for students at different stages of development (see Hastings, 1977).

The primary importance of Bloom's taxonomy is in its reminder that we want students to have many levels of skills. All too often teachers focus on measurable knowledge and comprehension objectives and forget that students cannot be considered proficient in many skills until they can apply or synthesize the skill. On the other side of the coin, some teachers fail to make certain that students are well rooted in the basics before heading off into higher-order objectives.

Using a Behavior Content Matrix.   One way to be sure that your objectives cover many levels is to write a **behavior content matrix** (Gage and Berliner, 1984). This is simply a chart that shows how a particular concept or skill will be taught and assessed at different cognitive levels. Examples of objectives in a behavior content matrix appear in Table 13.3. Note that for each topic, objectives are listed for some but not all of Bloom's taxonomy. Some topics do not lend themselves to some levels of the taxonomy, and there is no reason that every level should be covered for every topic. However, using a behavior content matrix in setting objectives forces you to consider objectives above the knowledge and comprehension levels.

> **behavior content matrix:**
> a chart that classifies lesson objectives according to cognitive level.

Type of Objective	Example 1: The Area of a Circle	Example 2: Main Idea of a Story	Example 3: The Colonization of Africa
Knowledge	Give the formula for area of a circle.	Define "main idea."	Make a timeline showing how Europeans divided Africa into colonies.
Comprehension		Give examples of ways to find the main idea of a story.	Interpret a map of Africa showing its colonization by European nations.
Application	Apply the formula for area of a circle to real-life problems.		
Analysis		Identify the main idea of a story.	Contrast the goals and methods used in colonizing Africa by the different European nations.
Synthesis	Use knowledge about the areas of circle and volumes of cubes to derive a formula for the volume of a cylinder.	Write a new story based on the main idea of the story read.	Write an essay on the European colonization of Africa from the perspective of a Bantu chief.
Evaluation		Evaluate the story.	

Table 13.3   Examples of Objectives in a Behavior Content Matrix

A behavior content matrix can remind teachers to develop instructional objectives that address skills at various cognitive levels.

Taxonomies of Affective Objectives.   Learning facts and skills is not the only important goal of instruction. Sometimes the feelings that students have about a subject or about their own skills are at least as important as how much information they learn. Instructional goals related to attitudes and values are called **affective objectives.** Many would argue that a principal purpose of a U.S. history or civics course is to promote values of patriotism and civic responsibility, and one purpose of any mathematics is course to give students confidence in their ability to use mathematics.

Krathwohl *et al.* (1964) designed a taxonomy of affective objectives, which can be summarized as follows:

1. *Receiving:* Students show awareness of and willingness to receive information or other stimuli (for example, "I'm willing to receive math instruction").
2. *Responding:* Students indicate a willingness to participate in a given activity, accept certain ideas, and show satisfaction in participating in activities (for example, "I'm eager to participate in group discussions").
3. *Valuing:* Students indicate that they value certain propositions, and express commitment to ideas or activities (for example, "I believe in the importance of civic responsibility in our society").

> **affective objectives:** objectives concerned with student attitudes and values.

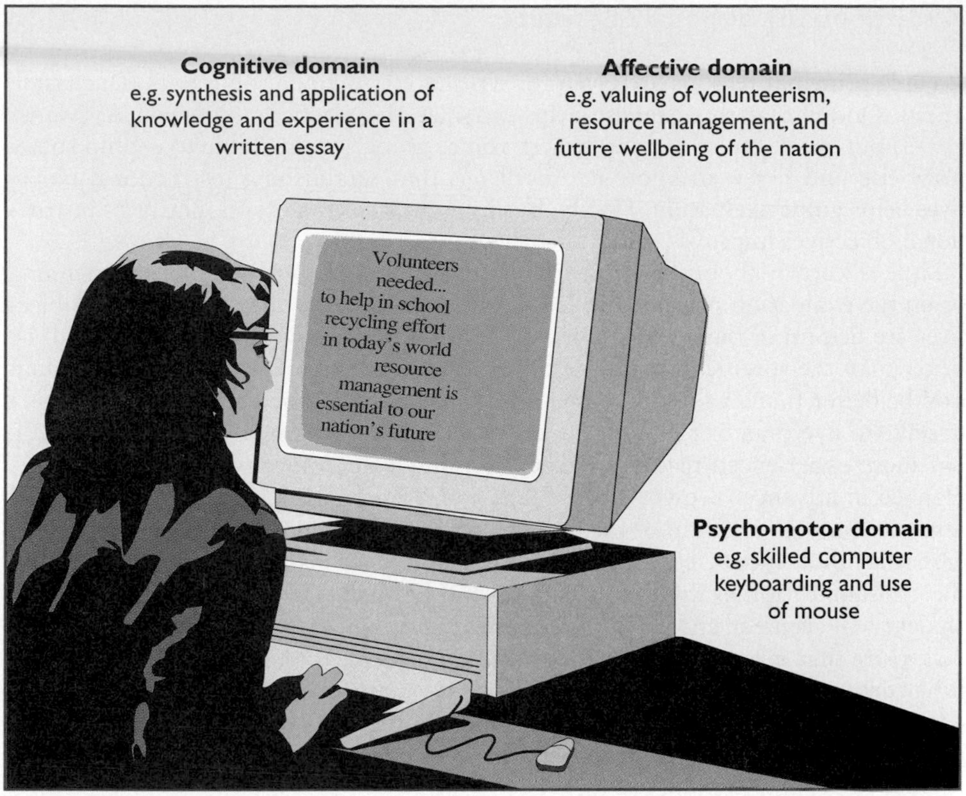

Figure 13.2
The Interplay of Different Kinds of Educational Objectives

4. *Organization:* Students integrate and reconcile different values and develop value systems. For example, students might reconcile love for living things and dislike of hunting with the need to avoid overpopulation of deer herds and with their own preference for eating meat.

5. *Characterization by Value:* A set of values becomes a way of life. Students develop a generalized predisposition to act in a certain way, such as to approach problems confidently and rationally or to put others' needs above their own.

This taxonomy of affective objectives is a reminder that affective objectives should be considered in planning and carrying out instruction (see Eisner, 1969). Love of learning, confidence in learning, and development of prosocial, cooperative attitudes are among the most important objectives teachers should have for their students.

Taxonomies of Psychomotor Objectives. The psychomotor domain refers to activities that involve physical performance or skill—sports, drama, driving, typing, and so on. Bloom's taxonomy can be adapted to physical performances, but Harrow (1972), Simpson (1972), and others have described specific taxonomies for **psychomotor objectives.** The main elements of Harrow's taxonomy are as follows:

1. reflex movements (*e.g.,* blinking)
2. basic fundamental movements (*e.g.,* running)
3. perceptual abilities (*e.g.,* skipping rope, writing individual letters)
4. physical abilities (*e.g.,* weight lifting, long-distance bicycling)
5. skilled movements (*e.g.,* playing tennis, dancing, typing, driving)
6. nondiscursive communication (*e.g.,* demonstrating emotions or other information with body language).

psychomotor objectives: objectives concerned with physical skills that students must master.

Research on Instructional Objectives

Three principal reasons are given for writing instructional objectives (Duchastel, 1979). One is that this exercise helps organize the teacher's planning. As Mager (1975) puts it, if you're not sure where you're going, you're liable to end up someplace else and not even know it. Another is that establishing instructional objectives helps guide evaluation. Finally, it is hypothesized that development of instructional objectives improves student achievement.

Little is known about the effects of instructional objectives on teachers' planning or on the evaluation process, but it is intuitively apparent that instructional objectives are helpful in these areas. How could fuzzy planning or no planning at all be better than the specification of clear, concrete objectives? How could fuzzy evaluation be better than evaluation based on well-thought-out objectives? It would be a mistake to overplan or to rigidly adhere to an inflexible plan (see Shavelson, 1987), but most experienced teachers create, use, and value objectives and assessments planned in advance (Brown, 1988; Clark and Yinger , 1986). Despite some mixed research findings, the sum of the research on instructional objectives generally suggests that they should be used. The establishment of instructional objectives and the communication of these objectives to students have never been found to reduce student achievement and have often been found to increase it. It is important to make sure that instructional objectives communicated to students be broad enough to encompass everything the lesson or course is supposed to teach; there is some danger that giving students too narrow a set of objectives may focus them on some information to the exclusion of other facts and concepts (see Duchastel, 1979; Klauer, 1984; and Melton, 1978).

Perhaps the most convincing support for the establishment of clear instructional objectives is indirect. Cooley and Leinhardt (1980) found that the strongest single factor predicting student reading and math scores was the degree to which students were actually taught the skills tested. This implies that instruction is effective to the degree that objectives, teaching, and assessment are coordinated with one another. Specification of clear instructional objectives is the first step in ensuring that classroom instruction is directed toward giving students critical skills, those that are important enough to test.

Self-Check

In a subject area of your choice at a level you plan to teach, attempt the procedures this section describes, and then review the section to see how you can improve on your results. Specifically, practice writing instructional objectives based on Mager's model, perform a task analysis, and use backward planning to sketch out a unit of study. Develop a behavior content matrix with one objective each in the cognitive, affective, and psychomotor domains.

---

evaluation: decision making about student performance and about appropriate teaching strategies.

Why Is Evaluation Important?

Evaluation refers to all the means used in schools to formally measure student performance. These include quizzes and tests, written evaluations, and grades. Student evaluation usually focuses on academic achievement, but many schools also evaluate behaviors and attitudes. For example, one national survey of report cards found that most elementary schools provided descriptions of students' behavior (such as "follows directions," "listens attentively," "works with others," "uses time wisely"). In upper elementary, middle, and high school the prevalence of behavior reports successively diminishes, but even many high schools rate students on such criteria as "works up to ability," "is prepared," and "is responsible" (Chansky, 1975).

Why do we use tests and grades? We use them because, one way or another, we must periodically check students' learning. Tests and grades tell teachers, students, and parents how students are doing in school. Teachers can use tests to see whether their instruction was effective and to find out which students need additional help. Students can use them to see whether their studying strategies are paying off. Parents need grades to find out how their children are doing in school; grades serve as the one consistent form of communication between school and home. Schools need grades and tests to make student placements. States and school districts need tests to evaluate schools and, in some cases, teachers. Ultimately, colleges use grades and standardized test scores to decide whom to admit. We must evaluate student learning, therefore; few would argue otherwise. Research on the use of tests finds that students learn more in courses that use tests than in those that do not (Bangert-Drowns *et al.*, 1986).

Student evaluations serve six primary purposes:

1. feedback to students
2. feedback to teachers
3. information to parents
4. information for selection and certification
5. information for accountability
6. incentives to increase student effort

Evaluation as Feedback

Imagine that a store owner tried several strategies to increase business—first advertising in the newspaper, then sending fliers to homes near the store, and finally holding a sale. However, suppose that after trying each strategy, the store owner failed to record and compare the store's revenue. Without taking stock this way, the owner would learn little about the effectiveness of any of the strategies and might well be wasting time and money.

Student Feedback.   Like the store owner, students need to know the results of their efforts (Bangert-Drowns *et al.*, 1991; Kulhavy and Stock, 1989). Regular evaluation gives them feedback on their strengths and weaknesses. For example, suppose a teacher had students write compositions and then gave back written evaluations. Some students might find out that they need to work more on content, others on the use of modifiers, still others on language mechanics. This information would help students improve their writing much more than would a grade with no explanation.

To be useful as feedback, evaluations should be as specific as possible. For example, Cross and Cross (1980–81) found that students who received written feedback in addition to letter grades were more likely than other students to feel that their efforts, rather than luck or other external factors, determined their success in school.

Teacher Feedback.   One of the most important (and often overlooked) functions of evaluating student learning is to provide feedback to teachers on the effectiveness

---

Connections

Recall the definition and discussion of feedback as a component of effective teaching in Chapter 8.

of their instruction. Teachers cannot expect to be optimally effective if they do not know whether students have grasped the main points of their lessons. Asking questions in class gives the teacher some idea of how well students have learned, but in many subjects brief, frequent quizzes are necessary to provide more detailed indications of students' progress.

Evaluation as Information

Information to Parents.   A report card is called a report card because it reports information on student progress to parents. This reporting function of evaluation is important for several reasons. First, routine school evaluations of many kinds (test scores, stars, and certificates as well as report card grades) keep parents informed about their children's schoolwork. For example, if a student's grades are dropping, the parents may know why and may be able to help the student get back on track. Second, grades and other evaluations set up informal home-based reinforcement systems. Recall from Chapter 11 that many studies have found that reporting regularly to parents when students do good work, and asking parents to reinforce good reports, improves student behavior and achievement (Barth, 1979). Without much prompting, most parents naturally reinforce their children for bringing home good grades, thereby making grades more important and more effective as incentives (Natriello and Dornbusch, 1984).

Information for Selection.   Some sociologists see as a primary purpose of schools the sorting of students into societal roles; if schools do not actually determine who will be a butcher, a baker, or a candlestick maker, they do substantially influence who will be a laborer, a skilled worker, a white-collar worker, or a professional. This sorting function takes place gradually over years of schooling. In the early grades students are sorted into reading groups and, in many cases, into tracks that may remain stable over many years (Slavin, 1987c, 1990a). Tracking becomes more widespread and systematic by junior high or middle school, when students begin to be selected into different courses (McPartland *et al.*, 1987). For example, some ninth-graders are allowed to take Algebra I, while others take pre-algebra or general mathematics. In high school, students are usually steered toward college preparatory, general, or vocational tracks, and of course a major sorting takes place when students are accepted into various colleges and training programs. Throughout the school years some students are selected into special education or gifted programs or into other special programs with limited enrollments.

Closely related to selection is certification, a use of tests to qualify students for promotion or for access to various occupations. For example, many states and local districts have minimum competency tests that students must pass to advance from grade to grade or to graduate from high school. Bar exams for lawyers, board examinations for medical students, and tests for teachers, such as the National Teachers' Examination, are examples of certification tests that control access to professions.

Information for Accountability.   Often, evaluations of students are used to evaluate teachers, schools, districts, or even states. Many states have statewide testing programs that allow the states to rank every school in terms of student performance. Most school districts use these tests for similar purposes. These test scores are often used in making decisions about the hiring and firing of principals and sometimes even superintendents. Consequently, these tests are taken very seriously. In addition, student test scores are often used to evaluate teachers.

Evaluation as Incentive

One important use of evaluations is to motivate students to give their best efforts. In essence, high grades, stars, and prizes are given as rewards for good work. These are primarily valued by elementary students because they are valued by their parents, and by some high school students because they are important for getting into college.

Natriello and Dornbusch (1984) and Natriello (1989) have suggested criteria that must be satisfied if evaluations are to increase student effort (see also Crooks, 1988). An adaptation of their criteria follows.

1. *Important Evaluations:* Evaluations are effective to the degree that they are important to students. For example, grades will be less effective as incentives for students whose parents pay little attention to their grades. They will be more effective for students planning to go to competitive colleges (which require high grades for admission). Natriello and Dornbusch (1984) state that evaluations will be important to students to the degree that they are seen as *central* to their attainment of valued objectives and *influential* in attaining those objectives.

2. *Soundly Based Evaluations:* Evaluations must be closely related to a student's actual performance. Students must feel that evaluations are fair, objective measures of their performance. To the degree that students believe they can outfox the system and get away with shoddy efforts or that the system is rigged against them, evaluations will have little impact on their efforts. Students should have every opportunity to show what they really know on tests. Reducing test anxiety, a serious problem for many students (Hembree, 1988; Hill and Wigfield, 1984), is one way to increase the soundness of evaluations. This can be done by giving plenty of time for tests, by reducing pressure, and by closely linking tests to course content.

3. *Consistent Standards:* Evaluations will be effective to the degree that students perceive them to be equal for all students. For example, if students feel that some of their classmates are evaluated more leniently than others, this will reduce the effectiveness of the evaluation system.

4. *Clear Criteria:* The criteria for success must be clear to students; they should know precisely what is required to obtain a good grade or other positive evaluation (see Schunk, 1983).

5. *Reliable Interpretations of Evaluations:* Appropriate interpretations must be made clear. Students often interpret evaluations (and their own efforts) in light of social contexts. For example, some students may believe that doing any homework at all shows a high level of effort when their classmates are doing none, or that a C is a good grade when many of their classmates are failing.

6. *Frequent Evaluations:* There is evidence that the more frequently evaluations take place, the more students generally achieve (Crooks, 1988; Kulik and Kulik, 1988; Peckham and Roe, 1977). Frequent, brief quizzes are better than infrequent, long tests because they require that students pay attention all the time rather than cram for the occasional exam, because they give students more timely feedback, and because they provide reinforcement for hard work closer in time to when the work was done.

Connections

Recall the discussion of the limitations of using grades as incentives in Chapter 10.

7. *Challenging Evaluations:* Evaluations should be challenging for all students, but impossible for none. This can be done by evaluating students according to their improvement over their own past performance, a strategy found to increase their achievement (Slavin, 1980). Evaluation systems should be set up to encourage students always to be reaching for success, just as runners set goals for finishing a mile a little bit faster than their previous best time.

Self-Check

Identify six primary purposes of evaluating student learning and give examples of each.

How Is Student Learning Evaluated?

As implied in the previous sections, evaluation strategies effective for any one purpose may be ineffective for other purposes. To understand how evaluations can be used most effectively in classroom instruction, you will need to know the differences between formative and summative evaluation, and between norm-referenced and criterion-referenced evaluation.

Formative and Summative Evaluations

The distinction between formative and summative evaluation was introduced in the discussion of mastery learning in Chapter 9, but this distinction also applies to a broader range of evaluation issues. Essentially, a **formative evaluation** asks "How are you doing?" while a **summative evaluation** asks "How did you do?" Formative, or diagnostic, tests are given to discover strengths and weaknesses in learning, to make midcourse corrections in pace or content of instruction. Formative evaluation is useful to the degree that it is informative, closely tied to the curriculum being taught, timely, and frequent. For example, frequent quizzes given and scored immediately after specific lessons might serve as formative evaluations, providing feedback to teachers and students that they can use to improve students' learning.

In contrast, summative evaluation refers to final tests of student knowledge. Summative evaluation may or may not be frequent, but it must be reliable and (in general) should allow for comparisons among students. Summative evaluations should also be closely tied to formative evaluations and to course objectives.

In mastery learning, both formative and summative tests are given frequently. However, in other instructional approaches the term "formative evaluation" usually refers to routine quizzes that evaluate students' progress during instruction, while "summative evaluation" refers to grading, standardized testing, or other final assessments of student achievement.

Norm-Referenced and Criterion-Referenced Evaluations

Norm-referenced evaluations focus on comparisons of a student's scores to those of other students. Within a classroom, grading on the curve gives us an idea of how

---

Connections

The concepts of formative and summative evaluation were initially defined in Chapter 9 in the context of mastery learning. The use of mastery criteria in grading is discussed later in this chapter.

---

formative evaluation: tests or assessments administered during units of instruction that measure progress and guide the content and pace of lessons.

summative evaluation: assessments that follow instruction and evaluate knowledge or skills.

norm-referenced evaluations: assessments that compare the performance of one student against the performance of others.

	Norm-Referenced Testing	Criterion-Referenced Testing
Principal use	Survey testing	Mastery testing
Major emphasis	Measures individual differences in achievement	Describes tasks students can perform
Interpretation of results	Compares performance to that of other individuals	Compares performance to a clearly specified achievement domain
Content coverage	Typically covers a broad area of achievement	Typically focuses on a limited set of learning tasks
Nature of test plan	Table of specifications is commonly used	Detailed domain specifications are favored
Item selection procedures	Items selected that provide maximum discrimination among individuals (to obtain high score variability); easy items typically eliminated from the test	Includes all items needed to adequately describe performance; no attempt made to alter item difficulty or to eliminate easy items to increase score variability
Performance standards	Level of performance determined by *relative* position in some known group (ranks fifth in a group of twenty)	Level of performance commonly determined by *absolute* standards (demonstrates mastery by defining 90 percent of the technical terms)

Table 13.4   Comparison of Two Approaches to Achievement Testing
Norm-referenced tests and criterion-referenced tests serve different purposes and have different features.

SOURCE: Gronlund, 1988, p. 15.

a student has performed in comparison with classmates. A student may also have a grade-level or school rank, and in standardized testing, student scores may be compared with those of a nationally representative norm group (see Chapter 14).

Criterion-referenced evaluations focus on assessing students' mastery of specific skills, regardless of how other students did on the same skills. Criterion-referenced evaluations are closely tied to the curriculum being taught and to the lesson or course objectives. Table 13.4 (from Gronlund, 1988) compares the principal features and purposes of criterion-referenced and norm-referenced testing (also see Shepard, 1989a; Popham, 1988).

Formative evaluation is almost always criterion-referenced. In formative testing, we want to know, for example, who is having trouble with Newton's Laws of Thermodynamics, not which student is first, fifteenth, or thirtieth in the class in physics knowledge. Summative testing, however, may be either criterion-referenced or norm-referenced. Even if it is criterion-referenced, however, we usually want to know on a summative test how each student did compared to other students.

criterion-referenced evaluations: assessments that rate how thoroughly students have mastered specific skills or areas of knowledge.

This teacher is discussing a student's individual performance on a daily quiz. What match between evaluation goals and the type of evaluation has he chosen? What match might he choose for comparing this student's performance with that of classmates at the end of the unit of instruction?

Connections

Recall the discussion in Chapter 8 of authentic assessment as a goal of humanistic approaches in education. Portfolio and performance assessments as types of authentic, or alternative, assessments are discussed in Chapter 14.

authentic assessment: measurement of important abilities using procedures that simulate the application of these abilities to real-life problems.

Authentic Assessments

Criterion-referenced evaluations, both formative and summative, may be based on evidence of student achievement in forms other than traditional paper-and-pencil tests. In recent years there has been a movement toward innovative forms of testing, called **authentic assessment,** that focus more on what students can actually do (Herman *et al.,* 1992; Wolf *et al.,* 1991; Tittle, 1991). Because of their growing importance, student portfolios and performance assessments are discussed in detail in Chapter 14.

Matching Evaluation Strategies with Goals

Considering all the factors discussed up to this point, what is the best strategy for evaluating students? The first answer is that there is clearly no *one* best strategy. The best means of accomplishing any one objective of evaluation may be inappropriate for other objectives. Therefore teachers must choose different types of evaluation for different purposes. At a minimum, two types of evaluation should be used, one directed at providing incentive and feedback and the other at ranking individual students relative to the larger group.

Evaluation for Incentive and Feedback.   Traditional grades are often inadequate as incentives to encourage students to give their best efforts and as feedback to teachers and students (see Slavin, 1978a). The principal problem is that grades are given too infrequently, are too far removed in time from student performance, and are poorly tied to specific student behaviors. Recall from Chapter 5 that the effectiveness of reinforcers and of feedback diminishes rapidly if there is much delay between behavior and consequences. By the same token, research has found that achievement is higher in classrooms where students receive immediate feedback on their quizzes than in those classrooms where feedback is delayed (Crooks, 1988; Kulik and Kulik, 1988).

Another reason grades are less than ideal as incentives is that they are usually based on comparative standards. In effect, it is relatively easy for high-ability students to achieve A's and B's but very difficult for low achievers to do so. As a result, high achievers do less work than they are capable of doing, and low achievers give up. As noted in Chapter 10, a reward that is too easy or too difficult to attain, or that is felt to be a result of ability rather than of effort, is a poor motivator (Atkinson and Birch, 1978; Weiner, 1989).

For these reasons, traditional grades should be supplemented by evaluations better designed for incentive and feedback. For example, teachers might give daily quizzes of five or ten items that are scored in class immediately after completion. These would give both students and teachers the information they need to adjust their teaching and learning strategies and to rectify any deficiencies revealed by their evaluations. If the quiz results were made important by having them count toward course grades or by giving students with perfect papers special recognition or certificates, then they would serve as effective incentives, rewarding effective studying behavior soon after it occurs. Use of the Individual Learning Expectations (ILE) strategy (Slavin, 1980) by itself or as part of Student Teams Achievement Divisions (see Chapter 8) adds the element of having students measured against their own past achievement. The emphasis is on improvement through increased effort rather than on high scores attained largely through ability or prior knowledge.

→   **Focus On**

Alternative Assessment

Critics of traditional formal tests that attempt to measure achievement or aptitude in a multiple-choice format point out that these tests cannot measure certain important skills, such as the ability to write competently and think creatively. So the search continues for better ways of finding out what students know and can do. Proposals for alternative assessment have included the use of portfolios, performances, and exhibitions.

Education critic Theodore Sizer suggests that high schools should design a series of exhibitions that would allow students to display what an informed and thoughtful student should know. The exhibitions could be projects that require the application of various skills for their successful completion. Unlike traditional tests, exhibitions would stretch over an extended period. They would challenge students to apply knowledge in realistic, real-world situations and also stimulate dialogue between students and their teachers.

Growing advocacy of alternative assessment has stimulated reforms in traditional and standardized testing. The National Center on Education and the Economy, a leading organization in the movement to establish national school standards, calls for administering a one-time examination as a final assessment of what students have learned. The national examination would be an in-depth investigation of student achievement for which students could directly study beforehand and to which teachers could directly teach. In reforms of the Scholastic Aptitude Test, meanwhile, the math section provides for student-derived answers, and the language section tests critical reading skills and adds an optional 20-minute essay.

Critical Thinking

What situation does the alternative assessment movement address? What exhibitions could you require as a summative test of a unit you would be likely to teach? How far do the national examination proposal and SAT reform go in addressing criticisms of traditional approaches to assessment?

Daniel Gursky, "Ambitious Measures," *Teacher,* April 1991; Theodore Sizer, *Horace's School.* Boston: Houghton Mifflin, 1992.

Evaluation for Group Comparison.   There are times when we do need to know how well students are doing in comparison to others. This information is important to give parents and students themselves a realistic picture of student performance. For example, students who have outstanding skills in science ought to know that they are exceptional, not only in the context of their class or school, but also in a broader state or national context. In general, students need to form accurate perceptions of their strengths and weaknesses to guide their decisions about their futures.

Comparative evaluations are traditionally provided by grades and by standardized tests (see Chapter 14). Unlike incentive/feedback evaluations, comparative evaluations need not be conducted frequently. Rather, the emphasis in comparative evaluations must be on fair, unbiased, reliable assessment of student performance. Comparative evaluations should assess what students can do and nothing else. Student grades should be based on demonstrated knowledge of the course content, not on politeness, good behavior, neatness, or punctuality, because the purpose of a grade is to give an accurate assessment of student performance, not to reward or punish students for their behavior. However, grades are imperfect as comparative evaluators because many teachers consider subjective factors when assigning grades. One solution in secondary schools is for teachers in a given department to get together to write departmental exams for each course. For example, a high school science department might decide on common objectives for all chemistry classes and then make up common unit or final tests. This would ensure that students in all classes are evaluated on the same criteria.

Comparative evaluations and other summative assessments of student performance must be firmly based on the objectives established at the beginning of the course and must be consistent with the formative incentive/feedback evaluations. We would certainly not want a situation in which students who are doing well on week-to-week assessments fail the summative evaluations because there is a lack of correspondence between the two forms of evaluation. For example, if the summative test uses essay questions to assess higher-order skills, then similar essay questions must be used all along as formative tests.

Self-Check

Construct a four-square matrix comparing formative and summative testing on one axis and norm-referenced and criterion-referenced testing on the other axis. In each box write a brief description of optimal conditions for using each combination.

How Are Tests Constructed?

Once you know the concept domains to be tested in a test of student learning, it is time to write test items. From 5 to 15 percent of all class time is used in written testing (Dorr-Bremme and Herman, 1986; Haertel, 1986). Writing good achievement tests is thus a critical skill for effective teaching. This section presents some basic principles of achievement testing and practical tools for test construction. Achievement testing is taken up again in Chapter 14 in relation to standardized tests.

Principles of Achievement Testing

Gronlund (1991) listed six principles to keep in mind in preparing achievement tests:

1. *Achievement tests should measure clearly defined learning objectives that are in harmony with instructional objectives:* Perhaps the most important principle of achievement testing is that the tests should correspond with the course objectives and with the instruction actually provided (Fuchs *et al.*, 1991; Linn, 1983). An achievement test should never be a surprise for students; rather, it should assess the students' grasp of the most important concepts or skills the lesson or course is supposed to teach. Further, assessments should tap the true objectives of the course, not easy-to-measure substitutes. For example, a course on twentieth-century art should probably use a test in which students are asked to discuss or to compare art works, not to match artists with their paintings (see Fredericksen, 1984).

2. *Achievement tests should measure a representative sample of the learning tasks included in the instruction:* With rare exceptions (such as multiplication facts),

Connections

The characteristics and uses of standardized achievement tests are discussed in Chapter 14.

achievement tests do not assess every skill or fact students are supposed to have learned. Rather, they sample from among all the learning objectives. If students do not know in advance which questions will be on a test, then they must study the entire course content to do well. However, the test items must be *representative* of all the objectives and content covered. For example, if an English literature course spent eight weeks on Shakespeare and two weeks on other Elizabethan authors, the test should have about four times as many items relating to Shakespeare as to the others.

Items chosen to represent a particular objective must be central to that objective. There is no place in achievement testing for tricky or obscure questions. For example, a unit test on the American Revolution should ask questions relating to the causes, principal events, and outcomes of that struggle, not who rowed George Washington across the Delaware.*

3. *Achievement tests should include the types of test items that are most appropriate for measuring the desired learning outcomes:* Items on achievement tests should correspond as closely as possible to the ultimate instructional objectives. For example, in mathematics problem solving our goal is to enable students to solve problems they will encounter outside of school. Thus multiple-choice items might be inappropriate for this kind of exam because in real life we are rarely presented with four options as possible solutions to a problem.

4. *Achievement tests should fit the particular uses that will be made of the results:* Each type of achievement test has its own requirements. For example, a test used for diagnosis would focus on particular skills students might need help with. A diagnostic test of elementary arithmetic might contain items on subtraction involving zeros in the minuend (for example, 307 - 127), a skill with which many students have trouble. In contrast, a test used to predict future performance might assess a student's general abilities and breadth of knowledge. Formative tests should be very closely tied to material recently presented, while summative tests should survey broader areas of knowledge or skills.

5. *Achievement tests should be as reliable as possible and should be interpreted with caution:* A test is reliable to the degree that students tested a second time would fall in the same rank order (see Chapter 14, "Reliability"). In general, **reliability** of achievement tests is increased by using relatively large numbers of items and by using few items that almost all students get right or that almost all students miss. The use of clearly written items that focus directly on the objectives actually taught also enhances test reliability. Still, no matter how rigorously reliability is built into a test, there will always be some error of measurement. Students have good and bad days or may be lucky or unlucky guessers. Some students are test-wise and usually test well; others are text-anxious and test far below their actual knowledge or potential. Therefore, no single test score should be viewed with excessive confidence. Any test score is only an approximation of a student's true knowledge or skills, and should be interpreted as such.

6. *Achievement tests should improve learning:* Achievement tests of all kinds, particularly formative tests, provide important information on students' learning progress. Achievement testing should be seen as part of the instructional process and used to improve instruction and guide student learning (Foos and

reliability: a measure of the consistency of test scores obtained from the same students at different times.

*Answer: John Glover and his Marblehead Marines.

A. Knowledge of Terms	B. Knowledge of Facts	C. Knowledge of Rules and Principles	D. Skill in Using Processes and Procedures	E. Ability to Make Translations	F. Ability to Make Applications
Atom ①		Boyle's law ⑫			
Molecule ②		Properties of a gas ⑬		Substance into diagram ㉒	
Element ③		Atomic theory ⑯			Writing and solving equations to fit experimental situations
Compound ④	Diatomic gases ⑪	Chemical formula ⑲		Compound into formula ㉑	㉘
Diatomic ⑤					
Chemical formula ⑥		Avogadro's hypothesis ⑭			㉓
Avogadro's number ⑦		Gay-Lussac's law ⑮			㉔
Mole ⑧		Grams to moles ⑱			㉕
Atomic weight ⑨		Molecular weight ⑰	Molecular weight ⑳		㉖
Molecular weight ⑩					㉗
					㉙

Table 13.5　Table of Specifications for a Chemistry Unit

This table of specifications classifies test items (circled numbers) and objectives according to six categories ranging from knowledge of terms to ability to apply knowledge.

SOURCE: Bloom et al., 1971, p. 121.

Fisher, 1988). This means that achievement test results should be clearly communicated to students soon after the test is taken; in the case of formative testing, students should be given the results immediately. Teachers should use the results of formative as well as summative tests to guide instruction, to locate strong and weak points in students' understandings, and to set an appropriate pace of instruction. Including review items on each test (and telling students you will do so) provides distributed practice of course content, an important aid for learning and retaining knowledge (Dempster, 1987).

Using a Table of Specifications

Gronlund's (1991) first principle—that achievement tests should measure well-specified objectives—is an important guide to the content of any achievement test. The first step in the test development process is to decide which concept domains the test will measure and how many test items will be allocated to each concept. Gronlund (1991) and Bloom *et al.* (1971) suggest teachers make up a **table of specifications** listing the various objectives taught and different levels of understanding to be assessed. The levels of understanding may correspond to Bloom's taxonomy of educational objectives (Bloom *et al.*, 1956). Bloom *et al.* (1971) suggest classifying test items for each objective according to six categories, shown in Table 13.5, a table of specifications for a chemistry unit.

Note that the table of specifications varies for each type of course and is nearly identical to behavior content matrixes, discussed earlier in this chapter. This is as it should be: A behavior content matrix is used to lay out objectives for a course, and the table of specifications tests those objectives.

Once you have written items corresponding to your table of specifications, look over the test in its entirety and evaluate it against the following standards:

1. Do the items emphasize the same things you emphasized in day-to-day instruction? (Recall how Mr. Sullivan, in the scenario presented at the beginning of this chapter, ignored this common sense rule.)
2. Has an important area of content or any objective been overlooked or underemphasized?
3. Does the test cover all levels of instructional objectives included in the lessons?
4. Does the language of the items correspond to the language and reading level you used in the lessons?
5. Is there a reasonable balance between what the items measure and the amount of time that will be required for students to develop a response?
6. Did you write model answers or essential component outlines for the short essay items? Does the weighting of each item reflect its relative value among all the other items?

Evaluation restricted to information acquired from paper-and-pencil tests provides only certain kinds of information about children's progress in school. Other sources and strategies for appraisal of student work must be used, including checklists, interviews, classroom simulations, role-playing activities, and anecdotal records. To do this systematically, you may keep a journal or log to record concise and cogent evaluative information on each student throughout the school year.

Writing Objective Test Items

Tests that can be evaluated in terms of the number of items that are correct or incorrect—without the need for interpretation—are referred to as objective tests. Multiple choice, matching, fill-in, and true-false are the most common forms. This section discusses these types of test items and their advantages and disadvantages.

Considered by some educators to be the most useful and flexible of all test forms (Lindeman and Merenda, 1979; Gronlund, 1991), multiple-choice items can be used in tests for most school subjects. The basic form of the **multiple-choice item** is a stem followed by choices, or alternatives. The **stem** may be a question or a partial

table of specifications: list of instructional objectives and expected levels of understanding that guide test development.

multiple-choice item: test item usually consisting of a stem followed by choices, or alternatives.

stem: a question or a partial statement in a test item that is completed by one of several choices.

statement that is completed by one of several choices. There is no truly optimum number of choices, but four or five are most common—one correct response and others referred to as **distractors.**

Here are two types, one with a question stem and the other a completion stem:

1. What color results from the mixture of equal parts of yellow and blue paint?
    a. red
    b. green (correct choice)
    c. gray
    d. black
2. The actual election of the U.S. president to office is done by
    a. all registered voters.
    b. the Supreme Court.
    c. the Electoral College. (correct choice)
    d. our Congressional representatives.

Theory Into Practice
Writing Multiple-Choice Tests

When writing a multiple-choice item keep two goals in mind. First, a knowledgeable student should be able to choose the correct answer and not be distracted by the wrong alternatives. Second, you should minimize the chance that a student ignorant of the subject matter can guess the correct answer. To achieve this, the distractors (the wrong choices) must look plausible to the uninformed: Their wording and form must not identify them readily as bad answers. Hence, one of the tasks in writing a good multiple-choice item is to identify two or three plausible, but not tricky, distractors. Here are some guidelines for constructing multiple-choice items.

1. Make the stem sufficiently specific to stand on its own without qualification.

In other words, the stem should contain enough information to set the context for the concepts in it. At the same time, the stem should not be too wordy; a test is not the place to incorporate instruction that should have been given in the lessons.

Here is an example of a stem for which insufficient context has been established:

Behavior modification is
a. punishment.
b. classical conditioning.
c. self-actualization.
d. reinforcement contingencies.

An improved version of this stem is

Which of the following alternatives best characterizes the modern clinical use of behavior modification?
a. punishment
b. classical conditioning
c. self-actualization
d. reinforcement contingencies (correct choice)

distractors: incorrect responses offered as alternative answers to a multiple-choice question.

2. Do not put too much information into the stem or require too much reading. Avoid complicated sentences unless the purpose of the item is to measure a student's ability to deal with new information or to interpret a paragraph.

3. The stem and every choice in the list of potential answers ought to fit grammatically. In addition, phrases or words that would commonly begin each of the alternatives should be part of the stem. It is also a sound idea to have the same grammatical form (say, a verb) at the beginning of each choice.

For example:

   The task of statistics is to
   a. *make* the social sciences as respectable as the physical sciences.
   b. *reduce* large masses of data to an interpretable form. (correct choice)
   c. *predict* human behavior.
   d. *make* the investigation of human beings more precise and rigorous.

4. Special care must be taken when using no-exception words such as "never," "all," "none," and "always." In multiple-choice items these words often give clues to the test-wise but concept-ignorant student. However, by including these no-exception words in *correct* choices, it is possible to discriminate knowledgeable from ignorant students.

   Hill (1977) notes that such qualifying words as "often," "sometimes," "seldom," "usually," "typically," "generally," and "ordinarily" are most often found in correct responses (or ones that are true) and, along with the no-exception words, should be avoided whenever possible.

5. Avoid making the correct choice either the longest or shortest of the alternatives (usually the longest, because absolutely correct answers often require qualification and precision).

6. Be cautious in using "none of the above" as an alternative because it too often reduces the possible correct choices to one or two items (Lindeman and Merenda, 1979).

Here is an example illustrating how a student may know very little and get the correct answer. By knowing only one of the choices is incorrect, a student will reduce the number of plausible choices from four to two:

   Research suited to investigate the effects of a new instructional program on mathematics achievement is
   a. historical.
   b. experimental. (correct choice)
   c. correlational.
   d. all of the above.

The student who knows that "historical" is not a good choice also knows that d must be incorrect, and the answer must be b or c.

7. After a test, discuss the items with students and note their interpretations of the wording of the items. Students often interpret certain phrases quite differently from what the teacher intended. Such information is very useful in revising items for the next test, as well as for learning about students' understandings.

8. Do not include a choice that is transparently absurd. All choices should sound plausible to a student who has not studied or otherwise become familiar with the subject.

Example with an absurd choice:

During the Civil War the main philosophical differences between the North and the South focused on
a. religious values.
b. agricultural and industrial interests.
c. secular human values.
d. the climate. (not a philosophical choice)

In effect this item has only three choices.

Besides these guidelines for writing multiple-choice items, here are some suggestions about format:

• List the choices vertically rather than side by side.
• Use letters rather than numerals to label the choices, especially on scientific and mathematical tests.
• Use word structures that make the stem agree with the choices according to acceptable grammatical practice. For example, a completion-type stem would require that each of the choices begin with a lower-case letter (unless it begins with a proper noun).
• Avoid overusing one letter position as the correct choice; instead, correct choices should appear in random letter positions.

True-False Items.   **True-false items** can be seen as one form of multiple choice. They are most useful when a comparison of two alternatives is called for, as in the following: Controversy over the use of behavioral objectives in setting goals is caused more by differences in terminology than by real differences in philosophies. (False)

The main drawback of true-false items is that students have a 50 percent chance of guessing correctly. For this reason, multiple-choice or other formats are generally preferable.

Fill-in-the-Blank Items.   When there is only one possible correct answer, the best item format is completion, or "fill in the blank," as in the following examples:

1. The largest city in Germany is _____.
2. What is 15% of $198.00? _____
3. The measure of electric resistance is the _____.

The advantage of **completion items** is that they can reduce the element of test-wiseness to near zero. For example, compare the following items:

1. The capital of Maine is _____.
2. The capital of Maine is:
a. Sacramento.
b. Augusta.
c. Juneau.
d. Boston.

true-false item: one form of multiple-choice test item, most useful when a comparison of two alternatives is called for.

completion items: fill-in-the-blank items on tests.

A student who has no idea what the capital of Maine is could pick Augusta from the list in item 2 because it is easy to rule out the other three cities. In item 1, however, the student has to know the answer. Completion items are especially useful in mathematics, where use of multiple-choice may help give the answer away or reward guessing. For example:

4037
−159

a. 4196
b. 4122
c. 3878 (correct answer)
d. 3978

If students subtract and get an answer other than any of those listed, they know they have to keep trying. In some cases, they can narrow the alternatives by estimating rather than knowing how to compute the answer. It is critical to avoid ambiguity in completion items. In some subject areas this can be difficult because two or more answers will reasonably fit a fragment that does not specify the context. Here are two examples:

1. The Battle of Hastings was in _____. (Date or place?)
2. "H_2O" represents _____. ("Water" or "two parts hydrogen and one part oxygen"?)

Matching Items. **Matching items** are commonly presented in the form of two lists, say A and B. For each item in List A, the student has to select one item in List B. The basis for choosing must be clearly explained in the directions. Matching items can be used to cover a large amount of content; that is, a large number of concepts should appear in the two lists. The primary cognitive skill being tested by matching exercises is recall.

A logistical difficulty with matching items is deciding on the number of concepts to put in each list. If both lists have the same number of items, and no item in B may be used more than once, then a student is able to answer at least one item by default. Or the student may be uncertain about one matching pair and become confused, switch a correct pair, and thus mismatch two items. Since the student cannot mismatch only one pair under these conditions, a "double jeopardy" situation has been created. It is possible to get around this problem by making List B contain more alternatives than the items in List A, and by allowing the alternatives in List B to be selected more than once as correct choices to match with items in List A.

Finally, each list of items to be matched should have no more than six items. Longer lists only confuse students and tend to measure perseverance rather than knowledge. If you find you have too many matched pairs for one question, divide the list into two questions.

Writing and Evaluating Essay Tests

Short essay questions allow students to respond in their own words. The most common form for a **short essay item** includes a question for the student to answer. The answer may range from a sentence or two to a page of, say, 100 to 150 words.

The essay form can elicit a wide variety of responses, from giving definitions of terms to comparing and contrasting important concepts or events. These items are

matching items: given two lists, each item in one list will match with one item in the other list.

short essay item: test item that includes a question for the student to answer, which may range from a sentence or two to a page of, say, 100 to 150 words.

These students took a poorly written classroom test containing short essay items. What mistakes in test construction did the novice student teacher probably make?

especially suited for assessing the ability of students to analyze, synthesize, and evaluate. Hence teachers may use them to appraise a student's progress in organizing data and applying concepts at the highest levels of instructional objectives. Of course, these items depend heavily on writing skills and the ability to phrase ideas.

One of the crucial faults teachers make in writing essay items is failing to clearly specify the approximate detail required in the response and its expected length. Stating how much weight an item has relative to the entire test is generally not sufficient to tell students how much detail must be incorporated in a response. Here's an illustration of this point:

Bad essay item: Discuss Canadian politics.

Improvement: In a 400-word essay, identify at least three ways in which the Canadian prime minister and the U.S. president differ in their obligations to their respective constituencies.

A short essay item, like all test items, should be linked directly to instructional objectives taught in the lessons. Consequently, the short essay item should contain specific information that students are to address. Some teachers seem reluctant to name the particulars that they wish the student to discuss, as if they believe that recalling a word or phrase in the instructions is giving away too much information. But if recall of a name is what you are attempting to measure, then use other, more suitable forms of test items.

Short essay items have a number of advantages in addition to letting students state ideas in their own words. Essay items are not susceptible to correct guesses. They can be used to measure creative abilities, such as writing talent or imagination in constructing hypothetical events. Short essay items may require students to combine several concepts in their response.

On the negative side is the problem of reliability in scoring essay responses. Some studies demonstrate that independent marking of the same essay response by several teachers results in appraisals ranging from excellent to a failing grade. This gross difference in evaluations indicates a wide range of marking criteria and standards among teachers of similar backgrounds (Lindeman and Merenda, 1979).

A second drawback of essay items is that essay responses take considerable time to evaluate. The time you might have saved by writing one essay item instead of several other kinds of items must be paid back when grading the essays.

Here are some additional suggestions for writing short essay items:

1. Match items with the instructional objectives.
2. Write a response to the item before you give the test to estimate the time students will need to respond. About four times the teacher's time is a fair gauge.
3. Do not use such general directives in an item as "discuss," "give your opinion about . . . ," "tell all you know about. . . ." Rather, carefully choose specific response verbs such as "compare," "contrast," "identify," "list and define," and "explain the difference."

After writing a short essay item—and clearly specifying the content that is to be included in the response—you must have a clear idea of how you will mark various pieces of a student's response. Of course, you want to use the same standards and criteria for all students' responses to that item.

The first step is to write a model response or a detailed outline of the essential elements students are being directed to include in their responses. You will compare students' responses to this model. If you intend to use evaluative comments but no letter grades, your outline or model will serve as a guide for pointing out to students' omissions and errors in their responses, as well as the good points of their answers. If you are using letter grades to mark the essays, you will compare elements of students' responses with the contents of your model and give suitable credit to responses that match the relative weights of elements in the model.

If possible, you should ask a colleague to assess the validity of the elements and their weights in your model response. Going a bit further and having the colleague apply the model criteria to one or more student responses could increase the reliability of your marking.

One issue relating to essay tests is whether and how much to count grammar, spelling, and other technical features. If you do count these, give students separate grades in content and in mechanics so that they will know the basis on which their work was evaluated.

Theory Into Practice
Writing and Evaluating Problem-Solving Items

In many subjects, such as mathematics and the physical and social sciences, instructional objectives include the development of skills in problem solving. Many academic disciplines have specific and unique procedures for problem solving. Unlike some school tasks with rigid procedures and right or wrong answers, a **problem-solving item** involves organizing, selecting, and applying complex procedures that have at least several important steps or components. It is important to appraise the students' work in each of these steps or components.

Here are a seventh-grade-level mathematical problem and a seventh-grader's response to it. In the discussion of evaluating problem solving to follow, the

problem-solving item:
problem solving involves organizing, selecting, and applying complex procedures that have at least several important steps or components.

essential components are described in specific terms, but they can be applied to all disciplines.

Problem:

Suppose two gamblers are playing a game in which the loser must pay an amount equal to what the other gambler has at the time. Now, if Player A won the first and third games, and Player B won the second game, and they finished the three games with $12 each, with how much money did each begin the first game?

A Student's Response:

After game	A had	B had
3	$12.00	$12.00
2	6.00	18.00
1	15.00	9.00
In the beginning	$7.50	$16.50

When I started with Game 1, I guessed and guessed but I couldn't make it come out to 12 and 12. Then I decided to start at Game 3 and work backwards. It worked!

How will you objectively evaluate such a response? As should be done when evaluating short essay items, a plan to appraise problem-solving responses should begin by writing either a model response or, perhaps more practically, an outline of the essential components or procedures involved in problem solving. As with essays, problem-solving responses may take several different yet valid approaches. The outline must be flexible enough to accommodate all valid possibilities.

In problem solving there are several important components that fit most disciplines. These include understanding the problem to be solved, attacking the problem systematically, and arriving at a reasonable answer. Following is a detailed list of elements common to most problem solving that can guide your weighting of elements in your evaluation of a student's problem-solving abilities.

Problem-Solving Evaluation Elements:

1. Problem organization
   a. Representation by table, graph, chart, etc. _____
   b. Representation fits the problem _____
   c. Global understanding of the problem _____

2. Procedures (mathematical: trial-and-error, working backward, experimental process, empirical induction)
   a. A viable procedure was attempted _____
   b. Procedure was carried to a final solution _____
   c. Computation (if any) was correct _____

3. Solution (mathematical: a table, number, figure, graph, etc.)
   a. Answer was reasonable _____
   b. Answer was checked _____
   c. Answer was correct _____

4. Logic specific to the detail or application of the given information was sound _____

Connections

Recall the steps in problem solving, discussed in Chapter 7, on which measures of problem solving are based.

If you wish to give partial credit for an answer that contains correct elements, or want to inform students about the value of their responses, you must devise ways to do this consistently. The following points offer some guidance:

1. Write model responses before giving partial credit for such work as essay writing, mathematical problem solving, laboratory assignments, or any work that you evaluate according to the quality of its various stages.

2. Tell students in sufficient detail the meaning of the grades you give in order to communicate the value of the work.

The following examples illustrate outlines of exemplary student work from mathematics and social studies or literature.

From Mathematics: Students are given this problem:

In a single-elimination tennis tournament 40 players are to play for the singles championship. Determine how many matches must be played.

Evaluation

a. evidence that the student understood the problem; demonstrated by depicting the problem with a graph, table, chart, equation, etc. (3 points)

b. use of a method for solving the problem that had potential for yielding a correct solution—for example, systematic trial-and-error, empirical induction, elimination, working backward (5 points)

c. generalization to other problems of this kind (1 point)

d. arrival at a correct solution (3 points)

The four components in the evaluation were assigned points according to the weight the teacher judged each to be worth in the context of the course of study and the purpose of the test. Teachers can give full credit for a correct answer even if all the work is not shown in the response, provided they know that students can do the work in their heads.

From Social Studies or Literature. Students are asked to respond with a 100-word essay to this item:

Compare and contrast the development of Inuit and Navajo tools on the basis of the climates in which these two peoples live.

Evaluation

a. The response gives evidence of specific and accurate recall of the climates in which the Inuit and Navajos live (1 point) and of Inuit and Navajo tools. (1 point)

b. The essay develops with continuity of thought and logic. (3 points)

c. An accurate rationale is provided for the use of the various tools in the respective climates. (3 points)

d. An analysis comparing and contrasting the similarities and differences between the two groups and their tool development is given. (8 points)

e. The response concludes with a summary and closure. (1 point)

Teachers on Teaching

What has been your experience with alternatives to traditional forms of assessment?

When a teacher stops feeling tied down to traditional pencil-and-paper tests, he or she discovers a whole new approach to teaching and evaluating students' actual mastery of skills. I follow these steps: 1. Identify the concepts I want to test for mastery. I use a multisensory approach when presenting the concepts to ensure that one method or another will capture each student's attention. 2. Examine each concept and the methods used to present it to determine further what I want to test for mastery. 3. Develop variations of tests for different classes and situations. When developing tests, I also ask myself the following questions: Would conventional methods measure mastery best Am I being flexible? What is a unique method I could use? Is it practical? Could it be modified to work? How do my learners learn best? What motivates them? Do I have hands-on materials to use in testing? Is it possible to test in a multisensory way? How can I modify assessment to meet individual needs? A multisensory approach helps all students acknowledge responsibility for their learning. After a story about Helen Keller I invited the Educational Interpreter at our school to help me present sign language as an alternative way of communicating. We chose a popular song and taught the students to sign that song with the music. Then we presented our "sign-song" to other classes. The experience and actual mastery of the sign-song was evaluation in itself, and I was able to award each student a grade based on participation. It is important to change students' ways of thinking about testing, to constantly reevaluate approaches to classroom measurement and evaluation.

Margaret Ball, Teacher of English
Stratford High School, Stratford, Wisconsin

I began many years ago keeping folders of student work that displayed each child's progress. Daily notes were added to the folder with information about each student's performance or behavior for the day. Since I don't keep numerical grades on a "learning first-grader," I couldn't always rely on my memory at grade-card time. This meant that the folders were invaluable. As the years have passed, the evaluation folders have developed to include even more information. This year's folders I made specifically with parents in mind. Like a baby book, the folders allow me to present to parents their child's specific growth during any grading period. I have also included student ownership in the folders this year. Weekly, each child gets to choose what he or she thinks is the best work to be included in the folder. Any paper that a child considers better than a previous paper can be substituted. This has worked very well. My students are aware of improvement. They try hard to make each piece of work better than the last. We've been collecting art work, math projects, writing samples, oral readings on tape, photos, and anecdotes. Folders reveal whatever level of achievement a child is capable of accomplishing. Daily and weekly work show continual learning. Also, I send these folders on to second grade so that teacher can trace each student's growth. Children lacking specific skills will have the advantage of showing next year's teacher what they've actually accomplished, and that teacher will know exactly where to begin instruction. This assessment process is motivating to students, nonambiguous to parents, and practical to teachers.

Elonda Hogue, Teacher, Grade 1
Cordley Elementary School, Lawrence, Kansas

These two examples should suggest ways to evaluate items in other subject areas as well. Giving partial credit for much of the work students do certainly results in a more complete evaluation of student progress than marking the work merely right or wrong. The examples show how to organize an objective style for evaluating work that does not lend itself to the simple forms of multiple -choice, true-false, completion, and matching items. Points do not have to be used to evaluate components of the responses. In many situations some kind of evaluative descriptors might be more meaningful. Evaluative descriptors are statements describing strong and weak features of a response to an item, a question, or a project. In the mathematics example, a teacher's evaluative descriptor for (a) might read "You have *drawn an excellent chart showing that you understand the meaning of the problem,* and that is very good, but it seems *you were careless* when you entered several important numbers in your chart."

Self-Check

Write items for a test on the unit of study you developed in the first Self-Check in this chapter, based on the instructional objectives you developed. Write a variety of test items, including multiple choice, true-false, completion, matching, short essay, and problem solving. After you have written at least one item of each type, review the section to see how you might improve them. List the criteria you will use for evaluating the essay and problem-solving items you have written.

How Are Grades Determined?

One of the most perplexing and often controversial tasks a teacher faces is grading student work (Kirschenbaum *et al.,* 1971; Aiken, 1983). Is grading necessary? It is clear that *some* form of summative student evaluation is necessary, and grading of one kind or another is the predominant form used in most American schools.

Traditional grading systems are probably less necessary in elementary than in secondary school. According to a study conducted by Burton (1983), primary, intermediate, and secondary school teachers view the *purpose* of grading differently. More than half (52 percent) of the primary grade teachers in the study said that their main reason for giving grades was that the school district required it; the evaluative and other functions of grades were not most important in their view. Furthermore, many of the primary teachers tended to blame grading practices on the college systems. In contrast, middle school and high school teachers listed "to inform students" as the most important reason for grading. They cited letter grading as a service to students and said that teachers owed it to them as part of their education.

As for methods used to assign grades, about as many elementary school teachers used numerical scores to give overall grades in school work as depended on "their own professional judgments." Elementary teachers also listed student participation and enthusiasm as an important second criterion for grading. By comparison, about 85 percent of the middle and high school teachers said they assign grades according to paper-and-pencil test results (Burton, 1983).

Establishing Grading Criteria

There are many sets of grading criteria, but regardless of the level of school teachers teach in, they generally agree on the need to explain the meaning of grades they give (Burton, 1983). Grades should communicate at least the relative value of a student's work in a class. They should also help students understand better what is expected of them and how they might improve.

Teachers and schools that use letter grades attach the following general meanings to the letters:

- A = superior; exceptional; outstanding attainment
- B = very good, but not superior; above average
- C = competent, but not remarkable work or performance; average
- D = minimum passing, but weaknesses are indicated; below average
- F = failure to pass; serious weaknesses demonstrated

Assigning Letter Grades

All school districts have a policy or common practice for assigning report card grades. Most use A–B–C–D–F or A–B–C–D–E letter grades, but many (particularly at the elementary level) use various versions of outstanding–satisfactory–unsatisfactory. Some simply report percentage grades. The criteria upon which grades are based vary enormously from district to district. Secondary schools usually give one grade for each subject taken, but most elementary schools and some secondary schools include ratings on effort or behavior as well as on performance.

The criteria for giving letter grades may be specified by a school administration, but most often grading criteria are set by individual teachers using very broad guidelines. In practice, few teachers could get away with giving half their students A's or with failing too many students, but between these two extremes teachers may have considerable leeway.

Absolute Grading Standards. Grades may be given according to absolute or relative standards. Absolute grading standards might consist of preestablished percentage scores required for a given grade, as in the following example:

Grade	% Correct
A	90–100%
B	80–89%
C	70–79%
D	60–69%
F	less than 60%

In another form of absolute standards, called criterion-referenced grading, the teacher decides in advance what performance constitutes outstanding (A), above-average (B), average (C), below-average (D), and inadequate (F) mastery of the instructional objective.

Absolute percentage standards have one important disadvantage: Student scores may depend on the difficulty of the tests they are given. For example, on a true-false test a student can pass (if a passing grade is 60 percent) by knowing only 20 percent of the answers and guessing on the rest (getting 50 percent of the remaining 80 percent of the items by chance). On a difficult test where guessing is impos-

This teacher plans to use a relative grading standard to establish letter grades for her students' report cards. What information does that give the students and parents about their achievement? What are some disadvantages of this method, and what are some alternatives?

sible, 60 percent could be a respectable score. For this reason, use of absolute percentage criteria should be tempered with criterion-referenced standards. That is, a teacher might use a 60–70–80–90 percent standard in most circumstances but establish (and announce to students) tougher standards for tests students are likely to find easy and easier standards for tests on which an average score might indicate adequate mastery.

Relative Grading Standards.   A **relative grading standard** exists whenever a teacher gives grades according to the students' rank in their class or grade. The classic form of relative grading is specifying what percentage of students will be given A's, B's, and so on. This practice is called "grading on the curve" because it typically allocates grades to students on the basis of their position on a normal curve of scores, as follows (Cureton, 1971):

Grade	% of Students
A	7
B	24
C	38
D	24
F	7

Grading on the curve and other relative grading standards have the advantage of placing students' scores in relation to one another, without regard to the difficulty of a particular test. However, relative grading standards have serious drawbacks. One is that because they hold the number of A's and B's constant, students in a class of high achievers must get much higher scores to earn an A or B than students in low-achieving classes—a situation that is likely to be widely seen as unfair. This problem is often dealt with by giving relatively more A's and B's in high-achieving classes than in others. Another disadvantage of grading on the curve is that it creates competition among students; when one student earns an A, this diminishes the chances that others may do so. Competition can inhibit students from helping one another and can hurt social relations among classmates (see Ames *et al.,* 1977).

relative grading standard: grading on the basis of how well other students performed on the same test rather in terms of preestablished absolute standards.

Strict grading on the curve, as well as guidelines for numbers of A's and B's, has been disappearing in recent years. For one thing, there has been a general grade inflation, so that more A's and B's are given now than in the past; C is no longer the expected average grade but often indicates below-average performance. The most common approach to grading involves teachers looking at student scores on a test, taking into account test difficulty and the overall performance of the class, and assigning grades in such a way that about the "right number" of students earn A's and B's and the "right number" fail. Teachers vary considerably in their estimates of what these right numbers should be, but schools often have unspoken norms about how many students should be given A's and how many should fail (see Hoge and Coladarci, 1989; Fitzpatrick, 1989).

Alternative Grading Systems.   Several other approaches to grading are used in conjunction with innovative instructional approaches. In contract grading, students negotiate a particular amount of work or level of performance they will achieve to receive a certain grade. For example, a student might agree to complete five book reports of a given length in a marking period to receive an A. **Mastery grading,** an important part of mastery learning (see Chapter 9), involves establishing a standard of mastery, such as 80 or 90 percent correct, on a test. All students who achieve that standard receive an A; students who do not achieve it the first time receive corrective instruction and then retake the test to try to achieve the mastery criterion. Individualized instructional programs (see Chapter 9) often use **continuous-progress grading,** in which students' evaluations depend on how many units they complete in a given time period, regardless of the level of the units. Sometimes continuous progress evaluation involves simply reporting to students and parents the specific skills students have mastered, without any indication of how the student is doing in relation to other students.

Assigning Report Card Grades

Most schools give report cards four or six times per year, that is, every nine or six weeks (Chansky, 1975). Report card grades are most often derived from some combination of the following factors (Jussim, 1991):

- average scores on quizzes and tests
- average scores on homework
- average scores on seatwork
- class participation (academic behaviors in class, answers to class questions, etc.)
- deportment (classroom behavior, tardiness, attitude)
- effort

One important principle in report card grading is that grades should never be a surprise to students. Students should always know how their grades will be computed, and whether classwork and homework are included, whether class participation and effort are taken into account. Being clear about standards for grading helps avoid many complaints about unexpectedly low grades and, more importantly, lets students know exactly what they must do to improve their grades.

Another important principle is that grades should be private. There is no need for students to know one another's grades, and making grades public only invites invidious comparisons among students (see Simpson, 1981). Finally, it is important to restate that grades are only one method of student evaluation. Written

---

Connections

Distinguish the goals and procedures for assigning report card grades from those used with daily report cards, described in Chapter 11.

---

mastery grading: absolute grading based on criteria for mastery.

continuous-progress grading: absolute grading based on the number of units completed or skills mastered.

evaluations that add information can provide useful information to parents and students (Burton, 1983).

Self-Check

Describe the grading system you will preferably use at the level you plan to teach. Briefly outline the advantages and drawbacks of no grades, letter grades, absolute grading standards, grading on the curve, contract grading, mastery grading, and continuous-progress grading.

Case to Consider

Making the Grade

Rachel Greenberg is a beginning social studies teacher in a large urban high school. In preparation for a social studies department meeting, she talks with Toni Sue Garrick in the teachers' lounge.

RACHEL: Toni, do you have a minute to tell me about the school's grading policy?

TONI SUE: Sure. Where do you want to begin?

RACHEL: Well, we do have a policy, I assume?

TONI SUE: I guess you could say so. If you look on the report cards, you'll notice that 94 to 100 is an A, 88 to 94 is a B, and so forth. Anything below 70 is failing.

RACHEL: What if no one gets in the 94 to 100?

TONI SUE: Then you either don't give any A's, if you think the test was fair, or you adjust the scale by adding on points to every student's score. There's no rigid policy, but if you give too many A's and B's that could become a problem.

RACHEL: How many are too many?

TONI SUE: Well, certainly there should be more B's than A's, and more C's than either A's or B's. You try to approximate the normal bell-shaped curve in a general, flexible way. It all depends on the students' ability level. In an advanced placement history course, I seldom give D's or F's. In the sophomore-level world history course, however, the number of D's and F's fairly closely approximates A's and B's.

RACHEL: What if a teacher puts a mastery learning plan into effect, and it works so well that everyone achieves at practically 100 percent? What happens to the bell-shaped curve then?

TONI SUE: Well, that happened a few years back. One young teacher did give almost all A's and B's. It came to light when the students began comparing grades at report card time. Some other teachers and parents were quite upset. The administration smoothed things over with the parents and other teachers. As for the young teacher, he's at another school now. I hear he's doing a fine job.

RACHEL: Oh. Well, another question: In my history classes I plan to emphasize individual and small-group projects. I am interested in cooperative learning approaches with mixed-ability groups. . . .

TONI SUE: Group projects are nice, but grading them can be very subjective and hard to defend. I'd go easy on that.

RACHEL: So you'd recommend objective tests, not essay tests?

TONI SUE: Right. Good objective tests are hard to write, but they're worth it. Because students and parents have a hard time arguing grading bias, favoritism, or subjectivity when you give objective tests. Also, I figure that objective tests help prepare the kids to succeed on standardized achievement tests.

RACHEL: I see what you mean, but I try to keep outcomes in mind—overall objectives like verbal information, intellectual skills, cognitive strategies, and so on. But teaching for those outcomes may not always leave time for teaching to objective tests. What if some of my students get D's and F's? I'm a little afraid of some of the parents.

TONI SUE: I think communication is the key. If the students—and their parents—think you're fair, you'll have few problems . Spell out very clearly what you expect and what the grading procedures are. After all, our society was founded on competition. Our kids have to learn how to deal with failure as well as success. And parents should understand that too.

RACHEL: Thanks, Toni Sue! I don't know if I altogether agree with you about the value of failure, but I really appreciate your support.

Problem Solving

1. Do you agree with the advice Rachel received? Why or why not? For the grade level you plan to teach, what departmentwide evaluation strategy would you propose for your subject area?

2. If you were on a committee to evaluate and revise this school's evaluation and grading policies and procedures, what would you recommend and why?

3. Extend the dialogue to express an evaluation approach that would work best for the way Rachel wants to teach.

Summary

What Are Instructional Objectives and How Are They Used?

Research supports the use of instructional, or behavioral, objectives, which are clear statements about what students should know and be able to do at the end of a lesson, unit, or course. These statements also specify the conditions of performance and the criteria for assessment. In planning lessons, task analysis contributes to the formulation of objectives, while backward planning is used to develop specific objectives from general objectives in a course of study. Objectives are closely linked with assessment. Bloom's taxonomy classifies educational objectives from simple to complex, including knowledge, comprehension, application, analysis, synthesis, and evaluation. A behavior content matrix helps to plan objectives, while a table of specification helps to plan corresponding tests. Taxonomies also exist for affective and psychomotor objectives.

Why Is Evaluation Important?

Formal measures of student performance or learning are important as feedback to students and teachers, as information to parents, as evidence for selection and certification, as incentives for increasing student effort, and as information for assessing school accountability.

How Is Student Learning Evaluated?

Strategies for evaluation include formative evaluation; summative evaluation; norm-referenced evaluation, in which a student's scores are compared with other students' scores; and criterion-referenced evaluation, in which students' scores are based on mastery. Students are evaluated through tests or performances. The appropriate method of evaluation is based on the goal of evaluation. For example, if the goal of testing is to find out if students have mastered a key concept in a lesson, a criterion-referenced, formative quiz or performance would be the most appropriate.

How Are Tests Constructed?

Tests are constructed to elicit evidence of student learning in relation to the instructional objectives. Each test form has optimal uses, advantages, and disadvantages. For example, if you want to learn how students think about, analyze, synthesize, or evaluate some aspect of course content, a short essay test may be most appropriate, provided you have time to administer and evaluate students' responses. Writing test items is a complex skill, including multiple-choice, true-false, completion, matching, short essay, and problem-solving items.

How Are Grades Determined?

Grading systems differ in elementary and secondary education. For example, informal assessments may be more appropriate at the elementary level, while letter grades become increasingly important at the secondary level. Grading standards may be absolute or relative (grading on the curve). Other systems include contract grading, mastery grading, and continuous-progress grading. Report card grades typically average scores on tests, homework, seatwork, class participation, deportment, and effort. There are ethical considerations in the use and reporting of grades.

Key Terms

affective objectives, 496
assessment, 493
authentic assessment, 504
backward planning, 490
behavior content matrix, 495
completion items, 512
continuous-progress grading, 522
criterion-referenced evaluations, 503
distractors, 510
evaluation, 498
formative evaluation, 502
instructional objective, 486
learning objectives, 493
mastery grading, 522
matching items, 513

multiple-choice item, 509
norm-referenced evaluations, 502
problem-solving item, 515
psychomotor objectives, 497
relative grading standard, 521
reliability, 507
short essay item, 513
stem, 509
summative evaluation, 502
table of specifications, 509
task analysis, 489
taxonomy of educational objectives, 494
teaching objectives, 493
true-false item, 512

Self-Assessment

1. Which of the following objectives satisfies the criteria proposed by Mager?

   a. The student will learn to solve long-division problems involving two-digit numbers.

   b. Without using a calculator, the student will correctly solve 10 out of 12 division problems involving up to two-digit numbers.

   c. The student will understand how to use a calculator in solving long-division problems containing up to two-digit numbers.

   d. Using a calculator, the student will demonstrate mastery of long division by solving problems involving up to two-digit numbers.

2. A student is shown a model of a space shuttle and asked to explain what its different components are and how they interact . What type of learning is most clearly being emphasized?

   a. knowledge

   b. evaluation

   c. synthesis

   d. analysis

3. A chart showing how a concept or skill will be taught at different cognitive levels in relation to instructional objectives is

   a. a result of task analysis.

   b. a result of backward planning.

   c. an example of a behavior content matrix.

   d. an example of a table of specifications.

4. Write a short essay on the importance of evaluation with examples of several ways that evaluations are used.

5. Gronlund's principles of achievement testing make all of the following points *except:*

   a. Tests should measure learning objectives that relate to instructional objectives.

   b. Tests should measure a representative sample of taught content.

   c. Tests should have items of the objective type.

   d. Tests should improve learning.

6. Match the following types of evaluations with the correct descriptions.

   ___ norm-referenced

   ___ criterion-referenced

   ___ formative

   ___ summative

   a. follows conclusion of instructional unit as a final test of knowledge

   b. measures performance against standard of mastery

   c. given during instruction; can guide lesson presentations

   d. measures achievement of one student relative to others

7. The purpose of devising a table of specifications in testing is to

   a. indicate the types of learning to be assessed for different instructional objectives.

   b. indicate the make-up of a test with regard to number of multiple-choice items, essay questions, etc.

   c. define clear scoring criteria for each essay or open-ended question used in a test.

   d. compare the students' scores on a standardized test to those of the national sample.

   e. define the normal curve percentile ranks for different letter grades.

8. Which of the following is recommended in constructing multiple-choice items?

   a. making the stem short and general, such as "Testing is:"

   b. frequently using "none of the above" as a distractor

   c. listing choices horizontally rather than vertically

   d. making distractors plausible

   e. using numbers, wherever feasible, instead of letters in listing distractors

14

Performance Assessments and Standardized Tests

Chapter Outline	Chapter Objectives
What Are Standardized Tests and How Are They Used? Selection and Placement Diagnosis Evaluation School Improvement Accountability	▲ Discuss five significant uses of standardized tests and ways to prepare students for taking standardized and formal classroom tests.
What Types of Standardized Test Are Given? Aptitude Tests Norm-Referenced Achievement Tests Criterion-Referenced Achievement Tests	▲ Compare and contrast the types of standardized aptitude and achievement tests used in schools, and describe their appropriate use.
How Are Standardized Test Scores Interpreted? Percentile Scores Grade Equivalent Scores Standard Scores	▲ Interpret the meaning of standardized test scores, including percentiles, grade equivalents, and the different types of standard scores.
What Are Some Issues Concerning Standardized and Classroom Testing? Validity and Reliability Test Bias and Test Ethics Authentic Assessment How Well Do Performance Assessments Work?	▲ Argue issues concerning standardized and classroom tests, including issues of validity, reliability, bias, ethics, and alternative testing, including the use of portfolios and performances as forms of authentic assessment.

J ennifer Tranh is a fifth-grade teacher at Lincoln Elementary School. Today she
is preparing to meet with the parents of one of her students, Anita McKay.

"Hello, Mr. and Mrs. McKay," said Ms. Tranh when Anita's parents
arrived. "I'm so glad you could come. Please take a seat, and we'll start right in.

"First, I wanted to tell you what a delight it is to have Anita in my class. She is
always so cheerful, so willing to help others. Her work is coming along very well in
most subjects, although there are a few areas I'm a bit concerned about. Before I
start, though, do you have any questions of me?"

Mr. and Mrs. McKay explained to Ms. Tranh that they thought Anita was having a good year, and that they were eager to hear how she was doing.

"All right. First of all, I know you've seen the results of Anita's California
Achievement Tests. We call those 'CATs' for short. Most parents don't understand
these test scores, so I'll try to explain them to you.

"First, let's look at math. As you know, Anita has always been a good math student, and her scores reflect this. She got a percentile score of 90 on math computations. That means that she scored better than 90 percent of all students in the
country. She did almost as well on math concepts and applications—her score is in
the 85th percentile."

"What does this 'grade equivalent' mean?" asked Mrs. McKay.

"That's a score that's supposed to tell how a child is achieving in relation to his or her grade level. For example, Anita's grade equivalent of 6.9 means that she is scoring more than a year ahead of the fifth-grade level."

"Does this mean she could skip sixth-grade math?" asked Mr. McKay.

Ms. Tranh laughed. "I'm afraid not. It's hard to explain, but a grade equivalent score of 6.9 is supposed to be what a student at the end of sixth grade would score on a fifth-grade test. It doesn't mean Anita already knows all the sixth-grade material. Besides, we take all of this testing information with a grain of salt. We rely much more on day-to-day performance and classroom tests to tell how students are doing. In this case, the standardized CAT scores are pretty consistent with what we see Anita doing in class. But let me show you another example where there is less consistency.

"I'm sure you noticed that Anita's scores in reading comprehension were much lower than her scores in most other areas. She got a percentile score of only 30. This is almost a year below grade level. I think Anita is a pretty good reader, so I was surprised. I gave her another test, the Gray Oral Reading Test. This test is given one-on-one, so it gives you a much better indication of how well students are reading. On the Gray, Anita scored at grade level. This score is more indicative of where I see her reading in class, so I'm not concerned about her in this area.

"On the other hand, there is a concern I have about Anita that is not reflected in her standardized tests. She scored near the 70th percentile in both language mechanics and language expression. This might make you think Anita's doing great in language arts, and she *is* doing well in many ways. However, I'm concerned about Anita's writing. I keep a portfolio of student writing over the course of the year. This is Anita's here. She's showing some development in writing, but I think she could do a lot better. As you can see, her spelling, punctuation, and grammar are excellent, but her stories are very short, factual, and stilted. I'd like to see her write more and really let her imagination loose. She tells great stories orally, but I think she's so concerned about making a mistake in mechanics that she writes very conservatively. On vacation you might encourage her to write a journal or to do other writing wherever it makes sense."

"But if her standardized test scores are good in language," said Mrs. McKay, "doesn't that mean that she's doing well?"

"Test scores tell us some things, but not everything," said Ms. Tranh. "The CAT is good on simple things like math computations and language mechanics, but it is not so good at telling us what children can actually do. That's why I keep portfolios of student work in writing, in math problem solving, and in science. I want to see how children are really developing in their ability to apply their skills to doing real things and solving real problems. In fact, now that we've gone over Anita's standardized tests, let's look at her portfolios, and I think you'll get a much better idea of what she's doing here in school!"

Jennifer Tranh's conversation with the McKays illustrates some of the uses and limitations of standardized tests. The CATs and the Gray Oral Reading Test give her information that does relate Anita's performance in some areas to national norms, but they do not provide the detail or comprehensiveness reflected in her portfolios of Anita's work and other observations of Anita's performance. Taken together, the cautiously interpreted standardized tests, the portfolios of Anita's work, and other classroom assessments provide a good picture of Anita's performance. Do you remember taking SATs, ACTs, or other college entrance examinations? Did you ever wonder how those tests were constructed, what the scores meant, and to what degree your scores represented what you really knew or could really do?

The SATs and other college entrance examinations are examples of **standardized tests**. Unlike the teacher-made tests discussed in Chapter 13, a standardized test is typically given to thousands of students who are similar to those for whom the test is designed. This allows the test publisher to establish norms, or standards, against which any individual score can be compared. For example, if a representative national sample of fourth-graders had an average score of thirty-seven items correct on a fifty-item standardized test, then we might say that fourth-graders who score above thirty-seven are "above national norms" on this test, while those who score below thirty-seven are "below national norms."

Traditional standardized tests are under attack throughout the U.S. and Canada, and entirely new forms of broad-scale tests are being developed and used. However, standardized tests of many kinds are used for a wide range of purposes at all levels of education. This chapter discusses how and why standardized tests are used, and how scores on these tests can be interpreted and applied to make important educational decisions. It also includes information on criticisms of standardized testing and on alternatives currently being developed, debated, and applied.

What Are Standardized Tests and How Are They Used?

Standardized tests are usually used to provide a yardstick against which to compare individuals or groups of students that teacher-made tests cannot provide. For example, suppose a child's parents asked a teacher how their daughter is doing in math. The teacher says, "Fine, she got a score of 81 percent on our latest math test." For some purposes, this information would be adequate. But for others, we might want to know much more. How does 81 percent compare to the scores of other students in this class? How about other students in the school, the district, the state, or the whole country? In some contexts the score of 81 percent might help qualify the girl for a special program for the mathematically gifted; in others it might suggest the need for remedial instruction. Also, suppose the teacher found that the class averaged 85 percent correct on the math test. How is this class doing compared to other math classes or to students nationwide? A teacher-made test cannot yield this information.

Standardized tests are typically carefully constructed to provide accurate information on students' levels of performance . Most often curriculum experts establish what students at a particular age should know about a subject or should be able to do. Then questions are written to assess the various skills or information students are expected to possess. The questions are tried out on various groups of students. Items that almost all students get right or almost all miss are usually dropped, as are items that students find unclear or confusing. Patterns of scores are carefully examined. If students who score well on most items do no better than lower-scoring students on a particular item, that item will probably be dropped.

Eventually a final test will be developed and given to a large selected group of students from all over the country. Usually attempts are made to ensure that this

> **standardized tests:** tests that are usually commercially prepared for nationwide use to provide accurate and meaningful information on students' level of performance relative to others at their age or grade levels.

group resembles the larger population of students who will ultimately use the test. For example, a test of geometry for eleventh-graders might be given to a sampling of eleventh-graders in urban, rural, and suburban locations, in different regions of the country, in public as well as private schools, and to students with different levels of preparation in mathematics. This step establishes the **norms** for the test, which provide an indication of how an average student will score. Finally, a testing manual is prepared, explaining how the test is to be given, scored, and interpreted. This particular standardized test is now ready for general use.

The test development process creates tests whose scores have meaning outside the confines of a particular classroom or school. These scores are used in a variety of ways. Explanations of some of the most important functions of standardized testing follow.

Selection and Placement

Standardized tests are often used to select students for entry or placement in specific programs. For example, the SATs (Scholastic Aptitude Test) or ACTs (American College Testing Program) you probably took in high school were used to help your college admissions board decide whether to accept you as a student. Similarly, admission to special programs for gifted and talented students might depend on standardized test scores. Standardized tests might also be used to decide whether to place students in special education programs or to assign students to tracks or ability groups. For example, high schools may use standardized tests to decide which students to place in college preparatory, general, or vocational programs, while elementary schools may use them to place students in reading groups (see Chapter 9 for between- and within-class ability grouping). Standardized tests are sometimes used to determine eligibility for grade-to-grade promotion, graduation from high school, or entry into an occupation.

Diagnosis

Often standardized tests are used to diagnose learning problems or strengths. For example, a student who is performing poorly in school might be given a battery of tests to determine whether the student has a learning disability or is mentally retarded. At the same time the testing might identify specific deficits in need of remediation. Diagnostic tests of reading skills, such as the Gray Oral Reading Test used by Ms. Tranh, are frequently used to identify a student's particular reading problem. For example, a diagnostic test might indicate that a student's decoding skills are fine, but that his or her reading comprehension is poor.

Evaluation

Perhaps the most common use of standardized testing is to evaluate the progress of students and the effectiveness of teachers and schools. For example, parents often want to know how their children are doing in comparison with what is expected of children at their grade level. Of course, standardized test scores are meaningful as evaluation only if used along with other information, such as students' actual performance in school and in other contexts, as was done by Ms. Tranh.

norms: standards derived from giving a test to a sample of people similar to those who will take the test and that can be used to interpret scores of future test takers.

Many students who score poorly on standardized tests excel in school, college, or occupations; either they have trouble taking tests well or they have important skills that are not measured by such tests.

School Improvement

Standardized tests can contribute to improving the schooling process. The results of some standardized tests provide information regarding appropriate student placement and diagnostic information important in remediation. In addition, achievement tests can guide curriculum development and revision where areas of weakness appear (see Ebel, 1980a). A broader view of the role of standardized tests in the schools suggests uses in guidance and counseling as well. This is true not only in the areas of achievement and aptitude testing but also for more specialized types of measures such as vocational interest inventories and other psychological scales that are used in the counseling of students in the schools.

Standardized tests also have some administrative roles. Academic achievement tests, for instance, are often used to evaluate the relative success of competing educational programs or strategies. For example, if a teacher or school tries out an innovative teaching strategy, tests can be used to find out whether it was more successful than previous methods. Also, district-wide test results often serve as a yardstick for citizens to judge the success of their local schools. Tests can also contribute to accountability, to evaluate relative teaching strengths and weaknesses of faculty. In all of these uses it is important to remember that educating students is a complex process and that standardized tests provide only a small portion of the information that is necessary for evaluating teachers, programs, or schools.

Accountability

A growing trend over the past twenty years has been to hold teachers and schools accountable for what students learn. Most states and school districts have implemented regular standardized testing programs and publish the results on a school-by-school basis (see Kirst, 1990). Not surprisingly, principals and other administrators watch these scores the way business owners watch their profit sheets. In many districts the scores of each teacher's students are made available to the school administration and may be used in decisions about hiring, firing, promotion, and transfer.

Many states and districts have established **minimum competency** tests that students must pass either to graduate from high school or to be promoted from grade to grade (see Lerner, 1981). These are typically criterion-referenced tests focusing on important skills students are expected to have mastered. School districts using minimum competency tests also usually establish special remedial programs—often during the summer—to help students pass the tests and qualify for promotion or graduation.

The accountability movement stems in part from the public's loss of confidence in American education. State legislators (among others), upset by examples of students graduating from high school unable to read or compute, have demanded that schools establish higher standards and that students achieve them.

The accountability movement has its critics, however. Many argue that minimum competency testing focuses schools on minimums rather than maximums. Others are concerned that schools will teach only what is tested, emphasizing reading and

> **Connections**
> Recall the discussion of accountability in Chapter 13 as a purpose of evaluation.

> **minimum competency tests:** criterion-referenced tests focusing on important skills students are expected to have mastered to qualify for promotion or graduation.

mathematics at the expense of, for instance, science and social studies. Teachers and principals point out that accountability assessments fail to take into account differences among students; a school or classroom may test low because the students are from disadvantaged backgrounds rather than because they were given poor instruction.

Regardless of these criticisms, accountability is probably here to stay. One advantage of accountability is that it does force schools and teachers to pay attention to students who might otherwise fall between the cracks and to help those who need the most help. Another is that it encourages schools to search out improved instructional methods and guarantees routine evaluation of any innovations they try. For example, one principal had several teachers using an effective reading program. A new teacher said she didn't like the program and preferred to use her own.

"Fine," the principal said, "if your program produces as much gain as ours, more power to you." As it turned out, the teacher's program did not increase reading scores as much as the principal's, so she dropped her own method and used his. The standardized tests of reading skills gave the principal and the teacher a fair standard against which to evaluate their programs, so (presumably) they ended up with the better program.

As standardized testing has taken on increasing importance in the evaluation of students, teachers, and schools, so too has the preparation of students to take these tests. Of course, the best way to prepare students for tests is to do a good job of teaching them the material. However, there is also a need to help many students become test-wise, to help them show what they really know on standardized tests and to help them get as good a score as possible.

Theory Into Practice

Teaching Test-Taking Skills

There are many ethical issues involved in helping students do well on standardized tests (Teddlie and Stringfield, 1989; Smith, 1991). For example, one way to help students score well is to know the test items in advance and teach them the answers. This clearly is cheating. A much more ethically ambiguous case arises when teachers know what is on the test and teach only objectives that they know will be tested. For example, if a standardized test did not assess Roman numerals, a math teacher might skip this topic in order to spend more time on an objective that is tested. This practice is criticized as "teaching to the test." On one hand it could be argued that it is unfair to test students on material that they have not been taught, and that instruction should therefore be closely aligned with tests (Cohen, 1987). On the other hand, a standardized test can only assess a small sample of all objectives taught in school. Gearing instruction toward those objectives that will be on the test, to the exclusion of all others, would produce a very narrow curriculum. An ethical compromise might be to teach the full range of objectives, not just those on the test.

Beyond matching instructional content with test objectives there are many ways to help students learn to do well on tests in general. Research has found that students can be taught to be test-wise, and that this increases their standardized test scores (Anastasi, 1981; Kulik *et al.*, 1984; Scruggs *et al.*, 1986). Questions

Connections

Consider the teaching of test-taking skills in the context of teaching metacognitive awareness and study skills, discussed in Chapter 7.

have been raised about the effectiveness of programs that prepare students for the Scholastic Aptitude Test. The consensus among researchers is now that coaching is effective, particularly for minority and low-achieving students (B.J. Becker, 1990; Messick, 1982).

Some ways of helping students to prepare for standardized tests follow (see Hill and Wigfield, 1984; Sarnacki, 1979):

1. Give students practice with similar item formats. For example, if a test will use multiple-choice formats, give students practice with similar formats in routine classroom quizzes and tests. If tests use unusual formats, such as verbal analogies (*i.e .,* BIG:SMALL::HONEST: _____, give students practice with this type of item.

2. Suggest that students skip over difficult or time-consuming items and return to them later.

3. If there is no penalty for guessing on a test, suggest to students that they always fill in some answer. If there is a penalty for guessing, students should still be encouraged to guess if they can narrow down the options to two.

4. Suggest that students read all options on a multiple-choice test before choosing one. Sometimes one answer is correct, but there may be a better answer.

5. Suggest to students that they use all available time. If they finish early, they should go back over their answers.

Self-Check

What is the main difference between standardized and nonstandardized tests? How are standardized test results used in student selection, placement, diagnosis, and evaluation? How are results used in education improvement and accountability?

What Types of Standardized Tests Are Given?

Three kinds of standardized tests are commonly used in school settings: aptitude tests, norm-referenced achievement tests, and criterion-referenced achievement tests.

An **aptitude test** is designed to assess students' abilities. It is meant to predict the ability of students to learn or perform particular types of tasks rather than to measure how much the students have already learned. The most widely used aptitude tests measure general intellectual aptitude, but many other, more specific tests measure particular aptitudes such as mechanical or perceptual abilities or reading readiness. The SAT, for example, is meant to predict a student's aptitude for college studies. An aptitude test is successful to the degree that it predicts performance. For example, a reading readiness test given to kindergartners that did not accurately predict how well the students would read when they reached first or second grade would be of little use.

Achievement tests are used (1) to predict student performance in a course of study, (2) to diagnose student difficulties, (3) to serve as formative tests of student progress, and (4) to serve as summative tests of learning.

aptitude test: a test designed to measure general abilities and to predict future performance.

achievement testing: standardized tests measuring how much students have learned in a given context.

A norm-referenced achievement test, which was discussed in Chapter 13, is an assessment of a student's knowledge of a particular content area, such as mathematics, reading, or Spanish. It provides scores that can be compared with those of a representative group of students, and it is constructed to show differences among students. Typically, norm-referenced achievement tests assess some but not all of the skills taught in any one school. A norm-referenced achievement test cannot be too specific because it is designed for nationwide use even though the curricula for any given subject vary from district to district. For example, if some seventh-graders learn about base-two arithmetic or Venn diagrams and others do not, then these topics would be unlikely to appear on a standardized mathematics test. A criterion-referenced achievement test also assesses a student's knowledge of subject matter, but rather than comparing the achievement of an individual student against national norms, it is designed to measure the degree to which the student has mastered certain well-specified skills. The information produced by a criterion-referenced test is quite specific: "Thirty-seven percent of Arkansas fifth-graders can fill in the names of the major Western European nations on an outline map" or "Ninety-three percent of twelfth-graders at Alexander Hamilton High School know that increasing the temperature of a gas in a closed container increases the gas's pressure." Sometimes criterion-referenced test scores are used to make comparisons from school to school or from district to district, but there is typically no representative norming group used. If a group of curriculum experts decides that every fifth-grader in Arkansas should be able to fill in an outline map of Western Europe, then the norm for that item is 100 percent; it is of less interest whether Arkansas fifth-graders score better or worse on this item than students in other states. What is more important is that, overall, students improve each year on this item.

Aptitude Tests

While aptitude tests, norm-referenced achievement tests, and criterion-referenced tests are each distinct in theory, there is, in fact, considerable overlap among them. For example, school learning definitely affects students' aptitude test scores, and a student who scores well on one type of test will usually score well on another. In fact, many testing theorists claim that aptitude and achievement tests are so highly correlated that both should be considered achievement tests (see, for example, Sternberg and Detterman, 1986; Ebel, 1980a; Anastasi, 1981).

The following sections discuss the types of aptitude and achievement tests most often given in schools.

General Intelligence Tests. The most common kind of aptitude tests given in school are tests of **intelligence**, or general aptitude for school learning. The intelligence quotient, or IQ, is the score most often associated with intelligence testing, but other types of scores are also used.

Intelligence tests are designed to provide a general indication of individuals' aptitudes in many areas of intellectual functioning. Intelligence itself is seen as the ability to deal with abstractions, to learn, and to solve problems (Estes, 1982; Snyderman and Rothman, 1987; Sternberg, 1982, 1986a,b), and tests of intelligence focus on these skills. Intelligence tests give students a wide variety of questions to answer and problems to solve.

The Measurement of IQ. The measurement of **intelligence quotient,** or IQ, was introduced in the early 1900s by Alfred Binet, a French psychologist, to identify

Connections

Recall the aspects of intelligence as a learner characteristic that were discussed in Chapter 4. Also, for a discussion of the use of IQ scores in the classification of exceptional learners for special-education services, see Chapter 12.

intelligence: general aptitude for learning, often measured by ability to deal with abstractions and to solve problems.

intelligence quotient: an intelligence test score that for people of average intelligence should be near 100.

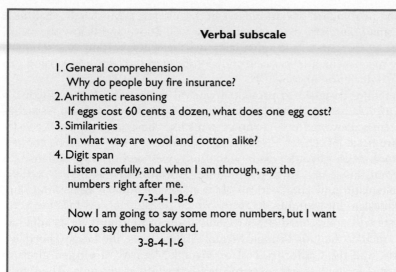

Verbal subscale

1. General comprehension
   Why do people buy fire insurance?
2. Arithmetic reasoning
   If eggs cost 60 cents a dozen, what does one egg cost?
3. Similarities
   In what way are wool and cotton alike?
4. Digit span
   Listen carefully, and when I am through, say the
   numbers right after me.
            7-3-4-1-8-6
   Now I am going to say some more numbers, but I want
   you to say them backward.
            3-8-4-1-6

Performance subscale

5. Digit-Symbol Substitution

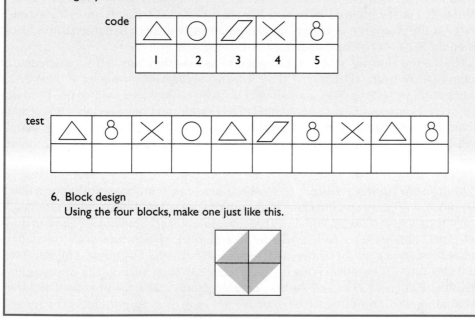

6. Block design
   Using the four blocks, make one just like this.

Figure 14.1

Illustrations of Items Used in Intelligence Testing

Intelligence tests focus on skills such as dealing with abstractions and solving problems. This sample of items resembles those used on the Wechsler Adult Intelligence Scale.

From Thorndike and Hagen, 1977, pp. 302–303.

children who were unlikely to profit from regular classroom instruction. The scale he developed to measure intelligence assessed a wide range of mental characteristics and skills, such as memory, knowledge, vocabulary, and problem solving. Binet tested a large number of students of various ages to establish norms (expectations) for overall performance on his tests. He expressed IQ as a ratio of **chronological age** to **mental age** (the average test scores received by students of a particular age), multiplied by 100. For example, six-year-olds (chronological age [CA] = 6) who score at the average for all six-year-olds (mental age [MA] = 6) would have an IQ of 100 (6/6 x 100 = 100). Six-year-olds who scored at a level typical of seven-year-olds (MA = 7) would have IQs of about 117 (7/6 x 100 = 117).

Over the years the chronological age/mental age comparison has been dropped, and IQ is now defined as having a mean of 100 and a standard deviation of 15

chronological age: the age of an individual in years.

mental age: the average test score received by individuals of a given chronological age.

(see the definition of standard deviation later in this chapter). Most scores fall near the mean, with small numbers of scores extending well above and below the mean. In theory, about 68 percent of all individuals will have IQs within one standard deviation of the mean, which is to say from 85 (one standard deviation below) to 115 (one standard deviation above).

Intelligence tests are designed to provide a general indication of an individual's aptitudes in many areas of intellectual functioning. The most widely used tests contain many different scales. Figure 14.1 shows items like those used on the Wechsler Adult Intelligence Scale (Wechsler, 1955). Each scale measures a different component of intelligence. Most often, a person who scores well on one scale will also do well on others, but this is not always so; the same person might do very well on general comprehension and similarities, less well on arithmetic reasoning, and poorly on block design, for example.

Intelligence tests are administered either to individuals or to groups. Tests administered to groups, such as the Otis-Lennon Mental Ability Tests, the Lorge-Thorndike Intelligence Tests, and the California Test of Mental Maturity, are often given to large groups of students as general assessments of intellectual aptitude. These tests are not as accurate or detailed as intelligence tests administered individually to people by trained psychologists, such as the Wechsler Intelligence Test for Children–Revised (WISC–R) or the Stanford-Binet test. For example, when students are being assessed for possible placement in special education, an individually administered test (most often the WISC–R) is usually administered, along with other tests.

The reason that IQ scores are important is that they are highly predictive of school performance (DeMyer, 1975). That is, students with higher IQs tend, on average, to get better grades, score higher on achievement tests, and so on. By about age six, IQ estimates tend to become relatively stable, and most people's IQs remain about the same into adulthood (Hopkins and Bracht, 1975). However, some people will experience substantial changes in their estimated IQ, often because of schooling or other environment influences (Ceci, 1991; Petty and Field, 1980).

Multifactor Aptitude Tests.   One other form of the aptitude test that provides a breakdown of more specific skills is the **multifactor aptitude battery.** A number of such tests are available, with a range of content and emphases. They include scholastic abilities tests such as the SAT; a number of elementary and secondary school tests, such as the Differential Aptitude Test, the Cognitive Abilities Test, and the Test of Cognitive Skills; reading readiness tests, such as the Metropolitan Reading Readiness Test, and various developmental scales for preschool children. At a minimum, most of these tests provide not only overall aptitude scores but also subscores for verbal and nonverbal aptitudes. Often subscores are even more finely divided to describe more specific abilities.

Norm-Referenced Achievement Tests

While aptitude tests focus on knowledge acquired both in school and out, achievement tests focus on skills or abilities that are traditionally taught in the schools. In general, standardized achievement tests fall into one of four categories: achievement batteries, diagnostic tests, single-subject achievement measures, and criterion-referenced achievement measures.

Achievement Batteries.   Standardized **achievement batteries,** such as the California Achievement Test, the Iowa Tests of Basic Skills, the Comprehensive

---

Connections

Recall the definitions of norm-referenced and criterion-referenced testing, given in Chapter 13.

---

multifactor aptitude battery: test that predicts ability to learn a variety of specific skills and types of knowledge.

achievement batteries: standardized tests that include several subtests designed to measure knowledge of particular subjects.

Test of Basic Skill, the Stanford Achievement Test, and the Metropolitan Achievement Tests, are used to measure individual or group achievement in a variety of subject areas. These survey batteries include several small tests, each on a different subject area, and are usually administered to a group over a period of several days. Many of the achievement batteries available for use in the schools are similar in construction and content. However, because of slight differences between the tests in the instructional objectives and subject matter sampled within the subtests, it is important before selecting a particular test to examine it carefully for its match with a specific school curriculum and for its appropriateness relative to school goals. Often achievement batteries have several forms for various age or grade levels so that achievement can be monitored over a period of several years.

These students will later be tested on their ability to identify animals by name, image, sound, and word. What type of achievement test will they be taking?

Diagnostic Tests. **Diagnostic tests** differ from achievement batteries in that they generally focus on a specific content area and emphasize those skills thought to be important for mastery of that subject matter. Diagnostic tests produce much more detailed information than other achievement tests. For example, a standardized mathematics test often produces scores for math computations, concepts, and applications, whereas a diagnostic test would give scores on more specific skills, such as adding decimals or solving two-step word problems. Diagnostic tests are mostly available for reading and mathematics and are intended to show specific areas of strength and weakness in these skills. The results can be used to guide remedial instruction or to structure learning experiences for students who are expected to learn the skill.

Subject Area Achievement Tests. Most classroom tests for assessing skills in specific subjects are made up by teachers. However, schools can purchase specific subject achievement tests for almost any subject. A problem with many of these tests is that unless they are tied to the particular curriculum and instructional strategies used in the classroom, they may not adequately represent the content that has been taught. If standardized achievement tests are considered for evaluating learning in specific areas, the content of the test should be closely examined for its match with the curriculum, instruction, and general teaching goals.

Criterion-Referenced Achievement Tests.

Criterion-referenced tests differ from norm-referenced standardized tests in a number of ways (see Popham, 1988; Shepard, 1989a). Such tests can take the form of a survey battery, a diagnostic test, or a single-subject test. In contrast to norm-referenced tests that are designed for use by schools with varying curricula, criterion-referenced tests are often constructed around a well-defined set of objectives. For many tests, these objectives can be chosen by the school district, building administrator, or teacher, to be applied in a specific situation. The items on the test are selected to match specific instructional objectives, often with three to five items measuring each objective. For this reason, these tests are sometimes referred to as objective-referenced tests. Criterion-referenced tests also differ from norm-referenced tests in that measurement with the criterion-referenced test often focuses on students' performance with regard to specific objectives rather than on the test as a whole. Therefore the tests can indicate which objectives individual students or the class as a whole have mastered. Test results can be used to guide future instruction or remedial activities.

> **diagnostic tests:** tests of specific skills used to identify students' needs and to guide instruction.

Finally, criterion-referenced tests differ from other achievement tests in the way they are scored and how the results are interpreted. With criterion-referenced tests, it is generally the score for each objective that is important. Results could show, for example, how many students can multiply two digits by two digits or how many can write a business letter correctly. Moreover, students' scores on the total test or on objectives are interpreted with respect to some criterion of adequate performance independent of group performance. Examples of criterion-referenced tests include tests for drivers and pilots, when we want to know who can drive or fly, not who is in the top 20 percent of drivers or pilots.

Score reports for criterion-referenced tests are frequently in the form of the number of items that the student got correct on each objective. From these data, the teacher can gauge whether the student has mastered the objective.

When criterion-referenced tests are used for making decisions about mastery of a subject or topic, some procedure must be employed to determine the test score cutoff point for mastery. Most procedures for the establishment of a **cutoff score** rely on the professional judgment of teachers and other school personnel. Qualified professionals examine each item in a test and judge the probability that a student with an acceptable level of proficiency would get the item correct. They then base the cutoff score for mastery or proficiency on these probabilities. See Berk (1986) for more on the setting of performance standards for criterion-referenced tests.

Self-Check

Compare and contrast aptitude and achievement tests, and give as many specific examples of each type as you can. How are aptitude and achievement measured? Compare and contrast norm-referenced achievement tests and criterion-referenced achievement tests. Think of an example of an optimally appropriate use for each type of test described in this section.

---

cutoff score: score designated as the minimum necessary to demonstrate mastery of a subject.

derived scores: values computed from raw scores that relate students' performances to those of a norming group; examples are percentiles and grade equivalents.

percentile score: derived score that designates what percent of the norming group earned raw scores lower than a particular score.

How Are Standardized Tests Interpreted?

After students take a standardized test, one of two things happens. The tests are sent for computer scoring to the central office or the test publisher or, less often, teachers or other school staff score the tests themselves, consulting test manuals to interpret the scores. In either case, the students' raw scores (the number correct on each subtest) are translated into one or more **derived scores**, such as percentiles, grade equivalents, or normal curve equivalents, which relate the students' scores to those of the group on which the test was normed. Each of these statistics has its own meaning, described in the following sections.

Percentile Scores

A **percentile score,** or percentile rank (sometimes abbreviated in test reports as %ILE), indicates the percentage of students in the norming group who scored lower than a particular score. For example, students who achieve at the median for

This parent would like an explanation of the percentiles, grade equivalents, and standard test scores on her daughter's CTBS test results. As her daughter's teacher, what will you say?

the norming group (that is, equal numbers of students scored better or worse than that score) would have a percentile rank of 50, because their scores exceeded those of 50 percent of the students in the norming group. If you ranked a group of thirty students from bottom to top on test scores, the twenty-fifth student from the bottom would score in the 83rd percentile (25/30 x 100 = 83.3).

Grade-Equivalent Scores

Grade-equivalent scores relate students' scores to the average scores obtained by students at a particular grade level. Let's say a norming group achieved an average raw score of 20 on a reading test at the beginning of fifth grade. This score would be established as a grade equivalent of 5.0. If a sixth-grade norming group achieved a fall test score of 30, this would be established as a grade equivalent of 6.0. Now let's say a fifth-grader achieved a raw score of 25. This is halfway between the score for 5.0 and that for 6.0, so this student would be assigned a grade equivalent of 5.5. The number after the decimal point is referred to as "months," so a grade equivalent of 5.5 would be read "five years, five months." In theory, a student in the third month of fifth grade should have a score of 5.3 (five years, three months), and so on.

The advantage of grade equivalents is that they are easy to interpret and make some intuitive sense. For example, if an average student gains one grade equivalent each year, we call this achieving at expected levels. If we know a student is performing two years below grade level (say, a ninth-grader who scores at a level typical of seventh-graders), this gives us some understanding of how poorly the student is doing.

However, grade-equivalent scores should be interpreted only as a rough approximation. For one thing, students do not gain steadily in achievement from month to

> **grade-equivalent scores:** standard scores that relate students' raw scores to the average scores obtained by norming groups a t different grade levels.

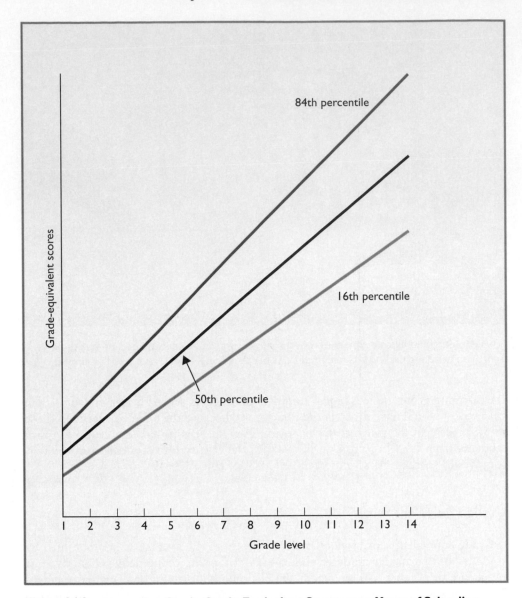

Figure 14.2   Increasing Gap in Grade-Equivalent Scores over Years of Schooling

A student who scores at the 16th percentile on a test in elementary school will have a corresponding grade-equivalent score relatively close to that of a student in the 84th percentile. However, two students who rank correspondingly high and low as measured by percentile in secondary school would find their grade-equivalent scores relatively far apart.

From Coleman and Karweit, 1972, p. 97.

month. For another, scores far from the expected grade level do not mean what they appear to mean. A fourth-grader who scores at, say, 7.4 grade equivalents is by no means ready for seventh-grade work; this score just means that the fourth-grader has thoroughly mastered fourth-grade work, and has scored as well as a seventh-grader would *on a fourth-grade test*. Obviously, the average seventh-grader knows a great deal more than what would be on a fourth-grade test, so there is no real comparison between a fourth-grader who scores at 7.4 grade equivalents and a seventh-grader who does so.

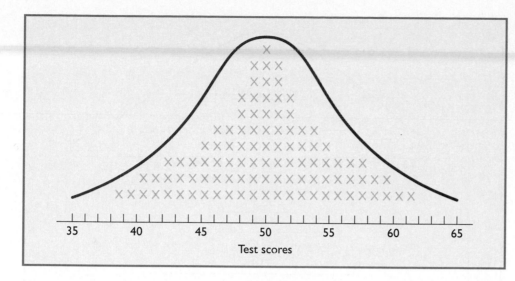

Figure 14.3

Frequency of Scores Forming a Normal Curve

If 100 people take a test and the score for each is marked by an x on a graph, the result could suggest a normal curve. In a normal distribution most scores are at or near the mean (in this case, 50) and the number of scores further from the mean progressively decreases.

From Slavin, 1992, p. 146.

Shifting definitions of grade-level expectations can also confuse the interpretation of scores. For example, New York City school administrators were pleased during the late 1980s to report that 67 percent of students were reading at or above grade level. However, after national concern about the "Lake Wobegon Effect," wherein much more than 50 percent of students were scoring "above average" (Cannell, 1987), test makers renormed their tests. As a result, administrators in New York City could then claim only 49 percent of their students were reading at or above grade level (Fiske, 1989).

Another common misinterpretation of grade-equivalent scores is that if the gap between low-achieving and average students increases over time, the low achievers are getting worse. In fact, achievement scores become more variable over the school years. A student who stays at the 16th percentile throughout elementary and secondary school will fall behind in grade equivalents, as illustrated in Figure 14.2, but that student is remaining at the same point relative to age-mates. When all these cautions are kept in mind, grade-equivalent scores are a useful and understandable shorthand for describing students' scores.

Standard Scores

Several kinds of scores describe test results according to their place on the normal curve. A normal curve describes a distribution of scores in which most fall near the mean, or average, with a smaller number of scores appearing the farther we go above or below the mean. A frequency graph of a **normal distribution** produces a bell-shaped curve. For example, Figure 14.3 shows a frequency distribution from a test with a mean score of 50. Each "x" indicates one student who got a particular score; there are 10 x's at 50, so we know that ten students got this score. Nine students got 49s and 51s, and so on, with very few students making scores above 60 or below 40. Normal distributions like the one shown in Figure 14.3 are common in nature; for example, height and weight are normally distributed throughout the general population of biologically normal people. Standardized tests are designed so that extremely few students will get every item or no item correct, so scores on them are typically normally distributed.

Connections

Scores based on normal distributions in standardized testing are analogous to grading on the curve in classroom assessment, described in Chapter 13.

normal distribution: bell-shaped symmetrical distribution of scores in which most scores fall near the mean, with progressively fewer occurring as distance from the mean increases.

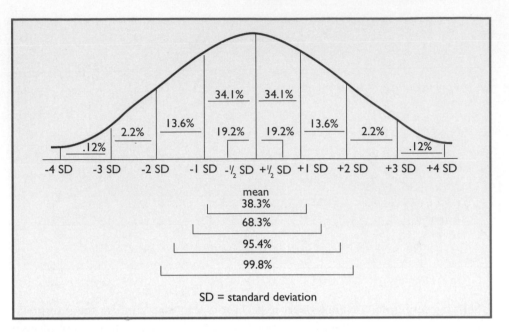

Figure 14.4   Standard Deviation

When test scores are normally distributed, knowledge of how far a given score lies from the mean in terms of standard deviations indicates what percent of scores are higher and lower.

From Slavin, 1992, p. 147.

Standard Deviation.   One important concept related to normal distributions is the **standard deviation,** a measure of the dispersion of scores. The standard deviation is, roughly speaking, the average amount that scores differ from the mean. For example, consider these two sets of scores:

SET A		SET B
85		70
70		68
65	← Mean →	65
60		62
45		60
Standard deviation: 14.6		Standard deviation: 4.1

Note that both sets have the same mean (65), but otherwise they are quite different, with Set A being more spread out than Set B. This is reflected in that Set A has a much larger standard deviation (14.6) than Set B (4.1). The standard deviation of a set of normally distributed scores indicates how spread out the distribution will be. Furthermore, when scores or other data are normally distributed, it allows us to predict how many scores will fall a given number of standard deviations from the mean. This is illustrated in Figure 14.4, which shows that in any normal distribution about 34.1 percent of all scores fall between the mean and one standard deviation above the mean (+1 SD), and a similar number fall between the mean and one standard deviation below the mean (–1 SD).

Scores on standardized tests are often reported in terms of how far they lie from the mean as measured by standard deviation units. For example, IQ scores are normed so that there is a mean of 100 and a standard deviation of 15. This means

standard deviation: a statistical measure of the degree of dispersion in a distribution of scores.

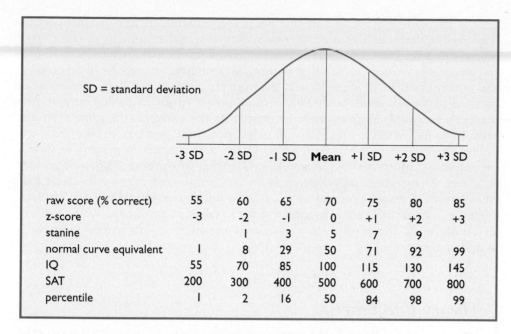

Figure 14.5 Relationship between Various Types of Scores
Raw scores that are normally distributed can be reported in a variety of ways. Each reporting method is characterized by its mean, by the range between high and low scores, and by the standard deviation interval.

that the average person will score 100; someone scoring one standard deviation above the mean will score 115; someone scoring one standard deviation below will score 85; and so on. Thus, about 68.2 percent of all IQ scores (that is, more than two-thirds) fall between 85 (-1 SD) and 115 (+1 SD). SAT scores are also normed according to standard deviations, with the mean set at 500 and a standard deviation of 100. That puts more than two-thirds of all scores between 400 and 600.

Stanines. One standard score that is sometimes used is the **stanine score** (from the words "standard nine"). Stanines have a mean of 5 and a standard deviation of 2, so each stanine represents .5 standard deviations. Stanine scores are reported as whole numbers, so a person who earned a stanine score of 7 (+1 SD) actually fell somewhere between .75 SD and 1.25 SD above the mean.

Normal Curve Equivalents. Another form of a standard score that is being increasingly used is the **normal curve equivalent,** or NCE. A normal curve equivalent can range from 1 to 99, with a mean of 50 and a standard deviation of approximately 21. NCE scores are similar to percentiles, except that, unlike percentile scores, intervals between NCE scores are equal. Another standard score, used more often in statistics than in reporting standardized test results, is the **z-score,** which sets the mean of a distribution at zero and the standard deviation at 1. Figure 14.5 shows how a set of scores with a mean percent correct of 70 percent and a standard deviation of 5 would be represented in z-scores, stanines, normal curve equivalents, percentile scores, and equivalent IQ and SAT scores.

Note the difference in the figure between percentile scores and all standard scores (z-score, stanine, NCE, IQ, and SAT). Percentile scores are bunched up

stanine scores: a type of standardized score ranging from 1 to 9, having a mean of 5 and a standard deviation of 2.

normal curve equivalent: set of standardized scores ranging from 1 to 99, having a mean of 50 and a standard deviation of about 21.

z-score: standard score having a mean of zero and a standard deviation of 1.

around the middle of the distribution because most students score near the mean. This means that small changes in raw scores near the mean can produce large changes in percentiles. In contrast, changes in raw scores make a smaller difference in percentiles far above or below the mean. For example, an increase of 5 points on the test from 70 to 75 moves a student from the 50th to the 84th percentile, an increase of 34 percentile points, but 5 more points (from 75 to 80) increases the student's percentile rank by only 14 points. At the extreme, the same 5 points, from 80 to 85, results in an increase of only 1 percentile point, from 98 to 99.

This characteristic of percentile ranks means that changes in percentiles should be cautiously interpreted. For example, one teacher might brag, "My average kids increased 23 percentile points (from 50 to 73), while your *supposedly* smart kids only gained 15 points (from 84 to 99). I really did a great job with them!" In fact, the bragging teacher's students gained only 3 points in raw score, or .6 standard deviation, while the other teacher's students gained 10 points in raw score, or 2 standard deviations!

Theory Into Practice

Interpreting CTBS/4 Test Scores

This section presents a guide to interpreting test reports for one widely used standardized test of academic performance, the Comprehensive Tests of Basic Skills (CTBS/4).

Class Record Forms

Figure 14.6 shows a sample CTBS Pre-Post class record sheet for a third-grade class. The letters on the sample refer to the principal parts of the record sheet, as follows:

- A   *Identification Data:* This section identifies the class that took the tests.

    - The grade (3.9) indicates that the students were in the ninth month of the third grade.

    - This section also indicates the form and level of the tests students took.

    - Most achievement batteries make available two parallel forms of the same test, consisting of different items but identical in every other respect.

- B   *Scores:* The data columns include pre- and post-test scores. For scale scores and normal curve equivalents, they also include differences. This arrangement makes it easy to determine individual growth attained between testing dates. In the sample, normal curve equivalents (NCE) and national percentiles (NP) were selected for reporting. Scores are listed for each test (such as reading) and subject (such as vocabulary and comprehension).

- C   *Summary:* A summary section reports mean scores—pretest scores, post-test scores, and differences— for the group as a whole.

Individual Reports

An individual test record is usually provided for each student. An example of a Student Interpretive Report (SIR) for the CTBS/4 appears in Figure 14.7. The meanings of the letters in the figure are as follows:

♦ CTBS/4 Comprehensive Tests of Basic Skills, Fourth Edition

PRE-POST CLASS RECORD SHEET

PRE TEST: CTBS/4 BENCHMARK
POST TEST: CTBS/4 BENCHMARK GRADE 3.9

CLASS: ADAMS
NORMS: ADAMS

PAGE 1

****TOTAL BATTERY INCLUDES TOTAL READING, TOTAL LANGUAGE, AND
TOTAL MATHEMATICS.**
MNCE: MEAN NORMAL CURVE EQUIVALENT
MDNP: MEDIAN NATIONAL PERCENTILE
MNPC: NATIONAL PERCENTILE OF MEAN NORMAL CURVE EQUIVALENT
DIFF: DIFFERENCE BETWEEN PRE AND POST SCORES LISTED ABOVE
DIFFERENCES ARE NOT REPORTED FOR NATIONAL PERCENTILE
**PRE-TEST GRADE 2 ONLY

PRE TEST DATE: 4/ 8/88
QUARTER MONTH: 29
NORMS: 1988 CTBS/4
PATTERN (IRT)
POST TEST DATE: 4/ 8/89
QUARTER MONTH: 29
NORMS: 1988 CTBS/4
PATTERN (IRT)

SCHOOL: WILDROSE
DISTRICT: WINFIELD
CITY: WINFIELD
STATE: ANYSTATE

CTBID: 89115811114000103-00004-000015

COPYRIGHT © 1989 BY MCGRAW-HILL, INC. ALL RIGHTS RESERVED

CTB/MCGRAW-HILL

Figure 14.6   Sample Class Record Sheet for a Standardized Test

When a class of students takes a standardized test as a pretest and a post-test, the results may be compared using a form similar to the one shown here. From CTB/McGraw Hill, 1990.

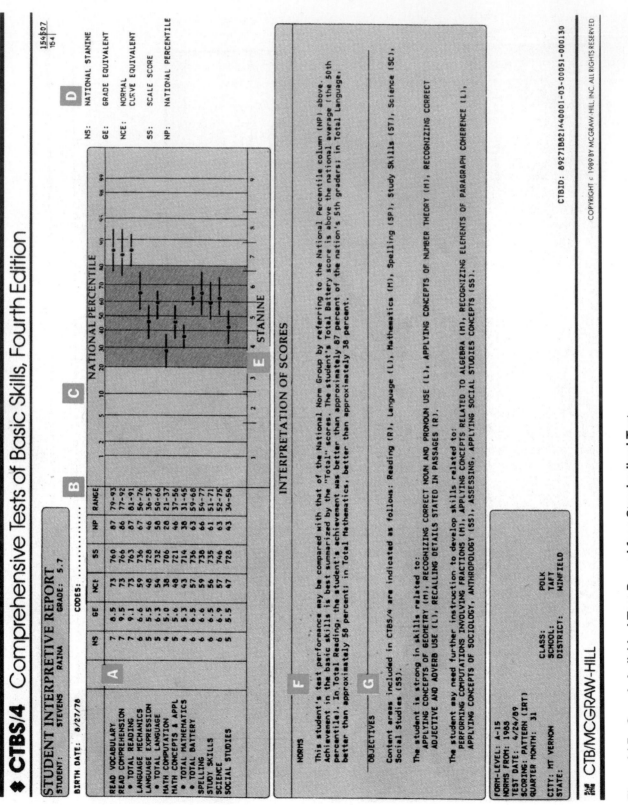

Figure 14.7   Sample Individual Test Record for a Standardized Test

Reports for individuals who take standardized tests may include overall scores and scores on specific content objectives. From CTB/McGraw Hill, 1989.

- *A   Identification Data and Scores:* The SIR includes as many as six norm-referenced scores, including the national percentile (NP). For each test and subtest in the content areas, this sample reports (from left to right) the national stanine, grade equivalent, normal curve equivalent, scale score, and national percentile.

- *B   Range:* The range column gives the numerical range of each national percentile "confidence band" shown on the graph. The student's score, which is subject to standard error and may vary by chance, falls within this range.

- *C   Confidence Band:* Each score's confidence band is represented on the graph by the bars extending to either side of the dot, which represents the reported score. The bands help you take into account the standard error of measurement when you are interpreting scores. The reported score is not an absolute measure of the student's performance; rather, it is a point within a range that probably includes the student's true score.

- *D   Legend:* The legend explains the acronyms for the names of the different types of scores.

- *E   Stanine Band:* The scale at the bottom of the graph displays national stanine bands, which have a constant relation to the national percentile. Stanines 4, 5, and 6 are generally regarded as the average range of achievement. In the sample, Raina Stevens's scores were all in the average range except for her reading scores, which were above average.

- *F   Norms:* This part of the report explains how to interpret the student's national percentile scores.

- *G   Objectives:* This part of the report analyzes the student's strengths and needs in terms of the subject objectives measured by the test battery, information that can help the teacher plan effective instruction.

Self-Check

Describe how the following kinds of scores are derived from standardized test results, and explain how the scores are interpreted: percentiles, grade-equivalent scores, standard scores. How are the concepts of normal distribution and standard deviation related to standard scores? How are the following standard scores interpreted: stanines, normal curve equivalents, z-scores? How do IQ scores and SAT scores relate to standard scores?

What Are Some Issues Concerning Standardized and Classroom Testing?

The use of standardized tests to assess teachers, schools, and districts has increased dramatically in recent years. Most states now have statewide testing programs, in which students at selected grade levels take standardized achievement tests and/or minimum competency tests. Scores on these tests are used to evaluate the state's educational program as a whole and to compare the performance of

Teachers on Teaching

What is the best way to prepare students for standardized tests?

The best preparation for taking standardized tests is a sound program of teaching and learning all year long. All lessons should teach pupils to think logically. This will build confidence to attack unfamiliar problems. This in turn improves test performance. Test-taking skills can be learned. Understanding how the test is structured gives the test-taker an advantage. The teacher can familiarize students with the format of the test. Pupils can practice items similar to those that appear on the standardized test. They also can learn to deal with the type of directions given on these tests. Another way the teacher can help students be prepared for the rigors of testing week is through good home–school communication. We advise parents to encourage proper diet, exercise, and a reasonable bedtime, to avoid scheduling major family events during testing week, and to make perfect attendance the goal. While today's educators should prepare students for standardized tests, they must not teach directly to the test. Although pressure is mounting to increase test scores, if the teacher teaches only to improve test scores, everyone involved loses. The results of these tests become meaningless. Many learning activities not easily measured by a standardized test will not be undertaken. Pupils will not discover their full potential. Future teachers will not be able to improve each child's pool of knowledge by using the previous year's test results to discover pupil needs. A professional educator should be able to prepare the students for the challenge of standardized tests without resorting to teaching to the test.

Richard C. Thorne, Jr., Teacher, Grade 4, and Assistant Principal
South Elementary School, Stoughton, Massachusetts
1992 Massachusetts Teacher of the Year

As a teacher, most of my experience with classroom tests comes from the State of North Carolina end-of-course (EOC) chemistry test, which all my students take each June. This test, among others, was put into place to ensure accountability on the part of the schools. The test is designed to measure how well students know the state's curriculum in chemistry. In my teaching, I feel pulled to give my students the most challenging, relevant, and enjoyable class possible to provide a solid base on which students can be successful in college chemistry classes; and have my students score well on the EOC test. The difficulties come when I do not have time to teach all of the material I'd like to, an annual event. Do I cover a topic that I know will be on the test? Or should I let my students do another lab that I know they will learn more from and will find interesting? My approach is to give students the best possible course and to cover as many topics as I can, whether or not they are on the test. I want to teach not only chemistry facts but also how chemistry affects students' lives. In addition, I am trying to help my students develop more positive attitudes toward science. Good test scores, while important, are secondary to these other goals. The EOC tests are useful in that they provide me with information on how my students did on different parts of the curriculum, which reflects on how well I did teaching the material. I can use this information to revise my course content and my teaching methods. Well-designed tests that measure higher-level thinking skills and a true understanding of a subject are a rarity. I do my students a great disservice if I let standardized tests dictate what and how I teach.

Louis J. Gotlib, High School Chemistry; Science, Grades 3–5
South Granville High School, Creedmore, North Carolina
Co-coordinator of the TRAVELING SCIENCE Project
1991 North Carolina Teacher of the Year

These students will take nation-wide standardized aptitude and achievement tests this year. Will the results be equally fair to them all? Why or why not?

individual school districts, schools, and teachers. These comparisons go under the general heading of accountability programs. Accountability is one of several issues about uses and abuses of standardized tests. Issues around testing, standards, and related topics are among the most hotly debated questions in American education (see Office of Technology Assessment, 1992). In recent years there have been many developments and proposals for change in testing. These are discussed in the following sections.

Validity and Reliability

The **validity** of a test refers to whether the test provides the type of information desired. The criteria used to evaluate the validity of a test vary according to the test's purpose. For example, if a test is being selected to help teachers and administrators determine which students are likely to have some difficulty with one or more aspects of instruction, the primary concern will be how the test predicts future academic performance. On the other hand, if the concern is a description of current achievement levels of a group of students, primary interest will focus on the accuracy of that description. In short, validity deals with the relevance of a test for its intended purpose.

Because of the various roles that tests are expected to play in the schools and their education process, there are several types of validity that may be of concern

> **validity:** a measure of the degree to which a test is appropriate for its intended use.

to test users. These fall into one of three basic classes: content validity, predictive validity, and construct validity (see Nimmer, 1989).

Content Validity.   The most important criterion for the usefulness of a test—especially an achievement test—is whether it assesses what the user wants it to assess (Popham, 1988). This criterion is called **content validity**. Content validity in achievement testing refers to the degree of overlap between what is taught (or what should be taught) and what is tested. Content validity is determined by carefully comparing the content of a test with the objectives of a course or program. Of course, the instructional activities in a classroom are guided largely by curriculum. Consequently, the three factors relevant to the evaluation of content validity are the test content, the instructional content, and the curriculum content.

Predictive Validity.   The **predictive validity** of a test refers to its contribution to the prediction of future behavior. For example, if we are using a test to predict future school performance, one way to examine its accuracy is to relate the test scores to some measure of performance in the future. If an appropriate level of correspondence exists between the test and future performance, the test could then be used to provide predictive information for students.

For example, test scores on SATs and ACTs have been shown to relate, to a reasonable degree, to performance in college, and are therefore used (along with high school grades and other information) by many college admissions officers in deciding which applicants to accept. Reading readiness tests and other school **readiness tests** are often used to route children into transitional first grades, extra-year kindergarten programs, and so on, a practice that has come under fire in recent years in large part because of the poor predictive validity of these measures (see Ellwein *et al.,* 1991; Shepard, 1991; Wodtke *et al.,* 1989).

Construct Validity.   **Construct validity** refers to the degree to which test scores relate to other scores and whether this correspondence makes sense in terms of what the test is supposed to measure (see Haertel, 1985). For example, consider a test of mechanical aptitude. Of course, such a test should be strongly related to a student's ability to build things. However, general intelligence might also predict (to some degree) how well a student can build things, so it is possible that what appears to be a test of mechanical aptitude is in fact a test of general intelligence. To document the construct validity of the mechanical aptitude test, the test designer might show that the test predicts actual mechanical performance much better than does a test of general intelligence.

Reliability.   While the validation process relates to the skills and knowledge measured by a test, the **reliability** of a test relates to the accuracy with which these skills and knowledge are measured. When a test is administered, there are a number of aspects related to both the test itself and the circumstances surrounding its administration that could cause the results to be inaccurate. In theory, if a student were to take the same test twice, we would expect the student to obtain the same score both times. The extent to which this would not occur is the subject of reliability. Ambiguous test items, testing experience, inconsistent motivation, and anxiety all affect test scores and could cause scores for different administrations of the same test to differ. If it could be shown that individuals receive similar scores on two administrations of the same test, then some confidence could be placed in the test's reliability. If the scores were greatly inconsistent, it would be difficult to place much faith in a particular test score. Generally, the longer the test and the greater the range of

---

content validity: a measure of the match between the content of a test and the content of the instruction that preceded it.

predictive validity: a measure of the ability of a test to predict future behavior.

readiness tests: tests to assess the student's level of skills and knowledge necessary for a given activity.

construct validity: degree to which test scores reflect what the test is intended to measure.

reliability: a measure of the consistency of test scores obtained from the same students at different times.

Testing Ethics

A better-than-average score on the Scholastic Aptitude Test will significantly broaden the number of colleges to which a student can successfully apply. Better-than-average scores on standardized tests make a school system look good in the eyes of the tax-paying citizens. With so much riding on test results, it is not surprising that students, teachers, and administrators are at times sorely tempted to do whatever is necessary to achieve the highest possible scores. Enter, ethics!

One ethical concern is that the content of the tests will determine what is taught. Instead of offering a comprehensive curriculum, schools might concentrate selectively on skills that standardized tests are known to measure. These tests do not permit an in-depth assessment of a student's general knowledge or ability; rather, they tend to concentrate on a small range of knowledge and number of skills. If teachers taught only those skills, students would not learn other less testable skills that could prove more valuable in the long run. Aside from being concerned that teachers will teach to the test, critics fear that schools will alter their curricula to conform to test content. They point out that standardized aptitude and achievement tests have made little effort to assess students' higher-level thinking and performance skills. Critics also point out that those who create the tests generally are not educators with a stake in the schools, nor do they represent various professional subject-area organizations. The tests are constructed by affiliates of textbook publishers or by non-profit organizations.

Other ethical issues concern the validity and reliability of the tests. Culture, class, and gender bias invalidate some items, according to critics. They charge that a passage intended to test reading comprehension discriminates against minority-group students if the passage is about a Greek mythological figure or a regatta or some other subject remote from their experiences. Similarly, passages on football and military life might place many female students at a disadvantage.

Critical Thinking

What influence do you think standardized testing has on the teaching of prep courses? On the curriculum? How should test content be determined? How would you describe an instance of culture, class, or gender bias you may recall from your own experience?

Lynn Olsen, "National Standards and Assessments," *Teacher,* May/June 1992; Diane Ravitch, "The Gender Gap in Math and Science," *Network News and Views,* March 1990.

---

items, the greater the reliability. In criterion-referenced testing, because a person's proficiency on specific skills is of primary interest, variability of scores between different test administrations or test takers is less important (see Berk, 1986).

Test Bias and Test Ethics

Some major criticisms of traditional multiple choice and standardized tests relate to issues of validity and reliability. Critics argue that such tests:

- give false information about the status of learning in the nation's schools;
- are unfair to (or biased against) some kinds of students (*e.g.,* minority students, those with limited proficiency in English, females, and students from low-income families);
- tend to corrupt the processes of teaching and learning, often reducing teaching to mere preparation for testing; and
- focus time, energy, and attention on the simpler skills that are easily tested and away from higher-order thinking skills and creative endeavors. (From Haney and Madaus, 1989, p. 684.)

These children are making decisions about which examples of their work to include in their portfolios before handing them in for evaluation. They have also decided to replace their handwriting samples with improved versions and to include an example of a recently mastered mathematical procedure. What benefits of portfolio assessment does this situation reflect?

One major issue in the interpretation of standardized test scores is the possibility of **test bias** against low-income or minority-group students (Jones, 1988; Scheuneman, 1984). In one sense, this is a question of test validity; a test that gave an unfair advantage to one or another category of student could not be considered valid for general use. Of greatest concern is the possibility that tests may be biased because their items assess knowledge or skills common to one culture but not another. It should go without saying that a test with any kind of overt cultural or gender bias should be rejected. For example, a test whose items always refer to doctors as "he" or give Hispanic names only to menial workers should not be used. Recent forms of widely used tests have almost always been edited to remove cultural or gender bias, but tests should nevertheless be carefully read to detect stereotyping or other unfair elements.

Authentic Assessment

After two decades of criticism of standardized testing (see Marzano and Costa, 1988), critics have finally succeeded in proposing, developing, and implementing alternative assessment systems that are designed to avoid the problems of typical multiple-choice tests. The key idea behind the new tests or testing alternatives is that students should be asked to document their learning or demonstrate that they can actually do something real with the information and skills they have learned in school. For example, students might be asked to keep a portfolio, set up an experiment, solve a complex problem in mathematics, or write something for a real audience. Such tests are referred to as *authentic assessments* (Herman *et al.*, 1992; Wiggins, 1989). In reading, the authentic assessment movement has led to development of tests in which students are asked to read longer sections and show their metacognitive awareness of reading strategies (Roeber and Dutcher, 1989; Valencia *et al.*, 1989). The new tests are also likely to require students to integrate knowledge from different domains.

Portfolio Assessment.   An approach to assessment often discussed along with authentic assessment is the collection of student **portfolios,** samples of student work over an extended period. For example, teachers might collect student compositions, projects, and other evidence of higher-order functioning and use this evidence to evaluate student progress over time.

For example, many teachers maintain portfolios of student writings that show the development of a composition from first draft to final product, journal entries, book reports, art work, computer printouts, or papers showing breakthroughs in problem solving (Arter, 1991; Wolf *et al.*, 1991; Wolf, 1989).

Portfolio assessment has important uses when teachers want to evaluate students for grades or other within-school purposes. An added benefit is that giving students a role in determining the contents of their portfolios may provide greater incentive to learn and encourage a greater sense of responsibility for their own learning. Innovators have proposed that portfolio assessment also be used as part of assessments for school accountability. This use is more controversial, as a student's product can be greatly influenced by his or her teacher's or classmates' input. However, portfolio assessments may be used in combination with other on-demand assessments that students do in a structured testing setting. The state of Vermont is currently implementing just such a combined system. The next Theory Into Practice

test bias: an undesirable characteristic of tests in which item content discriminates against certain students on the basis of socioeconomic status, race, ethnicity, or gender.

portfolio assessment: assessment of a collection of the student's work in an area, showing growth, self-reflection, and achievement.

offers practical tips to classroom teachers for planning, organizing, implementing, and using portfolio assessments.

Connections

Recall the definition and discussions of authentic assessment in Chapters 7 and 13.

Theory Into Practice
Making Portfolios Work for You

Planning and Organization

- Develop an overall flexible plan for student portfolios. What purposes will the portfolio serve? What items will be required? When and how will they be obtained? What criteria will be applied for reflection and evaluation?

- Plan sufficient time for students to prepare and discuss portfolio items. Portfolio assessments take more time and thought than correcting paper-and-pencil tests.

- Begin with one aspect of student learning and achievement, and gradually include others as you and the students learn about portfolio procedures. The writing process, for instance, is well suited to documentation through portfolios.

- Choose items to be included in portfolios that will show progress toward or mastery of important goals and objectives. Items that address multiple objectives help make portfolio assessments more efficient.

- Collect at least two types of items: required indicators (Arter, 1990) or core items (Meisels and Steele, 1991), and optional work samples. Required or core indicators are items collected for every child that will show how each child is progressing. Optional work samples show individual students' unique approaches, interests, and strengths.

- Experiment with different forms of organization and procedures until you find one that works for you.

- Place a list of goals and objectives in the front of each portfolio, along with a list of required indicators and a place for recording optional items, so that you and the students can keep track of contents.

Implementation

- Imbed the development of portfolio items into ongoing classroom activities to save time, ensure that portfolio items are representative of children's work, and increase authenticity.

- Give students responsibility for preparing, selecting, evaluating, and filing portfolio items and keeping portfolios up to date. Young children will need much more guidance, high school students much less.

- For selected portfolio items, model reflection and self-assessment for students to help them become aware of the processes they used, what they learned and have yet to learn, and what they may do differently next time.

- Record student and teacher comments about a portfolio item immediately, and attach them to the item. Let younger children dictate their comments.

- Be selective. A portfolio is not a haphazard collection of work samples, audiotapes, pictures, and other products. It is a thoughtful selection of items that

Figure 14.8

Example of a Performance Assessment Activity

From Shavelson et al., 1992.

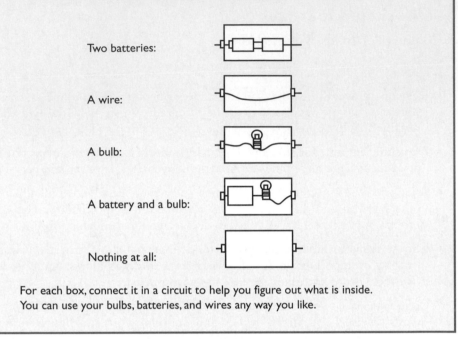

Find out what is in the six mystery boxes A, B, C, D, E, and F. They have five different things inside, shown below. Two of the boxes will have the same thing. All of the others will have something different inside.

Two batteries:

A wire:

A bulb:

A battery and a bulb:

Nothing at all:

For each box, connect it in a circuit to help you figure out what is inside. You can use your bulbs, batteries, and wires any way you like.

exemplify children's learning. Random inclusion of items quickly becomes overwhelming.

Use

- Analyze portfolio items for insight into students' knowledge and skills. As you do this, you will understand more of their strengths and needs, thinking processes, preconceptions, misconceptions, error patterns, and developmental benchmarks.

- Use portfolio information to document and celebrate students' learning, to share with parents and other school personnel, and to improve and target classroom instruction. If portfolios are not linked to improving instruction, they are not working.

Performance Assessment.   Authentic tests involving actual demonstrations of knowledge or skills in real life are called **performance assessments.** For example, ninth-graders might be asked to conduct an oral history by reading about a significant recent event and then interviewing the individuals involved. The quality of the oral histories, done over a period of weeks, would indicate the degree of the students' mastery of the social studies concepts involved (Wiggins, 1989).

A model for this type of exhibition of mastery assessment (Sizer, 1984) is the doctoral thesis, an extended project required for Ph.D.s that is intended to show not only what students know, but what they can do (Archibald and Newmann, 1988).

performance assessment: assessment of students' ability to perform tasks, not just knowledge necessary for a given activity.

How Well Do Performance Assessments Work?

One of the most important criticisms of traditional standardized testing is that it can focus teachers on teaching a narrow range of skills that happen to be on the test (see Slavin and Madden, 1991; Shepard, 1989b). How would performance assessments be better? At least in theory, it should be possible to create tests that require such a broad understanding of subject matter that the test would be worth teaching to. Wiggins (1989, p. 41) puts it this way:

> We *should* "teach to the test." The catch is to design and then teach to . . . tests so that practicing for and taking the tests actually enhances rather than impedes education.

This student is working as a cashier for the school restaurant, run by special education students. How could you use this context to assess her academic learning?

For example, consider the authentic test in science shown in Figure 14.8. Imagine that you know your students will have to conduct an experiment to solve a problem like the one posed in the figure (but not that exact problem). The only way to teach to such a test would be to expose students to a broad range of information about electricity, experimentation, and problem-solving strategies.

Several states, including Vermont, Connecticut, Maryland, and California, are now piloting or starting to use new, performance assessments in their state assessment programs (Aschbacher, 1991; Tittle, 1991). These programs are causing controversy, but appear to be meeting with general acceptance by educators and the public as soon as their bugs are worked out. Performance assessments are far more expensive than traditional multiple-choice measures, but most experts and policy makers are coming to agree that the investment is worthwhile if it produces markedly better tests and therefore leads to better teaching and learning.

Beyond all the practical problems and expense of administering and scoring performance tests (Maeroff, 1991), it is not yet clear whether the new tests will solve all the problems of standardized testing. For example, Shavelson *et al.* (1992) studied performance assessments in science (Figure 14.8 is taken from their study). They found that student performance on such assessments could be reliably rated, but different performance assessments produced very different patterns of scores, and student scores were still more closely related to student aptitude than to what students were actually taught.

The next Theory Into Practice offers classroom teachers practical suggestions for conducting a performance assessment.

Theory Into Practice
Conducting a Performance Assessment

Performance assessment has the potential of capturing student interest, improving student achievement, raising academic standards, and promoting the development of more integrated curricula. But how does one do a performance assessment? It begins with careful planning (see Herman *et al., 1992*).

1. *Identify a valued educational outcome:* Desired outcomes are derived from instructional objectives. The relevant question is, "What do we want students to know and be able to do?" As an example, consider a social studies teacher who wants students to understand and apply democratic principles, such as the protection of civil rights.

2. *Develop tasks students can perform to support their learning of the outcome:* After identifying an outcome, the next step is to ask, "What will we have the students do to support their learning of this outcome?" Students may learn and demonstrate the desired outcome in a variety of ways, for example, by reading, listening, speaking, discussing, role playing, writing, decision making, or problem solving. The following assignment is an example of a complex task students could perform to support their knowledge of the historical importance of protecting civil rights in a democracy:

> Imagine that Martin Luther King, Jr., was living now, and that you were helping him write a speech about progress in the protection of civil rights since his 1963 *I Have a Dream* speech. What will you advise? What evidence will you use to support the advice you give? What conclusions can you draw? Answer these questions in a long letter to Dr. King advising him of what you think he should include in his speech.

3. *Identify additional desired educational outcomes that are supported by the task:* This complex task concerns more than demonstrating and applying knowledge of civil rights as a democratic principle. It subsumes several prerequisite tasks, including basic skills such as reading a speech, gathering information, and writing a letter; and critical thinking skills, such as evaluating evidence and drawing conclusions. Because performance tasks are "authentic," they tend to support learning in more than one domain and for more than one outcome. It is the natural occurrence of multiple interrelated outcomes that allows for effective curriculum integration.

4. *Establish criteria and performance levels for evaluating student performances:* In this step, the relevant question is, "How will I know how well the students have performed?" One way to systematically assess student performance is to develop the criteria by which performances are to be judged and levels of performance are described. In the example above of advising a historical figure in the writing of a speech, criteria for evaluation could relate to each outcome-related task, and levels of performance in each one could be categorized as expert, intermediate, or novice. For example, an "expert" letter might require an "expert" rating on eight or more of the following outcomes.

- knowledge and examples of the concept of civil rights

- recognition and valuing of the role of civil rights protections in a democracy

- comprehension of the meaning of Martin Luther King's famous speech and knowledge of his ideas about civil rights

- knowledge of the historical and social contexts in which King made his speech

- use of facts on the developments in civil rights since 1963

- use of information resources and research strategies

- accuracy of interpretation and expression of facts

- use of selected facts as examples to support ideas or to provide evidence in an argument

- presentation of a coherent argument or plan

- use of generalizations or conclusions based on evidence

- integration of prior knowledge and experience, statement of personal relevance, or evidence of transfer

- appropriate written expression in letter form

- credibility and empathy in written role playing

Planning for performance assessments takes time, and rating performances takes practice to avoid the pitfalls of subjectivity. However, a single, well-thought-out, well-written item for a performance assessment could serve as a summative evaluation, for example, for all or most of your educational objectives for an entire unit.

Self–Check

Use all of the following terms in a discussion or essay about issues in standardized and classroom testing. Include one or more concrete example of each one.

validity
reliability
authentic assessment
test bias
test ethics

The Great Testing Controversy

Jerry Natkin is beginning his seventh year of teaching English; Roscoe Carnes is beginning his fourth year as an art teacher. It is early September, and the two friends sit talking in the teachers' lounge of the only high school in a medium-sized city.

ROSCOE: What's on your agenda in the English Department this year, Jerry? Any new plans or projects?

JERRY: Well, it may seem early to be worrying about this, but we're determined to do something about the standardized test results in this school.

ROSCOE: What's the matter with them?

JERRY: The scores are still declining. We looked back over ten years of results. On average, last year's students scored a couple of percentage points below the kids of five years ago, and even farther below the scores from ten years ago. I wonder if these kids just aren't learning.

ROSCOE: Did you consider that they might be learning a lot but can't show what they know on standardized achievement tests?

JERRY: Maybe. But regardless, the issue is how to get the scores up. I think that in the English department, at least we should make sure that our courses are covering the content of the state standardized test. As I see it, with some changes in course content and classroom testing procedures, we can easily increase the school's overall average score and also our number of state finalists each year.

ROSCOE: But, Jerry, that sounds like teaching to the test.

JERRY: It is. What's wrong with that?

ROSCOE: Is it ethical? Should tests determine curriculum? Is doing well on standardized tests the reason kids go to school? Is testing fair to all students? Those tests contain cultural and class biases, you know. And anyway, the state exam is practically all multiple choice. If you teach to the exam, you run the risk of lowering your standards—minimums do have a way of becoming maximums. What about higher-order learning like problem solving and creative thinking?

JERRY: Higher-order thinking is always part of English, Roscoe; don't worry! But I'm convinced we can include higher-order objectives *and* cover the test better. Also, we need to push the kids more.

ROSCOE: How?

JERRY: I'd like to involve the parents. Get them to work with their kids at home, using sample test items and such. You know, kids who score higher on tests make better grades and do better in life. We've got to coach them.

ROSCOE: I'd argue with you on that. How would you coach all the kids? Would it be fair to pick only some for special treatment? And what does "doing better in life" mean? Better income? Isn't there more to life than that?

JERRY: Sure, sure. Of course achievement tests aren't everything. And they aren't perfect either. But they're there, and we need them—for feedback! How else can we as teachers know what we've accomplished? We get to see kids make measurable progress.

ROSCOE: But I don't think standardized tests are a good measure of students' actual abilities or meaningful knowledge. Maybe your scores tell you something about English proficiency, but I can't measure my kids' progress that way.

JERRY: I bet you *could*. You could measure creativity. . . .

ROSCOE: And then teach to the creativity test? Jerry, do you really think standardized test scores should be guiding your instructional goals as an English teacher?

Problem Solving

1. Using a problem-solving approach, address Jerry's concerns about declining test scores. How would you evaluate Jerry's plan to improve scores? Is it a good idea? Will it work? What could his department do to increase parents' involvement? How could students be coached?

2. Using a problem-solving approach, address Roscoe's concerns about overrelying on test scores. Do standardized tests lead to lower minimum standards? How could that be avoided? Where should the line be drawn—should achievement tests be used for diagnosis? Prediction? Placement? Why or why not? Can cultural and class biases be removed? How else could student achievement be measured? How else could teachers get feedback?

3. Model your solutions by adding one or more new characters and extending the dialogue in writing or roleplay.

Summary

What Are Standardized Tests and How Are They Used?
The term "standardized" describes tests that are uniform in content, administration, and scoring, and therefore allow for the comparison of results across classrooms, schools, and school districts. Standardized tests, such as the SAT and CTBS, measure individual performance or ability against standards or norms established for many other students in the school district, state, or nation for whom the test was designed. Standardized test scores are used for selection and placement, such as grade promotion or college admission, for diagnosis and remediation, for evaluation of student proficiency or progress in content areas, and for evaluation of teachers and schools. Uses of standardized tests may be controversial, such as readiness testing of preschoolers and national testing for teacher certification. Other issues concern accountability, test bias, test ethics, and performance assessment.

What Types of Standardized Test Are Given?
Aptitude tests, such as tests of general intelligence or multifactor batteries, predict students' general abilities and preparation to learn. IQ tests administered to individuals or groups attempt to measure individual aptitude in the cognitive domain. Achievement tests assess student proficiency in various subject areas. Diagnostic tests focus on specific subject matter to discover strengths or weaknesses in mastery. Norm-referenced testing is an interpretation of scores in comparison with other people who took the test, while criterion-referenced testing is an interpretation of scores based on fixed performance levels.

How Are Standardized Test Scores Interpreted?
Scores derived from raw scores include percentiles, the percentage of scores in the norming group that fall below a particular score; grade equivalents, the grade and month at which a particular score is thought to represent typical performance; and standard scores, the students' performance in relation to the normal distribution of scores. Standard scores include stanines (based on the standard deviation of scores); normal curve equivalents (based on a comparison of scores with the normal distribution); and z-scores (the location of scores above or below the mean).

What Are Some Issues Concerning Standardized and Classroom Testing?
Tests and test items must have validity, the quality of testing what is intended to be tested. Content validity means that what is tested corresponds to what has been taught. Predictive validity means that the test accurately predicts future performance. Construct validity means that the test measures precisely what it is supposed to measure. Reliability means that test results are consistent when the test is administered at different places or times. Test bias in any form compromises validity. Test ethics in the content of standardized tests, student preparation for them, the uses of test scores, and the relationship of tests to the curriculum are other issues. The trend toward authentic assessment addresses some of these issues and presents both benefits and challenges. Performance assessment, portfolios, and exhibitions avoid the negative aspects of pencil-and-paper multiple-choice tests by requiring students to demonstrate their learning through work samples or direct real-world applications.

Key Terms

achievement batteries, 538

achievement testing, 535

aptitude test, 535

chronological age, 537

construct validity, 552

content validity, 552

cutoff score, 540

derived scores, 540

diagnostic tests, 539

grade-equivalent scores, 541

intelligence, 536

intelligence quotient, 536

mental age, 537

minimum competency tests, 533

multifactor aptitude battery, 538

normal curve equivalent, 545

normal distribution, 543

norms, 532

percentile score, 540

performance assessment, 556

portfolio assessment, 554

predictive validity, 552

readiness tests, 552

reliability, 552

standard deviation, 544

standardized tests, 531

stanine score, 545

test bias, 554

validity, 551

z-score, 545

Self-Assessment

1. Which of the following types of standardized test is designed to predict future performance?

   a. norm-referenced achievement test

   b. criterion-referenced achievement test

   c. aptitude test

   d. diagnostic test

2. Which of the following score reports would apply to a sixth-grade student who has scored at the national mean on a standardized test?

   a. %ILE = 40, Stanine = 9, z = 0

   b. NCE = 50, z = 0, %ILE = 50

   c. GE = 7.2, Stanine = 5, NCE = 100

   d. z = 3, NCE = 60, %ILE = 50

3. Both the first-period and fifth-period classes averaged 75 on the math final, but student scores in the first class were much more spread out. The first-period class therefore has a larger

   a. mean.

   b. median.

   c. standard deviation.

   d. normal curve equivalent.

4. A seventh-grader earns a grade equivalent of 9.4 on a standardized exam. Which of the following can be assumed?

   a. She is ready to tackle ninth-grade work.

   b. The standardized exam is too easy and needs to be renormed.

   c. She has scored as well on the test as the average ninth-grader would.

   d. All of the above.

5. When students take a certain aptitude test twice they score about the same both times. This result implies that the test has high

   a. predictive validity.

   b. content validity.

   c. construct validity.

   d. reliability.

6. IQ is measured today on the basis of

   a. Binet's ratio method.

   b. a formula involving chronological age and mental age.

   c. a mean of 100 and a standard deviation of 15.

   d. an average of scores on intelligence tests.

7. Tests that contain cultural or gender bias lack

   a. validity.

   b. authenticity.

   c. reliability.

   d. accountability.

8. Write a short essay describing performance assessment and discussing the advantages and disadvantages of performance assessment as a substitute for standardized testing.

ANSWER FEEDBACK

CHAPTER 1

1. Your answer should refer to the importance of teachers' problem–solving skills and their ability to translate information from educational psychology into sound classroom practice. See pages 8–9; 14–16.
2. **b** This is a definition for a principle; see page 13.
3. **a** See pages 17–22.
4. **d, a, e, c** See pages 18–24.
5. **b** The more checks the lower the score. See page 21.
6. **b**, because laboratory experiments permit the greatest control over all variables. See page 18.
7. **d** The more days absent the lower the rank. See pages 21–22.
8. A good research design might involve both observation and a series of single–case experiments to test the effects of random calling on student attention and to test the effects of both random calling and calling in order on student achievement. Similar research suggests Mr. Traub is right on the first assumption but not necessarily on the second one. Random calling seems to increase both attention and anxiety, but the predictability of being called in order may help younger students and poor readers to practice their reading skills more and thus to show higher achievement. Common sense alone, therefore, is not enough. See pages 15–16.

CHAPTER 2

1. **a** Decentration and reversible thinking appear in the concrete operational stage; see page 37; 39–41.
2. **c** The ability to perform conservation tasks was a concern of Piaget's but is not a part of Vygotsky's theory of cognitive development; see pages 48–49.
3. **a** Establishing an identity is the chief task of adolescence; see page 55.
4. **d** The use of an existing scheme in a new context is called assimilation; see pages 32–33.
5. **d** Piaget did not favor acceleration, believing that students would be harmed by being pushed to perform above their levels of cognitive development; see pages 45–47.
6. **c** If performance is strongly influenced by the way tasks are administered, then classification into stages may be unreliable; see page 44.
7. **d, c, b, a**; see pages 34–43 for description of each piagetian stage.
8. **a, c, b**; see pages 61–64 for descriptions of Kohlberg's stages.

CHAPTER 3

1. **b** Once children acquire vocabulary and the basic rules of sentence construction and grammar, they can understand an almost infinite variety of sentences. See page 75.
2. **a** Research shows that play enhances creative problem solving and other cognitive abilities. See pages 82–83
3. **b** Research suggests that Compensatory preschool programs benefit disadvantaged children, even very young ones, more than other groups. Readiness for and achievement in kindergarten and first grade are enhanced, but for greatest sustained benefit, compensatory education needs to be continued in subsequent grades. See pages 84–85.
4. **c** Preoperational thought is more characteristic of children in early childhood Children in middle childhood begin Piaget's concrete operational stage. See pages 89and 90.
5. **a** A minority of adolescents choose identity foreclosure as a solution to the discomfort of identity diffusion. See pages 101–102.
6. Males are twelve to eighteen months behind girls in development. Girls usually reach puberty by age 13, boys between 13 and 16. See page 89.
7. Your outline should refer to selected physical, cognitive, and socioemotional characteristics of preschool, primary school, and secondary school students. Examples of accommodating classroom instruction to the selected characteristics should also appear in the outline. See, for example, pages 90, 92, and 98.
8. **c, b, a, c, a, a, b**; for descriptions of developmental periods see sections beginning on pages 73, 87, and 96.

CHAPTER 4

1. Your essay might refer to modifications in the curriculum, adaptations of instruction, or changes in the communication of attitudes and expectations in the areas of socioeconomic status, race and ethnicity, religion and culture, bilingualism, gender and sex roles, or intelligence and learning styles. See pages 142–146.
2. **b**; SES cuts across all racial and ethnic distinctions; see page 116.
3. **d**; for information on family characteristics that affect achievement see pages 116–117.
4. See examples of multicultural education on pages 142–146.
5. **a**; for information on factors affecting achievement see pages 120–121
6. **a**; for information comparing approaches to bilingual

education see pages 127–129.

7. **c**; Males show more variability than females in academic performance; see pages 130–131

8. **a**, **b**; for information on intelligence see pages 134–138.

CHAPTER 5

1. **d**, feeling anxiety. Avoiding pain, startling, and experiencing thirst are all reflexes, but anxiety responses are all learned See pages 152–153.

2. **e**, Pavlov's classic experiment; **d**, Thorndike's work; **a**, Skinner box experiments; **b**, Bandura's research. See pages 155, 156, 157, and 174.

3. **a**, safety or security is a basic human need, while grades, money, praise, and access to toys are all secondary reinforcers. See page 158.

4. The Premack Principle states that activities less desired by learners can be increased by linking them to more desired activities. An example is "Those who complete their worksheets will be allowed 15 minutes to play a computer game of their choice." See page 159.

5. **c**, because praise is an example of positive reinforcement; **b**, because extra homework is an example of an undesirable consequence that is being removed; **a**, because the task is an example of presentation punishment. See pages 159, 160, and 161.

6. **b**, because it is an example of an FR 10 schedule; **c**, because the consequence is unpredictable though certain; **d**, because the time of reinforcement is predictable; **a**, because the time of reinforcement is not predictable. See pages 166–168.

7. **a**, Bandura's model of observational learning; the other choices refer to other ideas in social learning theory developed by Meichenbaum and others. See page 000.

8. **c**, According to Bandura, vicarious learning is a consequence of unintentional modeling in observational learning. All the other elements relate specifically to cognitive behavior modification. See page 174.

CHAPTER 6

1. **e**; See page 187.

2. **d**, **b**, **c**, **a**; Memories of experiences are stored in episodic memory; networks of schemata are stored in semantic memory; new and retrieved information is processed in short–term memory; and information is most easily lost from the sensory register. See pages 190–197.

3. **a** Using the same methods to teach similar concepts would increase confusion. See page 201.

4. retroactive, proactive; see pages 201–202.

5. To support the claim, your answer could refer to research on overlearning, automaticity, and enactment, for example. Your answer could refute the claim by pointing out that not all forms of practice are equally effective. Distributed practice is preferred to massed practice, for example. See pages 203–204.

6. **d**, **a**, **c**; See pages 205–209.

7. **b**, **a**, **c**; See pages 205–209.

8. **d**, schema theory. See pages 214–215.

CHAPTER 7

1. **c** For information on assisted learning, see page 231.

2. **c**, Bottom–up processing is the traditional approach. Constructive advocate presenting a general problem or whole task first and letting students discover what they need to know and be able to do in order to solve the problem or perform the task (top–down processing). See pages 225 and 227.

3. **a** Scaffolding is an instructional model based on constructivist theory, whereas metacognition is knowing about knowing and intentionally using knowledge about thinking to learn. See page 232.

4. PQ4r stands for Preview, Question, Read, Reflect, Recite, Review. These are steps in an effective method of studying. See page 244.

5. **b**, to make new information meaningful. The other choices are other teaching strategies based on cognitive views of learning. See page 237.

6. **b** Students are transferring and applying knowledge from one field to another. See page 247.

7. **c** Functional fixedness actually interferes with problem solving by preventing people from seeing problems in a new way or seeing all possible solutions. See pages 250–253.

8. **a** For information on expository teaching, see pages 230–232.

CHAPTER 8

1. **d** Teacher control is a feature of direct instruction. See page 265.

2. **g**, **f**, **c**, **b**, **e**, **a**, **d** See pages 265–266.

3. **d** Group discussion is an alternative instructional model and not a part of Hunter's program. See pages 283 and 290.

4. **d** Research supports the view that critical thinking requires learning modes that are not emphasized in direct instruction. See pages 282–286.

5. **a** Research recommends against all the other choices. See pages 267–282.

6. **d** Cooperative learning groups work best with mixed–ability groupings. See pages 287–288.

7. **c**, inquiry training. The other choices all relate to cooperative learning rather than to whole–class discussion. See page 292.

8. Your paragraph about humanistic education should include several of the following terms: open education, affective education, student–directed classes, alternative assessment, diagnostic assessment, team teaching, cross–age tutoring, individualized instruction, experiential learning, learning stations, independent learning skills, thinking and group decision–making skills. In comparing humanistic and direct approaches to instruction, you should be able to point out how both have appropriate uses. See pages 296–301.

CHAPTER 9

1. **e**; Unlike the elements in Carroll's model, all the elements in the QAIT model are alterable. See page 310.

2. **d**, **a**, **c**, **b**, **e**; for information on Carroll's instructional model see page 309.

3. **b**, **a**, **d**, **c**; for information on grouping strategies see pages 113–119.

4. Your answer could refer to research showing greater effec-

tiveness for higher student achievement. In addition, within–class ability grouping allows greater instructional flexibility and does not stigmatize students. See page 318.

5. d; mastery learning is defined on page 322.
6. a; quizzes for master learning are criterion–referenced, not norm–referenced See page 325.
7. True; for information on cross–age tutoring see page 331.
8. a; for a listing of types of CAI programs and their uses see pages 337–338.

CHAPTER 10

1. e, f, b, c, d, a, g. For information on Maslow's theory see page 350.
2. b, a, c See pages 351 (dissonance), 353 (attribution), and 357 (expectancy).
3. c; careful studying is a personal choice, an internal unstable locus of control involving effort. The other options are examples of stable or unstable internal loci of control. See page 355.
4. b; the teacher is trying to promote internal sources of motivation based on effort. See page 356.
5. b; for information on achievement goals see page 361.
6. a; taking a challenging course is an example of a learning goal, while the other options are all examples of performance goals. See page 359.
7. c; for information on the ILE model see page 379.
8. c, a, b; for information on goal structuring see page 381.

CHAPTER 11

1. c; It is engaged, or instructional, time that needs to be increased Increasing engaged time to 100 percent, however, would leave no school time for noninstructional events of activities. See pages 389–391.
2. d; according to Kounin, the teacher should have alerted the whole group that they would shortly be answering questions about what they have read See page 397.
3. d, b, a, c; see pages 396–398.
4. c, d, a, b; nonverbal to verbal cues, then repeated reminders, then administering consequences. See pages 405–407.
5. c, a, b; praise is a feature of teacher attention (page 408), being sent to time out removes the reinforcement of peer attention (page 409), and providing interesting instruction at an appropriate level may relieve frustration (page 410).
6. d, b, a, e, c; the steps for applied behavior analysis appear on pages 410–414.
7. c Behavior learning theory underlies all the strategies based on applied behavior analysis. See pages 415–416.
8. Your essay might make the points that behavior modification techniques can be misused to humiliate, manipulate, overcontrol, incorrectly motivate, and inappropriately punish students. See pages 423–425.

CHAPTER 12

1. b; special education programs are for all students without regard to socioeconomic status. Compensatory education, intervention programs, and federally mandated Chapter 1 programs target students from low income families and communities. See page 437.
2. Your answer should emphasize the importance of distin-

guishing a disability (a functional limitation that interferes with a person's physical or mental abilities) and a handicap (a condition imposed on a person with disabilities by society, the physical environment, or the person's attitude). Handicap is not a synonym for disability. For example, a student who hates school is handicapped by his or her attitude and a student who uses a wheelchair is handicapped by a lack of access ramps. See page 445.
3. c; A person with an IQ of 50 to 75 is regarded as mildly retarded See page 449.
4. c, d, b, a; see pages 450, 451, and 453. Attention deficits, memory disorders, and lack of coordination often point to specific learning disabilities; anxiety, phobias, aggression, and acute shyness may be symptoms of emotional disorders; a common type of speech disorders involves the articulation of sounds; and difficulty receiving and expressing verbal knowledge is often a sign of the presence of a language disorder.
5. Two common options for adapting educational programs to the needs of gifted and talented students are acceleration and enrichment. See page 460.
6. The order should be 2, 1, 4, and 3. Of the options, regular classroom placement is the least restrictive and self–contained special education classrooms are the most restrictive. See pages 463–465.
7. The order should be 4, 1, 3, and 2; among these options, referral for evaluation is the first step and signed parental approval of the IEP is last. See page 446.
8. Effective teaching of mainstreamed special–needs students in regular classrooms involves cooperative learning, computerized instruction, buddy systems, peer tutoring, consultation with special education professionals, and team teaching. In addition, mainstreamed students respond well to teaching practices that are effective for all students, such as managing time, capturing attention, giving positive feedback, and staying on task. See pages 474–479.

CHAPTER 13

1. b; this is the only objective that has all three parts of Mager's model. The statement includes the conditions under which learning will be assessed, what students will be able to do, and the criterion for success. See page 487.
2. d; analysis is the cognitive function involved in identifying components and explaining their interaction. See page 495.
3. c; a behavior content matrix relates content to instructional objectives in the cognitive or other domains, while a table of specifications relates test items to those objectives. See pages 495 and 509.
4. your essay on the importance of evaluation should refer to the uses of evaluation in student feedback, teacher feedback, information to parents, information for selection, information for accountability, and incentive for achievement. See pages 498–502.
5. c; Groundlund states that the type of test items should be consistent with the uses that will be made of the test results. See page 506.
6. d, b, c, a; norm–referenced tests measure the achievement of one student compared to others, while criterion–referenced tests measure performance against a standard of mastery. Formative tests are given during instruction and

guide lesson preparation, while summative tests are given at the end of an instructional unit. See pages 502–503.

7. **a**; "table of specification" is defined on page 509.

8. **d**; as a general rule in multiple choice tests, distractors should be plausible, stems should be long, "none of the above" should be avoided, and choices should be listed vertically by letter. See pages 509–512.

CHAPTER 14

1. **c** Aptitude tests are designed to predict future performance. See pages 535–538.

2. **b** For information on standard scores see page 543 and Figure 14.5.

3. **c** The spread of score reflects standard deviation; see pages 544–545.

4. **c** Higher grade–equivalent scores do not invalidate tests or student placements. See page 543.

5. **d** The replication of test scores in successive administration is a measure of reliability; see page 552.

6. **c** The ratio method described in options (a) and (b) is no longer in use; (d) is not an option. See page 538.

7. **a** For information on validity of tests, see pages 551–552.

8. Your short essay should refer to the qualities of performance assessment as a form of authentic assessment. Performance assessments avoid some pitfalls of traditional multiple–choice tests but may be difficult and expensive to create, administer, and score. Performance tests may also be greatly influenced by teacher input and student aptitude. See pages 556–559.

References

Abrami, P.C., Leventhal, L., and Perry, R.P. (1982). Educational seduction. *Review of Educational Research, 52,*446–462.

Abt Associates (1977). *Education as experimentation: A planned variation model,* Vol. IV. Cambridge, Mass.: Abt Associates.

Achenbach, T.M., and McConaughy, S.H. (1987). *Empirically based assessment of child and adolescent psychopathology: Practical applications.* Beverly Hills, CA: Sage.

Adams, A., Carnine, D., and Gersten, R. (1982). Instructional strategies for studying content area texts in the intermediate grades. *Reading Research Quarterly, 18,* 27–53.

Adams, J.L. (1974). *Conceptual blockbusting.* San Francisco, Calif.: Freeman.

Adams, M.J. (1989). Thinking skills curricula: Their promise and progress. *Educational Psychologist, 24,* 25–77.

Adams, M.J. (1990). *Beginning to read: Thinking and learning about print.* Cambridge, Mass: MIT Press.

Aiken, L.R. (1983). Determining grade boundaries on classroom tests. *Journal of Educational and Psychological Measurement, 43,* 759–762.

Aleman, S.R. (1990). *Attention deficit disorder.* Washington, D.C.: Education and Public Welfare Division of the Congressional Research Service.

Alexander, C., and Strain, P. (1978). A review of educators' attitudes toward handicapped children and the concept of mainstreaming. *Psychology in the Schools, 15,* 390–396.

Alexander, K.L., Entwisle, D.R., and Thompson, M.S. (1987). *School performance, status relations, and the structure of sentiment: Bringing the teacher back in* (Technical Report No. 9). Baltimore, Md.: Johns Hopkins University, Center for Research on Elementary and Middle Schools.

Allen, J., Clark, F., Gallagher, P., and Scofield, F. (1982). *Classroom strategies for accommodating exceptional learners.* Minneapolis: University of Minnesota, National Support Systems Project.

Allen, J.D. (1986). Classroom management: Students' perspectives, goals, and strategies. *American Educational Research Journal, 23,* 437–459.

Allington, R.L., and McGill-Franzen, A. (1989). School response to reading failure: Instruction for Chapter 1 and special education students in grades two, four, and eight. *Elementary School Journal, 89*(5), 529–542.

Allport, G. (1954). *The nature of prejudice.* Cambridge, Mass.: Addison-Wesley.

Alvermann, D.E., *et al.* (1985). Prior knowledge activation and the comprehension of compatible and incompatible text. *Reading Research Quarterly, 20,* 420–436.

American Association of University Women (1992). *How schools short change girls.* Washington, D.C.: Author.

American Institutes for Research (1977). *Evaluations of the impact of ESEA Title VII Spanish/English bilingual education programs.* Palo Alto, Calif.: AIR.

American Psychiatric Association (1982). *Diagnostic and statistical manual of mental disorders* (3rd ed. DSM III). Washington, D.C.: American Psychiatric Association.

American Psychiatric Association (1987). *Diagnostic and statistical manual of mental disorders* (3rd ed. rev.). Washington, D.C.: Author.

Ames, C. (1984). Achievement attributions and self-instruction under competitive and individualistic goal structures. *Journal of Educational Psychology, 76,* 478–487.

Ames, C. (1986). Effective motivation: The contribution of the learning environment. In R.S. Feldman (ed.), *The social psychology of education.* Cambridge, England: Cambridge University Press.

Ames, C. (ed.) (1987). The enhancement of student motivation. In D.A. Kleiber and M.L. Maehr, *Enhancing motivation.* Greenwich, Conn.: JAI.

Ames, C. (1992). Classrooms: Goals, structures, and student motivation. *Journal of Educational Psychology, 84,* 261–271.

Ames, C., and Ames, R. (1984). Systems of student and teacher motivation: Toward a qualitative definition. *Journal of Educational Psychology, 76,* 535–556.

Ames, C., Ames, R., and Felker, D.W. (1977). Effects of competitive reward structure and valence of outcome on children's achievement attributions. *Journal of Educational Psychology, 69,* 1–8.

Ames, C., and Archer, J. (1988). Achievement goals in the classroom: student's learning strategies and motivation processes. *Journal of Educational Psychology, 80,* 260–267.

Ames, R., and Ames, C. (1989). *Research on motivation in education,*Vol. 3. New York: Academic Press.

Anastasi, A. (1981). Abilities and the measurement of achievement. In W.B. Schrader (ed.), *New directions for testing and measurement,* Vol. 5. San Francisco: Jossey-Bass.

Anderson, J.R. (1985). *Cognitive psychology and its implications* (2nd ed.). San Francisco, Cal.: Freeman.

Anderson, J.R. (1990). *Cognitive psychology and its implications* (3rd ed.). New York: Freeman.

Anderson, J.R., and Bower, G. (1983). *Human associative memory.* Washington, D.C.: Winston.

Anderson, L.M. (1989). Learners and learning. In M. Reynolds (ed.), *Knowledge base for beginning teachers* (pp. 85–1000). New York: Pergamon.

Anderson, L.M., Brubaker, N.L., Alleman-Brooks, J., and Duffy, G.G. (1985). A qualitative study of seatwork in first-grade classrooms. *Elementary School Journal, 86,* 123–140.

Anderson, L.M., Evertson, C.M., and Brophy, J.E. (1979). An experimental study of effective teaching in first-grade reading groups. *Elementary School Journal, 79,* 193–223.

Anderson, L.M., Evertson, C.M., and Brophy, J.E. (1982). Principles of small group instruction in elementary reading (Occasional Paper No. 58). Institute for Research on Teaching, Michigan State University.

Anderson, L.W. (1984). *Time and school learning: Theory, research, and practice.* London: Croom Helm.

Anderson, L.W., and Pellicer, L.O. (1990). Synthesis of research on compensatory and remedial education. *Educational Leadership, 48*(1), 10–16.

Anderson, R.C., and Hidde, J.L. (1971). Imagery and sentence learning. *Journal of Educational Psychology, 62,* 81–94.

Anderson, R.C., and Pichert, J.W. (1978). Recall of previously unrecallable information following a shift in perspective. *Journal of Verbal Learning and Verbal Behavior, 17,* 1–12.

Anderson, R.C., Spiro, R.J., and Montague, W.E. (eds.) (1977). *Schooling and the acquisition of knowledge.* Hillsdale, N.J.: Erlbaum.

Anderson, T.H., and Armbruster, B.B. (1984). Studying. In P.D. Pearson (ed.), *Handbook of reading research.* New York: Longman.

Andre, T. (1973). Retroactive inhibition of prose and change in physical or organizational context. *Psychological Reports, 32,* 781–782.

Andre, T. (1979). Does answering higher-level questions while reading facilitate productive learning? *Review of Educational Research, 49,* 280–318.

Andre, T. (1984). Problem-solving. In G. Phye and T. Andre (eds.), *Cognitive instructional psychology.* New York: Academic Press.

Andre, T., Anderson, R.C., and Watts, G.H. (1976). Item-specific interference and list discrimination in free recall. *Journal of General Psychology, 72, 533–543.*

Andre, T., and Sola, J. (1976). Imagery, verbatim and paraphrased questions and retention of meaningful sentences. *Journal of Educational Psychology, 68,* 661–669.

Andre, T., and Womack, S. (1978). Verbatim and paraphrased questions and learning from prose. *Journal of Educational Psychology, 70,* 796–802.

Andrews, G.R., and Debus, R.L. (1978). Persistence and the casual perception of failure: Modifying cognitive attributions. *Journal of Educational Psychology, 70,* 154–166.

Archambault, F.X. (1989). Instructional setting and other design features of compensatory education programs. In R.E. Slavin, N.L. Karweit, and N.A. Madden (eds.), *Effective programs for students at risk.* Boston: Allyn & Bacon.

Archibald, D. and Newmann, F. (1988). *Beyond standardized testing: Authentic academic achievement in the secondary school.* Reston, Va.: NASSP Publications.

Arias, M.B. (1986). The context of education for Hispanic students: An overview. *American Journal of Education, 95,* 26–57.

Arlin, M. (1979). Teacher transitions can disrupt time flow in classrooms. *American Educational Research Journal, 16,* 42–56.

Arlin, M. (1984a). Time, equality, and mastery learning. *Review of Educational Research, 54,* 65–86.

Arlin, M. (1984b). Time variability in mastery learning. *American Educational Research Journal, 21,* 103–120.

Arlin, M., and Webster, J. (1983). Time costs of mastery learning. *Journal of Educational Psychology, 75,* 187–195.

Arnold, W.R., and Brungardt, T.M. (1983). *Juvenile misconduct and delinquency.* Boston: Houghton Mifflin.

Aron, I.E. (1977). Moral philosophy and moral education: A critique of Kohlberg's theory. *School Review, 85,* 197–217.

Aronfreed, J., and Reber, A. (1965). Internal behavioral suppression and the timing of social punishment. *Journal of Personality and Social Psychology, 1,* 3–16.

Aronson, E., Blaney, N., Stephan, C., Sikes, J., and Snapp, M. (1978). *The jigsaw classroom.* Beverly Hills, Calif.: Sage.

Arter, J. (1991). *Using portfolios in instruction and assessment: State of the art summary.* Portland, Ore.: Northwest Regional Educational Laboratory.

Arter, J.A. (1990). *Using portfolio in instruction and assessment.* Portland, Ore.: Northwest Regional Educational Laboratory.

Aschbacher, P.R. (1991). *Alternative assessment: State activity, interest, and concerns.* Los Angeles: UCLA Center for Research on Evaluation, Standards, and Student Testing.

Asher, S.R., Oden, S.L., and Gottman, J.M. (1977). Children's friendships in school settings. In L.G. Katz (ed.), *Current topics in early childhood education,* Vol. 1, pp. 33–62. Norwood, N.J.: Ablex Publishing Corp.

Asher, S.R., Renshaw, P.D., and Hymel, S. (1982). Peer relations and the development of social skills. In S.G. Moore and C.R. Cooper (eds.), *The young child: Reviews of research,* Vol. 3, pp. 137–158. Washington, D.C.: National Association for the Education of Young Children.

Atkinson, J.W. (1958). Towards experimental analysis of human motivation in terms of motive expectancies, and incentives. In J.W. Atkinson (ed.), *Motives in fantasy, action, and society.* Princeton, N.J.: Van Nostrand.

Atkinson, J.W. (1964). *An introduction to motivation.* Princeton, N.J.: Van Nostrand.

Atkinson, J.W., and Birch, D. (1978). *An introduction to motivation* (2nd ed.). New York: Van Nostrand.

Atkinson, J.W., and Litwin, G.H. (1960). Achievement motive and test anxiety as motives to approach success and avoid failure. *Journal of Abnormal and Social Psychology, 60,* 52–63.

Atkinson, M.I. (1984). Computer-assisted instruction: Current state of the art. *Computers in the Schools, 1,* 91–99.

Atkinson, R.C. (1968). Computerized instruction and the learning process. *American Psychologist, 12,* 225–239.

Atkinson, R.C. (1975). Mnemonotechnics in second language learning. *American Psychologist, 30,* 821–828.

Atkinson, R.C., and Fletcher, J.D. (1972). Teaching children to read with a computer. *The Reading Teacher, 25,* 319–327.

Atkinson, R.C., and Raugh, M.R. (1975). An application of the mnemonic keyword method to the acquisition of Russian vocabulary. *Journal of Experimental Psychology: Human learning and memory, 104,* 126–133.

Atkinson, R.C., and Shiffrin, R.M. (1968). Human memory: A proposed system and its component processes. In K. Spence and J. Spence (eds.), *The psychology of learning and motivation,* Vol. 2. New York: Academic Press.

Atwood, R. (1983, April). The interacting effects of task form and activity structure on students' task involvement and teacher evaluations. Paper presented at the annual meeting of the American Educational Research Association, Montreal.

Ausubel, D.P. (1960). The use of advanced organizers in the learning and retention of meaningful verbal material. *Journal of Educational Psychology, 51,* 267–272.

Ausubel, D.P. (1963). *The psychology of meaningful verbal learning.* New York: Grune and Stratton.

Ausubel, D.P. (1968). *Educational psychology: A cognitive view.* New York: Holt, Rinehart, & Winston.

Ausubel, D.P. (1978). In defense of advance organizers: A reply to the critics. *Review of Educational Research, 48,* 251–258.

Ausubel, D.P., and Youssef, M. (1963). Role of discriminability in meaningful parallel learning. *Journal of Educational Psychology, 54,* 331–336.

Ayllon, T., Garber, S., and Pisor, K. (1975). The elimination of discipline problems through a combined school-home motivation system. *Behavior Therapy, 6,* 616–626.

Ayllon, T., and Roberts, M.D. (1974). Eliminating discipline problems by strengthening academic performance. *Journal of Applied Behavior Analysis, 7,* 71–76.

Bain, B., and Yu, A. (1980). Cognitive consequences of raising children bilingually, "one parent, one language." *Canadian Journal of Psychology, 34,* 304–313.

Baldwin, J., and Baldwin, J. (1986). *Behavioral principles in everyday life* (2nd ed). Englewood Cliffs, N.J.: Prentice-Hall.

Ball, S., and Bogatz, G.A. (1970). *The first

year of Sesame Street: An evaluation. Princeton, N.J.: Educational Testing Service.

Ball, S., and Bogatz, G.A. (1972). *Reading and television: An evaluation of the Electric Company* (PR-72-2). Princeton, N.J.: Educational Testing Service.

Ballard, M., Corman, L., Gottlieb, J., and Kauffman, M. (1977). Improving the social status of mainstreamed retarded children. *Journal of Educational Psychology, 69,* 605–611.

Balow, I.H. (1964). The effects of homogeneous grouping in seventh grade arithmetic. *Arithmetic Teacher, 11,* 186–191.

Baltimore Public Schools (1972). A report of the study group on school attendance/dropouts. Baltimore, Md.

Bandura, A. (1965). Influence of models' reinforcement contingencies on the acquisition of imitative responses. *Journal of Personality and Social Psychology, 1,* 589–595.

Bandura, A. (1969). *Principles of behavior modification.* New York: Holt, Rinehart, & Winston.

Bandura, A. (1977). *Social learning theory.* Englewood Cliffs, N.J.: Prentice-Hall.

Bandura, A. (1986). *Social foundations of thought and action: A social-cognitive theory.* Englewood Cliffs, N.J.: Prentice-Hall.

Bangert, R., Kulik, J., and Kulik, C. (1983). Individualized systems of instruction in secondary schools. *Review of Educational Research, 53,* 143–158.

Bangert-Drowns, R.L., Kulik, C.C., Kulik, J.A., and Morgan, M. (1991). The instructional effect of feedback in test-like events. *Review of Educational Research, 61*(2), 213–238.

Bangert-Drowns, R.L., Kulik, J.A., and Kulik, C.-L. (1986, April). Effects of frequent classroom testing. Paper presented at the annual convention of the American Education Research Association, San Francisco.

Banks, J.A. (1988). *Multiethnic education: Theory and practice.* Boston: Allyn & Bacon.

Banks, J.A. (1993). Multicultural education: Characteristics and goals. In J.A. Banks and C.A.M. Banks (eds.), *Multicultural education: Issues and perspectives* (2nd ed.). Boston: Allyn & Bacon.

Banks, J.A., and Banks, C.A.M. (1993). *Multicultural education: Issues and perspectives* (2nd ed.). Boston: Allyn & Bacon.

Barber, R.M., and Kagey, J.R. (1977). Modification of school attendance for an elementary population. *Journal of Applied Behavior Analysis, 10,* 41–48.

Barnes, E., Berrigan, C., and Biklen, D. (1978). *What's the difference? Teaching positive attitudes toward people with disabilities.* Syracuse, N.Y.: Human Policy Press.

Baron, J.B. (1989). Performance testing in Connecticut. *Educational Leadership, 46*(7), 8.

Baron, R., Tom, D., and Cooper, H. (1985). Social class, race, and teacher expectations. In J. Duser (ed.), *Teacher expectations.* Hillsdale, N.J.: Erlbaum.

Baron, R.A. (1992). *Psychology* (2nd ed.). Boston: Allyn & Bacon.

Barr, R. (1987). Content coverage. In M.J. Dunkin (ed.), *International encyclopedia of teaching and teacher education.* New York: Pergamon.

Barr, R. (1990). The social organization of literacy instruction. In S. McCormick and J. Zutell (eds.), *Thirty-ninth yearbook of the National Reading Conference.* Chicago: National Reading Conference.

Barr, R. (1992). Teachers, materials, and group composition in literacy instruction. In M.J. Dreher and W.H. Slater (eds.), *Elementary school literacy: Critical Issues.* Norwood, Mass.: Christopher-Gordon.

Barr, R., and Dreeben, R. (1983). *How schools work.* Chicago: University of Chicago Press.

Barringer, C., and Gholson, B. (1979). Effects of type and combination of feedback upon conceptual learning by children: Implications for research in academic learning. *Review of Educational Research, 49,* 459–478.

Barrish, H.H., Saunders, M., and Wolf, M.M. (1969). Good behavior game: Effects of individual contingencies for group consequences on disruptive behavior in a classroom. *Journal of Applied Behavior: Analysis, 2,* 119–124.

Bar-Tal, D. (1979). Interactions of teachers and pupils. In I.H. Frieze, D. Bar-Tal, and J.S. Carroll (eds.), *New approaches to social problems: Applications of attribution theory.* San Francisco: Jossey-Bass.

Barth, R. (1979). Home-based reinforcement of school behavior: A review and analysis. *Review of Educational Research, 49,* 436–458.

Barton, K. (1973). Recent data on the culture-fair scales. In *Information Bulletin 16.* Champaign, Ill.: Institute for Personality and Ability Testing.

Baruth, L.G., and Manning, M.L. (1992). *Multicultural education of children and adolescents.* Boston: Allyn & Bacon.

Baskin, B.H., and Harris, K.H. (1977). *Notes from a different drummer: A guide to juvenile fiction portraying the handicapped.* New York: R.R. Bowker.

Bates, J.A. (1979). Extrinsic reward and intrinsic motivation: A review with implications for the classroom. *Review of Educational Research, 19,* 557–576.

Bates, J.A. (1987). Reinforcement. In M.J. Dunkin (ed.), *The international encyclopedia of teaching and teacher education.* New York: Pergamon.

Baumrind, D. (1973). The development of instrumental competence through socialization. In A. Pick (ed.), *Minnesota symposium on child psychology,* Vol. 7, pp. 3–46. Minneapolis: University of Minnesota Press.

Baumrind, D. (1980). New directions in socialization research. *American Psychologist, 35,* 639–652.

Beady, L.L., Slavin, R.E., and Fennessey, G.M. (1981). Alternative student evaluation structures and a focused schedule of instruction in an inner-city junior high school. *Journal of Educational Psychology, 73,* 518–523.

Bear, G.G., Clever, A., and Proctor, W.A. (1991). Self-perceptions of nonhandicapped children and children with learning disabilities in integrated classes. *Journal of Special Education, 24,* 409–426.

Bear, T., Schenk, S., and Buckner, L. (1992/93). Supporting victims of child abuse. *Educational Leadership, 50*(4), 42–47.

Becker, B.J. (1990). Coaching for the scholastic aptitude test: Further synthesis and appraisal. *Review of Educational Research, 60*(3), 373–417.

Becker, H.J. (1986). *Instructional uses of computers: Reports from the 1985 national survey* (Issue No. 1). Baltimore, Md.: Johns Hopkins University. Center for Research on Elementary and Middle Schools.

Becker, H.J. (1990a, April). *Computer use in United States schools: 1989.* Paper presented at the annual convention of the American Educational Research Association, Boston.

Becker, H.J. (1990b, April). *Effects of computer use on mathematics achievement: Field findings from a nationwide field experiment in grade five to eight classes.* Paper presented at the annual meeting of the American Educational Research Association, Boston.

Becker, H.J. (1990c). Curriculum and instruction in middle-grade schools. *Phi Delta Kappan, 71*(6), 450–457.

Becker, H.J. (1992). Computer-based integrated learning systems in the elementary and middle grades: A critical review and synthesis of evaluation reports. *Journal of Educational Computing Research, 8,* 1–41.

Becker, W., and Carnine, D. (1980). Direct instruction: An effective approach for educational intervention with the disadvantaged and low performers. In B. Lahey and A. Kazdin (eds.), *Advances in child clinical psychology.* New York: Plenum.

Becker, W.C., Madsen, C.H., Arnold, C.R., and Thomas, D.R. (1967). The contingent use of teacher attention and praise in reducing classroom behavior problems. *Journal of Special Education, 1,* 287–307.

Beezer, B. (1985). Reporting child abuse and neglect: Your responsibilities and your protections. *Phi Delta Kappan, 66,* 434–436.

Behnke, G.J. (1979). *Coping with classroom distractions: The formal research study.* (Tech. Ref. No. 79-2). San Francisco: Far West Laboratory.

Belgard, M., Rosenshine, B., and Gage, N.L. (1971). Effectiveness in explaining: Evidence on its generality and correlation with pupil rating. In I. Westbury and A. Bellack (eds.), *Research into classroom processes: Recent developments and next steps.* New York: Teachers College Press.

Belleza, F.S. (1981). Mnemonic devices classification, characteristics, and criteria. *Review of Educational Research, 51,* 247–275.

Benbow, C.P., and Stanley, J.C. (1980). Sex differences in mathematical ability: Fact or artifact? *Science, 210,* 1262–1264.

Bereiter, C., and Englemann, S. (1966). *Teaching disadvantaged children in the preschool.* Englewood Cliffs, N.J.: Prentice-Hall.

Bereiter, C., and Scardamalia, M. (1987). *The psychology of written composition.* Hillsdale, N.J.: Erlbaum.

Berg, C.A., and Clough, M. (1990/91). Hunter lesson design: The wrong one for science teaching. *Educational Leadership, 48*(4), 73–78.

Berk, L.E. (1991). *Child development* (2nd ed.). Boston: Allyn & Bacon.

Berk, L.E. (1993). *Infants, children, and adolescents.* Needham, Mass.: Allyn & Bacon.

Berk, L.E., and Garvin, R.A. (1984). Development of private speech among low-income Appalachian children. *Developmental Psychology, 20,* 271–286.

Berk, R. (1986). A consumer's guide to setting performance standards on criterion referenced tests. *Review of Educational Research, 56,* 137–172.

Berk, R.A. (1980). *Criterion-referenced testing: State of the art.* Baltimore, Md.: Johns Hopkins University Press.

Berko, J. (1985). The child's learning of English morphology. *Word, 14,* 150–177.

Berlyne, D.E. (1965). Curiosity and education. In J.D. Krumboltz (ed.), *Learning and the educational process.* Chicago: Rand McNally.

Berndt, T.J. (1982). The features and effects of friendship in early adolescence. *Child Development, 53,* 1447–1460.

Berrueta-Clement, J.R., Schweinhart, L.J., Barnett, W.S., Epstein, A.S. and Weikart, D.P. (1984). *Changed lives.* Ypsilanti, Mich.: High/Scope.

Bershon, B.L. (1992). Cooperative problem solving: A link to inner speech. In R. Hertz-Lazarowitz and N. Miller (Eds.), *Interaction in cooperative groups.* New York: Cambridge University Press.

Bersoff, D.N. (1981). Testing and the law. *American Psychologist, 36,* 1047–1056.

Beyer, B.K. (1988). *Developing a thinking skills program.* Boston: Allyn & Bacon.

Birman, B.F., Oraland, M.E., Jung, R.K., Anson, R.J., Garcia, G.N., Moore, M.T., Funkhouser, J.E., Morrison, D.R., Turnbull, B.J., and Reisner, E.R. (1987). *The current operation of the Chapter 1 program.* Washington, D.C.: Office of Educational Research and Improvement, U.S. Department of Education.

Bivens, J.A., and Berk, L.E. (1990). A longitudinal study of the development of elementary school children's private speech. *Merrill-Palmer Quarterly, 36,* 121–127.

Black, J.K. (1981). Are young children really egocentric? *Young Children, 36,* 51–55.

Blackadar, A.R., and Nachtigal, P. (1986). *Cotapaxi/Westcliffe follow-through project: Final evaluation report.* Denver: Mid-Continental Regional Educational Laboratory.

Blackhurst, A.E., and Berdine, W.H. (1981). *An introduction to special education.* Boston: Little, Brown.

Blasi, A. (1983). Moral cognition and moral action: A theoretical perspective. *Developmental Review, 3,* 178–210.

Blechman, E.A. (1985). *Solving child behavior problems at home and at school.* Champaign, Ill.: Research Press.

Bleier, R. (1988). Sex differences in research: Science or belief? In R. Bleier (ed.), *Feminist approaches to science* (pp. 147–164). New York: Pergamon.

Block, J.H., and Anderson, L.W. (1975). *Mastery learning in classroom instruction.* New York: Macmillan.

Block, J.H., and Burns, R.B. (1976). Mastery learning. In L.S. Shulman (ed.), *Review of research in education* (Vol. 4, pp. 3–49). Itasca, Ill.: F.E. Peacock, Inc.

Block, K.K., and Peskowitz, N.B. (1990). Metacognition in spelling: Using writing and reading to self-check spelling. *Elementary School Journal, 91,* 151–164.

Bloom, B.S. (1964). *Stability and change in human characteristics.* New York: Wiley.

Bloom, B.S. (1968). Learning for mastery (UCLA-CSEIP). *Evaluation Comment, 1,* 2.

Bloom, B.S. (1976). *Human characteristics and school learning.* New York: McGraw-Hill.

Bloom, B.S. (1984). The 2 sigma problem: The search for methods of instruction as effective as one-to-one tutoring. *Educational Researcher, 13,* 4–16.

Bloom, B.S. (1986). Automaticity: The hands and feet of genius. *Educational Leadership, 43,* 70–77.

Bloom, B.S., Englehart, M.B., Furst, E.J., Hill, W.H., and Krathwohi, O.R. (1956). *Taxonomy of educational objectives: The classification of educational goals. Handbook 1: The cognitive domain.* New York: Longman.

Bloom, B.S., Hastings, J.T., and Madaus, G.F. (1971). *Handbook on formative and summative evaluation of student learning.* New York: McGraw-Hill.

Bloome, D., Puro, P., and Theodorou, E. (1989). Procedural displays and classroom lessons. *Curriculum Inquiry, 19*(3), 265–291.

Blos, P. (1979). *The adolescent passage.* New York: International Universities Press.

Blume, G.W. (1984, April). *A review of research on the effects of computer programming on mathematical problem solving.* Paper presented at the annual convention of the American Educational Research Association, New Orleans.

Blumenfeld, P.C. (1992). Classroom learning and motivation: Clarifying and expanding goal theory. *Journal of Educational Psychology, 84,* 272–281.

Boden, M.A. (1980). *Jean Piaget.* New York: Viking Press.

Bogdan, R.C., and Biklen, S.K. (1982). *Qualitative research for education: An introduction to theory and methods.* Boston: Allyn & Bacon.

Boocock, S.S. (1980). *Sociology of education* (2nd ed.). Boston: Houghton Mifflin.

Bookbinder, S.R. (1978). *Mainstreaming: What every child needs to know about disabilities.* Providence: Rhode Island Easter Seal Society.

Bornstein, P.H. (1985). Self-instructional training: A commentary and state-of-the-art. *Journal of Applied Behavior Analysis, 18,* 69–72.

Borstein, M., and Quevillon, R. (1976). The effects of a self-instructional package with overactive preschool boys. *Journal of Applied Behavior Analysis, 9,* 179–188.

Bos, C.S., and Vaughn, S. (1988). *Strategies for teaching students with learning and behavior problems.* Boston: Allyn & Bacon.

Botvin, G. (1984). Prevention of alcohol misuse through the development of personal and social competence: A pilot study. *Journal of Alcohol Studies, 45,* 37.

Bower, G.H., Clark, M.C., Lesgold, A.M., and Winzenz, D. (1969). Hierarchical retrieval schemes in recall of categorized word lists. *Journal of Verbal Learning and Verbal Behavior, 8,* 323–343.

Bower, G.H., and Karlin, M.B. (1974). Depth of processing pictures of faces and recognition memory. *Journal of Experimental Psychology, 103,* 751–757.

Bowerman, C.E., and Kinch, J.W. (1969). Changes in family and peer orientation of children between fourth and tenth grades. In M. Gold and E. Douvan (eds.), *Adolescent development.* Boston: Allyn & Bacon.

Boykin, A.W. (1986). The triple quandary and the schooling of Afro-American children. In U. Neisser (ed.), *The school achievement of minority children.*

Hillsdale, N.J.: Erlbaum.

Braddock, J.H. (1985). School desegregation and black assimilation. *Journal of Social Issues, 41,* 9–22.

Braddock, J.H. (1989). *Tracking of Black, Hispanic, Asian, Native American, and White students: National patterns and trends.* Baltimore, Md.:Johns Hopkins University Center for Research on Effective Schooling for Disadvantaged Students.

Braddock, J.H., and Slavin, R.E. (1992). *Why ability grouping must end: Achieving excellence and equity in American education.* Baltimore, MD: Johns Hopkins University, Center for Research on Effective Schooling for Disadvantaged Students.

Brainin, S.S. (1985). Mediated learning: Pedagogical issues in the improvement of cognitive functioning. In E.W. Gordon (ed.), *Review of research in education,* Vol. 12. Washington, D.C.: American Educational Research Association.

Bransford, J.D. (1979). *Human cognition: Learning, understanding, and remembering.* Belmont, Calif.: Wadsworth.

Bransford, J.D., Burns, M.S., Delclos, V.R., and Vye, N.J. (1986a). Teaching thinking: Evaluating evaluations and broadening the data base. *Educational Leadership, 44(2),* 68–70.

Bransford, J.D., Sherwood, R.D., Vye, N.J., and Rieser, J. (1986b). Teaching thinking and problem solving: Research foundations. *American Psychologist, 41,* 1078–1087.

Bransford, J.D., Stein, B.S., Vye, N.J., Franks, J.J., Auble, P.M., Mezynski, K.J., and Perfetto, G.A. (1982). Differences in approaches to learning: An overview. *Journal of Experimental Psychology: General, III,* 390–398.

Bransford, L.A., Baca, L., and Lane, K. (1973). *Cultural diversity and the exceptional child.* Reston, Va.: Council for Exceptional Children.

Bretzing, B.B., and Kulhavy, R.W. (1979). Note taking and depth of processing. *Contemporary Educational Psychology, 4,* 145–153.

Bretzing, B.B., and Kulhavy, R.W. (1981). Note taking and passage style. *Journal of Educational Psychology, 73,* 242–250.

Brewer, W.F., and Nakamura, G.V. (1984). The nature and function of schemas. In R.S. Wyer and T.K. Srull (eds.), *Handbook of social cognition* (pp. 119–160). Hillsdale, N.J.: Erlbaum.

Brigham, T.A., Hopper, C., Hill, B., deArmas, A.D., and Newsom, P. (1985). A self-management program for disruptive adolescents in the school. *Behavior Theory, 16,* 99–115.

Broden, M., Bruce, C., Mitchell, M.A., Carter, V., and Hall, R.V. (1970b). Effects of teacher attention on attending behavior of two boys at adjacent desks.

Journal of Applied Behavior Analysis, 3, 199–203.

Broden, M., Hall, R.V., Dunlap, A., and Clark, R. (1970a). Effects of teacher attention and a token reinforcement system in a junior high school special education class. *Exceptional Children, 36,* 341–349.

Broden, M., Hall, R.V., and Mitts, B. (1971). The effects of self-recording on the classroom behavior of two eighth-grade students. *Journal of Applied Behavior Analysis, 4,* 191–199.

Bronfenbrenner, U. (1989). Ecological systems theory. In R. Vasta (ed.), *Annals of child development* (Vol. 6, pp. 187–251). Greenwich, Conn.: JAI Press.

Brookover, W., Beady, C., Flood, P., Schweister, J., and Wisenbaker, J. (1979). *School social systems and student achievement.* New York: Praeger.

Brooks, B.D. (1975). Contingency management as a means of reducing school truancy. *Education, 95,* 206–211.

Brooks, D.M. (1985). Beginning of the year in junior high: The first day of school. *Educational Leadership, 42,* 76–78.

Brooks, J.G. (1990). Teachers and students: Constructivists forging new connections. *Educational Leadership, 47(5),* 68–71.

Brophy, J. (1981). Teacher praise: A functional analysis. *Review of Educational Research, 51,* 5–32.

Brophy, J. (1987). Synthesis of research on strategies for motivating students to learn. *Educational Leadership, 45* October, 1987), 40–48.

Brophy, J. (1992). Probing the subtleties of subject-matter teaching. *Educational Leadership, 49(7),* 4–8.

Brophy, J.E. (1982, April). Fostering student learning and motivation in the elementary school classroom. Occasional Paper No. 51, East Lansing, Mich.: Institute for Research on Teaching.

Brophy, J.E. (1988). Research on teacher effects: Uses and abuses. *Elementary School Journal, 89,* 3–21.

Brophy, J.E., and Evertson, C.M. (1974). Process-product correlations in the Texas teacher effectiveness study: Final report (Research Reports No. 74-4). Austin: Research and Development Center for Teacher Education. University of Texas.

Brophy, J.E., and Evertson, C.M. (1976). *Learning from teaching: A developmental perspective.* Boston: Allyn & Bacon.

Brophy, J.E., and Evertson, C.M. (1981). *Student characteristics and teaching.* New York: Longman.

Brophy, J.E., and Good, T.L. (1974). *Teacher-student relationships: Causes and consequences.* New York: Holt, Rinehart & Winston.

Brophy, J.E., and Good, T.L. (1986). Teacher behavior and student achievement. In M.C. Wittrock (ed.), *Handbook of research on teaching* (3rd ed.). New

York: Macmillan.

Brown, A.L. (1978). Metacognitive development and reading. In R.J. Spiro, B.C. Bruce, and G.W.F. Brewer (eds.), *Theoretical issues in reading comprehension.* Hillsdale, N.J.: Erlbaum.

Brown, A.L. (1984, April). Learner characteristics and scientific texts. Paper presented at the annual meeting of the American Educational Research Association, New Orleans.

Brown, A.L., Bransford, J.D., Ferrara, R.A., and Campione, J.C. (1983). Learning, remembering, and understanding. In J. Flavell and E.M. Markman (eds.), *Handbook of child psychology,* 4th ed., Vol. 3, 515–629. New York: Wiley.

Brown, A.L., Campione, J.C., and Day, J.D. (1981). Learning to learn: On training students to learn from texts. *Educational Researcher, 10,* 14–21.

Brown, A.L., Smiley, S.S., Day, J.D., Townsend, M.A.R., and Lawson, S.C. (1977). Intrusion of a thematic idea in children's comprehension and retention of stories. *Child Development, 48* (1), 454–466.

Brown, D.S. (1988). Twelve middle-school teachers' planning. *Elementary School Journal, 89,* 69–88.

Brown, J.S., Collins, A., and Duguid, P. (1989). Situated cognition and the culture of learning. *Educational Research, 18,* 32–42.

Bruner, J.S. (1966). *Toward a theory of instruction.* New York: Norton.

Bryan, J.H. (1975). Children's cooperation and helping behaviors. In E.M. Hetherington (ed.), *Review of child development research,* Vol. 5, pp. 127–181. Chicago: The University of Chicago Press.

Bryant, D.M., Clifford, R.M., and Peisner, E.S. (1991). Best practices for beginners: Developmental appropriateness in kindergarten. *American Educational Research Journal, 28(4),* 783–803.

Burnette, J. (1987). *Adapting instructional materials for mainstreamed students.* Reston, Va.: Council for Exceptional Children.

Burns, M. (1986). Teaching "what to do" in arithmetic vs. teaching "what to do and why." *Educational Leadership, 43(7),* 34–38.

Burns, R.B. (1984). How time is used in elementary schools: The activity structure of classrooms. In L.W. Anderson (ed.), *Time and school learning: Theory, research, and practice.* London: Croom Helm.

Burton, F. (1983). *A study of the letter grade system and its effects on the curriculum.* ERIC No. 238143.

Burton, R.V. (1976). Honesty and dishonesty. In T. Lickona (ed.), *Moral development and behavior.* New York: Holt, Rinehart, & Winston.

Burtt, H.E. (1932). The retention of early

memories. *Journal of Genetic Psychology, 40,* 287–295; *50,* (1937), 187–192; *58,* (1941), 435–439. Articles abridged in W. Dennis (ed.), *Readings in child psychology.* Englewood Cliffs, N.J.: Prentice-Hall, 1963.

Butterfield, E.C. (1988). On solving the problem of transfer. In M.M. Grunesberg, P.E. Morris, and R.N. Sykes (eds.), *Practical aspects of memory* (Vol. 2, pp. 377–382). London, England: Academic Press.

Byrnes, J.P. (1988). Formal operations: A systematic reformulation. *Developmental Review, 8,* 66–87.

Cairns, J.P. (1987). Behavior problems. In M.J. Dunkin (ed.), *International encyclopedia of teaching and teacher education.* New York: Pergamon.

Caldwell, B. (1977). Aggression and hostility in young children. *Young Children, 32,* 4–13.

Calhoun, G., and Elliott, R. (1977). Self-concept and academic achievement of educable retarded and emotionally disturbed children. *Exceptional Children, 44,* 379–380.

California State Department of Education (1983). *Basic principles for the education of language-minority students: An overview.* Sacramento: California State Department of Education.

Calkins, L.M. (1983). *Lessons from a child: On the teaching and learning of writing.* Exeter, N.H.: Heinemann.

Camp, E., Islom, G., Herbert, F., and Van Doornick, W. (1977). "Think aloud": A program for developing self-control in young aggressive boys. *Journal of Abnormal Child Psychology, 5,* 157–169.

Campbell, V.N. (1964). Self-direction and programmed instruction for five different types of learning objectives. *Psychology in the Schools, 1,* 348–359.

Canfield, J. (1990). Improving students' self-esteem. *Educational Leadership, 48*(1), 48–50.

Cannell, J.J. (1987). *Nationally normed elementary achievement testing in America's public schools: How all fifty states are above the national average.* Daniels, W.Va.: Friends for Education.

Canter, L. (1989). Assertive discipline— More than names on the board and marbles in a jar. *Phi Delta Kappan, 71*(1), 41–56.

Canter, L., and Canter, M. (1976). *Assertive discipline.* Los Angeles: Lee Canter and Associates.

Cantrell, R., and Cantrell, M. (1976). Preventive mainstreaming: Impact of a supportive services program on pupils. *Exceptional Children, 46,* 381–386.

Caplan, P.J., MacPherson, G.M., and Tobin, P. (1985). Do sex-related differences in spatial abilities exist? A multilevel critique with new data. *American Psychologist, 40,* 786–799.

Carbo, M., Dunn, R., and Dunn, K. (1986). *Teaching students to read through their individual learning styles.* Englewood Cliffs, N.J.: Prentice-Hall.

Cardelle-Elawar, M. (1990). Effects of feedback tailored to bilingual students' mathematics needs on verbal problem solving. *Elementary School Journal, 91,* 165–175.

Carlsen, W. (1991). Questions in classrooms: A sociolinguistic perspective. *Review of Educational Research, 61*(2), 157–178.

Carnegie Council on Adolescent Development (1989). *Turning points: Preparing American youth for the 21st century.* New York: Carnegie Corporation.

Carpenter, T.P., Fennema, E., Peterson, P.L., Chiang, C.-P., and Loef, M. (1989). Using knowledge of children's mathematics thinking in classroom teaching: An experimental study. *American Educational Research Journal, 26,* 499–531.

Carroll, J.B. (1963). A model of school learning. *Teachers College Record, 64,* 723–733.

Carroll, J.B. (1987). The national assessments in reading: Are we misreading the findings? *Phi Delta Kappan, 68,* 424–430.

Carroll, J.B. (1989). The Carroll model: A 25-year retrospective and prospective view. *Educational Researcher, 18,* 26–31.

Carter, K., Cushing, K., Sabers, D., Stein, P., and Berliner, D. (1988). Expert-novice differences in perceiving and processing visual classroom information. *Journal of Teacher Education, 39*(3), 25–31.

Carter, L.F. (1984). The sustaining effects study of compensatory and elementary education. *Educational Researcher, 13*(7), 4–13.

Carter, T.P., and Segura, R.D. (1979). *Mexican Americans in school: A decade of change.* Princeton, N.J.: College Entrance Examination Board.

Case, R. (1984). The process of stage transition: A neo-Piagetian view. In R.J. Sternberg (ed.), *Mechanisms of cognitive development.* New York: W.H. Freeman.

Case, R. (1985). *Intellectual development: A systematic reinterpretation.* New York: Academic Press.

Casto, G., and Mastropieri, M.A. (1986). The efficacy of early intervention programs: A meta-analysis. *Exceptional Children, 52,* 417–424.

Cattell, R.B. (1957). *Culture-fair intelligence test.* Champaign, Ill.: Institute for Personality and Ability Testing.

Ceci, S.J. (1991). How much does schooling influence general intelligence and its cognitive components? A reassessment of the evidence. *Developmental Psychology, 27,* 703–722.

Chan, C.K.K., Burtis, P.J., Scardamalia, M., and Bereiter, C. (1992). Constructive activity in learning from text. *American Educational Research Journal, 29,* 97–118.

Chance, P. (1992). The rewards of learning. *Phi Delta Kappan, 74,* 200–207.

Chang, T.M. (1986). Semantic memory: Facts and models. *Psychological Bulletin, 99,* 199–220.

Chansky, N.M. (1975). A critical examination of school report cards from K through 12. *Reading Improvement, 12,* 184–192.

Chapman, J.W. (1988). Learning disabled children's self-concepts. *Review of Educational Research, 58,* 347–371.

Charles, C.M. (1989). *Building classroom discipline: From models to practice* (3rd ed.). New York: Longman.

Chi, M.T.H., and Ceci, S. (1987). Content knowledge: Its role, representation, and restructuring in memory development. In H.W. Reese (ed.), *Advances in child development and behavior* (vol. 20, pp. 91–142). Orlando, Fla.: Academic Press.

Chobot, R., and Garibaldi, A. (1982). In-school alternatives to suspension: A description of ten school district programs. *The Urban Review, 14,* 71–75.

Chomsky, C. (1969). *The acquisition of syntax in children from 5 to 10.* M.I.T. Press Research Monogram No. 57. Cambridge, Mass.: M.I.T. Press.

Christie, J.F. (1980). The cognitive significance of children's play: A review of selected research. *Journal of Education, 162,* 23–33.

Christoplos, F., and Renz, P. (1969). A critical examination of special education programs. *Journal of Special Education, 3,* 371–379.

Clarizio, H., and McCoy, G. (1976). *Behavior disorders in children* (2nd ed.). New York: Crowell.

Clark, C.M. (1987). The Carroll model. In M.J. Dunkin (ed.), *International encyclopedia of teaching and teacher education.* New York: Pergamon.

Clark, C.M., Gage, N.L., Marx, R. W., Peterson, P.L., Stayrook, N.G., and Winne, P.H. (1979). A factorial experiment on teacher structuring, soliciting, and reacting. *Journal of Educational Psychology, 71,* 534–552.

Clark, C.M., and Peterson, P.L. (1986). Teachers' thought processes. In M.C. Wittrock (ed.), *Handbook of research on teaching* (3rd ed.). New York: Macmillan.

Clark, C.M., and Yinger, R. (1986). Teacher planning. In D. Berliner and B. Rosenshine (eds.), *Talks to teachers* (pp. 342–365). New York: Random House.

Clark, J., (1990). *Patterns of thinking: Integrating learning skills with content teaching.* Boston: Allyn & Bacon.

Clark, J.M., and Paivio, A. (1991). Dual coding theory and education. *Educational Psychology Review, 3*(3), 149–210.

Clark, R.E. (1985). Evidence for confounding in computer-based instruction studies: Analyzing the meta-analyses. *Educational Communication and Technology Journal, 33*, 249–262.

Clarke, A.M., and Clarke, A.D.B. (eds.) (1976). *Early experience: Myth and evidence.* New York: The Free Press.

Clements, D.H. (1986). Effects of Logo and CAI environments on cognition and creativity. *Journal of Educational Psychology, 78*, 309–318.

Clements, D.H., and Gullo, D.F. (1984). Effects of computer programming on young children's cognition. *Journal of Educational Psychology, 76*, 1051–1058.

Clifford, M.M. (1984). Thoughts on a theory of constructive failure. *Educational Psychologist, 19*, 108–120.

Clifford, M.M. (1990). Students need challenge not easy success. *Educational Leadership, 48*(1), 22–26.

Cloward, R.A., and Ohlin, L.E. (1960). *Delinquency and opportunity.* New York: The Free Press.

Cloward, R.D. (1967). Studies in tutoring. *Journal of Experimental Education, 36*, 14–25.

Coats, W.D., and Smidchens, U. (1966). Audience recall as a function of speaker dynamism. *Journal of Educational Psychology, 57*, 189–191.

Cochran-Smith, M. (1991). Word processing and writing in elementary classrooms: A critical review of related literature. *Review of Educational Research, 61*(1), 107–155.

Cohen, E., Intill, J., and Robbins, S. (1978). Teachers and reading specialists: Cooperation or isolation? *Reading Teacher, 32*, 281–287.

Cohen, E.G. (1984). Talking and working together: Status, interaction, and learning. In P. Peterson, L.C. Wilkinson, and M. Hallinan (eds.), *The social context of instruction: Group organization and group processes.* New York: Academic Press.

Cohen, E.G. (1986). *Designing groupwork: Strategies for the heterogeneous classroom.* New York: Teachers College Press.

Cohen, E.G., and Anthony, B. (1982, March). Expectation states theory and classroom learning. Paper presented at the annual convention of the American Educational Research Association, New York.

Cohen, N.J., and Squire, L.R. (1980). Preserved learning and retention of pattern analyzing skill in amnesia: Dissociation of knowing how and knowing that. *Science, 210*, 207–209.

Cohen, R.L. (1989). Memory for action events: The power of enactment. *Educational Psychology Review, 1*(1), 57–80.

Cohen, S., and Debettencourt, L. (1983). Teaching children to be independent learners: A step-by-step strategy. *Focus on Exceptional Children, 16*(3), 1–12.

Cohen, S.A. (1987). Instructional alignment: Searching for a magic bullet. *Educational Researcher, 16*, 16–20.

Colby, C., and Kohlberg, L. (1984). Invariant sequence and internal consistency in moral judgment stages. In W. Kurtines and J. Gewirts (eds.), *Morality, moral behavior, and moral development.* New York: Wiley-Interscience.

Cole, D.A., and Meyer, L.H. (1991). Social integration and severe disabilities: A longitudinal analysis of child outcomes. *Journal of Special Education, 25*, 340–351.

Cole, N.S. (1981). Bias in testing. *American Psychologist, 36*, 1067–1077.

Coleman, J. (1961). *The adolescent society.* New York: Free Press.

Coleman, J.S., Campbell, E.Q., Hobson, C.L., McPartland, J.M., Mood, A.M., Weinfeld, F.D., and York, R.L. (1966). *Equality of educational opportunity.* Washington, D.C.: U.S. Department of Health, Education and Welfare.

Coleman, J.S., and Harris, T.R. (1969). *Economic system* (Simulation Game). Indianapolis: Bobbs-Merrill.

Coleman, M.C. (1986). *Behavior disorder: Theory and practice.* Englewood Cliffs, N.J.: Prentice-Hall.

College Entrance Examination Board (1985). *Equality and excellence: The educational status of Black Americans.* New York: CEEB.

Collins, A.M., and Loftus, E.I. (1975). A spreading-activation theory of semantic processing. *Psychological Review, 82*, 407–428.

Colson, S. (1980). The evaluation of a community-based career education program for gifted and talented students. *Gifted Child Quarterly, 24*, 101–106.

Combs, A.W. (ed.) (1967). *Humanizing education: The person in the process.* Washington, D.C.: Association for Supervision and Curriculum Development, National Education Association.

Commons, M.L., Richards, F.A., and Kuhn, D. (1982). Systematic and metasystematic reasoning: A case for levels of reasoning beyond Piaget's stage of formal operations. *Child Development, 53*, 1058–1069.

Conger, J.J., and Petersen, A.C. (1984). *Adolescence and youth: Psychological development in a changing world.* New York: Harper & Row.

Cooley, W.W. (1981). Effectiveness in compensatory education. *Educational leadership, 38*, 298–301.

Cooley, W.W., and Leinhardt, G. (1980). The instructional dimensions study. *Educational Evaluation and Policy Analysis, 2*, 7–26.

Cooper, H. (1989). Synthesis of research on homework. *Educational Leadership, 47*(3), 85–91.

Cooper, H.M., and Good, T.L. (1983). *Pygmalion grows up: Studies in the expectation communication process.* New York: Longman.

Cooper, H.M., and Tom, D.Y.H. (1984). Teacher expectation research: A review with implications for classroom instruction. *Elementary School Journal, 85*, 77–89.

Copeland, W.D. (1983, April). Classroom management and student teachers' cognitive abilities: A relationship. Paper presented at the annual convention of the American Educational Research Association, Montreal.

Corkill, A.J. (1992). Advance organizers: Facilitators of recall. *Educational Psychology Review, 4*, 33–67.

Corno, L., and Rohrkemper, M. (1985). The intrinsic motivation to learn in classrooms. In C. Ames and R. Ames (eds.), *Research on motivation to learn in classrooms, Vol II: The classroom milieu.* Orlando, Fla.: Academic Press.

Corno, L., and Snow, R.E. (1986). Adapting teaching to individual differences among learners. In M.C. Wittrock (ed.), *Handbook of research on teaching* (3rd ed.). New York: Macmillan.

Costanzo, P.R., and Shaw, M.E. (1966). Conformity as a function of age level. *Child Development, 37*, 967–975.

Covington, M.V. (1984). The self-worth theory of achievement motivation: Findings and implications. *Elementary School Journal, 85*, 5–20.

Craig, G.J. (1989). *Human development* (5th ed.). Englewood Cliffs, N.J.: Prentice-Hall.

Craik, F.I.M. (1979). Human memory. *Annual Review of Psychology, 30*, 63–102.

Craik, F.I.M., and Lockhart, R.S. (1972). Levels of processing: A framework for memory research. *Journal of Verbal Thinking and Verbal Behavior, 11*, 671–684.

Crain, R., and Mahard, R. (1983). The effect of research methodology on desegregation-achievement studies: A meta-analysis. *American Journal of Sociology, 88*, 839–855.

Crain, R.L., Mahard, R.E., and Narot, R.E. (1982). *Making desegregation work: How schools create social climate.* Cambridge, Mass.: Ballinger.

Crain, W.C. (1985). *Theories of development: Concepts and applications.* Englewood Cliffs, N.J.: Prentice Hall.

Cratty, B.J. (1970). *Perceptual and motor development in infants and children.* New York: Macmillan.

Cratty, B.J. (1982). Motor development in early childhood: Critical issues for researchers in the 1980's. In B. Spodek (ed.), *Handbook of research in early childhood education*, pp. 27–46. New York: The Free Press.

Crawford, J. (1983). *A study of instructional processes in Title I classes: Executive summary*. Oklahoma City: Oklahoma City Public Schools.

Crawford, J. (1989). Instructional activities related to achievement gain in Chapter 1 classes. In R.E. Slavin, N.L. Karweit, and N.A. Madden (eds.), *Effective programs for students at risk*. Boston: Allyn & Bacon.

Crawford, R.P. (1954). *Techniques of creative thinking*. Englewood Cliffs, N.J.: Hawthorne.

Crocker, R.K., and Brooker, G.M. (1986). Classroom control and student outcomes in grades 2 and 5. *American Educational Research, 23*, 1–11.

Cronbach, L.J. (1990). *Essentials of psychological testing* (5th ed.). New York: Harper & Row.

Crooks, T.J. (1988). The impact of classroom evaluation practices on students. *Review of Educational Research, 58*, 438–481.

Cross, L.H., and Cross, G.M. (1980–1981). Teachers' evaluative comments and pupil perception of control. *Journal of Experimental Education, 49*, 68–71.

Csikszentmihalyi, M., and Larson, R. (1984). *Being adolescent*. New York: Basic Books.

CTB/McGraw-Hill (1982). *Examination materials: An illustrated overview of the comprehensive tests of basic skills*. Monterey, Calif.: CTB/McGraw-Hill.

Cummins, J. (1984). *Bilingualism and special education*. San Diego, Calif.: College Hill.

Cummins, J. (1986). Empowering minority students: A framework for intervention. *Harvard Educational Review, 96*, 18–36.

Cureton, L.E. (1971). The history of grading practice. *Measurement in Education, 2*, 1–8.

Damon, W. (1983). *Social and personality development: Infancy through adolescence*. New York: Norton.

Damon, W. (1984). Peer education: The untapped potential. *Journal of Applied Developmental Psychology, 5*, 331–343.

Damon, W., and Hart, D. (1982). The development of self-understanding from infancy through adolescence. *Child Development, 53*, 841–864.

Dansereau, D.F. (1985). Learning strategy research. In J. Segal, S. Chipman, and R. Glaser (eds.), *Thinking and learning skills: Relating instruction to basic research*, Vol. 1. Hillsdale, N.J.: Erlbaum.

Dansereau, D.F., McDonald, B.A., Collins, K.W., Garland, J.C., Holley, C.T., Liekhoff, G.M., and Evans, S.H. (1979). Evaluation of a learning strategy system. In H.F. O'Neill, Jr., and C.D. Spielberger (eds.), *Cognitive and affective learning strategies*. New York: Academic Press.

Das Gupta, P., and Bryant, P.E. (1989). Young children's causal inferences. *Child Development, 60*, 1138–1146.

Davis, G.A. (1983). *Educational psychology: Theory and practice*. Reading, Mass.: Addison-Wesley.

Davis, H. (1970). Abnormal hearing and deafness. In H. Davis and R. Silverman (eds.), *Hearing and deafness*. New York: Holt, Rinehart, & Winston.

Deaux, K. (1984). From individual differences to social categories: Analysis of a decade's research on gender. *American Psychologist, 39*, 105–116.

DeCharms, R. (1976). *Enhancing motivation*. New York: Irvington Press/Wiley.

DeCharms, R. (1980). The origins of competence and achievement motivation in personal causation. In L.J. Fyons, Jr. (ed.), *Achievement motivation*. New York: Plenum.

DeCharms, R. (1984). Motivation enhancement in educational settings. In R. Ames and C. Ames (eds.), *Research on motivation in education, Vol. 1: Student motivation*. New York: Academic Press.

Deci, E., and Ryan, R. (1985). *Intrinsic motivation and self-determination in human behavior*. New York: Plenum.

Deci, E., and Ryan, R. (1987). The support of autonomy and the control of behavior. *Journal of Personality and Social Psychology, 53*, 1024–1037.

Deci, E.L. (1975). *Intrinsic motivation*. New York: Plenum.

Delandsheere, V. (1977). On defining educational objectives. *Evaluation in Education, 1*, 73–150.

Delclos, V.R., and Harrington, C. (1991). Effects of strategy monitoring and proactive instruction on children's problem-solving performance. *Journal of Educational Psychology, 83*, 35–42.

Delin, P.S. (1969). The learning to criterion of a serial list with and without mnemonic instructions. *Psychomatic Science, 16*, 169–170.

De Lisi, R., and Straudt, J. (1980). Individual differences in college students' performance on formal operations tasks. *Journal of Applied Developmental Psychology, 1*, 201–208.

Delprato, D.J., and Midgley, B.D. (1992). Some fundamentals of B.F. Skinner's behaviorism. *American Psychologist, 47*, 1507–1520.

Dempster, F.N. (1987). Time and the production of classroom learning: Discerning implications from basic research. *Educational Psychologist, 22*, 1–21.

Dempster, F.N. (1989). Spacing effects and their implications for theory and practice. *Educational Psychology Review, 1*, 309–330.

Dempster, F.N. (1991). Synthesis of research on reviews and tests. *Educational Leadership, 72*(8), 71–76.

Demyer, M.K. (1975). The nature of neuropsychological disability in autistic children. *Journal of Autism and Childhood Schizophrenia, 5*, 109–128.

Deno, S.L. (1985). Curriculum-based measurement: The emerging alternative. *Exceptional Children, 52*, 219–232.

Derry, S.J., and Murphy, D.A. (1986). Designing systems that train learning ability: From theory to practice. *Review of Educational Research, 56*, 1–39.

Deshler, D.D., and Schumaker, J.B. (1986). Learning strategies: An instructional alternative for low-achieving adolescents. *Exceptional Children, 52*, 583–590.

Deutsch, M. (1949). A theory of cooperation and competition. *Human Relations, 2*, 129–152.

Devin-Sheehan, L., Feldman, R.S., and Allen, V.L. (1976). Research on children tutoring children: A critical review. *Review of Educational Research, 46*, 355–385.

Devries, D.L., and Edwards, K.J. (1974). Student teams and learning games: Their effects on cross-race and cross-sex interaction. *Journal of Educational Psychology, 66*, 741–749.

Devries, D.L, and Slavin, R.E. (1978). Teams-Games-Tournament (TGT): Review of ten classroom experiments. *Journal of Research and Development in Education, 12*, 28–38.

Dick, W., and Reiser, R.A. (1989). *Planning effective instruction*. Englewood Cliffs, N.J.: Prentice-Hall.

Dickerson, D., Spellman, C.R., Larsen, S., and Tyler, L. (1973). Let the cards do the talking: A teacher-parent communication program: Daily report card system. *Teaching Exceptional Children, 5*, 170–178.

Diener, C.I., and Dweck, C.S. (1978). An analysis of learned helplessness: Continuous changes in performance, strategy, and achievement cognitions following failure. *Journal of Personality and Social Psychology, 36*, 451–462.

Dimino, J., Gersten, R., Carnine, D., and Blake, G. (1990). Story grammar: An approach for promoting at-risk secondary students' comprehension of literature. *Elementary School Journal, 91*, 19–32.

Dolan, L.J., Kellam, S.G., Brown, C.H., Werthamer-Larsson, L., Rebok, G.W., Mayer, L.S., Laudolff, J., Turkkan, J.S., Ford, C., and Wheeler, L. (in press). The short-term impact of two classroom-based preventive interventions on aggressive and shy behaviors and poor achievement. *Journal of Applied Developmental Psychology*.

Donaldson, M. (1978). *Children's minds*. New York: Norton.

Donovan, J.F., Sousa, D.A., and Walberg, H.J. (1987). The impact of staff development on implementation and student achievement. *Journal of Educational Research, 80*, 348–351.

Dooling, D.J., and Lachman, R. (1971). Effects of comprehension on retention of prose. *Journal of Experimental Psychology, 8,* 216–222.

Dornbusch, S.M., Carlsmith, J.M., Bushwall, S.J., Ritter, P.L., Leiderman, H., Hastorf, A.H., and Gross, R.T. (1985). Single parents, extended households, and the control of adolescents. *Child Development, 56,* 326–341.

Dorr-Bremme, D.W., and Herman, J. (1986). *Assessing school achievement: A profile of classroom practices.* Los Angeles: Center for the Study of Evaluation, UCLA.

Dougherty, E., and Dougherty, A. (1977). The daily report card: A simplified and flexible package for classroom behavior management. *Psychology in the Schools, 14,* 191–195.

Downing, J., Coughlin, R.M., and Rich, G. (1986). Children's invented spellings in the classroom. *Elementary School Journal, 86,* 295–303.

Doyle, W. (1983). Academic work. *Review of Educational Research, 53,* 159–199.

Doyle, W. (1984). How order is achieved in classrooms: An interim report. *Journal of Curriculum Studies, 16,* 259–277.

Doyle, W. (1986). Classroom organization and management. In M.C. Wittrock (ed.), *Handbook of research on teaching* (3rd ed.), pp. 392–431. New York: Macmillan.

Doyle, W., and Carter, K. (1984). Academic tasks in classrooms. *Curriculum Inquiry, 14,* 129–149.

Drabman, R., Spitalnik, R., and O'Leary, K. (1973). Teaching self-control to disruptive children. *Journal of Abnormal Psychology, 82,* 10–16.

Dreher, M.J., and Slater, W.H. (eds.) (1992). *Elementary school literacy: Critical issues.* Norwood, Mass.: Christopher-Gordon.

duBoulay, J.B.H., and Howe, J.A.M. (1984). Logo building blocks: Student teachers using computer-based mathematics apparatus. *Computers and Education, 6,* 93–98.

Duchastel, P. (1979). Learning objectives and the organization of prose. *Journal of Educational Psychology, 71,* 100–106.

Duell, O.K. (1978). Overt and covert use of objectives of different cognitive levels. *Contemporary Educational Psychology, 3,* 239–245.

Duffy, G.G., and Roehler, L.R. (1986). The subtleties of instructional mediation. *Educational Leadership, 43*(7), 23–27.

Dukes, R., and Seidner, C. (1978). *Learning with simulations and games.* Beverly Hills, Calif.: Sage.

Duncker, K. (1945). On problem solving. *Psychological Monographs, 58* (Whole No. 270).

Dunkin, M. (1978). Student characteristics, classroom processes, and student achieve-ment. *Journal of Educational Psychology, 70,* 998–1009.

Dunkin, M.J., and Biddle, B.J. (1974). *A study of teaching.* New York: Holt, Rinehart, and Winston.

Dunkin, M.J., and Doenau, S.J. (1987). Students' ethnicity. In M.J. Dunkin (ed.), *International encyclopedia of teaching and teacher education.* New York: Pergamon.

Dunn, K., and Dunn, R. (1987). Dispelling outmoded beliefs about student learning. *Educational Leadership, 44*(6), 55–62.

Dunn, L.M. (1968). Special education for the mentally retarded—Is it justified? *Exceptional Children, 35,* 5–22.

Dunn, R., Beaudrey, J.S., and Klavas, A. (1989). Survey of research on learning styles. *Educational Leadership, 46*(6), 50–58.

Duran, R.P. (1983). *Hispanics' education and background.* New York: College Entrance Examination Board.

Durso, F.T., and Coggins, K.A. (1991). Organized instruction for the improve-ment of word knowledge skills. *Journal of Educational Psychology, 83,* 108–112.

Dweck, C. (1975). The role of expectations and attributions in the alleviation of learned helplessness. *Journal of Personality and Social Psychology, 31,* 674–685.

Dweck, C.S. (1986). Motivational processes affecting learning. *American Psychologist, 41,* 1040–1048.

Dweck, C.S., and Elliot, E.S. (1983). Achievement motivation. In E.M. Hetherington (ed.), *Socialization, person-ality, and social development.* New York: Wiley.

Dyer, H.S. (1967). The discovery and devel-opment of educational goals. *Proceedings of the 1966 Invitational Conference on Testing Problems.* Princeton, N.J.: Educational Testing Service.

Dyson, A.H. (1984). Teachers and young children: Missed connections in teaching/learning to write. *Language Arts, 59,* 674–680.

Ebel, R.L. (1972). *Essentials of educational measurement* (3rd ed.). Englewood Cliffs, N.J.: Prentice-Hall.

Ebel, R.L. (1980a). Achievement tests as measures of developed abilities. In W.B. Schrader (ed.), *New directions for testing and measurement,* Vol. 5. San Francisco: Jossey-Bass.

Ebel, R.L. (1980b). Evaluation of students: Implications for effective teaching. *Educational Evaluation and Policy Analysis, 2,* 47–51.

Edgerton, R.B. (1984). Mental retardation: An anthropologist's changing view. In B. Blatt and R. Morris (eds.), *Perspectives in special education,* Vol. 1. Glenview, Ill.: Scott, Foresman.

Edlund, C. (1969). Rewards at home to pro-mote desirable school behavior. *Teaching Exceptional Children, 1,* 121–127.

Edwards, P.E., Logue, M.E., and Russell, A.S. (1983). Talking with young children about social ideas. *Young Children, 39,* 12–20.

Edwards, W. (1954). The theory of decision making. *Psychology Bulletin, 51,* 380–417.

Egan, K. (1989). Memory, imagination, and learning: Connected by the story. *Phi Delta Kappan, 70,* 455–459.

Ehly, S.W., and Larsen, S.C. (1980). *Peer tutoring for individualized instruction.* Boston: Allyn & Bacon.

Ehri, L. (1991). Development of the ability to read words. In R. Barr, M. Kamil, P. Mosenthal, and P.D. Pearson (eds.), *Handbook of Reading Research* (Vol. II, pp. 383–417). New York: Longman.

Ehrlick, D., Gutiman, J., Schonback, P., and Mills, J. (1957). Postdecision exposure to relevant information. *Journal of Abnormal Social Psychology, 54,* 98–102.

Eiben, R.M., and Crocker, A.C. (1983). Cerebral palsy within the spectrum of developmental disabilities. In G.H. Thompson, I.L. Rubin, and R.M. Bilenker (eds.), *Comprehensive manage-ment of cerebral palsy.* New York: Grune & Stratton.

Eichorn, D. (1966). *The middle school.* New York: Center for Applied Research in Education.

Eisner, E.W. (1969). Instructional and expressive educational objectives: Their formulation and use in curriculum. In W.J. Popham, E.W. Eisner, H.J. Sullivan, and L.L. Tyler (eds.), *Instructional objec-tives.* AERA. Monograph Series on Curriculum Evaluation, No. 3. Chicago: Rand McNally, pp. 1–31.

Eisner, E.W. (1982). The contribution of painting to children's cognitive develop-ment. *Journal of Education, 164,* 227–237.

Elashoff, J.D., and Snow, R.E. (1971). *Pygmalion reconsidered.* Worthington, Ohio: Charles A. Jones.

Elawar, M.C., and Corno, L. (1985). A fac-torial experiment in teachers' written feedback on student homework: Changing teacher behavior a little rather than a lot. *Journal of Educational Psychology, 77,* 162–173.

Elbers, S. (1991). The development of com-petence and its social context. *Educational Psychology Review, 3*(2), 73–94.

Elkind, D. (1981). *The hurried child: Growing up too fast, too soon.* Reading, Mass.: Addison-Wesley.

Elkind, D. (1984). *All grown up and no place to go.* Boston: Addison-Wesley.

Elkind, D. (1986a). Helping parents make healthy educational choices for their chil-dren. *Educational Leadership, 44*(3), 36–38.

Elkind, D. (1986b, May). Formal education and preschool education: An essential difference. *Phi Delta Kappan,* 631–636.

Elkind, D. (1989). Developmentally appropriate practice: Philosophical and practical implications. *Phi Delta Kappan, 71*(2), 113–117.

Ellson, D.G. (1976). Tutoring. In N.L. Gage (ed.), *The psychology of teaching methods* (pp. 130–165). Chicago: University of Chicago Press.

Ellson, D.G., Harris, P., and Barber, L. (1968). A field test of programmed and directed tutoring. *Reading Research Quarterly, 3,* 307–367.

Ellwein, M.C., Walsh, D. J., Eads II, G.M., and Miller, A. (1991). Using readiness tests to route kindergarten students: The snarled intersection of psychometrics, policy, and practice. *Educational Evaluation and Policy Analysis, 13*(2), 159–175.

Emmer, E. (1987). Classroom management and discipline. In V. Richardson-Koehler (ed.), *Educator's handbook: A research perspective* (pp. 233–258). White Plains, N.Y.: Longman.

Emmer, E., Everton, C., and Anderson, L. (1980). Effective classroom management at the beginning of the school year. *Elementary School Journal, 80,* 219–231.

Emmer, E.T., and Aussiker, A. (1990). School and classroom discipline programs: How well do they work? In O.C. Moles (ed.), *Student discipline strategies.* Albany: State University of New York Press.

Emmer, E.T., Everton, C.M., Sanford, J.P., Clements, B.S., and Worsham, M.E. (1984). *Classroom management for secondary teachers.* Englewood Cliffs, N.J.: Prentice-Hall.

Emmer, E.T., Sanford, J., Clements, B., and Martin, J. (1982). *Improving classroom management and organization in junior high schools: An experimental investigation.* Austin: University of Texas, Research and Development Center for Teacher Education.

Engle, R.W., Nations, J.K., and Cantor, J. (1990). Is "working memory capacity" just another name for word knowledge? *Journal of Educational Psychology, 82*(4), 799–804.

Englert, C.S., Raphael, T.E., Anderson, L.M., Anthony, H.M., and Stevens, D.D. (1991). Making strategies and self-talk visible: Writing instruction in regular and special education classrooms. *American Educational Research Journal, 28,* 337–372.

Ennis, R. (1989). Critical thinking and subject specificity. *Educational Researcher 18*(3), 4–10.

Ensminger, M.E., and Slusarcick, A.L. (1992). Paths to high school graduation or dropout: A longitudinal study of a first grade cohort. *Sociology of Education, 65,* 95–113.

Entwistle, D., and Hayduk, L. (1981). Academic expectations and the school achievement of young children. *Sociology of Education, 54,* 34–50.

Entwistle, N. (1981). *Styles of learning and teaching.* New York: Wiley.

EPIE Institute (1990). *The integrated instructional systems report.* Water Mill, N.Y.: Author.

Epstein, C. (1980). Brain growth and cognitive functioning. In *The emerging adolescent: Characteristics and implications.* Columbus, Ohio: NMSA.

Epstein, H.T. (1990). Stages in human mental growth. *Journal of Educational Psychology, 82*(4), 876–880.

Epstein, J.L. (1985). After the bus arrives: Resegregation in desegregated schools. *Journal of Social Issues, 41,* 23–43.

Epstein, J.L. (1988). *Homework practices, achievements, and behaviors of elementary school students* (Tech. Rep. No. 26). Baltimore, Md.: Johns Hopkins University, Center for Research on Elementary and Middle Schools.

Epstein, J.L. (1992). School and family partnerships. In M. Alkin (ed.), *Encyclopedia of Educational Research* (pp. 1139–1151). New York: Macmillan.

Epstein, J.L., and Dauber, S.L. (1989). *Effects of the Teachers Involve Parents in Schoolwork (TIPS) social studies and art program on student attitudes and knowledge.* Baltimore, MD: Johns Hopkins University, Center for Research on Elementary and Middle Schools.

Epstein, J.L., and Dauber, S.L. (1991). School programs and teacher practices of parent involvement in inner-city elementary and middle schools. *Elementary School Journal, 91,* 289–303.

Epstein, J.L., and McPartland, J.M. (1975). *The effects of open school organization on student outcomes.* Baltimore, Md.: Center for Social Organization of Schools, Johns Hopkins University.

Epstein, M.H., and Cullinan, D. (1992). Emotional/behavioral problems. In M.C. Alkin (ed.), *Encyclopedia of educational research* (6th ed.) (pp. 430–432). New York: Macmillan.

Erikson, E.H. (1963). *Childhood and society* (2nd ed.). New York: Norton.

Erikson, E.H. (1968). *Identity, youth and crisis.* New York: Norton.

Erikson, E.H. (1980). *Identity and the life cycle* (2nd ed.). New York: Norton.

Estes, N.K. (1982). Learning, memory, and intelligence. In R.J. Sternberg (ed.), *Handbook of human intelligence.* New York: Cambridge University Press.

Ethington, C.A. (1991). Testing a model of achievement behaviors. *American Educational Research Journal, 28,* 155–172.

Evertson, C.M. (1982). Differences in instructional activities in higher- and lower-achieving junior high English and match classes. *Elementary School Journal, 82,* 329–350.

Evertson, C.M. (1989). Improving classroom management: A school-based program for beginning the year. *Journal of Educational Research, 83,* 82–90.

Evertson, C.M., and Emmer, E.T. (1982). Effective management at the beginning of the year in junior high classes. *Journal of Educational Psychology, 74,* 485–498.

Evertson, C.M., Emmer, E.T., and Brophy, J.E. (1980). Predictors of effective teaching in junior high mathematics classrooms. *Journal for Research in Mathematics Education, 11,* 167–178.

Evertson, C.M., Emmer, E.T., Clements, B.S., Sanford, J.P., and Worsham, M.E. (1984). *Classroom management for elementary teachers.* Englewood Cliffs, N.J.: Prentice-Hall.

Evertson, C.M., Emmer, E.T., Sanford, J., and Clements, B. (1983). Improving classroom management: An experiment in elementary school classrooms. *Elementary School Journal, 84,* 173–188.

Evertson, C.M., and Harris, A.H. (1992). What we know about managing classrooms. *Educational Leadership, 49*(7), 74–78.

Evertson, C.M., Weade, R., Green, J., and Crawford, J. (1985). *Effective classroom management and instruction: An exploration of models.* Nashville, Tenn.: Vanderbilt University.

Fagan, E.R., Hassler, D.M., and Szabo, M. (1981). Evaluation of questioning strategies in language arts instruction. *Research in the Teaching of English, 15,* 267–273.

Fantuzzo, J.W., Polite, K., and Grayson, N. (1990). An evaluation of reciprocal peer tutoring across elementary school settings. *Journal of School Psychology, 28,* 309–323.

Feather, N. (ed.) (1982). *Expectations and actions.* Hillsdale, N.J.: Erlbaum.

Federal Register (1977, August). Washington, D.C.: U.S. Government Printing Office.

Fein, G.G. (1979). Play and acquisition of symbols. In L.G. Katz (ed.), *Current topics in early childhood education,* Vol. 2, pp. 195–226. Norwood, N.J.: Ablex Publishing Corp.

Fein, G.G. (1981). The physical environment: Stimulation or evocation. In R.M. Lerner and N.A. Busch-Rossnagel (eds.), *Individuals as producers of their development: A lifespan perspective,* pp. 257–279. New York: Academic Press.

Feingold, A. (1992). Sex differences in variability in intellectual abilities: A new look at an old controversy. *Review of Educational Research, 62*(1), 61–84.

Feldhusen, J.F. (1989). Synthesis of research on gifted youth. *Educational Leadership, 46*(6), 6–12.

Feldhusen, J.F., and Sokol, L. (1982). Extra-school programming to meet the needs of gifted youth: Super Saturday. *Gifted Child Quarterly, 21,* 450–476.

Fennema, E., and Sherman, J. (1977). Sex-related differences in mathematics achievement, spatial visualization, and affective factors. *American Educational Research Journal, 14,* 51–71.

Festinger, L.A. (1957). *A theory of cognitive dissonance.* Evanston, Ill.: Ron, Peterson.

Feuerstein, R., (1980). *Instrumental enrichment: An intervention program for cognitive modifiability.* Baltimore: University Park Press.

Feuerstein, R. and Jensen, M.R. (1980, May). Instrumental enrichment: Theoretical basis, goals, and instruments. *Educational Forum,* 401–423.

Feuerstein, R., Miller, R., Hoffman, M.B., Rand, Y., Mintzker, Y., and Jensen, M.R. (1981). Cognitive modifiability in adolescence: Cognitive structure and the effects of intervention. *Journal of Special Education, 15,* 269–287.

Fielding, L.G., Anderson, R.C., and Pearson, P.D. (1990). *How discussion questions influence children's story understanding* (Tech. Rep. No. 490). Champaign, Ill.: University of Illinois, Center for the Study of Reading.

Finn, J.D., and Cox, D. (1992). Participation and withdrawal among fourth-grade pupils. *American Educational Research Journal, 29*(1), 141–162.

Fiordaliso, R., Lordeman, A., Filipczak, J., and Friedman, R.M. (1977). Effects of feedback on absenteeism in the junior high school. *Journal of Educational Research, 70,* 188–192.

Fishburne, P., Abelson, H., and Cisin, I. (1980). *The national survey on drug abuse: Main findings, 1979.* Washington, D.C.: U.S. Government Printing Office.

Fisher, C.W., Berliner, D.C., Filby, N.N., Marliave, R., Cahen, L.S., Dishaw, M.M., and Moore, J.E. (1978). *Teaching behaviors, academic learning time, and student achievement: Final report of Phase III-B, beginning teacher evaluation study.* (Tech. Report V-1.) San Francisco: Far West Laboratory for Educational Research and Development.

Fiske, E.B. (1989, July 12). The misleading concept of "average" on reading tests changes, and more students fall below it. *New York Times.*

Fitzpatrick, A.R. (1989). Social influences in standard setting: The effects of social interaction on group judgments. *Review of Educational Research, 59*(3), 315–328.

Flavell, J.H. (1985). *Cognitive development* (2nd ed.). Englewood Cliffs, N.J.: Prentice-Hall.

Flavell, J.H. (1986, January). Really and truly. *Psychology Today,* 38–44.

Fletcher, J.D. (1992). Individualized systems of instruction. In M.C. Alkin (ed.), *Encyclopedia of educational research* (6th ed.) (pp. 612–620). New York: Macmillan.

Floden, R.E., and Klinzing, H.G. (1990). What can research on teacher thinking contribute to teacher preparation? A second opinion. *Educational Research, 19*(4), 15–20.

Florida State Department of Education (1990). *Multicultural teaching strategies* (Tech. Rep. No. 9). Tallahassee: Author.

Foos, P.W., and Fisher, R.P. (1988). Using tests as learning opportunities. *Journal of Educational Psychology, 80,* 179–183.

Forehand, G., and Ragosta, M. (1976). *A handbook for integrated schooling.* Washington, D.C.: U.S. Department of Education.

Forman, E., and McPhail, J. (1989). *What have we learned about the cognitive benefits of peer interaction? A Vygotskian critique.* Paper presented at the annual meeting of the American Educational Research Association, San Francisco.

Forman, G.E., and Fosnot, C.T. (1982). The use of Piaget's constructivism in early childhood programs. In B. Spodek (ed.), *Handbook of research in early childhood education,* pp. 185–211. New York: The Free Press.

Forsterling, F. (1985). Attribution retraining: A review. *Psychological Bulletin, 98,* 495–512.

Forsyth, D.R. (1986). An attributional analysis of students' reactions to success and failure. In R.S. Feldman (ed.), *The social psychology of education.* Cambridge, England: Cambridge University Press.

Fox, L.H. (1979). Programs for the gifted and talented: An overview. In A.H. Passow (ed.), *The gifted and talented: Their education and development.* Chicago: University of Chicago Press.

Frankenburg, W.K., and Dodds, J.B. (1970). *Denver Developmental Screening Test.* Denver: University of Colorado Medical Center.

Frederick, W., and Walberg, H. (1980). Learning as a function of time. *Journal of Educational Research, 73,* 183–194.

Frederiksen, N. (1984a). Implications of cognitive theory for instruction in problem solving. *Review of Educational Research, 54,* 363–407.

Frederiksen, N. (1984b). The real test bias: Influences of testing on teaching and learning. *American Psychologist, 39,* 193–202.

French, E.G. (1956). Motivation as a variable in work partner selection. *Journal of Abnormal and Social Psychology, 55,* 96–99.

French, E.G., and Thomas, F. (1958). The relation of achievement motivation to problem-solving effectiveness. *Journal of Abnormal and Social Psychology, 56,* 45–48.

Friedman, L. (1989). Mathematics and the gender gap: A meta-analysis of recent studies on sex differences in mathematical tasks. *Review of Educational Research, 59*(2), 185–213.

Frieze, I., and Weiner, B. (1971). Cue utilization and attributional judgments for success and failure. *Journal of Personality, 39,* 91–109.

Fuchs, D., and Fuchs, L.S. (1989). Exploring effective and efficient preferral interventions: A component analysis of behavioral consultation. *School Psychology Review, 18,* 258–281.

Fuchs, D., Fuchs, L.S., Bahr, M.W., Fernstrom, P., and Stecker, P.M. (1990). Mainstream assistance teams: A scientific basis for the art of consultation. *Exceptional Children, 56,* 493–513.

Fuchs, L.S., Fuchs, D., Hamlett, C.L., and Stecker, P.M. (1991). Effects of curriculum-based measurement and consultation on teacher planning and student achievement in mathematics operations. *American Educational Research Journal, 28*(3), 617–641.

Fudor, E.M. (1971). Resistance to social influence among adolescents as a function of level of moral development. *Journal of Social Psychology, 85,* 121–126.

Furey, P. (1986). A framework for cross cultural analysis of teaching methods. In P. Byrd (ed.), *Teaching across cultures in the university ESL program.* Washington, D.C.: National Association for Foreign Student Affairs.

Furman, W., and Bierman, K.L. (1984). Children's concepts of friendship: A multi-method study of developmental changes. *Developmental Psychology, 21,* 1016–1024.

Furst, E.J. (1981). Bloom's taxonomy of educational objectives for the cognitive domain: Philosophical and educational issues. *Review of Educational Research, 51,* 441–453.

Fyans, L.J., Jr., and Maehr, M.L. (1980). Attributional style, task selection and achievement. In L.J. Fyans, Jr. (ed.), *Achievement motivation.* New York: Plenum.

Gadow, K. (1981). Effects of stimulant drugs on attention and cognitive deficits. *Exceptional Educational Quarterly, 2,* 83–93.

Gage, N.L. (1978). *The scientific basis of the art of teaching.* New York: Teachers College Press.

Gage, N.L., and Berliner, D.C. (1984). *Educational psychology* (3rd ed.). Boston: Houghton Mifflin.

Gage, N.L., and Needels, M.C. (1989). Process-product research on teaching: A review of criticism. *Elementary School Journal, 89,* 253–300.

Gagné, R. (1977). *The conditions of learning* (3rd ed.). New York: Holt, Rinehart, &

Winston.

Gagné, R., and Briggs, L. (1979). *Principles of instructional design* (2nd ed.). New York: Holt, Rinehart & Winston.

Gagné, R.M. (1974). *Essentials of learning for instruction.* Hinsdale, Ill.: Dryden.

Gagné, R.M. (1984). Learning outcomes and their effects. *American Psychologist, 39,* 377–385.

Gagné, R.M., and Driscoll, M.P. (1988). *Essentials of learning for instruction* (2nd ed.), Englewood Cliffs, N.J.: Prentice-Hall.

Gall, M. (1984). Synthesis of research on teachers' questioning. *Educational Leadership, 42,* 40–47.

Gall, M., Ward, B., Berliner, D., Cahen, L., Winne, P., Glashoff, J., and Stanton, G. (1978). Effects of questioning techniques and recitation on student learning. *American Educational Research Journal, 15,* 175–199.

Gall, M.D. (1970). The use of questions in teaching. *Review of Educational Research, 40,* 707–721.

Gall, M.D. (1987). Discussion methods. In M.J. Dunkin (ed.), *International encyclopedia of teaching and teacher education.* New York: Pergamon.

Gall, M.D., Fielding, G., Schalock, D., Charters, W.W., and Wilczynski, J.M. (1984). *Involving the principal in teachers' staff development: Effects on the quality of mathematics instruction in elementary schools.* Eugene, Oreg.: Center for Educational Policy and Management, University of Oregon.

Gallagher, J.J. (1992). Gifted persons. In M.C. Alkin (ed.), *Encyclopedia of educational research* (6th ed.) (pp. 544–549). New York: Macmillan.

Gamoran, A. (1984, April). Egalitarian versus elitist use of ability grouping. Paper presented at the annual convention of the American Educational Research Association, New Orleans.

Garber, H.L. (1988). *The Milwaukee Project: Preventing mental retardation in children at risk.* Washington, D.C.: American Association on Mental Retardation.

Garcia, E.E. (1992). "Hispanic" children: Theoretical, empirical, and related policy issues. *Educational Psychology Review, 4*(1), 69–93.

Garcia, R.L. (1991). *Teaching in a pluralistic society.* New York: Harper-Collins.

Gardner, H. (1982). *Development psychology* (2nd ed.). Boston: Little, Brown.

Gardner, H., and Hatch, T. (1989). Multiple intelligences go to school. *Educational Researcher, 18*(8), 4–10.

Gardner, M.K. (1985). Cognitive psychological approaches to instructional task analysis. In E.W. Gordon (ed.), *Review of research in education,* Vol. 12, pp. 157–195. Washington, D.C.: American Educational Research Association.

Garner, R., and Alexander, P.A. (1989). Metacognition: Answered and unanswered questions. *Educational Psychologist, 24,* 143–158.

Garner, R., Alexander, P.A., Gillingham, M.G., Kulikowich, J.M., and Brown, R. (1991). Interest and learning from text. *American Educational Research Journal, 28*(3), 643–659.

Gartner, A., and Lipsky, D.K. (1987). Beyond special education: Toward a quality system for all students. *Harvard Educational Review, 57,* 367–395.

Garza, S.A., and Barnes, C.P. (1989). Competencies for bilingual multicultural teachers. *The Journal of Educational Issues of Language Minority Students, 5,* 1–25.

Gelman, R. (1979). Preschool thought. *American Psychologist, 34,* 900–905.

Gelman, R., and Baillargeon, R. (1983). A review of some Piagetian concepts. In J.H. Flavell and E.M. Markman (eds.), *Handbook of child psychology,* Vol. 3: Cognitive development (4th ed., pp. 167–230). New York: Wiley.

Genesee, F. (1985). Second language learning through immersion: A review of U.S. programs. *Review of Educational Research, 55,* 541–561.

Genter, D. (1989). The mechanisms of analogical reasoning. In S. Vosniadou and A. Ortony (eds.), *Similarity and analogical reasoning.* Cambridge, England: Cambridge University Press.

Geoffrion, L.D., and Goldenberg, E.P. (1981). Computer based exploratory learning systems for communication-handicapped children. *Journal of Special Education, 15,* 325–331.

George, P. (1993, March). *Examining the culture of the classroom.* Paper presented at the Comparative and International Education Society, Kingston, Jamaica.

Gerard, H.B., and Miller, N. (1975). *School desegregation: A long-range study.* New York: Plenum.

Gerber, M.M., and Semmel, M.I. (1984). Teacher as imperfect test: Reconceptualizing the referral process. *Educational Psychologist, 19,* 137–148.

Gern, T., and Gern, P. (1986). *Substance abuse prevention activities for elementary children.* Englewood Cliffs, N.J.: Prentice-Hall.

Gersten, R., and Carnine, D. (1984). Direct instruction mathematics: A longitudinal evaluation of low-income elementary students. *Elementary School Journal, 84,* 395–407.

Gersten, R., and Keating, T. (1987). Long-term benefits from direct instruction. *Educational Leadership, 44*(6), 28–31.

Getsie, R.L., Langer, P., and Glass, G.V. (1985). Meta-analysis of the effects of type and combination of feedback on children's discrimination learning. *Review of Education Research, 55,* 9–22.

Gettinger, M. (1989). Effects of maximizing time spent and minimizing time needed for learning on pupil achievement. *American Educational Research Journal, 26,* 73–91.

Getzels, J.W., and Jackson, P.W. (1962). *Creativity and intelligence.* New York: Wiley.

Giaconia, R.M., and Hedges, L.V. (1982). Identifying features of effective open education. *Review of Educational Research, 52,* 579–602.

Gibbs, J.C., Arnold K.D., and Burkhart, J.F. (1984). Sex differences in the expression of moral judgment. *Child Development, 55,* 1040–1043.

Gilles, C., Bixby, M., Crowley, P., Crenshaw, S., Henrichs, M., Reynolds, F., and Pyle, D. (1988). *Whole language strategies for secondary students.* New York: Richard C. Owen.

Gilligan, C. (1982). *In a different voice: Sex differences in the expression of moral judgment.* Cambridge, Mass.: Harvard University Press.

Gilligan, C. (1985). Remapping development. Paper presented at the biennial meeting of the Society for Research in Child Development, Toronto.

Ginott, H. (1972). *Teacher and child.* New York: Macmillan.

Ginsburg, H.P., and Opper, S. (1988). *Piaget's theory of intellectual development* (3rd ed.). Englewood Cliffs, N.J.: Prentice-Hall.

Glanzer, M. (1982). Short-term memory. In C.R. Puff (ed.), *Handbook of research methods in human memory and cognition.* New York: Academic Press.

Glass, G.V., and Smith, M.L. (1977). *Pull out in compensatory education.* Washington, D.C.: Department of Health, Education, and Welfare.

Glasser, W.L. (1969). *Schools without failure.* New York: Harper & Row.

Glavin, J., Quay, H., Annesly, F., and Werry, J. (1971). An experimental resource room for behavior problem children. *Exceptional Children, 38,* 131–138.

Gleason, J.B. (1981). Code switching in children's language. In E.M. Hetherington and R.D. Parke (eds.), *Contemporary reading in child psychology* (2nd ed.), pp. 134–138. New York: McGraw-Hill.

Glover, J.A., Bullock, R.G., and Dietzer, M.L. (1990). Advance organizers: Delay hypotheses. *Journal of Educational Psychology, 82,* 291–297.

Godden, D., and Baddeley, A.D. (1975). Context-dependent memory in two natural environments: On land and under water. *British Journal of Psychology, 66,* 325–331.

Goffin, S.G., and Tull, C.Q. (1984, March). *Encouraging possibilities for cooperative behavior with young children.* Paper presented at the annual meeting of the Southern Association for Children under

Six, Lexington, Ky.

Goffin, S.G., and Tull, C.Q. (1985). Problem solving: Encouraging active learning. *Young Children*, 40(3), 28–32.

Gold, M. (1970). *Delinquent behavior in an American city*. Belmont, Calif.: Brooks/Cole.

Gold, R.M., Reilly, A., Silberman, R., and Lehr, R. (1971). Academic achievement declines under pass-fail grading. *Journal of Experimental Education*, 39, 17–21.

Goldberg, M., Passow, A., and Justman, J. (1966). *The effects of ability grouping*. New York: Teacher's College Press.

Goldhaber, D. (1979). Does the changing view of early experience imply a changing view of early development? In L.G. Katz (ed.), *Current topics in early childhood education*, Vol. 2, pp. 117–140. Norwood, N.J.: Ablex Publishing Co.

Goldstein, H., Moss, J., and Jordan J. (1966). *The efficacy of special class training on the development of mentally retarded children* (Cooperative Research Project No. 619). Washington, D.C.: U.S. Office of Education.

Good, T. (1983a, April). Classroom research: A decade of progress. Paper presented at the annual meeting of the American Educational Research Association, Montreal.

Good, T. (1987). Teacher expectations. In D. Berliner and B. Rosenshine (eds.), *Talks to Teachers* (pp. 159–200). New York: Random House.

Good, T.L. (1983b). Classroom research: Past and future. In F. Sykers and L.S. Shulman (eds.), *Handbook of teaching and policy*. New York: Longman.

Good, T., and Findley, N. (1985). Sex role expectations and achievement. In J. Dusek (ed.), *Teacher expectations*. Hillsdale, N.J.: Erlbaum.

Good, T., and Grouws, D. (1977). Teaching effects: A process-product study in fourth grade mathematics classes. *Journal of Teacher Education*, 28, 49–54.

Good, T., and Grouws, D. (1979). The Missouri Mathematics Effectiveness Project: An experimental study in fourth-grade classrooms. *Journal of Educational Psychology*, 71, 355–362.

Good, T., Grouws, D., and Ebmeier, H. (1983). *Active mathematics teaching*. New York: Longman.

Good, T., and Marshall, S. (1984). Do students learn more in heterogeneous or homogeneous groups? In P. Peterson, L.C. Wilkinson, and M. Hallinan (eds.), *The social context of instruction: Group organization and group processes*, pp. 15–38. New York: Academic Press.

Good, T.L., and Brophy, J.E. (1973). *Looking in classrooms*. New York: Harper & Row.

Good, T.L., and Brophy, J.E. (1984). *Looking in classrooms* (3rd ed.). New York: Harper & Row.

Good, T.L., and Brophy, J.E. (1989). Teaching the lesson. In R.E. Slavin (ed.), *School and classroom organization*. Hillsdale, N.J.: Erlbaum.

Goodlad, J.I. (1983). *A place called school*. New York: McGraw-Hill.

Goodman, K.S. (1986). *What's whole in whole language?* Portsmouth, N.H.: Heinemann.

Goodman, K.S., and Goodman, Y.M. (1989). Introduction: Redefining education. In L.B. Bird (ed.), *Becoming a whole language school: The Fair Oaks story* (pp. 3–10). Katonah, NY: Richard C. Owen.

Goodman, P. (1964). *Compulsory miseducation*. New York: Horizon Press.

Gordon, E.W. (1991). Human diversity and pluralism. *Educational Psychologist*, 26(2), 99–108.

Gordon, I. (1975). *Human development: A transactional perspective*. New York: Harper & Row.

Gottfredson, G.D. (1984). *How schools, families, and justice agencies can reduce youth crime*. Baltimore, Md.: Center for Social Organization of Schools, Johns Hopkins University.

Gottfredson, G.D., Karweit, N.L., and Gottfredson, G.D. (1989). *Reducing disorderly behavior in middle schools*. Baltimore, Md.: Johns Hopkins University, Center for Research on Elementary and Middle Schools.

Gottfried, A.E. (1985). Academic intrinsic motivation in elementary and junior high school students. *Journal of Educational Psychology*, 77, 631–645.

Gottfried, A.E. (1990). Academic intrinsic motivation in young elementary school children. *Journal of Educational Psychology*, 82(3), 525–538.

Gottlieb, J., Alter, M., and Gottlieb, B.W. (1991). Mainstreaming academically handicapped children in urban schools. In J.W. Lloyd, A.C. Repp, and N. Smith (eds.), *The regular education initiative: Alternative perspectives on concepts, issues, and models* (pp. 95–112). Sycamore, Ill.: Sycamore Press.

Gottlieb, J., and Leyser, Y. (1981). Friendship between mentally retarded and nonretarded children. In S. Asher and J. Gottman (eds.), *The development of children's friendships*. Cambridge, England: Cambridge University Press.

Graden, J.L., Casey, A., and Bonstrom, O. (1985). Implementing a preferral intervention system: Part II. The data. *Exceptional Children*, 51, 487–496.

Graham, S. (1991). A review of attribution theory in achievement contexts. *Educational Psychology Review*, 3(1), 5–39.

Graham, S., and Golan, S. (1991). Motivational influences on cognition: Task involvement, ego involvement, and depth of information processing. *Journal of Educational Psychology*, 83(2), 187–194.

Graubard, P.S. (1969). Utilizing the group in teaching disturbed delinquents to learn. *Exceptional Children*, 36, 267–272.

Graves, D. (1983). *Writing: Teachers and children at work*. Exeter, N.H.: Heinemann.

Green, G., and Osborne, J.G. (1985). Does vicarious instigation provide support for observational learning theories? A critical review. *Psychological Bulletin*, 97, 3–16.

Greenblat, C.S. (1982). Games and simulations. In H.E. Mitzel (ed.), *Encyclopedia of educational research*, pp. 713–716. New York: Free Press.

Greenbowe, T., Herron, J.D., Nurrenbern, S., Staver, J.R., and Ward, C.R. (1981). Teaching preadolescents to act as scientists: Replication and extension of an earlier study. *Journal of Educational Psychology*, 73, 705–711.

Greene, D., and Lepper, M.R. (1974). How to turn play into work. *Psychology Today*, 8, 49–54.

Greene, R.L. (1986). Sources of recency effects in free recall. *Psychological Bulletin*, 99, 221–228.

Greenfield, P.M. (1984). Theory of the teacher in learning activities. In B. Rogoff and J. Lave (eds.), *Everyday cognition: Its development in social context*, pp. 117–138. Cambridge, Mass.: Harvard University Press.

Gregory, I.D. (1975). A new look at the lecture method. *British Journal of Educational Technology*, 6, 55–62.

Greif, E.B., and Ulman, K.J. (1982). The psychological impact of menarche on early adolescent females: A review of the literature. *Child Development*, 53, 1413–1430.

Gresham, F. (1981). Social skills training with handicapped children: A review. *Review of Educational Research*, 51, 139–176.

Gresham, F.M. (1986). Strategies for enhancing the social outcomes of mainstreaming. In C.J. Meisel (ed.), *Mainstreaming handicapped children: Outcomes, controversies, and new directions* (pp. 193–218). Hillsdale, N.J.: Erlbaum.

Gronlund, N.E. (1985). *Measurement and evaluation in teaching* (5th ed.). New York: Macmillan.

Gronlund, N.E. (1988). *Constructing achievement tests* (4th ed.). Englewood Cliffs, N.J.: Prentice-Hall.

Gronlund, N.E. (1991). *How to write and use instructional objectives* (4th ed.). Englewood Cliffs, N.J.: Prentice-Hall.

Grossman, H. (1983). *Classification in mental retardation*. Washington, D.C.: American Association of Mental Deficiency.

Grusec, J., and Arnason, L. (1982). Consideration for others: Approaches to understanding altruism. In S.G. Moore and C.P. Cooper (eds.), *The young child: Reviews of research*, Vol. 3, pp. 159–174. Washington, D.C.: National Association for the Education of Young Children.

Guilford, J.P. (1939). *General psychology.* New York: Van Nostrand.

Guilford, J.P. (1988). Some changes in the Structure-of-Intellect model. *Educational and Psychological Measurement, 48*, 1–4.

Gump, P.V. (1982). School settings and their keeping. In D.L. Duke (ed.), *Helping teachers manage classrooms*, pp. 98–114. Alexandria, Va.: Association for Supervision and Curriculum Development.

Gunderson, D.V. (1982). Bilingual education. In H.E. Mitzel (ed.), *Encyclopedia for educational research*. New York: Free Press.

Guralnick, M.J., and Weinhouse, E. (1984). Peer-related social interactions of developmentally delayed young children: Development characteristics. *Developmental Psychology, 20*, 815–827.

Guskey, T.R. (1990). Cooperative mastery learning strategies. *The Elementary School Journal, 91*(1), 33–42.

Guthrie, J.T., Bennett, S., and Weber, S. (1991). Processing procedural documents: A cognitive model for following written directions. *Educational Psychology Review, 3*, 249–265.

Gutiérrez, R., and Slavin, R.E. (1992). Achievement effects of the nongraded elementary school. A best-evidence synthesis. *Review of Educational Research, 62*, 333–376.

Hacker, A. (ed.) (1983). *U/S: A statistical portrait of the American people.* New York: Viking Press.

Haertel, E. (1985). Construct validity and criterion-referenced testing. *Review of Educational Research, 55*, 23–46.

Haertel, E. (1986, April). *Choosing and using classroom tests: Teachers' perspectives on assessment.* Paper presented at the annual meeting of the American Educational Research Association, San Francisco.

Hakuta, K., and Garcia, E.E. (1989). Bilingualism and education. *American Psychologist, 44*, 374–379.

Hakuta, K., and Gould, L.J. (1987). Synthesis of research on bilingual education. *Educational Leadership, 44*(6), 38–45.

Hales, L.W., Bain, P.T., and Rand, L.P. (1971, February). An investigation of some aspects of the pass-fail grading system. Paper presented at the annual meeting of the American Educational Research Association, New York.

Hall, J.W. (1991). More on the utility of the keyword method. *Journal of Educational Psychology, 83*(1), 171–172.

Hall, R.V., Axelrod, S., Foundopoulos, M.,

Shellman, J., Campbell, R.A., and Cranston, S. (1971). *The effective use of punishment to modify behavior in the classroom. Educational Technology, 11*, 24–26.

Hall, R.V., Lund, D., and Jackson, D. (1968). Effects of teacher attention on study behavior. *Journal of Applied Behavior Analysis, 1*, 1–12.

Hallahan, D.P., and Kauffman, J.M. (1991). *Exceptional children* (5th ed.). Englewood Cliffs, N.J.: Prentice-Hall.

Halpern, D.F., Hansen, C., and Riefer, D. (1990). Analogies as an aid to understanding and memory. *Journal of Educational Psychology, 82*, 298–305.

Hamaker, C. (1986). The effects of adjunct questions on prose learning. *Review of Educational Research, 56*, 212–242.

Hamblin, R.L., Buckholdt, D., Ferritor, D., Kozloff, M., and Blackwell, L. (1971). *The humanization processes.* New York: Wiley-Interscience.

Hamburg, D.A. (1992). *Today's children: Creating a future for a generation in crisis.* New York: Times Books.

Hamilton, R.J. (1985). A framework for the evaluation of the effectiveness of adjunct questions and objectives. *Review of Educational Research, 55*, 47–85.

Haney, W., and Madaus, G. (1989). Searching for alternatives to standardized tests: Whys, whats, and whithers. *Phi Delta Kappan, 70*(9), 683–687.

Hanson, S.L., Morrison, D.R., and Ginsburg, A.L. (1989). The antecedents of teenage fatherhood. *Demography, 26*, 579–596.

Hardman, M.L., Drew, C.J., Egan, M.W., and Wolf, B. (1993). *Human exceptionality* (4th ed.). Boston: Allyn & Bacon.

Harpring, S.A. (1985, April). Inclass alternatives to traditional Chapter I pullout programs. Paper presented at the annual meeting of the American Educational Research Association, Chicago.

Harris, J.R., and Liebert, R.M. (1987). *The child: Development from birth through adolescence* (2nd ed.). Englewood Cliffs, N.J.: Prentice-Hall.

Harris, K.R. (1990). Developing self-regulated learners: The role of private speech and self-instruction. *Educational Psychologist, 21*, 35–50.

Harris, K.R., and Pressley, M. (1992). The nature of cognitive strategy instruction: Interactive strategy construction. *Exceptional Children, 58*.

Harrison, G.V. (1972). *Beginning reading. I: A professional guide for the lay tutor.* Provo, Utah: Brigham Young University Press.

Harrop, A., and McCann, C. (1983). Behavior modification and reading attainment in the comprehensive school. *Educational Research, 25*, 191–195.

Harrow, A. (1972). *A taxonomy of the psychomotor domain.* New York: McKay.

Harste, J.C., and Burke, C.L. (1980). Examining instructional assumptions: The child as informant. *Theory into Practice, 19*, 170–178.

Harter, S. (1982). The perceived competence scale for children. *Child Development, 53*, 87–97.

Harter, S. (1990). Issues in the assessment of the self-concept of children and adolescents. In A. LaGreca (ed.), *Through the eyes of a child* (pp. 292–325). Boston: Allyn & Bacon.

Hartley, S.S. (1978). *Meta-analysis of the effects of individually paced instruction in mathematics* (doctoral dissertation, University of Colorado, 1977). Dissertation Abstracts International, 38, 4003A (University Microfilms No. 77-29, 926).

Hartshorne, H., and May, M.A. (1928). *Studies in the nature of character. I: Studies in deceit.* New York: Macmillan.

Hass, A. (1979). *Teenage sexuality.* New York: Macmillan.

Hastings, W.M. (1977). In praise of regurgitation. *Intellect, 105*, 349–350.

Hawkins, J., and Sheingold, K. (1986). The beginning of a story: Computers and the organization of learning in classrooms. In J. Albertson and L. Cunningham (eds.), *Microcomputers and education* (pp. 40–57). Chicago: University of Chicago Press.

Hawkins, J.D., Doueck, H.J., and Lishner, D.M. (1988). Changing teaching practices in mainstream classrooms to improve bonding and behavior of low achievers. *American Educational Research Journal, 25*, 31–50.

Hawley, W.D., Crain, R.L., Russell, C.H., Smylie, M.A., Fernandez, R.R., Schofield, J.W., Tompkins, R., Trent, W.T., and Zlotnik, M.S. (1983). *Strategies for effective desegregation.* Lexington, Mass.: D.C. Heath.

Hayes, J.R., Rosenfarb, I., Wulfert, E., Munt, E.D., Korn, Z., and Zettle, R.D. (1985). Self-reinforcement effects: An artifact of social standard setting? *Journal of Applied Behavior Analysis, 18*, 201–214.

Hayes, L. (1976). The use of group contingencies for behavioral control: A review. *Psychological Bulletin, 83*, 628–648.

Hembree, R. (1988). Correlates, causes, effects, and treatment of test anxiety. *Review of Educational Research, 58*, 47–77.

Henry, S.L., and Pepper, F.C. (1990). Cognitive, social, and cultural effects on Indian learning style: Classroom implications. *The Journal of Educational Issues of Language Minority Students, 7*, 85–97.

Herb, D.O. (1972). *A textbook of psychology* (3rd ed.). Philadelphia: Saunders.

Herman, J.L., Aschbacher, P.R., and Winters, L. (1992). *A practical guide to alternative assessment.* Alexandria, Va.: Association for Supervision and Curriculum Development.

Herman, S.H., and Tramontana, J. (1971). Instructions and group versus individual reinforcement in modifying disruptive group behavior. *Journal of Applied Behavior Analysis, 4,* 113–119.

Hernandez, H. (1990). *Multicultural education: A teacher's guide to content and practice.* Columbus, Oh.: Merrill.

Hersen, M. (ed.) (1986). *Pharmacological and behavioral treatment: An integrative approach.* New York: Wiley.

Hersen, M., and Barlow, D. (1976). *Single-case experimental designs.* Elmsford, N.Y.: Pergamon Press.

Hess, R.D., and McDevitt, T.M. (1984). Some cognitive consequences of maternal intervention techniques: A longitudinal study. *Child Development, 55,* 2017–2030.

Hess, R.D., and Shipman, V.C. (1970). Early experiences and the socialization of cognitive modes in children. In M.W. Miles and W.W. Charters, Jr. (eds.), *Learning in social settings.* Boston: Allyn & Bacon.

Heward, W., and Orlansky, M. (1980). *Exceptional children.* Columbus, Ohio: Charles E. Merrill.

Heyns, B. (1978). *Summer learning and the effects of schooling.* New York: Academic Press.

Hidi, S., and Anderson, V. (1986). Producing written summaries: Task demands, cognitive operations, and implications for instruction. *Review of Educational Research, 56,* 473–493.

Hiebert, E. (1983). An examination of ability groupings for reading instruction. *Reading Research Quarterly, 18,* 231–255.

Hiebert, J., Wearne, D., and Taber, S. (1991). Fourth graders' gradual construction of decimal fractions during instruction using different physical representations. *Elementary School Journal, 91,* 321–341.

Higbee, K.L. (1978). Some pseudo-limitations of mnemonics. In M.M. Gruneberg, P.E. Morris, and R.N. Sykes (eds.), *Practical aspects of memory.* New York: Academic Press.

Higbee, K.L. (1979). Recent research on visual mnemonics: Historical roots and educational fruits. *Review of Educational Research, 49,* 611–629.

Higbee, K.L., and Kunihira, S. (1985). Cross-cultural applications of Yodai mnemonics in education. *Educational Psychologist, 20,* 57–64.

Hilgard, E.R., and Bower, G.H. (1966). *Theories of learning.* New York: Appleton-Century-Crofts.

Hill, J.R. (1977). *Measurement and evaluation in the classroom.* Columbus, Oh.: Merrill.

Hill, K., and Horton, M. (1985, April).

Validation of a classroom curriculum teaching elementary school students test-taking skills that optimize test performance. Paper presented at the annual meeting of the American Educational Research Association, Chicago.

Hill, K., and Wigfield, A. (1984). Test anxiety: A major educational problem and what can be done about it. *Elementary School Journal, 85,* 105–126.

Hilliard, A.G. (1989). Teachers and cultural styles in a pluralistic society. *NEA Today, 7*(6), 65–69.

Hilliard, A.G. (1991/92). Why we must pluralize the curriculum. *Educational Leadership, 49*(4), 12–16.

Hilliard, A.G. (1992). The pitfalls and promises of special education practice. *Exceptional Children, 59,* 168–172.

Hillocks, G. (1984). What works in teaching composition: A meta-analysis of experimental treatment studies. *American Journal of Education, 93,* 133–170.

Hiroto, D.S., and Seligman, M.E.P. (1975). Generality of learned helplessness in man. *Journal of Personality and Social Psychology, 31,* 311–327.

Hirsch, B.J., and Radkin, B.D. (1987). The transition to junior high school: A longitudinal study of self-esteem, psychological symptomatology, school life, and social support. *Child Development, 58,* 1235–1243.

Hirschi, T. (1969). *Causes of delinquency.* Berkeley: University of California Press.

Hitchcock, D. (1983). *Critical thinking: A guide to evaluating information.* Toronto: Methven.

Hixon, T.J., Shriberg, L.D., and Saxman, J.H. (eds.) (1980). *Introduction to communication disorders.* Englewood Cliffs, N.J.: Prentice-Hall.

Hodges, W., and Sheehan, R. (1978). Follow through as ten years of experimentation: What have we learned? *Young Children, 34,* 4–14.

Hodges, W., and Smith, L. (1978, August). Retrospect and prospect in early childhood and special education. Paper presented at the annual meeting of the American Psychological Association, Toronto.

Hodgkinson, H.L. (1985). *All one system: Demographics of education, kindergarten through graduate school.* Washington, D.C.: Institute for Educational Leadership.

Hoffman, M.L. (1979). Development of moral thought, feeling and behavior. *American Psychologist, 34,* 958–966.

Hogan, R., and Emler, N.P. (1978). Moral development. In M.E. Lamb (ed.), *Social and personality development,* pp. 200–233. New York: Holt, Rinehart, & Winston.

Hoge, R.D., and Coladarci, T. (1989). Teacher-based judgments of academic achievement: A review of literature.

Review of Educational Research, 59(3), 297–313.

Holt, J. (1964). *How children fail.* New York: Pitman.

Hopkins, K.D., and Bracht, G.H. (1975). Ten-year stability of verbal and nonverbal IQ scores, *American Educational Research Journal, 12,* 469–477.

Horn, R.E., and Cleaves, A. (1980). *The guide to simulations/games for education and training* (4th ed.). Beverly Hills, Calif.: Sage.

Hornberger, N.H. (1989). Continua of biliteracy. *Review of Educational Research, 59*(3), 271–296.

Horwitz, R. (1979). Psychological effects of the "open classroom." In H.J. Walberg (ed.), *Educational environments and effects: Evaluation, policy and productivity.* Berkeley: McCutchen.

Howard, E.R. (1978). *School discipline desk book.* West Nyack, N.Y.: Parker.

Hull, F.M., and Hull, M.E. (1973). Children with oral communication disabilities. In L.M. Dunn (ed.), *Exceptional children in the schools: Special education in transition.* New York: Holt, Rinehart, & Winston.

Hull, F.M., Mielke, P.W., Timmons, R.J., and Willeford, J.A. (1971). The national speech and hearing survey: Preliminary results. *ASHA, 13,* 501–509.

Humphreys, L.G. (1986). Describing the elephant. In R.J. Sternberg and D.K. Detterman (eds.), *What is intelligence?* (pp. 97–100). Norwood, N.J.: Ablex.

Hunter, M. (1982). *Mastery teaching.* El Segundo, Calif.: TIP Publications.

Hunter, M. (1990/91). Hunter lesson design helps achieve the goals of science instruction. *Educational Leadership, 48*(4), 79–81.

Hunter, M., and Barker, G. (1989). If at first . . . : Attribution theory in the classroom. *Annual editions: Educational psychology 89/90.* Guilford, Conn.: Duskin.

Hyde, T.S., and Jenkins, J.J. (1969). Differential effects of incidental tasks on the organization of recall of highly associated words. *Journal of Experimental Psychology, 82,* 472–481.

Individually Prescribed Instruction (1972). *Individually prescribed instruction.* New York: Appleton-Century-Crofts.

Inhelder, B., and Piaget, J. (1958). *The growth of logical thinking from childhood to adolescence.* New York: Basic Books.

Isaacson, R.L. (1964). Relation between achievement, test anxiety, and curricular choices. *Journal of Abnormal and Social Psychology, 64,* 447–452.

Isenberger, J., and Quisenberry, N.L. (1988). Play: A necessity for all children. *Childhood Education,* February, 138–144.

Iversen, I.H. (1992). Skinner's early research: From reflexology to operant conditioning. *American Psychologist, 47,* 1318–1328.

Jacklin, C.N. (1983). Boys and girls entering school. In M. Marland (ed.), *Sex differentiation and schooling.* London: Heinemann.

Jacklin, C.N. (1989). Female and male: Issues of gender. *American Psychologist, 44,* 127–133.

Jackson, P., and Lahaderne, H. (1967). Inequalities of teacher-pupil contacts. *Psychology in the Schools, 4,* 204–208.

Jacobs, J.E., and Wigfield, A. (1989). Sex equity in mathematics and science education: Research-policy links. *Educational Psychology Review, 1*(1), 39–56.

Jagacinski, C.M., and Nicholls, J.G. (1990). Reducing effort to protect perceived ability: "They'd do it but I wouldn't." *Journal of Educational Psychology, 82,* 15–21.

James, W. (1912). *Talks to teachers on psychology: And to students on some of life's ideals.* New York: Holt.

Jenkins, J.R., and Jenkins, L.M. (1987). Making peer tutoring work. *Educational Leadership, 44*(6), 64–68.

Jensen, A.R. (1980). *Bias in mental testing.* New York: The Free Press.

Jenson, W., Sloane, H., and Young, K. (1988). *Applied behavior modification in education.* Englewood Cliffs, N.J.: Prentice-Hall.

Johnson, D., and Johnson, R. (1991). *Learning together and alone* (3rd ed.). Englewood Cliffs, N.J.: Prentice-Hall.

Johnson, D.W., and Johnson, R.T. (1974). Instructional goal structure: Cooperative, competitive, or individualistic. *Review of Educational Research, 44,* 213–240.

Johnson, D.W., and Johnson, R.T. (1979). Conflict in the classroom: Controversy and learning. *Review of Educational Research, 49,* 51–70.

Johnson, D.W., and Johnson, R.T. (1987). *Learning together and alone* (2nd ed.). Englewood Cliffs, N.J.: Prentice-Hall.

Johnson, D.W., and Johnson, R.T. (1989). *Cooperation and competition: Theory and Research.* Edina, Minn.: Interaction Book Co.

Johnson, G.O. (1950). A study of the social position of the mentally retarded child in the regular grades. *American Journal of Mental Deficiency, 55,* 60–89.

Johnson, J.E., and Hooper, F.E. (1982). Piagetian structuralism and learning: Two decades of educational application. *Contemporary Educational Psychology, 7,* 217–237.

Johnson, L.C., and Waxman, H.C. (1985, March). *Evaluating the effects of the "Groups of Four" program.* Paper presented at the annual convention of the American Educational Research Association, Chicago.

Johnson-Laird, P.N., Herrmann, D.J., and Chaffin, R. (1984). Only connections: A critique of semantic networks.

Psychological Bulletin, 96, 292–315.

Johnston, P., Allington, R., and Afflerbach, P. (1985). The congruence of classroom and remedial instruction. *Elementary School Journal, 85,* 465–477.

Jones, J. (1961). *Blind children: degree of vision mode of reading.* Washington, D.C.: U.S. Department of Health, Education and Welfare.

Jones, R.L. (1988). *Psychoeducational assessment of minority group children.* Berkeley, Calif.: Cobb & Henry.

Jones, R.M. (1968). *Fantasy and feeling in education.* New York: Harper & Row.

Joyce, B., and Weil, M. (1986). *Models of teaching* (3rd ed.). Englewood Cliffs, N.J.: Prentice-Hall.

Juel, C. (1991). Beginning reading. In R. Barr, M. Kamil, P. Mosenthal, and P.D. Pearson (eds.), *Handbook of reading research* (Vol. I, pp. 759–788). New York: Longman.

Jussim, L. (1991). Grades may reflect more than performance: Comment on Wentzel (1989). *Journal of Educational Psychology, 83*(1), 153–155.

Kagan, D. (1988). Teaching as clinical problem solving: A critical examination of the analogy and its implications. *Review of Educational Research, 58,* 482–505.

Kagan, J. (1964). Acquisition and significance of sex typing and sex-role identity. In M.L. Hoffman and L.W. Hoffman (eds.), *Review of child development research.* New York: Sage.

Kagan, J., Klein, R.E., Finley, G.E., Rogoff, B., and Nolan, E. (1979). A cross-cultural study of cognitive development. *Monographs of the Society for Research in Child Development, 44,* No. 5.

Kagan, S. (1983). Social orientation among Mexican-American children: A challenge to traditional classroom structures. In E.E. Garcia (ed.), *The Mexican-American child: Language, cognition, and social development.* Tempe, Ariz.: Center for Bilingual Education.

Kagan, S. (1989). *Cooperative learning resources for teachers.* San Juan Capistrano, Calif.: Resources for Teachers.

Kagan, S., Zahn, G.L., Widaman, K.F., Schwartzwald, J., and Tyrrell, G. (1985). Classroom structural bias: Impact of cooperative and competitive classroom structures on cooperative and competitive individuals and groups. In R.E. Slavin *et al.* (eds.), *Learning to cooperate, cooperating to learn.* New York: Plenum.

Kallison, J.M. (1986). Effects of lesson organization on achievement. *American Educational Research Journal, 23,* 337–347.

Kamii, C., and Devries, R. (1978). *Physical knowledge in preschool education: Implications of Piaget's theory.* Englewood Cliffs, N.J.: Prentice-Hall.

Kamii, C., and Devries, R. (1980). *Group*

games in early education: Implications of Piaget's theory. Washington, D.C.: National Association for the Education of Young Children.

Kamin, L.J. (1975). *The science and politics of IQ.* New York: Wiley.

Kaplan, R.M., and Pascoe, G.C. (1977). Humorous lectures and humorous examples: Some effects upon comprehension and retention. *Journal of Educational Psychology, 69,* 61–65.

Karraker, R. (1972). Increasing academic performance through home managed contingency programs. *Journal of School Psychology, 10,* 173–179.

Karweit, N. (1976). A reanalysis of the effect of quantity of schooling on achievement. *Sociology of Education, 49,* 236–246.

Karweit, N., and Slavin, R.E. (1981). Measurement and modeling choices in studies of time and learning. *American Educational Research Journal, 18,* 157–171.

Karweit, N.L. (1981). Time in school. *Research in Sociology of Education and Socialization, 2,* 77–110.

Karweit, N.L. (1989a). Effective kindergarten programs and practices for students at risk of academic failure. In R.E. Slavin, N.L. Karweit, and N.A. Madden (eds.), *Effective programs for students at risk.* Boston: Allyn & Bacon.

Karweit, N.L. (1989b). Preschool programs for students at risk of school failure. In R.E. Slavin, N.L. Karweit, and N.A. Madden (eds.), *Effective programs for students at risk.* Boston: Allyn & Bacon.

Karweit, N.L. (1989c). Time and learning: A review. In R.E. Slavin (ed.), *School and classroom organization.* Hillsdale, N.J.: Erlbaum.

Karweit, N.L. (1994a). Can preschool alone prevent early reading failure? In R.E. Slavin, N.L. Karweit, and B.A. Wasik (eds.), *Preventing early school failure.* Boston: Allyn & Bacon.

Karweit, N.L. (1994b). Issues in kindergarten organization and curriculum. In R.E. Slavin, N.L. Karweit, and B.A. Wasik (eds.), *Preventing early school failure.* Boston: Allyn & Bacon.

Karweit, N.L., and Wasik, B.A. (1994). Extra-year kindergarten programs and transitional first grades. In R.E. Slavin, N.L. Karweit, and B.A. Wasik (eds.), *Preventing early school failure.* Boston: Allyn & Bacon.

Katz, L.G., Evangelou, D., and Hartman, J.A. (1991). *The case for mixed-age grouping in early childhood education.* Washington, D.C.: National Association for the Education of Young Children.

Kauffman, J.M. (1989). *Characteristics of behavioral disorders of children and youth* (4th ed.). Columbus, OH: Merrill.

Keith, T.Z., Reimers, T.M., Fehrmann, P.G., Pottebaum, S.M., and Aubey, L.W. (1986). Parental involvement, homework, and TV time: Direct and indirect effects on high school achievement. *Journal of Educational Psychology, 78,* 373–380.

Kellam, S.G., and Werthamer-Larsson, L. (1986). Developmental epidemiology: A basis for prevention. In M. Kessler and S.E. Goldston (eds.), *A decade of progress in primary prevention* (pp. 154–180). Hanover, N.H.: University Press of New England.

Keller, F.S. (1968). "Good-bye, teacher . . ." *Journal of Applied Behavior Analysis, 1,* 78–89.

Kendall, P.C. (1981). Cognitive-behavioral interventions with children. In B.B. Lahey and A.E. Kazdin (eds.), *Advances in clinical psychology,* Vol. 4. New York: Plenum.

Kennedy, M.M., Birman, B.F., and Demaline, R.E. (1986). *The effectiveness of Chapter 1 services.* Washington, D.C.: Office of Educational Research and Improvement, U.S. Department of Educational Research and Improvement, U.S. Department of Education.

Kessen, W. (1979). The American child and other cultural inventions. *American Psychologist, 34,* 815–820.

Keyser, D.J., and Sweetland, R.C. (eds.) (1984–85). *Test critiques* (Vols. 1–4). Kansas City: Test Corporation of America.

Kierstead, J. (1985). Direct instruction and experiential approaches: Are they really mutually exclusive? *Educational Leadership, 42*(8), 25–30.

Kiewra, D.A. (1985). Providing the instructor's notes: An effective addition to student notetaking. *Educational Psychologist, 20,* 33–39.

Kiewra, K.A. (1983). The process of review: A levels-of-processing approach. *Contemporary Educational Psychology, 8,* 366–374.

Kiewra, K.A. (1991). Aids to lecture learning. *Educational Psychologist, 26,* 37–53.

Kiewra, K.A., DuBois, N.F., Christian, D., McShane, A., Meyerhoffer, M., and Roskelley, D. (1991). Note-taking functions and techniques. *Journal of Educational Psychology, 83,* 240–245.

Kimball, M.M. (1989). A new perspective on women's math achievement. *Psychological Bulletin, 105,* 198–214.

King, A. (1991). Effects of training in strategic questioning on children's problem-solving performance. *Journal of Educational Psychology, 83,* 307–317.

King, A. (1992a). Facilitating elaborative learning through guided student-generated questioning. *Educational Psychologist, 27,* 111–126.

King, A. (1992b). Comparison of self-questioning, summarizing, and note taking-review as strategies for learning from lectures. *American Educational Research Journal, 29,* 303–323.

King, N.J., and Ollendick, T.H. (1989).

Children's anxiety and phobic disorders in school settings: Classification, assessment, and intervention issues. *Review of Educational Research, 59*(4), 431–470.

Kirby, F.D., and Shields, F. (1972). Modification of arithmetic response rate and attending behavior in a seventh-grade student. *Journal of Applied Behavior Analysis, 5,* 79–84.

Kirk, S.A. (1972). *Educating exceptional children* (2nd ed.). Boston: Houghton Mifflin.

Kirkpatrick, C. (1926). *Intelligence and immigration.* Mental Measurement Monographs, Serial No. 2. Baltimore: The Williams and Wilkins Co.

Kirschenbaum, H. (1992). A comprehensive model for values education and moral education. *Phi Delta Kappan, 73*(10), 771–776.

Kirschenbaum, H., Simon, S.B., and Napier, R.W. (1971). *Wad-ja-get? The grading game in American education.* New York: Hart Publishing Co.

Kirst, M.W. (1990). *Accountability: Implications for state and local policymakers.* Washington, D.C.: U.S. Department of Education.

Klauer, K. (1984). Intentional and incidental learning with instructional texts: A meta-analysis for 1970–1980. *American Educational Research Journal, 21,* 323–339.

Klausmeier, H.J., and Harris, C.W. (1966). *Analysis of concept learning.* New York: Academic Press.

Klausmeier, H.J., Jeter, J.T., Quilling, M.R., Fryer, D.A., and Allen, P.S. (1975). *Individually guided motivation.* Madison, Wisc.: Research and Development Center for Cognitive Learning.

Klein, S. (1985). *Handbook for achieving sex equality through education.* Baltimore, Md.: Johns Hopkins University Press.

Klieber, D.A., and Barnett, L.A. (1980). *Leisure in childhood. Young Children, 35,* 47–52.

Kline, S. (1977). *Child abuse and neglect: A primer for school personnel.* Reston, Va.: Council for Exceptional Children.

Knapczyk, D.R. (1988). Reducing aggressive behaviors in special and regular classes by training alternative social responses. *Behavioral Disorders, 14,* 27–39.

Knapp, M.S., and Shields, P.M. (1990). Reconceiving academic instruction for the children of poverty. *Phi Delta Kappan, 71,* 753–758.

Knapp, M.S., Turnbull, B.J., and Shields, P.M. (1990). New directions for educating the children of poverty. *Educational Leadership, 48*(1), 4–8.

Kneedler, R. (1984). *Special education for today.* Englewood Cliffs, N.J.: Prentice-Hall.

Knight, C.B., Halpin, G., and Halpin, G. (1992, April). *The effects of learning environment accommodations on the*

achievement of second graders. Paper presented at the annual meeting of the American Educational Research Association, San Francisco.

Kohlberg, L. (1963). The development of children's orientations toward moral order. I: Sequence in the development of human thought. *Vita Humana, 6,* 11–33.

Kohlberg, L. (1969). Stage and sequence: The cognitive-developmental approach to socialization. In D.A. Golsin (ed.), *Handbook of socialization theory and research,* pp. 347–380. Chicago: Rand McNally.

Kohlberg, L. (1978). Revisions in the theory and practice of moral development. In W. Damon (ed.). *New directions for child development* (No. 2, pp. 83–87). San Francisco: Jossey-Bass.

Kohlberg, L. (1984). *Essays on moral development.* San Francisco: Harper & Row.

Kornetsky, C. (1975). Minimal brain dysfunction and drugs. In W.M. Cruickshank and D.P. Hallahan (eds.), *Perceptual and learning disabilities in children, Vol 2: Research and Theory.* Syracuse, N.Y.: Syracuse University Press.

Kounin, J. (1970). *Discipline and group management in classrooms.* New York: Holt, Rinehart, & Winston.

Kozma, R. (1991). Learning with media. *Review of Educational Research, 61*(2), 179–211.

Kozol, J. (1991). *Savage inequalities: Children in America's schools.* New York: Crown.

Krasnor, L.R., and Pepler, D.J. (1980). The study of children's play: Some suggested future directions. *New Directions for Child Development, 9,* 85–95.

Krathwohl, D.R., Bloom, B.S., and Masia, B.B. (1964). *Taxonomy of educational objectives: The classification of educational goals. Handbook II: Affective domain.* New York: David McKay.

Kratochwill, T.R., and Bijou, S.W. (1987). The impact of behaviorism on educational psychology. In J.A. Glover, and R.R. Ronning (eds.), *Historical foundations of educational psychology.* New York: Plenum.

Kreinberg, N., and Thompson, V. (1986). *Family math: Report of activities.* Berkeley: University of California Press.

Krueger, W.C.F. (1929). The effect of overlearning on retention. *Journal of Experimental Psychology, 12,* 71–128.

Krug, D., Davis, T.B., and Glover, J.A. (1990). Massed versus distributed reading: A case of forgetting helping recall? *Journal of Educational Psychology, 82,* 366–371.

Kuhara-Kojima, K., and Hatano, G. (1991). Contribution of content knowledge and learning ability to the learning of facts. *Journal of Educational Psychology, 83*(2), 253–263.

Kukla, A. (1972a). Attributional determinants of achievement-related behavior. *Journal of Personality and Social Psychology, 21,* 166–174.

Kukla, A. (1972b). Foundations of an attributional theory of performance. *Psychological Review, 79,* 454–470.

Kulhavy, R.W., and Stock, W.A. (1989). Feedback in written instruction: The place of response certitude. *Educational Psychology Review, 1*(4), 279–308.

Kulik, C.L., Kulik, J.A., and Bangert-Drowns, R. L. (1984, April). Effects of computer-based education of elementary school pupils. Paper presented at the annual convention of the American Educational Research Association, New Orleans.

Kulik, C.L., Kulik, J.A., and Bangert-Drowns, R.L. (1986, April). Effects of testing for mastery on student learning. Paper presented at the annual convention of the American Educational Research Association, San Francisco.

Kulik, C.L., Kulik, J.A., and Bangert-Drowns, R.L. (1990). Effectiveness of mastery learning programs: A meta-analysis. *Review of Educational Research, 60*(2), 265–299.

Kulik, J.A., and Kulik, C.L. (1984). Effects of accelerated instruction on students. *Review of Educational Research, 54,* 409–425.

Kulik, J.A., and Kulik, C.L. (1988). Timing of feedback and verbal learning. *Review of Educational Research Journal, 21,* 79–97.

Kulik, J.A., Kulik, C.L., and Bangert, R.L. (1984). Effects of practice on aptitude and achievement test scores. *American Educational Research Journal, 21,* 435–447.

Kulik, J.A., Kulik, C.L., and Cohen, P.A. (1979). A meta-analysis of outcome studies of Keller's Personalized System of Instruction. *American Psychologist, 34,* 307–318.

Kunihira, S., Kuzma, R., Meadows, G., and Lotz, T. (1981, April). Effects of visually aided verbal mnemonics in developing computational skills with fractional numbers. Paper presented at the annual meeting of the Western Psychological Association, Los Angeles.

Kutnick, P.J. (1988). *Relationships in the primary school classroom.* London: Paul Chapman.

Laboratory of Comparative Human Cognition. (1983). Culture and cognitive development. In P. Mussen (ed.), *Handbook of child psychology,* Vol. 1. New York: Wiley.

Laboratory of Comparative Human Cognition (1989). Kids and computers: A positive vision of the future. *Harvard Educational Review, 59,* 73–86.

Lahaderne, H. (1968). Attitudinal and intellectual correlates of attention: A study of four sixth-grade classrooms. *Journal of Educational Psychology, 59,* 320–324.

Lahey, B., Gendrich, J., Gendrich, S., Schnelle, L., Gant, D., and McNee, P. (1977). An evaluation of daily report cards with minimal teacher and parent contacts as an efficient method of classroom intervention. *Behavior Modification, 1,* 381–394.

Lam, T.C.M. (1992). Review of practices and problems in the evaluation of bilingual education. *Review of Educational Research, 62*(2), 181–203.

Lambie, R.A. (1980). A systematic approach for changing materials, instruction, and assignments to meet individual needs. *Focus on Exceptional Children, 6*(8), 1–14.

Laminack, L.L. (1990). "Possibilities, Daddy, I think it says possibilities": A father's journal of the emergence of literacy. *The Reading Teacher, 43,* 536–540.

Lampert, M. (1986). Knowing, doing, and teaching multiplication. *Cognition and Instruction, 3,* 305–342.

Land, M.L. (1987). Vagueness and clarity. In M.J. Dunkin (ed.), *International encyclopedia of teaching and teacher education.* New York: Pergamon.

Landy, F.J. (1984). *Psychology: The science of people.* Englewood Cliffs, N.J.: Prentice-Hall.

Larrivee, B. (1985). *Effective teaching behaviors for successful mainstreaming.* New York: Longman.

Larrivee, B., and Horne, M.D. (1991). Social status: A comparison of mainstreamed students with peers of different ability levels. *Journal of Special Education, 25,* 90–101.

Laurie, T.E., Buchwach, L., Silverman, R., and Zigmond, N. (1978). Teaching secondary learning disabled students in the mainstream. *Learning Disability Quarterly, 1,* 62–72.

Lavatelli, C. (1970). *Piaget's theory applied to an early childhood curriculum.* Cambridge, Mass.: American Science and Engineering.

Lave, J. (1988). *Cognition in practice.* Boston: Cambridge Press.

Lawson, G., Peterson, J., and Lawson, A. (1983). *Alcoholism and the family.* Rockville, Md.: Aspen Systems.

Lawton, J.T., and Wanska, S.K. (1977). Advance organizers as a teaching strategy: A reply to Barnes and Clawson. *Review of Educational Research, 47,* 233–244.

Lay, M.Z., and Dopyera, J.E. (1977). *Becoming a teacher of young children.* Lexington, Mass.: D.C. Health.

Leach, D.M., and Graves, M. (1973). The effects of immediate correction on improving seventh grade language arts performance. In A. Egner (ed.), *Individualizing junior and senior high instruction to provide special education within regular classrooms.* Burlington,

Vt.: University of Vermont.

Leeper, R.W. (1935). A study of a neglected portion of the field of learning: The development of sensory organization. *Pedagogical Seminary and Journal of Genetic Psychology, 46,* 41–75.

Lefcourt, H. (1976). *Locus of control: Current trends in research and theory.* Hillsdale, N.J.: Erlbaum.

Lefkowitz, W. (1975). Communication grows in a "magic circle." In D.A. Read and S.B. Simon (eds.), *Humanistic education sourcebook,* pp. 457–459. Englewood Cliffs, N.J.: Prentice-Hall.

Leinhardt, G. (1992). What research on learning tells us about teaching. *Educational Leadership, 49*(7), 20–25.

Leinhardt, G., and Bickel, W. (1989). Instruction's the thing wherein to catch the mind that falls behind. In R.E. Slavin (ed.), *School and classroom organization.* Hillsdale, N.J.: Erlbaum.

Leinhardt, G., and Greeno, J.D. (1986). The cognitive skill of teaching. *Journal of Educational Psychology, 78,* 73–95.

Leinhardt, G., and Pallay, A. (1982). Restrictive educational settings: Exile or haven? *Review of Educational Research, 52,* 557–578.

Lepper, M.R. (1983). Extrinsic reward and intrinsic motivation: Implications for the classroom. In J.M. Levine and M.C. Wang (eds.), *Teacher and student perceptions: Implications for learning,* pp. 281–317. Hillsdale, N.J.: Erlbaum.

Lepper, M.R. (1985). Microcomputers in education. Motivational and social issues. *American Psychologist, 40,* 1–18.

Lepper, M.R. (1988). Motivational considerations in the study of instruction. *Cognition and Instruction, 5,* 289–309.

Lepper, M.R., Greene, D., and Nisbett, R.E. (1973). Undermining children's intrinsic interest with extrinsic rewards: A test of the overjustification hypothesis. *Journal of Personality and Social Psychology, 28,* 129–137.

Lerner, B. (1981). The minimum competency testing movement: Social, scientific, and legal implications. *American Psychologist, 36,* 1057–1066.

Lesgold, A. (1988). Problem solving. In R.J. Sternberg and E.E. Smith (eds.), *The psychology of human thought* (pp. 188–213). New York: Cambridge University Press.

Lever, J. (1978). Sex differences in the complexity of children's play and games. *American Sociological Review, 43,* 471–483.

Levin, J.R. (1981). The mnemonic 80's: Keywords in the classroom. *Educational Psychologist, 16,* 65–82.

Levin, J.R., Morrison, C.R., McGivern, J.E., Mastropieri, M.A., and Scruggs, T.E. (1986). Mnemonic facilitation of text-embedded science facts. *American Educational Research Journal, 23,*

489–506.

Levin, J.R., Shriberg, L.K., Miller, G.E., McCormick, C.B., and Levin, B.B. (1980). The keyword method as applied to elementary school children's social studies content. *Elementary School Journal, 80,* 185–191.

Levin, M.E., and Levin, J.R. (1990). Scientific mnemonics: Methods for maximizing more than memory. *American Educational Research Journal, 27,* 301–321.

Levine, C., Kohlberg, L., and Hewer, A. (1985). The current formulation of Kohlberg's theory and a response to critics. *Human Development, 28,* 94–100.

Levine, D.U. (ed.) (1985). *Improving student achievement through mastery learning programs.* San Francisco: Jossey-Bass.

Levine, D.V., and Havinghurst, R.S. (1989) *Society and education* (7th ed.). Boston: Allyn & Bacon.

Levine, D.V., and Stark, J. (1982). Instructional and organizational arrangements that improve achievement in inner-city schools. *Educational Leadership, 39,* 41–46.

Lewandowsky, S., and Murdock, B.B. (1989). Memory for serial order. *Psychological Review, 96,* 25–57.

Lewin, K. (1947). Group decision and social change. In T.M. Newcomb and E.L. Hartley (eds.), *Readings in social psychology.* New York: Holt, Rinehart, & Winston.

Liebert, R.M., and Wicks-Nelson, R. (1981). *Developmental psychology* (3rd ed.). Englewood Cliffs, N.J.: Prentice-Hall.

Lindeman, R.H., and Merenda, P.F. (1979). *Educational measurement.* Glenview, Ill.: Scott Foresman.

Linn, A.J. (1983). Testing and instruction: Links and distinctions. *Journal of Educational Measurement, 20,* 179–189.

Linn, M.C., and Hyde, J.S. (1989). Gender, mathematics, and science. *Educational Researcher, 18*(8), 17–27.

Litow, L., and Pumroy, D.K. (1975). A brief review of classroom group-oriented contingencies. *Journal of Applied Behavior Analysis, 8,* 341–347.

Livson, N., and Peskin, H. (1980). Perspectives on adolescence from longitudinal research. In J. Adelson (ed.), *Handbook of adolescent psychology.* New York: Wiley.

Lloyd, D.N. (1978). Prediction of school failure from third-grade data. *Educational and Psychological Measurement, 38,* 1193–1200.

Locke, E., and Latham, G.P. (1990). *A theory of goal setting and task performance.* Englewood Cliffs, N.J.: Prentice-Hall.

Locke, E.A., Cartledge, N., and Koeppel, J. (1968). Motivational effects of knowledge of results: A goal-setting phenomenon? *Psychological Bulletin, 70,* 474–485.

Lockheed, M.E. (1984). Sex segregation and male preeminence in elementary classrooms. In E. Fennema and M.J. Ayer (eds.), *Women and education: Equity or equality?* Berkeley: McCutchan.

Lockheed, M.E., and Harris, A.M. (1982). Classroom interaction and opportunities for cross-sex peer learning in science. *Journal of Early Adolescence, 2,* 135–143.

Lockheed, M.E., Harris, A.M., and Finkelstein, K.J. (1979). *Curriculum and research for equity: A training manual for promoting sex equity in the classroom.* Princeton, N.J.: Educational Testing Service.

Lohman, D.E. (1989). Human intelligence: An introduction to advances in theory and research. *Review of Educational Research, 59*(4), 333–373.

Long, B. (1967). Developmental changes in the self-concept during middle childhood. *Merrill Palmer Quarterly, 13.*

Longfellow, C. (1979). Divorce in context: Its impact on children. In G. Levinger and O. Moles (eds.), *Divorce and separation.* New York: Basic Books.

Luckasson, R., Coulter, D., Polloway, E., Reiss, S., Schalock, R., Snell, M., Spitalnik, D., and Stark, J. (1992). *Mental retardation: Definitions, classification, and systems of supports* (9th ed.). Washington, D.C.: American Association on Mental Retardation.

Lueckemeyer, C.L., and Chiappetta, E.L. (1981). An investigation into the effects of a modified mastery learning strategy on achievement in a high school human physiology unit. *Journal of Research in Science Teaching, 18,* 269–273.

Lysynchuk, L.M., Pressley, M., & Vye, N.J. (1990). Reciprocal teaching improves standardized reading-comprehension performance in poor comprehenders. *Elementary School Journal, 90,* 469–484.

Machida, K., and Carlson, J. (1984). Effects of a verbal mediation strategy on cognitive processes in mathematics learning. *Journal of Educational Psychologist, 76,* 1382–1385.

MacIver, D.J. (1992). *Motivating disadvantaged early adolescents to reach new heights: Effective evaluation, reward, and recognition structures* (No. 32). Baltimore: Johns Hopkins University, Center for Research on Effective Schooling for Disadvantaged Students.

MacMillan, D.L., and Forness, S.R. (1992). Mental retardation. In M.C. Alkin (ed.), *Encyclopedia of educational research* (6th ed.). New York: Macmillan.

MacMillan, D.L., Keough, B.K., and Jones, R.L. (1986). Special educational research on mildly handicapped learners. In M.C. Wittrock (ed.), *Handbook of research on teaching* (3rd ed.). New York: Macmillan.

MacMillan, D.L., Meyers, C.E., and

Morrison, G.M. (1980). System-identification of mildly mentally retarded children: Implications for interpreting and conducting research. *American Journal of Mental Deficiency, 85,* 108–115.

Madden, N.A., and Slavin, R.E. (1983a). Effects of cooperative learning on the social acceptance of mainstreamed academically handicapped students. *Journal of Special Education, 17,* 171–182.

Madden, N.A., and Slavin, R.E. (1983b). Mainstreaming students with mild academic handicaps: Academic and social outcomes. *Review of Educational Research, 53,* 519–569.

Madden, N.A., Slavin, R.E., Karweit, N.L., Dolan, L.J., and Wasik, B.A. (1993). Success for All: Longitudinal effects of a restructuring program for inner-city elementary schools. *American Educational Research Journal, 30.*

Madden, N.A., Slavin, R.E., and Stevens, R.J. (1986). *Cooperative integrated reading and composition: Teacher's manual.* Baltimore, Md.: Johns Hopkins University, Center for Research on Elementary and Middle Schools.

Maddox, H., and Hoole, F. (1975). Performance decrement in the lecture. *Educational Review, 28,* 17–30.

Maddux, C.D., Johnson, D.L, and Willis, J.W. (1992). *Educational computing.* Boston: Allyn & Bacon.

Madison, C.H., Becker, W.C., and Thomas, D.R. (1986). Rules, praise, and ignoring: Elements of elementary classroom control. *Journal of Applied Behavior Analysis, 1,* 139–150.

Madsen, C.H., Becker, W.C., and Thomas, D.R. (1968). Rules, praise, and ignoring: Elements of elementary classroom control. *Journal of Applied Behavior Analysis, 1,* 139.

Maeroff, G.I. (1991). Assessing alternative assessment. *Phi Delta Kappan, 73*(4), 272–281.

Mager, R.F. (1975). *Preparing instructional objectives.* Belmont, Calif.: Fearon.

Maheady, L., Harper, G.F., and Mallette, B. (1991). Peer-mediated instruction: Review of potential applications for special education. *Reading, Writing, and Learning Disabilities, 7,* 75–102.

Mahone, C.H. (1960). Fear of failure and unrealistic vocational aspiration. *Journal of Abnormal and Social Psychology, 60,* 253–261.

Maier, N.R. (1930). Reasoning in humans. I. On direction. *Journal of Comparative Psychology, 10,* 115–143.

Maier, S.F., Seligman, M.E.P., and Solomon, R.L. (1969). Pavlovian fear conditioning and learned helplessness. In B.A. Campbell and R.M. Church (eds.), *Punishment and adverse behavior.* New York: Appleton-Century-Crofts.

Maker and Schiever (eds.) (1989). *Critical issues in gifted education: Defensible pro-*

grams for cultural and ethnic minorities. Austin, Tex.: Pro-Ed.

Malina, R.M. (1982). Motor development in the early years. In S.G. Moore and C.R. Cooper (eds.), *The young child: Reviews of research,* Vol. 3, pp. 211–230. Washington D.C.: National Association for the Education of Young Children.

Malone, T., and Lepper, M. (1988). Making learning fun: A taxonomy of intrinsic motivation for learning. In R. Snow and M. Farr (eds.), *Aptitude, learning, and instruction, Vol. III: Cognitive and affective process analysis.* Hillsdale, N.J.: Erlbaum.

Malouf, D.B., Wizer, D.R., Pilato, V.H., and Grogan, M.M. (1990). Computer-assisted instruction with small groups of mildly handicapped students. *Journal of Special Education, 24,* 51–68.

Mandeville, G. (1988, April). *An evaluation of PET using extant achievement test data.* Paper presented at the annual convention of the American Educational Research Association, New Orleans.

Mandeville, G.K., and Rivers, J.L. (1991). The South Carolina PET study: Teachers' perceptions and student achievement. *Elementary School Journal, 91,* 377–407.

Manning, B.H. (1988). Application of cognitive behavior modification: First and third graders' self-management of classroom behaviors. *American Educational Research Journal, 25,* 193–212.

Manning, B.H. (1991). *Cognitive self-instruction of classroom processes.* Albany: SUNY Press.

Manning, M.L., and Boals, B.M. (1987). In defense of play. *Contemporary Education, 58,* 206–210.

Mantzicopoulos, P., and Morrison, D. (1992). Kindergarten retention: Academic and behavioral outcomes through the end of second grade. *American Educational Research Journal, 29*(1), 182–198.

Maple, S.A., and Stage, F.K. (1991). Influences on the choice of math/science major by gender and ethnicity. *American Educational Research Journal, 28*(1), 37–60.

Margolis, H., and Schwartz, E. (1989, January). Facilitating mainstreaming through cooperative learning. *The High School Journal,* 83–88.

Marland, M. (ed.) (1983). *Sex differentiation and schooling.* London: Heinemann.

Marland, S.P. (1972). *Education of the gifted and talented.* Washington, D.C.: U.S. Government Printing Office.

Marliave, R., Fisher, C., and Dishaw, M. (1978). Academic learning time and student achievement in the B–C period. Far West Laboratory for Educational Research and Development, Technical note v-29.

Marsh, H.W. (1986). Self-serving effect (bias?) in academic attributions: Its relation to academic achievement and self-concept. *Journal of Educational Psychology, 78,* 190–200.

Marsh, H.W. (1989). Age and sex effects in multiple dimensions of self-concept: Preadolescence to early adulthood. *Journal of Educational Psychology, 81,* 417–430.

Marsh, H.W. (1990a). The structure of academic self-concept. The Marsh/Shavelson model. *Journal of Educational Psychology, 82*(4), 623–636.

Marsh, H.W. (1990b). Causal ordering of academic self-concept and academic achievement: A multiwave, longitudinal panel analysis. *Journal of Educational Psychology, 82*(4), 646–656.

Marsh, H.W., Craven, R.G., and Debus, R. (1991). Self-concepts of young children 5 to 8 years of age: Measurement and multidimensional structure. *Journal of Educational Psychology, 83*(3), 377–392.

Marshall, H. (1981). Open classroom: Has the term outlived its usefulness? *Review of Educational Research, 51,* 181–192.

Marshall, P.M. (1982) *Homework and social facilitation theory in teaching elementary school mathematics.* Unpublished doctoral dissertation, Stanford University.

Marshall, S.P. (1984). Sex differences in children's mathematics achievement: Solving computations and story problems. *Journal of Educational Psychology, 76,* 194–204.

Martin, G., and Pear, J. (1992). *Behavior modification: What it is and how to do it* (4th ed.). Englewood Cliffs, N.J.: Prentice-Hall.

Martin, J.E., Rusch, F.R., and Heal, L.W. (1982). Teaching community survival skills to mentally retarded adults: A review and analysis. *Journal of Special Education, 16,* 243–267.

Marzano, R.J., and Costa, A.L. (1988). Question: Do standardized tests measure general cognitive skills? Answer: No. *Educational Leadership, 45*(8), 66–73.

Maslow, A.H. (1954). *Motivation and personality.* New York: Harper & Row.

Maslow, A.H. (1968). *Toward a psychology of being* (2nd ed.). New York: Van Nostrand Reinhold.

Mason, J.M., Peterman, C.L., Dunning, D.D., and Stewart, J.P. (1992). Emergent literacy: Alternative models of development and instruction. In M.J. Dreher and W.H. Slater (eds.), *elementary school literacy: Critical issues.* Norwood, MA: Christopher-Gordon.

Masterson, J.F. (1967). *The psychiatric dilemma of adolescence.* Boston: Little, Brown.

Matson, J.L., and Mulick, J.A. (eds.) (1988). *Handbook of mental retardation* (2nd ed.). New York: Pergamon.

Mayer, R.E. (1979). Can advance organizers influence meaningful learning? *Review of Educational Research, 49,* 371–383.

Mayer, R.E. (1984). Twenty-five years of research on advance organizers. *Instructional Science, 8,* 133–169.

Mayer, R.E. (1989). Models for understanding. *Review of Educational Research, 59,* 43–64.

Mayer, R.E., and Anderson, R.B. (1991). Animations need narrations: An experimental test of dual-coding hypothesis. *Journal of Education Psychology, 83*(4), 484–490.

Mayer, R.E., and Gallini, J.K. (1990). When is an illustration worth ten thousand words? *Journal of Educational Psychology, 82,* 715–726.

Mazur, J. (1990). *Learning and behavior* (2nd ed.). Englewood Cliffs, N.J.: Prentice-Hall.

McAfee, O., and Leong, D. (1993). *Assessing and guiding young children's development and learning.* Boston: Allyn & Bacon.

McAllister, L.W., Stachowiak, J.G., Baer, D.M., and Conderman, L. (1969). The application of operant conditioning techniques in a secondary school classroom. *Journal of Applied Behavior Analysis, 2,* 277–285.

McCaleb, J., and White, J. (1980). Critical dimensions in evaluating teacher clarity. *Journal of Classroom Interaction, 15,* 27–30.

McClelland, D. (1985). *Human motivation.* Glenview, Ill.: Scott-Foresman.

McClelland, D.C. (1969). The role of educational technology in developing achievement motivation. *Educational Technology, 9*(10), 7.

McClelland, D.C., and Atkinson, J.W. (1948). The projective expression of needs: II. The effect of different intensities of the hunger drive on thematic apperception. *Journal of Experimental Psychology, 38,* 643–658.

McClelland, D.C., Atkinson, J.W., Clark, R.T., and Lowell, E.L. (1953). *The achievement motive.* New York: Appleton-Century-Crofts.

McCombs, B.L. (1984). Processes and skills underlying continuing motivation to learn: Toward a definition of motivational skills training interventions. *Educational Psychologist, 19,* 199–218.

McCombs, B.L. (1991). Motivation and lifelong learning. *Educational Psychologist, 26*(2), 117–127.

McCormick, C.B., and Levin, J.R. (1984). A comparison of different prose-learning variations of the mnemonic keyword method. *American Educational Research Journal, 21,* 379–398.

McDonald, B.A., Larson, C.D., Dansereau, D.I., and Spurlin, J.E. (1985). Cooperative dyads: Impact on text learning and transfer. *Contemporary Educational Psychology, 10,* 369–377.

McGroarty, M. (1992). The societal context of bilingual education. *Educational Researcher, 21*(2), 7–9.

McKenzie, G. (1979). Effects of questions and testlike events on achievement and on-task behavior in a classroom concept learning presentation. *Journal of Educational Research, 72,* 348–350.

McKenzie, G.R., and Henry, M. (1979). Effects of testlike events on on-task behavior, test anxiety, and achievement in a classroom rule-learning task. *Journal of Educational Psychologist, 71,* 370–374.

McKenzie, M. (1977). The beginnings of literacy. *Theory into Practice, 10,* 315–324.

McKey, R., Condelli, L., Ganson, H., Barrett, B., McConkey, C., and Plantz, M. (1985). *The impact of Head Start on children, families, and communities.* Washington, D.C.: CSR, Inc.

McKinney, J.D., and Speece, D.L. (1986). Academic consequences and longitudinal stability of behavioral subtypes of learning disabled children. *Journal of Educational Psychology, 78,* 365–372.

McPartland, J.M., Coldiron, J.R., and Braddock, J.H. (1987). *School structures and classroom practices in elementary, middle, and secondary schools (Tech. Rep. No. 14).* Baltimore, Md.: Johns Hopkins University, Center for Research on Elementary and Middle Schools.

Medland, M., and Vitale, M. (1984). *Management of classrooms.* New York: Holt, Rinehart, & Winston.

Medley, D.M. (1979). The effectiveness of teachers. In P.L. Peterson and H. Walberg (eds.), *Research on teaching: Concepts, findings, and implications,* pp. 11–27. Berkeley: McCutchan.

Meichenbaum, D. (1977). *Cognitive behavior modification: An integrative approach.* New York: Plenum.

Meichenbaum, D., and Goodman, J. (1971). Training impulsive children to talk to themselves: A means of developing self-control. *Journal of Abnormal Psychology, 77,* 115–126.

Meisels, S., and Steele, D. (1991). *The early childhood portfolio collection process.* Center for Human Growth and Development. Ann Arbor, Mich.: University of Michigan.

Melton, R.F. (1978). Resolution of conflicting claims concerning the effect of behavioral objectives on student learning. *Review of Educational Research, 18,* 291–302.

Menyuk, P. (1982). Language and development. In C.B. Kapp and J.B. Krakow (eds.), *The child: Development in a social context,* pp. 282–331. Reading, Mass.: Addison-Wesley.

Mercer, J.R. (1973). *Labeling the mentally retarded.* Berkeley: University of California Press.

Messick, S. (1982). Issues of effectiveness and equity in the coaching controversy: Implications for educational and testing practice. *Educational Psychologist, 17,*

67–91.

Messick, S. (1984). The nature of cognitive styles: Problems and promise in educational practice. *Educational Psychologist, 19,* 59–74.

Metfessel, N.S., Michael, W.B., and Kirsner, D.A. (1969). Instrumentation of Bloom's and Krathwohl's taxonomies for the writing of educational objectives. *Psychology in the Schools, 6,* 227–231.

Metz, M.H. (1978). *Classrooms and corridors: The crisis of authority in desegregated secondary schools.* Berkeley: University of California Press.

Mevarech, Z.R. (1985). The effects of cooperative mastery learning strategies on mathematics achievement. *Journal of Educational Research, 78,* 372–377.

Meyer, L., Gersten, R.M., and Gutkin, J. (1983). Direct instruction: A project follow-through success story in an inner-city school. *Elementary School Journal, 84,* 241–252.

Meyer, L.A. (1984). Long-term academic effects of the Direct Instruction Project Follow-Through. *Elementary School Journal, 84,* 380–394.

Meyer, L.A. (1987). Strategies for correcting students' wrong answers. *Elementary School Journal, 87,* 227–241.

Meyer, W.J., and Thompson, G.G. (1963). Teacher interaction with boys contrasted with girls. In R.G. Kuhlen and G.G. Thompson (eds.), *Psychological studies of human development.* New York: Appleton-Century-Crofts.

Meyers, J., Gelzheiser, L., Yelich, G., Gallagher, M. (1990). Classroom, remedial and resource teachers' views of pull-out programs. *Elementary School Journal, 90*(5), 531–545.

Mielle, F. (1979). Cultural bias in the WISC. *Intelligence, 3,* 149–164.

Miller, A., and Hom, Jr., H.L. (1990). Influence of extrinsic and ego incentive value on persistence after failure and continuing motivation. *Journal of Educational Psychology, 82*(3), 539–545.

Miller, G.A. (1956). The magical number seven, plus or minus two: Some limits on our capacity for processing information. *Psychological Review, 63,* 81–97.

Miller, G.A., Galanter, E., and Pribram, K.H. (1960). *Plans and the structure of behavior.* New York: Holt, Rinehart, & Winston.

Miller, G.E., Levin, J.R., and Pressley, M. (1980). An adaptation of the keyword method to children's learning of verbs. *Journal of Mental Imagery, 4,* 57–61.

Miller, P.H. (1983). *Theories of developmental psychology.* San Francisco: W.H. Freeman.

Miller, R.L. (1976). Individualized instruction in mathematics: A review of research. *The Mathematics Teacher, 69,* 345–351.

Miller, T.L., and Sabatino, D. (1978). An

evaluation of the teacher-consultant model as an approach to mainstreaming. *Exceptional Children, 45,* 86–91.

Mitchell, B.M. (1984). An update on gifted/talented education in the U.S. *Roeper Review, 6,* 161–163.

Mitchell, J.V. (ed.) (1985). *The ninth mental measurements yearbook.* Lincoln: University of Nebraska, Buros Institute of Mental Measurement.

Mitchell, P., and Erickson, D.K. (1980). The education of gifted and talented children: A status report. *Exceptional Children, 45,* 12–16.

Moles, O. (1984, April). In-school alternatives to suspension: stability and effects. Paper presented at the annual convention of the American Educational Research Association, New Orleans.

Moles, O.C. (1990). *Student discipline strategies: Research and practice.* Albany: State University of New York Press.

Moll, L.C. (ed.) (1990). *Vygotsky and education.* Cambridge, England: Cambridge University Press.

Morgan, M. (1984). Reward-induced decrements and increments in intrinsic motivation. *Review of Educational Research, 54,* 5–30.

Morine-Dershimer, G. (1983). Instructional strategy and the "creation" of classroom status. *American Educational Research Journal, 20,* 645–661.

Morris, C.C., Bransford, J.D., and Franks, J.J. (1977). Levels of processing versus transfer appropriate processing. *Journal of Verbal Learning and Verbal Behavior, 16,* 519–533.

Morris, D., Shaw, B., and Perney, J. (1990). Helping low readers in grades 2 and 3: An after-school volunteer tutoring program. *Elementary School Journal, 91,* 133–150.

Morris, L.G. (1985). *Psychology: An introduction* (5th ed.). Englewood Cliffs, N.J.: Prentice-Hall.

Morrison, D.M. (1985). Adolescent contraceptive behavior: A review. *Psychological Bulletin, 98,* 538–568.

Moshman, D. (1990). Rationality as a goal of education. *Educational Psychology Review, 2*(4), 335–364.

Moss, H.A. (1967). Sex, age, and state as determinants of mother-infant interaction. *Merrill-Palmer Quarterly, 13,* 19–36.

Mullis, I., Dossey, J., Foertsch, M., Jones, L., and Gentile, C. (1991). *Trends in academic progress.* Washington, D.C.: National Center for Education Statistics, U.S. Department of Education.

Murphy, R.T., and Appel, L.R. (1984). *Evaluation of the writing to read instructional system, 1982–1984.* Princeton, N.J.: Educational Testing Service.

Murray, F.B. (1982). Teaching through social conflict. *Contemporary Educational Psychology, 7,* 257–271.

Nafpaktitis, M., Mayer, G.R., and Butterworth, T. (1985). Natural rates of teacher approval and disapproval and their relation to student behavior in intermediate school classrooms. *Journal of Educational Psychology, 77,* 362–367.

Nagy, P., and Griffiths, A.K. (1982). Limitations of recent research relating Piaget's theory to adolescent thought. *Review of Educational Research, 52,* 513–556.

Nakane, M. (1981). *Yodai.* Kyota, Japan: New Teaching Method Research Center, Ryoyo Schools.

Naremore, R.C. (1980). Language disorders in children. In T.J. Hixon, L.D. Shriberg, and J.H. Saxman (eds.), *Introduction to communication disorders.* Englewood Cliffs, N.J.: Prentice-Hall.

Nash, W.R., Borman, C., and Colson, S. (1980). Career education for gifted and talented students: A senior high school model. *Exceptional Children, 46,* 404–405.

National Association for the Education of Young Children (1989). *Appropriate education in the primary grades.* Washington, D.C.: Author.

National Center for Educational Statistics (1988). *Digest of educational statistics.* Washington, D.C.: U.S. Department of Education, NCES.

National Clearinghouse for Drug Abuse Information (1986). *Teen involvement for drug abuse prevention.* Rockville, Md.: NCDAI.

National Commission on Excellence in Education (1983). *A nation at risk.* Washington, D.C.: U.S. Department of Education.

National Institute of Education (1978). *Compensatory education study.* Washington, D.C.: NIE.

National Institute on Drug Abuse, U.S. Department of Health and Human Services. (1987). *National trends in drug use and related factors among American high school students and young adults.* Rockville, Md.: Author.

National Society for the Prevention of Blindness (1966). *Estimated statistics on blindness and vision problems.* New York: NSPB.

National Society for the Prevention of Blindness (1969). *Vision screening in the schools* (Pub. #257). New York: National Society for the Prevention of Blindness.

Natriello, G. (1989). The impact of evaluation processes on students. In R.E. Slavin (ed.), *School and classroom organization,* Hillsdale, N.J.: Erlbaum.

Natriello, G., and Dornbusch, S.M. (1984). *Teacher evaluative standards and student effort.* New York: Longman.

Naveh-Benjamin, M. (1991). A comparison of training programs intended for different types of test-anxious students: Further support for an information-pro-

cessing model. *Journal of Educational Psychology 83,* 134–139.

Neale, D.C., Smith, D., and Johnson, V.G. (1990). Implementing conceptual change teaching in primary science. *Elementary School Journal, 91,* 109–131.

Neill, A.S. (1960). *Summerhill: A radical approach to child rearing.* New York: Hart.

Nettles, S.M. (1991). Community involvement and disadvantaged students: A review. *Review of Educational Research, 61,* 379–406.

Newell, A., and Simon, H. (1972). *Human problem solving.* Englewood Cliffs, N.J.: Prentice-Hall.

Newmann, F.M. and Thompson, J. (1987). *Effects of cooperative learning on achievement in secondary schools: A summary of research.* Madison, Wisc.: University of Wisconsin, National Center on Effective Secondary Schools.

Nicholls, J.G. (1984). Conceptions of ability and achievement motivation. In R. Ames and C. Ames (eds.), *Research on motivation in education,* Vol. 1. New York: Academic Press.

Niemiec, R.P., and Walberg, H.J. (1985). Computers and achievement in the elementary schools. *Journal of Educational Computering Research, 1,* 435–440.

Nimmer, D.M. (1989). Measures of validity, reliability, and item-analysis for classroom tests. In *Annual editions: Educational psychology 89/90* (pp. 204–205). Guilford, Conn.: Duskin.

Nist, S.L., Simpson, M.L., Olejnik, S., and Mealey, D.L. (1991). The relation between self-selected study processes and test performance. *American Educational Research Journal, 28,* 849–874.

Nitsch, K.E. (1977). Structuring decontextualized forms of knowledge. Unpublished doctoral dissertation, Vanderbilt University.

Noddings, N. (1992). Variability: A pernicious hypothesis. *Review of Educational Research, 62,* 85–88.

Noll, V.H., Scannel, D.P., and Craig, R.C. (1979). *Introduction to educational measurement* (4th ed.). Boston: Houghton Mifflin.

Norris, S.P. (1985). Synthesis of research on critical thinking. *Educational Leadership, 42,* 40–45.

Nowicki, S., Duke, M.P., and Crouch, M.P.D. (1978). Sex differences in locus of control and performance under competitive and cooperative conditions. *Journal of Educational Psychology, 70,* 482–486.

Nucci, L. (1987). Synthesis of research on moral development. *Educational Leadership, 44,* 86–92.

Nurss, J.R., and Hodges, W.L. (1982). Early childhood education. In H.E. Mitzel (ed.) *Encyclopedia of Educational Research* (5th ed.), pp. 477–513. New York: Free Press.

Nuthall, G. (1987). Reviewing and recapitulating. In M.J. Dunkin (ed.), *International encyclopedia of teaching and teacher education.* New York: Pergamon.

Oakes, J. (1985). *Keeping track: How schools structure inequality.* New Haven, Conn.: Yale University Press.

Oakes, J. (1989). Tracking in secondary schools: A contextual perspective. In R.E. Slavin (ed.), *School and classroom organization.* Hillsdale, N.J.: Erlbaum.

Oakes, J. (1992). Can tracking research inform practice? Technical, normative, and political considerations. *Educational Researcher, 21*(4), 12–21.

Oakland, T. (ed.) (1977). *Psychological and educational assessment of minority children.* New York: Brunner/Mazel.

Oakley, D.A. (1981). Brain mechanisms of mammalian memory. *British Medical Bulletin, 37,* 175–180.

Oakley, D.A. (1983). The varieties of memory: A phylogenetic approach. In A. Mayes (ed.), *Memory in animals and humans,* pp. 20–82. Woringham, England: Van Nostrand Reinhold.

Oden, S. (1982). Peer relationship development in childhood. In L.G. Katz (ed.), *Current topics in early childhood education,* Vol. 4, pp. 87–117. Norwood, N.J.: Ablex Publishing Corp.

Odle, S.J., and Galtelli, B. (1980). The Individualized Education Program (IEP): Foundation for appropriate and effective instruction. In J.W. Schifani, R.M. Anderson, and S.J. Odle (eds.), *Implementing learning in the least restrictive environment.* Baltimore: University Park Press.

O'Donnell, H. (1982). Computer literacy. II: Classroom applications. *Reading Teacher, 35,* 614–617.

Office of Technology Assessment (1992). *Testing in American schools: Asking the right questions.* Washington, D.C.: U.S. Congress, Office of Technology Assessment.

Ogbu, J. (1987). Variability in school performance: A problem in search of an explanation. *Anthropology and Education Quarterly, 18,* 312–334.

Oishi, S., Slavin, R.E., and Madden, N.A. (1983, April). Effects of student teams and individualized instruction on cross-race and cross-sex friendships. Paper presented at the annual meeting of the American Educational Research Association, Montreal.

O'Leary, K.D. (1980). Pills or skills for hyperactive children. *Journal of Applied Behavior Analysis, 13,* 191–204.

O'Leary, K.D., and Becker, W.C. (1967). The effects of the intensity of a teacher's reprimands on children's behavior. *Journal of School Psychology, 7,* 8–11.

O'Leary, K.D., Kaufman, K.F., Kass, R.E., and Drabman, R.S. (1970). The effects of loud and soft reprimands on the behavior of disruptive students. *Exceptional Children, 37,* 145–155.

O'Leary, K.D., and O'Leary, S.G. (1972). *Classroom management: The successful use of behavior modification.* New York: Pergamon.

O'Leary, K.D., and O'Leary, S.G. (eds.) (1977). *Classroom management: The successful use of behavior modification* (2nd ed.), New York: Pergamon.

Olson, D.R., and Pau, A.S. (1966). Emotionally loaded words and the acquisition of a sight vocabulary. *Journal of Educational Psychology, 57,* 174–178.

O'Neil, J. (1991). A generation adrift? *Educational Leadership, 49*(1), 4–10.

Orlick, T. (1978). *Winning through cooperation.* Washington, D.C.: Acropolis Books.

Ormell, C.P. (1979). The problem of analyzing understanding. *Educational Research, 22,* 32–38.

Osborn, A.F. (1963). *Applied imagination* (3rd ed.). New York: Scribner's.

Osborn, J.D., and Osborn, P.K. (1983). *Cognition in early childhood.* Athens, Ga.: Education Associates.

Osguthorpe, R.T. (1984). Handicapped students as tutors for nonhandicapped peers. *Academic Therapy, 19,* 473–483.

Osguthorpe, R.T., and Scruggs, T.E. (1986). Special education students as tutors: A review and analysis. *Remedial and Special Education, 7*(4), 15–25.

O'Shea, T., and Self, J. (1983). *Learning and teaching with computers: Artificial intelligence in education.* Englewood Cliffs, N.J.: Prentice-Hall.

Ottenbacher, K.J., and Cooper, H.M. (1983). Drug treatment of hyperactivity in children. *Developmental Medicine and Child Neurology, 25,* 358–366.

Overton, W.F. (1984). World views and their influence on psychological theory and research. In H.W. Reese (ed.), *Advances in child development and behavior.* New York: Academic Press.

Owen, S.L., Froman, R.D., and Moscow, H. (1981). *Educational psychology* (2nd ed.). Boston: Little, Brown.

Paivio, A. (1971). *Imagery and verbal processes.* New York: Holt.

Palincsar, A.S. (1984, April). Reciprocal teaching: Working within the zone of proximal development. Paper presented at the annual convention of the American Educational Research Association, New Orleans.

Palincsar, A.S. (1986a). The role of dialogue in providing scaffolded instruction. *Educational Psychologist, 21,* 73–98.

Palincsar, A.S. (1986b). *Reciprocal teaching teacher's manual.* East Lansing: Michigan State University, Institute for Research on Teaching.

Palincsar, A.S. (1987, April). Reciprocal teaching: Field evaluations in remedial and content-area reading. Paper presented at the annual convention of the American Educational Research Association, Washington, D.C.

Palincsar, A.S., and Brown, A.L. (1984). Reciprocal teaching of comprehension fostering and comprehension monitoring activities. *Cognition and Instruction, 2,* 117–175.

Palincsar, A.S., Brown, A.L, and Martin, S.M. (1987). Peer interaction in reading comprehension instruction. *Educational Psychologist, 22,* 231–253.

Palumbo, D.B. (1990). Programming language/problem-solving research: A review of relevant issues. *Review of Educational Research, 60*(1), 65–89.

Papert, S. (1980). *Mindstorms: Children, computers, and powerful ideas.* New York: Basic Books.

Paris, S., Cross, D., and Lipson, M. (1984). Informal strategies for learning: A program to improve children's reading awareness and comprehension. *Journal of Educational Psychology, 76,* 1239–1252.

Paris, S.G., Wixson, K.K., and Palincsar, A. (1986). Instructional approaches to reading comprehension. In E.Z. Rothkopf (ed.), *Review of research in education,* Vol. 13, pp. 91–128. Washington, D.C.: American Educational Research Association.

Parke, B.N. (1983). Use of self-instructional materials with gifted primary aged students. *Gifted Child Quarterly, 27,* 29–34.

Parsons, J., Adler, T., and Kaczala, C. (1982). Socialization of achievement attitudes and beliefs: Parental influences. *Child Development, 53,* 310–339.

Passow, A.H. (ed.) (1979). *The gifted and talented: Their education and development.* Chicago: University of Chicago Press.

Pavan, B.N. (1992). The benefits of nongraded schools. *Educational Leadership, 50*(2), 22–25.

Pea, R.D., and Kurland, D.M. (1984). *Logo programming and the development of planning skills.* (Tech. Rep. No. 16). New York: Bank Street College of Education, Center for Children and Technology.

Peckham, P.D., and Roe, M.D. (1977). The effects of frequent testing. *Journal of Research and Development in Education, 10,* 40–50.

Penfield, W. (1969). Consciousness, memory, and man's conditioned reflexes. In K.H. Pribram (ed.), *On the biology of learning.* New York: Harcourt Brace Jovanovich.

Pepitone, E.A. (1980). *Children in cooperation and competition: Toward a developmental social psychology.* Lexington, Mass.: D.C. Heath.

Pepitone, E.A. (1985). Children in cooperation and competition: Antecedents and consequences of self-orientation. In R.E. Slavin, S. Sharan, S. Kagan, R. Hertz-Lazarowitz, C. Webb, and R. Schmuck

(eds.). *Learning to cooperate, cooperating to learn.* New York: Plenum.

Perfetto, G.A., Bransford, J.D., and Franks, J.J. (1983). Constraints on access in a problem solving context. *Memory and Cognition, 11,* 24–31.

Perkins, D.N., and Salomon, G. (1988). Teaching for transfer. *Educational Leadership, 46*(1), 22–32.

Perkins, D.N., and Salomon, G. (1989). Are cognitive skills context-bound? *Educational Researcher, 18,* 16–25.

Perkins, W.H. (1980). Disorders of speech flow. In T.J. Hixon, L.D. Shriberg, and J.H. Saxman (eds.), *Introduction to communication disorders.* Englewood Cliffs, N.J.: Prentice-Hall.

Perl, E., and Lambert, W.E. (1962). The relation of bilingualism to intelligence. *Psychological Monographs, 76,* 1–23.

Peskin, H. (1967). Pubertal onset and ego functioning. *Journal of Abnormal Psychology, 72,* 1–15.

Peters, E.E., Levin, J.R., McGivern, J.E., and Pressley, M. (1985). Further comparison of representational and transformational prose-learning imagery. *Journal of Educational Psychology, 77,* 129–136.

Peterson, L.R., and Peterson, M.J. (1959). Short-term retention of individual verbal items. *Journal of Experimental Psychology, 58,* 193–198.

Peterson, P.L. (1979). Direct instruction reconsidered. In P. Peterson and H. Walberg (eds.), *Research on teaching: Concepts, findings, and implications,* pp. 57–69. Berkeley: McCutchan.

Peterson, P.L., and Fennema, E. (1985). Effective teaching, student engagement in classroom activities, and sex-related differences in learning mathematics. *American Educational Research Journal, 22,* 309–335.

Petrie, C.R. (1963). Informative speaking: A summary and bibliography of related research. *Speech Monography, 30,* 79–91.

Petty, M.F., and Field, C.J. (1980). Fluctuations in mental test scores. *Educational Research, 22,* 198–202.

Peverly, S.T. (1991). Problems with the knowledge-based explanation of memory and development. *Review of Educational Research, 61*(1), 71–93.

Pfiffer, L., Rosen, L., and O'Leary, S. (1985). The efficacy of an all positive approach to classroom management. *Journal of Applied Behavior Analysis, 18,* 257–261.

Phillips, B., Pitcher, G., Worsham, M., and Miller, S. (1980). Test anxiety and the school environment. In I. Sarason (ed.), *Test anxiety: Theory, research, and applications.* Hillsdale, N.J.: Erlbaum.

Phillips, J.L. (1975). *The origins of intellect: Piaget's theory* (2nd ed.). San Francisco: W.H. Freeman.

Piaget, J. (1932). *The moral judgment of the child.* Glencoe, Ill.: Free Press.

Piaget, J. (1952a). *The language and thought of the child*. London: Routledge and Kegan-Paul.

Piaget, J. (1952b). *The origins of intelligence in children*. New York: Basic Books.

Piaget, J. (1962). *Play dreams and imitation in childhood*. New York: Norton.

Piaget, J. (1964). *The moral judgment of the child*. New York: Free Press.

Piaget, J. (1972). Intellectual evolution from adolescence to adulthood. *Human Development, 15*, 1–12.

Piaget, J. (1973). *The psychology of intelligence*. Totowa, N.J.: Littlefield, Adams.

Piaget, J., and Inhelder, B. (1956). *The child's conception of space*. Boston: Routledge and Kegan Paul.

Piaget, J., and Inhelder, B. (1969). *The psychology of the child*. New York: Basic Books.

Piaget, J., and Inhelder, B. (1973). *Memory and intelligence*. New York: Basic Books.

Pine, G.J., and Hilliard, A.G. (1990). Rx for racism: Imperatives for America's schools. *Phi Delta Kappan, 71*(8), 593–600.

Pinnell, G.S. (1989). Reading Recovery: Helping at-risk children learn to read. *Elementary School Journal, 90*, 161–182.

Pinnell, G.S. (1990). Success for low achievers through Reading Recovery. *Educational Leadership, 48*(1), 17–21.

Pinnell, G.S., DeFord, D.E., and Lyons, C.A. (1988). *Reading Recovery: Early intervention for at-risk first graders*. Arlington, Va.: Educational Research Service.

Pintrich, P.R., and Blumenfeld, P. (1985). Classroom experience and children's self-perceptions of ability, effort, and conduct. *Journal of Educational Psychology, 77*, 646–657.

Pittman, T.S., Boggiano, A.K., and Ruble, D.N. (1983). Intrinsic and extrinsic motivational orientations: Limiting conditions on the undermining and enhancing effects of reward on intrinsic motivation. In J.M. Levine and M.C. Wang (eds.), *Teacher and student perceptions: Implications for learning*, pp. 319–340. Hillsdale, N.J.: Erlbaum.

Play (1982, December). Play: Practical applications of research. Newsletter of Phi Delta Kappa's Center on Evaluation, Development and Research, Bloomington, Ill.

Plumb, J.H. (1974). The great change in children. In S. Coopersmith and L. Feldman (eds.), *The formative years: Principles of early childhood education*, pp. 28–37. San Francisco: Albion Publishing Co.

Poest, C.A., Williams, J.R., Witt, D.D., and Atwood, M.R. (1990). Challenge me to move: Large muscle development in young children. *Young Children, 45*(5) 4–10.

Polloway, E.A., Cronin, M.E., and Patton, J.R. (1986). The efficiency of group versus one-to-one instruction. *Remedial and Special Education, 7*, 22–30.

Polya, G. (1957). *How to solve it* (2nd ed.). New York: Doubleday.

Popham, W.J. (1981). *Modern educational measurement*. Englewood Cliffs, N.J.: Prentice-Hall.

Popham, W.J. (1988). *Educational evaluation* (2nd ed.). Englewood Cliffs, N.J.: Prentice-Hall.

Porter, A.C., and Brophy, J.E. (1988). Synthesis of research on good teaching: Insights from the work of the Institute for Research on Teaching. *Educational Leadership, 45*, 74–85.

Postman, L., and Underwood, B.J. (1973). Critical issues in interference theory. *Memory and Cognition, 1*, 19–40.

Postman, N. (1982). *The disappearance of childhood*. New York: Delacorte Press.

Potter, E.F. (1977, April). Children's expectancy of criticism for classroom achievement efforts. Paper presented at the annual convention of the American Educational Research Association, New York.

Powers, S.I., Hauser, S.T., and Kilner, L.A. (1989). Adolescent mental health. *American Psychologist, 44*, 200–208.

Prawat, R.S. (1991). The value of ideas: The immersion approach to the development of thinking. *Educational Researcher, 20*(2), 3–10, 30.

Premack, D. (1965). Reinforcement theory. In D. Levine (ed.), *Nebraska symposium on motivation*. Lincoln, Neb.: University of Nebraska Press.

Presseisen, B.Z. (ed.) (1988). *At-risk students and thinking*. Washington, D.C.: National Education Association.

Pressley, M. (1979). Increasing children's self-control through cognitive interventions. *Review of Educational Research, 49*, 319–370.

Pressley, M. (1991). Comparing Hall (1988) with related research on elaborative mnemonics. *Journal of Educational Psychology, 83*(1), 165–170.

Pressley, M., Goodchild, F., Fleet, J., Zajchowski, R., and Evans, E.D. (1989). The challenges of classroom strategy instruction. *Elementary School Journal, 89*, 301–342.

Pressley, M., and Harris, K.R. (1990). What we really know about strategy instruction. *Educational Leadership, 48*(1), 31–34.

Pressley, M., Harris, K.R., and Marks, M.B. (1992a). But good strategy instructors are constructivists! *Educational Psychology Review, 4*, 3–31.

Pressley, M., and Levin, J.R. (1978). Developmental constraints associated with children's use of the keyword method of foreign language vocabulary learning. *Journal of Experimental Child Psychology, 26*, 359–372.

Pressley, M., and Levin, J.R. (eds.) (1983). *Cognitive strategy research: Educational applications*. New York: Springer-Verlag.

Pressley, M., Levin, J.R., and Delaney, H. (1982). The mnemonic keyword method. *Review of Educational Research, 52*, 61–92.

Pressley, M., Tannenbaum, R., McDaniel, M.A., and Wood, E. (1990). What happens when university students try to answer prequestions that accompany textbook material? *Contemporary Educational Psychology, 15*, 27–35.

Pressley, M., Woloshyn, V., Lysynchuk, L.M., Martin, V., Wood, E., and Willoughby, T. (1990). A primer of research on cognitive strategy instruction: The important issues and how to address them. *Educational Psychology Review, 2*, 1–58.

Pressley, M., Wood, E., Woloshyn, V.E., Martin, V., King, A., and Menke, D. (1992b). Encouraging mindful use of prior knowledge: Attempting to construct explanatory answers facilitates learning. *Educational Psychologist, 27*, 91–109.

Price, G.G. (1982). Cognitive learning in early childhood education: Mathematics, science, and social studies. In B. Spodek (ed.), *Handbook of research in early childhood education*, pp. 264–294. New York: The Free Press.

Quay, H., and Werry, J. (eds.) (1979). *Psychopathological disorders of children* (2nd ed.). New York: Wiley.

Quay, H.C., and Werry, J.S. (eds.) (1986). *Psychopathological disorders of childhood* (3rd ed.). New York: Wiley.

Raffini, J.P. (1986). Student apathy: A motivational dilemma. *Educational Leadership, 44* (1), 53–55.

Rafoth, M.A., Leal, L., and De Fabo, L. (1993). *Strategies for learning and remembering: Study skills across the curriculum*. Washington, D.C.: National Education Association Professional Library.

Ramey, C.T., and Campbell, F.A. (1984). Preventive education for high-risk children: Cognitive consequences of the Carolina Abecedarian Project. *American Journal of Mental Deficiency, 88*, 515–523.

Ramey, C.T., and Ramey, S.L. (1992). *At risk does not mean doomed*. Birmingham, Ala.: Civitan International Research Center, University of Alabama.

Ramirez, J.D. (1986). Comparing structured English immersion and bilingual education: First-year results of a national study. *American Journal of Education, 95*, 122–148.

Rappaport, M.D., Murphy, M.A., and Bailey, J.E. (1982). Ritalin vs. response cost in the control of hyperactive children. A within-subject comparison. *Journal of Applied Behavior Analysis, 5*, 205–216.

Raudenbush, S.W. (1984). Magnitude of

teacher expectancy effects on pupil IQ as a function of the credibility of expectancy induction: A synthesis of finds from 18 experiments. *Journal of Educational Psychology, 76,* 85–97.

Read, C. (1975). Lessons to be learned from the preschool orthographer. In E.H. Lennenberg and E. Lennenberg (eds.), *Foundations of language development,* pp. 329–346. New York: Academic Press.

Reder, L.M. (1980). The role of elaboration in the comprehension and retention of prose. *Review of Educational Research 50,* 5–54.

Redfield, D.L., and Rousseau, E.W. (1981). A meta-analysis of experimental research on teacher questioning behavior. *Review of Educational Research, 51,* 237–245.

Reigeluth, C.M. (ed.) (1983). *Instructional design theories and models: An overview of their current status.* Hillsdale, N.J.: Erlbaum.

Reiss, S., and Cellerino, M. (1983). Guiding gifted students through independent study. *Teaching Exceptional Children, 15,* 136–139.

Rekrut, M.D. (1992, April). *Teaching to learn: Cross-age tutoring to enhance strategy acquisition.* Paper presented at the annual meeting of the American Educational Research Association, San Francisco.

Renzulli, J.S. (1977). *The enrichment trial model: A guide for developing defensible programs for the gifted and talented.* Wethersfield, Conn.: Creative Learning Press.

Renzulli, J.S. (1978). What makes giftedness? Re-examining a definition. *Phi Delta Kappan, 60*(3), 180–184, 261.

Renzulli, J.S. (ed.) (1986). *Systems and models for developing programs for the gifted and talented.* Mansfield Center, Conn.: Creative Learning Press.

Reynolds, A.J. (1991). Early schooling of children at risk. *American Educational Research Journal, 28*(2), 392–422.

Rhodes, L.K. (1977). Predictable books: An instructional resource for meaningful reading and writing. In D. Strickland (ed.), *The affective dimension of reading,* pp. 195–202. Bloomington: Indiana University Press.

Richardson, F., and Woolfolk, R. (1980). Mathematics anxiety. In I. Sarason (ed.), *Test anxiety: theory, research, and applications.* Hillsdale, N.J.: Erlbaum.

Richer, S. (1977). *The kindergarten as a setting for sex-role socialization.* Ottawa: Carlton University, Department of Sociology, unpublished paper.

Rickards, J.P. (1979). Adjunct postquestions in text: A critical review of methods and processes. *Review of Educational Research, 49,* 181–196.

Rist, R. (1970). Student social class and teacher expectations: The self-fulfilling prophecy in ghetto education. *Harvard Educational Review, 40,* 411–451.

Rist, R.C. (1978). *The invisible children: School integration in American society.* Cambridge, Mass.: Harvard University Press.

Robins, L.N. (1974). Antisocial behavior disturbances of childhood: Prevalence, prognosis, and prospects. In E.J. Anthony and C. Koupernik (eds.), *The child in his family: Children at psychiatric risk.* New York: Wiley.

Robinson, F.P. (1961). *Effective study.* New York: Harper & Row.

Robinson, N., and Robinson, H. (1976). *The mentally retarded child* (2nd ed.). New York: McGraw-Hill.

Roblyer, M.D., Castine, W.H., and King, F.J. (1988). *Assessing the impact of computer-based instruction.* New York: Haworth.

Rocklin, T. (1987). Defining learning: Two classroom examples. *Teaching of Psychology, 14,* 228–229.

Roeber, E., and Dutcher, P. (1989). Michigan's innovative assessment of reading. *Educational Leadership 46*(7), 64–69.

Rogers, C. (1969) *Freedom to learn.* Columbus, Ohio: Charles E. Merrill.

Rogow, S.M. (1988). *Helping the visually impaired child with developmental problems: Effective practice in home, school, and community.* New York: Teachers College Press.

Rohrkemper, M.M. (1984). The influence of teacher socialization style on students' social cognition and reported interpersonal classroom behavior. *Elementary School Journal, 85,* 245–275.

Rohrkemper, M.M., and Bershon, B.L. (1984). Elementary school students' reports of the causes and effects of problem difficulty in mathematics. *Elementary School Journal, 85,* 127–147.

Rosaen, C. (1990). Improving writing opportunities in elementary classrooms. *Elementary School Journal, 90,* 419–434.

Rose, B.C. (1980). Child abuse and the educator. *Focus on exceptional children, 12*(9), 1–13.

Rose, T.L. (1984). Current uses of corporal punishment in American public schools. *Journal of Educational Psychology, 76,* 427–441.

Rosenbaum, J. (1980). Social implications of educational grouping. *Review of Research in Education, 8,* 361–401.

Rosenbaum, M.S., and Drabman, R.S. (1982). Self-control training in the classroom: A review and critique. *Journal of Applied Behavior Analysis, 12, 467–485, 264,* 266.

Rosenblatt, D.B. (1982). Play. In M. Rutter (ed.), *Scientific foundations of developmental psychiatry.* Baltimore: University Park Press.

Rosenfield, D., Folger, R., and Adelman, H.F. (1980). When rewards reflect competence: A qualification of the overjustification effect. *Journal of Personality and Social Psychology, 39,* 368–376.

Rosenholtz, S.J., and Simpson, C. (1984). The formation of ability conceptions: Developmental trend or social construction? *Review of Educational Research, 54,* 31–63.

Rosenholtz, S.J., and Wilson, B. (1980). The effects of classroom structure on shared perceptions of ability. *American Educational Research Journal, 17,* 175–182.

Rosenshine, B. (1971). Objectively measured behavioral predictors of effectiveness in explaining. In I.D. Westburg and A.A. Bellack (eds.), *Research in classroom processes.* New York: Teachers College Press.

Rosenshine, B. (1979). The third cycle of research on teacher effects: Content covered, academic engaged time, and direct instruction. In P.L. Peterson and H.L. Walberg (eds.), *Research on teaching: Concepts, findings, and implications.* Berkeley, Calif.: McCutchan.

Rosenshine, B. (1982, April). The master teacher and the master developer. Paper presented at the annual convention of the American Educational Research Association, New York.

Rosenshine, B., and Chapman, S. (1992, April). *Teaching students to generate questions: A review of research on the effectiveness of different concrete prompts.* Paper presented at the annual meeting of the American Educational Research Association, San Francisco.

Rosenshine, B., and Meister, C. (1991, April). *Reciprocal teaching: A review of nineteen experimental studies.* Paper presented at the annual meeting of the American Educational Research Association, Chicago.

Rosenshine, B., and Meister, C. (1992). The use of scaffolds for teaching higher-level cognitive strategies. *Educational Leadership, 49*(7), 26–33.

Rosenshine, B.V. (1980). How time is spent in elementary classrooms. In C. Denham and A. Lieberman (eds.), *Time to learn.* Washington, D.C.: National Institute of Education.

Rosenshine, B.V. (1986). Synthesis of research on explicit teaching. *Educational Leadership, 43*(7), 60–69.

Rosenshine, B.V., and Stevens, R.J. (1986). Teaching functions. In M.C. Wittrock (ed.), *Third handbook of research on teaching.* Chicago: Rand McNally.

Rosenthal, R., and Jacobson, L. (1968). *Pygmalion in the classroom.* New York: Holt, Rinehart, & Winston.

Rossell, C.H. (1983). Desegregation plans, racial isolation, white flight, and community response. In C.H. Rossell and W.D. Hawley (eds.), *The consequence of school desegregation.* Philadelphia: Temple University Press.

Rothenberg, J. (1989). The open classroom reconsidered. *Elementary School Journal, 90,* 68–86.

Rothkopf, E.Z. (1970). The concept of mathemagenic activities. *Review of Educational Research, 40,* 325–326.

Rothrock, D. (1982). The rise and decline of individualized instruction. *Educational Leadership, 39,* 528–531.

Rotter, J. (1954). *Social learning and clinical psychology.* Englewood Cliffs, N.J.: Prentice Hall.

Rowan, B., and Miracle, A. (1983). Systems of ability grouping and the stratification of achievement in elementary schools. *Sociology of Education, 56,* 133–144.

Rowe, M.B. (1974). Wait time and rewards as instructional variables, their influence on language, logic, and fate control. I: Wait time. *Journal of Research in Science Teaching, 11,* 81–94.

Royer, J.M., and Feldman, R.S. (1984). *Educational psychology: Applications and theory.* New York: Alfred A. Knopf.

Rubin, D.C. (1985). Flashbulb memories. *Psychology Today,* September, 63–68.

Rubin, J.H., and Everett, B. (1982). Social perspective-taking in young children. In S.G. Moore and C.R. Cooper (eds.), *The young child: Reviews of research,* Vol. 3, pp. 97–114. Washington, D.C.: The National Association for the Education of Young Children.

Rubin, Z. (1980). *Children's friendships.* Cambridge, Mass.: Harvard University Press.

Ruiz, C.J. (1985). *Effects of Feuerstein instructional enrichment program on pre-college students.* Guayana, Venezuela: University of Guayana.

Rumelhart, D.E., and Ortony, A. (1977). The representation of knowledge in memory. In R.C. Anderson, R.J. Spiro, and W.E. Montague (eds.), *Schooling and the acquisition of knowledge,* pp. 99–135. Hillsdale, N.J.: Erlbaum.

Rundus, D., and Atkinson, R.C. (1970). Rehearsal processes in free recall: A procedure for direct observation. *Journal of Verbal Learning and Verbal Behavior, 9,* 99–105.

Runge, A., Walker, J., and Shea, T.M. (1975). A passport to positive parent-teacher communications. *Teaching Exceptional Children, 7,* 91–92.

Russell, R.G., (1991, April). *A meta-analysis of word processing and attitudes and the impact on the quality of writing.* Paper presented at the annual meeting of the American Educational Research Association, Chicago.

Ryan, R., and Stiller, J. (1991). The social contexts of internalization: Parent and teacher influences on autonomy motivation, and learning. In P. Pintrich and M. Maehr (eds.), *Advances in Motivation*

and Achievement, Vol. 7 (pp. 115–149). Greenwich, Conn.: JAI Press.

Sabers, D.S., Cushing, K.S., and Berliner, D.C. (1991). Differences among teachers in a task characterized by simultaneity, multidimensionality, and immediacy. *American Educational Research Journal, 28,* 68–87.

Sadker, M., and Sadker, D. (1985, March). Sexism in the schoolroom of the '80s. *Psychology Today, 19,* 54–57.

Sadker, M., Sadker, D., and Steindam, S. (1989). Gender equity and educational reform. *Educational Leadership, 46*(6), 44–47.

Sadker, M.P., and Sadker, D.M. (1982). *Sex equity handbook for schools.* New York: Longman.

Safer, D.J. (1982). *School programs for disruptive adolescents.* Baltimore, Md.: University Park Press.

Safer, D.J., Heaton, R.C., and Parker, F.C. (1981). A behavioral program for disruptive junior high school students: Results and follow-up. *Journal of Abnormal Child Psychology, 9,* 483–494.

Sailor, W. (1991). Special education in the restructured school. *Remedial and Special Education, 12*(6), 8–22.

Salganik, M.W. (1980, January 27). Teachers busy teaching make city's 16 "best" schools stand out. *Baltimore Sun,* p. A4.

Salomon, G., and Gardner, H. (1986). The computer as educator: Lessons from television research. *Educational Researcher, 15,* 13–19.

Salomon, G., and Perkins, D.N. (1989). Rocky roads to transfer: Rethinking mechanisms of a neglected phenomenon. *Educational Psychologist, 24,* 113–142.

Salomon, G., Perkins, D.N., and Globerson, T. (1991). Partners in cognition: Extending human intelligence with intelligent technologies. *Educational Researchers, 20*(3), 2–9.

Sameroff, A. (1975). Early influences on development: Fact or fancy. *Merrill-Palmer Quarterly, 21,* 267–294.

Samson, G.E., Strykowski, B., Weinstein, T., and Walberg, H.J. (1987). The effects of teacher questioning levels on student achievement: A quantitative synthesis. *Journal of Educational Research, 80,* 290–295.

Samuels, S.J. (1981). Some essentials of decoding. *Exceptional Education Quarterly, 2,* 11–25.

Sanford, J.P., and Evertson, C.M. (1981). Classroom management in a low SES junior high: Three case studies. *Journal of Teacher Education, 32,* 34–38.

Sarnacki, R.E. (1979). An examination of test-wiseness in the cognitive test domain. *Review of Educational Research, 49,* 252–279.

Sater, G.M., and French, D.C. (1989). A comparison of the social competencies of

learning disabled and low achieving elementary-aged children. *Journal of Special Education, 23,* 29–42.

Savell, J.M., Twohig, P.T., and Rachford, D.L. (1986). Empirical status of Feuerstein's "Instrumental Enrichment" (FIE) technique as a method of teaching thinking skills. *Review of Educational Research, 56,* 381–409.

Scarr, S. (1981). *Race, social class, and individual differences in I.Q.* Hillsdale, N.J.: Erlbaum.

Scarr, S., and McCartney, K. (1983). How people make their own environments: A theory of genotype-environmental effects. *Child Development, 54,* 424–435.

Scarr, S., and Weinberg, R.A. (1976). I.Q. Test performances of black children adopted by white families. *American Psychology, 31,* 726–739.

Scarr, S., and Weinberg, R.A. (1986). The early childhood enterprise: Care and education of the young. *American Psychologist, 41,* 1140–1146.

Schafer, W.E., and Olexa, C. (1971). *Tracking and opportunity.* Scranton, Pa.: Chandler.

Schallert, D.L. (1976). Improving memory for prose: The relationship between depth of processing and context. *Journal of Verbal Learning and Verbal Behavior, 15,* 621–632.

Scheuneman, J.D. (1984). A theoretical framework for the exploration of causes and effects of bias in testing. *Educational Psychologist, 19,* 219–225.

Schickedanz, J.A. (1978). "Please read that story again!" Exploring relationships between story reading and learning to read. *Young Children, 33,* 48–55.

Schickedanz, J.A. (1981). "Hey! This book's not working right." *Young Children, 37,* 18–27.

Schickedanz, J.A. (1982). The acquisition of written language in young children. In B. Spodek (ed.), *Handbook of research in early childhood education,* pp. 242–263. New York: Free Press.

Schickedanz, J.A., Schickedanz, D.I., and Forsyth, P.D. (1982). *Toward understanding children.* Boston: Little, Brown.

Schif, M., Duyme, M., Dumaret, A., and Tomkiewicz, S. (1982). How much could we boost scholastic achievement and IQ scores? A direct answer from a French adoption study. *Cognition, 12,* 165–196.

Schifani, J.W., Anderson, R.M., and Odle, S.J. (eds.) (1980). *Implementing learning in the least restrictive environment.* Baltimore, Md.: University Park Press.

Schmuck, R.A. and Schmuck, P.A. (1971). *Group processes in the classroom.* Dubuque, Iowa: Wm. C. Brown.

Schneider, W., and Pressley, M. (1989). *Memory development between 2 and 20.* New York: Springer-Verlag.

Schoen, H.L. (1976). Self-paced mathematics instruction: How effective has it been?

Arithmetic Teacher, 23, 90–96.

Schunk, D.H. (1981). Modeling and attributional effects on children's achievement: A self-efficacy analysis. *Journal of Educational Psychology, 73,* 93–105.

Schunk, D.H. (1982). Effects of effort attributional feedback on children's perceived self-efficacy and achievement. *Journal of Educational Psychology, 74,* 548–556.

Schunk, D.H. (1983). Reward contingencies, and the development of children's skills and self-efficacy. *Journal of Educational Psychology, 75,* 511–518.

Schunk, D.H. (1990). Introduction to the special section on motivation and efficacy. *Journal of Educational Psychology, 82,* 1–6.

Schwartz, B., and Reisberg, D. (1991). *Learning and memory.* New York: Norton.

Schwartz, J.I. (1981). Children's experiments with language. *Young Children, 36,* 16–26.

Science Research Associates, Inc. (1972). *Using test results: A teacher's guide.* Chicago: Science Research Associates, Inc.

Scott-Jones, D. (1984). Family influences on cognitive development and school achievement. In E. Gordon (ed.), *Review of research in education* (Vol. 11, pp. 259–304). Washington, D.C.: American Educational Research Association.

Scruggs, T.E., and Richter, L. (1986). Tutoring learning disabled students: A critical review. *Learning Disability Quarterly, 9,* 2–14.

Scruggs, T.E., White, K.R., and Bennion, K. (1986). Teaching test-taking skills to elementary-grade students: A meta-analysis. *Elementary School Journal, 87,* 69–82.

Seddon, G.M. (1978). The properties of Bloom's taxonomy of educational objectives for the cognitive domain. *Review of Educational Research, 48,* 303–323.

Seligman, M.E.P. (1975). *Helplessness: On depression, development, and death.* San Francisco: Freeman.

Seligman, M.E.P. (1981). A learned helplessness point of view. In L.P. Rehm (ed.), *Behavior therapy for depression: Present status and future directions,* pp. 123–141. New York: Academic Press.

Selman, R.L. (1981). The child as a friendship philosopher. In S.R. Asher and J.M. Gottman (eds.), *The development of children's friendships,* pp. 242–272. Cambridge, England: Cambridge University Press.

Selman, R.L., and Selman, A.P. (1979). Children's ideas about friendship: A new theory. *Psychology Today, 13,* 71–72, 74, 79–80, 114.

Sharan, S. (1980). Cooperative learning in small groups: Recent methods and effects on achievement, attitudes, and ethnic relations. *Review of Educational Research, 50,* 241–249.

Sharan, S., Kussell, P., Hertz-Lazarowitz, R., Bejarano, Y., Raviv, S., and Sharan, Y. (1984). *Cooperative learning in the classroom: Research in desegregated schools.* Hillsdale, N.J.: Erlbaum.

Sharan, S., and Shachar, C. (1988). *Language and learning in the cooperative classroom.* New York: Springer.

Sharan, S., and Sharan, Y. (1976). *Small-group teaching.* Englewood Cliffs, N.J.: Educational Technology Publications.

Sharan, Y., and Sharan, S. (1989/90). Group investigation expands cooperative learning. *Educational Leadership, 47*(4), 17–21.

Sharan, Y., and Sharan, S. (1992). *Group investigation: Expanding cooperative learning.* New York: Teacher's College Press.

Shavelson, R.J. (1987). Planning. In M. Dunkin (ed.), *The international encyclopedia of teaching and teacher education* (pp. 483–486). New York: Pergamon.

Shavelson, R.J., Baxter, G.P., and Pine, J. (1992). Performance assessments: Political rhetoric and measurement reality. *Educational Researcher, 21*(4), 22–27.

Shaywitz, S.E., and Shaywitz, B.A. (1988). Attention deficit disorder: Current perspectives. In J.F. Kavanagh and T.J. Truss (eds.), *Learning disabilities: Proceedings of the National Conference.* Parkton, Md.: York.

Shepard, L.A. (1989a). Norm-referenced vs. criterion-referenced tests. In *Annual editions: Educational psychology 89/90,* (pp. 198–203). Guilford, Conn.: Duskin.

Shepard, L.A. (1989b). Why we need better assessments. *Educational Leadership, 46*(7), 4–9.

Shepard, L.A. (1991). The influence of standardized tests on early childhood curriculum, teachers, and children. In B. Spodek and O.N. Saracho (eds.), *Yearbook in early childhood education.* New York: Teachers College Press.

Shepard, L.A., and Smith, M.L. (1986). Synthesis of research on school readiness and kindergarten retention. *Educational Leadership, 44,* 78–86.

Shiffrin, R.M., and Schneider, W. (1977). Controlled and automatic human information processing: Perceptual learning, automatic attending, and a general theory. *Psychological Review, 84,* 127–190.

Shimmerlik, S.M. (1978). Organization theory and memory for prose: A review of the literature. *Review of Educational Research, 48,* 103–120.

Shimmerlik, S.M., and Nolan, J.D. (1976). Organization and the recall of prose. *Journal of Educational Psychology, 68,* 779–786.

Shirey, L.L., and Reynolds, R.E. (1988). Effect of interest on attention and learning. *Journal of Educational Psychology, 80,* 159–166.

Shriberg, L.D. (1980). Developmental phonological disorders. In T.J. Hixon, L.D. Shriberg, and J.H. Saxman (eds.), *Introduction to communication disorders.* Englewood Cliffs, N.J.: Prentice-Hall.

Shuell, T.J. (1981). Dimensions of individual differences. In F.H. Farley and N.J. Gordon (eds.), *Psychology and education: The state of the Union.* Berkeley, Calif.: McCutchan.

Shulman, L. (1987). Knowledge and teaching: Foundations of the new reform. *Harvard Educational Review, 19*(2), 4–14.

Shulman, L., and Keislar, R. (eds.) (1966). *Learning by discovery: A critical appraisal.* Chicago: Rand-McNally.

Siegler, R.S. (1983). Information processing approaches to development. In W. Kessen (ed.), *Handbook of child psychology: Vol. 1. History, theory, and methods* (pp. 129–212). New York: Wiley.

Siegler, R.S. (1985). Encoding and the development of problem solving. In S.F. Chipman, J.W. Segal, and R. Glaser (eds.), *Thinking and learning skills* (Vol. 2). Hillsdale, N.J.: Erlbaum.

Siegler, R.S. (1988). Mechanisms of cognitive development. *Annual Review of Psychology, 40,* 353–379.

Siegler, R.S. (1991). *Children's thinking.* (2nd ed.). Englewood Cliffs, N.J.: Prentice-Hall.

Sikes, J.N. (1972, July). Differential behavior of male and female teachers with male and female students. *Dissertation Abstracts International, 33,* 217A.

Silver, A.A., and Hagin, R.A. (1990). *Disorders of learning in childhood.* New York: Wiley.

Silver, E.A. (1985). *Teaching and learning mathematical problem solving: Multiple research perspective.* Hillsdale, N.J.: Erlbaum.

Silverman, R.E. (1985). *Psychology* (5th ed.). Englewood Cliffs, N.J.: Prentice-Hall.

Simmons, R.G., Burgeson, R., Carleton-Ford, S., and Blyth, D. (1987). The impact of cumulative change in early adolescence. *Child Development, 58,* 1220–1234.

Simmons, W. (1985). Social class and ethnic differences in cognition: A cultural practice perspective. In S.F. Chipman, J.W. Segal, and R. Glaser (eds.), *Thinking and learning skills,* Vol. 2. Hillsdale, N.J.: Erlbaum.

Simon, S.B., and Bellanca, J.A. (eds.) (1976). *Degrading the grade myths: A primer of alternatives to grades and marks.* Washington, D.C.: Association for Supervision and Curriculum Development.

Simpson, C. (1981). Classroom structure and the organization of ability. *Sociology of Education, 54,* 120–132.

Simpson, E. (1972). The classification of educational objectives in the psychomotor domain. *The psychomotor domain*, vol. 3. Washington, D.C.: Gryphon House.

Simpson, E.J. (1966). *The classification of educational objectives: Psychomotor domain*. Urbana, Ill.: University of Illinois Press.

Simpson, R.L. (1980). Modifying the attitudes of regular class students toward the handicapped. *Focus on Exceptional Children, 13*(3), 1–11.

Single Parent (1979). 22, 31–33.

Sizer, T. (1984). *Horace's compromise: The dilemma of the American high school*. Boston: Houghton Mifflin.

Skiba, R., and Raison, J. (1990). Relationship between the use of timeout and academic achievement. *Exceptional Children, 57*, 36–47.

Skinner, B.F. (1953). *Science and human behavior*. New York: Macmillan.

Skinner, B.F. (1968). *The technology of teaching*. New York: Appleton-Century-Crofts.

Skinner, B.F. (1987). *Upon further reflection*. Englewood Cliffs, N.J.: Prentice-Hall.

Slavin, R.E. (1977a, April). A new model of classroom motivation. Paper presented at the annual convention of the American Educational Research Association, New York.

Slavin, R.E. (1977b). Classroom reward structure: An analytic and practical review. *Review of Educational Research, 47*, 633–650.

Slavin, R.E. (1978a). Separating incentives, feedback, and evaluation: Toward a more effective classroom system. *Educational Psychologist, 13*, 97–100.

Slavin, R.E. (1978b). Student teams and achievement divisions. *Journal of Research and Development in Education, 12*, 38–49.

Slavin, R.E. (1979). Effects of biracial learning teams on cross-racial friendships. *Journal of Educational Psychology, 71*, 381–387.

Slavin, R.E. (1980). Effects of individual learning expectations on student achievement. *Journal of Educational Psychology, 72*, 520–524.

Slavin, R.E. (1983a). *Cooperative learning*. New York: Longman.

Slavin, R.E. (1983b). *Student team learning*. Washington, D.C.: National Education Association.

Slavin, R.E. (1984a). Component building: A strategy for research-based instructional improvement. *Elementary School Journal, 84*, 255–269.

Slavin, R.E. (1985a). Team Assisted Individualization: A cooperative learning solution for adaptive instruction in mathematics. In M. Wang and H. Walberg (eds.), *Adapting instruction to individual difference*. Berkeley: McCutchan.

Slavin, R.E. (1985b). Team Assisted Individualization: Combining cooperative learning and individualized instruction in mathematics. In R.E. Slavin, S. Sharan, S. Kagan, R. Hertz-Lazarowitz, C. Webb, and R. Schmuck (eds.), *Learning to cooperate, cooperating to learn*, pp. 177–209. New York: Plenum.

Slavin, R.E. (1985c). Cooperative learning: Applying contact theory in desegregated schools. *Journal of Social Issues, 41*, 45–62.

Slavin, R.E. (1986a). The Napa evaluation of Madeline Hunter's ITIP: Lessons learned. *Elementary School Journal, 87*, 165–171.

Slavin, R.E. (1986b). *Using student team learning* (3rd ed.). Baltimore, Md.: The Johns Hopkins University, Center for Research on Elementary and Middle Schools.

Slavin, R.E. (1987a). A theory of school and classroom organization. *Educational Psychologists, 22*, 89–108.

Slavin, R.E. (1987b). Grouping for instruction in the elementary school. *Educational Psychologist, 22*, 109–127.

Slavin, R.E. (1987c). Ability grouping and student achievement in elementary schools: A best-evidence synthesis. *Review of Educational Research, 57*, 293–336.

Slavin, R.E. (1987d). Mastery learning reconsidered. *Review of Educational Research, 57*, 175–213.

Slavin, R.E. (1987e). Cooperative learning: Where behavioral and humanistic approaches to classroom motivation meet. *Elementary School Journal, 88*, 29–37.

Slavin, R.E. (1987f). Grouping for instruction: Equity and effectiveness. *Equity and Excellence, 23*, 31–36.

Slavin, R.E. (1988). Synthesis of research on grouping: In elementary and secondary schools. *Educational Leadership, 46*(1), 67–77.

Slavin, R.E. (1989). Achievement effects of substantial reductions in class size. In R.E. Slavin (ed.), *School and Classroom Organization*. Hillsdale, N.J.: Erlbaum.

Slavin, R.E. (1990a). Ability grouping and student achievement in secondary schools: A best-evidence synthesis. *Review of Educational Research, 60*, 471–499.

Slavin, R.E. (1990b). *Cooperative learning: Theory, research, and practice*. Englewood Cliffs, N.J.: Prentice-Hall.

Slavin, R.E. (1991). Synthesis of research on cooperative learning. *Educational Leadership, 48*(5), 71–82.

Slavin, R.E. (1992). *Research methods in education: A practical guide* (2nd ed.). Boston: Allyn & Bacon.

Slavin, R.E., Braddock, J.H., Hall, C., and Petza, R.J. (1989). *Alternatives to ability grouping*. Baltimore, Md.: The Johns Hopkins University, Center for Research on Effective Schooling for Disadvantaged Students.

Slavin, R.E., and Karweit, N.L. (1982a, August). School organizational vs. developmental effects on attendance among young adolescents. Paper presented at the annual convention of the American Psychological Association, Washington, D.C.

Slavin, R.E., and Karweit, N.L. (1982b). *Ability-Grouped Active Teaching (AGAT): Teacher's manual*. Baltimore, Md.: Center for Social Organization of Schools, Johns Hopkins University.

Slavin, R.E., and Karweit, N. (April 1984a). Within-class ability groupings and student achievement: Two field experiments. Paper presented at the annual convention of the American Educational Research Association, New Orleans.

Slavin, R.E., and Karweit, N. (1984b). Mastery learning and student teams: A factorial experiment in urban general mathematics classes. *American Educational Research Journal, 21*, 725–736.

Slavin, R.E., and Karweit, N. (1985). Effects of whole class, ability grouped, and individualized instruction on mathematics achievement. *American Educational Research Journal 22*, 351–368.

Slavin, R.E., Karweit, N.L., and Wasik, B.A. (1994). *Preventing early school failure: Research on effective strategies*. Boston: Allyn & Bacon.

Slavin, R.E., Leavey, M.B., and Madden, N.A. (1984). Combining cooperative learning and individualized instruction: Effects on student mathematics achievement, attitudes, and behaviors. *Elementary School Journal, 84*, 409–422.

Slavin, R.E., Leavey, M.B., and Madden, N.A. (1985). *Team Assisted Individualization: Mathematics*. Watertown, Mass.: Charlesbridge.

Slavin, R.E., and Madden, N.A. (1979). School practices that improve race relations. *American Educational Research Journal, 16*(2), 169–180.

Slavin, R.E., and Madden, N.A. (1987, April). Effective classroom programs for students at risk. Paper presented at the annual convention of the American Educational Research Association, Washington, D.C.

Slavin, R.E., and Madden, N.A. (1991). Modifying Chapter 1 program improvement guidelines to reward appropriate practices. *Educational Evaluation and Policy Analysis, 13*, 369–379.

Slavin, R.E., Madden, N.A., and Karweit, N.L. (eds.) (1989). *Effective programs for students at risk*. Boston: Allyn & Bacon.

Slavin, R.E., Madden, N.A., Karweit, N.L., Dolan, L., and Wasik, B.A. (1992). *Success for All: A relentless approach to prevention and early intervention in elementary schools*. Arlington, Va.: Educational Research Service.

Slavin, R.E., Madden, N.A., and Leavey, M.B. (1984a). Effects of cooperative learning and individualized instruction on mainstreamed students. *Exceptional Children, 84,* 409–422.

Slavin, R.E., Madden, N.A., and Leavey, M.B. (1984b). Effects of Team-Assisted Individualization on the mathematics achievement of academically handicapped and nonhandicapped students. *Journal of Educational Psychology, 76,* 813–819.

Slavin, R.E., and Stevens, R.J. (1991). Cooperative learning and mainstreaming. In J.W. Lloyd, N.N. Singh, and A.C. Repp (eds.). *The regular education initiative: Alternative perspectives on concepts, issues, and models* (pp. 177–191). Sycamore, Ill.: Sycamore.

Sleeter, C.E., and Grant, C.A. (1988). *Making choices for multicultural education: Five approaches to race, class, and gender.* Columbus, Oh.: Merrill.

Sluyter, D., and Hawkins, R. (1972). Delayed reinforcement of classroom behavior by parents. *Journal of Learning Disabilities, 5,* 16–24.

Smith, C., and Lloyd, B. (1978). Maternal behavior and perceived sex of infant: Revisited. *Child Development, 49,* 1263–1265.

Smith, D.D. (1989). *Teaching students with learning and behavior problems* (2nd ed.). Englewood Cliffs, N.J.: Prentice-Hall.

Smith, D.D., and Luckasson, R. (1992). *Introduction to special education: Teaching in an age of challenge.* Boston: Allyn & Bacon.

Smith, D.D., and Luckasson, R. (1993). *Introduction to special education.* Boston: Allyn & Bacon.

Smith, J.K., and Katims, M. (1977). Reading in the city: The Chicago Mastery Learning Reading Program. *Phi Delta Kappan, 59,* 199–202.

Smith, L., and Land, M. (1981). Low-interference verbal behaviors related to teacher clarity. *Journal of Classroom Interaction, 17,* 37–42.

Smith, L.R., and Cotten, M.L. (1980). Effect of lesson vagueness and discontinuity on student achievement and attitudes. *Journal of Educational Psychology, 72,* 670–675.

Smith, M.L. (1991). Meanings of test preparation. *American Educational Research Journal, 28*(3), 521–542.

Smith, P.K. (1978). A longitudinal study of social participation in preschool children: Solitary and parallel play re-examined. *Developmental Psychology, 14,* 517–523.

Snarey, J.R. (1985). Cross-cultural universality of socio-moral development: A critical review of Kohlbergian research. *Psychological Bulletin, 97,* 202–232.

Snow, R.E. (1986). Individual differences and the design of educational programs.

American Psychologist, 41, 1029–1039.

Snow, R.E. (1992). Aptitude theory: Yesterday, today, and tomorrow. *Educational Psychologist, 27*(1), 5–32.

Snow, R.E., and Lohman, D.F. (1984). Toward a theory of cognitive aptitude for learning from instruction. *Journal of Educational Psychology, 76,* 347–376.

Snowman, J. (1984). Learning tactics and strategies. In G. Phye and T. Andre (eds.), *Cognitive instructional psychology.* New York: Academic Press.

Snyderman, M., and Rothman, S. (1987). Survey of expert opinion on intelligence and aptitude testing. *American Psychologist, 42,* 137–144.

Solomon, R.L., Turner, L.H., and Lessac, M.S. (1968). Some effects of delay of punishment on resistance to temptation in days. *Journal of Personality and Social Psychology, 8,* 233–238.

Solso, R.L. (1991). *Cognitive psychology* (3rd ed.). Boston: Allyn & Bacon.

Somerville, J.C. (1982). *The rise and fall of childhood.* Beverly Hills, Calif.: Sage Publications.

Spady, W.G. (1988). Organizing for results: The basis of authentic restructuring and reform. *Educational Leadership, 46*(2), 4–8.

Spector, J.E. (1992). Predicting progress in beginning reading: Dynamic assessment of phonemic awareness. *Journal of Educational Psychology, 84*(3), 353–363.

Sperling, G.A. (1960). The information available in brief visual presentations. *Psychological Monographs, 74,* No. 498.

Spivak, G., Marcus, J., and Swift, M. (1986). Early classroom behaviors and later misconduct. *Developmental Psychology, 22,* 124–131.

Sprigle, J.E., and Schaeffer, L. (1985). Longitudinal evaluation of the effects of two compensatory preschool programs on fourth through sixth-grade students. *Developmental Psychology, 21,* 702–708.

Spurlin, J.E., Dansereau, D.F., Larson, C.O., and Brooks, L.W. (1984). Cooperative learning strategies in processing descriptive text: Effects of role and activity level of the learner. *Cognition and Instruction, 1,* 451–463.

Stahl, S.A., and Miller, P.D. (1989). Whole language and language experience approaches for beginning reading: A quantitative research synthesis. *Review of Educational Research, 59,* 87–116.

Stallings, J., and Krasavage, E.M. (1986). Program implementation and student achievement in a four-year Madeline Hunter follow-through project. *Elementary School Journal, 87,* 117–138.

Stallings, J.A. (1979). How to change the process of teaching reading in secondary schools. *Educational Horizons, 57,* 196–201.

Stallings, J.A., and Kaskowitz, D. (1974). *Follow-through classroom observation*

evaluation 1972–73. Menlo Park, Calif.: Standard Research Institute.

Stallings, J.A., and Stipek, D. (1986). Research on early childhood and elementary school teaching programs. In M.C. Wittrock (ed.), *Handbook of research on teaching* (3rd ed.). New York: Macmillan.

Stanley, J.C. (1979). The study and facilitation of talent for mathematics. In A.H. Passow (ed.), *The gifted and talented: Their education and development.* Chicago: University of Chicago Press.

Stanley, J.C., and Benbow, C.P. (1986). Extremely young college graduates: Evidence of their success. *College and University, 58,* 361–371.

Stein, B.S., Littlefield, J., Bransford, J.D., and Persampieri, M. (1984). Elaboration and knowledge acquisition. *Memory and Cognition, 12,* 522–529.

Stein, M.K., Leinhardt, G., and Bickel, W. (1989). Instructional issues for teaching students at risk. In R.E. Slavin, N.L. Karweit, and N.A. Madden (eds.), *Effective programs for students at risk.* Boston: Allyn & Bacon.

Steinberg, L.D., and Hill, J.P. (1978). Patterns of family interaction as a function of age, the onset of puberty, and formal thinking. *Developmental Psychology, 14,* 683–684.

Sternberg, R. (1990). *Metaphors of mind: Conceptions of the nature of intelligence.* New York: Cambridge University Press.

Sternberg, R.J. (1982). Reasoning, problem solving, and intelligence. In R.J. Sternberg (ed.), *Handbook of human intelligence.* New York: Cambridge University Press.

Sternberg, R.J. (ed.) (1986a). *Advances in the psychology of human intelligence,* Vol. 3. Hillsdale, N.J.: Erlbaum.

Sternberg, R.J. (1986b). Intelligence, wisdom, and creativity: Three is better than one. *Educational Psychologist, 21,* 175–190.

Sternberg, R.J., and Bhana, K. (1986). Synthesis of research on the effectiveness of intellectual skills programs: Snake-oil remedies or miracle cures? *Educational Leadership, 44*(2), 60–67.

Sternberg, R.J., and Detterman, D.K. (eds.) (1986). *What is intelligence?* Norwood, N.J.: Ablex.

Stevens, R.J., Madden, N.A., Slavin, R.E., and Farnish, A.M. (1987). Cooperative Integrated Reading and Composition: Two field experiments. *Reading Research Quarterly, 22,* 433–454.

Stevens, R.J., and Slavin, R.E. (1991). *A cooperative learning approach to accommodating student diversity in reading and writing: Effects on handicapped and non-handicapped students.* Baltimore, Md.: Johns Hopkins University, Center for Research on Effective Schooling for Disadvantaged Students.

Stevens, R.J., and Slavin, R.E. (1992). *The cooperative elementary school: Effects on students' achievement, attitudes, and social relations.* Baltimore, Md.: Johns Hopkins University, Center for Research on Effective Schooling for Disadvantaged Students.

Stiggins, R.J. (1985). Improving assessment where it means the most: In the classroom. *Educational Leadership, 43*(2), 69–74.

Stiggins, R.J., and Bridgeford, N.J. (1985). The ecology of classroom assessment. *Journal of Educational Measurement, 22,* 271–286.

Stigler, S.M. (1978). Some forgotten work on memory. *Journal of Experimental Psychology: Human Learning and Memory, 4,* 1–4.

Stipek, D.J. (1981). Children's perceptions of their own and their classmates' ability. *Journal of Educational Psychology, 73,* 404–410.

Stipek, D.J. (1993). *Motivation to learn: From theory to practice* (2nd ed.). Boston: Allyn & Bacon.

Stitelman, L., and Coplin, W. (1969). *American government simulation series.* Chicago: Science Research Associates.

St. John, N.H. (1975). *School desegregation: Outcomes for children.* New York: John Wiley and Sons.

Strain, P., and Kerr, M.M. (1981). *Mainstreaming of children in schools.* New York: Academic Press.

Straus, M.A., Gelles, R.J., and Steinmetz, S.K. (1980). *Behind closed doors: Violence in the American family.* New York: Doubleday.

Strauss, A., and Corbin, J. (1990). *The basics of qualitative research: Grouped theory research: Grounded theory procedures and techniques.* Newbury Park, Calif.: Sage.

Strike, K.A. (1975). The logic of learning by discovery. *Review of Educational Research, 45,* 461–483.

Stringfield, S., and Hartman, A. (in press). The detection of group level irregularities on standardized achievement tests. *Journal of Educational Measurement.*

Suhor, C. (1989). "English Only" movement emerging as a major controversy. *Educational Leadership, 46*(6), 80–82.

Sullivan, H.S. (1953). *Interpersonal theory of psychiatry.* New York: Norton.

Sulzby, E., and Teale, W. (1991). Emergent literacy. In R. Barr, M.L. Kamil, P. Moselthal, and P.D. Pearson (eds.), *Handbook of reading research,* Vol. II (pp. 727–757). New York: Longman.

Sulzer-Azaroff, B., and Mayer, G.R. (1986). *Achieving educational excellence using behavioral strategies.* New York: Holt, Rinehart, & Winston.

Sund, R. (1976). *Piaget for educators.* Columbus, Ohio: Merrill.

Suransky, U.P. (1982). *The erosion of child-*

hood. Chicago: University of Chicago Press.

Suransky, U.P. (1983). Tale of rebellion and resistance: The landscape of early institutional life. *Journal of Education, 165,* 135–157.

Sutton, R.E. (1991). Equity and computers in the schools: A decade of research. *Review of Educational Research, 61*(4), 475–503.

Swanson, H., O'Connor, J.E., and Cooney, J.B. (1990). An information processing analysis of expert and novice teachers' problem solving. *American Educational Research Journal, 27,* 533–556.

Swanson, H.L. (1980). Auditory and visual vigilance in normal and learning disabled readers. *Learning Disabilities Quarterly, 3,* 70–78.

Swanson, H.L. (1990). Influence of metacognitive knowledge and aptitude on problem solving. *Journal of Educational Psychology, 82,* 306–314.

Swiatek, M.A., and Benbow, C.P. (1991). Ten-year longitudinal follow-up of ability-matched accelerated and unaccelerated gifted students. *Journal of Educational Psychology, 83*(4), 528–538.

Sylvester, R. (1985). Research on memory: Major discoveries, major educational challenges. *Educational Leadership, 42,* 69–75.

Taba, H. (1967). *Teacher's handbook for elementary social studies.* Reading, Mass.: Addison-Wesley.

Taft, R. (1987). Ethnographic methods. In M.J. Dunkin (ed.), *International encyclopedia of teaching and teacher education.* Oxford: Pergamon.

Tanner, J.M. (1978). *Foetus into man: Physical growth from conception to maturity.* Cambridge, Mass.: Harvard University Press.

Tavris, C. (1992). *The mismeasure of woman.* New York: Simon and Schuster.

Taylor, D. (1983). *Family literacy: Young children learning to read and write.* Exeter, N.H.: Heinemann.

Taylor, R. (1984). *Assessment of exceptional students: Educational and psychological procedures.* Englewood Cliffs, N.J.: Prentice-Hall.

Teddlie, C., and Stringfield, S. (1989). Ethics and teachers: Implications of research on effective schools. *Ethics in Education, 9*(2), 12–14.

TenBrink, T.D. (1986). Writing instructional objectives. In J. Cooper (ed.), *Classroom teaching skills* (3rd ed.). Lexington, Mass.: D.C. Heath.

Tenenbaum, G. (1982). A method of group instruction which is as effective as one-to-one tutorial instruction (doctoral dissertation, University of Chicago, 1982). *Dissertation Abstracts International, 43,* 1822A.

Tennyson, R.D., and Park, O. (1980). The teaching of concepts: A review of instruc-

tional design literature. *Review of Educational Research, 50,* 55–70.

Terman, L. (1926). *Genetic studies of genius. Vol. 1: Mental and physical traits of a thousand gifted students* (2nd ed.). Stanford, Calif.: Stanford University Press.

Terman, L.M., and Merrill, M.A. (1960). *Stanford-Binet Intelligence Scale, Manual for the Third Revision Form L-M.* Boston: Houghton Mifflin.

Terman, L.M., and Oden, M.H. (1959). The gifted group in mid-life. In *Genetic studies of genius,* Vol. 5. Stanford, Calif.: Stanford University Press.

Tharp, R.G., and Gallimore, R. (1988). *Rousing minds to life.* New York: Cambridge University Press.

Thelen, H.A. (1967). *Classroom grouping for teachability.* New York: Wiley.

Thibault, J.W., and Kelley, H.H. (1959). *The social psychology of groups.* New York: Wiley.

Thieme-Busch, C.A., and Prom, S.E. (1983, April). Impact of teacher use of time training on student achievement. Paper presented at the annual convention of the American Educational Research Association, Montreal.

Thistlewaite, D.L., Dehaan, H., and Kamenetzky, J. (1955). The effects of "directive" and "nondirective" communication procedures on attitudes. *Journal of Abnormal and Social Psychology, 51,* 107–118.

Thoma, S.J. (1986). Estimating gender differences in the comprehension and preference of moral issues. *Developmental Review, 6,* 165–180.

Thomas, A. (1981). Current trends in developmental theory. *American Journal of Orthopsychiatry, 51,* 580–609.

Thomas, E.L., and Robinson, H.A. (1972). *Improving reading in every class: A sourcebook for teachers.* Boston: Allyn & Bacon.

Thomas, J.W., and Rohwer, W.D. (1986). Academic studying: The role of learning strategies. *Educational Psychologist, 21,* 19–41.

Thomas, R.M. (1979). *Comparing theories of child development.* Belmont, Calif.: Wadsworth.

Thompson, M.S., Entwisle, D.R., Alexander, K.L., and Sundius, M.J. (1992). The influence of family composition on children's conformity to the student role. *American Educational Research Journal, 29*(2), 405–424.

Thornburg, H. (1979). *The bubblegum years: Sticking with kids from 9–13.* Tucson, Ariz.: HELP Books.

Thorndike, E.L., and Woodworth, R.S. (1901). The influence of improvement in one mental function upon the efficiency of other functions. *Psychological Review, 8,* 247–261.

Thorndike, R.L., and Hagen, E. (1969).

Measurement and evaluation in psychology and education (3rd ed.). New York: Wiley.

Timpson, W.M., and Tobin, D.N. (1982). *Teaching as performing: A guide to energizing your public presentation.* Englewood Cliffs, N.J.: Prentice-Hall.

Tittle, C.K. (1991). Changing models of student and teacher assessment. *Educational Psychologist, 26*(2), 157–165.

Tobias, S. (1981). Adaptation to individual differences. In F.H. Farley and N.J. Gordon (eds.), *Psychology and education: The state of the Union,* pp. 60–81. Berkeley, Calif.: McCutchan.

Tobias, S. (1985). Test anxiety: Interference, defective skills, and cognitive capacity. *Educational Psychologist, 20,* 135–142.

Tobin, K. (1986). Effects of teacher wait time on discourse characteristics in mathematics and language arts classes. *American Educational Research Journal, 23,* 191–200.

Tobin, K. (1987). The role of wait time in higher cognitive level learning. *Review of Educational Research, 57,* 69–95.

Tobin, K.G., and Capie, W. (1982). Relationships between classroom process variables and middle-school science achievement. *Journal of Educational Psychology, 74,* 441–454.

Toll, D. (1970). *Ghetto* (Simulation Game). Indianapolis, Ind.: Bobbs-Merrill.

Tompkins, G.E. (1981). Writing without a pencil. *Language Arts, 58,* 823–833.

Top, B.L., and Osguthorpe, R.T. (1987). Reverse-role tutoring: The effects of handicapped students tutoring regular class students. *Elementary School Journal, 87,* 413–423.

Top, F. (ed.) (1970). *Report of the Committee on Infectious Diseases.* Evanston, Ill.: American Academy of Pediatrics.

Torrance, E.P. (1981). Ten ways of helping young children gifted in creative writing and speech. In J.C. Gowan, J. Khatena, and E.P. Torrance (eds.), *Creativity: Its educational implications.* Dubuque, Iowa: Kendall/Hunt.

Torrance, E.P. (1986). Teaching creative and gifted learners. In M.C. Wittrock (ed.), *Handbook of research on teaching* (3rd ed.). New York: Macmillan.

Towson, S. (1985). Melting pot or mosaic: Cooperative education and interethnic relations. In R.E. Slavin, S. Sharan, S. Kagan, R. Hertz-Lazarowitz, C. Webb, and R. Schmuck (eds.), *Learning to cooperate, cooperating to learn.* New York: Plenum.

Tulving, E. (1972). Episodic and semantic memory. In E. Tulving and W. Donaldson (eds.), *Organization of memory.* New York: Academic Press.

Tulving, E. (1985). How many memory systems are there? *American Psychologist, 40,* 385–398.

Turnbull, A.P., and Brantley, J.C. (1982). *Mainstreaming: Developing and implementing individualized education programs* (2nd ed.). Columbus, Ohio: Charles E. Merrill.

Turnbull, A.P., and Schulz, J.B. (1979). *Mainstreaming handicapped students: A guide for the classroom teacher.* Boston: Allyn & Bacon.

Tyler, L.E. (1965). *The psychology of human differences.* New York: Appleton-Century-Crofts.

U.S. Census Bureau (1981, July). *Race of the population by states.* Washington, D.C.: U.S. Government Printing Office.

U.S. Commission on Civil Rights (1975). *A better chance to learn: Bilingual bicultural education.* Washington, D.C.: Government Printing Office.

U.S. Department of Education (1991). *Youth indicators.* Washington, D.C.: Author.

U.S. Department of Education (1992). *Fourteenth annual report to Congress on the implementation of the Individuals with Disabilities Education Act.* Washington, D.C.: Author.

U.S. Department of Health, Education and Welfare (1969). *The problem of mental retardation.* Washington, D.C.: U.S. Government Printing Office.

U.S. Department of Health, Education and Welfare (1978). *Height and weight of children.* United States: NC for HS, Series 11 (104). Rockville, Md., September 1970, Pp. 2 and 4.

U.S. Department of Health and Human Services (1991). *Drug use among American high school students and young adults, 1975–1990.* Washington, D.C.: Author.

U.S. Department of Labor, Bureau of Labor Statistics (1988, September). *Labor force participation, unchanged among mothers with young children* (Bureau of Labor Statistics press release). Washington, D.C.: U.S. Government Printing Office.

U.S. Office of Education (1970). *Manual for project applicants and grantees.* Washington, D.C.: USOE.

Valencia, S.W., Pearson, P.D., Peters, C.W., and Wixson, K.K. (1989). Theory and practice in statewide reading assessment: Closing the gap. *Educational Leadership, 46*(7), 57–63.

Vander Zanden, J.W. (1978). *Human development.* New York: Alfred A. Knopf.

Van Patten, J., Chao, C.-I., and Reigeluth, C.M. (1986). A review of strategies for sequencing and synthesizing instruction. *Review of Educational Research, 56,* 437–471.

VanSickle, R.L. (1986, April). *A quantitative review of research on instructional simulation gaming: A twenty-year perspective.* Paper presented at the annual convention of the American Educational Research Association, San Francisco.

Van Tassel-Baska (1989). Appropriate curriculum for gifted learners. *Educational Leadership 46*(6), 13–15.

Vellutino, F.R. (1991). Introduction to three studies on reading acquisition: Convergent findings on theoretical foundations of code-oriented versus whole-language approaches to reading instruction. *Journal of Educational Psychology, 83,* 437–443.

Vosniadou, S., and Schommer, M. (1988). Explanatory analogies can help children acquire information from expository text. *Journal of Educational Psychology, 80,* 524–536.

Vukelich, C., and Golden, J. (1984). Early writing: Development and teaching strategies. *Young Children, 39,* 3–8.

Vygotsky, L.S. (1978). *Mind in society* (M. Cole, V. John-Steiner, S. Scribner, and E. Souberman, eds.). Cambridge, Mass.: Harvard University Press.

Vygotsky, L.S. (1987). *The collected works of L.S. Vygotsky* (translated by Rieber and Carton). New York: Plenum.

Wadsworth, B. (1978). *Piaget for the classroom teacher.* New York: Longman.

Wadsworth, B. (1989). *Piaget's theory of cognitive and affective development* (4th ed.). New York: Longman.

Walberg, H. (1988). Synthesis of research on time and learning. *Educational Leadership, 45*(6), 76–80.

Walden, E.L., and Thompson, S.A. (1981). A review of some alternative approaches to drug management of hyperactive children. *Journal of Learning Disabilities, 14,* 213–217.

Walker, H.M., Severson, H., Stiller, B., Williams, G., Haring, N., Shinn, M., and Todis, B. (1988). Systematic screening of pupils in the elementary range for behavior disorders: Development and trial testing of a multiple rating model. *Remedial and Special Education, 9*(3), 8–14.

Walker, J.E., and Shea, T.M. (1980). *Behavior modification: A practical approach for educators* (2nd ed.). St. Louis: C.V. Mosby.

Walker, L.J. (1989). A longitudinal study of moral reasoning. *Child Development, 60,* 157–166.

Walker, L.J., DeVries, B., and Trevethan, S.D. (1987). Moral stages and moral orientations in real-life and hypothetical dilemmas. *Child Development, 58,* 842–858.

Wallach, G.P., and Miller, L. (1988). *Language intervention and academic success.* Boston: Little, Brown.

Wallach, M.A., and Kogan, N. (1965). *Modes of thinking in young children: A study of the creativity-intelligence distinction.* New York: Holt, Rinehart, & Winston.

Waller, P., and Gaa, J. (1974). Motivation in the classroom. In R. Coop and K. White (eds.), *Psychological concepts in the classroom.* New York: Harper & Row.

Wallerstein, J., and Ketty, J. (1980). California's children of divorce. *Psychology Today, 11,* 67–76.

Walters, R.H., Parke, R.D., and Cane, V.A. (1965). Timing of punishment and the observation of consequences to others as determinants of response inhibition. *Journal of Experimental Child Psychology, 2,* 10–30.

Wang, M.C., and Stiles, B. (1976). Effects of the self-schedule system on teacher and student behaviors. In M.C. Wang (ed.), *The self-schedule system for instructional-learning management in adaptive school learning environments.* Pittsburgh: Learning Research and Development Center, University of Pittsburgh.

Ward, M.H., and Baker, B.L. (1968). Reinforcement therapy in the classroom. *Journal of Behavior Analysis, 1,* 323–328.

Wasik, B.A., and Karweit, N.L. (1994). Off to a good start: Effects of birth-to-three interventions on early school success. In R.E. Slavin, N.L. Karweit, and B.A. Wasik (eds.), *Preventing early school failure.* Boston: Allyn & Bacon.

Wasik, B.A., and Slavin, R.E. (1993). Preventing early reading failure with one-to-one tutoring: A review of five programs. *Reading Research Quarterly.*

Waters, M.C. (1990). *Ethnic options: Choosing identities in America.* Berkeley: University of California Press.

Watson, D.J. (1989). Defining and describing whole language. *Elementary School Journal, 90,* 129–141.

Wattenberg, W.W., and Clifford, C. (1964). Relationship of self-concepts to beginning achievement in reading. *Child Development, 35,* 461–467.

Weade, R., and Evertson, C.M. (1988). The construction of lessons in effective and less effective classrooms. *Teaching and Teacher Education, 4,* 189–213.

Weber, E. (1973). The function of early childhood education. *Young Children, 28,* 265–274.

Wechsler, D. (1955). *Wechsler Adult Intelligence Scale.* New York: Psychological Corporation.

Weikart, D.P., Rogers, L., and Adlock, C. (1971). *The cognitively oriented curriculum.* Urbana, Ill.: University of Illinois Press.

Weiner, B. (1979). A theory of motivation for some classroom experiences. *Journal of Educational Psychology, 71,* 3–25.

Weiner, B. (1986). *An attributional theory of motivation and emotion.* New York: Springer.

Weiner, B. (1989). *Human motivation.* Hillsdale, N.J.: Erlbaum.

Weiner, B. (1990). History of motivational research in education. *Journal of Educational Psychology, 82*(4), 616–622.

Weiner, B., and Rosenbaum, R.M. (1965). Determinants of choice between achieve-

ment and nonachievement-related activities. *Journal of Experimental Research of Personality, 1,* 114–121.

Weinstein, C., and Mignano, A. (1993). *Organizing the elementary school classroom: Lessons from research and practice.* New York: McGraw-Hill.

Weinstein, C., Ridley, D.S., Dahl, T., and Weber, E.S. (1988/89). Helping students develop strategies for effective learning. *Educational Leadership, 46*(4), 17–19.

Weinstein, C.S. (1979). The physical environment of the school: A review of the research. *Review of Educational Research, 49,* 557–610.

Weinstein, C.S. (1987). Seating patterns. In M.J. Dunkin (ed.), *International encyclopedia of teaching and teacher education.* New York: Pergamon.

Weinstein, R.S. (1976). Reading group membership in first grade: Teacher behaviors and pupil experience over time. *Journal of Educational Psychology, 68,* 103–116.

Weir, S. (1981, September). Logo and exceptional children. *Microcomputing,* 76–82, 84.

Weis, J.G., and Sederstrom, J. (1981). *The prevention of serious delinquency: What to do?* Center for Law and Justice, University of Washington.

Weiss, S. (1989). The Ritalin controversy. *NEA Today, 8*(1), 10–11.

Wendt, A.W. (1955). Motivation, effort, and performance. In D.C. McClelland (ed.), *Studies in motivation.* New York: Appleton-Century-Crofts.

Wentzel, K.R. (1991). Classroom competence may require more than intellectual ability: Reply to Jussim (1991). *Journal of Educational Psychology, 83,* 156–158.

Wertsch, J. (1986, April). *Mind in context: A Vygotskian approach.* Paper presented at the annual meeting of the American Educational Research Association, San Francisco.

Wertsch, J.V. (1991). *Vygotsky and the social formation of mind.* Cambridge, Mass.: Harvard University Press.

Whalen, C.K. (1983). Hyperactivity, learning problems, and attention deficit disorders. In T.H. Ollendick and M. Hersen (eds.), *Handbook of child psychopathology,* pp. 151–199. New York: Plenum.

White, S.H., and Buka, S.L. (1987). Early education: Programs, traditions, and policies. In E.Z. Rothkopf (ed.), *Review of research in education* (Vol. 14). Washington, D.C.: American Educational Research Association.

Whitley, B.E., and Frieze, I.H. (1985). Children's causal attributions for success and failure in achievement settings: A meta-analysis. *Journal of Educational Psychology, 77,* 608–616.

Wigfield, A., and Eccles, J. (1989). Test anxiety in elementary and secondary students. *Educational Psychologist, 24,* 159–183.

Wiggins, G. (1989). Teaching to the (authen-

tic) test. *Educational Leadership 46*(7), 41–47.

Wiig, E.H. (1982). Communication disorders. In H. Haring (ed.), *Exceptional children and youth.* Columbus, Ohio: Charles E. Merrill.

Wilcox, R.T. (1989). Rediscovering discovery learning. In *Annual editions: Educational psychology.* Guilford, Conn.: Duskin.

Wilhite, S.C. (1990). Self-efficacy, locus of control, self-assessment of memory ability, and study activities as predictors of college course achievement. *Journal of Educational Psychology Review, 82*(4), 696–700.

Wilkerson, R.M., and White, K.P. (1988). Effects of the 4Mat system of instruction on students' achievement, retention, and attitudes. *Elementary School Journal, 88,* 357–368.

Will, M. (1986). *Educating students with learning problems: A shared responsibility.* Washington, D.C.: U.S. Department of Education.

Williams, L. (1974). Black pride, academic relevance, and individual achievement. In R.W. Taylor and R.M. Wolf (eds.), *Crucial issues in testing.* Berkeley: McCutchan.

Willig, A.C. (1985). A meta-analysis of selected studies on the effectiveness of bilingual education. *Review of Educational Research, 55,* 269–317.

Willis, D.H. (1976). *A study of the relationship between visual acuity, reading mode, and school systems for blind students—1976.* Louisville, Ky.: American Printing House for the Blind.

Wilson, B.G. (1971). Evaluation of learning in art education. In B.S. Bloom, J.T. Hastings, and G.F. Madaus (eds.), *Handbook on formative and summative evaluation of student learning.* New York: McGraw-Hill.

Wilson, R. (1984). A review of self-control treatments for aggressive behavior. *Behavioral Disorders, 9,* 131–140.

Wilson, S. (1977). The use of ethnographic techniques in educational research. *Review of Educational Research, 47,* 245–265.

Wine, J.D. (1980). Cognitive-attentional theory of test anxiety. In I. Sarason (ed.), *Test anxiety: Theory, research, and applications.* Hillsdale, N.J.: Erlbaum.

Winett, R.A., and Vachon, E.M. (1974). Group feedback and group contingencies in modifying behavior of fifth graders. *Psychological Reports, 34,* 1283–1292.

Winett, R.A., and Winkler, R.C., (1972). Current behavior modification in the classroom: Be still, be quiet, be docile. *Journal of Applied Behavior Analysis, 5,* 499–504.

Winn, W. (1991). Learning from maps and diagrams. *Educational Psychology Review, 3,* 211–247.

Winne, P.H. (1979). Experiments relating teachers' use of higher cognitive questions to student achievement. *Review of Educational Research, 49*, 13–50.

Withall, J. (1987). Teacher-centered and learner-centered teaching. In M.J. Dunkin (ed.), *International encyclopedia of teaching and teacher education*. New York: Pergamon.

Witkin, H.A., and Goodenough, D.R. (1981). *Cognitive styles: Essence and origins*. New York: International Universities Press.

Witkin, H.A., Moore, C.A., Goodenough, D.R., and Cox, P.W. (1977). Field-dependent and field-independent cognitive styles and their educational implications. *Review of Educational Research, 47*, 1–64.

Wittrock, M.C. (1974). Learning as a generative process. *Educational Psychologist, 11*, 87–95.

Wittrock, M.C. (1978). The cognitive movement in instruction. *Educational Psychologist, 13*, 15–29.

Wittrock, M.C. (1986). Students' thought processes. In M.C. Wittrock (ed.), *Handbook of research on teaching* (3rd ed.). New York: Macmillan.

Wittrock, M.C. (1991). Generative teaching of comprehension. *Elementary School Journal, 92*, 169–184.

Wittrock, M.C., and Alesandrini, K. (1990). Generation of summaries and analogies and analytic and holistic abilities. *American Educational Research Journal, 27*, 489–502.

Wodtke, K.H., Schommer, and Brunelli, P. (1989). How standardized is school testing? An exploratory observational study of standardized group testing in kindergarten. *Educational Evaluation and Policy Analysis, 11*(3), 223–235.

Wolf, D., Bixby, J., Glenn, J., and Gardner, H. (1991). To use their minds well: New forms of student assessment. *Review of Research in Education, 17*, 31–74.

Wolf, D.P. (1989). Portfolio assessment: Sampling student work. *Educational Leadership, 46*(7), 35–40.

Wolf, M., Birnbauer, J.S., Williams, T., and Lawler, J. (1965). A note on apparent extinction of vomiting behavior of a retarded child. In L. Ullmann and L. Krassner (eds.), *Case studies in behavior modification*. New York: Holt, Rinehart, & Winston.

Wolfgang, D.C., and Sanders, S. (1981). Defending young children's play as the ladder to literacy. *Theory into Practice, 20*, 116–120.

Wolfgang, M.E., Figlio, R.M., and Sellin, T. (1972). *Delinquency in a birth cohort*. Chicago: University of Chicago Press.

Wong, B.Y.L. (1985). Self-questioning instructional research: A review. *Review of Educational Research, 55*, 227–268.

Wong, H.D., Bernstein, L., and Shevick, E. (1978). *Life science* (2nd ed.). Englewood Cliffs, N.J.: Prentice-Hall.

Wong-Fillmore, L., and Valadez, C. (1986). Teaching bilingual learners. In M.C. Wittrock (ed.), *Handbook of research on teaching* (3rd ed.). New York: Macmillan.

Wood, D.J., Bruner, J.S., and Ross, G. (1976). The role of tutoring in problem solving. *Journal of Child Psychology and Psychiatry, 17*, 89–100.

Woodward, J., Carnine, D., and Gersten, R. (1988). Teaching problem solving through computer simulations. *American Educational Research Journal, 25*, 72–86.

Woolfolk, A.E., and Brooks, D. (1982). Nonverbal communication in teaching. In E. Gordon (ed.), *Review of research in education* (Vol. 10). Washington, D.C.: American Educational Research Association.

Woolfolk, A.E., and Brooks, D.M. (1985). Beyond words: The influence of teachers' nonverbal behaviors on students' perceptions and performances. *Elementary School Journal, 85*, 513–528.

Woolfolk, A.E., and McCune-Nicolich, L. (1984). *Educational psychology for teachers* (2nd ed.). Englewood Cliffs, N.J.: Prentice-Hall.

Wyckoff, W.L. (1973). The effect of stimulus variation on learning from lecture. *Journal of Experimental Education, 41*, 85–90.

Yawkey, T.D. (1980). More on play as intelligence in children. *Journal of Creative Behavior, 13*, 247–258, 262.

Ysseldyke, J., and Algozzine, B. (1982). *Critical issues in special and remedial education*. Boston: Houghton Mifflin.

Zellermayer, M., Salomon, G., Globerson, T., and Givon, H. (1991). Enhancing writing-related metacognitions through a computerized writing partner. *American Educational Research Journal, 28*, 373–391.

Ziegler, S. (1981). The effectiveness of cooperative learning teams for increasing cross-ethnic friendship: Additional evidence. *Human Organization, 40*, 264–268.

Zigler, E., and Seitz, V. (1982). Head Start as a national laboratory. *Annals American Academy of Political and Social Science, 461*, 81–90.

Zigler, E., Taussig, C., and Black, K. (1992). Early childhood intervention: A promising preventative for juvenile delinquency. *American Psychologist, 47*, 997–1006.

Zigler, E., and Valentine, J. (1979). *Project Head Start: A legacy of the war on poverty*. New York: Free Press.

Zimmerman, B.J., Bandura, A., and Martinez-Pons, M. (1992). Motivation for academic attainment: The role of self-efficacy beliefs and personal goal setting. *American Educational Research Journal, 29*, 663–676.

Zimmerman, B.J., and Kleefeld, C.F. (1977). Toward a theory of teaching: A social learning view. *Contemporary Educational Psychology, 2*, 158–171.

Zimmerman, B.J., and Schunk, D.H. (eds.) (1989). *Self-regulated learning and academic achievement: Theory, research, and practice*. New York: Springer.

Zimmerman, E.H., and Zimmerman, J. (1962). The alteration of behavior in a special classroom situation. *Journal of the Experimental Analysis of Behavior, 5*, 59–60.

Ziv, A. (1988). Teaching and learning with humor: Experiment and replication. *Journal of Experimental Education, 57*, 5–18.

Zook, K.B. (1991). Effects of analogical processes on learning and misrepresentation. *Educational Psychology Review, 3*, 41–72.

Zucker, R. (1979). Development aspects of drinking through the young adult years. In H. Blane and M. Chafetz (eds.), *Youth, alcohol, and social policy*. New York: Plenum.

Name Index

Subject Index

Photo Credits

This page constitutes an extension of the copyright page.

Stephen Marks: pp. 16, 18, 29, 71, 81, 91, 129, 140, 143, 162, 170, 202, 216, 223, 235, 241, 279, 345, 362, 387, 392, 399, 403, 455, 471, 489, 492, 552;

Jim Pickerell: pp. 7, 8, 44, 53, 77, 85, 113, 118, 132, 160, 198, 208, 247, 253, 268, 282, 288, 307, 315, 319, 328, 331, 374, 413, 441, 461, 483, 537, 539

Brian Smith: pp. 56, 98, 105, 126, 151, 185, 225, 263, 276, 311, 354, 376, 424, 435, 502, 512, 527, 549, 555

Elizabeth Crews: p.37; Jim Argo/Picture Group:p. 64; Eliot Elisofon/LIFE: p. 156 ; Sisse Brimberg/Woodfin Camp & Assoc. p. 176; Lawrence Migdale /Photo Researchers p. 190; George Goodwin/Monkmeyer Press p.349 ; Lew Merrim/ Monkmeyer Press p. 449;